Celebration Bar Review

Multistate Personal Trainer™ Book 1

©1995-2010 Celebration Bar Review   ALL RIGHTS RESERVED
No part of this publication may be reproduced, stored in a retrieval system, or transmitted in any form or by any means, electronic, mechanical, photocopying, recording or otherwise without the prior written permission of the publishers.
PRINTED IN THE USA
NO RESALE PERMITTED

Questions Numbered 101 through the end of each section are reprinted herein with the permission of NCBE, the copyright owner and are copyright ©1995-2010 by the National Conference of Bar Examiners. Permission to use the NCBE's questions does not constitute an endorsement by NCBE or otherwise signify that NCBE has reviewed or approved any aspect of these materials or the company or individuals who distribute these materials.

All other questions, and answers are © 1995 - 2010 Celebration Bar Review All rights reserved

SUMMARY OF CONTENTS

INTRODUCTION	1
CONSTITUTIONAL LAW QUESTIONS	3
CRIMINAL LAW & PROCEDURE QUESTIONS	99
PROPERTY QUESTIONS	215

INTRODUCTION

The Multistate Personal Trainer Books 1 and 2 contain MBE-type practice questions for use in preparation for the Multistate Bar Exam. Follow your syllabus with regard to when to practice with these questions.

Please note that the answer to each question immediately follows the question. Immediate feedback for each question you answer at the time the question is answered is the best way to learn from these questions. We suggest that you take steps to cover the answer immediately following each question before you begin answering the question so as not to inadvertently "cheat."

Under exam conditions, answering 100 questions will take the average student approximately 2 1/2 to 3 hours. Taking the time to review your answers and fully understanding the answers and the reasoning for the answer will probably double that time. **Accordingly, you should probably allow approximately six hours to work with 100 questions. Timing will vary by student.**

Working with all of the questions provided, including the 1991 MBE and the accompanying Workshop should take the average student approximately 70 hours. This will be time well spent.

It is important to understand that the National Conference of Bar Examiners are constantly creating new question types and fact patterns in their attempts to keep the exam fresh. Accordingly, you should view these questions as a learning tool to help you learn and understand the applicable legal rules in actual fact patterns rather than look at these questions as indicative of the type you will actually see on the exam. Furthermore, with regard to **very few** question throughout this text, you may find that "old" law is used and thus may make a particular question and/or answer "outdated". When appropriate, we try to edit in order to make the question more relevant, but we prefer not to change what the NCBE has created. Again, the most updated law is contained in your materials and these trainer questions are to be used to help you apply the law (whether old or new) to a set of facts.

Although performance on these questions is no guarantee of an equivalent performance on the MBE, experience shows that there is great value to practicing with these types of questions. For a rule of thumb on how you are performing, we suggest the following rough guide:

- 75% or more of the questions correct in any given subject is an indication that you are well-prepared for the MBE for that subject.
- 60% - 74% or more of the questions correct in any given subject is an indication that you are doing well but should concentrate on your weak areas for that particular subject.
- 59% or less of the questions correct in any given subject is an indication that you should do additional study in that subject generally.

Again these are rough guides, and how you should prepare can vary from state to state. Never hesitate to call your Bar Review Mentor for additional assistance.

Questions Numbered 101 through the end of each section are reprinted herein with the permission of NCBE, the copyright owner and are copyright ©1995-2010 by the National Conference of Bar Examiners. Permission to use the NCBE's questions does not constitute an endorsement by NCBE or otherwise signify that NCBE has reviewed or approved any aspect of these materials or the company or individuals who distribute these materials.

All other questions, and answers are © 1995-2010 Celebration Bar Review All rights reserved

CONSTITUTIONAL LAW QUESTIONS

Question 1

The State of Vermaine is operating a large nuclear power plant on the Vermaine River. The plant uses river water for cooling and discharges water back into the river, ten degrees warmer than it was at point of entry. While this temperature differential quickly dissipates, it has adversely affected the business of Igg Loo ("Iggy"), a downstream ice cutting operator, located in the State of New Hampster. Primarily as a result of Iggy's urging, New Hampster has sued Vermaine in the United States Supreme Court, alleging damage to its environment and seeking an injunction against thermal discharge. The United States Supreme Court should

(A) hear the matter on the merits because New Hampster is suing in its own right and jurisdiction is proper.
(B) dismiss the action because it does not have original jurisdiction.
(C) dismiss the suit because the suit is really one by Iggy against Vermaine and is barred by the Eleventh Amendment.
(D) remand the case to the district court for trial because it does not have the time to function as a trial court.

Answer to Question 1

Under Article III, §2(2) of the Constitution, the Supreme Court has original and exclusive jurisdiction over controversies between two states. Since this is a controversy between New Hampster and Vermaine, Supreme Court jurisdiction is proper, and (B) is incorrect.

(C) is incorrect because New Hampster is a real party in interest, and thus the Eleventh Amendment, which bars suits by citizens of one state against another state in federal court, is inapplicable.

(D) is incorrect because, by definition, a court with original jurisdiction is a trial court. Since the constitution gives the Supreme Court original jurisdiction over such matters, Congress may not limit that jurisdiction, and the Court has no discretion in determining whether to exercise that jurisdiction. In other words, the Court not only **may**, but **must** function as a trial court. See *Marbury v. Madison*, 1 Cranch 137 (1803).

A state can sue another state to protect its natural resources for the benefit of its own citizens under the *parens patriae* doctrine. *Pennsylvania v. West Virginia*, 262 U.S. 553 (1923). New Hampster is suing Vermaine under this doctrine in seeking to protect its natural resources. Therefore, (A) is correct.

Question 2

Congress duly enacted legislation preventing any state-supported university system from firing or refusing to hire a person on the basis of his or her gender. In its preamble, the Act states that it is enacted pursuant to both the power of Congress to regulate commerce among the states and Section 5 of the Fourteenth Amendment, which grants Congress the power to enforce that Amendment. The Act creates a cause of action in the person aggrieved by a violation of this law to sue the state in federal district court. Amanda, a citizen of the state of Alabania, has brought suit under the statute against the state of Alabania to reinstate her as the dean of Alabania State University's School of Law, alleging that her dismissal was an act of sexual discrimination. The state of Alabania brings a motion to dismiss on the ground that Congress cannot confer federal jurisdiction on such a suit.

If the motion to dismiss is denied, it will most likely be because

(A) since Congress has the power to control the jurisdiction of the federal courts under Article III of the Constitution, it can

authorize jurisdiction over remedial damage suits against a state.
(B) the Eleventh Amendment does not apply to suits by citizens against their own states.
(C) despite the Eleventh Amendment, Congress, acting pursuant to the Commerce Clause and/or the Fourteenth Amendment, can permit suits against a state in federal court.
(D) pursuant to the Supremacy Clause, Congress can limit the sovereign immunity of states.

Answer to Question 2

The Eleventh Amendment prohibits suits against a state in the federal court by a citizen of another state and has also been construed to prohibit a suit in federal court against a state by one of its own citizens. *Hans v. Louisiana*, 134 U.S. 1 (1890). As a result, the power of Congress under Article III of the Constitution to control the jurisdiction of federal courts is limited by the specific prohibition concerning suits against states contained in the Eleventh Amendment. However, Congress can act pursuant to its power to enforce a later Amendment, here the Fourteenth, to authorize such suits, because the later Amendments limit the scope of the Eleventh Amendment. *Fitzpatrick v. Bitzer*, 427 U.S. 445 (1976). (D) is incorrect. Congress does not have the authority under the Supremacy Clause to limit state sovereign immunity by permitting suits against a state in the federal court. The Supremacy Clause is limited by the Eleventh Amendment. There must be a specific authorization by the state to waive its immunity under the Eleventh Amendment or an act of Congress pursuant to a later Amendment, such as the Fourteenth, because a later Amendment limits the scope of the Eleventh Amendment, just as the Eleventh Amendment limits the Supremacy Clause.

Since the given statute relied in part on the Fourteenth Amendment, this is the clearest authority for Congress to authorize such a suit. Therefore, (C) is the best answer and under this analysis, (A) and (B) are incorrect. (C) is not perfect, though, because the Commerce Clause is followed by and thus limited by the Eleventh Amendment.

Question 3

The state of Calegon has passed a tort claims statute which permits suits in the courts of the state of Calegon against the state based upon the doctrine of respondeat superior for damages caused by the negligence of state employees in the course of their employment. The state of Nevazona has a long-arm statute which permits suits against nonresidents for "causing tortious injury in the state of Nevazona." Irit, the Commissioner of Revenue in Calegon, was driving her state-owned vehicle in Nevazona to attend a convention of state revenue commissioners when she was involved in an automobile accident with Harriet, a resident of Nevazona. In addition to suing in the Calegon state court, Harriet can sue the state of Calegon for damages incurred in the automobile accident with Irit in

I. a state court of general jurisdiction in the state of Nevazona.
II. in the federal district court of Nevazona.

(A) I only
(B) II only
(C) either I or II
(D) neither I nor II

Answer to Question 3

A suit in state court is proper, but a suit in federal court is improper. In *Nevada v. Hall*, 440 U.S. 410 (1979), the United States Supreme Court held that if a state has waived its sovereign immunity, the state can be sued in the state court of another state, provided that the other state can assert personal jurisdiction. This jurisdiction extends to another state's court even if the waiver statute attempts to require that suits be brought in that state's court. The *Nevada* Court stated that another state court is not constitutionally required to recognize any limitations on a state's waiver of sovereign immunity. They may do so as a matter of comity, but may also assume jurisdiction to vindicate an important state policy such as compensating victims of car accidents. In this case, where an agent of the state of Calegon was operating a state-owned car in the state of Nevazona, Calegon has waived its immunity and Nevazona has properly exercised long-arm jurisdiction. Therefore, under *Nevada*, there is proper jurisdiction in the Nevazona state court.

However, the Eleventh Amendment prohibits a suit against a state in the federal court. A waiver of sovereign immunity in state court proceedings is not a waiver of the protection provided by the Eleventh Amendment. See *Clark v. Barnard*, 108 U.S. 436 (1883) (a state's waiver of its Eleventh Amendment immunity must be unmistakably clear). Therefore, a suit in the federal district court of Nevazona would not be constitutional.

Because Harriet may sue in Nevazona only in a state court, (A) is correct.

Question 4

Federal legislation was enacted setting forth new requirements concerning the permitted variance in the size of Congressional districts. Because many of the Congressional districts from which Congresspersons had traditionally run would be changed by these requirements, and because Congress desired a speedy determination of the constitutionality of the statute, the statute specifically granted standing to any sitting Congressperson to sue the relevant state redistricting commission to determine the constitutionality of the act as it affected that Congressperson's district. Original jurisdiction for such suits was mandated in the United States Supreme Court. The portion of the statute establishing exclusive original jurisdiction in the United States Supreme Court is

(A) constitutional, because Congress has the power to determine the jurisdiction of federal courts.
(B) constitutional, because it is authorized pursuant to the power of Congress to enforce the Fifteenth Amendment.
(C) unconstitutional, because by granting standing only to sitting Congresspersons, it denies equal protection of the laws to other individuals who may wish to run for Congress.
(D) unconstitutional, because it is inconsistent with Article III of the United States Constitution.

Answer to Question 4

Even though Congress does have the authority to prescribe the jurisdiction of lower federal courts, one clear limitation on the power of Congress to determine the jurisdiction of federal courts is that the United States Constitution expressly and exclusively establishes the original jurisdiction of the United States Supreme Court and Congress cannot supplement or limit that jurisdiction. *Marbury v. Madison*, 1 Cranch 137 (1803). (A) is incorrect because it is too broad a statement.

Congress clearly has the power to pass voting legislation concerning issues of race pursuant to the Fifteenth Amendment. However, at issue here is not the validity of the statute itself, but only the provision creating exclusive original jurisdiction in the U.S. Supreme Court to hear claims raised by redistricting. The fact that the rest of the statute may be valid under the Fifteenth Amendment does not save the jurisdictional provision from constitutional attack. (B) is incorrect.

(C) is incorrect because Congress does have the power to specifically confer standing in cases brought in the federal court. There is clearly a logical nexus between a sitting Congressperson and the composition of the electoral district, and no constitutional requirement that other individuals be granted similar standing.

(D) is correct because Congress cannot enact a statute that alters the *original* jurisdiction of the Supreme Court as established in Article III of the United States Constitution.

Questions 5 and 6 are based on the following fact situation.

The State of New Dakotah recently adopted anti-pollution legislation to prohibit certain levels of industrial smoke emission, under standards to be set by the state administrator and to become effective six months after promulgation. The Rubbermade Company decided that it could not comply with the somewhat vague standards as announced, and therefore advised its employees that it would have to go out of business on the effective date of the standards. Before the effective date of the state legislation and regulations, Local 57 of the Rubberworkers Union, representing employees of the plant, sued for declaratory judgment and injunction in federal court, claiming that the state statute violated the Commerce Clause of the Constitution of the United States, and that the regulations were adopted in violation of the due process requirements of the Fourteenth Amendment.

5. Assume that the federal court took jurisdiction and held the statute unconstitutional on Commerce Clause grounds, stating that smoke abatement requires nationally uniform regulation; further assume affirmance by the Court of Appeals. Review in the Supreme Court, at the instance of the state, should be

(A) granted as a matter of right.
(B) accepted for discretionary review if four members of the Court so vote.
(C) accepted for discretionary review if no fewer than five members of the Court so vote.
(D) denied for lack of justiciability.

6. Which of the following defenses is most likely to be successful in federal court?

(A) The issues are not ripe.
(B) The issues are moot.
(C) Local 57 lacks standing.
(D) The suit should have been brought first in a state court.

Answer to Question 5

The question is how the case will go to the Supreme Court, by appeal or by certiorari.

(A) is incorrect because current law restricts review by appeal to judgments of a three-judge federal district court created under 28 U.S.C. § 2284. A direct appeal is not available from judgments of United States courts of appeal.

Review of a United States Court of Appeal judgment is by certiorari. 28 U.S.C.§ 1254. The concurrence of only four judges is required to grant a writ of certiorari. Therefore, (B) is correct and (C) is incorrect.

(D) is incorrect because the case is justiciable. There is a genuine controversy between two adversarial parties. This is not a political question, or an issue otherwise committed exclusively to the executive or legislative departments. It is part of the function of the courts to review legislation for constitutionality.

Answer to Question 6

(A) is incorrect because the statute has been passed, regulations have been promulgated under it, and the company is about to close because of these regulations. The case is sufficiently concrete for the court to decide whether or not, as applied in this situation, the statute is unconstitutional. Therefore, the case is ripe. The court will not wait for the plant to close before determining the validity of the act. At that point, it will be too late to prevent the harm.

(B) is incorrect because circumstances have not changed, and the decision will affect the parties. A case only becomes moot if, after the suit is brought, circumstances change to such an extent that the decision will not affect the parties.

(C) is incorrect because the Court has held that when there is a close relationship between the party and a third person, and there is a special need to vindicate the rights of the third person, a party is permitted to raise the constitutional rights of a third party. See *NAACP v. Alabama*, 357 U.S. 449 (1958). Under this analysis, Local 57 does have standing to bring suit. It represents individuals who might not be allowed or able to bring their own suit; therefore Local 57 will probably be allowed standing because the statute infringes upon its members' rights.

Discretionary abstention is the applicable doctrine here. The state statute has not been construed by the state courts. A narrow state court construction may reduce the statute's burden on commerce and may resolve problems as to the manner in which the regulations were adopted, thus avoiding a decision on the federal constitutional issues. Under these circumstances, the federal court probably will defer to the state courts. (D) is correct.

Question 7

The legislature of the Commonwealth of Oklatucky has passed a statute under the authority of its police power which would prohibit Oklatucky Edison, the state's only electric utility, from operating its current nuclear power plant and from building any new nuclear power plants. Because the legislature is concerned with the constitutionality of the statute, and because of the political controversy surrounding the statute, the legislature has exercised the power given to it under the Oklatucky Constitution to submit the statute to the Oklatucky Supreme Court to obtain a ruling on its constitutionality.

Pursuant to a statutory provision, Oklatucky Edison is permitted to intervene in the proceedings before the Oklatucky Supreme Court. It files a brief in that court and in oral argument vigorously asserts that the statute is unconstitutional. The Oklatucky Supreme Court holds that the statute is constitutional.

If Oklatucky Edison should appeal the decision to the United States Supreme Court, the U.S. Supreme Court should

(A) decline to decide the case on the basis that there is no case or controversy.
(B) decline to decide the case on the basis that this is a nonjusticiable political question.
(C) uphold the decision of the Oklatucky Supreme Court because the state has broad authority under the police power to regulate and prohibit dangerous activities within the state.
(D) reverse the decision of the Oklatucky Supreme Court because the Oklatucky statute constitutes a taking without just compensation in violation of the Fourteenth Amendment.

Answer to Question 7

(B) is incorrect. The matter does not present a political question because it is the type of issue regularly decided by courts and has not been exclusively committed to another branch of the government. If the legislation were in effect and Edison sued to enjoin its enforcement, the Court could decide the matter. Since the legislation is not in effect, though, this is only an advisory opinion and thus does not constitute an actual case or controversy, as required in the federal courts.

(C) and (D) present possible rationales to uphold or reverse the decision, but the Court will not reach the merits of the case and therefore they are incorrect.

(A) is correct. The decision of the Oklatucky Supreme Court was an advisory opinion to the state legislature. Therefore, there is no case or controversy as required for federal court jurisdiction under Article III of the U.S. Constitution. Thus, the decision of the Oklatucky Supreme Court cannot be reviewed in the United States Supreme Court.

Question 8

Congress has passed a statute which provides that no federal court, including the United States Supreme Court, shall have jurisdiction to decide any case involving the validity under the Constitution of any law limiting the rights of children under age 15 to obtain an abortion without parental consent. If properly challenged, the statute would be held

(A) constitutional, if prior Supreme Court decisions have upheld the constitutionality of similar statutes.

(B) constitutional, because of the plenary power of Congress to determine jurisdiction of the federal courts.
(C) unconstitutional, because it seriously interferes with the attainment of a supreme and uniform federal constitutional law.
(D) unconstitutional, because Congress cannot regulate the jurisdiction of the United States Supreme Court.

Answer to Question 8

This statute would make final the various decisions of the state courts concerning the validity of abortion statutes under the federal Constitution. However, the Constitution gives the federal courts (and not Congress) the power to finally interpret the federal Constitution. Congress may not take away this power and change the framework set up by the Constitution by altering the jurisdiction of the federal courts. Congress's power to alter the federal courts' jurisdiction is better characterized as "substantial" than as "plenary" (which means "full" or "absolute"). Therefore, (B) is incorrect.

(A) would allow state courts to interpret the federal Constitution, perhaps ignoring or distinguishing prior Supreme Court decisions, without further review by the Supreme Court.

(D) is incorrect because Congress **may** regulate the *appellate* jurisdiction of the Supreme Court, provided such regulation does not undermine the role of the Court in the general constitutional structure.

(C) is correct. To deny federal jurisdiction over a constitutional issue would be to subvert one of the basic purposes of the Supreme Court, which is to ensure uniformity of interpretation of the federal Constitution.

Question 9

The state of Halaski, which was admitted to the Union after the Civil War, inserted language identical to the Fourth Amendment into the state constitution.

Margaret was indicted by the state for murder. The police searched her home and found a gun which proved to be the murder weapon. Margaret's attorney brought a motion to suppress the gun, which was denied. Margaret was convicted and appealed her case to the Supreme Court of Halaski.

In its decision, the Halaski Supreme Court stated that its task was to determine if the evidence was properly suppressed under the provisions of the Halaski Constitution. In making that determination, it said that, in the interests of comity, it intended to construe the Halaski Constitution in harmony with the United States Constitution. Relying solely on federal precedent, the court concluded that the provisions of the state constitution required that the gun be suppressed and reversed the conviction. The district attorney now seeks a writ of certiorari to the United States Supreme Court. What action should the Court take?

(A) The Court may, in its discretion, grant the writ of certiorari, because an interpretation of the Fourth Amendment of the U.S. Constitution, as applicable to the state through the Fourteenth Amendment, is essential to the disposition of the case.
(B) The Court may, in its discretion, grant the writ of certiorari, because there was no separate state issue as the basis for the decision.
(C) Refuse to hear the case, even though the state court purported to rely on federal law, because the state supreme court interpreted the state, not the federal, constitution.
(D) Refuse to hear the case, because the state court's interpretation of the Halaski constitution's search and seizure provision is dispositive of the case.

Answer to Question 9

(A) is incorrect. If the state supreme court had upheld the conviction, then the issue of whether the search violated federal search and seizure rules would have been essential for a decision, because the conviction could be overturned if there had been a federal constitutional violation, even if there had not been a violation of the state constitution. That analysis was not required in this case, because the state supreme court **overturned** the conviction based on the state constitution, making a determination of the federal constitutional issues unnecessary. The federal claim is now moot.

(C) is incorrect. If the state court had interpreted its own constitution independent of federal law, then no federal question would have been presented and (C) would have been correct. However, here the court purported to interpret federal precedents in order to reach its decision and therefore the decision is reviewable by the United States Supreme Court.

(D) is incorrect. This choice states correctly that the interpretation of the state constitutional provision is dispositive of the case. However, the interpretation at issue is based on federal law and, in such cases, the Supreme Court may review state court decisions by certiorari to ensure uniformity of interpretation of federal laws and the Constitution. See *Martin v. Hunter's Lessee*, 14 U.S. (1 Wheat) 304 (1816) and 28 U.S.C. § 1257.

(B) is correct. In this case, the state supreme court was purporting to construe the Fourth Amendment of the federal constitution in order to construe its state constitutional provision in harmony with it. Therefore, the state decision is not really upon separate and independent state grounds. As a result, the U.S. Supreme Court has the right to review the decision, because it is in fact an application of federal precedents, in order to assure that the decision is in conformity with the Court's interpretation.

Question 10

Congress has passed a statute, known as the Federal Beekeepers' Act, requiring that beekeepers be licensed, regulating the cleanliness of apiaries, and establishing safety standards for the removal of honey from the hives. Congress has appropriated $1,000,000 to fund the Act.

Assume that a federal taxpayer tried to challenge the validity of the Beekeepers' Act. What is the most likely disposition by the federal court?

(A) The court would dismiss for failure to state a cause of action.
(B) The court would dismiss for lack of standing.
(C) The court would determine the validity of the statute if the taxpayer could show a direct benefit from a determination that the Act was unconstitutional.
(D) The court would determine the validity of the statute if the appropriation in support of the Act's regulatory requirements were a separate appropriation.

Answer to Question 10

There is a cause of action which may be adjudicated if brought by a plaintiff with standing. For example, a beekeeper might be able to challenge the act as an improper exercise of Congress' commerce powers. Therefore, (A) is incorrect.

The beekeeper would probably not be successful, but could try to establish standing by showing direct economic harm as a result of the legislation. Federal taxpayer standing is limited to a challenge to a substantial exercise of Congressional power under the Taxing and Spending Clause, and the taxpayer must establish a direct nexus between her status as a taxpayer and the wrong she is alleging. *Flast v. Cohen*, 392 U.S. 83 (1968). (C) and (D) misstate the requirement for federal taxpayer standing. Moreover, an ordinary taxpayer is not likely to be able to show the direct benefit from the challenge that is required for taxpayer standing; the mere fact that she may benefit indirectly from saving the government some money is not enough. Likewise, the severability of the appropriation provision of the Act is irrelevant. Because taxpayer standing is so limited, it is highly unusual for the taxpayer to have standing to challenge an Act of Congress.

In this case, a federal taxpayer would not have standing to challenge the Act's validity because the court will view the Act as a regulatory rather than a spending statute. Therefore, the suit will be dismissed, and (B) is correct.

Question 11

A City ordinance requires that 10% of the dollar amount spent on city contracts each fiscal year be awarded to businesses owned by racial minorities, also known as Minority Business Enterprises (MBE's). The United General Contractor Association (UGCA) filed suit on behalf of its nonminority members challenging the ordinance as violative of the Equal Protection Clause of the Fourteenth Amendment. UGCA claimed that many of its members regularly bid on and performed construction work for City and would have bid on designated contracts but for the restrictions imposed by the ordinance.

Prior to trial, the city files a motion to dismiss. The court in this case should

(A) deny the motion; UGCA has standing because in equal protection cases injury in fact is not just a denial of a benefit, but also a denial of equal treatment imposed by a barrier to obtaining the benefit.
(B) deny the motion; race-based statutes which operate as quotas are facially invalid under the Equal Protection Clause of the Fourteenth Amendment.
(C) grant the motion; UGCA lacks standing because it has not shown a sufficient nexus between itself and its individual members' claims to satisfy the requirements for associational standing.
(D) grant the motion; UGCA lacks standing because it failed to show that, but for the program, a member would have successfully been awarded any additional contract work.

Answer to Question 11

(B) is incorrect because, although race-based statutes are subject to strict scrutiny, it is too broad to state that every such program, no matter what the facts and circumstances, is unconstitutional.

Standing requires a plaintiff to allege injury in fact. (D) is incorrect because UGCA can raise the rights of its members so long as at least one of them alleges an injury in fact and so long as the relief granted does not have to be tailored to individual members. Both requirements are satisfied because we have the requisite injury in fact (an unequal opportunity to get a benefit) and a ruling striking down the statute does not require the presence of individual members.

The question is whether UGCA can allege injury in fact when it is unable to show that it actually lost any business by the operation of the statute. In equal protection cases, including *Bakke* and more recently in *Northeastern Florida Chapter of Associated General Contractors*, 113 S.Ct. 2297 (1993), it was held that an allegation that the plaintiff faced an unequal opportunity to get a benefit was enough to establish prima facie evidence of injury in fact. The plaintiff need not show that he or she would have necessarily gotten the benefit. (A) is correct. (C) is incorrect because it states too stringent a test to establish standing.

Question 12

The Town of High Brow has passed a zoning ordinance that permits only single-family homes to be built in the town. Each home must be built on a two-acre lot, and must have 200 feet of frontage on an approved street. The ordinance effectively prevents low-income housing from being built in the town. An action has been brought by three low-income persons alleging that the town's exclusionary zoning practices have effectively excluded persons of low and moderate income from living in the town in violation of the constitutional rights of the petitioners.

If the Town were to bring a motion to dismiss on the ground that the petitioners lack standing, which of the following facts would be most helpful to the Town?

(A) There was no showing of discrimination against minorities because of the exclusion of low-income housing from the town.
(B) There was adequate low-income housing available in the adjoining city.
(C) The petitioners were not residents of High Brow.

(D) The petitioners would be unable to make a showing that they would be likely to use low-income housing in High Brow if it were built.

Answer to Question 12

The focus of this question is standing. (A) and (B) each articulate defenses that might go to the merits of the case but are not relevant on the issue of standing. The petitioners need only show direct and actual harm to have standing. Whether they have grounds to defeat the town policy is another matter entirely.

(C) is incorrect because the petitioners need not show present residence in High Brow. In fact, it is the basis of their claim that they cannot presently reside in High Brow. Therefore, the fact that the petitioners are not now residents of High Brow would not be helpful to the Town.

To have standing in this type of case, the petitioners must show that they would be affected by a decision in their favor. Specifically, they must show that they would be likely to take advantage of an opportunity to live in High Brow. If the petitioners could not show that they would live in High Brow, they would lack standing and so the argument in (D) would be most helpful to the Town. (D) is therefore correct.

Question 13

Congress passed a national medical insurance program to provide medical care to all citizens in states which opted to participate in the program. Substantial federal expenditures were involved. To participate, states were required to comply with federal health care and recordkeeping standards. The State of Florabama has decided not to participate in the program. Dr. Mort is a prominent physician practicing in Florabama.

If Dr. Mort, as a federal taxpayer, brought suit in the federal district court to enjoin expenditure under the program, the court would hold he had standing if he could show

(A) that he has a personal stake in the outcome of the litigation.
(B) that he would be economically harmed by the proposed legislation.
(C) that the particular program is in derogation of a constitutional provision which restricts the taxing and spending power.
(D) that a significant part of his tax dollars would be used to support the program.

Answer to Question 13

(A) and (B) would be arguments to establish Dr. Mort's standing as a physician harmed by the statute. But Dr. Mort probably cannot establish standing as anything other than a taxpayer since the federal statute does not apply directly to him. Florabama, where Dr. Mort practices, has opted out of the program. Therefore, the only effect on Dr. Mort is as a federal taxpayer. Since Dr. Mort can only sue as a federal taxpayer, showings of direct economic harm or of a personal stake in the outcome are irrelevant, and (A) and (B) are incorrect.

(D) is incorrect because the mere fact that his tax dollars will be used to support the program is too remote an interest to confer taxpayer standing. If that were enough, every taxpayer in the United States would have standing to challenge every federal program.

To establish federal taxpayer standing under *Flast v. Cohen*, 392 U.S. 83 (1968), there must be a logical nexus between the plaintiff's asserted status as a taxpayer and the claim sought to be adjudicated, and the challenge must be to a spending statute which is allegedly in derogation of the congressional taxing and spending power under Article I. (C) most closely articulates the requirement for federal taxpayer standing under *Flast* and is therefore correct.

Question 14

Harry Krishna sought to distribute handbills in the mall of the ABC Shopping Center, a four-acre plaza owned by ABC, Inc. The handbills urged attendance at a large spiritual gathering, scheduled at the county fairgrounds for the following month. Requested by the plaza manager to stop handbilling while on ABC property, Harry persisted. The manager summoned a policeman and repeated the request in the officer's presence. When Harry continued his effort to distribute the handbills, he was placed under arrest by the officer for criminal trespass. Following his release on bail by the municipal court, Harry promptly filed suit in federal district court to enjoin the pending prosecution against him, and for declaratory judgment that the trespass ordinance is unconstitutional as applied.

The federal district court is most likely to avoid decision on the merits because

(A) the case lacks adequate ripeness to meet the requirements of Article III.
(B) this kind of case can only be heard by a three-judge court.
(C) the political question doctrine applies.
(D) the doctrine of equitable abstention may apply.

Answer to Question 14

(A) is incorrect. All the events pertinent to the adjudication have already occurred and the case is ripe. Harry is being prosecuted under the statute. There is an actual case or controversy.

(B) is incorrect because a three-judge federal court is not required in a suit to enjoin enforcement of a state criminal statute. In fact, the three-judge federal district court is a court of very limited jurisdiction and, absent an Act of Congress specifically conferring jurisdiction in such a case, would not have the authority to hear the case presented in this question.

(C) is incorrect because a suit to enjoin a state statute on First Amendment grounds comes within none of the categories of a political question. It is not an issue committed for final resolution to another branch of government, it will not provoke an embarrassing confrontation between branches of government, there is no need to adhere to a political decision already made, and it is possible to order appropriate relief against the state officials.

However, the federal court will dismiss this suit because of the doctrine of abstention. Because a state criminal proceeding has commenced, the federal court will abstain from hearing the case. Under the case of *Younger v. Harris*, 401 U.S. 37 (1971), the federal court, as a matter of comity, will not enjoin the prosecution of a state criminal proceeding when the case has already commenced, unless there is bad faith on behalf of the prosecution or other extraordinary circumstances. The defendant must raise his constitutional defenses in the state criminal proceeding. Therefore, (D) is the correct answer.

Question 15

An ordinance of the Town of Newberry making it criminal for "five or more persons to congregate in a public place so as to disturb the peace" has been part of the town ordinances for 100 years. Although the ordinance has not been enforced in over 50 years, the sheriff of Newberry announced that he would arrest groups of five or more persons who demonstrated in front of the barbershop, a popular hangout for the town's male residents. Because they had planned a demonstration in front of the barbershop to support gay and lesbian awareness and were concerned about the threatened prosecutions, the League of Lesbian Voters announced that its members might schedule a protest demonstration in front of the barbershop, urging the repeal of the ordinance. The sheriff stated that he would arrest the demonstrators if they violated the ordinance. The League organization then brought an action in federal court to enjoin the prosecution of the barbershop demonstrators. The best defense for the Town in that action is

(A) there is no standing because the rights of these plaintiffs are not affected in any manner which is different from the public at large.
(B) the case is not ripe because the character of the barbershop demonstration is not known.
(C) there is no case or controversy because there have been no prosecutions under the ordinance for 50 years.
(D) the Town is immune from suit under the Eleventh Amendment.

Answer to Question 15

The plaintiffs' injury need not be one which they have suffered in a different manner than the public at large, so long as they have suffered specifically. *Duke Power Co. v. Carolina Environmental Study Group*, 438 U.S. 59 (1978). Therefore, (A) is not a good defense and is incorrect.

(C) is incorrect. If there is a substantial indication that the government will prosecute the plaintiffs, the past failure of the Town to prosecute cases under the ordinance does not render a current dispute nonjusticiable, provided a concrete dispute exists.

The Eleventh Amendment is not applicable because only states, not subdivisions of a state, enjoy immunity from suit under the Amendment and therefore (D) is incorrect.

Here, there is only a generalized threat of prosecution and there is only a possibility that the demonstrators will hold a protest in front of the barbershop. Further, it is not clear that the actual demonstration will in fact violate the ordinance. If the group had made definite plans to conduct a demonstration that would subject them to prosecution under the ordinance, they would be able to show that they were harmed specifically because their right to free speech has been denied. Thus, (B), which recognizes that the case is not ripe and therefore the best defense, is correct.

Question 16

The city of Somerbridge in the state of Masshire has enacted an ordinance which prevents the owner of a dwelling unit which has been converted to a condominium from evicting a tenant from the premises for a period of two years following the conversion.

Patty is the purchaser of a condominium unit. Duke, the tenant, refuses to vacate the unit, even though he is only a tenant at sufferance. Patty has commenced an action in federal district court, alleging that the operation of the ordinance has resulted in a taking of her property without just compensation. Which of the following may be a reason that the federal district court will abstain from deciding the case?

(A) There is doubt under the state law of Masshire whether a community has the authority to adopt the ordinance.
(B) A Masshire state trial court held a similar ordinance in another city unconstitutional under the Fourteenth Amendment as a taking without just compensation.
(C) The mayor of the city of Somerbridge has urged that the ordinance not be enforced.
(D) The attorney for the city of Somerbridge has urged that the statute not be enforced.

Answer to Question 16

Under the abstention doctrine, a federal court has discretion to refuse to hear a case which alleges the unconstitutionality of a state statute if there are undecided issues of state law which will resolve the issue without applying federal constitutional principles. (B) is incorrect because the state court in the other trial based its decision on federal constitutional law, rather than state law.

The purpose of the abstention doctrine is to promote principles of federalism by giving deference to state court decisions. The positions of the mayor and the city attorney regarding enforcement of the ordinance have no bearing on abstention doctrine analysis. The fact that a particular city official has urged that the ordinance not be enforced would only go to issues of ripeness, if it is relevant at all in the case. It would not relate to the issue of abstention, which is what the question specifically asks. (C) and (D) are therefore incorrect.

(A) is the correct answer because state resolution of the issue would obviate the need for federal action.

Question 17

The State of New Canada has a retirement system under which a fixed percentage of an employee's pay is deducted each payday. Retirement benefits are paid beginning at age 65 for the life of the employee. Actuarial statistics indicate that those who completely abstain from alcohol have a greater life expectancy than those who use alcohol. Those who abstain therefore receive smaller monthly retirement benefits than those who use alcohol.

If a person who did not use alcohol challenged on constitutional grounds the lower monthly benefit standard applicable to persons in his class, what is the appropriate burden of proof?

(A) The nondrinker should be required to show the lack of a compelling state need.
(B) The nondrinker should be required to show that the benefit standard is not related to a rational state purpose.
(C) The state should be required to show that the classification was justified by a compelling state need.
(D) The state should be required to show that the benefit standard was related to a rational state purpose.

Answer to Question 17

When the burden of proof requires a showing of compelling need, that burden is always on the state. However, such a burden of proof is only applicable when the statute involves race, alienage, or fundamental interests. When the challenge involves an area of economic regulation (as is the case here), the burden is on the challenger to show that no rational purpose exists for the statute.

(A) and (C) are incorrect because they apply the wrong standard (compelling state need) in the area of economic regulation and, even if that were the proper standard, (A) incorrectly places the burden on the challenger.

(D) is incorrect because when a rational purpose must be shown, the challenger, not the state, shoulders the burden of proof.

(B) is correct because it states the correct test and proper burden of proof.

Question 18

Connie, a former high school and college student body president, wanted to become a Congresswoman. She collected enough valid signatures under the law of Illiwa to require the registrar to place her name on the ballot. One of her opponents, Bennie, challenged Connie's right to be on the ballot on the ground that Connie would not achieve her 25th birthday before the day she would be required to take office. The state ballot law commission found that Connie would not satisfy the age requirement and ordered her name stricken from the ballot. On appeal, the Illiwa Supreme Court affirmed the decision. Further review in the United States Supreme Court was not sought. Instead, Connie ran a sticker and write-in campaign and received more votes than any of her opponents.

Both Connie and Bennie, the candidate who received the second highest number of votes, sought to be seated as members of Congress. A congressional committee held hearings and found that Connie did not meet the age requirement and recommended that Bennie be seated. Congress adopted the recommendations and voted to seat Bennie.

If Connie should bring suit in the federal district court to require that she be seated, the court would

(A) refuse to decide the case on the merits because the decision reached by the state supreme court is res judicata because U.S. Supreme Court review was not sought.
(B) refuse to hear the case because it is within the exclusive and original jurisdiction of the U.S. Supreme Court.
(C) refuse to hear the case because of the political question doctrine.
(D) hear and decide the case on the merits.

Answer to Question 18

The issue presented in this case raises federal constitutional issues, and except for the political question doctrine, would be decided by the federal court. Although the decision of the state supreme court may have some collateral estoppel effect on the instant case, it is not a matter of res judicata because the two claims are different and the parties are different. The first case was between Connie and the state, and the decision was that Connie could not be on the state ballot. This case will be between Connie and the U.S. Congress, and the issue will be whether she should be seated. Thus, (A) is incorrect.

(B) is incorrect because this is not a case within the exclusive original jurisdiction of the Supreme Court. The cases over which the Supreme Court has original and exclusive jurisdiction (versus original and concurrent jurisdiction) are those involving controversies between two or more states. In fact, this case is not within the jurisdiction of the federal courts at all, because it involves a political question.

The political question doctrine prevents judicial review of the merits of a question when the Constitution vests the final decision on a particular matter in a branch of the federal government other than the courts. The Constitution sets out qualifications of age and citizenship for members of Congress. Article I, § 5 provides that "Each house shall be the judge of elections, returns and qualifications of its own members." Therefore, the court cannot decide the merits of this case because the matter is reserved to the legislative branch of government, making (C) correct and (D) incorrect.

Question 19

Because of renewed hostilities by the nation of North Namrea against the United States ally of South Namrea, the President has decided to terminate the U.S. treaty with North Namrea. The President and his advisors have reviewed the law on treaties and the relevant constitutional provisions and have determined that the President can terminate the treaty without the Senate's approval. In fact, the Constitution addresses treaty approval, but is silent on the termination process. Senator Commitose and a few of his colleagues learned of the President's plan to terminate the treaty and brought suit in federal court to enjoin that action. The court should

(A) dismiss the complaint because it is up to the President and Congress to determine the process to terminate a treaty.
(B) decide the case, because when the Constitution is silent on an issue, it is within the powers of the Court, as the interpreter of the Constitution, to decide which branch of the federal government has the power to terminate a treaty.
(C) hold that the President's plenary power over foreign policy matters includes the power to terminate treaties without the advice and consent of the Senate.
(D) hold for the plaintiffs because it is constitutionally presumed that if the Senate is required to approve a treaty, then the Senate also must vote to end a treaty.

Answer to Question 19

This question is based on the case of *Goldwater v. Carter*, 444 U.S. 996 (1979), where President Carter sought to unilaterally terminate the treaty with Taiwan. In that case, the Court found that this constituted a nonjusticiable political question. The Court held that, since the Constitution did not address treaty terminations, this was a problem that should be resolved by the President and Congress.

(B) represents one of the arguments made in a dissenting opinion in *Goldwater* where Justice Brennan argued that if there was a question as to who had the constitutional authority in a particular area, the political question doctrine should not apply. However, that argument did not prevail and so is not correct here.

Although one of the factors in determining that a political question existed in *Goldwater* was the fact that this controversy involved the area of foreign relations, which is not an area of judicial intervention, the Court did not reach the merits of the case and therefore (C) is incorrect.

(D) is incorrect because, in *Goldwater*, the Court further argued that when the Constitution is silent in an area, the political process should determine what procedures should be followed. In other words, there are no constitutional presumptions applicable here.

(A) is correct because it states the *Goldwater* holding that would be applicable to this case.

Question 20

The Nova state legislature received numerous petitions from voters in the state who wanted more input into the Presidential nomination process. The voters believe that if their choice is binding on the delegates to the Democratic and Republican Presidential Conventions, the state's nominees will more accurately reflect the desires of the state's citizens and not just the preference of the party delegates. After much debate, the state legislature passed the Binding Primary Vote Act. The Act requires that the state's party delegates vote in accordance with the outcome of the state's Presidential primary results.

For once, both national parties agreed, and refused to seat the delegates from Nova at their respective Presidential Conventions, arguing that it was against party rules and a violation of their constitutional rights to force delegates to vote in conformance with the state primary results. The Nova Supreme Court upheld the Binding Primary Vote Act because it complied with the state Constitution and ordered both parties to comply with Nova state law and seat the delegates from Nova.

On appeal to the United States Supreme Court, which of the following is the most likely outcome of the case?

(A) The Court will decline to hear the case because the decision of the Nova Supreme Court was based on an independent and adequate state ground.
(B) The Court will decline to hear the case because the issues in this case present a nonjusticiable political question.
(C) The Court will hear the case and find for the petitioners unless the state can show a compelling state interest which is vindicated by the Act.
(D) The Court will hear the case and find for the state unless the petitioners prove there is no rational purpose for the Act.

Answer to Question 20

(A) is incorrect because although the state supreme court decided the issue based on state constitutional law, there is an outstanding federal constitutional issue that must be resolved. The Supreme Court must decide whether the First Amendment associational rights of the parties under the federal Constitution have been violated by the state statute.

While an argument can be made that this is a nonjusticiable political question and the state and political parties should resolve their differences without judicial intervention, the First Amendment associational rights of the party delegates override the need for judicial restraint and (B) is incorrect.

The state statute infringes on the political parties' First Amendment associational rights, i.e., their ability to determine the terms and conditions of their membership, and may implicate their fundamental rights to vote. Therefore, the state must prove a compelling state interest to justify interference with this fundamental right. When a fundamental right is at issue, the burden is always on the state to prove a compelling state need. The burden is never on the petitioners and the rational basis test is too low a standard. Therefore, (C) is correct and (D) is incorrect.

Question 21

A statute of the State of Enchantment requires that, six months after enactment, all automobiles sold in the state shall be equipped with a passive restraint system to protect passengers in the event of a collision.

Assume that the United States Supreme Court invalidates the statute as an undue burden on interstate commerce. After that decision, Congress passes a statute permitting each state to require passive restraint systems in motor vehicles sold in that state. If a plaintiff with proper standing challenges the Congressional statute, the Supreme Court will hold

(A) for the plaintiff, because the Supreme Court is the final arbiter of the Constitution.
(B) for the plaintiff, because the Court's prior decision is *res judicata* on the issue.
(C) for the state, because an act of Congress is the supreme law of the land.
(D) for the state, because Congress has the authority to limit the scope of the Commerce Clause.

Answer to Question 21

While the Court is the final arbiter of the Constitution, Congress has the ultimate authority regarding the Commerce Clause. Congress may nullify a Supreme Court decision that a state regulation is an undue burden on interstate commerce by passing legislation authorizing a state to regulate interstate commerce in the manner found unconstitutional by the Court. Congress determines both the positive and the negative impact of the Commerce Clause. The Court must defer to Congress' action because of Congress' plenary power to regulate interstate commerce and must follow these laws despite the Court's earlier decision to the contrary. (A) and (B) are incorrect.

(C) is incorrect because it misstates the reason the Court must defer to an act of Congress under the Commerce Clause. The reason the Court will defer to Congress is because of Congress' plenary power to regulate interstate commerce. Courts can make decisions under the Commerce Clause only when Congress has not spoken. However, in other areas, the Supreme Court does have the power to overturn legislation of Congress, and thus an act of Congress is not necessarily the "supreme law of the land."

(D), which correctly states Congress' authority, is correct.

Question 22

Concerned by the need throughout the country to provide proper disposal facilities for low-level radioactive waste, Congress mandated that each state either provide for such facilities within the boundaries of that state or, in the alternative, be required to take title to all low-level nuclear waste generated in that state and dispose of it in accordance with federal regulations. The State of New Delaware has brought suit against the United States, alleging that the statute is unconstitutional because it mandates that a state carry out federal policy. In the suit, the Court should hold that the act is

(A) constitutional, because Congress can regulate state conduct where it does not affect the core of state sovereignty.
(B) constitutional, because the act regulates an important area of interstate commerce.
(C) unconstitutional, because Congress cannot mandate that a state implement a federal program.
(D) unconstitutional, unless the act regulates only state conduct and does not affect conduct of private individuals.

Answer to Question 22

(A) is incorrect. If Congress has the power to regulate a matter, the fact that it involves the core of state sovereignty is not a valid objection. Moreover, Congress does not have the power to use the commerce power to command that a state implement a federal regulation. *New York v. United States*, 112 S.Ct. 2408 (1992). Congress must either regulate the matter itself or use the spending power to coerce compliance. It cannot order the states to comply.

(B) is incorrect. *New York v. U.S.* held that Congress does not have the power to command that a state implement a federal regulation, even in an important area of interstate commerce. In essence, Congress has the authority under the Commerce Clause to regulate, but cannot use that authority to force a state to regulate.

(D) is incorrect because it is opposite the holding in *New York v. U.S.* This statute is unconstitutional because it applies only to state governments and constitutes an attempt to force the states to regulate, which Congress cannot do. If the statute applied to both private individuals and government entities, it would not come within the narrow exception carved out by *New York v. U.S.* and would likely be constitutional.

(C) is correct because the holding of the Court in *New York v. U.S.* is that the Constitution bars the federal government from commanding that the states implement a federal program, even if similar results could be achieved through incentives under the taxing and spending power.

Question 23

Jonah, a black male fashion model, entered a private restaurant which was frequented almost entirely by local residents. All other customers in the restaurant at the time Jonah entered were white male construction workers. The restaurant purchased a substantial portion of its food from local suppliers who obtained their goods from a variety of sources, both in state and out of state. Jonah was refused service. There was no state statute prohibiting this type of discrimination. If Jonah brought suit in federal court for damages resulting from the refusal of the restaurant to serve him, he would

(A) prevail if Congress had enacted a statute prohibiting such activity under the commerce power.
(B) prevail even in the absence of a Congressional statute, because the activities of the restaurant owner violate the privileges and immunities granted to all citizens under the Fourteenth Amendment.
(C) prevail even if Congress had not acted in the area, because this constitutes a denial of the equal protection of the law under the Fourteenth Amendment.
(D) not prevail even if Congress had enacted a statute prohibiting this activity, because this is local activity which cannot be regulated under the commerce power.

Answer to Question 23

(B) is incorrect. The Privileges and Immunities Clause of the Fourteenth Amendment is a prohibition against state interference with attributes of national citizenship and is inapplicable in a suit against a private individual.

(C) is incorrect. Neither the Fourteenth Amendment nor any other section of the Constitution, except for the Thirteenth Amendment ban on involuntary servitude, prohibits private acts of racial discrimination. Since the Fourteenth Amendment does not provide a cause of action against private individuals, Jonah cannot prevail for this reason.

The modern interpretation of the Commerce Clause permits federal regulation of almost all types of local activity if that local activity affects interstate commerce. The Supreme Court has held that Congress has the power to enact legislation prohibiting even private discrimination under the Commerce Clause. For example, in *Katzenbach v. McClung*, 379 U.S. 294 (1964), the Court sustained that portion of the Civil Rights Act of 1964 which prohibited discrimination in private restaurants, if a substantial amount of the food consumed in the restaurant moved in interstate commerce, on the ground that discrimination in restaurants impeded interstate travel. Therefore, (A) is correct and (D) is not.

Question 24

The Federal Wage and Hour Law provides that all nonsalaried employees are entitled to be paid at one and one-half times their regular hourly rate of pay for each hour which they work in any week in excess of 40 hours. The Commonwealth of Colony provides by statute that state police officers shall be compensated for hours worked in excess of 40 in any week at their regular rate of pay and shall have their work hours in the subsequent week reduced by the hours in excess of 40 which they worked the previous week.

If the United States Department of Labor challenges the validity of the law of the Commonwealth, the court would find it

(A) invalid because Congress has the power under the Commerce Clause to regulate the wages and hours of employees who are engaged in essential functions of state government.

(B) invalid because Congress can ensure that police officers earn adequate pay under its police power.
(C) valid as an exercise of the power reserved to the state under the Tenth Amendment.
(D) valid because the police officers perform a local function and do not affect interstate commerce.

Answer to Question 24

(B) is incorrect. Congress has no "police power." The police power belongs to the states. Congress' only comparable power is the power to spend (not regulate) in support of the general welfare.

(D) is incorrect. The Supreme Court decisions in the 1930's broadly expanded the scope of activities which can be regulated by Congress under the Commerce Clause. The "local function" analysis is no longer applicable. *San Antonio Metropolitan Transit Authority*, 469 U.S. 528 (1985), held that the federal minimum wage law applies even to state employees. The Supreme Court thereby essentially removed any judicially imposed limits on the power of Congress to regulate state activity under the Commerce Clause. The Tenth Amendment will not bar the application of a federal statute promulgated under the commerce power from applying to the state. Thus, if Congress can legitimately regulate a particular area, as it can here, those regulations are applicable to the state and its agencies. (C) is incorrect and (A) is correct.

Question 25

In an attempt to conquer lung cancer, Congress passed a law which imposes a seventy-five cents per pack tax on each pack of cigarettes sold in the United States and directs that the proceeds of the tax be paid to three leading cancer research hospitals in Boston, New York and San Francisco. A court would most likely rule the act

(A) constitutional under the Commerce Clause.
(B) constitutional under the taxing and spending power.
(C) unconstitutional because of the unreasonable amount of the tax compared to the value of the product.
(D) unconstitutional because a revenue source has been directly tied to a spending project.

Answer to Question 25

(A) is incorrect. The Commerce Clause is always a good answer when it comes to supporting federal legislation, unless there is a provision of the Constitution more specifically related to the legislation in question. This statute does not involve regulation of interstate commerce and is clearly authorized under the taxing and spending power. Therefore, the Commerce Clause is not the best answer.

(D) is incorrect. Under Article 1, Section 8 of the Constitution, Congress is empowered to impose taxes. As part of this taxing authority, Congress may dedicate the tax revenues to a specific purpose.

There are very few limitations on the taxing and spending power. Congress can make a judgment concerning which institutions might best use cancer research funds and that judgment, if rational, will not be overturned by the courts. Therefore, this legislation is constitutional under the taxing and spending power, and (B) is correct. Congress can further impose a tax on cigarettes which might be almost confiscatory, but it would still be constitutional if it has a revenue purpose. Therefore, (C) is incorrect.

Question 26

State U. is a state university in the State of Purgatory. The State U. Pharmacy School manufactures a drug called "Campusil" in its pharmaceutical school laboratories to help students safely stay awake while studying for exams. State U. sells the drug through its campus bookstore only to members of the college community.

Congress has passed a law levying a tax on the sale of "Campusil." The State of Purgatory

19

brings suit against the United States challenging the validity of the imposition of the tax. A federal judge hearing the case should rule that the tax is

(A) an interference with the sovereign function of the state.
(B) unconstitutional, as the imposition of sales taxes is a method of taxation which is proper only for the states.
(C) unconstitutional as a direct tax which must be apportioned among the states.
(D) a valid exercise of the federal taxing power.

Answer to Question 26

The federal government has the power to levy a tax upon instrumentalities of a state as long as the instrumentality is not one that can only be operated by a sovereign. Since the pharmaceutical business can also be run by private entities, the federal government has the power to tax it. Thus, (A) is incorrect.

(C) is incorrect because the tax is not a direct tax and therefore does not fall under the constitutional mandate that it be levied proportionately among the states. The only types of taxes which are direct are "head" taxes on population and ad valorem property taxes. A sales tax is neither.

Article I, Section 8 of the Constitution gives Congress the power to impose taxes subject to the uniformity, direct tax, and export tax limitations. A federal sales tax would not violate any of these three limitations. Therefore, sales taxes are not a method of taxation exclusively reserved to the states and the federal government may impose a sales tax on the sale of the drug Campusil. Thus, (B) is incorrect and (D) is correct.

Question 27

Congress has passed an election reform law after holding hearings in which it gathered extensive evidence concerning the corruption of the political process by the presence of large contributors and by the cost of political campaigns. The legislation sets overall spending limits on political contributions by individuals and organizations, requires contributions and expenditures to be reported to a body that makes the reports public, and provides financing for political campaigns.

Another section of the act provides for payments by the United States to individual candidates, on the condition that they agree to limit their overall spending in accordance with amounts prescribed in the statute. Assume that Dork, a candidate for the United States Senate, accepted the funds from the U.S. Treasury, spent more on the campaign than was prescribed in the statute, and raised the unconstitutionality of this provision as a defense. Which of the following statements best describes the constitutional principle appropriate to the decision?

(A) The General Welfare Clause is a limitation upon the power of Congress to regulate individuals.
(B) Congress may spend for the general welfare and condition those expenditures so as to limit an individual's freedom in a way it could not accomplish by direct regulation.
(C) Congress has the power to place expenditure limitations on candidates because of its power to regulate federal elections.
(D) Congress has no power to limit the expenditure of funds in a political campaign because such a limitation unreasonably restricts the core of First Amendment freedoms.

Answer to Question 27

(A) is incorrect. The spending power for the general welfare is not a **limitation** on the power of Congress, but rather is a grant of power.

(C) is incorrect. The Court in *Buckley v. Valeo*, 424 U.S. 1 (1976), held that a direct limitation on expenditure of a candidate's own funds was unconstitutional. Thus, it appears that Congress does not have the authority to regulate a candidate's expenditures, except indirectly, through its spending power.

(D) is incorrect. This is a correct statement of the limitations on the congressional regulatory power, not the spending power. Congress can condition the expenditure of federal funds on the recipient's compliance with stated requirements, even if those requirements impinge on the rights of the recipient.

(B) is correct. Congress may condition the receipt of funds upon the candidate's agreement to act in a manner in which it could not require him to act. Although the Court in *Buckley v. Valeo*, 424 U.S. 1 (1976), held that a direct limitation on expenditure of a candidate's own funds was unconstitutional, it sustained Congress' power to finance federal elections, and to condition the payment of these election funds on the voluntary acceptance of the expenditure limitations.

Question 28

Congress has enacted a law making it a federal crime for an individual to negotiate a contract with a foreign government without permission of the President. Davidson, without the authority of the President, went to Syria to negotiate the withdrawal of Americans in captivity and was indicted for his actions. Which of the following is the strongest argument that the indictment is valid?

(A) Congress may enact the statute pursuant to its power to regulate foreign commerce.
(B) Congress may enact the statute pursuant to its power to regulate for the general welfare.
(C) Congress may define prohibited actions to effectuate the exclusive power of the national government to conduct foreign relations.
(D) The President has inherent power to conduct the foreign relations of the United States. By negotiating with a foreign government without the President's permission, Davidson is infringing on that power.

Answer to Question 28

(A) is incorrect because this Act is not directed toward Congress's role in regulating foreign commerce. It is an act designed to deter interference with the President's power over foreign affairs.

(B) is incorrect because Congress may only spend, not regulate, for the general welfare.

Since this question involves an indictment for a crime, the defendant is entitled to notice that his action is criminal. He could only be indicted for violation of a statute, not for infringing on the President's inherent power. Therefore, (D) is incorrect.

Congress has a role in foreign relations in that it must appropriate funds necessary to carry out foreign policy. Incident to its defined powers, it has the right to further the power of the President and preserve the monopoly of the federal government over foreign relations. Therefore, (C) is correct.

Question 29

Congressman Green has been indicted for conspiracy to use improper influence on the Justice Department to prevent a tax fraud investigation of his former business partner. The government desires to show that, as part of the conspiracy, the Congressman made a speech on the floor of the House at a relevant time urging a cutback in appropriations for the Internal Revenue Service. White is Congressman Green's legislative aide and speechwriter. The prosecution has called him as a witness and has inquired concerning the circumstances of the preparation of that speech.

Upon objection, the Court should hold that White

(A) need not answer the questions because a Congressional aide is protected by the Speech or Debate Clause when preparing a speech for the floor of the Congress.
(B) need not answer the questions because the Speech or Debate Clause protects all confidential communications between a Congressperson and his or her aide.
(C) must answer the questions because the Speech or Debate Clause does not protect speeches when they are the subject of a criminal prosecution.

(D) must answer the questions because the Speech or Debate Clause only protects speeches made on the floor of the Congress and not relations with Congressional aides.

Answer to Question 29

(B) is incorrect because the Speech or Debate Clause does not create a general privilege between a member of Congress and his or her aides.

(C) is incorrect because, under the Speech or Debate Clause, the deliberative process on the floor of Congress is a protected activity even when it is relevant to a criminal investigation. This immunity extends to civil as well as criminal proceedings. *Doe v. McMillan*, 412 U.S. 306 (1973).

A Congressional aide who assists with the legislative process by preparing a speech to be delivered during a legislative session is protected under the Speech or Debate Clause. *Gravel v. United States*, 408 U.S. 606 (1972). Therefore, (D) is incorrect and (A) is correct. Notice also that (A) and (D) are opposites. When two answers are directly opposed to each other, one of them is usually the correct answer.

Question 30

Congress has enacted a statute which gives individuals the right to view any file which the government has assembled concerning that individual. The President is considering the appointment of Iliya Kuryakin as an ambassador to East Slavia, and has requested that appropriate government agencies conduct a background investigation. The investigation revealed some derogatory information, and the President declined to appoint Kuryakin. After his attempts to view the file were refused by the White House staff, Kuryakin brought an action to inspect his personnel file under the aforementioned act.

What is the strongest argument in favor of the constitutionality of the statute?

(A) Individuals must have access to their own personnel files to protect their rights against government deprivation.

(B) The right of inspection by the subject is necessary to maintain the accuracy of government personnel files.

(C) An individual who is the subject matter of a government personnel file has a constitutional right to view it.

(D) Congress may establish reasonable rules dealing with custody of and access to government files.

Answer to Question 30

(A) and (B) are incorrect because they are general policy arguments and do not identify a specific constitutional source of congressional power to enact the statute. Therefore, they are not good answers since there is an answer which more directly supports this legislation.

(C) is incorrect because no constitutional right of access to government personnel files exists.

The federal property power gives Congress the authority to dispose of government property, including personal property such as government personnel files, and to regulate its use, and therefore (D) is correct.

Question 31

Because of severe budget restraints, state officials of Calizona have reviewed every possible cost-cutting measure. Everyone agrees that the state can save a substantial amount of money if changes are made in the state election process in the many Hispanic communities by eliminating the need for ballots and instructions printed in both Spanish and English and just having Spanish-speaking officials at the registration and polling sites. To accomplish this objective, the state legislature passes an election statute which requires that all citizens in communities with a population that is 55% or more Hispanic take and pass a Spanish literacy test to be eligible to vote. The Asian-American community is outraged. They argue that they are in effect disenfranchised by this legislation because there is also a large Asian-American population in the predominantly Hispanic communities, and most Asian-Americans are not fluent in Spanish and so would not be able to vote. A group of concerned Asian-American citizens brings their complaint to the U.S. Attorney General, who orders the state to cease and desist the tests. The state files suit in the Supreme Court against the Attorney General alleging that her orders are unconstitutional.

Which of the following arguments supports the state's claim that the Attorney General's actions are not authorized by the Fifteenth Amendment?

   I. The Supreme Court has upheld the constitutionality of literacy tests for voting.
   II. Only the courts can provide remedies for violations of the Fifteenth Amendment.

(A) I only
(B) II only
(C) both I and II
(D) neither I nor II

Answer to Question 31

The Voting Rights Act of 1965, passed pursuant to Congress's power under the Fifteenth Amendment, gave the primary responsibility for enforcing voting rights to the Justice Department. The Act also suspended literacy tests for voting. Although the Supreme Court had previously upheld the constitutionality of literacy tests in *Lassiter v. Northampton County Board of Elections*, 360 U.S. 45 (1959), the provisions of the Act supersede prior caselaw and literacy tests are now unlawful. The constitutionality of the Act was challenged in *South Carolina v. Katzenbach*, 383 U.S. 301 (1966), but the Court upheld these provisions under the congressional power to implement the Fifteenth Amendment, which guarantees that the right to vote may not be denied because of race. Therefore, the Attorney General is authorized to remedy the infringement on the Asian-American community's right to vote in Caligonia and the tests are unlawful. Since both arguments will fail, (D) is correct and the remaining choices are incorrect.

Question 32

Reza, an Iranian national, attempted to kill the former Shah of Iran while the Shah was confined to a New York hospital. Reza was tried in New York for the crime of attempted murder, and sentenced to ten years in prison. Meanwhile, opponents of the Shah took hostages at the American embassy in Teheran to protest the entry of the Shah into the United States. One of the conditions for release of the hostages was the release of Reza from a New York jail. The President, to comply with this condition, pardoned Reza and ordered him released. The strongest argument available to the Governor of New York in declining to release the prisoner is that

(A) when the governor of a state acts pursuant to the state constitution, he is exempted from regulation by the federal government.
(B) the President, under the constitutional mandate to execute the laws, must honor any valid judgments of state courts.
(C) the President's power as Commander in Chief does not extend to state prisoners.
(D) the presidential pardon power does not extend to Reza.

Answer to Question 32

(A) is incorrect. The issue in this question is not a conflict between state and federal law, but the scope of the Presidential pardon power. Moreover, even if there was a conflict between state and federal regulations, the federal law would prevail over the state constitution under the Supremacy Clause.

(B) is incorrect because the President has an obligation to execute the laws of the United States, not those of any individual state. Therefore, this choice has no relevance to the President's constitutional authority.

(C) is incorrect because the President's power as Commander in Chief extends to the criminal justice system, but only in time of war and only to military personnel. This is not a good argument because the President is not acting in his capacity as Commander in Chief, but is attempting to exercise his Presidential pardon power under the Constitution.

Article II, Section 2 of the Constitution gives the President the power to grant pardons only for offenses against the United States. Therefore, the Presidential pardon power extends to federal crimes only, not to state crimes. Since Reza committed a state crime, attempted murder, the President has no power to release him and (D) is correct.

Question 33

Congress has enacted the War Powers Act (over a presidential veto), providing that the President must withdraw any troops from foreign hostilities within 60 days of committing them, unless he receives congressional authorization to continue the hostilities. The President has sent troops into the foreign state of Libran, where they have engaged in hostilities for a period of 60 days. A resolution was presented to each branch of Congress to continue the hostilities beyond the 60-day period, but the resolution was defeated in each branch. The President refuses to withdraw the troops at the end of the 60-day period. If this controversy is referred to the judicial branch and the court decides in the President's favor, it will most likely be on the basis that

(A) the President has plenary power to engage the U.S. in foreign hostilities short of declaring war.
(B) the President has the power to continue foreign hostilities pursuant to his power over foreign relations.
(C) the President has the power to continue foreign hostilities pursuant to his power as Commander in Chief.
(D) U.S. statutes cannot reach actions in foreign countries.

Answer to Question 33

(A) is incorrect because it takes an unnecessarily expansive view of the President's power and it does not relate that power to specific constitutional authority.

(B) is more definite and therefore better. Nevertheless, (B) is incorrect because, while the President has considerable power over foreign relations, that power is not as closely related to this action as the power as Commander in Chief.

(D) is incorrect because Congress does have the power in many cases, such as the regulation of foreign commerce, to reach actions in foreign countries. Further, the War Powers Act is legislation directed towards the authority of the President to deploy troops and not the foreign actions themselves.

The answer to this unresolved issue depends upon the scope of the President's power to deploy troops without the approval of Congress. The most obvious source of that power is his constitutional power as Commander in Chief of the Armed Forces. Therefore, (C) is correct.

Questions 34 and 35 are based on the following fact situation.

As a result of an ongoing Congressional investigation into attempted assassinations of foreign leaders, the President authorized the Attorney General to appoint a special prosecutor with broad powers to investigate and prosecute anyone committing criminal conduct relating to those acts. The Attorney General appointed Brenda Starr to this position. After a lengthy investigation, Starr presented evidence to the grand jury which resulted in the indictment of Carey, the ex-director of the CIA, for conspiracy to kill the Prince of Wales. Carey has indicated that his principal defense is that he was specifically ordered to develop an assassination plot on the Prince by the President at a meeting in the President's office. Carey also alleges that the President kept notes of the meeting, showing that Carey was so ordered. To prepare the case, the special prosecutor has summonsed the notes of that meeting.

34. The President's counsel filed a motion to quash that subpoena, but the district court

denied the motion. On appeal, the United States Supreme Court should

(A) quash the subpoena, because the subject matter relates to diplomatic and military secrets.
(B) quash the subpoena, because this is a dispute within factions of the executive branch, and therefore not a justiciable controversy.
(C) quash the subpoena, because a President has the right to confidential and unbiased advice from his subordinates.
(D) uphold the district court, because executive privilege must give way when matters relevant and admissible in pending criminal trials are summonsed.

35. If the President removed the special prosecutor from office for serving a summons upon him, and the dismissal were challenged in court, the court would hold

(A) for the special prosecutor, because she was appointed by the Attorney General, who thus had the sole power to remove her.
(B) for the special prosecutor, because the removal was an act of attainder.
(C) for the President, because of his constitutional authority to appoint executive officers.
(D) for the President, because Congress has authorized the removal of executive officers of the United States by the President.

Answer to Question 34

(B) is incorrect because the Court in *United States v. Nixon*, 418 U.S. 683 (1974) held that it is possible for a special prosecutor to sue the President in certain circumstances and present a justiciable controversy.

(C) sets forth the elements of the qualified executive privilege, but that privilege will not protect these documents.

(D) correctly states the holding of *Nixon*. However, the *Nixon* Court said in dicta that courts will not make further inquiry if the claim of privilege is made in the areas of military and diplomatic secrets. Unlike the case of *Nixon*, this case involves the operation of the foreign policy of the United States. Therefore, it appears that such material is absolutely privileged. (A) is correct and (D) is incorrect.

Answer to Question 35

(A) is incorrect because any power the Attorney General has as a subordinate of the President to remove individuals is derived from the power of the President.

(B) is incorrect because an act of attainder is an act by the legislature which punishes a specific individual or class of persons. Thus, only a removal or punishment by Congress would be an act of attainder, not a removal by the President. Unless Congress constitutionally limits the removal authority, the President enjoys broad removal power over federal officers (except judges). *Meyers v. United States*, 272 U.S. 52 (1926).

(D) is incorrect because the source of the removal authority is constitutional. It is an incident of the appointment power and it is not based on an act of Congress. *Meyers v. United States*.

Pursuant to the appointment power, the President has complete constitutional authority to remove all high-ranking executive officers of the United States, whether appointed by him or by a subordinate. Therefore, (C) is correct.

Question 36

After a lengthy investigation of the activities of the Counter-Intelligence Agency ("CIA"), Congress decided that, in order to control the agency effectively, greater Congressional participation in agency affairs was required. It therefore amended the CIA's enabling legislation to provide that whoever holds the position of Chief of Staff of the Joint House and Senate Intelligence Committee shall be the deputy director of the CIA.

Assuming a challenge by the CIA reaches the Supreme Court on the merits, the Court would hold

(A) that the statute is unconstitutional because no Senator or Representative can hold an office in the executive branch of government.
(B) that the statute is unconstitutional because of the doctrine of separation of powers.
(C) that the statute is constitutional because the deputy director is not an officer of the United States.
(D) that the statute is constitutional because Congress has specific authority to oversee the CIA and therefore has the power to appoint a person to regulate it.

Answer to Question 36

(A) is incorrect. While it is true that senators and representatives cannot hold office in the executive branch, the deputy director whose appointment is in issue is neither a senator nor a representative, but an employee of Congress, so this statement is inapplicable to this case.

The deputy director of the CIA **is** an officer of the United States because the CIA is part of the executive branch. Article II, § 2 of the Constitution vests the appointment of officers of the United States in the President alone. Congress may not vest itself with the power to appoint individuals unless such appointments are incident to the legislative function, because such an exercise of power would violate the principle of separation of powers under *Buckley v. Valeo*, 424 U.S. 1 (1976). Therefore, since only the President has the power to appoint the deputy director of the CIA, who is an officer of the United States, (B) is correct and (C) and (D) are incorrect.

Question 37

The Securities and Exchange Act of 1990 authorized the Securities and Exchange Commission to issue rules regarding the identity of all participants in any hostile takeover attempt. The Act provides that, before issuing those rules, the agency must publish the proposed rule in the Federal Register at least 60 days before it becomes effective, and must hold hearings in at least Washington DC, New York, and Los Angeles at which interested parties can comment on the proposed rule. In a severable provision, the statute also provides that otherwise valid rules issued by the agency under authority delegated to it by this statute may be set aside by a majority vote of a designated standing joint committee of Congress.

The provision of this statute relating to the power of the designated standing joint committee of Congress is

(A) unconstitutional, because it authorizes a legislative change of legal rights and obligations by means other than those specified in the Constitution for the enactment of laws.
(B) unconstitutional, because it denies due legislative process to members of Congress who are not appointed to the joint legislative committee authorized to set aside rules of this agency.
(C) constitutional, because rulemaking is essentially a legislative function and, therefore, Congress has greater freedom to intervene in the adoption of rules than it has to intervene in the adjudicatory functions of an administrative agency.
(D) constitutional, because it is a necessary and proper means of ensuring that the rules issued by this agency are actually consistent with the will of Congress.

Answer to Question 37

(B) is incorrect because it is the lack of appropriate legislative process, rather than the denial of due process to the members of Congress who are not on the joint committee, which makes the veto procedure unconstitutional.

Even though rulemaking is a legislative function, Congress cannot retain control over rulemaking by an agency by any means other than the constitutional process by which it enacts legislation. Therefore, (C) is incorrect.

Congress has the power to delegate rulemaking authority to an independent federal agency. It likewise has the power to limit that rulemaking authority and to change rules by

26

legislation. However, Congress cannot delegate this legislative function to a committee. (A) is correct and (D) is incorrect.

Question 38

Armand, the leader of an international drug cartel, was tried and convicted on various federal drug trafficking and conspiracy charges, and his mansion in Florida was seized by drug enforcement officials.

Aside from his drug activities, Armand is also a very successful businessperson and has advised the President in many of the President's personal business affairs. To show his gratitude to Armand, the President pardoned him, but the government officials refused to return his Florida property under the rationale that, although Armand was pardoned, he was still guilty and they could keep the fruits of his crimes.

Armand filed suit in federal court for the return of his property and the federal court held, in accordance with previous Supreme Court decisions, that the Presidential pardon proved his innocence. The court therefore ordered that the property be returned to Armand. The federal government immediately appealed to the Supreme Court.

Congress was dismayed that all the efforts and money spent to capture Armand were for naught and, while the appeal was pending, Congress passed a statute which declared that a Presidential pardon was not proof of innocence and that any property taken as a result of illegal drug activity should remain the property of the government with no right of appeal to the Supreme Court.

If Armand challenges the constitutionality of the statute, the Supreme Court will most likely hold that the statute is

(A) constitutional, because the Court is not authorized to review an act of Congress.
(B) constitutional, because under Article III, § 2 of the constitution, Congress has unlimited authority to make exceptions to the appellate jurisdiction of the United States.
(C) unconstitutional, because Congress is infringing on the role of the judicial branch.
(D) unconstitutional, because it is an impermissible ex post facto law.

Answer to Question 38

(A) is incorrect. Although there is no specific constitutional authorization for the Supreme Court to review an act of Congress, the Court in *Marbury v. Madison*, 1 Cranch 137 (1803), held that the power of judicial review stems from the Court's power to decide cases. If a case comes before the Court, and that law is challenged as repugnant to the Constitution, it is the duty of the Court to determine the constitutionality of the legislation (even if the act concerns the Court's own jurisdiction). Therefore, the Court can properly exercise jurisdiction in this case.

(B) is incorrect because, as described above, Congress' power is not "unlimited." In *Ex parte McCardle*, 7 Wall. 506 (1869), the Court gave a broad interpretation to Congress's power to make exceptions to the appellate jurisdiction of the Supreme Court, but it did not confer upon Congress unlimited power in this area.

(D) is incorrect because this is not an ex post facto law. This law does not make an activity criminal that was lawful at the time of performance. Here, Armand's activities were unlawful at the time of performance and continue to be. Therefore, this is not a ground for holding the statute invalid.

The Supreme Court in *United States v. Klein*, 13 Wall. 128 (1872), held that although Congress has broad power to control the appellate jurisdiction of the Supreme Court, it cannot use that power to control the outcome of a particular case. In essence, the statute in question is an attempt by Congress to decide the merits of the case and is an unconstitutional infringement on the authority vested in the judicial branch. Therefore, (C) is correct.

Question 39

There is a high demand for U.S. arms in many third world countries. Vice President

Grouse saw an opportunity in that fact to become a billionaire overnight. He conspired with various Pentagon and CIA officials to sell arms to the country of El Vis, which was a bitter enemy of many United States allies. Once the money started to roll in, Grouse began to brag about his success to "trusted" aides and Congresspersons. When President Hedge heard of these activities, he launched a full-scale investigation into the matter. After obtaining a substantial amount of evidence against Vice President Grouse, he presented the findings to Congress, which immediately commenced impeachment proceedings.

Which of the following is the only correct statement about these proceedings?

(A) The House of Representatives has the sole power to impeach.
(B) A two-thirds vote of Congress is required to convict.
(C) Only the President, not the Vice President, may be impeached.
(D) A criminal prosecution is not constitutionally permitted after an impeachment proceeding.

Answer to Question 39

(B) is incorrect because a two-thirds vote of the Senate, not the entire Congress, is required for conviction. (After impeachment, the case is tried in the Senate.)

(C) is incorrect because the Vice President can be impeached. Article II, §4 of the Constitution provides that the President, Vice President, and all civil officers of the United States can be removed from office by impeachment and conviction.

The Constitution provides that an impeachment conviction results in no more than removal from office and disqualification from holding any other federal office. However, the Constitution also provides that the officer can still be subject to criminal prosecution in addition to the impeachment proceeding. Therefore, (D) is an incorrect statement.

The House of Representatives has the sole power to impeach, an action akin to indictment in a criminal case. Therefore, (A) is the only correct statement about these proceedings.

Question 40

The State of Nirvana has adopted a state Clean Air Act, which both imposes limits on the amount of sulfur dioxide which can be emitted from electrical generating stations in the state powered by oil, and prescribes that limestone scrubbers meeting precise specifications be installed on every oil-fueled generator in the state capable of generating more than ten megawatts of electricity. Assume that there is no contradictory federal statute on this matter.

The federal government operates an oil-fueled generating station in the state under a contract with a private corporation. The plant has 11 megawatts of capacity, but is maintained solely to power federal government facilities. The station does not exceed the sulfur dioxide emission requirements because it uses a low-sulfur fuel, but it has not installed limestone scrubbers.

If the state environmental agency charged with enforcement of the state statute prosecuted the private operator of the power plant for violation of the state statute, the court would find the operator

(A) guilty, because the regulation of pollution is a joint concern of the federal government and the state and, therefore, both of them may regulate conduct which causes pollution.
(B) guilty, because the regulation of pollution is a legitimate state police power concern.
(C) not guilty, because the violations of the state pollution-control standards involved here are so *de minimis* that they are beyond the legitimate reach of state law.
(D) not guilty, because the operations of the federal government are immune from state regulation in the absence of federal consent.

Answer to Question 40

(A) and (B) are incorrect because the state cannot use its police power to regulate a federal activity absent federal consent.

(C) is incorrect because it does not matter whether the violation of the law is great or *de minimis*.

In this question, the state has passed the regulatory legislation but the federal government owns the facility the legislation seeks to regulate. Here, the Supremacy Clause comes into play, making the federal government immune from state regulation unless it consents to be regulated. (D) is correct.

Question 41

When it closed the Clinton Navy Yard in the city of Hope, the federal government leased a portion of the repair facility to the Inhalation Company, an air filtration firm. The lease provided that if the company were required to pay real estate taxes, it could deduct the amount so paid from the rent, but the lessor would have the right to contest the tax. The city immediately imposed a tax upon the Inhalation Company's use and occupation of the premises. The tax was measured by multiplying the value of the buildings leased by the local real estate tax rate. If the Inhalation Company and the federal government were to contest the tax,

(A) they would not prevail because the city has an absolute right to tax the possession of real estate within the city limits in a nondiscriminatory manner.
(B) they would not prevail if the tax was nondiscriminatory, unless Congress specifically exempted this type of transaction from local taxes.
(C) they would prevail because it is actually a tax on the federal government because of the tenant's right to deduct the tax payments.
(D) they would prevail because it is actually a tax on the federal government because it is measured by the value of the government buildings.

Answer to Question 41

(A) is incorrect because the doctrine of intergovernmental immunity would prevent the municipality from levying even a nondiscriminatory tax on the federal government. *McCulloch v. Maryland*, 17 U.S. (4 Wheat) 316 (1819). Moreover, Congress could specifically exempt this type of leasehold from taxation, and the state taxing statute would then be unconstitutional because of the Supremacy Clause.

(C) is incorrect because, although a state or a municipality is not permitted to levy a tax which falls directly on the federal government, it is permitted to levy a tax on a private individual, even if that taxing statute places an economic burden upon the federal government. *City of Detroit v. Murray Corp.*, 355 U.S. 489 (1958).

(D) is incorrect because the tax is on the leasehold interest of the tenant. Therefore, the tax is not legally on the federal government.

The tax is not directly on the federal government and the method of taxation is nondiscriminatory. Only if Congress had exempted this type of transaction from local taxes would the federal government be able to defeat this tax under the Supremacy Clause. Therefore, (B) is correct.

Question 42

The State of Oklahoma - citing the low sulfur content of coal mined in the state of Oklahoma, the necessity to protect the air quality in the state, and the energy wasted if coal is transported over great distances when there is a local supply available - mandated by statute that 10% of the coal used in any coal-fired power plant in the state capable of generating in excess of 100 megawatts of electricity be mined in the state of Oklahoma.

The State of Wyoming is not in the business of mining coal, but imposes a severance tax of three dollars per ton on the coal mined in Wyoming. It has brought an original action in the Supreme Court of the United States asking that the Oklahoma statute be declared

29

unconstitutional. The State of Oklahoma has filed all necessary motions to dismiss the case prior to a hearing on the merits. What is the most likely resolution by the United States Supreme Court?

(A) Dismiss the action because the State of Wyoming will not be directly harmed by the statute and therefore does not have standing to challenge it.
(B) Dismiss the action because the State of Wyoming is bringing this action on behalf of its coal producers, and the *parens patriae* doctrine does not extend to the protection of economic interests in a state.
(C) Hear the case on the merits and find that the statute is a valid health and safety measure.
(D) Hear the case on the merits and hold the statute unconstitutional because it is in violation of the Commerce Clause.

Answer to Question 42

In the case of *Wyoming v. Oklahoma*, 112 S.Ct. 789 (1992), the United States Supreme Court found that Wyoming had both standing and the right to invoke the original jurisdiction of the Court, because it was directly harmed by the loss of severance tax revenue. Therefore, (A) is incorrect.

(B) is incorrect because Wyoming does not need to rely on the *parens patriae* doctrine here. The state itself will suffer direct loss from the statute.

The health and safety concerns of Oklahoma can be accomplished by less restrictive means than mandating use of local resources, and the statute directly discriminates in favor of local commerce and against interstate commerce. *Wyoming v. Oklahoma*, 112 S.Ct. 789 (1992). Therefore, (D) is correct and (C) is incorrect.

Question 43

The state of Merryland is the home of preeminent medical research and testing facilities. The blood test for AIDS antibodies was developed at Janes Hotchkiss University in that state. Anxious to prevent the use of blood transfusions which have been contaminated with the AIDS virus, the legislature of Merryland enacted a statute prohibiting the use in any medical facility in the state of Merryland of any blood or blood derivative which has not been tested and declared to contain no AIDS antibodies by a testing facility located in the state of Merryland and approved by the Commissioner of Health of the state of Merryland.

The Mayonaze Clinic is an established, reputable hospital system with a large hospital in Merryland, as well as hospitals in several other states. The Mayonaze Clinic has a long-term contractual relationship with a large, state-of-the-art blood-testing facility located in the state of Road Eyeland to perform blood tests for all of the hospitals associated with the Mayonaze Clinic.

The clinic petitioned the Commissioner of Health of the state of Merryland for her approval to use blood which is tested at the Road Eyeland facility at its Merryland hospital. The Commissioner, citing the statute, refused. The Mayonaze Clinic, alleging that the statute as applied to it was unconstitutional, sued to enjoin her from preventing the use of blood tested for the AIDS virus at the Road Eyeland facility from being used in its Merryland hospital. In that suit, the court will find for

(A) the plaintiff, because the statute imposes an unreasonable burden on interstate commerce.
(B) the plaintiff, because the statute impairs the obligation of contract.
(C) the defendant, because the statute is valid under the police power, since it is directly related to public health.
(D) the defendant, because the statute is reasonably related to the integrity of the blood supply in the state of Merryland.

Answer to Question 43

A state has the right to take reasonable measures to protect the health and safety of its citizens under the state police power. However, a state does not have the power to discriminate against out-of-state entities, even to meet valid police power goals, unless the state regulations are the least restrictive means available to achieve a proper goal. *Dean Milk v. City of Madison*, 340 U.S. 349 (1951).

(B) is incorrect because a valid exercise of the police power may validly abrogate preexisting contracts without impairing their obligation in a constitutional sense. For example, if the state of Merryland reasonably found that the Road Eyeland facility was not performing proper tests for the AIDS virus, it could refuse to accept tests from that facility despite the preexisting contract. Here, we have an exercise of police power which is only invalid on Commerce Clause grounds.

(C) and (D) are incorrect. Even though blood testing is a valid exercise of the police power, it must be done within the limitations of the negative implications of the Commerce Clause. That is, it cannot discriminate against out-of-state commerce in favor of local commerce. This statute violates that principle, because there is no showing that an out-of-state entity could not provide the same quality of service.

Restriction of testing to in-state facilities is not the least restrictive means available to accomplish Merryland's goal, since testing facilities in other states may be able to provide the same services just as well. (A) is correct.

Question 44

After the legislature in North Virginia, an East Coast jurisdiction, made an investigation of the amount of gasoline consumed in automobile racing, it passed a statute prohibiting automobile racing in North Virginia. For the past ten years, the Western Auto Racing Association has rented the Doomsday Dragway in North Virginia to stage its Eastern Regional Elimination Tournament, in which members of the association from the western states competed in a preliminary elimination tournament. If the association should bring suit to challenge the constitutionality of the statute, the court should hold it

(A) unconstitutional unless authorized by Congress.
(B) unconstitutional, because all of the participants in the race are engaging in interstate commerce.
(C) constitutional, because the local interest in conservation outweighs the burden on interstate commerce.
(D) constitutional, because the business of racing is operated for a profit.

Answer to Question 44

The regulation at issue is not an unconstitutional burden on interstate commerce because it applies equally to in-state and out-of-state automobile racers. Its constitutionality is not determined by whether the commerce affected is a profit-making industry. Furthermore, a state does not need authorization from Congress to regulate based on health and safety interests of the state. The source of authority to regulate for health and safety is the state police power and any regulation passed pursuant to that authority is constitutional as long as it is rational and does not violate other constitutional provisions. Thus, neither (A) nor (B) nor (D) sets forth the proper holding in this case and all are incorrect.

(C) is the correct answer. A uniform regulation which is designed for a valid state purpose, and which affects both in-state and out-of-state persons or entities equally, will be upheld if it has a rational purpose, such as conservation.

Questions 45 and 46 are based on the following fact situation.

The State of No. Fear provides by statute: "No person may be awarded any state construction contract without agreeing to employ only citizens of the state and of the United States in performance of the contract."

45. In evaluating the constitutionality of this state statute under the Supremacy Clause, which of the following would be most directly relevant?

(A) the number of aliens currently residing in No. Fear
(B) the treaties and immigration laws of the United States
(C) the need of the state for this particular statute
(D) the general unemployment rate in the nation

46. If the No. Fear statute is attacked as violating the Commerce Clause, which of the following defenses is the WEAKEST?

(A) The statute will help assure that workers with jobs directly affecting the performance of public contracts are dedicated to their jobs.
(B) The statute will help assure a continuously available and stable work force for the execution of public contracts.
(C) The statute will help assure that only the most qualified individuals work on public contracts.
(D) The statute will help protect the workers of the State of No. Fear from competition by foreign workers.

Answer to Question 45

This question asks you to evaluate the state statute under the Supremacy Clause. Therefore, there must be a federal law, constitutional provision or treaty against which to evaluate the state statute. Choices (A) and (C) provide possible reasons why a legislator might vote for the statute, but neither gives a reason to invoke Supremacy Clause principles. (C) is incorrect because there is no balancing test in Supremacy Clause analysis - the state's need for a statute is irrelevant.

The national unemployment rate may be relevant in evaluating the statute's constitutionality under the Commerce Clause, but not under the Supremacy Clause. The Supremacy Clause controls those situations where there is a conflict between federal law, interests, or policies on the one hand and state law on the other. (D) is incorrect.

If the treaties and immigration laws of the United States grant aliens or foreigners the right to work, the state statute would be in conflict with federal law and therefore would be invalid under the Supremacy Clause. (B) is correct.

Answer to Question 46

(A), (B) and (C) all deal with public contracts. When a state acts as a market participant and not a regulator, it has the right to discriminate between in-state and out-of-state commerce for any rational reason. Thus, if the attack on the statute were in relationship to a public contract, the state might prevail for this reason. See *White v. Massachusetts Council of Construction Employers, Inc.*, 460 U.S. 204 (1983). Therefore, these choices are all incorrect.

(D) is the weakest defense for the statute, because it is directly contrary to the common-market principles for which the Commerce Clause stands, namely, that workers should be able to travel freely from state to state, and that local workers should not be protected to the detriment of other workers. Therefore, (D) is correct.

Question 47

Scientists have recently discovered that a chemical which can be synthesized from the sap of the tropical yew tree is very effective in treating upper respiratory infections. The chemical cannot yet be synthesized in a laboratory and tropical yew trees will grow only in the swampy marshes of Florida. Florida has passed legislation imposing a substantial tax on the sap extracted from tropical yew trees in the state. The sap is often then processed outside of the state for distribution to patients who are predominantly not citizens of Florida. Is the Florida tax statute constitutional?

(A) Yes.
(B) Yes, if the money raised by the tax is dedicated to the expenses of maintaining the tropical yew tree forests.
(C) No, because of the Equal Protection Clause.

32

(D) No, because of the Privileges and Immunities Clause of Article IV, Section 2.

Answer to Question 47

(B) is incorrect because there is no requirement that the revenue raised by the tax be used to maintain the forests. Since Florida can tax this activity and the only purpose appears to be to generate revenue, there are no restrictions on the expenditure of that revenue (provided that the expenditures do not violate some other provision of the federal constitution, such as guaranteed fundamental rights).

This state tax statute does not violate the federal constitution. The fact that the state is the sole supplier of a product does not affect its ability to tax the item, if the tax is not designed to discriminate against nonresidents. As long as the tax applies equally to residents and nonresidents, it will not fail as a result of the application of the Privileges and Immunities Clause of Article IV, Section 2. Even though there may be a disproportionate effect on nonresidents as a result of their disproportionate use of the chemical, the fact remains that a nonresident can extract sap and purchase the chemical at the same price as a resident of the state. The fact that the state may have chosen to tax this item heavily because the burden would fall more heavily on nonresidents is not relevant. See *Commonwealth Edison Co. v. Montana*, 453 U.S. 609 (1981) (a tax on coal mined in-state was upheld, despite 90% of the coal being shipped out-of-state, where the coal consumed in-state was taxed at the same rate as the coal consumed out-of-state). Since the statute does not discriminate against a suspect class or affect a fundamental right, the statute need only pass the rational basis test to satisfy the Equal Protection Clause. This statute would seem to pass that test. This is not the type of tax statute which would require the application of the Commerce Clause, since it does not appear to unconstitutionally burden interstate commerce. Thus, (A) is correct and (C) and (D) are incorrect.

Question 48

Competition between milk producers in the State of Madison is generally between smaller, less efficient local producers and larger, out-of-state concerns that can produce milk more efficiently and cheaply. In which of the following situations would the action of the state in controlling milk prices violate the Commerce Clause?

(I) Madison establishes a minimum retail price at which milk can be sold in Madison. The statute applies by its terms to milk produced both in Madison and outside of Madison.

(II) Madison establishes a minimum price which wholesale buyers must pay for milk from the milk producers if the milk is to be sold at retail in Madison. The statute applies by its terms to milk produced both in Madison and outside of Madison.

(A) (I) only
(B) (II) only
(C) both (I) and (II)
(D) neither (I) nor (II)

Answer to Question 48

In situation (1), the state is only establishing a floor on the retail price at which milk can be sold in its own state. It hurts the consumers in Madison and helps producers whether or not they are local or out-of-state. Moreover, both local and out-of-state producers have complete freedom of price competition. Therefore, there is no effect of discrimination against out-of-state producers in (I) and this statute thus would not violate the Commerce Clause.

On the other hand, in situation (II), the state, in an attempt to protect inefficient in-state producers, is attempting to place a floor on the price at which out-of-state **producers** can sell milk in Madison. Since the statute has the effect of insulating the inefficient local producers from more efficient out-of-state competition, it violates the Commerce Clause in (II). See *H.P. Hood v. Dumond*, 336 U.S. 525 (1949).

Since the statute in (I) is constitutional and the statute in (II) is not, (B) is the correct answer.

Question 49

In recent years, various organizations have formed throughout the United States whose stated purpose is to relocate all minority groups to areas outside the United States. They have attempted to accomplish this goal through violence and physical transport of minority persons across U.S. borders. They ultimately plan to take over local and state governments, as well as the federal government, so that they can "legally" realize their objectives. In response to these activities, various states have passed statutes making it unlawful to conspire to use any elected government position for discriminatory purposes. The federal government has a similar statute making these activities a federal crime.

A newly elected senator who is a member of the group called Aryans Rule is prosecuted under the state statute of Wyomaine and seeks an injunction in federal court to enjoin prosecution under the state statute, arguing that the federal statute preempts prosecution under the state statute. The federal court will

(A) deny the injunction because there is no conflict between the federal and state law and therefore the Supremacy Clause does not apply.
(B) deny the injunction because the federal law does not specifically prohibit state legislation in this area.
(C) grant the injunction because the state statute is at odds with a federal interest.
(D) grant the injunction because, when there is a federal and state law governing the same activity, the federal law always takes precedence under the Supremacy Clause.

Answer to Question 49

(A) is incorrect because a direct conflict between a state and federal statute is only one way to invalidate the state statute under the Supremacy Clause. State statutes also will be invalidated if the federal government has preempted the field, if the statute inhibits federal policies, or, as in this case, there is an overriding federal interest in the field which supersedes the state interest.

Likewise, federal regulation does not have to specifically prohibit state regulation to preempt that field, making (B) an incorrect answer. For example, the Court can find preemption if the federal regulation is complete and comprehensive, thereby proving congressional intent to retain exclusive control in that area.

There are situations where a federal and state law can regulate the same area without implicating the Supremacy Clause. Unless the federal government has preempted the field and permitted no state regulation in an area, a state act which furthers the general policies of a federal act is usually upheld. For example, although Congress has enacted numerous statutes prohibiting racial discrimination, state statutes prohibiting discriminatory practices in other situations have been upheld because they further an important federal policy. See *Colorado Anti-Discrimination Commission v. Continental Air Lines, Inc.*, 372 U.S. 714 (1963). Thus, (D) is incorrect.

If this statute only involved state and local governments, it would not be invalid under the Supremacy Clause. However, in *Pennsylvania v. Nelson*, 350 U.S. 497 (1956), the Court invalidated a state statute which attempted to regulate subversive activity aimed at overthrowing the state and federal governments. The Court reasoned that the need for uniformity and the federal interest in protecting its government superseded any similar state interest in that area and therefore (C) is correct.

Question 50

The Federal Aviation Administration (FAA) has enacted a regulation which prohibits firearms from being carried on any plane in interstate travel. However, a state law of the state of Las Venas requires all Las Venas police officers to carry their service revolvers with them at all times while they are on duty. Officer Keno, a detective on the state police force of Las Venas, is scheduled to fly to a neighboring state to pick up a prisoner who is being extradited to the state of Las Venas to stand for trial. If, in the proper proceeding, Officer Keno objects to the application of the FAA regulation to her on the basis of the Las Venas state law, will she succeed?

(A) Yes, because state law will prevail over an agency rule.
(B) Yes, because the federal government is prohibited by principles of federalism from interfering in necessary state matters.
(C) No, unless the agency rule is not properly adopted.
(D) No, under the Commerce Clause.

Answer to Question 50

The former rule that the U.S. Congress could not use the Commerce Clause and the Supremacy Clause to enact legislation which interfered with traditional state governmental functions has been reversed. The current rule is that federal law will prevail over state law, even in areas of traditional state governmental functions, as long as the effect on the state is only incidental and the federal legislation was not enacted specifically to apply to state governments alone. See *Garcia v. San Antonio Metropolitan Transit Authority*, 469 U.S. 528 (1985). This rule was not enacted to apply specifically to state officers; it applies to all airline passengers. Therefore, it will not fail for the reason set forth in (B) and that choice is incorrect.

(D) is an incorrect answer. The Commerce Clause may be the source of Congressional power to establish the Federal Aviation Administration, and thus the indirect authority for this agency rule. However, the question is not whether the rule is valid, but whether it will prevail over a contradictory state law. The correct answer is that it will, **under the Supremacy Clause.**

(C) states that the federal agency rule will prevail over the state statute if the rule was properly adopted. That is true. A regulation of a federal agency, if it is properly adopted, has the status of federal law. Since this choice contains the fact which gives the agency rule the status of federal law, it will prevail over any conflicting state law under the Supremacy Clause. Therefore, (C) is correct and (A) is incorrect.

Question 51

In order to extend the working lives of citizens of the United States, a federal statute prohibits discrimination on account of age for all persons between the ages of 50 and 70 in matters relating to employment. A Sunshine State constitutional provision requires that all state judges retire at age 65. Solomon, a respected judge in the Sunshine State trial court, has reached his 65th birthday, and the governor of the State has named his replacement. If Solomon refuses to retire and brings suit in federal court to enjoin the governor of Sunshine from replacing him on the bench,

(A) Solomon will prevail because the Supremacy Clause invalidates the state constitutional provision.
(B) Solomon will prevail only if Congress can legislate under the Fourteenth Amendment to protect a class if discrimination against that class would be subject to the strict scrutiny test.
(C) Sunshine State will prevail because the Eleventh Amendment prohibits the suit.
(D) Sunshine State will prevail, because federalism requires that the federal government not interfere with matters central to the efficient administration of state government.

Answer to Question 51

(B) is incorrect because the Fourteenth Amendment is not the only source of power for Congress to pass such legislation. Congress could enact this legislation under the commerce power, for instance.

(C) is incorrect. Under *Ex parte Young*, 209 U.S. 123 (1908), a suit against a state officer to prevent him from enforcing a state statute that is contrary to federal law does **not** violate the Eleventh Amendment.

Under the holding of *Garcia v. San Antonio Metropolitan Transit Authority*, 469 U.S. 528 (1985), federal legislation which is generally applicable to both private and state entities is constitutional, even if it has the incidental effect of controlling the operation of state governments. Therefore, (A) is correct and (D) is incorrect.

Question 52

Congress has passed a statute authorizing the President to issue executive orders controlling the price of gasoline. The President then issues an executive order revoking all price controls on gasoline, stating that she finds all such price controls to be detrimental. Thereafter, Mary Island passes a law which provides that gasoline distributors cannot sell imported gasoline at a lower price than locally produced gasoline. If a corporate distributor of gasoline from outside of Mary Island sues to have this statute held unconstitutional, the corporation's best argument would be

(A) the Equal Protection Clause.
(B) the negative power of the Commerce Clause.
(C) the Supremacy Clause.
(D) the Privileges and Immunities Clause of the Fourteenth Amendment.

Answer to Question 52

(A) is incorrect because this is economic regulation, which need only satisfy the rational basis test. If there is any rational basis to support this statute, it will survive that test. Since the statute does not seem wholly irrational, (A) is not the best argument to defeat it.

A statement by the President that price controls are detrimental is not the same as a federal statute either occupying the field or declaring that states may not regulate the price of gasoline. Therefore, although a Supremacy Clause argument could be made, it is not a terribly persuasive one, and since there is a better choice, (C) is not the corporation's best argument.

The Privileges and Immunities Clause of the Fourteenth Amendment protects only those rights guaranteed as an incident of national citizenship. Therefore, (D) is incorrect, although it may be noted that the Privileges and Immunities Clause of Article IV, §2 would have provided a good argument to defeat this statute.

Even where Congress has not acted, a state statute may violate the negative (or "dormant") power of the Commerce Clause by discriminating against interstate commerce. The case may be even stronger here where Congress has given the President (and presumably **only** the President) the power to regulate the price of gasoline. This statute acts to discriminate against interstate commerce, because it insulates local distributors from the effects of competition from out-of-state distributors who may be more efficient. Therefore, this statute could be held unconstitutional under the Commerce Clause. (B) is correct.

Question 53

A zoning ordinance of Oldtown, an urban community in Calexico (a western state), requires that in every parcel of land that is subdivided for residential purposes, one acre of contiguous open space shall be provided for each ten dwelling units. The ordinance provides that the open space either be left in its natural condition or be used for playgrounds, golf or tennis. There is no requirement that either lot owners in the subdivision or the public at large have access to the open space.

James has just completed a subdivision with 1,000 residential units and, in accordance with the ordinance, transferred 100 acres to the Swingers Country Club, a private club, under terms which require them to develop the land for a golf and tennis facility.

After the recreational facilities had been constructed, Indira, a citizen of India who owned one of the dwelling units in the subdivision, applied for membership in the Swingers Country Club. Although many owners of dwelling units in the subdivision are members of the golf club, ownership is not an automatic qualification for membership.

The board of directors of the Country Club refused to admit Indira to membership. The reason stated by the directors is that membership is open only to citizens of the United States and, as an alien, Indira is ineligible for membership.

If Indira brings suit in federal court challenging Swingers' refusal to grant her membership,

(A) Indira will prevail, because she has not been granted the privileges and immunities afforded to the citizens of the state of Calexico.
(B) Indira will prevail, because the Equal Protection Clause of the Fourteenth Amendment forbids discrimination on the basis of alienage except in sensitive governmental positions.
(C) Swingers Country Club will prevail, because alienage is not a suspect classification under the Fourteenth Amendment when the discrimination does not involve employment.
(D) Swingers Country Club will prevail, because constitutional restrictions are inapplicable to its rights to admit members.

Answer to Question 53

(A) is incorrect. The Article IV Privileges and Immunities Clause protects a nonresident from discrimination by the state based upon the fact that he does not reside in the state. This Clause is not applicable here because the facts here do not indicate that the discrimination was based upon out-of-state residence and, even if there was discrimination based on nonresidence, it is on the part of a private organization, not the state.

(C) incorrectly states the scope of alienage as a suspect classification. It extends to areas beyond employment. In any event, the Equal Protection Clause is inapplicable because this is not state action.

To find a violation of the Equal Protection Clause, Indira must show state action. Here, there is no state action because the discrimination is an act of a private organization which had no public franchise or support. Furthermore, the ordinance requiring that land be set aside for recreational purposes does not encourage or require discrimination on the basis of alienage and will not satisfy the state action requirement. Therefore, since there was no state action as is required for the Fourteenth Amendment to be applicable, (D) is correct and (B) is incorrect.

Question 54

African-Americans comprise 70% of the school population in the city of Jackson in the State of Dixie. That city is surrounded by four suburbs in which blacks comprise only 5% of the school population. The four suburbs and the city of Jackson comprise Lee County. After lengthy hearings, a federal district court judge found that the Lee County school system was segregated as a result of deliberate actions by public officials. The judge may order a remedy which includes busing between Jackson and the four suburban communities

(A) if she finds the action reasonably necessary to achieve integration of the Lee County schools.
(B) if she can devise a reasonable plan to allocate the costs of the plan fairly, and can set up an appropriate administration between previously independent school districts.
(C) if she finds that actions of Lee County officials caused the segregation.
(D) under no circumstances, because they are separate governmental units.

Answer to Question 54

The correct answer to this question depends upon the origin of the official action which resulted in the unconstitutional segregation. If the official action was confined to one municipality, the remedy is likewise confined to that municipality. See *Milliken v. Bradley*, 418 U.S. 717 (1974). On the other hand, if the county were a participant in the official action which caused the segregation, then a remedy beyond the municipal boundary would be appropriate. Therefore, (C) is correct and (A) and (B) are incorrect.

(D) is incorrect because a remedy which includes more than one community is permissible if the segregation was caused by officials of a governmental unit comprising more than one municipality.

Question 55

The City of Athenea makes a large commitment to the physical fitness of its youth. It has constructed public skating rinks which are available free of charge to both public and private high schools for both practice and interscholastic competition. Each public and private high school in the city is given an allowance for hockey uniforms and a grant to help defray coaching salaries.

Spartan High School was founded in the 1930's by a group of Athenean businessmen who established Spartan as an all-male school based on the rigorous physical discipline and austerity of ancient Sparta. Spartan High School is exempt from federal and state taxation. It is funded in part by private donations, and in part by a city-funded "school choice" program which provides the parent(s) of each student who attends a private secular school with a tuition tax credit. Spartan sports teams excelled and the school took full advantage of the public aid to athletic activities.

When Spartan High won the state hockey tournament, the team's coach, Garry Heart, was interviewed on television. When asked about life at Spartan High School, Coach Heart said, "My boys sure wish they had some girls for classmates and I don't blame them."

When the chairman of the board of trustees of Spartan saw the television interview, he immediately fired Heart as coach.

Coach Heart has sued Spartan High School in the appropriate federal district court, alleging that the termination violated his constitutional rights. The most likely outcome of that suit is that

(A) Spartan High School will succeed because it did not violate Heart's constitutional rights with respect to either free speech or due process.
(B) Heart will succeed because Spartan High School violated his right to free speech by firing him based upon the content of his remarks.
(C) Heart will succeed because Spartan High School denied him procedural due process by failing to afford him a hearing before terminating his employment.
(D) Spartan High School will be held to have violated Heart's constitutional rights unless Heart was an at-will employee.

Answer to Question 55

Before an individual's Fourteenth Amendment rights can be violated, there must be a finding that the entity alleged to be violating those rights has engaged in "state action." State action is shown when the entity is either engaged in a strictly public function or took actions which had significant state involvement. *Gilmore v. City of Montgomery*, 417 U.S. 556 (1974).

If the state action requirement were satisfied in this case, (B), (C) and (D) might support Heart's claim. If Heart had an employment contract sufficient to give him a property right, then the school would have been required to give Heart a hearing regarding his termination. Also, the school would not have been able to terminate Heart's employment on the basis of his exercise of his right to speak on a public matter which did not reflect directly on his job performance.

However, the Spartan School is a private educational institution. Its non-exclusive use of a public hockey rink and its acceptance of public assistance in its athletic program do not constitute significant state involvement with the school. Since state action cannot be shown, the school has not violated Heart's constitutional rights. (A) is the correct answer and the other choices are wrong.

Question 56

Anciano, elderly and infirm, was a patient in the Last Stop Nursing Home. He was receiving "level-three" care for which the United States government, through the state, reimbursed the nursing home at the regulated rate of $60 per day. The licensure, staffing levels, and physical facilities at the home are regulated by the state. When Anciano's health improved slightly, the administration of the home transferred him to a portion of the home where "level-four" care was given, and the Medicaid reimbursement was reduced to $50 per day. Anciano demanded a hearing, which was denied, and he sued the nursing home, alleging that his transfer was improper. In that action, he will be

(A) successful, because his right to remain in level-three care is a "property" right protected by the Due Process Clause.
(B) successful, because his federal Medicaid benefits were reduced without a hearing required by the Due Process Clause.
(C) unsuccessful, because the action of the administration of the home does not constitute state action.
(D) unsuccessful, because the transfer does not constitute the loss of either a property or liberty right.

Answer to Question 56

Prior to determining whether there are any property or liberty rights at issue in a question, the precedent issue of state action must be considered. The due process rights of the Fourteenth Amendment are not triggered unless the state acts to deprive a person of a guaranteed right. The state funding of a private entity does not in itself constitute state action. See *Blum v. Yaretsky*, 457 U.S. 991 (1982) (state not implicated when patients discharged or transferred from nursing home funded by state). Since there is no state action, there are no due process protections and therefore (C) is correct and the remaining choices are incorrect.

Question 57

State A has recently enacted a statute making it a misdemeanor for any teacher in the public school system to teach any theory of human origin except those which can be supported by demonstrable scientific evidence. Scopes, a public school biology teacher in State A who has satisfied the requirements of standing and who desires to teach the Biblical theory of human origin, has challenged the constitutionality of that statute.

The best argument for the state to uphold the constitutionality of the statute would be

(A) the statute will protect children of families who do not subscribe to the Biblical theory of human origin from exposure to anything but a scientific theory.
(B) the control of the curriculum of the public school is within the power reserved to the states, as long as that curriculum does not violate fundamental constitutional rights.
(C) the statute discriminates against no particular religious sect and prefers the teaching of no particular sect.
(D) the purpose of the statute is only to ensure that theories of human origin will be based upon demonstrable scientific evidence.

Answer to Question 57

(A) and (D) are policy arguments that do not address the source of state power to control the curriculum and are therefore incorrect. (A) is also incorrect on the law because the statute restricts the First Amendment rights of teachers who want to teach **and** students who want to learn Biblical theory.

(C) demonstrates that this statute does not constitute an establishment of religion, but does not deal with the tougher issue of whether this statute violates the First Amendment rights of schoolteachers to free expression and free exercise of religion. The argument in (C) does not address the source of state power to control the curriculum and is therefore incorrect.

The state has the constitutional authority to control the content of the curriculum within the public schools, provided state involvement does not violate any constitutional rights. *Everson v. Board of Education*, 330 U.S. 1 (1947). Therefore, this is the best argument and (B) is correct.

Question 58

Mike and Robin wanted to get married because as soon as Robin is married she will be eligible to inherit a trust fund established by her grandfather. Unfortunately, Mike, who was previously married and has two children by that marriage, was prosecuted under a new state statute designed to go after deadbeat dads who fail to pay child support. He is now serving a one-year sentence in the county jail. Mike and Robin plan to pay the back child support from the trust fund once they are married.

Mike and Robin scheduled their wedding for next Sunday during jail visiting hours, but are informed that they cannot get married until they get permission from the court because the statute under which Mike was prosecuted requires that the court give permission before the father remarries to ensure that the new marriage will not be an obstacle to his child support obligations. The jail administrator also has a policy that requires that an inmate receive his permission to marry, which permission will be withheld if the administrator believes that the ceremony will cause security problems at the facility. To avoid numerous requests, it is his practice to give permission only in those situations where one of the parties to the marriage is terminally ill. The security issue is of some concern because the administrator's budget has been severely cut and he does not have the funds to call in additional officers to monitor the event and the guests. Despite Mike's assurances that he will pay the child support when due and that only Robin and her 80-year-old parents will be present at the ceremony, both the court and the administrator have denied Mike permission to marry.

Under current due process analysis, will Mike and Robin be successful if they bring suit to assert their right to get married as planned?

(A) No, because the state's interest in protecting the welfare of Mike's children and their right to continued support prevails over Mike's desire to marry.
(B) No, because as a prisoner, Mike's rights are subordinate to the effective administration of the facility.
(C) Yes, because the child support law retroactively affects Robin's vested property rights in the trust fund.
(D) Yes.

Answer to Question 58

(C) is incorrect because the issue in this case is Mike's right to marry without interference from the state, not access to Robin's trust fund. The child support law is not intended to interfere with anyone's inheritance rights, but rather to ensure that a father be able to pay his child support obligations. To trigger due process, the statute must directly target a vested property right, as in the case of *Binney v. Long*, 299 U.S. 280 (1936), where a statute that retroactively taxed a vested remainder interest was held unconstitutional.

The right to marry is a fundamental right that is constitutionally protected under the due process clause. Both the denial by the court and the jail administrator are unconstitutional. In *Zablocki v. Redhail*, 434 U.S. 374 (1978), the Court invalidated a state statute which required that persons under a support order obtain the court's permission before marrying. The Court said that the statute was an unconstitutional interference with a fundamental right. Therefore, the requirement that Mike receive the court's permission is invalid and not an obstacle to the ceremony. Likewise, in *Turner v. Safley*, 482 U.S. 78 (1987), the Court held that a prison regulation that prohibited any inmate from marrying except with the permission of the superintendent unconstitutionally interfered with the prisoner's right to marry. Although the Court did leave open whether the prisoner could be denied the right to marry if a serious threat to security existed, the issue of security does not appear to be of concern in this case, given the small number and age of the attendees. Thus, (D) is correct and (A) and (B) are incorrect.

Question 59

The State of Pax has a statute on the books making it a Class 1 criminal misdemeanor to disturb the peace. Anyone found guilty of disturbing the peace is subject to a fine of up to $50. Recently, one of the independent churches in the state has become a scene of picketing because of the outspoken views of the church's pastor in favor of racial discrimination. Thereafter, the Pax state legislature duly enacted a new statute which stated, in relevant part, "Because of the disruption specific to these types of disturbances, it will now be a Class 2 misdemeanor to disrupt a house of worship or other such assembly."

Denise, who was participating in an organized protest on the public sidewalk in front of the church, was arrested and charged with the Class 2 misdemeanor of disturbing the peace. This is the first prosecution under either statute in their entire history. If Denise raises the unconstitutionality of the ordinance as a defense in her criminal prosecution, her best argument would be that the statute is unconstitutional

(A) as applied to Denise's conduct.
(B) as a violation of the Due Process Clause.
(C) as a violation of the Establishment Clause.
(D) as an invalid content-based regulation of speech.

Answer to Question 59

(A) is incorrect because if a statute regulating speech is unconstitutional (e.g., because it is vague or overbroad), it is unconstitutional as to all conduct. It is incorrect to say that it is unconstitutional only as to one person's conduct.

(C) is incorrect because, although an argument could be made, there is no strong evidence that this statute is intended to or has the primary effect of promoting a particular religion or religion in general. Rather, it appears that the statute was enacted to protect the rights of citizens during worship, a time often traditionally reserved for quiet reverie. Also, there does not appear to be excessive entanglement between the church and the state as a result of this statute.

Also, this is not a content-based regulation of speech. It is merely a time, place or manner regulation because it restricts speech on the basis of its location, rather than its content. Therefore, (D) is incorrect as well.

The substantive strand of the Due Process Clause requires that a criminal statute fairly notify a person of reasonable intelligence that the statute forbids certain conduct before the person can be prosecuted under that statute for the conduct. *United States v. Harris*, 347 U.S. 612 (1954). This statute criminalizes disturbing the peace without defining what conduct is thereby criminalized. Also, there are no state court opinions clarifying the conduct criminalized by the statute. Although the facts do not state what type of picket Denise was participating in, the statute does not provide any guidance as to what types of protests would be criminal. This should be sufficient to render the statute unconstitutional and (B) is correct.

Question 60

There are many new members in the state legislature of North Jersey, many of whom campaigned in support of pro-life legislation. To fulfill their campaign promises, these legislators introduced a bill which would make it unlawful to use state money to pay for abortions. They also included the requirement that, before a female can have an abortion, she must obtain the consent of the biological father of the fetus and, if she is a minor, she must obtain the consent of at least one parent. After much debate, the legislation was passed by a narrow margin.

Maria is a 16-year-old girl who is pregnant. Both she and her boyfriend, Tony, acknowledge that he is the father. Although Maria and Tony both come from conservative Catholic families, they have opposing views on the abortion issue. Maria believes that she is too young to care for a child and that it would not be in her or the fetus' best interest for her to see the pregnancy to term. On the other hand, Tony believes that abortion is murder and a mortal sin. Maria does not dare tell her parents because she knows that they will be angry about her behavior and that they will never condone an abortion because of their religious beliefs. With nowhere else to turn, Maria went to the local welfare office and applied for emergency financial assistance to pay for her abortion. At this visit, a social worker advised Maria of the new law and told her that there is no way she will get money from the state to pay for the abortion and, even if she did have the money, she would not be able to get the abortion without the consent of one of her parents and Tony.

If Maria challenges the constitutionality of the abortion law, which of the following provisions will pass constitutional muster?

I. the parental consent requirement
II. the requirement that the biological father consent to the abortion
III. the prohibition against use of state funds to pay for abortions

(A) I only
(B) II only
(C) III only
(D) I and II only

Answer to Question 60

With regard to parental consent requirements, the Court has held that there must be a "judicial bypass" procedure when parental consent is required to protect the interests of the minor child should the parent fail or refuse to give consent. Therefore, to be constitutional, the statute must provide for a judicial hearing as an alternative to the parental consent. *Planned Parenthood of S.E. Penn. v. Casey*, 120 L.Ed.2d 674 (1992). Since the parental consent provision (I) in this statute does not provide for a "judicial bypass," it is unconstitutional.

Likewise, in *Planned Parenthood of Central Missouri v. Danforth*, 428 U.S. 52 (1976), the Court struck down legislation which required that the father give consent to an abortion. The Court said that this requirement was an unconstitutional infringement on the woman's right to privacy, and the decision to have an abortion was hers alone and could not be delegated to another. Thus, provision (II) is unconstitutional.

The Court has upheld prohibitions on the use of public money, both federal and state, to fund abortions. The Court has also upheld the state's right to prohibit use of public facilities and public employees to provide abortions. *Webster v. Reproductive Health Services*, 492 U.S. 469 (1989). Therefore, provision (III) is constitutional.

Since Provision (III) is the only constitutional provision, (C) is correct and all other choices are wrong.

Question 61

The State of Calexico has a policy of hiring new state employees on a provisional basis for a six-month period. If the job performance is satisfactory and a permanent position is available, the employee is then given civil service status. Calexico has followed no consistent pattern with respect to the termination of provisional employees. Some never received permanent positions. Others were given hearings after notice, during which their job performance as provisional employees was discussed. If a provisional employee who was terminated without a hearing challenged the constitutionality of the state's action, the court should rule that

(A) the employee would succeed, because the inconsistent nature of the state's discharge procedure denies her equal protection of the law.
(B) the employee would succeed, because the state's action is an act of attainder.
(C) the employee would not succeed, because a state's procedure with respect to state employees is a matter reserved to the state under the Tenth Amendment.
(D) the employee would not succeed, because she does not have a right to notice and a hearing protected by the Due Process Clause of the Fourteenth Amendment.

Answer to Question 61

(B) is incorrect. A bill of attainder is the punishment of an individual by a legislative act. In this case, there is no statute directed towards any individual, so this constitutional prohibition is inapplicable.

(C) is also incorrect. The state is not immune under the Tenth Amendment to the demands of the federal constitution. Thus, due process must be accorded any state employees who have a property right in continued employment. The state does not need constitutional authority for its discharge procedure here because no property right exists.

An employee who has no expectation of continued employment (i.e., one who has been hired on a probationary basis) has no due process rights regarding termination. Here, because provisional employees have no expectation of a permanent job when they are hired by the state, they have no property right and therefore no entitlement to a hearing and the state's discharge procedure need not be consistent. Thus, (D) is correct and (A) is incorrect.

Question 62

On the day following the United Nations vote condemning Zionism, the parents of ten Jewish children who attended the fourth grade in a local public school gave their children armbands with the emblem of the State of Israel, which the children wore to school that day. During the school day, there was some uneasiness in the classroom, and some other children in the class directed ethnic slurs at the Jewish children. At the close of school, the principal, as a representative of the school committee, appeared in the classroom and told the children not to wear the armbands to school the next day. When the children appeared the next day with the armbands, they were immediately suspended. If the parents of one of the children challenged the suspension on due process grounds, the court would hold for

(A) the school committee, because the students were deprived of neither liberty nor property.
(B) the school authorities, because the principal's warning satisfied the due process requirements.
(C) the parents, because damage to reputation coupled with suspension from school together constitute a property interest of sufficient magnitude for a hearing to be constitutionally required.
(D) the parents, because the damage to reputation is by itself a property interest of sufficient magnitude for a hearing to be constitutionally required.

Answer to Question 62

In *Goss v. Lopez*, 419 U.S. 565 (1975), the Court held that the right to continued attendance at a public school, together with the damage caused to one's reputation by being suspended, is a property right. Therefore, the state must comply with procedural due process before it can suspend a student. The principal's warning does not satisfy due process. The students have a right to a hearing at which they are confronted with charges and a determination is made. Thus, (C), which sets forth the proper due process principles, is correct, and (A) and (B) are incorrect.

(D) is incorrect because it deals only with reputation. One's reputation alone is not enough of a property right for a hearing to be required before the state impugns that reputation.

Question 63

The state of New Z-land has the highest rate of alcohol-related traffic fatalities in the nation. Various automobile associations have even warned their membership to avoid traveling in the state because of the danger on the highways. Seeing a marked decrease in its tourism, the state has become aggressive in its campaign to arrest drunk drivers. As part of this effort, the local and state law enforcement agencies have set up roadblocks on a daily basis to encourage public awareness of the problem and to arrest those who are under the influence.

Soupy is a salesman who travels throughout New Z-land, and he cannot work without his car and his license. Along with his usual sales pitch, he always takes new clients to a local drinking and eating establishment and treats them to dinner and as many drinks as they care to indulge in. It is not uncommon for Soupy himself to consume seven or eight drinks in one evening.

One night, after a long evening with a new client who took full advantage of Soupy's hospitality, Soupy was stopped at one of the roadblocks. He was visibly intoxicated and failed the field sobriety test and was asked to take a breathalyzer test. He was coherent enough to know that he would fail the test and would lose his livelihood, so he refused. Upon his refusal, his license was immediately suspended. Since it was Friday night and there was a large number of arrests clogging the court calendar, the first day that a hearing could be scheduled in the matter was the following Tuesday. Because of the suspension, Soupy was unable to make the sales calls he had scheduled that weekend and lost a number of clients as a result.

Soupy sues the state for violations of his right to due process. In that suit, the court will hold for

(A) the state, because the suspension furthered the state interest in highway safety.
(B) the state, because a driver's license is a privilege granted by the state and therefore is not subject to due process requirements.
(C) Soupy, because he has a property interest in the license and was entitled to a pre-suspension hearing.
(D) Soupy, because he has a constitutional right to refuse to incriminate himself by taking a breathalyzer test.

Answer to Question 63

(D) is incorrect for two reasons. First, this choice does not address a due process issue and therefore is unresponsive to the question presented. Moreover, it is an incorrect statement of law. A breathalyzer test is evidence of physical condition and not testimonial in nature. Therefore, such evidence is not protected by the right against self-incrimination.

Although there was a time when driver's licenses were considered a privilege granted by the state and therefore could be terminated without formal process, current caselaw now holds otherwise. See *Bell v. Burson*, 402 U.S. 535 (1971). Since driver's licenses are frequently necessary for employment, the Court has recognized a property interest in the license, and therefore due process is required to **terminate** the license. However, where the state has a compelling interest in highway safety and there is a right to a hearing after suspension, such as is the case here, the Court has upheld a short-term **suspension** of a driver's license when a person refused to take a breathalyzer test. *Mackey v. Montrym*, 443 U.S. 1 (1979). Therefore, (A) is correct and (B) and (C) are incorrect.

Question 64

Rob and Laura were college students who had a brief but passionate relationship. A few months after the affair ended, Laura gave birth to a son, Richie. On Richie's birth certificate, Laura listed the father as unknown. Laura soon found that baby Richie interfered with her school work and career ambitions and asked Rob to raise Richie. Rob readily agreed.

All was well for a number of years until Rob lost his job as a television comedy writer. After months of unemployment, Rob became clinically depressed and suffered from violent mood swings. The person who suffered the most from these episodes was little Richie, who was hospitalized frequently for contusions and broken bones. Although hospital officials, teachers and neighbors told the state social service agency of their suspicions that Richie was a victim of child abuse, the agency took no action.

Eventually, Richie ran away from home and was found wandering the streets, where he was picked up by the police and sent to Social Services. Richie was placed with a foster family, the Cleavers, who now want to adopt Richie.

While Richie was in foster care, Rob sought psychiatric help and has been able to turn his life around. He is able to control his depression through medication and is gainfully employed in the movie industry. Rob wants Richie to return home. Unbeknownst to Rob, the Cleavers have begun adoption proceedings and received Laura's consent to the adoption. No one has contacted Rob because he is not listed as the father on the birth certificate and there has never been any other proceeding acknowledging that he is Richie's father. Further, because of his past behavior, the social services agency considers him an unfit custodian.

Under current due process standards, which of the following statement(s) is correct?

I. The state did not violate Richie's rights because, even though it was informed of the alleged abuse, it was under no obligation to remove him from the home.

II. The state did not violate Rob's rights because he was never legally named as Richie's father and has proven that he is an unfit custodian, and therefore has no right to notice of the adoption proceeding.

(A) I only
(B) II only
(C) both I and II
(D) neither I or II

Answer to Question 64

The Due Process Clause prohibits a government to act to deprive an individual of a liberty interest, but does not impose an affirmative duty for the government to protect an individual from a deprivation of that interest by another. In *DeShaney v. Winnebago County Department of Social Services*, 489 U.S. 189 (1989), the Court held that since the state had no affirmative obligation to protect a child from physical abuse where the state did not have physical custody of the child, there was no violation of the child's liberty interest in bodily integrity by leaving the child in the custody of an abusive parent. Thus, under *DeShaney*, the social service agency was under no obligation to remove Richie from the home, regardless of their knowledge of the situation.

On the other hand, a parent of a child has a right to notice of any proceeding which will terminate those parental rights, if the parent has either been legally named or has participated in the rearing of the child. Further, that parent has a right to a hearing on whether he is fit to assume the role of parenting the child. *Stanley v. Illinois*, 405 U.S. 645 (1972); cf. *Lehr v. Robertson*, 463 U.S. 248 (1983) (there are no due process protections when the parent of an illegitimate child has not assumed any parenting responsibilities). Since Rob assumed responsibility for Richie for many years, Rob has a right to both notice of the adoption and a hearing on whether he is now capable of caring for Richie.

Since statement (I) is the only correct statement, (A) is the right choice and the other choices are wrong.

Question 65

The State of Vabaria has created a corporation, Wasteco, which is wholly owned by the state, for the purpose of owning and operating sanitary landfills throughout the state. The state Secretary of Environmental Affairs is the holder of all of the capital stock on behalf of the state. The corporation has set up two categories of waste. It charges $10 per cubic yard for Type A waste, and $50 per cubic yard for Type B waste. Property owners in the Town of Frankfurter pay a substantially higher rate for waste disposal than those in the Town of Wiener because their rubbish contains a much higher portion of Type B waste than Type A waste.

If a group of citizens from Frankfurter bring an action in federal court to enjoin Wasteco from charging the differential between Type A trash and Type B trash on an equal protection theory, the court would most likely

(A) hear the suit on the merits, and find for the defendants only if the differential is justified by a compelling state purpose.

(B) hear the suit on the merits, and find for the defendants if the rate differential is rational.
(C) dismiss the suit, because Wasteco is acting like a private corporation and is not subject to Fourteenth Amendment limitations.
(D) dismiss the suit because of the Eleventh Amendment.

Answer to Question 65

The State of Vabaria is involved in the business of providing sanitary landfills for its citizens, and therefore any suit brought in federal court challenging rate differentials will be based on a state action theory. The citizens of Frankfurter may challenge the differentials as a violation of the Equal Protection Clause.

(A) is incorrect. Because categories of waste set up by the corporation are a form of economic regulation, the state's purpose need only be rational, not compelling.

(C) is incorrect. Vabaria's participation in the business constitutes state action and therefore Wasteco is subject to Fourteenth Amendment limitations.

(D) is incorrect because Eleventh Amendment immunity would apply only to a suit by the citizens against Vabaria itself. This immunity does not protect the corporation from a suit by the citizens of Frankfurter.

Because the categories of waste set up by the corporation are a form of economic regulation, the court will uphold the differentials if they serve a rational purpose. Therefore, (B) is correct.

Question 66

In which of the following situations would the United States Supreme Court hold that the state election and districting laws do not violate the Equal Protection Clause?

(A) State A provides that an individual must be a resident in a locality for 90 days before he is eligible to vote.
(B) Town X, in State B, provides that only persons with children in the school system and persons owning property in the school district are eligible to vote in elections for the local school board.
(C) State C elects the lower branch of its state legislature from single-member districts in which the population is approximately equal, and elects its upper branch by having two senators per county.
(D) State D provides that approximately one-half of the legislative districts in the lower branch of the legislature shall have two representatives, and the remaining districts shall have one representative. Those districts having two representatives are in areas which are racially and ethnically homogeneous, and have precisely twice as many registered voters as the average number of voters in districts having one representative.

Answer to Question 66

(A) is incorrect. A durational residency requirement for voting is consistent with equal protection only if it allows only the reasonable time necessary to process voting lists. Fifty days is the longest period which has been upheld. *Marston v. Lewis*, 410 U.S. 679 (1973).

(B) is incorrect. The one person-one vote rule applies even to municipal offices with legislative policy-making functions. All persons in the geographic district who meet minimal residence and age requirements must be eligible to vote for candidates for such offices. This rule applies even to school boards. *Kramer v. Union Free School District*, 395 U.S. 621 (1969).

(C) is incorrect. The one person-one vote rule applies to both branches of a state legislature. The apportionment scheme in State C violates this rule because it does not give equal weight to the vote of each person for the upper branch. The upper branch is based on counties, which may not be equal in population.

(D) is correct. Since there is no racial or ethnic motivation in the creation of multi-member districts, they are constitutional as long as they are proportional in size to single-member districts. It is permissible to use registered voters as well as population as a measure of the equality of districts. *Whitcomb v. Chavis*, 403 U.S. 124 (1971).

Question 67

The city of New Orleans, pursuant to a state enabling act, has prohibited all pushcart vendors of food products from operating in the French Quarter, an important tourist area, unless they have operated in that area for at least eight years prior to the enactment of the ordinance. Connie Croissant, a pushcart vendor who was selling pastries for only two years prior to the adoption of the ordinance, was denied a license to operate a pushcart in the French Quarter, while Bonnie Brioche, who has been vending pastries for twenty years, was granted a license. Connie has brought suit in federal court attacking the validity of the grandfather clause.

What would be the best theory for the city to justify the ordinance?

(A) It is essential to limit the number of vendors to preserve the economic vitality of the French Quarter.
(B) It is in the nature of a zoning ordinance, and therefore reasonable.
(C) It is more likely that vendors with long experience will operate in a manner conducive to the charm of the area.
(D) There is a compelling state need to improve the charm of the French Quarter.

Answer to Question 67

(A) is incorrect because it does not address the issue of discrimination between vendors, which would at least subject the ordinance to scrutiny under the rational basis test.

(B) is incorrect because the question addresses economic regulation, not land use regulation. Moreover, not all zoning ordinances are reasonable by definition, as this choice implies.

(D) is incorrect. Since the ordinance in question is an economic regulation, it need only pass the rational basis test. This choice defines the burden on the state if the ordinance were subject to strict scrutiny.

In the area of economic regulation, a state regulation implicating the Equal Protection Clause is upheld as long as there is a rational purpose to the statute. The Supreme Court held in *New Orleans v. Dukes*, 427 U.S. 297 (1976), that a statute regulating street vendors in the French Quarter and prohibiting vendors who had been in business for less than eight years was reasonable (and therefore valid) based on the state's legitimate interest in preserving the charm of the French Quarter. Therefore, (C) is correct.

Question 68

The intestacy statute of Illini permits illegitimate children whose paternity has been established in judicial proceedings to inherit from their fathers, and denies all other illegitimate children the status of heirs of their fathers.

If Perry's illegitimate daughter Debbie, whose paternity was never adjudicated but who lived with Perry during her entire minority, brought suit to challenge the constitutionality of the Illini statute, the Supreme Court would be most likely to hold the statute

(A) constitutional, because the state has the right to provide for the orderly administration of decedent's estates.
(B) constitutional, because the state has the right to promote family life by encouraging couples to marry and legitimize children.
(C) unconstitutional, because the state has failed to show a compelling need for the classification.
(D) unconstitutional, because the statute impermissibly excludes from inheritance those persons whose paternity can be easily established.

Answer to Question 68

In *Trimble v. Gordon*, 430 U.S. 762 (1977), the promotion of family life was held to be an improper reason to classify on the ground of illegitimacy where the paternity of the child had been judicially determined during the decedent's lifetime, and therefore (B) is incorrect.

This question is based upon a New York intestacy statute, the constitutionality of which was upheld by a closely divided Court in *Lalli v. Lalli*, 439 U.S. 259 (1978). While the reasoning of choice (D) was strongly argued as the reason to hold the New York statute unconstitutional, the orderly administration of estates was held to be a sufficiently compelling state purpose to permit the state to distinguish between illegitimates whose paternity had been established by court decree during the father's lifetime, and those whose paternity had not been so established. Therefore, (A) is correct and (C) and (D) are incorrect.

Question 69

The state university of Academia is comprised of the undergraduate schools of management, arts and sciences, engineering, and education. Although all of the other university schools are open to both males and females, it is the policy of the university to only admit women to its school of medicine because it wants to ensure that no woman who is interested in the field of medicine be denied an opportunity to get a degree in that area. The justification for this policy is that it compensates for past discrimination against women by providing them with a competitive advantage in the school's admission process. Kildare, who is a resident of Academia and cannot afford to attend a private institution, although he has been accepted at a number of them, applied to the Academia school of medicine. He was denied admission based on the "women only" policy.

If Kildare challenges the constitutionality of the admission policy, he will most likely

(A) win, because the policy does not serve an important state need.
(B) win, because there is no compelling state need for the policy.
(C) lose, because the policy remedies the effects of past discrimination against women.
(D) lose, because Kildare's poverty is not subject to a higher degree of scrutiny and therefore the admission policy must only have a rational purpose.

Answer to Question 69

(B) is incorrect because, when there is a claim of gender discrimination, the courts apply an intermediate level of scrutiny, not strict scrutiny, as this choice incorrectly suggests. If there is a gender-based classification, as is the case in this admission policy, the state must show an important state need for that classification. *Craig v. Boren*, 429 U.S. 190 (1976).

(D) does not address the nature of the discrimination involved in this case. The admission policy does not discriminate against Kildare because of his financial status, but discriminates against him because of his gender.

While the Court held in *Mississippi University for Woman v. Hogan*, 458 U.S. 718 (1982), that the woman-only admissions policy of a state-run nursing school violated a male applicant's right to equal protection, the Court has found some gender-based classifications constitutional because they remedy the effects of past discrimination. The Court in *Hogan* rejected the state's argument that it remedied the effects of past discrimination because it did nothing more than perpetuate the stereotype of nursing as a woman's job and failed to enhance the position of women in society.

This analysis could be applied to the case at hand. Because medicine is not considered traditionally a woman's job, (C) is correct and (A) is incorrect (although (A) might be successful if the undergraduate school in question were one that traditionally encouraged female applicants versus male, such as nursing).

Question 70

Because of the threat of terrorist attacks and the hostilities towards Americans in general, the U.S. State Department has implemented a new policy whereby all foreign service personnel in the Middle East must retire at age 55 (versus the mandatory retirement age of 60 for all other foreign service personnel stationed in countries other than the Middle East). All other federal personnel are subject to mandatory retirement at age 70. The government believes that it is in the foreign service employees' best interest to force early retirement so that the older staff is not subject to stressful and dangerous situations and so that the United States is assured that the Middle East positions in particular will be staffed by the strongest and most physically and mentally able persons available.

Ararat, who is age 55, considers himself a very healthy person. He runs 6 miles a day, works out in the gym 2 hours a day and is the most knowledgeable person in the foreign service corps in regard to Middle East history and politics, not to mention the fact that he is fluent in a number of the local languages and dialects. Despite his qualifications, he is advised that he will be subject to the early retirement policy and should be prepared to return to the States in one month.

When Ararat returns to the United States, he sues the federal government and numerous federal officers in their official capacity. The basis of his constitutional claim is that the retirement policy is discriminatory and in violation of equal protection of the laws. Assuming that there is no applicable Congressional legislation in this area, the court will hold the policy

(A) unconstitutional, because it discriminates against personnel in the Middle East versus other foreign service and federal employees.
(B) unconstitutional, because it impermissibly discriminates on the basis of age.
(C) unconstitutional, because the policy is over-inclusive, particularly as it applies to Ararat.
(D) constitutional, because it is rationally related to a government objective.

Answer to Question 70

(A) and (B) are incorrect because age is not a suspect classification and, absent congressional legislation to the contrary, statutes which discriminate based on age have been upheld. See *Massachusetts Board of Retirement v. Murgia*, 427 U.S. 307 (1976) (statute requiring uniformed police officers to retire at age 50 upheld); and *Vance v. Bradley*, 440 U.S. 93 (1979) (requirement that foreign service officers retire at age 60 upheld even though retirement age for federal civil service employees was 70). The fact that there is discrimination also on the basis of the branch of the service does not add to the analysis.

(C) presents an argument advanced in *Murgia*, where the Court upheld a statute requiring uniformed police officers to retire at age 50. The officers argued that the retirement age did not take into consideration those officers over 50 who might be in great condition and capable of working. The Court rejected this argument because it found that, although the state could provide for case-by-case evaluation, it was not constitutionally required to do so.

(D) is correct. In *Vance v. Bradley*, 440 U.S. 93 (1979), the government requirement that foreign service officers retire at age 60 was upheld even though retirement age for federal civil service employees was 70. The Court found that the earlier retirement age was rationally related to the United States' goal of assuring the professional competence, as well as the physical and mental reliability, of the foreign service corps.

Question 71

Jim was a member of the U.S. Army who was stationed in the foreign county of East Slavia for a number of years. He grew to love the country and the people and eventually established a home with one of the local women, Olga, who worked at the base where he was stationed. During their time together, Jim and Olga had two children. When the defense department decided to close the base and send the army personnel home, Jim was devastated. He could not take Olga with him because he still had a wife in the United States. Although he and his wife were estranged, they had not been formally divorced and army policy prohibited him from bringing a foreign woman into the country while he was still married to another.

When the time came to leave, Jim promised Olga that he would immediately divorce his wife and send for her and the children. Shortly after Jim left East Slavia, Olga was killed by sniper fire and the children were placed in an orphanage. When Jim learned of this, he began to make arrangements to have the children sent to the U.S., but was informed that the children could not immigrate to the U.S. because they were illegitimate and the immigration quota for East Slavia had been satisfied. The applicable law stated that when a country's immigration quota was reached, the illegitimate children of a father could not be admitted to the U.S. However, this restriction did not apply to the illegitimate children of a mother.

Jim sought to have this law invalidated as unconstitutional. The federal appeals court agreed with him, and the federal government appealed to the Supreme Court. On appeal, the Court will

(A) uphold the lower court decision because the statute does not serve an important governmental interest.
(B) uphold the lower court decision because the statute does not serve a compelling governmental interest.
(C) overturn the lower court decision because the statute is a constitutional exercise of congressional authority.
(D) overturn the lower court decision because the statute is rationally related to a governmental purpose.

Answer to Question 71

(B) and (D) are incorrect because, in cases involving gender-based discrimination, statutes are generally subject to an intermediate level of scrutiny, not strict scrutiny. Therefore, if this statute were subject to gender-based scrutiny, this would be an incorrect burden of proof. Although the Court has applied the intermediate level of scrutiny to statutes which have afforded greater rights to mothers of illegitimate children than the fathers, the Court has refused to apply this same scrutiny in cases involving immigration. In *Fiallo v. Bell*, 430 U.S. 787 (1977), the Court found a statute similar to this one constitutional based on Congress' broad constitutional authority in the area of immigration. Therefore, (C) is correct and (A) is incorrect.

Question 72

The Police Department of the City of Metro desires to hire an undercover agent to infiltrate a radical gang of African-American revolutionaries which advocates the violent overthrow of the present political system. A confidential memorandum is circulated among police officers interested in undercover details. The job carries a hardship differential equal to 50% of the officer's base pay.

White, a white police officer with substantial experience in undercover work, applies for the position. His application is rejected and he remains on cruiser patrol at base pay. Black, a black police officer, new to the force with no experience in undercover work, is selected for the position. White files suit against the department, alleging that he is the most qualified officer in undercover investigations and that he was rejected solely because of his race. The department admitted that race was the determinative criteria in filling the position. The result of that suit will most likely be that

(A) the department's decision will be upheld as necessary to achieve a compelling interest.
(B) the department's decision will be upheld as rationally related to a legitimate state interest.
(C) the department's decision will be overturned because race cannot be used as a criterion in public job assignments.
(D) the department's decision will be overturned as a violation of the Equal Protection Clause of the Fourteenth Amendment.

Answer to Question 72

The primary criterion for the public job assignment in this case is race. Under the Equal Protection Clause, that classification is only valid when necessary to achieve a compelling interest. This is one of the rare cases which meets this standard. A white police officer would be totally ineffective penetrating an organization in which race is the primary criterion for membership. Since the racial classification in this case will be upheld, (A) is correct and (C) and (D) are incorrect.

(B) is incorrect because the compelling interest standard, rather than the rational purpose standard, is applicable when the classification is by race, as it is here.

Question 73

State X has established a manpower retraining program at the regional vocational high schools in the state, which permits State X residents to obtain vocational skills at night for nominal tuition. Resident aliens are not eligible for the program. Xu is a legal resident of State X, but is not a citizen of the United States. He has been denied admission to the program because of his alien status, unless he pays a tuition which fully reflects the cost of the program. If Xu should challenge the constitutionality of his exclusion from the program, he will

(A) prevail, because the action of the state violates the Privileges and Immunities Clause of Article IV of the Constitution.
(B) prevail, because there is not sufficient justification to discriminate against aliens as a class.
(C) not prevail, because aliens are not per se a discreet and insular minority; therefore, a classification excluding them is valid.
(D) not prevail, because the exclusion is rationally related to legitimate state purposes.

Answer to Question 73

(A) is incorrect because the Privileges and Immunities Clause of Article IV protects nonresidents from discrimination by a state, but Xu is a resident of State X. Therefore, Xu has no claim under the Privileges and Immunities Clause.

The state may discriminate against aliens only in specific matters relating to the governmental process, such as the denial of a right to run for elective office or to hold a position as a police officer or probation officer or a public school teacher. In all other cases, a state's attempt to discriminate against persons based on alienage will be subject to the strict scrutiny test because alienage is a suspect classification. Therefore, (C) and (D) are incorrect and (B) is correct because there is no compelling justification for denying Xu the same educational opportunities offered to other residents of State X.

Question 74

Baker, a 21-year-old white male, applied to law school at Peach State University, a prominent southern university which had been found in 1970 to have unlawfully refused applicants on account of their race in the past. His law school aptitude test score and grade point average were below the lowest score of white applicants admitted. They were substantially above 15 of the 20 black students admitted. The university agreed to hold 20 places in each class for black students, pursuant to a consent decree entered in 1970. If Baker brings suit to require that he be admitted because the university has unlawfully discriminated against him because of his race, the Court would

(A) grant relief because a state may not use race as a criterion in making admissions decisions.
(B) grant relief because a classification solely by race, even to achieve a worthy purpose, is not necessary to satisfy a compelling state need, and therefore violates the Equal Protection Clause.
(C) deny relief because a state may consider race as a factor in admissions when it is attempting to aid disadvantaged minorities and penalizes no particular group.
(D) deny relief because the racial classification is designed to remedy past unlawful discrimination.

Answer to Question 74

(A) is incorrect because race may be used as a criterion for making admissions decisions, provided it is not the conclusive criterion.

Classification by race is permissible if (and only if) it is necessary to remedy past unlawful discrimination. Here, past unlawful discrimination has been found and, therefore, the racial classification does not violate the Equal Protection Clause. Therefore, (B) is incorrect.

(C) is incorrect because it is factually wrong. Peach State University is not merely using race as a factor in admissions, which it may admittedly do; rather, it has set up a quota system and is using race as the primary criterion for admission. Therefore, if the statute is to be upheld, it must be upheld on the basis of the right to use such a racial classification.

Race may be used as a criterion for admissions without violating the Equal Protection Clause and racial quotas may be used to remedy past unlawful racial discrimination. This case is different from *University of California Regents v. Bakke*, 438 U.S. 265 (1978), because the University of California had not been found guilty of past discrimination and was not under a court order to integrate, whereas Peach State could be required to use the quota system because of its past discrimination. (D) is correct.

Question 75

The Federal Center for Disease Control sponsored a study which demonstrated that immigrants to the United States from a particular country, Zengandu, were almost 90% more likely to carry a certain deadly, highly infectious disease than other immigrants. As a result, one state passed a law which provides that persons who have immigrated from this particular country are prohibited from handling food in eating establishments. If an immigrant from the country in question is fired from her job at a restaurant in the state because of the statute and brings suit to challenge its constitutionality, the decision will be

(A) that the plaintiff has no standing, if she is not a legal resident alien.
(B) for the plaintiff, because the statute violates a fundamental right.
(C) for the plaintiff, if there is any less restrictive means to achieve the state's purpose.
(D) for the state, because this is a reasonable application of the state's police power.

Answer to Question 75

(A) is incorrect because even an illegal alien has standing to object to a violation of rights under the U.S. Constitution. A strict scrutiny test would not apply to the analysis, as it would if the alien were a legal resident, but the illegal alien would still have standing and something more than a rational basis test would likely apply.

(B) is incorrect because there is no fundamental right involved here. The United States Supreme Court has not recognized a fundamental right to work. The only other fundamental right that might be involved is the fundamental right to travel, but this statute does not directly limit the right to travel. It does not prevent these immigrants from moving into the state; it only restricts what jobs they can hold once they arrive. The more serious aspect of this statute is that it may affect the rights of foreign nationals to move to this country. This would constitute discrimination on the basis of alienage, which would trigger the application of a strict scrutiny standard.

The fact that this statute is a reasonable application of the state's police power will not save it. This state statute discriminates against persons on the basis of their alienage. Such a statute is subject to a strict scrutiny test. Therefore, this statute is valid only if it is narrowly tailored to meet a compelling government interest. The fact that this statute is "reasonable" would satisfy the rational basis test, but not the strict scrutiny test. It may also help to note that the state probably could validly discriminate against persons with this disease in this arena under constitutional principles, but the fact that they chose to discriminate against aliens invokes a much higher standard of review.

Therefore, (C), which recognizes this higher standard of review, is correct and (D), which would only apply the rational purpose test, is incorrect.

Question 76

Crabby, a resident of Delawhere, was a commercial crab fisherman who crabbed for two months per year in the Chessapeek Bay in Merryland. Effective this year, due to a decline in the number of mature crabs in the bay, the legislature provided that the fee for a commercial crabbing license was $50 per year for a resident and $500 per year for a nonresident. If Crabby challenged the constitutionality of the law under the Privileges and Immunities Clause of Article IV, the Court would find that

(A) it is unconstitutional because a state may not deny a nonresident a livelihood unless that action is necessary to satisfy a compelling state need.
(B) it is unconstitutional discrimination against nonresidents because it does not bear a substantial relationship to the fact that there is a limited number of crabs.
(C) it was constitutional because the state has a proprietary interest in the crabs within its borders, and therefore may discriminate against nonresidents.
(D) it was constitutional because no fundamental interest was infringed.

Answer to Question 76

The United States Supreme Court has held that a state must show a substantial relationship between a statute which discriminates against nonresidents and the purpose for which the statute was enacted. *Hicklin v. Orbeck*, 437 U.S. 518 (1978).

(A) is incorrect because the showing of a compelling state interest is required only under the strict scrutiny standard. That standard is not applicable under the Article IV Privileges and Immunities Clause, where the Supreme Court has applied a "substantial relationship" test.

(C) is incorrect. If a proprietary right to a license is involved, a state may not discriminate against nonresidents merely because it has a proprietary interest in the resources within its borders. The substantial relationship test must be met.

(D) is incorrect because a commercial activity is involved, and therefore Crabby's fundamental right to earn a livelihood may be at stake. However, if this were a case of fishing for sport, the discrimination might be permissible. See *Baldwin v. Fish and Game Commission*, 436 U.S. 371 (1978) (right to hunt elk for sport not a fundamental right and state could discriminate against nonresidents).

This statute does not meet the substantial relationship test because it is not specifically nonresidents who are causing the problem in the crab population. Therefore, (B) is correct.

Question 77

Congress has passed a law requiring every male in the United States to register with the Selective Service System after attaining his eighteenth birthday. Because of widespread disregard of the law, Congress conditioned the eligibility of students to receive federal financial aid for higher education upon proof of their compliance with the registration requirements.

Manning, a 19-year-old male college student who would otherwise be eligible for federal financial aid, challenged the statute's constitutionality on the ground that it constituted a bill of attainder. Which of the following arguments is strongest in support of that contention?

(A) Congress has punished a specific group of persons for their past actions without a judicial trial.
(B) A student is required to incriminate himself if he applies for federal financial aid.
(C) Congress has discriminated against males by refusing to require females to register for the draft.
(D) The statute invidiously discriminates against students who are poor.

Answer to Question 77

(B) is incorrect because there is no issue of self-incrimination here. The student is under no obligation to apply for the aid in the first place.

(C) is incorrect because, in *Rostker v. Goldberg*, 453 U.S. 57 (1981), the registration of males and not females for the military was upheld against a Fifth Amendment equal protection challenge. The Court stated that since the decision not to use women as combat troops resulted from congressional and military findings and was not the byproduct of a traditional way of thinking about women, the discrimination was justified by the important governmental interest of raising and supporting an army.

(D) is incorrect because poverty is not a suspect classification for purposes of equal protection analysis unless a fundamental right is also infringed, which is not the case here. There is no fundamental right to federal financial aid for higher education.

The question asks for the reasoning in support of a bill of attainder argument. A bill of attainder occurs when the legislature punishes a specific individual or group of individuals for past conduct without a trial. (A), which describes this concept, is therefore the correct answer. This argument was sustained at the district court level in the case involving draft registration; however, it ultimately was rejected by the United States Supreme Court in *Selective Service System v. Minnesota Public Interest Research Group*, 468 U.S. 841 (1984). None of the other choices relate at all to an argument that this statute is a bill of attainder (i.e., a legislative punishment).

Question 78

The state of Delmont operated Delmont Law School. In the school year beginning September 1, 1995, the annual tuition at the school was $8,000 for bona fide residents of the state and $15,000 for out-of-state residents.

On March 1, 1996, the state board of regents, pursuant to its statutory authority to set yearly tuition at state institutions, announced a tuition increase of $500 for in-state residents and $1,000 for out-of-state residents for the school year beginning September 1, 1996. The regents held no public hearing on the proposal to increase tuitions.

Tom Kruse, an out-of-state law student who entered his second year of law school on September 1, 1996, challenged the validity of the increase in his tuition for the year beginning September 1, 1996. The most plausible basis on which to challenge this state scheme is

(A) the Impairment of the Obligations of Contract Clause.
(B) the Due Process Clause.
(C) the Equal Protection Clause.
(D) the Privileges and Immunities Clause of Article IV.

Answer to Question 78

(A) is incorrect because there is no existing contract for a specific price for more than one year of school. The change in tuition for an ensuing year is not a breach of a contract and, hence, not an impairment of the obligation of contract.

The state, in setting tuition for future years, is not depriving anyone of a property right protected by the Due Process Clause, since the tuition contract is an annual contract. Therefore, no hearings are necessary to meet the standards of procedural due process, and choice (B) is incorrect.

Although an argument might be constructed, the Equal Protection Clause has traditionally been invoked successfully only where the law challenged discriminated on the basis of race, alienage, gender or age, and therefore (C) is incorrect.

The Privileges and Immunities Clause protects a citizen of one state from discrimination by another state because of the individual's state citizenship. The Privileges and Immunities Clause of Article IV is a much better argument than Equal Protection because this state statute discriminates against nonresidents. While some difference in treatment may be constitutionally sanctioned, the state would be required to justify it. Therefore, (D) is correct.

Question 79

State X has recently enacted a statute requiring all teachers in the public school system who teach any theory of human origin based on Darwinian theory to also teach theories based on established religious doctrines. Scopes, a public school biology teacher in State X who has satisfied the requirements of standing and who does not want to teach religious theories of human origin, has challenged the constitutionality of that statute.

What should the court decide?

(A) The statute is constitutional because the state has an obligation to present to students all sides of a field of learning as important as human origin.
(B) The statute is constitutional because there is no entanglement of church and state.
(C) The statute is unconstitutional as an establishment of religion.
(D) The statute is unconstitutional because the state has no right to control school curriculum.

Answer to Question 79

(B) addresses a separation of church and state argument, which could be raised here, but it reaches the wrong conclusion - a court clearly **could** find entanglement here.

(D) is incorrect as a matter of law. The state **has** the right to control school curriculum. It just cannot do so in a way that violates the Constitution.

In *Edwards v. Aguillard*, 482 U.S. 578 (1987), the Court held unconstitutional a state statute requiring that public schools that teach evolution also teach "creation-science" as well. Such a requirement tends to promote religion and therefore violates the Establishment Clause. (C) is correct and (A) is incorrect.

Question 80

The bishop of a hierarchical church was summarily removed from her post as director of education for the church by those in authority on the ground that she was teaching church doctrine in an improper manner. She has brought suit in a state court against the church, alleging that her dismissal was illegal. The court should

(A) dismiss the case, because her action presents no case or controversy.
(B) dismiss the case, because the First and Fourteenth Amendments prevent the court from deciding such a case.
(C) hear the case, because the court can determine, on neutral principles, if she was in fact teaching church doctrines improperly.
(D) decide in her favor, because the church did not accord her due process when it dismissed her.

Answer to Question 80

A controversy exists, but it is not reviewable by a secular court. The First and Fourteenth Amendments prevent the state from adjudicating ecclesiastical issues. The state may not resolve church disputes in its courts because to do so would violate the Establishment Clause. *Jones v. Wolf*, 443 U.S. 595 (1979). Note, however, that neutral principles of law which do not involve ecclesiastical questions, such as the determination of the meaning and effect of a deed, can be used to resolve cases involving church property. Since this is a controversy that cannot be decided by the court, (B) is correct and (A) and (C) are incorrect.

(D) is incorrect because religious organizations need not accord their members due process rights. Due Process protections are available only when there is state action.

Question 81

Jones is the leader of a religious cult in the state of New Man. The cult has been in existence for over 100 years with a membership in excess of 20,000 people. As a regular part of their weekly worship, cult members kill a white-tailed deer as a sacrifice to atone for their sins.

The state of New Man recently conducted an in-depth wildlife study which concluded that white-tailed deer were dwindling in number and were in danger of becoming extinct. Following publication of the study, New Man passed a law proscribing "any religious, ritualistic animal sacrifice involving white-tailed deer." Hunting is a popular sport in New Man and white-tailed deer are a coveted breed. Although hunting is not affected by the new law, hunting is regulated under separate New Man statutes. The hunting statutes severely limit the times and locations where one can hunt and the number of animals, including white-tailed deer, which can be killed.

Jones has again presided over the sacrifice of a white-tailed deer, and he was arrested for violating the new law. If Jones challenges the constitutionality of the New Man statute, the trial court would

(A) uphold the statute because hunters are the only other group in New Man who kill white-tailed deer and their actions are severely restricted by other statutes.
(B) uphold the statute as a valid, facially neutral statute serving legitimate government interests in environmental protection.
(C) invalidate the statute because the protection of white-tailed deer is an attempt to hoard the species for the benefit of the state's hunters in violation of the Commerce Clause.
(D) invalidate the statute because it singles out religious sacrifice in violation of the Free Exercise Clause of the First Amendment.

Answer to Question 81

(A) suggests an equality of treatment between hunters and members of the religion with respect to the deer, but the equivalence is not established. Again, only religious killings are barred by the statute in question. Hunters, though regulated (and even if regulated severely), are still permitted to kill the deer. Such a restrictive application is impermissible and therefore (A) is wrong.

(C) is incorrect because there is no factual basis for the conclusion in the question. There is nothing to suggest that the statute is a hoarding statute and there is no mention that out-of-staters are barred from hunting. Therefore, the Commerce Clause is inapplicable.

The law violates the Free Exercise Clause because it restricts practices based on their religious motivation. This is not a law that simply bans the killing of white-tailed deer (with a consequent effect on religious practices). Rather, it prohibits only the religious or ritualistic killing of the deer, leaving hunters to kill them for sport. Such a restrictive application is impermissible. *Church of the Lukumi Babalu Aye, Inc. v. City of Hialeah*, 113 S.Ct. 2217 (1993). Thus, (D) is correct and (B) is incorrect because it states a misperception of the law: it is not neutral; it singles out religious killings.

Question 82

The State wants to open a pilot day-care program for abused children and to that end submits the project for open bids, as required by State law. The State can only afford to set up one such pilot program at this time. Of the various bids entered, the lowest bid which met the criteria established by the State was submitted by The Brotherhood of Peaceful Momentum, a religious organization. The Brotherhood's bid is low in part because the building in which the program will be housed is tax exempt under state law because it is owned by a religious group. The Brotherhood has agreed to operate under the conditions of the project contract, including that the program cannot be used to espouse or promote any particular religious views, but studies have shown that children in such situations tend to emulate their caregivers. If the State decides to award the contract to The Brotherhood, would that decision be susceptible to constitutional attack?

(A) Yes, because this would constitute secular aid to a religious group.
(B) Yes, because this would constitute an establishment of religion.
(C) Yes, because the First Amendment rights of freedom of religion and speech accorded to

The Brothers by the U.S. Constitution would be violated by the provision of the state contract prohibiting them from espousing their religious views.
(D) No, because this entanglement is not excessive.

Answer to Question 82

(A) is incorrect. This does not constitute unconstitutional secular aid to a religious group. The government is not in any way subsidizing the promotion of The Brothers' religious belief. The Brotherhood has merely agreed to provide secular services to the state in exchange for money received from the state to cover the expenses of providing those services. The Brothers likely would not provide those services unless the state paid them to do so, so there is no subsidy involved. This situation is most akin to the case of the state providing secular textbooks to religious schools free of charge, which is constitutional.

(B) is incorrect because this would not constitute an establishment of religion. The Brothers would not be allowed to promote their religion as part of their services to the state, and the mere fact that the children may consider the Brothers to be role models is not enough to constitute an establishment of religion.

(C) is incorrect because there is no violation of The Brothers' constitutional rights of free speech and freedom of religion. The government cannot condition the provision of fundamental rights on an individual's agreement to give up their constitutional rights. However, The Brotherhood has no right to this contract to provide day-care services. Therefore, the government can require them to comply with the terms of the contract if they desire to receive its benefits.

(D) is the correct answer. This situation would not constitute an establishment of religion because the primary purpose of the program is secular, its primary effect does not advance religion, and there is not excessive entanglement between the religious organization and the state. There is not excessive entanglement between the church and the state because the contract makes clear that The Brothers are not to use the program to espouse or promote their religious views.

Question 83

Bayside High School is scheduled to conduct its graduation ceremonies in a couple of weeks. Principal Belding is a good friend and follower of the Reverend Becky Grand and was able to convince the Reverend to attend the ceremonies, say an opening prayer and give the commencement address. Although Belding is a devout Christian, he is aware that not all students and parents share his religious beliefs and is sensitive to the constitutional issues surrounding prayer at schools. With this in mind, he has instructed the Reverend to make sure that his prayer is nonsectarian, just a general invocation of blessings, and has even provided the Reverend with a sample prayer which he believes will pass First Amendment scrutiny.

One of the students, Zach, is offended by the ceremony (having been raised in an atheist home) and sues the school for violation of his First Amendment rights. In that case, the court will hold the ceremonies

(A) constitutional, because attendance at graduation ceremonies is voluntary and therefore a student is not compelled to participate in the prayer reading.
(B) constitutional, because the prayer is nonsectarian and therefore does not promote any particular religion.
(C) unconstitutional only if the students are forced to participate in the prayer reading.
(D) unconstitutional, because the prayer is not exempt from Establishment Clause limitations.

Answer to Question 83

This question is based on the Supreme Court case of *Lee v. Weisman*, 120 L.Ed.2d 467 (1992). In that case, the Court held that a prayer at a high school graduation ceremony is not constitutional merely because it is nonsectarian. Even a nonsectarian prayer at a state-sponsored event violates the Establishment Clause because it may still promote religion in general, even if it does not promote any particular religion. The Court found that it was no defense that participation in the graduation or the prayer was voluntary. The Court reasoned that a high school graduation was a significant public, state-sponsored occasion and it was not constitutionally appropriate to subject someone to religious participation in order to attend the event. Further, although the student was not forced to participate per se, there was peer pressure to stand or at least maintain respectful silence and these factors taken together in essence forced the student to participate in the prayer.

The *Lee* Court rejected the arguments in support of the prayer set forth in (A), (B) and (C). (D), which finds the prayer unconstitutional, is correct.

Question 84

Regulations of the United States Postal Service establish certain minimum guidelines for items that may be mailed through the U.S. Postal System. One of these guidelines prohibits items from being mailed that are smaller than 3 inches by 5 inches. Unaware of this regulation, Perrier, a candidate for the United States Congress, has designed and printed a postcard announcing his candidacy and his views to be mailed to every voter in his district. The postcard measures only 2.5 inches by 4 inches. When the postcards are presented to the local U.S. Post Office for mailing, they are rejected by the local postmaster for failure to meet the U.S. Postal Service specifications. Perrier then brings suit to declare the regulation unconstitutional as it applies to this postcard. The outcome of this suit is most likely to be that the statute will be held

(A) constitutional if the postcard could be redesigned and reprinted to meet the Postal Service specifications.
(B) constitutional because it is reasonable.
(C) unconstitutional because this form of speech is highly protected under the constitutional scheme.
(D) unconstitutional because this constitutes a prior restraint on speech.

Answer to Question 84

(C) is incorrect because this is not a content-based regulation of speech. If it were, the fact that this speech is political would entitle it to be accorded a very high level of protection. However, in this case, the regulation is not content-based, but is content-neutral.

(D) is incorrect because there is no prior restraint on speech here. Perrier was not prevented from printing the postcards, and would not be prevented from handing them out on the street. The only problem is that the postcards cannot be mailed because their size does not meet the Postal Service specifications. This specification does not appear to have been designed to discriminate against a particular type of speech.

(B) is the correct answer. This is a time, place, or manner regulation of speech because it does not discriminate on the basis of the content of the speech. Such regulations are constitutional as long as they are reasonable. This regulation is reasonable because it is presumably designed to safeguard the efficient automated operations of the postal system. Further, the regulation is constitutional even if the postcard cannot be redesigned to fit within the specifications and therefore cannot be mailed. Thus, (A) is incorrect.

Question 85

The state of New Hampshire supplies textbooks on American History to all public high schools located in the state. The state education department has promulgated a rule requiring all high school students studying American History to cover their books with a state-supplied book cover which has the state motto "Live Free or Die" on the front and a picture of the Governor of New Hampshire on the back. A student refused to place this cover on his history book and was disciplined for violating the education department regulation. If he should challenge the validity of his discipline, the regulation would most likely be held

(A) valid, because the state is acting *in loco parentis*.
(B) valid, because the books are furnished at school expense.
(C) invalid, because the state cannot force an individual to advertise.
(D) invalid, because a state cannot prescribe the type of book cover to be placed on schoolbooks.

Answer to Question 85

The issue in this question is not the book covers per se, but the message the students are forced to convey. Since (D) does not properly characterize the constitutional problem, it is incorrect.

(A) is incorrect. Even if the state is acting *in loco parentis*, it has no right to impose a particular message on the students. In fact, because it is the state, the state cannot force students to display a message that the students' parents could unofficially force them to display.

(B) is incorrect. Even if the state is paying for the books (or covers), it has no right to impose a particular message on the students.

The government may not require an individual to display a message because to do so would be to regulate unconstitutionally the content of speech. *Wooley v. Maynard*, 430 U.S. 705 (1977). The education department may not impose state-ordained speech on the students and therefore (C) is correct.

Question 86

An ordinance of the City of Metropolis permits a parade on a public street when it is conducted pursuant to a license granted by the chief of police. The ordinance requires the chief to grant a license so long as the parade is conducted on a weekend or holiday and does not block a street for more than 30 minutes. The ordinance also provides that the chief of police shall first determine the cost of the police detail required to provide for order and security at the parade and then collect from the persons in charge of the parade a fee sufficient to reimburse the city for the cost of providing the detail.

"Let Live, or Die," a prominent and militant anti-abortion group, applied for a permit for a parade route which passed in front of a number of abortion clinics. Because the chief of police knew that several abortion rights groups would be present in front of the clinics and feared that a violent clash between the two groups might ensue, the chief determined that a police detail twice as large as was usually assigned was necessary for the parade. The chief conditioned the issuance of the permit on the payment in advance for the beefed-up police detail.

"Let Live, or Die" has brought suit to require the chief to issue the permit without the payment of the fee based upon the size of the police detail. In that lawsuit,

(A) the plaintiff should prevail unless the group intends to interfere with the fundamental right of a woman to an abortion.
(B) the plaintiff should prevail because the ordinance is a regulation based upon the content of speech.
(C) the defendant should prevail because the ordinance is a reasonable regulation of the time, place, and manner of speech.
(D) the defendant should prevail if the chief's determination of the need for additional security was reasonable.

Answer to Question 86

(A) is incorrect because the parade permit is a license to exercise rights of free speech. If the group exercising those rights violates the fundamental constitutional rights of others, the remedy is to punish them for such a violation, not to deny them the right of free speech.

The United States Supreme Court case of *Forsyth County v. Nationalist Movement*, 120 L.Ed.2d 101 (1992), held unconstitutional a statute which allowed a government official to establish, without guidelines, a parade permit fee based upon perceived security requirements, which would inevitably depend on the content of the speech. The Court held that this was an unconstitutional regulation of the content of speech, not a regulation of the time, place and manner of speech. (B) is correct and (C) and (D) are incorrect.

Moreover, note that (C) and (D) are virtually indistinguishable on the law - both state that this scheme is constitutional because it is reasonable. Whenever two choices are so close, the better guess is that they are both wrong.

Question 87

Dick, a 21-year-old white male, was convicted of aggravated battery for the severe beating of a 40-year-old black woman. The jury found that Dick had selected his victim based on race. Aggravated battery has a maximum sentence of two years. As a result of the jury's findings, however, Dick was sentenced to seven years. The basis for the longer sentence was a state statute which provides for enhancing or increasing a penalty whenever the defendant "intentionally selects the person against whom the crime is committed because of the race, religion, color, disability, sexual orientation, national origin or ancestry of that person." Dick appeals his longer sentence, challenging the constitutionality of the "penalty enhancement" statute.

On appeal, the Supreme Court would find the statute

(A) constitutional, because the state's law is not directed at expression, but at bias-motivated conduct which can inflict distinct individual and societal harm.
(B) constitutional, because blacks are a suspect class and the state has a compelling interest in protecting them from bias-motivated violence under the Equal Protection Clause of the Fourteenth Amendment.
(C) unconstitutional, because the statute is overbroad and punishes expression protected by the First Amendment.
(D) unconstitutional, because the statute is underinclusive and punishes only motivations directed against the groups listed in the statute.

Answer to Question 87

(B) is incorrect. Although the state may have a compelling interest in protecting blacks, the manner of that protection must not violate other constitutional provisions, and the real issue here is the validity of the law under the First Amendment. (B) also would not support the law in its entirety, to protect all of the listed groups.

In *R.A.V. v. City of St. Paul*, 112 S.Ct. 2538 (1992), the Supreme Court struck down a "hate speech" law that made it a crime to take actions or use symbols which would arouse anger, alarm, or resentment on the basis of race, color, creed, religion, or gender. This law was specifically directed at expression and thus was a form of content control and even viewpoint discrimination since it prohibited the communication of views on state-disfavored subjects. However, in *Wisconsin v. Mitchell*, 113 S.Ct. 2194 (1993), the Court distinguished *R.A.V.* and upheld a stiffer sentence law for bias-motivated crimes. The Court noted that the government can punish people for conduct even if the person was communicating a message, so long as the government is punishing the conduct, and not the message itself. For example, one cannot kill the president and claim protection from prosecution because the killing was meant to express opposition to government policies. In *Wisconsin*, the Court found that the law was aimed at conduct, not expression, and that the bias-motivated nature of the offense was relevant to sentencing because the state could conclude that bias-motivated crimes, inflict greater individual and societal harms than do other crimes. Therefore, (A) is correct and (C) is incorrect.

(D) also is incorrect. Although the Court in *Wisconsin v. Mitchell* did not directly address the issue, it concluded that the legislature could reasonably conclude that bias motivations of the kind described in the statute were more likely to provoke retaliatory crimes, cause distinct emotional harms, and incite community unrest. Thus, the law is not unconstitutional merely because it is underinclusive.

Question 88

The President of the United States is considering signing a treaty with Great Britain which would do away with all tariffs on goods shipped between the two countries. Opponents of the treaty who live in Boston stage a rally at which they criticize the treaty and dump boxes of tea biscuits into the harbor as a symbol of their denunciation of the subjugation of the United States to Great Britain. Unbeknownst to them, such dumping constitutes a violation of federal pollution statutes. The statutes in question provide for criminal penalties and substantial fines for violations, but also provide for special waiver permits in limited cases. The participants in the rally are charged with a violation of those statutes. The outcome of those proceedings would most likely be in favor of

(A) the government, because the First Amendment will not protect the defendants in this instance.
(B) the government, because the defendants could have made their criticism without violating the statute.
(C) the defendants, because their conduct was protected symbolic speech.
(D) the defendants, because they lacked the requisite mental intent.

Answer to Question 88

(D) is incorrect because the pollution statutes in question are likely to be regulatory statutes, where no particular mental intent is required. Moreover, a mistake of law is usually not a defense to any crime, except in the limited cases where a statute provides that the defendant must know that the conduct is illegal for it to constitute a crime. Last but not least, it should be clear that the rest of the choices involve principles of constitutional law, which makes it more likely that this question tests that subject, rather than criminal law.

(B) is incorrect. The fact that the defendants could have made their point without resorting to the conduct in question is irrelevant to the analysis. It is not for the government to decide which is the most appropriate manner in which to conduct free expression. All the government can do is regulate conduct in limited circumstances, where the regulation furthers an important or substantial governmental interest, is only incidentally related to free speech, and is no more restrictive than necessary to further the government's interest.

Even when analyzed as symbolic speech, conduct is not protected by the First Amendment from governmental regulation which (1) furthers an important or substantial governmental interest, (2) is only incidentally related to free speech, and (3) is no more restrictive than necessary to further the government's interest. In this case, the federal pollution statute meets all three criteria. Therefore, the defendants can be convicted under the statute despite the fact that this could be portrayed as symbolic speech, making (A) the correct answer and (C) incorrect.

Question 89

I.M. King was addressing an audience in a park in Philadelphia on the subject of salvation. He uttered words highly offensive to the religious crowd that gathered to hear him speak but objected to his views of himself as the Messiah. After a while the crowd became unruly, and there was muttering and pushing. Five spectators indicated that if the police did not get "that S.O.B." off the stand, they would do it themselves. At this point, a police officer stepped in to stop a fight from breaking out, and demanded that King cease speaking. When he refused, the police officer arrested King. He was convicted of disorderly conduct.

King applied for a permit to speak in a public park in Kansas City the following month, but the permit was denied, solely because of the outbreak in Philadelphia the month before. King addressed a group in a public park anyway without the permit, and was arrested and convicted for speaking without a permit in violation of a Kansas City municipal ordinance. Upon appeal to the United States Supreme Court, the conviction will be

(A) reversed because it violates the rights of an audience to assemble peaceably.
(B) reversed because King's arrest and conviction constitute a violation of his First Amendment rights.
(C) sustained as a reasonable regulation by the city of the public parks and streets.
(D) sustained because there was a clear and present danger of violence.

Answer to Question 89

(A) is incorrect because the First Amendment rights of the speaker are far more germane to the issue than the speculative rights of a potential audience. Also, be skeptical of any choice that involves raising the rights of a third party. The party to the lawsuit is King, not a member of the audience.

(D) is incorrect because there was no clear and present danger here. The decision to deny the permit was based on a crowd's response in another city the week previous.

Violence is not imminent in this fact situation. The state may not deny a speaker the right to use a public forum merely because violence has occurred when he has spoken previously. Instead, the state has the obligation to provide sufficient police protection to control violence. Under *Brandenburg v. Ohio*, 395 U.S. 444 (1969), the probability of harm is no longer the criterion for speech limitations. The focus is now on whether the language of the speaker is **directed towards** causing imminent harm and whether it is in fact likely to cause that harm. Therefore, (B) is correct and (C) is incorrect.

Question 90

An "anti-hate" ordinance of the Emerald City bans any writing or symbol which the defendant knows or should know arouses anger on the basis of race, color, creed, religion, or gender.

The Emerald City owns the Emerald City Regional Airport and has adopted by ordinance a ban on all solicitation in the airport terminal.

Esmerelda is the head of the local chapter of the Witches. She dressed in her usual basic black and went to the main terminal of the Emerald city Regional Airport. She stood silently in a corner of the terminal near the passenger gates with a large kettle on a tripod. A skull and crossbones was painted on the kettle and it supported a sign which said "Death to all Munchkins for blue is the color of mourning."

Esmerelda was arrested for violating both ordinances, and raises the defense that both are unconstitutional. In the prosecution, the court is likely to hold that

(A) the anti-hate ordinance is constitutional because it is reasonably related to the compelling state interest of protecting groups which have been the objects of discrimination.
(B) the anti-hate ordinance is unconstitutional unless the actions of Esmerelda can be construed as "fighting words."
(C) the airport ordinance is constitutional because it constitutes a reasonable regulation.
(D) the airport ordinance is unconstitutional because the exercise of free speech cannot be banned in a public forum.

Answer to Question 90

This question is based, in part, on *R.A.V. v. City of St. Paul*, 112 S.Ct. 2538 (1992), where the Court held that legislation directed towards "hate speech" violated the First Amendment. In that case, the Court further held that the statute would be unconstitutional even if construed to apply only to fighting words because, even though fighting words are unprotected speech, the government cannot regulate that speech in a content-based manner. Thus, both (A) and (B) are wrong.

In *International Society for Krishna Consciousness Inc. v. Lee*, the Court held that an airport terminal, even one owned by a public authority, is not a traditional public forum, but is instead a nonpublic forum where regulation of speech need only meet the standard of reasonableness. Therefore, (D) is incorrect. In *Lee*, a total (i.e., content-neutral) ban on solicitation was held reasonable and (C) is therefore correct.

Question 91

Masshire State University was established by the state of Masshire and is governed by a board of regents appointed by the governor. The university policy permits student organizations to use rooms on campus for meetings upon the payment of a nominal charge, but prohibits student religious groups of any denomination or belief from using any campus rooms for religious discussion or worship. The Masshire Catholic Club was denied use of a meeting room pursuant to this policy, and has sued to enjoin the university from denying the Club the use of campus facilities for religious meetings. In that suit, the university will

(A) prevail, because the policy is a reasonable time and place restriction of speech.
(B) prevail, because to permit use of the campus facilities would constitute an establishment of religion.
(C) not prevail, because it is restricting the organization's free exercise of religion.
(D) not prevail, because the restriction is a content-based restriction of speech not justified by a compelling state need.

Answer to Question 91

(A) is incorrect because this is not a time and place restriction. It is not content-neutral, but discriminates on the basis of content. Therefore, reasonableness is not the correct standard.

(C) is incorrect because the question addresses the issue of discrimination in access to a public forum based on content, rather than regulation of religious thought or belief itself. The group is not prohibited from the exercise of its religion by this policy; it is only restricted from meeting in a public forum.

A policy of equal access to school facilities for all groups, including religious groups, does not violate the Establishment Clause (as long as it does not otherwise run afoul of the *Lemon* three-pronged test - purpose, effect, and entanglement). If a public institution permits any group to use its facilities for the purpose of expressive activity, it may not deny access to a particular group based on the content of the group's speech. Such a policy is considered content-based discrimination and can only be justified by a compelling state interest. *Widmar v. Vincent*, 454 U.S. 263 (1981). Here, because the university permits student organizations to use its rooms, it may not discriminate against student religious groups without a **compelling** interest. The Court has yet to find such a compelling interest. Therefore, (D) is correct and (B) is incorrect.

Question 92

P.W. Herman was indicted in the State of Inhibition for exhibition and possession of obscene materials. Pursuant to a valid arrest warrant, Herman was arrested in the living room of his home, where he was charging admission for the showing of "Prurient Interest," a film which depicted nudity, but did not show the genitals of the actors or actresses during sex acts. While on the premises, the officers went upstairs and, unknown to Herman, seized from a bedside reading stand magazines explicitly depicting in great detail various types of unnatural sexual acts. At the trial, when she first learned of the seizure of the bedside material, Herman's attorney objected to the admissibility of the material found on the reading stand, but the objection was overruled on the ground that local rules of procedure only allow a search and seizure issue to be raised by a pretrial motion to suppress. Herman was convicted both for exhibiting the film and for possessing the material on the bedside stand, and has appealed to the United States Supreme Court.

With respect to the showing of the film "Prurient Interest," the Court should

(A) reverse the conviction because an individual has the right to possess obscene material in his own home.
(B) reverse the conviction because the film is not obscene and is entitled to First Amendment protection.

(C) affirm the conviction because the First Amendment does not apply to commercial motion pictures.
(D) affirm the conviction because the jury found that the film offended community standards in Inhibition and is therefore obscene.

Answer to Question 92

(A) is incorrect because the defendant was exhibiting the film for profit, and not possessing it privately.

(C) is incorrect because the First Amendment **does** protect commercial motion pictures. Motion pictures are a protected form of communication.

(B) is correct. The United States Supreme Court held in *Jenkins v. Georgia*, 418 U.S. 153 (1974), that, even though local rather than national standards controlled the definition of obscenity, juries did not have unbridled discretion to declare obscene a film which depicted nudity, but which did not display the genitals of the actors and actresses engaged in sexual acts. Such depiction is, by definition, not obscene. Therefore, (D) is incorrect.

Question 93

As part of its zoning ordinance, the city of Chicago forbids a theater which shows sexually explicit material to be located within 1,000 feet of any other theater exhibiting such sexually explicit material. Just prior to the effective date of the ordinance, Heffer signed a contract to lease a gas station which was within 500 feet of an existing adult theater. She planned to convert the gas station into an adult theater, but when he applied for a license to exhibit adult films in the building, the license was denied because of the zoning ordinance.

What is the strongest argument by the city in favor of the constitutionality of the ordinance?

(A) Zoning ordinances are constitutionally permissible under the police power.
(B) Sexually explicit movies are obscene and can be prohibited entirely.
(C) The city's concern for the character of the neighborhood outweighs the specific limitation on free speech.
(D) The plaintiff has no standing to attack the constitutionality of the ordinance.

Answer to Question 93

(A) is incorrect because zoning ordinances are constitutional only if they do not impermissibly infringe on guaranteed rights. Here, Heffer can argue that the zoning ordinance unconstitutionally restricts her free speech.

(B) is incorrect because sexually explicit material is not necessarily obscene. *Erznoznik v. City of Jacksonville*, 422 U.S. 205 (1975).

(D) is incorrect. The plaintiff has standing because he has a direct and substantial interest in the outcome of the dispute.

(C) is correct. The city may regulate the location of adult theaters because it has a valid interest in protecting the character of its neighborhood, provided reasonable access to such theaters is not denied to the public. *Young v. American Mini Theatres, Inc.*, 427 U.S. 50 (1976).

Question 94

Sodom, an alien, operates an adult theater in Gomorrah which shows films which are obscene in the constitutional sense. Pursuant to a narrowly drawn statute, Sodom is prosecuted for the exhibition of an obscene motion picture, and asserts as a defense the right of privacy. Which of the following is the best reason that the defense will not be successful?

(A) The right to possess obscene material does not extend beyond the home.
(B) The right of privacy does not extend to the possession of obscene motion pictures.
(C) The right of privacy does not extend to public theaters.
(D) An alien may not assert an invasion of privacy defense.

Answer to Question 94

(A) is incorrect. The right to possess obscene material may extend beyond the home as long as the obscene material is intended for personal use.

(B) is incorrect. The right to possess obscene material includes the right to possess obscene motion pictures. See *Stanley v. Georgia*, 394 U.S. 557 (1969).

(D) is incorrect because an alien may assert the First Amendment defense of invasion of privacy; the First Amendment (via the Fourteenth Amendment) protects the rights of "persons," and aliens are persons under the Fourteenth Amendment.

Exhibiting obscene films for profit is not a personal use of obscene material and is, therefore, not protected by the First Amendment. See *Paris Adult Theater I v. Slaton*, 413 U.S. 49 (1973). Therefore, (C) is correct.

Question 95

Eddie operates an "adult" theater; children under 18 are not allowed on the premises. The only moving pictures he shows are features, approximately five minutes in length, in which two or more persons perform acts of sexual intercourse or other sexual acts for the entire film. The films are in color and show the explicit function of the sexual organs. If the state, which has a narrowly drawn obscenity statute that follows the most recent United States Supreme Court decisions on the subject, prosecutes Eddie and he raises constitutional defenses, the most likely result is that he will be found

(A) guilty, because the statute as applied is a constitutional exercise of the police power.
(B) guilty, because the state may use local standards to determine if the picture has redeeming social value.
(D) not guilty because of the First Amendment.
(C) not guilty, because the statute violates the constitutional rights of the consenting adults in the audience.

Answer to Question 95

(B) is incorrect because local standards are applied to determine if the work is patently offensive, not whether it has redeeming social value. In fact, however, the film is obscene. The factual description of the film in this question leaves little doubt that it is obscene under the standard of *Miller v. California*, 413 U.S. 15 (1973). The work taken as a whole appeals to the prurient interest; it depicts, in a patently offensive way, sexual conduct specifically defined by the applicable state law; and it has no redeeming social value.

(C) is incorrect because there is no constitutional right for consenting adults to view obscene material in a public theater. *Paris Adult Theater I v. Slaton*, 413 U.S. 49 (1973).

Once material is adjudged obscene, it is outside the protection of the First Amendment and is subject to regulation under the police power. It therefore is not entitled to First Amendment protection. (A) is correct and (D) is incorrect.

Question 96

An instructor in the public school system in a municipality was required to sign two loyalty oaths as a condition of employment: the first to uphold and defend the Constitution, and the second to defend the government from overthrow by force or violence or any improper method. She has brought an appropriate suit in federal court to require that the municipality continue to employ her even if she does not sign either oath. The court will most likely hold

(A) that both of the loyalty oaths specified in the question are vague and overbroad, and therefore the requirement to take them is not a permissible condition of public service.
(B) that only the loyalty oath to uphold and defend the Constitution is a permissible condition of public employment.
(C) that the oath promising to defend the government from overthrow by force and violence or other improper method is a permissible condition of public service.

(D) that no loyalty oath is permissible as a condition of public employment.

Answer to Question 96

An oath to uphold and defend the Constitution is nothing more than a commitment to the constitutional process and is similar to the oaths prescribed in the Constitution for elected officials. Such oaths have been held to be constitutional as a prerequisite for public employment. *Cole v. Richardson*, 405 U.S. 676 (1972). Thus, both (A) and (D) are overbroad and incorrect.

On the other hand, the oath to oppose the overthrow of government is unconstitutional because of the overbreadth and vagueness of its wording. If it only had read that the affiant would swear to oppose the overthrow of the government of the United States by any illegal or unconstitutional method, the oath would be constitutional under *Cole v. Richardson*, 405 U.S. 676 (1972). However, the word "improper" used in the oath described in the question renders that oath unconstitutionally overbroad and vague. See, e.g., *Baggett v. Bullitt*, 377 U.S. 360 (1964) (an oath that employees "promote respect for the flag and reverence for law and order" held to be vague). Thus, (B) is correct and (C) is incorrect.

Question 97

Sons of the Boss, Inc. ("SOB"), a voluntary association, limits its membership to sons of chief executive officers of corporations whose gross sales exceed $20,000,000 annually who are engaged in the business in an executive capacity. Members meet regularly to discuss such topics as "Succession to the Presidency," "Relationships with Fellow Employees," and "Handling Dad in his Dotage."
State W has enacted a statute which requires that such organizations admit women to membership.
Helena Curley Frown, a resident of State W and the vice president of Fem Corp., is the daughter of the chief executive officer. The gross sales of Fem Corp. exceed $50,000,000 per year. Helena has brought suit against SOB, alleging that they have violated the State W statute and demanding that she be admitted to membership. The association has defended the suit by alleging that the state statute is unconstitutional.
Which of the following propositions is correct with respect to that suit?

I. The state has an important interest in eradicating discrimination against women.
II. The association has a First Amendment right to freedom of association.
III. The admission of women does not significantly impinge upon the association's freedom of speech.

(A) I only
(B) II only
(C) I and II only
(D) I, II and III

Answer to Question 97

Proposition I is correct; a state statute designed to prevent discrimination on account of sex satisfies an important state need.
Proposition II is correct because a private association has First Amendment associational rights.
Proposition III is also correct. Even though the statute satisfies an important state need, the association's First Amendment right to freedom of association can only be overcome upon a finding that the free speech rights of the association would not be significantly restricted by the admission of women. A state's important interest in eradicating sex discrimination justifies such a limited intrusion on the right to associate. *Roberts v. United States Jaycees*, 468 U.S. 609 (1984).
Since I, II, and III are correct, (D) is the right answer.

Question 98

Eldridge was a political activist during the 60's and 70's and joined and left many organizations through the years, such as Students for a Democratic Society, the Communist Party of America and the Black Panthers. Eventually, he abandoned all political activity and made his living growing organic vegetables.

At the age of 40, Eldridge suffered from mid-life crisis and decided to go to law school. There, he did extremely well, especially in the areas of corporate tax and anti-trust law. Upon graduation, he was offered a job as an associate with a prestigious firm in the District of Corrosion.

When it came time to complete the DC bar application, which is prepared in accordance with statutory requirements, Eldridge did not answer the question regarding membership in subversive organizations because he did not want to lie about his former membership, but he also did not want to jeopardize his chances for bar membership by answering in the affirmative. Because of this omission, his application was denied.

With the help of his future law firm, Eldridge challenges the constitutionality of the bar application in the appropriate court. In that case, Eldridge will

(A) prevail, because he is no longer a member of any organization and therefore the question is irrelevant.
(B) prevail, because the question unconstitutionally infringes on his freedom of association.
(C) not prevail, because the state has an important interest in denying bar admission to members of subversive organizations.
(D) not prevail, because the question serves a legitimate state interest.

Answer to Question 98

The state has the right to inquire into the character of candidates for admission to the bar and the Court has held that states may inquire into membership in subversive organizations, past and present. *Law Students Civil Rights Research Council, Inc. v. Wadmond*, 401 U.S. 154 (1972). While Eldridge's past activity is not a valid reason to deny him membership, there is no constitutional principle to support his refusal to answer the question. In *Konigsberg v. State Bar of California*, 366 U.S. 36 (1961), the Court held that an applicant could be denied admission to the bar for failure to answer the question about membership in subversive organizations. The Court reasoned that the state's interest in knowing the backgrounds and character of applicants to the bar outweighed the minimal effect on the applicant's free association. Therefore, since the question serves a legitimate state interest and does not infringe on Eldridge's constitutional rights, (D) is correct and (A) and (B) are incorrect.

(C) also is incorrect. While the state may ask about membership in subversive organizations, the state may not deny membership to the bar solely because of membership in a subversive organization. The state must also prove that the applicant had knowledge of the organization's illegal goals and intends to further those illegal goals. *Schware v. Board of Bar Examiners*, 353 U.S. 232 (1957).

Question 99

After the dissolution of the Soviet Union, Svetlana became disillusioned with the politics of her homeland and emigrated to the United States. Although she remained a card carrying member of the Communist Party, her political activities were limited to attending PTA meetings and organizing the labor union at the General Navigation plant ("GN"). She was employed by GN as an assembly line worker installing computer chips in navigation panels for navy war planes under contract with the federal government. Because of her experience in defense manufacturing, she was one of the candidates for the position of department manager. All candidates for this position were subject to background checks because of the high-level responsibility associated with the position. As a result of this investigation, the plant supervisor discovered that Svetlana was a member of the Communist Party. Upon the advice of company counsel, Svetlana was fired from her job because her employment was in violation of a federal statute which prohibits a member of any communist party from working in defense facilities.

Svetlana sues the federal government and GN, alleging that the termination violated her First Amendment rights. In that suit, Svetlana will

(A) win, because the statute unconstitutionally restricts her freedom of association.
(B) win, because the government may not deny an individual employment based on organization membership.
(C) lose, because Congress has plenary power over issues involving national security.
(D) lose, because Congress has the authority to regulate industry pursuant to its commerce power.

Answer to Question 99

In *United States v. Robel*, 389 U.S. 258 (1967), the Court held that the United States could not refuse a person employment in a defense facility solely because of membership in a communist group. In that case, the Court found a similar statute overly broad in that it was not tailored to meet the specific concerns of national security and established guilt by association without regard for First Amendment rights. Therefore, Congress' power over issues of national security is not plenary when an individual's First Amendment rights are affected.

(B) is incorrect. The government may deny a person employment if she is a member of a subversive organization and she knows of the illegal objectives of the organization and intends to further them. *Elfbrandt v. Russell*, 384 U.S. 11 (1966). Also, in *Robel*, the Court indicated that mere membership in a subversive organization might be cause to deny employment in a highly sensitive position. Since there are exceptions to the rule stated in this choice and another choice is correct without qualification, this choice is incorrect.

(D) is incorrect because the exercise of Congress' commerce power is subject to constitutional limitations. It may not improperly infringe on individual constitutional rights, such as freedom of association. Therefore, the commerce power is not a valid justification for this statute.

Applying the *Robel* holding to the case at hand, it appears that this principle would apply to Svetlana's termination as well, and therefore the application of the statute to her restricts her freedom of association. Note, however, that GN might have been able to deny her the management position based on the dicta in *Robel* which indicated that membership may be cause to deny a person a sensitive security position, but there are insufficient facts here to make that judgment call. Therefore, (A) is correct and (C) is incorrect.

Question 100

The federal maximum security prison in the state of Wachusetts has had ongoing problems with gang-related violence by the prisoners. Each gang is composed of a different ethnic group within the prison population. As a result, the prison officials devise a plan whereby the prison will be divided into several different units, each unit composed of one ethnic group. Interaction between the residents of different units will be severely curtailed and monitored. If subjected to constitutional attack, this plan will be held

(A) unconstitutional, because the classification by ethnic group is in violation of the Equal Protection Clause.
(B) unconstitutional, as a violation of the prisoners' First Amendment right to free association.
(C) constitutional, because prisoners do not have the same constitutional protections as ordinary citizens.
(D) constitutional, because it is reasonably related to a valid governmental objective.

Answer to Question 100

(A) is incorrect. It can be argued that no one class is treated any differently than another -- all groups are being segregated and treated equally. It is not clear that the Court's rejection of "separate but equal" theory in *Brown v. Board of Education* applies outside the context of schools. Therefore, there is probably no equal protection claim. If there is an equal protection claim, this scheme will probably survive strict scrutiny because of the state's compelling interest in maintaining security and order in prisons.

(B) is incorrect. To say that prisoners' First Amendment rights to freedom of association are often legitimately curtailed is to understate the case. This curtailment could easily be supported by the government's compelling state interest in protecting its agents and its charges from violence. Further, the groups have been housed together and may continue to associate as a group within their units. Moreover, membership in an organization with criminal purposes would not be a protected association under the First Amendment.

(C) is incorrect. The government is allowed more regulation of the rights of prisoners not because they have fewer rights, but because the government often has a more compelling interest in regulating their rights in the interest of security, safety, and law and order.

(D) is correct. Of the choices, this is the best answer because the regulation involves law enforcement operations. Even under the strict scrutiny test, race-conscious decisions would probably be upheld because maintaining order in the prison system could be perceived as a compelling state interest.

Question 101

A recently enacted state law forbids nonresident aliens from owning more than 100 acres of land within the state and directs the state attorney general to bring an action of ejectment whenever a nonresident alien owns such land.

Zane, a nonresident alien, has obtained title to 200 acres of land in the state, and he brings an action in federal court to enjoin the state attorney general from enforcing the statute. The attorney general moves to dismiss the complaint.

The federal court should

(A) dismiss the action, because under the Constitution, nonresident aliens may not sue in federal court.
(B) dismiss the action, because a state has plenary power to determine the qualifications for landholding within its boundaries.
(C) hear the action, because the United Nations Charter forbids such discrimination.
(D) hear the action, because a federal question is presented.

Answer to Question 101

Aliens have standing to sue in federal court. The Equal Protection Clause of the Fourteenth Amendment protects "persons," versus just citizens, and therefore an alien has standing to sue for violations of the Fourth Amendment guarantees of equal protection of the laws and due process. In this case, the plaintiff's action presents a federal question, that is, whether or not the state land statute is unconstitutional under the U.S. Constitution. Under Article III of the Constitution, federal courts have jurisdiction over cases arising under the U.S. Constitution. Therefore, (D) is correct and (A), which says that the plaintiff does not have standing, is incorrect.

(B) is incorrect because a state's power over land within its boundaries is not plenary. It is subject to any applicable limitation of the U.S. Constitution and federal law, such as the Equal Protection Clause.

(C) is incorrect. The United Nations Charter is a nonself-executing treaty and does not have the force of law in the United States. Nonself-executing treaties do not supersede existing federal and state law until there is federal legislation implementing their provisions. An example of this is the human rights provisions of the United Nations Charter that have not been implemented by federal legislation.

Question 102

Hobson was appointed to a tribunal established pursuant to a congressional act. The tribunal's duties were to review claims made by veterans and to make recommendations to the

Veterans Administration on their merits. Congress later abolished the tribunal and established a different format for review of such claims. Hobson was offered a federal administrative position in the same bureau at a lesser salary. He thereupon sued the government on the ground that Congress may not remove a federal judge from office during good behavior nor diminish his compensation during continuance in office. Government attorneys filed a motion to dismiss the action. The court should

(A) deny the motion, because the independence of the federal judiciary is guaranteed by the Constitution.
(B) deny the motion, because Hobson has established a property right to his federal employment on the tribunal.
(C) grant the motion, because Hobson lacked standing to raise the question.
(D) grant the motion, because Hobson was not a judge under Article III and is not entitled to life tenure.

Answer to Question 102

The tribunal established in this question was not an Article III court because its duties were not to decide cases or controversies. Rather, they made recommendations to an administrative agency. Therefore, the court should find that this was an Article I court created pursuant to Congress' legislative power. Since he is not an Article III judge, Hobson is not entitled to life tenure (i.e., the elimination of his job does not threaten the independence of the judiciary). Therefore, (D) is correct, and (A) is incorrect.

Even if Hobson had an employment contract with the government and thus a property right, he would have, at most, a right to a due process hearing before his transfer, not a right to a lifetime contract. See *Perry v. Sindermann*, 408 U.S. 593 (1972). Therefore, (B) is incorrect.

(C) is incorrect because direct and substantial interests of Hobson were affected. Therefore, he would have standing to litigate the government's attempt to harm those interests, if there was a legal basis for his cause of action.

Question 103

John Doe, the owner of a milk container manufacturing firm, sought to focus public attention on the milk packaging law of the State of Clinton in order to have it repealed. On a weekday at 12:00 noon, he delivered an excited, animated, and loud harangue on the steps of the state capitol in front of the main entryway. An audience of 200 onlookers, who gathered on the steps, heckled him and laughed as he delivered his tirade. Doe repeatedly stated, gesturing expressively and making faces, that "the g-dd--ed milk packaging law is stupid," and that "I will strangle every one of those g-dd--ed legislators I can get hold of because this law they created proves they are all too dumb to live." After about fifteen minutes, Doe stopped speaking, and the amused crowd dispersed.

The relevant statute of the State of Clinton prohibits "all speech making, picketing, and public gatherings of every sort on the Capitol steps in front of the main entryway between 7:45 a.m. - 8:15 a.m., 11:45 a.m. - 12:15 p.m., 12:45 p.m. - 1:15 p.m., and 4:45 p.m. - 5:15 p.m., on Capitol working days."

Which of the following possible plaintiffs other than Doe would be most likely to obtain an adjudication in a federal court on the validity of the "Capitol steps" statute?

(A) a state taxpayer in the highest tax bracket
(B) a politician intending to make a campaign speech on the Capitol steps during a prohibited time
(C) a legislator who voted against the statute because he thought it unconstitutional
(D) an organization the purpose of which was "to seek judicial invalidation of unconstitutional laws"

Answer to Question 103

A party is most likely to have standing when the party has suffered actual harm. This statute may presently have a chilling effect on the politician who is afraid to make a speech for fear of arrest. Since this politician is directly harmed, he or she has standing to obtain relief through judicial action. (B) is correct.

(A) is incorrect because there is no nexus between a person's status as a taxpayer and the alleged harm caused by the statute. The taxpayer is very unlikely to have been actually harmed.

(C) is incorrect because this legislator is not likely to be actually harmed by the legislation. A legislator has no special standing to challenge a statute in court merely because the legislator thought it unconstitutional and voted against it.

(D) is incorrect because an organization seeking judicial invalidation of unconstitutional laws is unlikely to have anything other than an abstract academic interest in any particular statute. This is insufficient to give a party standing.

Questions 104 and 105 are based on the following fact situation.

The state of Champlain enacts the Young Adult Marriage Counseling Act, which provides that, before any persons less than 30 years of age may be issued a marriage license, they must receive at least five hours of marriage counseling from a state-licensed social worker. This counseling is designed to assure that applicants for marriage licenses know their legal rights and duties in relation to marriage and parenthood, understand the "true nature" of the marriage relationship, and understand the procedures for obtaining divorces.

104. Pine, aged 25, contemplates marrying Ross, aged 25. Both are residents of the state of Champlain. Pine has not yet proposed to Ross because he is offended by the counseling requirement. Pine sues in federal court seeking a declaratory judgment that the Young Adult Marriage Counseling Act is unconstitutional. Which of the following is the clearest ground for dismissal of this action by the court?

(A) Pine and Ross are residents of the same state.
(B) No substantial federal question is presented.
(C) The suit presents a nonjusticiable political question.
(D) The suit is unripe.

105. In a case in which the constitutionality of the Young Adult Marriage Counseling Act is in issue, the burden of persuasion will probably be on

(A) the person challenging the law, because there is a strong presumption that elected state legislators acted properly.
(B) the person challenging the law, because the Tenth Amendment authorizes states to determine the conditions on which they issue marriage licenses.
(C) the state, because there is a substantial impact on the right to marry, and that right is fundamental.
(D) the state, because there is a substantial impact on the discrete and insular class of young adults.

Answer to Question 104

The doctrine of ripeness bars premature consideration of claims. This suit is not ripe because the plaintiff has not yet attempted to marry and therefore is not subject to the requirements of the statute. Therefore, (D) is correct.

(A) is incorrect because Pine and Ross are not adversarial parties and therefore do not have to show diversity of citizenship to establish federal court jurisdiction. Moreover, federal court jurisdiction in this case would be based on federal question jurisdiction, not diversity of citizenship, because Pine is challenging the constitutionality of the statute.

(B) is incorrect because the federal question presented is substantial, i.e., whether the Act violates the federal constitution.

(C) is incorrect because the suit does not present a political question. A suit to enjoin a state statute on First Amendment grounds comes within none of the categories of a political question. It is not an issue committed for final resolution to another branch of government, it will not provoke an embarrassing confrontation between branches of government, there is no need to adhere to a political decision already made, and it is possible to order appropriate relief against the state officials.

Answer to Question 105

While the burden is usually on the plaintiff to prove the unconstitutionality of a statute, the burden shifts to the state if a fundamental right, such as the right to marry, is involved. The Supreme Court has held invalid state laws which directly and substantially interfered with the right to marry, which was declared to be a fundamental right under the Fourteenth Amendment's Equal Protection Clause. Therefore, the state must show a compelling need to infringe upon it in order to sustain the law. (C) is correct.

(A) is incorrect because there is no evidentiary "presumption" that state legislators acted properly in any particular situation.

(B) is incorrect because the Tenth Amendment does not authorize state governments to infringe rights protected by the Constitution. The right to marry is a fundamental right protected by the Constitution.

(D) is partially correct in that the state does have the burden of proof in this case. But it is incorrect because it does not address the issue of marriage as a fundamental right and because it incorrectly categorizes young adults as a suspect class.

Question 106

A state statute requires the permanent removal from parental custody of any child who has suffered "child abuse." That term is defined to include "corporal punishment of any sort."

Zeller very gently spanks his six-year-old son on the buttocks whenever he believes that spanking is necessary to enforce discipline on him. Such a spanking occurs no more than once a month and has never physically harmed the child.

The state files suit under the statute to terminate Zeller's parental rights solely because of these spankings. Zeller defends only on the ground that the statute in question is unconstitutional as applied to his admitted conduct. In light of the nature of the rights involved, which of the following is the most probable burden of persuasion on this constitutional issue?

(A) The state has the burden of persuading the court that the application of this statute to Zeller is necessary to vindicate an important state interest.
(B) The state has the burden of persuading the court that the application of this statute to Zeller is rationally related to a legitimate state interest.
(C) Zeller has the burden of persuading the court that the application of this statute to him is not necessary to vindicate an important state interest.
(D) Zeller has the burden of persuading the court that the application of this statute to him is not rationally related to a legitimate state interest.

Answer to Question 106

The right of a parent to custody of a child is one of the privacy-based fundamental rights. Under a modern analysis, a statute which deprives an individual of such a fundamental right is constitutional only when the state proves that a compelling state interest is involved in applying the statute to the defendant. While (A) does not use the precise language of strict scrutiny ("important" vs. "compelling state interest"), it is the closest to the applicable burden of proof in cases involving fundamental rights and is therefore correct.

(B) is incorrect because when a fundamental right is involved, the state must prove more than a rational basis for the legislation. Further, when the rational basis standard is applied, the burden is on the challenger, not the state.

(C) and (D) are incorrect because, as discussed above, the defendant does not have the burden of proof in these circumstances.

Question 107

Congress enacted a law prohibiting the killing, capture, or removal of any form of wildlife upon or from any federally owned land.

Which of the following is the most easily justifiable source of national authority for this federal law?

(A) the Commerce Clause of Article I, §8
(B) the Privileges and Immunities Clause of Article IV
(C) the Enforcement Clause of the Fourteenth Amendment
(D) the Property Clause of Article IV, §3

Answer to Question 107

(A) is incorrect. This is a potential choice because Congress could regulate these activities under the Commerce Clause; however, the Property Clause of Article IV relates more directly to regulation of wildlife on federal lands and therefore (D) is the best answer. Article IV, Section 3 gives Congress plenary power to regulate and protect all real and personal property owned by the federal government, including federal lands and the animals inhabiting them.

(B) is incorrect because the Privileges and Immunities Clause of Article IV prohibits states from discriminating against nonresidents regarding the privileges of state citizenship. The law regarding wildlife involves federal regulatory power, not state action.

(C) is incorrect. The Enforcement Clause of the Fourteenth Amendment gives Congress the power to enforce the prohibition against state infringement on privileges of national citizenship, but is not the correct source of power over federal property.

Question 108

The strongest constitutional basis for the enactment of a federal statute requiring colleges and universities receiving federal funds to offer student aid solely on the basis of need is the

(A) police power.
(B) war and defense power.
(C) power to tax and spend for the general welfare.
(D) power to enforce the Privileges and Immunities Clause of the Fourteenth Amendment.

Answer to Question 108

The proposed statute is a federal one. Therefore, the correct answer must be one of the enumerated powers given to Congress in the Constitution. Answer (A), the police power, is incorrect because it is not a source of Congressional power. There is no federal police power. It is instead a source of power for the states through the Tenth Amendment, which hold residual sovereignty under our federal system.

(B) is incorrect. It is conceivable that Congress could impose such a restriction pursuant to the war and defense power, particularly during wartime. Since the question does not indicate a wartime setting and there are substantial limitations on the regulation of civilian activities during peacetime under the war powers, the spending power is much more suited to the exercise of this type of authority.

(C) is correct. The body of the question indicates that the statute is only to apply to colleges and universities receiving federal aid. Congress has extraordinarily broad power to spend for the general welfare, and may condition such expenditures upon the recipient complying with policy guidelines. Since the potential recipient need not accept the aid, the statute only regulates those who agree to the restriction.

(D) is incorrect. The Privileges and Immunities Clause of the Fourteenth Amendment has not been developed as a source of Congressional power. This Clause is a limitation on the states from interfering with the rights of national citizenship. Further, this Clause is of limited application and has very seldom been used to strike down legislation and is therefore usually the wrong answer.

Question 109

Congressional legislation regulating the conditions for marriages and divorces would be most likely upheld if it

(A) applied only to marriages and divorces by members of the armed services.
(B) applied only to marriages performed by federal judges and to divorces granted by federal courts.
(C) implemented an executive agreement seeking to define basic human rights.
(D) applied only to marriages and divorces in the District of Columbia.

Answer to Question 109

(A) is incorrect. Legislation controlling marriage and divorce of members of the armed services possibly could be upheld under the war power, but probably only during wartime. Since this choice is overbroad, it is incorrect.

(B) is incorrect. The federal courts do not have jurisdiction over marriages and divorces.

(C) is incorrect. Regulation of marriages and divorces outside the District of Columbia is left to the states under their police powers. There is no clear constitutional authority for the Congress (or the executive branch) to regulate such matters.

(D) is correct. The Constitution gives Congress the powers of a state legislature in the District of Columbia, including the control of marriages and divorces.

Question 110

Congress enacts a statute punishing "each and every conspiracy entered into by any two or more persons for the purpose of denying Black persons housing, employment, or education, solely because of their race." Under which of the following constitutional provisions is the authority of Congress to pass such a statute most clearly and easily justifiable?

(A) the Commerce Clause
(B) the General Welfare Clause of Article I, Section 8
(C) the Thirteenth Amendment
(D) the Fourteenth Amendment

Answer to Question 110

Under the theory that discriminatory practices affect interstate commerce, the Commerce Clause might be used to justify this statute. See *Heart of Atlanta Motel v. United States*, 379 U.S. 241 (1964) and *Katzenbach v. McClung*, 379 U.S. 294 (1964). However, the Commerce Clause is not as clear a justification for this statute as is the Thirteenth Amendment.

The Thirteenth Amendment, which abolished slavery, has been construed by the Supreme Court to authorize Congress to pass laws designed to abolish the incidents of slavery and, particularly, discrimination against African-Americans. Such legislation need not be directed against state action, but can govern individual conduct. *Jones v. Alfred H. Mayer Co.*, 392 U.S. 409 (1968). Therefore, the Thirteenth Amendment is the provision which most easily and clearly justifies the legislation that prohibits purely individual discrimination against African-Americans. Since the Thirteenth Amendment is the best justification for this statute, (C) is correct and (A) is incorrect.

(B) is incorrect because the General Welfare Clause of Article I, Section 8 authorizes **spending** by the federal government but is **not** a source of power to **regulate** individual activity.

(D) is incorrect. This legislation cannot be justified under the Equal Protection Clause of the Fourteenth Amendment because that amendment can be used only to support legislation dealing with state action.

Question 111

Green is cited for contempt of the House of Representatives after she refused to answer certain questions posed by a House committee concerning her acts while serving as a United States ambassador. A federal statute authorizes the Attorney General to prosecute contempts of Congress. Pursuant to this law, the House directs the Attorney General to begin the criminal proceedings against Green. A federal grand jury indicts Green, but the Attorney General refuses to sign the indictment.

Which of the following best describes the constitutionality of the Attorney General's action?

(A) illegal, because the Attorney General must prosecute if the House of Representatives directs
(B) illegal, because the Attorney General must prosecute those who violate federal law
(C) legal, because ambassadors are immune from prosecution for acts committed in the course of their duties
(D) legal, because the decision to prosecute is an exclusively executive act

Answer to Question 111

It is the obligation of the executive branch of government, including the attorney general, to execute the laws of the United States. The law at issue in this question authorizes, but does not require, the attorney general to prosecute. The decision to prosecute is therefore a discretionary act of the attorney general, and (D) is the correct answer and (B), which mandates prosecution, is incorrect.

The direction of the House of Representatives to prosecute is not a law, which the executive branch would be bound to obey. The House is in the position of a person who has been harmed and asks the attorney general for help. Therefore, (A) is incorrect.

(C) is incorrect. Appointed federal officials are not immune from prosecution because of their actions in office. The acts of an ambassador are probably a proper subject of a House committee inquiry, and it is doubtful that executive privilege will apply.

Question 112

A federal statute sets up a program of dental education. The statute provides that the Secretary of Health and Human Services "shall, on a current basis, spend all of the money appropriated for this purpose" and "shall distribute the appropriated funds" by a specified formula to state health departments that agree to participate in the program. In the current year, Congress has appropriated $100 million for expenditure on this program.

In order to ensure a budget surplus in the current fiscal year, the President issues an executive order directing the various cabinet secretaries to cut expenditures in this year by 10 percent in all categories. He also orders certain programs to be cut more drastically because he believes that "they are not as important to the general welfare as other programs." The President identifies the dental education program as such a program and orders it to be cut by 50 percent. Assume that no other federal statutes are relevant.

To satisfy constitutional requirements, how much money must the Secretary of Health and Human Services distribute for the dental education program this year?

(A) $50 million, because the President could reasonably determine that this program is not as important to the general welfare as other programs
(B) $50 million, because, as chief executive, the President has the constitutional authority to control the actions of all of his subordinates by executive order
(C) $90 million, because any more drastic cut for this program would be a denial of equal protection to beneficiaries of this program
(D) $100 million, because the President may not unilaterally suspend the effect of a valid federal statute imposing a duty to spend appropriated monies

Answer to Question 112

The statute involved in this case is mandatory, not discretionary, in nature. The use of the words "shall ... spend" and "shall distribute" take away the discretion of the executive branch as to whether to spend this money, because the executive branch is obligated to "execute the laws of the United States." The Secretary must therefore spend the $100 million and (D) is the correct answer.

(A) is incorrect because the President does not have discretion when legislation mandates spending. If Congress desires that a project go forward, it can mandate that appropriated funds be spent, and the President is required to spend them, because he has a constitutional obligation to execute the laws.

(B) is incorrect because the President's subordinates are also required to execute the laws and cannot be relieved of that responsibility by executive order.

(C) is incorrect because the issue here is not the dental program compared to other programs, but rather the mandatory nature of the congressional legislation.

Question 113

A recently enacted state law forbids nonresident aliens from owning more than 100 acres of land within the state and directs the state attorney general to bring an action of ejectment whenever a nonresident alien owns such land.

Zane, a nonresident alien, has obtained title to 200 acres of land in the state, and he brings an action in federal court to enjoin the state attorney general from enforcing the statute. The attorney general moves to dismiss the complaint.

The best argument for Zane is that

(A) states are forbidden by the Commerce Clause from interfering with the rights of nonresidents to own land.
(B) the state's power to restrict alien rights is limited by the federal power to control foreign relations.
(C) the state statute adversely affects Zane's right to travel.
(D) the 100-acre restriction means that aliens cannot engage in farming operations requiring larger amounts of land.

Answer to Question 113

The Commerce Clause would be an appropriate basis for challenging this statute if it discriminated against citizens of another state. This statute, though, constitutes discrimination against non-U.S. citizens. In that case, the plenary power of the federal government to control foreign nationals and foreign relations is the best basis to attack this statute because states may not enact legislation which interferes that power. See *Zschernig v. Miller*, 389 U.S. 429 (1968), where an intestacy statute restricting the property inheritance rights of certain foreign nationals was invalidated. Thus, (B) is correct and (A) is incorrect.

(C) is incorrect. Zane has a fundamental right to travel, even though he is a nonresident alien, because the Equal Protection Clause applies to all "persons." However, this is still not the best answer because it is not clear that this statute affects the right to travel, while it clearly violates the federal government's plenary power to regulate foreign nationals and foreign relations.

(D) is incorrect. There is no fundamental right to work. Moreover, (D) is factually untrue because aliens are not restricted from **leasing** land if they wish to engage in larger farming operations.

Question 114

A statute of the state of Tuscarora made it a misdemeanor to construct any building of more than five stories without an automatic fire sprinkler system.

A local construction company built in Tuscarora a ten-story federal office building. It constructed the building according to the precise specifications of a federal contract authorized by federal statutes. Because the building was built without the automatic fire sprinkler system required by state law, Tuscarora prosecutes the private contractor.

Which of the following is the company's strongest defense to that prosecution?

(A) The state sprinkler requirement denies the company property or liberty without due process.
(B) The state sprinkler requirement denies the company equal protection of the laws.
(C) As applied, the state sprinkler requirement violates the Supremacy Clause.
(D) As applied, the state sprinkler requirement violates the Obligation of Contracts Clause.

Answer to Question 114

(A) is incorrect. This type of regulation is permissible under the state's police power to protect the health and safety of the state's inhabitants, and does not constitute a taking unless it prevents almost all use of the property. Therefore, such a state statute is generally valid (except if it is in conflict with federal law).

(B) is incorrect. The statute cannot be successfully challenged on an equal protection basis because economic and social regulations require only a rational purpose, and the sprinkler law has a rational basis.

(C) is correct. The state sprinkler law is in conflict with the federal statute which authorized the specific construction details. Therefore, the federal regulation prevails under the Supremacy Clause.

(D) is incorrect. The construction company's contract with the federal government is not going to be abrogated by the state statute. The contract is still valid. The only question is whether the contractor is liable for the violation of the statute.

Question 115

Until 1954, the State of New Atlantic required segregation in all public and private schools, but all public schools are now desegregated. Other state laws, enacted before 1954 and continuing to the present, provide for free distribution of the same textbooks on secular subjects to students in all public and private schools. In addition, the state accredits schools and certifies teachers.

Little White School House, a private school that offers elementary and secondary education in the state, denies admission to all non-Caucasians.

Which of the following is the strongest argument against the constitutionality of free distribution of textbooks to the students at Little White School House?

(A) No legitimate educational function is served by the free distribution of textbooks.
(B) The state may not in any way aid private schools.
(C) The Constitution forbids private bias of any kind.
(D) Segregation is furthered by the distribution of textbooks to these students.

Answer to Question 115

Any discrimination on account of race by a state is forbidden by the Equal Protection Clause unless it is justified by a compelling state need. State aid to a segregated facility which benefits that facility to an extent greater than general governmental services constitutes forbidden state action. The distribution of textbooks is a distinct financial benefit to the segregated school, and is therefore in violation of the Equal Protection Clause. *Norwood v. Harrison*, 413 U.S. 455 (1973). (D) is correct. (Note, however, that this rule of law must be distinguished from the rule of law that allows the free distribution of secular textbooks to **religious** schools which do not discriminate on the basis of race.)

(A) is incorrect because it is factually wrong. The distribution of textbooks serves an important educational function and would be permitted if it did not aid segregation.

(B) is incorrect. The state may aid private education through grants, special programs, loan guarantees for students, money for the construction of dormitories, and many other ways, as long as it does not further a constitutionally forbidden purpose, such as supporting segregation. See *Norwood v. Harrison*, 413 U.S. 455 (1973).

(C) is incorrect because the Fourteenth Amendment only prohibits bias in the form of state action. Private bias outside of the state action concept is constitutionally permissible, although it may be prohibited by statute pursuant to the Thirteenth Amendment.

Question 116

A statute of the state of Lenape flatly bans the sale or distribution of contraceptive devices to minors. Drugs, Inc., a national retailer of drugs and related items, is charged with violating the Lenape statute. Which of the following is the strongest constitutional argument that Drugs, Inc. could make in defending itself against prosecution for violation of this statute?

(A) The statute constitutes an undue burden on interstate commerce.

(B) The statute denies minors one of their fundamental rights under due process of law.
(C) The statute denies Drugs, Inc. a privilege or immunity of state citizenship.
(D) The statute violates the First Amendment right to freedom of religion because it regulates morals.

Answer to Question 116

The right to have access to and use contraceptives is a fundamental privacy right protected by the Due Process Clause. State interference with that right can only be justified by a compelling state need not present here. *Carey v. Population Services International*, 431 U.S. 678 (1977) (prohibition on sale of contraceptives to persons under age 16 held invalid on due process grounds). Therefore, (B) is correct.

(A) is incorrect. The state has the right to regulate matters of the health of its citizens as long as it does not interfere with interstate commerce by discriminating between in-state and out-of-state business concerns. This statute is not discriminatory because it applies equally to all distributors of contraceptives wherever located and therefore is not an undue burden on interstate commerce.

(C) is incorrect because the statute of the state of Lenape does not deny citizens of other states any privilege or immunity which is granted to citizens of Lenape. This statute applies equally to all persons whatever their citizenship.

(D) is incorrect. There are no facts in the question which indicate that this statute interferes with any religious practices. Therefore, it does not interfere with the free exercise of religion.

Question 117

Barnes was hired as an assistant professor of mathematics at Reardon State College and is now in her third consecutive one-year contract. Under state law, she cannot acquire tenure until after five consecutive annual contracts. In her third year, Barnes was notified that she would not be re-hired for the following year. Applicable state law and college rules did not require either a statement of reasons or a hearing, and in fact neither was offered to Barnes.

Which of the following, if established, most strongly supports the college in refusing to give Barnes a statement of reasons or an opportunity for a hearing?

(A) Barnes's academic performance had been substandard.
(B) A speech she made that was critical of administration policies violated a college regulation concerning teacher behavior.
(C) Barnes worked at the college for less than five years.
(D) Barnes could be replaced with a more competent teacher.

Answer to Question 117

The strongest argument for the state college in refusing to grant a hearing is one which indicates that Barnes has no property right for the state to take away because she does not have tenure. A teacher who has less than five years' employment at the college does not have a renewable right to a teaching contract under state law. Therefore, no property interest was terminated and no hearing is required. *Perry v. Sindermann*, 408 U.S. 593 (1972). (C) is correct.

(A) and (D) are incorrect because they address only the issue of academic performance, rather than vested rights. Even if the academic performance of a tenured professor at a state school was substandard, the professor's employment could not be terminated without a hearing. *Perry v. Sindermann*, 408 U.S. 593 (1972).

(B) is incorrect because it gives a reason why a professor (even one with **no** property right) **is** entitled to a hearing. A professor cannot be disciplined for exercising freedom of speech rights under the First and Fourteenth Amendments. If the employment contract was terminated after such a speech, the college would be required to demonstrate that the professor was fired for reasons other than the exercise of rights of free speech. *Mt. Healthy School District v. Doyle*, 429 U.S. 274 (1977).

Question 118

The State of Missoula has enacted a new election code designed to increase voter responsibility in the exercise of the franchise and to enlarge citizen participation in the electoral process. None of its provisions conflicts with federal statutes.

Which of the following is the strongest reason for finding unconstitutional a requirement in the Missoula election code that each voter must be literate in English?

(A) The requirement violates Article I, §2 of the Constitution, which provides that representatives to Congress be chosen "by the People of the several States."
(B) The requirement violates Article I, §4 of the Constitution, which gives Congress the power to "make or alter" state regulations providing for the "Time" and "Manner" of holding elections for senators and representatives.
(C) The requirement violates the Due Process Clause of the Fourteenth Amendment.
(D) The requirement violates the Equal Protection Clause of the Fourteenth Amendment.

Answer to Question 118

Whether the state has a right to use literacy as a classification to interfere with the franchise would be argued under the Equal Protection Clause. The state must show a compelling interest to justify such a qualification, since the right to vote is a fundamental right, placed upon the highest tier of equal protection scrutiny. An equal protection, rather than due process, analysis is appropriate because literacy tests tend to discriminate against certain classes of persons. Therefore, (D) is correct.

Article I, §2 of the Constitution is the basis upon which the Court determined that the one person - one vote rule applies to congressional districts. However, it has not been held that that provision concerns qualifications for the franchise, and therefore (A) is not the correct answer.

(B) is incorrect for two reasons. First, this is a code which deals with state as well as federal offices. Article I, §4 only concerns congressional authority over federal elections. Second, this is not a "time" and "manner" qualification; it is based upon particular knowledge and skills. Therefore, Article I, §4 does not apply.

(C) is incorrect. The Due Process Clause, even the substantive due process rights found thereunder, is not the best reason to find the statute unconstitutional. When a statute involves a fundamental right and infringes more on the rights of one class of persons than on the rights of another class, then the Court applies an equal protection analysis in determining the constitutionality of the statute. The Due Process Clause is the best answer when the fundamental rights of **all** citizens are negatively impacted. Therefore, (C) is incorrect.

Question 119

A state statute provides that persons moving into a community to attend a college on a full-time basis may not vote in any elections for local or state officials that are held in that community. Instead, the statute provides that, for voting purposes, all such persons shall retain their residence in the community from which they came. In this state the age of majority is 18.

Which of the following is the strongest argument to demonstrate the unconstitutionality of this state statute?

(A) A state does not have an interest that is sufficiently compelling to justify the exclusion from voting of an entire class of persons.
(B) There are less restrictive means by which the state could assure that only actual residents of a community vote in its elections.
(C) Most persons moving to a community to attend college full-time are likely to have attained the age of majority under the laws of this state.
(D) On its face this statute impermissibly discriminates against interstate commerce.

Answer to Question 119

Because the right to vote is fundamental, the franchise may not be abridged unless justified by a compelling state need. (A) is too broad in stating that no state interest is sufficiently compelling to justify exclusion of a class of voters and is therefore incorrect. For example, states have excluded an entire class of voters on the basis of illiteracy, and the Supreme Court has upheld such an exclusion in *Lassiter v. Northampton Election Board*, 360 U.S. 45 (1959). [Note, however, that literacy tests are now unlawful (for the most part) under the Civil Rights Act of 1968.]

The state has the right to limit the franchise to residents of a community, but may impose only reasonable restrictions. A state may impose a reasonable durational residency requirement to ensure voters are bona fide residents. The Supreme Court found a 50-day residency requirement constitutional in *Marston v. Lewis*, 410 U.S. 679 (1973). However, a restriction which prohibits college students from voting in a community during the entire time they are enrolled at a local college would deny them the franchise, and less restrictive residency requirements could be imposed to ensure that the students are bona fide residents. Therefore, (B) is the strongest argument against the constitutionality of the statute and is the correct answer.

(C) is incorrect because the state statute is not denying students the franchise on the basis of age, but rather on the basis of residency.

(D) is incorrect. While it can be argued that the state statute in issue will have the effect of restricting the right to interstate travel as well as the right to vote of any out-of-state student, the Commerce Clause has not been used to remedy infringements on the right to travel except in the case of racial discrimination.

Questions 120 and 121 are based on the following fact situation.

The state of Aurora requires licenses of persons "who are engaged in the trade of barbering." It will grant such licenses only to those who are graduates of barber schools located in Aurora, who have resided in the state for two years, and who are citizens of the United States.

120. Which of the following is the strongest ground on which to challenge the requirement that candidates for barber licenses must have been residents of the state for at least two years?

(A) the Privileges and Immunities Clause of the Fourteenth Amendment
(B) the Due Process Clause of the Fourteenth Amendment
(C) the Equal Protection Clause of the Fourteenth Amendment
(D) the Obligation of Contracts Clause

121. The requirement that candidates for licenses must be citizens is

(A) constitutional as an effort to ensure that barbers speak English adequately.
(B) constitutional as an exercise of the state's police power.
(C) unconstitutional as a bill of attainder.
(D) unconstitutional as a denial of equal protection.

Answer to Question 120

The right to travel interstate is a fundamental right of the citizens of the United States. Any interference with that right by legislation - such as by penalizing individuals by imposing durational residential requirements before an individual can exercise rights or receive benefits, or by discriminating against out-of-state residents - must be justified by a compelling state need, or it will be unconstitutional under the Equal Protection Clause of the Fourteenth Amendment. This is such a statute because it effectively prevents citizens from other states from pursuing their livelihood in the state of Aurora without adequate justification. Therefore, (C) is correct.

The Privileges and Immunities Clause of the Fourteenth Amendment has never been used to invalidate a state statute. Its interpretation has been limited to those rights which are privileges of national citizenship. That issue is not present in this question. Therefore, (A) is incorrect.

(B) is incorrect as a matter of constitutional case law because this issue has traditionally been analyzed under the Equal Protection Clause of the Fourteenth Amendment, not the Due Process Clause.

(D) is incorrect. There is no contractual right or obligation which is impaired in this fact pattern.

Answer to Question 121

Under present interpretations of the Equal Protection Clause, alienage is a suspect classification. To discriminate on that basis, the state must show that the occupation is one where persons participate directly in the formulation, execution, and review of broad public policy. Since the occupation of barbering does not fit into that category, the statute is unconstitutional as a denial of equal protection, and (D) is correct and (B) is incorrect.

(A) is incorrect because ensuring that barbers speak English is not reasonably related to the requirement of citizenship, since there are citizens who do not speak English and noncitizens who do. Moreover, the purpose of requiring that barbers speak English is not an important enough state purpose to survive strict scrutiny under the Equal Protection Clause, which applies since this constitutes a classification based on alienage.

(C) is incorrect. The statute is not a bill of attainder (i.e., a legislative infliction of punishment on an identifiable individual without judicial trial), because no identifiable individual is affected, and the denial of a barbering license is probably not the infliction of punishment.

Question 122

John Doe, the owner of a milk container manufacturing firm, sought to focus public attention on the milk packaging law of the State of Clinton in order to have it repealed. On a weekday at 12:00 noon, he delivered an excited, animated, and loud harangue on the steps of the state capitol in front of the main entryway. An audience of 200 onlookers who gathered on the steps, heckled him and laughed as he delivered his tirade. Doe repeatedly stated, gesturing expressively and making faces, that "the g-ddamned milk packaging law is stupid," and that "I will strangle every one of those g-ddamned legislators I can get hold of because this law they created proves they are all too dumb to live." After about 15 minutes, Doe stopped speaking, and the amused crowd dispersed.

The relevant statute of the State of Clinton prohibits "all speech making, picketing, and public gatherings of every sort on the Capitol steps in front of the main entryway between 7:45 a.m. - 8:15 a.m., 11:45 a.m. - 12:15 p.m., 12:45 p.m. - 1:15 p.m., and 4:45 p.m. - 5:15 p.m., on Capitol working days."

The "Capitol steps" statute is probably

(A) constitutional both on its face and as applied to Doe.
(B) constitutional on its face but unconstitutional as applied to Doe.
(C) unconstitutional on its face, because it applies to all working days.
(D) unconstitutional on its face, because it concerns the state capitol.

Answer to Question 122

The first step in the analysis is to determine if the capitol steps statute is unconstitutional on its face. There are two theories on which it could be unconstitutional on its face: vagueness and overbreadth. The statute is not vague because it precisely limits the time and place of speech. It is not overbroad because it does not apply by its terms to speech which is constitutionally protected. It is content-neutral and does not completely prohibit speech. Therefore, the statute is valid on its face.

The statute is likewise constitutional as applied to the defendant. The state has a valid interest in providing unimpeded access to the capitol building during the hours when employees are coming and going to work. The statute is narrow in scope and designed to accomplish this purpose. While there is a limitation on the time and place of speech, it is a minor limitation justified by legitimate state interests. Since the statute is constitutional both on its face and as applied, (A) is correct and (B) is incorrect.

(C) is incorrect because the term "working days" is reasonably precise, and an individual would be able to determine the days on which it applied by consulting a schedule of holidays for state workers. These are also the days on which the state has a valid interest in restricting disruptive speech. The statute might be held unconstitutional if it applied to any **more** than working days. The statute is also not unreasonably limited by the fact that it applies to all working days, because it only restricts speech during a relatively narrow time on these days; speeches are otherwise allowed all day long.

(D) is incorrect. Even though the capitol steps are a public forum and even though this speech is highly protected, the statute is constitutional because it is narrowly drawn and provides for the minimum interference necessary to accomplish a valid state objective.

Question 123

A newly enacted criminal statute provides, in its entirety, "No person shall utter to another person in a public place any annoying, disturbing, or unwelcome language." Smith followed an elderly woman for three blocks down a public street, yelling in her ear offensive four-letter words. The woman repeatedly asked Smith to leave her alone, but he refused.

In the subsequent prosecution of Smith, the first under this statute, Smith will

(A) not prevail.
(B) prevail, because speech of the sort described here may not be punished by the state because of the First and Fourteenth Amendments.
(C) prevail, because, although his speech may be punished by the state, the state may not do so under this statute.
(D) prevail, because the average user of a public street would think his speech/action here was amusing and ridiculous rather than "annoying," etc.

Answer to Question 123

The statute is unconstitutional on its face because it is both vague and overly broad. The state may protect its citizenry from certain speech, but only if the statute is precisely drawn and a potential violator will be able to determine from the language of the statute what actions or speech is proscribed. In this statute, words such as "annoying" and "unwelcome" are subject to a number of subjective interpretations and therefore do not define precisely the proscribed speech. However, Smith's speech could be proscribed in a properly drawn statute. For these reasons, (C) is correct and (A) and (B) are incorrect.

Since this statute is unconstitutional because it is vague and overbroad, Smith does not need to rely on the dubious argument in (D) that the statute does not apply to his conduct.

Questions 124 and 125 are based on the following fact situation.

The state of Aurora requires licenses of persons "who are engaged in the trade of barbering." It will grant such licenses only to those who are graduates of barber schools located in Aurora, who have resided in the state for two years, and who are citizens of the United States.

124. The requirement that candidates for licenses must be graduates of barber schools in Aurora is probably

(A) unconstitutional as an undue burden on interstate commerce.
(B) unconstitutional as a violation of the Privileges and Immunities Clause of the Fourteenth Amendment.
(C) constitutional, because the state does not know the quality of out-of-state barber schools.
(D) constitutional, because barbering is a privilege and not a right.

125. Assume that a resident of the state of Aurora was denied a license because she had graduated from an out-of-state barber school.

82

Her suit in federal court to enjoin denial of the license on this ground would be

(A) dismissed, because there is no diversity of citizenship.
(B) dismissed, because of the abstention doctrine.
(C) decided on the merits, because federal jurisdiction extends to controversies between two states.
(D) decided on the merits, because a federal question is involved.

Answer to Question 124

Any state statute which discriminates in favor of an in-state activity and against an out-of-state one is suspect because the negative implications of the Commerce Clause require that a state open its borders to competition from other states. An act licensing only barbers who graduated from schools in the state gives the schools located in the state a substantial advantage over the out-of-state schools, and will be constitutional only if the state can justify it as a valid exercise of the police power.

(C) is not sufficient justification because less restrictive means are available to accomplish the same objective. The state could rely on an accrediting body and permit only graduates of accredited schools to obtain a license. Following the theory of *Dean Milk v. Madison* a the state might inspect out-of-state schools and charge them for the inspection. (C) is therefore incorrect.

(D) is incorrect because the right to earn a living through a lawful occupation is a property right under the Fourteenth Amendment, and may not be taken away arbitrarily on the theory that it is a privilege.

(B) is incorrect because the Privileges and Immunities Clause of the Fourteenth Amendment has been given very restrictive scope by the United States Supreme Court, and does not apply to discrimination by a state against out-of-state businesses.

(A) is correct because the negative implications of the power of Congress to regulate interstate commerce forbids the state to discriminate against interstate commerce when a less restrictive means of accomplishing a legitimate state objective is available.

Answer to Question 125

This question requires a knowledge of the bases of federal court jurisdiction.

(A) is incorrect because diversity of citizenship is not the sole basis of federal court jurisdiction. Even though the choice correctly states that there is no diversity of citizenship, that fact alone is not sufficient to deny jurisdiction.

(B) is incorrect because the abstention doctrine is inapplicable to this fact situation. The federal court will abstain when the state statute in question is ambiguous and has not been construed by the state court, and it is possible to avoid the federal constitutional question by construing the statute. This is called *Pullman*-type abstention, and is not appropriate here because the statute is unambiguous in its denial of a license to a graduate of an out-of-state school. The other type of abstention which involves the refusal of the federal court to enjoin the operation of state criminal or quasi-criminal statute is likewise inapplicable.

(C) is incorrect. Even though it is a correct statement of law in that the United States Supreme Court has original and exclusive jurisdiction in controversies between two states, this is not such a lawsuit. It is a suit between a resident of Aurora and the State of Aurora.

(D) is correct. The federal court has jurisdiction to determine lawsuits arising under the Constitution and laws of the United States. Since this lawsuit challenges the validity of the statute because it violates the Equal Protection Clause of the U.S. Constitution, the federal court has federal question jurisdiction.

Question 126

Doe is prosecuted for giving his 14-year-old daughter a glass of wine in violation of a state statute prohibiting any person from serving any alcoholic beverage to a minor. Doe defends on the ground that the state statute as applied in his case unconstitutionally interferes with his free exercise of religion.

In determining the constitutionality of this application of the state statute, the court may NOT properly

(A) require the state to bear the burden of persuading the court that the statute is constitutional as applied to Doe.
(B) determine the reasonableness of Doe's religious beliefs.
(C) ascertain whether Doe's religious beliefs require him to serve wine to his child.
(D) decide whether Doe is sincere in his religious beliefs - that is, whether he really believes them.

Answer to Question 126

The correct answer to this question is in the negative. Therefore, an appropriate court procedure will be an incorrect response.
(A) is incorrect because under *Sherbert v. Verner* the state has the burden of proving that an interference with the freedom of religion is justified by a compelling state need.
(B) is correct and (D) is incorrect because under *United States v. Seeger*, a conscientious objector case, the courts may inquire into whether a religious belief is sincerely held but may not inquire into the reasonableness of that belief.
(C) is incorrect because the court has the right to determine whether the conduct which is claimed to be protected by the right to free exercise of religion is in fact based upon a religious belief.

Question 127

An appropriations act passed by Congress over the President's veto directs that one billion dollars "shall be spent" by the federal government for the development of a new military weapons system, which is available only from the Arms Corporation. On the order of the President, the Secretary of Defense refuses to authorize a contract for purchase of the weapons system. The Arms Corporation sues the Secretary of Defense, alleging an unlawful withholding of these federal funds.

The strongest constitutional argument for the Arms Corporation is that

(A) passage of an appropriation over a veto makes the spending mandatory.
(B) Congress's power to appropriate funds includes the power to require that the funds will be spent as directed.
(C) the President's independent constitutional powers do not specifically refer to spending.
(D) the President's power to withhold such funds is limited to cases where foreign affairs are directly involved.

Answer to Question 127

(B) is the correct answer because Congress can require that the President execute a law by making it mandatory. It is the President's function and constitutional duty as the Chief Executive to execute such a law.
(A) is incorrect because the bill might be written in such a manner that the spending is discretionary even after the bill is passed. If it contains such discretion, and is passed over a veto, it is not a mandatory bill.
(C) is incorrect because this is not a question of the President's powers, but a question of the President's obligation to execute the laws passed by Congress.
(D) is incorrect because the President would be obligated to execute the law even if it related to foreign affairs. The President has much discretion in foreign affairs, but not with respect to expenditures mandated by Congress.

Question 128

Congress enacted a statute providing that persons may challenge a state energy law on the ground that it is in conflict with the federal constitution in either federal or state court. According to this federal statute, any decision by a lower state court upholding a state energy law against a challenge based on the federal constitution may be appealed directly to the United States Supreme Court.
The provisions of this statute that authorize direct United States Supreme Court review of

specified decisions rendered by lower state courts are

(A) constitutional, because congressional control over questions of energy usage is plenary.
(B) constitutional, because Congress may establish the manner by which the appellate jurisdiction of the United States Supreme Court is exercised.
(C) unconstitutional, because they infringe the sovereign right of states to have their supreme courts review decisions of their lower state courts.
(D) unconstitutional, because under Article III of the Constitution, the United States Supreme Court does not have authority to review directly decisions of lower state courts.

Answer to Question 128

Article III of the U.S. Constitution gives Congress the authority to regulate the appellate jurisdiction of the Supreme Court. Since the Supreme Court has the authority to review state court decisions involving federal questions, Congress has the authority to provide for direct review of lower state court decisions. (B) is therefore correct.

(A) is incorrect because the issue in the question is congressional control of Supreme Court appellate jurisdiction, not energy usage, and because Congress probably does not have plenary power over issues of energy usage. That power is shared with the states.

(C) is incorrect because the issues involved in these cases arise under federal law, namely the constitutionality of state law under the federal constitution, and the U.S. Supreme Court has ultimate review. Congress has the power to provide for a shorter appeal process.

(D) is incorrect because it misstates the authority of Congress over the appellate jurisdiction of the U.S. Supreme Court.

Question 129

The state of Rio Grande entered into a contract with Roads, Inc., for construction of a four-lane turnpike. Prior to commencement of construction, the legislature, in order to provide funds for parks, repealed the statute authorizing the turnpike and cancelled the agreement with Roads, Inc. Roads, Inc., sued the state to enforce its original agreement. In ruling on this case, a court should hold that the state statute cancelling the agreement is

(A) valid, because constitutionally the sovereign is not liable except with its own consent.
(B) valid, because the legislature is vested with constitutional authority to repeal laws it has enacted.
(C) invalid, because a state is equitably estopped to disclaim a valid bid once accepted by it.
(D) invalid, because of the constitutional prohibition against impairment of contracts.

Answer to Question 129

The state of Rio Grande has entered into a valid, binding contract with Roads, Inc. The state legislature passed a statute cancelling the contract even though the need for parks was apparent when the contract was made. There was no unforeseen emergency justifying the state's action. Therefore, the act is an unconstitutional impairment of contract, and (D) is the correct answer.

(C) is incorrect because state legislation, if constitutional, would override principles of equitable estoppel.

(B) is incorrect because the clause in the Constitution prohibiting a state from impairing the obligation of contract is a limitation on the state's ability to repeal a contract.

(A) is incorrect because a state's sovereignty is limited by the Constitution.

Question 130

Congress passes a law regulating the wholesale and retail prices of "every purchase or sale of oil, natural gas, and electric power made in the United States." The strongest argument in support of the constitutionality of this statute is that

(A) the Constitution expressly empowers Congress to enact laws for "the general welfare."

(B) Congress has the authority to regulate such products' interstate transportation and importation from abroad.
(C) Congress may regulate the prices of every purchase and sale of goods and services made in this country, because commerce includes buying and selling.
(D) in inseverable aggregates, the domestic purchases or sales of such products affect interstate or foreign commerce.

Answer to Question 130

This question tests the basis of the Congressional power over all commerce in the United States, including local commerce. The rule is that local transactions can be regulated because in the aggregate they affect interstate commerce. (D) is the correct answer.

(A) is incorrect because the General Welfare Clause gives Congress the power to spend, not to regulate.

(B) is incorrect because the power to regulate price is not incident to the power to regulate transportation.

(C) is incorrect because Congress was not given the authority in the Constitution to regulate all commerce, but rather only commerce among the states.

Questions 131 - 133 are based on the following fact situation.

Congress provides by statute that any state that fails to prohibit automobile speeds of over 55 miles per hour on highways within the state shall be denied federal highway construction funding. The state of Atlantic, one of the richest and most highway-oriented states in the country, refuses to enact such a statute.

131. Which of the following potential plaintiffs is most likely to be able to obtain a judicial determination of the validity of this federal statute?

(A) A taxpayer of the United States and the state of Atlantic who wants his state to get its fair share of his tax monies for highways, and fears that, if it does not, his state taxes will be increased to pay for the highway construction in the state of Atlantic that federal funds would have financed.
(B) Contractors who have been awarded contracts by the state of Atlantic for specified highway construction projects, which contracts are contingent on payment to the state of the federal funds to which it would otherwise be entitled.
(C) An automobile owner who lives in the state of Atlantic and regularly uses its highway system.
(D) An organization dedicated to keeping the federal government within the powers granted it by the Constitution.

132. The best argument that can be made in support of the constitutionality of this federal statute is that

(A) the states ceded their authority over highways to the national government when the states accepted federal grants to help finance the highways.
(B) the federal government can regulate the use of state highways without limitation because the federal government paid for most of their construction costs.
(C) reasonable legislators could believe that the 55 mile-an-hour speed limit will assure that the federal money spent on highways results in greater benefit than harm to the public.
(D) a recent public opinion survey demonstrates that 90% of the people in this country support a 55 mile-an-hour speed limit.

133. The federal statute relating to disbursement of highway funds conditioned on the 55 mile-an-hour speed limit is probably

(A) unconstitutional.
(B) constitutional only on the basis of the spending power.
(C) constitutional only on the basis of the commerce power.
(D) constitutional on the basis of both the spending power and the commerce power.

Answer to Question 131

The taxpayer in (A) has no standing to sue because the statute is a regulatory rather than a spending statute. Federal taxpayer standing exists only to challenge the Congressional spending power. Here, Congress seeks to regulate state highway speeds by conditioning receipt of federal funds on Atlantic's passage of state legislation.

The automobile owner in (C) does not have standing as a citizen because the injury suffered by this person is an injury shared with the citizens of Atlantic in general. There is no concrete personal injury.

The organization in (D) has no standing to sue because it has no direct and substantial interest in the outcome of the suit.

(B) is correct because the contractors are harmed specifically by the federal statute. The potential plaintiffs suffer direct economic harm because of the statute, and they may have a cause of action for impairment of contract. Therefore, they have standing to sue.

Answer to Question 132

Exercise of the congressional spending power need only be reasonably related to the grant of that power by the Constitution, and therefore (C) is correct.

(A) is incorrect because the states do not cede authority over highways to the federal government by accepting federal funds, even though their use of such funds may be conditioned upon compliance with congressional requirements.

(B) is incorrect because Congress does not have unlimited regulatory power.

A public opinion survey is irrelevant to the constitutionality of a federal statute, and therefore (D) is incorrect.

Answer to Question 133

Under the Commerce Clause, Congress may regulate highways because of their effect on interstate commerce. Congress may also use the spending power to regulate highways by attaching conditions to the receipt of federal funds by the states. Therefore, (D) is correct.

Question 134

Congress decides that the application of the Uniform Consumer Credit Code should be the same throughout the United States. To that end, it enacts the UCCC as a federal law directly applicable to all consumer credit, small loans, and retail installment sales. The law is intended to protect borrowers and buyers against unfair practices by suppliers of consumer credit.

A national religious organization makes loans throughout the country for the construction and furnishing of churches. The federal UCCC would substantially interfere with the successful accomplishment of that organization's religious objectives. The organization seeks to obtain a declaratory judgment that the federal law may not be applied to its lending activities. As a matter of constitutional law, which of the following best describes the burden that must be sustained?

(A) The federal government must demonstrate that the application of this statute to the lending activities of this organization is necessary to vindicate a compelling governmental interest.
(B) The federal government must demonstrate that a rational legislature could believe that this law helps to achieve a legitimate national interest when applied to both religious and secular lending activities.
(C) The organization must demonstrate that no reasonable legislator could think that application of the UCCC to this organization would be helpful in accomplishing a legitimate governmental objective.
(D) The organization must demonstrate a specific congressional purpose to inhibit the accomplishment of the organization's religious objectives.

Answer to Question 134

The position of the religious organization is that the act of Congress interferes with its free exercise of religion. When an act impinges upon that First Amendment right, it may be sustained only when the interference is necessary to satisfy a compelling governmental interest. Therefore, (A) is the correct answer.

(B) is incorrect because the burden of proof as articulated in *Sherbert v. Verner* is stricter than the rational belief standard set forth in (B).

(C) and (D) are both incorrect because the government, not the individual or organization, has the burden of proof when its statute restricts the free exercise of religion. If this were not a First Amendment case, (C) rather than (D) would set forth the appropriate standard in order to hold a statute unconstitutional.

Questions 135 and 136 are based on the following fact situation.

Three states, East Winnetka, Midland, and West Hampton are located next to one another in that order. The states of East Winnetka and West Hampton permit the hunting and trapping of snipe, but the state of Midland strictly forbids it in order to protect snipe, a rare species of animal, from extinction. The state of Midland has a state statute that provides, "Possession of snipe traps is prohibited. Any game warden finding a snipe trap within the state shall seize and destroy it." Snipe traps cost about $15 each.

Prentis is a resident of West Hampton and an ardent snipe trapper. She drove her car to East Winnetka to purchase a new improved snipe trap from a manufacturer there. In the course of her trip back across Midland with the trap in her car, Prentis stopped in a Midland state park to camp for a few nights. While she was in that park, a Midland game warden saw the trap, which was visible on the front seat of her car. The warden seized the trap and destroyed it in accordance with the Midland statute after Prentis admitted that the seized item was a prohibited snipe trap. No federal statutes or federal administrative regulations apply.

135. Assume that Prentis demonstrates that common carriers are permitted to transport snipe traps as cargo across Midland for delivery to another state and that, in practice, the Midland statute is enforced only against private individuals transporting those traps in private vehicles. If Prentis challenges the application of the Midland statute to her on the basis only of a denial of equal protection, this application of the statute will probably be found

(A) constitutional, because the traps constitute contraband in which Prentis could have no protected property interest.
(B) constitutional, because there is a rational basis for differentiating between the possession of snipe traps as interstate cargo by common carriers and the possession of snipe traps by private individuals.
(C) unconstitutional, because the state cannot demonstrate a compelling public purpose for making this differentiation between common carriers and such private individuals.
(D) unconstitutional, because interstate travel is a fundamental right that may not be burdened by state law.

136. Assume that a valid federal administrative rule, adopted under a federal consumer product safety act, regulates the design of snipe traps. The rule was issued to prevent traps from causing injury to human beings, e.g., by pinching fingers while persons were setting the traps. No other federal law applies. Which of the following best states the effect of the federal rule on the Midland state statute?

(A) The federal rule preempts the Midland state statute, because the federal rule regulates the same subject matter, snipe traps.
(B) The federal rule preempts the Midland state statute, because the federal rule does not contain affirmative authorization for continued state regulation.
(C) The federal rule does not preempt the Midland state statute, because the Midland state statute regulates wild animals, a field of exclusive state power.
(D) The federal rule does not preempt the Midland state statute, because the purposes of the federal rule and the Midland state statute are different.

Answer to Question 135

The differentiation in the enforcement of the Midland statute between personal carriers and commercial carriers constitutes a regulation of economic interests. If subjected to an equal protection challenge, the statute need only meet a rational basis test to be constitutional. Since the state could rationally assume that an individual possessing a trap within the state would use it within the state, while a commercial carrier would not, the statute is rational. (B) is the correct answer.

(A) is incorrect, because the issue is not whether the traps are contraband, but whether the state can properly seize traps held by individuals and not seize traps held by commercial carriers. Whether Prentiss had a property interest in the traps would be relevant only to a due process analysis.

(C) is incorrect because this differentiated enforcement of a statute involves neither a suspect class nor a fundamental right, and therefore the state need not demonstrate a compelling state need.

(D) is incorrect because the state is not burdening interstate travel, but rather enforcing its laws within the boundaries of the state.

Answer to Question 136

To decide this preemption question, you must focus on the purpose of Congress in passing the consumer product safety act and the purpose of the design regulation adopted under it. The purpose of the act and the regulation is to protect consumers from injury, not to protect wildlife. Such a statute does not preempt state statutes on the subject matter of every product regulated. Here, Congress intended only to protect consumers from hazardous products and it did not intend to preempt a state's authority to protect wildlife. (A) is therefore incorrect.

(B) is incorrect because a federal statute need not contain affirmative authorization for states to legislate on the subject matter when the purpose of the federal act is totally different from the state act.

(C) is incorrect because the federal government could also legislate to protect wild animals pursuant to the commerce power. This is not an area of exclusive state power.

(D) is correct because it properly discusses the differences in the purposes of the federal and state acts.

Question 137

Barnes was hired as an assistant professor of mathematics at Reardon State College and is now in his third consecutive one-year contract. Under state law, he cannot acquire tenure until after five consecutive annual contracts. In his third year, Barnes was notified that he would not be re-hired for the following year. Applicable state law and college rules did not require either a statement of reasons or a hearing, and in fact neither was offered to Barnes.

Which of the following, if established, sets forth the strongest constitutional argument Barnes could make to compel the college to furnish him a statement of reasons for the failure to rehire him and an opportunity for a hearing?

(A) There is no evidence that tenured teachers are any more qualified than he is.
(B) He leased a home in reliance on an oral promise of reemployment by the college president.
(C) He was the only teacher at the college whose contract was not renewed that year.
(D) In the expectation of remaining at the college, he had just moved his elderly parent to the town in which the college is located.

Answer to Question 137

The right to a hearing when an individual is dismissed from government employment depends upon whether the individual has been deprived of a property right. In the field of education, tenure or a contract which is either continuing or which the individual has an express or implied right to renew is the type of property interest which cannot be taken away without notice and a hearing. In this question, Barnes does not yet have tenure. Absent some special circumstance which creates a property right, he would have no claim to a hearing under the Due Process Clause. Therefore, the factual pattern which will give him a contract right to be rehired will be his strongest argument for a hearing.

(A) goes to the merits of why he should be rehired for an additional one-year contract, but does not establish any right to be rehired, and is therefore incorrect.

(B) is the correct answer. If the president has authority to enter into a teaching contract, Barnes might have an enforceable contract right because his reliance on the oral promise might take the promise out of the Statute of Frauds. Even if the contract is unenforceable because it cannot be performed in one year, it is still a contract and therefore a property interest.

(C) is incorrect because the fact that most teachers get rehired does not give any one teacher a right to be rehired, unless it amounts to an unwritten policy that all teachers are always rehired.

(D) is incorrect because, even though there was reliance on the expectation that he would be rehired, there was no action from the college which induced that reliance, and therefore no property right was created.

Question 138

The State of Missoula has enacted a new election code designed to increase voter responsibility in the exercise of the franchise and to enlarge citizen participation in the electoral process. None of its provisions conflicts with federal statutes.

The Missoula election code provides that in a special-purpose election for directors of a state watershed improvement district, the franchise is limited to landowners within the district, because they are the only ones directly affected by the outcome. Each vote is weighted according to the proportion of the holding of that individual in relation to the total affected property. The best argument in support of the statute and against the application of the one-person/one-vote principle in this situation is that the principle

(A) applies only to elections of individuals to statewide public office.
(B) does not apply where property rights are involved.
(C) does not apply, because the actions of such a district principally affect landowners.
(D) does not apply because of rights reserved to the states by the Tenth Amendment.

Answer to Question 138

(A) is incorrect because the one person/one vote principle applies to other elective offices, including county and municipal offices.

(B) is incorrect because the principle does apply where property rights are involved as, for example, on bond issues.

(C) is the correct answer because, in the Salyer Land Co. case, the state was permitted, in this limited situation, to allow only landowners to vote, since the election of the directors of a watershed improvement district principally affects landowners. This is highly unusual in franchise law.

(D) is incorrect because the federal government can regulate the right to the franchise under the Equal Protection Clause. The Tenth Amendment does not bar such regulation.

Question 139

A federal criminal law makes it a crime for any citizen of the United States, not specifically authorized by the President, to negotiate with a foreign government for the purpose of influencing the foreign government in relation to a dispute with the United States. The strongest constitutional grounds for the validity of this law is that

(A) under several of its enumerated powers, Congress may legislate to preserve the monopoly of the national government over the conduct of United States foreign affairs.
(B) Congress has the power to legislate in support of the President's power over foreign affairs.
(C) the law deals with foreign relations and therefore is not governed by the First Amendment.
(D) federal criminal laws dealing with international affairs need not be as specific as those dealing with domestic affairs.

Answer to Question 139

This question asks for the constitutional grounds for the validity of the law. Therefore, the proper inquiry is into the source of Congressional power to enact the statute. (A) is the only choice which deals with such a source of power and, therefore, is the correct answer.

(B) is an incorrect answer because Congress has no inherent or granted power to legislate in support of the powers of other branches. The Necessary and Proper Clause only justifies actions in support of Congress' enumerated powers.

(C) is incorrect because it deals with a response to a possible attack on the validity of the law, not the source of Congress' power to legislate.

(D) is incorrect because it deals with a response to a charge that the law is unconstitutionally vague, rather than the source of congressional power to enact it.

Question 140

The federal government has complete jurisdiction over certain park land located within the state of Plains. To conserve the wildlife that inhabits that land, the federal government has enacted a statute forbidding all hunting of animals in the federal park. That statute also forbids the hunting of animals that have left the federal park and entered the state of Plains.

Hanson has a hunting license from the state of Plains authorizing him to hunt deer anywhere in the state. On land within the state of Plains located adjacent to the federal park, Hanson shoots a deer he knows has recently left the federal land.

Hanson is prosecuted for violating the federal hunting law. The strongest ground supporting the constitutionality of the federal law forbidding the hunting of wild animals that wander off federal property is that

(A) this law is a necessary and proper means of protecting United States property.
(B) the animals are moving in the stream of interstate commerce.
(C) the police powers of the federal government encompass protection of wild animals.
(D) shooting wild animals is a privilege, not a right.

Answer to Question 140

Article IV of the Constitution gives the federal government broad rights with respect to its property. An incident of this constitutional property right is the power over wild animals that regularly inhabit but have strayed from federal property. (A) is correct.

It is likely that Congress could pass such a statute pursuant to its power to regulate interstate commerce. However, the question asked for the strongest ground supporting the constitutionality of the statute. Since the wild animals are federal property, the property power is a stronger argument. (B) is therefore incorrect, not because it is not a ground to uphold the statute, but because there is a stronger ground presented in another choice.

(C) is incorrect because there is no federal police power which would serve as a justification to uphold the constitutionality of statutes.

(D) is incorrect because it does not set forth the basis on which the constitutionality of the statute rests.

Question 141

A federal statute requires United States civil service employees to retire at age 75. However, that statute also states that civil service employees of the armed forces must retire at age 65.

Powell, a 65-year-old civil service employee of the Department of the Army, seeks a declaratory judgment that would forbid his mandatory retirement until age 75.

The strongest argument that Powell can make to invalidate the requirement that he retire at age 65 is that the law

(A) denies him a privilege or immunity of national citizenship.
(B) deprives him of a property right without just compensation.
(C) is not within the scope of any of the enumerated powers of Congress in Article I, §8.
(D) invidiously discriminates against him on the basis of age in violation of the Fifth Amendment.

Answer to Question 141

The Privileges and Immunities Clause of the Fourteenth Amendment applies only to state infringement on the privileges of national citizenship. Here, a federal statute requires Prentis to retire at age 65. No state discrimination is involved, and therefore (A) is incorrect.

(B) is incorrect because it addresses the wrong constitutional concepts. The issue is not whether the right to earn a living is a property right triggering the rights to procedural due process and compensation for a taking, but rather whether the classification of certain civil servants as a separate category by the legislature serves a rational purpose.

(C) is incorrect because under Article I, §8, Congress has the power to make rules for the regulation of the armed forces, and may also make any laws necessary and proper for carrying out that power.

Age is not a suspect classification; however, if Prentis can prove that the federal requirement of retirement at age 65 for civil servants of the armed forces is not rationally related to a legitimate U.S. goal, then the statute may be invalidated on the basis that it arbitrarily classifies a certain group of civil servants in violation of the Equal Protection Clause of the Fifth Amendment, which protects citizens against discriminatory federal action. Therefore, (D) is correct.

Question 142

Congress passes an Energy Conservation Act. The act requires all users of energy in this country to reduce their consumption by a percentage to be set by a presidential executive order. The act sets forth specific standards the President must use in setting the percentage and detailed procedures to be followed.

The provision that allows the President to set the exact percentage is probably

(A) constitutional, because it creates a limited administrative power to complement the statute.
(B) constitutional, because inherent executive powers permit such action even without statutory authorization.
(C) unconstitutional as an undue delegation of legislative power to the executive.
(D) unconstitutional, because it violates the Due Process Clause of the Fifth Amendment.

Answer to Question 142

Congress has the power to delegate to the President discretion in the administration of laws, as long as there are standards which set forth how that discretion is to be exercised. This statute sets forth such standards and is therefore constitutional. (A) is the correct answer.

(B) is incorrect because it does not focus on the issue presented by the question. You are asked whether the standard set forth in the statute meets constitutional muster, and should not pick an answer which deals with the inherent power of the President if the standard were not there. (A) is a more sharply focused choice, goes directly to the issue and is the better answer.

(C) is incorrect because such a limited delegation to the President is constitutional.

(D) is incorrect because there is no violation of due process when the President sets forth legislative-type standards pursuant to a proper delegation. There is no constitutional right to a hearing for any individual affected.

Question 143

Congress enacts a law providing that all disagreements between the United States and a state over federal grant-in-aid funds shall be settled by the filing of a suit in the federal district court in the affected state. "The judgment of that federal court shall be transmitted to the head of the federal agency dispensing such funds, who, if satisfied that the judgment is fair and lawful, shall execute the judgment according to its terms." This law is

(A) constitutional, because disagreements over federal grant-in-aid funds necessarily

involve federal questions within the judicial power of the United States.
(B) constitutional, because the spending of federal monies necessarily includes the authority to provide for the effective settlement of disputes involving them.
(C) unconstitutional, because it vests authority in the federal court to determine a matter prohibited to it by the Eleventh Amendment.
(D) unconstitutional, because it vests authority in a federal court to render an advisory opinion.

Answer to Question 143

Federal court jurisdiction under Article III of the Constitution extends only to cases and controversies - i.e, lawsuits where the court has the power to enter a binding judgment in a dispute between litigants. The lawsuit in this case has all of the characteristics of a case or controversy except that the judgment is only advisory, not binding on the federal agency. Therefore, (D) is the correct answer.

(C) is incorrect because the Eleventh Amendment only prevents a citizen of one state from suing a state in the federal court. It does not prevent a state from suing the United States.

(B) is incorrect because the federal court system cannot be used as a means to settle disputes unless the dispute is framed as a case or controversy.

(A) is incorrect because, even though the disputes raise a federal question, they are not resolved in this instance through the framework of a case or controversy.

Question 144

The city of Newtown adopted an ordinance providing that street demonstrations involving more than 15 persons may not be held in commercial areas during "rush hours." "Exceptions" may be made to the prohibition "upon 24-hour advance application to and approval by the police department." The ordinance also imposes sanctions on any person "who shall, without provocation, use to or of another, and in his presence, opprobrious words or abusive language tending to cause a breach of the peace." The ordinance has not yet had either judicial or administrative interpretation. Which of the following is the strongest argument for the facial unconstitutionality of both parts of the ordinance?

(A) No type of prior restraint may be imposed on speech in public places.
(B) Laws regulating, by their terms, expressive conduct or speech may not be overbroad or unduly vague.
(C) The determination whether public gatherings may be lawfully held cannot be vested in the police.
(D) The right of association in public places without interference is assured by the First and Fourteenth Amendments.

Answer to Question 144

A statute is unconstitutional on its face if it is overbroad or vague. If a statute is not precise, or if it covers protected conduct, people who would ordinarily exercise their right of free speech would be afraid to do so lest they violate the statute. Therefore, someone who is charged under the statute may attack it on its face. (B) is thus the correct answer.

(A) is incorrect because a narrowly drawn licensing statute, which regulates the time, place and manner of speech, and not its content, will be constitutional.

(C) is incorrect because determination of whether public gatherings may be lawfully held can be vested in the police if their discretion is narrowly restricted.

(D) is incorrect because, although it is a broad general statement that is largely true, the statement does not attack the statute on its face. Also, the right of association is subject to reasonable time, place and manner restrictions, which the statement does not recognize.

Notice that the fact pattern says that the ordinance had not been construed. If it had, and had been construed narrowly so that it told people what conduct it punished, and the state was allowed to punish people for such conduct, then the statute could not be attacked on its face.

Questions 145 and 146 are based on the following fact situation.

John Doe, the owner of a milk container manufacturing firm, sought to focus public attention on the milk packaging law of the State of Clinton in order to have it repealed. On a weekday at 12:00 noon, he delivered an excited, animated, and loud harangue on the steps of the state capitol in front of the main entryway. An audience of 200 onlookers, who gathered on the steps, heckled him and laughed as he delivered his tirade. Doe repeatedly stated, gesturing expressively and making faces, that "the g-ddamned milk packaging law is stupid," and that "I will strangle every one of those g-ddamned legislators I can get hold of because this law they created proves they are all too dumb to live." After about fifteen minutes, Doe stopped speaking, and the amused crowd dispersed.

There are three relevant statutes of the State of Clinton. The first statute prohibits "all speech making, picketing, and public gatherings of every sort on the Capitol steps in front of the main entryway between 7:45 a.m. - 8:15 a.m, 11:45 a.m. - 12:15 p.m., 12:45 p.m. - 1:15 p.m., and 4:45 p.m. - 5:15 p.m., on Capitol working days."

145. A second statute punishes "any person who shall intentionally threaten the life or safety of any public official for any act which he performed as part of his public office." Which of the following statements is correct concerning the possible punishment of Doe under the second statute?

(A) The statute is unconstitutional on its face.
(B) The statute is constitutional on its face, but Doe could not constitutionally be punished under it for this speech.
(C) Doe could constitutionally be punished under the statute for his speech.
(D) Doe could constitutionally be punished under the statute for his speech, but only if one or more legislators were actually present when he delivered it.

146. A third state statute, enacted in 1880, makes criminal "the utterance in any public place of any blasphemy or sacrilege." Assume that there have been only a few recorded prosecutions under the 1880 statute. Doe is charged with violating its proscriptions. The charge is based wholly on the speech he delivered on the steps of the Clinton state capitol. Which of the following constitutional defenses to this prosecution under the 1880 statute would be the LEAST likely to succeed?

(A) This statute is vague and therefore violates the Due Process Clause of the Fourteenth Amendment.
(B) This statute is an establishment of religion and therefore violates the Due Process Clause of the Fourteenth Amendment.
(C) Application of this statute to Doe denies him equal protection of the laws in violation of the Fourteenth Amendment.
(D) Application of this statute to Doe denies him freedom of speech in violation of the Fourteenth Amendment.

Answer to Question 145

The same considerations of vagueness and overbreadth are applicable in this question to an attack on the statute on its face. This statute is also quite specific. It requires a threat to the life of a public official on account of official actions. A vagueness attack might be made upon the word "threat," but it clearly indicates to an actor that a philosophical discussion of political issues is not covered. The statute does not threaten to punish protected speech, and therefore is not overbroad. Therefore, (A) is incorrect.

(B) is correct and (C) is incorrect because the statute could not be constitutionally applied to Doe. This statute is a regulation of content of speech rather than time, place, and manner. Since Doe's speech does not incite immediate harm, it is constitutionally protected and the statute cannot be constitutionally applied to Doe. Although Doe threatened the lives of the legislators voting for the Milk Act, there was no threat of imminent harm to any legislator or the audience.

(D) is incorrect because the speech, in the context in which it was made, cannot be reasonably construed as an immediate threat to a legislator, even if one were in the audience. It is mere hyperbole.

Answer to Question 146

The words "blasphemy" and "sacrilege" do not have precise meaning. They will be differently construed by individuals with different religious beliefs. "Blasphemy" is defined as speaking of something sacred in an irreverent manner. "Sacrilege" is the profanation of something sacred. Neither term satisfies the constitutional standards of preciseness. Therefore, (A) would be a good constitutional defense and is a wrong answer.

Since the statute criminalizes statements which attack religion, it could be construed as an establishment of religion. (B) is therefore a good constitutional defense and a wrong answer.

The statute regulates the content of speech and could only be valid if applied to situations where there is an imminent threat of serious harm. Therefore, (D) is a good constitutional defense and a wrong answer.

The statute involves neither a fundamental interest nor a suspect classification as those standards have developed under the Equal Protection Clause. Therefore, (C) would not be a good constitutional defense and is the correct answer.

Questions 147 and 148 are based on the following fact situation.

The Federal Automobile Safety Act establishes certain safety and performance standards for all automobiles manufactured in the United States. The Act creates a five-member "Automobile Commission" to investigate automobile safety, to make recommendations to Congress for new laws, to make further rules establishing safety and performance standards, and to prosecute violations of the act. The chairman is appointed by the President, two members are selected by the President pro tempore of the Senate, and two by the Speaker of the House of Representatives.

Minicar, Inc., a minor United States car manufacturer, seeks to enjoin enforcement of the Commission's rules.

147. The best argument that Minicar can make is that

(A) legislative power may not be delegated by Congress to an agency in the absence of clear guidelines.
(B) the commerce power does not extend to the manufacture of automobiles not used in interstate commerce.
(C) Minicar is denied due process of law because it is not represented on the Commission.
(D) the Commission lacks authority to enforce its standards because not all of its members were appointed by the President.

148. The appropriate decision for the court is to

(A) allow the Commission to continue investigating automobile safety and making recommendations to Congress.
(B) allow the Commission to prosecute violations of the act but not allow it to issue rules.
(C) forbid the Commission to take any action under the act.
(D) order that all members of the Commission be appointed by the President by and with the advice and consent of the Senate.

Answer to Question 147

Congress has broad power to delegate its legislative power to administrative agencies. The standards set forth in this act requiring the agency to make rules concerning safety and design standards of automobiles is sufficiently precise, and (A) is therefore incorrect.

Since 1937, the federal commerce power has extended to any manufacturing which affects interstate commerce. The manufacture of automobiles clearly does, so (B) is incorrect.

Procedural due process is required only when the state is depriving an individual of life, liberty, or property. It does not appear that any action has been taken against Minicar. Even if procedural due process were required, the requirements are for a notice and hearing, not for representation on the commission itself. Therefore, (C) is incorrect.

(D) is correct because only a member of the executive branch may prosecute. In order to hold an executive office, the holder must be appointed by the President. Since four out of five members of the Commission are appointed by Congress, the Commission may not legally enforce its standards.

Answer to Question 148

This question illustrates how the choices in a subsequent question can be a clue to the answer to a previous question. (D) and (A) clearly indicate that the problem with the act is the fact that Congress has appointed members of the Commission, which is the correct answer to the previous question.

The appropriate remedy when the act has improperly given Congress the power to appoint members of an independent agency is to construe the act so that the powers of the commission are restricted to those things which a body whose members are appointed by Congress may properly perform, namely, to advise Congress on appropriate legislation. (A) is therefore correct.

(B) is incorrect because prosecution of violations is the function of the executive, and can properly be conducted only if all members of the commission were appointed by the President.

(C) is incorrect because the commission, even if it contains members appointed by the President, may continue advising Congress on legislation, since this is neither an executive nor a legislative function.

(D) is incorrect because a court cannot change the substantive provisions of an act to make it constitutional. All it can do is declare that the act is unconstitutional as written. It is the function of the legislature to rewrite the act so that it is constitutional.

Question 149

Pursuant to a state statute, Clovis applied for tuition assistance to attend the Institute of Liberal Arts. He was qualified for such assistance in every way, except that he was a resident alien who did not intend to become a United States citizen.

The state's restriction of such grants to United States citizens or resident aliens seeking such citizenship is probably

(A) valid, because aliens are not per se "a discrete and insular minority" specially protected by the Fourteenth Amendment.
(B) valid, because the line drawn by the state for extending aid was reasonably related to a legitimate state interest.
(C) invalid, because the justifications for this restriction are insufficient to overcome the burden imposed on a state when it uses such an alienage classification.
(D) invalid, because the Privileges and Immunities Clause of Article IV does not permit such an arbitrary classification.

Answer to Question 149

Alienage is a somewhat suspect classification under the Equal Protection Clause. For a state to discriminate on that basis, it must show that an important state interest is protected by the classification. No such interest is protected by denying financial assistance to attend a state school. Therefore, the state action is unconstitutional and (C) is correct.

(B) is incorrect because the line drawn by the state did not relate to essential governmental functions, the area where the state can discriminate between aliens and citizens.

(D) is incorrect because the Privileges and Immunities Clause of Article IV protects citizens of other states, not aliens.

(A) is incorrect because aliens have been classified as a discrete and insular minority without political representation, and have been given protection under the Equal Protection Clause.

Questions 150 and 151 are based on the following fact situation.

An act of Congress provides that "no federal court shall order the implementation of a public school desegregation plan that would require the transportation of any student to a school other than the school closest or next closest to his place of residence."

150. Which of the following is the strongest argument for the constitutionality of the act?

(A) The Fourteenth Amendment authorizes Congress to define governmental conduct.
(B) Under Article III, Congress may restrict the jurisdiction of the federal courts.
(C) Transportation of students is subject to regulation by Congress because commerce is involved.
(D) Congress provides partial support for public education and is therefore entitled to establish conditions upon the expenditure of federal grants.

151. Which of the following is the strongest argument against the constitutionality of the act?

(A) This statute unduly burdens interstate commerce.
(B) Congress cannot limit the authority of federal courts to hear and decide cases properly presented for decision.
(C) The Privileges and Immunities Clause of the Fourteenth Amendment prohibits Congress from limiting the forms of relief afforded by federal courts.
(D) The courts, not Congress, have the primary responsibility for defining the minimum requirements of the Equal Protection Clause of the Fourteenth Amendment.

Answer to Question 150

The statute involved in this question is a limitation upon the type of remedy which can be decreed by a federal court in a school desegregation case.

Since this statute does not purport to be a regulation of commerce, but rather a limitation on court power, the Commerce Clause is not the strongest argument for its constitutionality, and (C) is incorrect.

(D) is incorrect because the statute is not a spending statute and does not attach conditions incident to the spending of federal funds. Moreover, if the statute were held to be an unconstitutional act which promoted segregation, authority under the spending power would be irrelevant.

There once was a theory based upon *Katzenbach v. Morgan* that Congress had the power to define the substantive content of the Equal Protection Clause. However, in *Oregon v. Mitchell*, the court retreated from that position and held that the substantive content of the Equal Protection Clause was a matter for court development, not congressional definition. Therefore, (A) is incorrect.

(B) is correct because the Constitution gives Congress the power to establish and prescribe the jurisdiction of lower federal courts and the power to limit the appellate jurisdiction of the Supreme Court. As long as Congress has not provided a rule of decision in a pending case or limited the inherent powers a court needs to operate as a court, such legislation will be upheld. (B) most clearly provides authority for what the act purports to do - limit the power of the courts.

Answer to Question 151

This statute does not purport to affect interstate commerce. In any event, Congress has the power to burden interstate commerce pursuant to the commerce power, and such activity is not really subject to judicial review. (A) is therefore incorrect.

(B) is incorrect because it is contrary to a specific constitutional provision which authorizes Congress to establish and set the jurisdiction of all federal courts except the original jurisdiction of the Supreme Court.

(C) is incorrect because the court has not developed the Privileges and Immunities Clause of the Fourteenth Amendment as a substantive protection of civil rights.

(D) is correct because in *Oregon v. Mitchell*, the Court reserved to the judiciary the power to determine the substantive content of the Equal Protection Clause. If the limitation on the busing remedy were held to be an invalid attempt to limit school desegregation, then the attempt by Congress to limit the federal courts would be invalid.

Question 152

The President of the United States recognizes the country of Ruritania and undertakes diplomatic relations with its government through the Secretary of State. Ruritania is governed by a repressive totalitarian government.

In an appropriate federal court, Dunn brings a suit against the President and Secretary of State to set aside this action on the ground that it is inconsistent with the principles of our constitutional form of government. Dunn has a lucrative contract with the United States Department of Commerce to provide commercial information about Ruritania. The contract expressly terminates, however, "when the President recognizes the country of Ruritania and undertakes diplomatic relations with its government."

Which of the following is the most proper disposition of the Dunn suit by the federal court?

(A) suit dismissed, because Dunn does not have standing to bring this action
(B) suit dismissed, because there is no adversity between Dunn and the defendants
(C) suit dismissed, because it presents a nonjusticiable political question
(D) suit decided on the merits

Answer to Question 152

Since this suit involves the conduct of foreign relations, an area of authority reserved by the Constitution to the President of the United States and not the federal courts, the political question doctrine requires that the suit be dismissed. (C) is therefore the correct answer. (D), which states that the suit should be decided on its merits, is wrong.
(A) is incorrect because Dunn has sufficient economic interest in the outcome of the litigation to have standing.
(B) is incorrect because Dunn and the defendants (the President and the Secretary of State) are in fact adversaries in this matter.

Question 153

Congress enacts a criminal statute prohibiting "any person from interfering in any way with any right conferred on another person by the Equal Protection Clause of the Fourteenth Amendment."

Application of this statute to Jones, a private citizen, would be most clearly constitutional if Jones, with threats of violence, coerces

(A) a public school teacher to exclude black pupils from her class, solely because of their race.
(B) black pupils, solely because of their race, to refrain from attending a privately owned and operated school licensed by the state.
(C) a bus driver, who operates a free school bus service under the sponsorship of a local church, to refuse to allow black pupils on the bus, solely because of their race.
(D) the federal official in charge of distributing certain federal benefits directly to students from distributing them to black pupils, solely because of their race.

Answer to Question 153

This statute, since it was passed under the authority of the Fourteenth Amendment, is most clearly constitutional when the person violating the statute causes state action to be taken which discriminates on the basis of race.
(A) is correct because the action of the public school teacher constitutes state action, whether coerced or not.
(B) is incorrect because the school involved is a private school and the state licensure does not transform the school into an agency of the state.
(C) is incorrect because the operation of the bus is private rather than state action.
(D) is incorrect because the actions of the federal official are federal rather than state action.

CRIMINAL LAW & PROCEDURE QUESTIONS

Question 1

After tryouts in which her daughter was not chosen to be a member of the local high school cheerleader squad, Mother shot at the leg of Vickie, the newly chosen head cheerleader for the school team, intending to injure her leg enough to hospitalize her for a few weeks during football season, but not to kill her. Vickie died of shock before she reached the hospital.

What is the most serious offense of which Mother could properly be convicted?

(A) murder
(B) voluntary manslaughter
(C) involuntary manslaughter
(D) none of the above

Answer to Question 1

(B) is incorrect because voluntary manslaughter requires provocation. Winning the competition for the head cheerleader position does not constitute provocation by Vickie.

(C), which offers the choice of involuntary manslaughter is incorrect because involuntary means unintentional and Mother did intend her actions.

(A) is correct. If there is intent to do serious bodily harm, and death results from the act committed, the crime is murder even though the defendant did not intend that the victim should die. The intent to do serious bodily harm constitutes sufficient malice to support a charge of murder. In this case, although Mother did not intend to kill Vickie, she did intend to commit serious bodily harm. She is liable for any consequences of her intended act. (D) is obviously incorrect because (A) is correct.

Question 2

Four case summaries appear below. Select the case that would be most applicable as a precedent to answer the following question:

Pro and Bro were driving on a city street en route to rob a store when a boy threw a rock at the car, denting it. Pro deliberately ran into the boy with the car, causing injuries from which the boy died 10 days later. Pro is charged with murder. Should he be convicted?

(A) Dolores saw her husband and a co-worker named Barbara go into a hotel under circumstances that made her suspect adultery. While following them after they came out of the hotel, Dolores was told by Fred, another co-worker whose help Dolores had enlisted, that he [Fred] had also seen them go into the same hotel the day before. Dolores took a handgun from the glove compartment of her car and shot Barbara dead. Dolores's conviction of murder was reversed, as the evidence showed guilt only of manslaughter.
(B) During an argument in the shop, Deadhead hit a fellow worker on the head with an iron crowbar, crushing his skull. Although Deadhead testified that he did not intend to kill, his conviction of murder was affirmed.
(C) Debtor owed Banker $5000. Impatient at Debtor's failure to pay, Banker went to Debtor's office. He demanded payment, brandished a revolver, and threatened to shoot Debtor if he did not pay up. All this occurred in the presence of Debtor's aged secretary, who as a result of the excitement, died of heart failure on the spot. Banker's conviction of manslaughter was affirmed.
(D) Duane and Wayne held up a store and tried to escape in their car. Shots from pursuing police disabled the car, and Duane was captured. Wayne fled on foot, commandeered a passing truck, and at gunpoint forced the driver to drive off. A

chase extending over 25 miles followed. In an exchange of shots, a policeman was killed and Wayne escaped. Duane's conviction of murder was affirmed.

Answer to Question 2

The process of answering a question where your task is to pick the most applicable of four precedents is first to decide the principle of law represented by each precedent and then choose the one that would most likely control the fact pattern at issue.

Precedent (A) holds that finding a spouse in the act of adultery, or being told of the same, is sufficient provocation to reduce an intentional killing to voluntary manslaughter if the killing takes place in the heat of passion. This choice can be eliminated easily because the throwing of the rock against Pro's car is not adequate provocation to reduce the crime to manslaughter and, therefore, precedent (A) is inapplicable.

Precedent (C) holds that a death occurring within the course of a misdemeanor *malum in se* is misdemeanor-manslaughter. Banker was owed the money. There was no robbery because there was no intent to steal. Thus, Banker was engaged at most in an assault. This choice can be eliminated easily because there is no misdemeanor present in the fact pattern in the question. If anything, Pro was involved in a felony. Therefore, precedent (C) is inapplicable.

Precedent (D) holds that a death occurring in the course of a dangerous felony is murder even if there was no intention to kill, and that the dangerous felony extends to the process of escaping from the scene of the crime even if the escape covers a great distance. In this case, the felony-murder precedent would be applicable if the death occurred in the attempted commission of a felony. Here, the death occurred several miles from where the felony was to occur, so it is at least arguable that the felons were not yet close enough to be in the attempted commission of a felony. Moreover, the fact that Pro deliberately drove the car into the boy shows an intent to do serious bodily injury, which qualifies as sufficient malice to make Pro guilty of murder. We need not rely on a felony-murder theory here as to Pro. (The felony-murder theory would be a better theory to hold Bro liable for murder, since it does not appear that Bro intended to harm the child. In that case, we would have to rely on Bro's guilty intent to commit the crime of robbery as a substitute for the *mens rea* required for murder.)

Precedent (B) holds that intent to inflict serious bodily harm is a sufficient *mens rea* (malice) for the homicide crime of murder if the victim dies from that serious bodily harm. Precedent (B) is the most applicable because deliberately driving a car into a person shows an intent to do great bodily harm and, therefore, the death occurring in such a case is murder.

Question 3

Mom and Dad are devout members of the Scientific Way, a religious sect that believes in the power of faith healing. They live in a state where the common-law rules concerning murder have not been altered by statute or decision. When their ten-year-old daughter Valerie suffered from acute appendicitis, they called in Marjorie, a religious practitioner, who instructed them about church teaching on this matter and told them that their child would not die. All three of them prayed over Valerie. Surgery would have saved her, but neither Mom nor Dad called for medical assistance. After the appendix ruptured, Valerie died of the resulting complications.

Mom and Dad have been indicted for the crime of murder. If they are acquitted, it will most likely be because

(A) they did not intend to kill or to harm Valerie.
(B) they neither premeditated nor deliberated.
(C) they in good faith relied upon what Marjorie told them, so if Marjorie was wrong, they have the defense of mistake of fact.
(D) the First Amendment Free Exercise Clause protects their sincerely held religious beliefs.

Answer to Question 3

A murder conviction requires an intentional killing, or the intentional infliction of serious bodily harm. If the defendants neither intended to harm Valerie, nor to kill her, they are not guilty of murder. It is clear from the facts of the question that they did not desire the death of their daughter, nor did they desire to do her great bodily harm. Therefore, if they are acquitted, it will be because they did not have the requisite intent to commit common-law murder. (A) is correct.

(B) is incorrect because deliberation and premeditation are not the required mental states for murder. Rather, they are the mental states required for first-degree murder in a jurisdiction that has divided murder into degrees, an issue not relevant to this question. Under the common law, which applies here, the defendants could be liable for murder even though premeditation or deliberation is not present, if they acted with the intent to kill or harm the victim.

(C) is incorrect because to take advantage of the defense of mistake of fact in regard to a general intent crime, the mistake must be reasonable in an objective sense. Here, the actions of the defendants in failing to obtain medical help for their seriously ill child were not reasonable in relation to societal standards. If mistake is to be a defense in this case, it is only because it negates the specific intent required to be guilty of murder.

(D) presents a tempting choice because of the religious aspect to the question. However, the First Amendment Free Exercise of Religion Clause protects only sincerely held religious beliefs; it does not protect actions based upon those beliefs if the government has a compelling interest in prohibiting those acts. Here, the state has a compelling interest in protecting the lives of the children within its jurisdiction, and therefore may punish parents who neglect to obtain medical aid for their children if a death results.

Question 4

What is the most serious crime for which Dave can be convicted in each case?

CASE I - Fearing home intruders, Dave put a mechanical device in his home that would fire a shotgun at close range at the front door of his house, if the door were forced open at a time when the device was operative. Dave set the device and left on a three-week vacation. Seeing two weeks' worth of newspapers piled in front of Dave's front door, Ned, a neighbor, was afraid that Dave had had a heart attack, and forced the front door open to investigate. The shotgun fired and killed Ned.

CASE II - Dave's Mom was suffering from terminal cancer and was in intense pain. Dave regularly injected the prescribed dosage of painkiller into Mom's arm by hypodermic needle. Mom pleaded with Dave to give her a double dosage of painkiller, which they both knew would be fatal. At first Dave refused, but after several days of pleading by Mom, Dave injected a double dosage of painkiller into her, and Mom died instantly.

The most serious crime for which Dave could be convicted is

(A) manslaughter in both Case I and Case II.
(B) manslaughter in Case I and murder in Case II.
(C) murder in Case I and manslaughter in Case II.
(D) murder in both Case I and Case II.

Answer to Question 4

Dave committed murder in both Case I and Case II. Where there is a killing by a mechanical device, the person who sets the device is responsible for its operation to the same extent as he would be if he were present and pulled the trigger at the time it went off. Since use of deadly force to protect property is not a defense to a murder charge, the killing in Case I was committed without justification, excuse or mitigation. The homicide in Case I was therefore murder, and not manslaughter.

Case II describes a mercy killing, which is an intentional killing -- a shortening of Mom's life. The victim's consent to homicide, absent a statute permitting such an act, is never a defense nor a mitigating factor that will reduce the homicide crime from murder to manslaughter. There is no evidence of provocation or an imperfect defense here that would reduce the crime to manslaughter. Therefore, (D) is correct and the other choices are incorrect.

Question 5

Dan is having a love affair with Gina, and lies to her about his marital status. Gina finds out that Dan is lying, and shoots him. Wanda, his wife, finds Dan in his wounded condition and asks him what happened. He says a woman shot him, and begs her forgiveness for his infidelity. Wanda walks away in anger. Dan dies of the wound, but would not have died if medical assistance had been summoned. Who is guilty of a homicide crime?

(A) Gina only
(B) Wanda only
(C) Both Wanda and Gina
(D) Either Wanda or Gina, but not both

Answer to Question 5

Both Wanda and Gina are guilty of a homicide crime. Wanda is guilty, despite the general rule that there is no affirmative duty to aid an individual in distress unless you are the cause of the distress. Although it was merely Wanda's inaction (refusing to summon medical assistance) which was a "but for" cause of Dan's death, she is nonetheless guilty of a homicide crime because the husband-wife relationship imposes on her a duty to aid her husband. A breach of that duty will result in imposition of criminal homicide liability if the intentional failure to summon aid causes death. Dan's adultery does not provide an excuse. Wanda's crime would probably be involuntary manslaughter based upon willful, wanton conduct in refusing to summon aid.

Gina also is guilty of a homicide crime, probably murder, since she shot Dan with the apparent intent to do at least great bodily harm, and the intervening conduct of Wanda did not break the chain of causation. (C) is correct because both may be convicted of a homicide crime, and the other answers are incorrect for this reason.

(D) is also incorrect because it suggests that the liability of one person for a murder provides a defense to another.

Question 6

Kimberly is a doctor at the County Hospital. Peter is her ex-lover who left her for another woman. John is a local drug dealer to whom Peter owes $50,000. One day, as Peter was walking across the street, John deliberately ran over him with his car. Peter was alive at the time he arrived at County Hospital, but would have died in an hour from the injuries inflicted by John. At the hospital, Peter was first seen by Kimberly, the emergency room doctor. Instead of treating him for his injuries, Kimberly gave him an unnecessary lobotomy knowing that he was unlikely to survive in his weakened state, and Peter died on the operating table as a result of the operation. As a result of these actions,

(A) both Kimberly and John are guilty of attempted murder.
(B) both Kimberly and John are guilty of murder.
(C) John is guilty of murder and Kimberly is guilty of attempted murder.
(D) Kimberly is guilty of murder and John is guilty of attempted murder.

Answer to Question 6

John assaulted Peter with the intent to kill him, but Peter's death was actually caused by a totally independent criminal act committed at the hospital. Since his actions did not result in

Peter's death, John is not guilty of murder, but is guilty of attempted murder. (B) and (C) are incorrect.

Kimberly's actions, however, were the "but for" and proximate cause of Peter's death. They were intentional. Thus, Kimberly is guilty of murder, and John is guilty of attempted murder. (D) is correct, and (A) is incorrect.

Question 7

Thelma and Louise planned to rob a convenience store. Thelma entered the convenience store while Louise waited in the car as a lookout. Louise noticed a police car arrive and honked her horn once, this being the prearranged signal. She then drove away. Thelma heard the signal but proceeded to present a note to the cashier demanding money. Thelma was killed as she tried to leave the convenience store, by an off-duty policeman hired by the store. Louise is tried for felony murder. The result is most likely

(A) not guilty, because she was not present at the time.
(B) not guilty, because she withdrew from the conspiracy.
(C) not guilty, because the killing was justifiable.
(D) guilty, because she was a conspirator.

Answer to Question 7

A conspirator is criminally responsible for every crime committed in the course of the felony, whether or not he or she is present. Specifically, a felon can be held responsible under a theory of felony murder for almost every death committed in the course of the felony, whether or not the felon actually did the killing or was even present. Therefore, (A) is incorrect.

(B) is incorrect because Louise did not withdraw from the conspiracy. The honk of the horn in this case could most reasonably be interpreted as a prearranged signal to the felon in the liquor store that there was trouble. It did not indicate to the co-felon, Thelma, that Louise withdrew from the conspiracy. Therefore, since Louise did not communicate her withdrawal, she remains a conspirator and is criminally responsible for any crimes committed within the scope of the conspiracy.

Ordinarily Louise would be liable for any death which occurred as a result of the felony, including the death of her co-conspirator. However, in this case the death was caused by a law enforcement officer. Under the majority *Redline* doctrine, the defendant is not guilty of felony murder in the death of a co-felon caused by a police officer. The rationale for the rule is that a killing committed to prevent a felon's escape is a justifiable homicide under the law. The fact that the officer was off-duty does not change the rule. Therefore, (C) is correct and (D) is incorrect.

Question 8

Al, an adult, induced Bob, an 16-year-old boy, to help him rob a liquor store in a jurisdiction where deliberate and premeditated murder and common-law felony murder are classified as first-degree murder and all other common-law murder is classified as second-degree murder. Al told Bob that all Bob would need to do would be to sit behind the wheel of Al's automobile outside the store, while Al went in and held up the clerk, and be ready to drive off as soon as Al came out with the money.

Al held up the clerk, who was alone in the store. But as he was taking the money from the cash register with one hand while holding a revolver on the clerk with the other, the clerk grabbed for the gun. They struggled for possession for a minute or more, during which time the revolver, still in Al's hand, was discharged, inflicting a fatal wound on the clerk. Al took some of the money, fled, and the two drove off, with Bob driving. Two hours later they were apprehended. They were tried for murder in the first-degree.

Al testified that the revolver was fired accidentally, solely in the course of the struggle for its possession, and that he did not intentionally or voluntarily pull the trigger. Bob testified that he had not seen a revolver in Al's possession, and that he was not told and did not know what means Al intended to use to hold up the clerk.

Assuming that Bob is being tried as an adult, the court's decision should be

(A) both defendants are guilty of murder in the first-degree.
(B) both are guilty of some form of homicide but not first-degree murder.
(C) Al is guilty of first-degree murder, but Bob is guilty of some lesser degree of homicide.
(D) Al is guilty of homicide in some degree, but Bob is not guilty.

Answer to Question 8

The death in this case, although unintentional, occurred in the course of a robbery and is therefore first-degree felony murder under the statute that divides murder into degrees. Al and Bob both committed first-degree murder, because they conspired to rob the liquor store, a dangerous felony, and a death resulted. Al is guilty of first-degree murder under the felony-murder rule, even though the killing itself was unintentional, since the killing occurred within the scope of and within the course of their dangerous felony.

Since they were conspirators, and since Bob was an accomplice to the actual felony of robbery, Al's crimes will be imputed to Bob. The fact that Al induced Bob to help him, or that Bob was only 16, is not a defense for Bob. Al's crime will be imputed to Bob even though he did not know of the gun, because a killing is a likely occurrence during a robbery.

(A) is correct.

Questions 9 and 10 are based on the following fact situation.

Roberta approached a teller at the Bank and slipped a note through the window that said, "This is a robbery, hand over the money." The teller handed her the money and she left the bank. Gary, the bank guard, rushed out of the bank in pursuit and fired one shot at Roberta. However, the bullet missed Roberta, and killed Bystander.

9. If Gary is charged with a homicide crime, he is likely to be found

(A) not guilty, because he did not possess the *mens rea* for a homicide crime.
(B) not guilty, unless his conduct in shooting the bullet was negligent.
(C) guilty of involuntary manslaughter.
(D) guilty of murder.

10. If Roberta is charged with felony murder, she is likely to be found

(A) not guilty because she was not in the commission of the robbery when the death occurred.
(B) not guilty because the killing by the bank guard was a justifiable homicide.
(C) guilty if and only if she was armed.
(D) guilty whether or not she was armed.

Answer to Question 9

The key to answering this question is a knowledge of the concept of *mens rea* and the doctrine of transferred intent. If shooting at Roberta would result in Gary's conviction of a homicide charge, his intent, or *mens rea*, would be transferred to the shooting of Bystander and would support a charge based on Bystander's death. However, Gary's actions in shooting at Roberta were justified and would not support any homicide charge.

(B) is incorrect only in that it gives the wrong reason for the acquittal. This choice states that Gary is not guilty of a homicide crime "unless" he was negligent, i.e., he is guilty "if and only if" he was negligent. The lowest standard that will support a homicide charge is gross negligence, which is the *mens rea* for involuntary manslaughter. The standard for every other homicide crime is higher. Gary was not guilty of gross negligence since he had the right to use deadly force against the bank robber. His conduct in this emergency situation was neither willful and wanton nor reckless and, therefore, also cannot satisfy the requirement for depraved heart murder.

(C) and (D) are incorrect because Gary's actions were justified and, therefore, would not support any homicide charge.

(A) is correct because Gary lacked the requisite *mens rea* to commit a homicide. In this case, Gary was pursuing a fleeing criminal who had just committed the dangerous felony of robbery, and thus he had the right to use deadly force to apprehend that felon. When the bullet killed Bystander by mistake, the doctrine of transferred intent applies the *mens rea* of the intended action to the unintended one. In this case, that *mens rea* will result in a finding that the killing is justified, and therefore Gary is not guilty.

Answer to Question 10

A defendant is guilty of felony murder if (1) a death occurs during the commission of the felony, and (2) the death is proximately caused by the commission of the felony, regardless of whether the defendant or a third person actually caused the death. The time span that is deemed within the commission of the felony starts when the felon is guilty of an attempt and continues through the escape.

Roberta committed the crime of robbery because she committed larceny from the bank by putting the teller in fear. Escape from the scene of the crime is included in the commission of the crime. Thus, (A) is incorrect.

(B) is incorrect. Even though Gary would not be guilty of murder because the shooting would be considered a justifiable homicide, Roberta is nevertheless guilty of felony murder. The *Redline* doctrine precludes felony-murder liability for the defendant only when a **co-felon** is killed by a person attempting to thwart the crime. It does not apply if the person killed is anyone but a co-felon.

The death of Bystander, even though proximately caused by the deliberate act of a third party (the bank guard) and not by Roberta, is related to the felony of robbery. Roberta is guilty of the underlying robbery crime, whether or not she was armed. Therefore, (C) is incorrect and (D) is correct.

Question 11

Sean bought a rifle for the purpose of killing Caitlin. He has learned that Caitlin will be marching in the annual St. Patrick's parade. Sean rents a hotel room overlooking the parade route and fires the rifle at Caitlin as her company of dancers marches by. The bullet just misses Caitlin, but hits and kills Maureen who is marching next to her. In addition to being convicted of murder based on a theory of an intentional killing under the doctrine of transferred intent, Sean

(A) could be convicted of murder only on a theory of extreme recklessness.
(B) could be convicted of murder only on a theory of felony murder.
(C) could be convicted of murder on a theory of both felony murder and extreme recklessness.
(D) could not be convicted of murder on any other theory.

Answer to Question 11

(A) correctly states that murder could be found on a theory of extreme recklessness - the abandoned and malignant heart doctrine. Even though there was no intent to kill Maureen, the firing of a rifle into a crowd of marchers carried with it a known, high risk of harm to those not intended to be killed, without any social benefit. However, this is not the only theory on which Sean could be convicted of murder, so (A) is incorrect.

(B) recognizes the theory of felony murder, which could also be used to convict Sean. At the time that Sean shot the bullet which killed Maureen, he was engaged in the attempted murder of Caitlin, a dangerous common-law felony. Ordinarily, a homicide crime such as manslaughter cannot be the underlying crime for felony murder because that would make every manslaughter a felony murder. But the attempted murder of Caitlin can be the underlying felony for the actual murder of

Maureen. Because this is not the only theory, (B) is incorrect.

(C) is correct and (D) is incorrect because Sean could be convicted on a theory of felony murder and on a theory of extreme recklessness.

Question 12

Michiko ran a successful raw fish restaurant in State X. However, business fell off dramatically when Toshio opened a competing restaurant on the same block. To hurt her competition, Michiko decided to spread a drug on some fish served by Toshio's restaurant, which in small quantities would cause numbness in a diner's mouth but in large quantities could be fatal. The drug can legally be sold only to licensed physicians and dentists, who use it as an anesthetic.

Michiko contacted Sam, who sold Michiko the condiments and spices used in her restaurant. She told him of her plan and asked him to obtain a supply of the drug. At first Sam refused, but reluctantly agreed when Michiko threatened to take her business elsewhere. Sam contacted his good friend Phil, a pharmacist, purchased a pound of the drug, and delivered it to Michiko. The next day, Michiko and Toshio attended the same fish auction. Michiko sprinkled enough of the drug on the fish purchased by Toshio so that consumption of one fish would leave the diner with a mild numbness in the mouth.

The next day in Toshio's restaurant, Glutton ordered three times the normal serving of fish. Each of the fish had been sprinkled with the drug. Instead of the mild numbness which would be caused by a normal serving of fish, the drug caused Glutton to suffer a cardiac arrest and die.

Statutes of State X define first-degree murder as "an intentional or premeditated killing of one occurring during the perpetration of a felony"; second-degree murder as a death resulting from an act intended to do bodily harm; and manslaughter as an unlawful killing committed with extreme recklessness. Assault with intent to inflict serious bodily harm is also a felony in the jurisdiction. Each degree of murder and manslaughter is a mutually exclusive crime.

Which of the following individuals would most likely be convicted of second-degree murder?

I. Michiko
II. Sam
III. Phil

(A) I only
(B) I and II only
(C) I and III only
(D) I, II and III

Answer to Question 12

Second-degree murder, under the statute, is a death resulting from an act intended to do bodily harm. Michiko (I) is guilty of second-degree murder because she intended to do bodily harm and did so. It does not matter that she did not know the identity of the person she would actually harm. Sam (II) was a conspirator with Michiko because he supplied the chemical knowing her purpose, and he did not withdraw. Sam is therefore guilty of the same crime as Michiko, second-degree murder.

Phil, on the other hand, did not know the purpose for which the chemical was to be used. He is therefore not guilty under a conspiracy theory for second-degree murder.

Because only Michiko and Sam are guilty of second-degree murder, (B) is correct.

Question 13

Dan and Barbara, who had lived together for many years, spent their summer vacations on a houseboat in Blue Bay. They would frequently leave their home port at the town of Cod and travel into the bay 12 miles to a favorite fishing spot, Fishermen's Reef, which is about one mile from the town of Bass.

When they were fishing on Fishermen's Reef one day, Dan began to complain of chest pains, and pleaded with Barbara to bring the boat to Bass so that he could see a doctor immediately. Although she could reach Bass in approximately 15 minutes and medical facilities were available at dockside, Barbara did not like the harbormaster in Bass, and therefore decided to head home to Cod, nearly an hour and a half away. Dan was in a coma when he arrived at the hospital in Cod, and died there about an hour after being admitted. An autopsy determined that he died of a blood clot in a coronary artery. Further tests showed that the clot could have been dissolved and Dan's life could have been saved if he had received the medical treatment available in Bass within an hour of his first symptoms.

After an investigation, the county attorney indicted Barbara for involuntary manslaughter.

Which of the following facts, if true, would be most helpful in defending Barbara on that charge?

(A) Barbara and Dan were not married.
(B) Dan had not been diagnosed with a heart condition, but had frequently complained to Barbara of severe chest pains caused by indigestion.
(C) If the doctor in Cod had used the drugs available to him as soon as Dan had arrived at the hospital in Cod, it is likely that the clot would have been dissolved and Dan would not have died.
(D) Dan had a serious case of coronary artery disease, and a second heart attack probably would have killed him within a few days anyway.

Answer to Question 13

(A) is a possible answer but is not the best answer. The issue of marriage is irrelevant to Barbara's defense. Under these circumstances, Barbara owed an affirmative duty to Dan to bring him to medical attention. The circumstances where the medical emergency occurred, at sea, where the only person capable of helping him is Barbara, would probably impose a duty.

(C) is incorrect. If Barbara had the *mens rea* necessary for involuntary manslaughter, the negligence of a doctor who later treated Dan would not be a defense. It would not be an intervening cause which would prevent Barbara's negligence from being the proximate cause of Dan's death, since it was Barbara's gross negligence which would have put Dan in a position where even slight negligence by the doctor would result in Dan's death. Therefore, this fact would not be helpful.

(D) is incorrect. A homicide crime occurs when a person with the appropriate *mens rea* shortens the life of the victim. The fact that the victim would soon die of other causes is irrelevant.

(B) is correct. Since Barbara has been indicted for involuntary manslaughter, the prosecution must prove that her conduct in not taking the boat to Bass constituted gross negligence or willful and wanton conduct. Her conduct in not seeking the fastest available medical attention would reach that level of culpability only if she knew or reasonably should have known about the seriousness of Dan's medical condition. The fact that Dan had not had any previous heart attacks and that the same symptoms had occurred in the past when his condition was not serious tend to show that Barbara was not grossly negligent in taking the boat back to Cod.

Question 14

Jim and Dave were fraternity brothers. Each was dating Pam. At the fraternity dining hall one evening, Jim approached Dave and punched him in the stomach in front of a number of their fraternity brothers. As other students separated them, Jim said, "I'm not through with you yet because you had the nerve to date my girl, Pam." Dave was enraged by his injury and the public humiliation of the incident.

Two days later, as Dave sat eating a steak in the dining hall, he saw Jim enter and a group of his friends began to tease Dave about the earlier incident. Shortly thereafter, a careless fellow diner, Vic, then accidentally hit Dave on the back of the head with a tray. Dave picked up his steak knife, wheeled around, and punctured Vic's abdomen, a wound which proved fatal.

Dave is tried for murder in the death of Vic, and the evidence described above is introduced. At the conclusion of the evidence, Dave's lawyer requests that the jury be given an instruction that they can find the defendant guilty of voluntary manslaughter. Should the trial judge so instruct the jury?

(A) Yes, because the jury could find that the defendant had an honest but unreasonable belief that he needed deadly force to defend himself.
(B) Yes, because the jury could find that the defendant possessed the *mens rea* for voluntary manslaughter with respect to Jim because he was adequately provoked and that *mens rea* is transferred to the killing of Vic.
(C) No. The trial court should refuse the instruction because Vic, not Jim, was the victim.
(D) No. The trial court should refuse the instruction because Dave is not entitled to an instruction on self-defense.

Answer to Question 14

There are two possible theories on which a jury can reduce an intentional killing from murder to voluntary manslaughter. The first, which is applicable here, is an imperfect defense. If the defendant has a right of self-defense but exercises it unreasonably by using excessive force, or is careless concerning the identity of the person against whom he has the right, then the imperfect defense will reduce the crime from murder to voluntary manslaughter.

The other theory, a killing in the heat of passion, should probably not be given as a jury instruction. The earlier fight was two days previous. No new provocation took place when Jim entered the dining hall. Even though the earlier fight was an adequate provocation for voluntary manslaughter, as a matter of law, Dave was not in the heat of passion at the time of the stabbing. Therefore, (B) is incorrect.

(C) can be eliminated because the doctrine of transferred intent will allow Dave to argue that his actions toward Vic were in reality directed, albeit unreasonably, against Jim. If Dave had the right of self-defense against Jim, but exercised it imperfectly (against Vic), the jury could consider this as a factor which would reduce the killing of Vic to voluntary manslaughter.

(D) is incorrect because Dave is entitled to have the jury consider voluntary manslaughter. In this case, the defendant had a right of self-defense to use nondeadly force against Jim, because Jim had hit him before and had warned Dave that he would try again. That right of self-defense was unreasonably exercised against Vic, but the jury is entitled to consider this issue in deciding if it should reduce murder to voluntary manslaughter. Therefore, (A) is correct.

Question 15

Natalie and Dean, married for twelve years with a ten-year-old daughter, Jessica, have recently divorced, primarily because of Natalie's relationship with Robert. Natalie has custody of Jessica. One Sunday afternoon, Dean returned to the marital domicile to take Jessica for their weekly visitation, and found her in bed sobbing. When Dean asked the reason for her emotional state, she truthfully told him that Robert had just sexually abused her and then left to go drinking in a neighborhood bar.

Enraged, Dean stormed into the living room and confronted Natalie. During the ensuing heated argument which lasted for 20 minutes, Dean threatened several times to "blow Robert's head off." Dean then demanded the key to his gun cabinet, which was still in the house. Natalie told him that she didn't have it. Dean then spent ten minutes prying open the gun cabinet to obtain his shotgun. He set out on foot to find Robert in one of the neighborhood bars.

Forty minutes later, after searching through three bars, Dean found Robert in a corner booth of Mae's Bar & Grill. Dean approached Robert, pointed the loaded shotgun at his head, and told him he was going to blow his head off for what he had done to Jessica. Robert desperately pleaded for his life, and then drew a knife from his pocket. When Dean saw the knife, he immediately pulled the trigger of the shotgun, instantly killing Robert.

If Dean is charged with a homicide crime for the death of Robert, what is the most likely result?

(A) He will be convicted of no homicide crime, because he killed Robert in self-defense.
(B) He will be convicted of voluntary manslaughter, because he killed Robert in the heat of passion.
(C) He will be convicted of voluntary manslaughter, because Robert's sexual assault on Jessica was adequate provocation.
(D) He will be convicted of murder.

Answer to Question 15

Dean intentionally killed Robert and is guilty of murder unless he either had a state of mind which reduces the crime to manslaughter or has a defense to reduce or preclude his criminal liability. Since, as will be seen below, none of these apply, Dean will be convicted of murder, and (D) is correct.

Dean may not use the defense of self-defense because he was the aggressor in possession of a deadly weapon. He entered the bar and approached Robert with a shotgun and pointed it at Robert's head. He never relinquished the aggressor role and therefore never had the right of self-defense. Therefore, (A) is incorrect.

(B) and (C), which invoke complementary portions of the voluntary manslaughter standard, are both incorrect because both are incomplete. A murder will be reduced to voluntary manslaughter only if the accused acted both in response to adequate provocation and in the heat of passion. (B) cannot be correct because a killing in the heat of passion alone is not enough. (B) is also incorrect because Dean did not kill in the heat of passion. These facts describe a long and purposeful series of acts which culminated in the confrontation at the bar. Dean engaged in a 20-minute argument with his wife, spent 10 minutes obtaining possession of the gun, and 40 minutes searching the neighborhood bars. This should have provided enough time for a reasonable person to cool off -- in other words, Dean had time to deliberate and premeditate this crime.
(C) correctly asserts that adequate provocation existed (the sexual abuse of the accused's daughter), but cannot be correct because that alone is not enough.

Although there is a possible judgment call in this question about whether Dean was in the heat of passion at the time of the killing, the question is structurally designed to make that answer wrong. If Dean were guilty of voluntary manslaughter, there would have to be both adequate provocation and a killing in the heat of passion. If you conclude that Dean committed voluntary manslaughter, it is impossible to pick rationally between (B) and (C).

Question 16

In which of the following cases is the defendant (Dan) guilty of murder?

(A) Vic slaps Dan's wife in Dan's presence. Dan becomes enraged and kills Vic.
(B) Dan observes Vic stealing the hood ornament from his car. Dan immediately shoots Vic.
(C) Vic, a police officer, insults a juvenile, Dan, age 16, by calling him a "dumb little bastard" without justification. Dan stabs and kills the officer.
(D) Dan and Vic have an argument in a bar. Vic throws whiskey in Dan's face. Dan wipes his face, pulls a knife, and fatally stabs Vic.

Answer to Question 16

In this question, all of the killings are intentional. The task is to pick the one **least** likely to be reduced to voluntary manslaughter.

While physical violence in (A) was not inflicted on the defendant personally, observing the infliction of physical violence on a close relative may also be sufficient provocation to reduce the crime to manslaughter.

The intentional killing in (B) may be reduced to voluntary manslaughter if the defendant had a right either to defend his property or to effect an arrest, and used excessive force. The stealing of personal property in his presence gave the defendant the right to use force, but not deadly force. Since he exercised his right imperfectly, the intentional killing will be reduced from murder to voluntary manslaughter.

The intentional killing in (D) may be reduced to voluntary manslaughter if it is found that Dan acted in the heat of passion after adequate provocation. It is possible that the physical violence of throwing the drink in D's face in the course of an argument is sufficient provocation to reduce the killing to voluntary manslaughter.

(C) is correct. The verbal insult by the police officer is not sufficient provocation to reduce murder to manslaughter. Moreover, a juvenile, age 16, is capable of possessing the *mens rea* necessary for murder and may be prosecuted for that crime, though he may be prosecuted in juvenile court.

Question 17

Rita, a leader in the "right to life" movement was seated at a luncheon table during a conference on women's rights next to Abby, a member of the abortion rights league. Just as the salad was served, Rita called Abby a "bloody murderer." Abby stood up and knocked over the chair in which Rita was sitting, sending Rita sprawling to the floor. Abby then went back to eating her salad. Rita picked herself up, took a sharp knife from the table and moved menacingly toward Abby. Abby tried to get out of the way but was cut on the leg when Rita swung the knife at her. Abby then picked up her knife from the table and inflicted a fatal stab wound on Rita.

If Abby is prosecuted for murder, which of the following facts, if true, would be least helpful to her defense?

(A) Rita intended to provoke Abby with her remark.
(B) Rita had no reason to fear serious bodily injury as she arose from the floor and seized the knife.
(C) The fight escalated between the incident with the chair and the slashing on the leg.
(D) Picketers from the "right to life" movement were at the entrance to the ballroom where the luncheon was held.

Answer to Question 17

This question requires the negative - that you choose the **least** effective fact in providing a defense to murder. Since she intentionally killed Rita, Abby's best defense is self-defense. In this case, however, Abby was the initial physical aggressor when she tipped over Rita's chair. Therefore, she will have to establish that she no longer was the aggressor at the time of Rita's attack and thus had regained the right to use deadly force in self-defense.

If Rita had no reason to fear bodily harm when she arose from the floor, then Abby's status as an aggressor is at least arguably over, and any escalation by Rita would give Abby the right of self-defense. This fact will be helpful and (B) is therefore a wrong answer.

The fact that the fight escalated from the use of nondeadly to deadly force will help Abby because it will make Rita the aggressor and will give Abby the right of self-defense. This fact will be helpful and (C) is therefore an incorrect answer.

Since at least some jurisdictions have adopted the "retreat doctrine," self-defense will not be available in those jurisdictions if Abby had an avenue of retreat. Thus, the fact that Abby had no easy escape because "right to life" activists were at the doorway will negate any possible use of the retreat doctrine to deny Abby a right of self-defense. This fact will be helpful and (D) is therefore a wrong answer.

(A) is correct because the fact that Rita verbally assaulted Abby by calling her a murderer will not help to establish Abby's right of self-defense. Such verbal abuse gave her no right at that time to use even nondeadly force against Rita, and will not prevent her from being considered the aggressor.

Question 18

Cramer holds a gun on Dolores and orders her to set fire to a boat owned by Valerie, which is sitting next to the dock. Because she fears that Cramer will shoot her if she refuses to obey, Dolores complies. Valerie sees the fire from the restaurant where she is having dinner, and runs down the dock and onto the boat in an attempt to recover some valuable personal property on the boat. The boat capsizes because of the fire, and Valerie drowns. The definition of arson has been expanded by statute to include boats. Dolores is charged with the murder of Valerie. She should be found

(A) guilty, because she could have taken the gun away from Cramer and avoided burning the boat.
(B) guilty, because duress is not a defense to murder.
(C) not guilty, because Valerie voluntarily put herself in danger.
(D) not guilty, because duress is a defense to arson.

Answer to Question 18

The only possible theory on which Dolores could be charged with the murder of Valerie is felony murder, since she did not intend to kill Valerie. If Dolores can show that she is not guilty of the underlying felony which forms the basis for the felony-murder charge, then she will not be guilty of the felony murder. In general, it is true that duress is not a defense to a homicide crime. But duress is a defense to lesser felonies which may be the basis for felony murder.

(A) is incorrect because the facts do not show that Dolores could have easily avoided complying with Cramer's demand by disarming him. The standard to invoke the defense of duress is that there be a threat of force against him which a reasonable person would have been unable to resist. An unarmed person does not usually have the opportunity to disarm a gunman and is under no duty to make the attempt.

Dolores did burn the property of another, but has a defense to the arson crime because there was the threat of force against her which a reasonable person would have been unable to resist. Since Dolores has a duress defense to the underlying felony, she is not guilty of felony murder. (B) generally states a correct principle of law, but that principle does not control the result in a felony murder case.

(C) is incorrect because the fact that Valerie voluntarily put herself in danger is irrelevant. Under a felony-murder theory, it does not make any difference if the victim voluntarily put himself in danger, as long as the death occurred in the commission of the felony.

(D) is correct.

Question 19

Dave is walking in front of a liquor store when Rob, who has just robbed the store at gunpoint, orders him to drive the getaway car parked at the curb. As Dave and Rob are approaching a red light at a busy intersection where pedestrians are crossing the street, the brakes fail. To avoid hitting the pedestrians, Dave swings his car across the sidewalk and into Val's house. The car strikes Val, who is watching television in his living room, killing him. If Dave is charged with manslaughter, his best defense is

(A) duress.
(B) necessity.
(C) self-defense.
(D) defense of others, the pedestrians on the crosswalk.

Answer to Question 19

Dave might have available a defense of duress (coercion) to any charge of participation in a robbery, because there was the threat of force against him which a reasonable person would have been unable to resist. However, that defense is irrelevant to this manslaughter charge because duress is unavailable as a matter of law as a defense to a homicide crime. Moreover, in driving the car into the house, he was not reacting to the threat from the gunman, but the danger which occurred because of a nonhuman factor, the bad brakes. Thus, (A) is incorrect.

Self-defense in the homicide context refers to the right to use force to protect oneself when one reasonably believes he is in danger of death or serious bodily harm. Here, the defendant was not himself in danger of serious bodily harm. Only the pedestrians were in any danger. Therefore, (C) is incorrect.

Defense of others refers to the right to use force to protect individuals from a threat by a third party, where the third party appears likely to cause death or serious bodily harm to those individuals. It does not refer to the right of the defendant to threaten the life of one group of individuals in order to save another group of individuals from a threat which he himself has put in motion. Thus, defense of others does not apply and (D) is incorrect.

A necessity to break the law exists where an illegal act must be committed in order to prevent a greater evil. Here, a reasonable person would have driven into Val's house because that would be less likely to cause a fatality than striking the pedestrians (a greater evil). Thus, the defense of necessity applies, and (B) is correct.

Question 20

Guru was the leader of a religious cult and David was a member of that cult. For 30 consecutive days, Guru preached a sermon in which he proclaimed that he had the power to call lightning down from the heavens to strike down followers whom he considered to be sinners. David believed Guru had this power. One day, Guru saw David's 13-year-old daughter Denise wearing eye makeup. Guru summoned David and David's daughter before him and proclaimed that he was about to strike Denise with lightning for her misdeed. David took a knife and stabbed Guru, killing him. If charged with a homicide crime, David's "defense of others" defense will

(A) be sustained, because he actually believed his daughter was in danger.
(B) be sustained, because reflection is not required when there is an imminent threat of death to others.
(C) not be sustained, because David's belief that his daughter was in danger was not reasonable.
(D) not be sustained, because his daughter was not in fact threatened.

Answer to Question 20

David's cult membership tends to show the sincerity of his belief that his daughter was in danger, but that is not enough to satisfy the legal test, as response (A) suggests it is. A **reasonable** person in this situation would not have believed that his daughter was in any danger from Guru's alleged power to invoke divine intervention. Therefore, David does not have the defense of defense of another to the homicide crime.

The theory that reflection is not required when there is an imminent threat of death to others is irrelevant. The issue is whether it was reasonable to believe that the danger was imminent. Since there was no reason to believe that there was an imminent danger of harm in this case, (B) is incorrect.

A person is justified in using deadly force in defense of another only if that person has an honest and reasonable belief that the other person is in imminent danger of death or great bodily harm. The other person need not in fact be threatened, but the person who comes to the defense must honestly and reasonably believe that the victim had a right to self-defense. Since the fact that the daughter was not in fact threatened is not dispositive, (D) is incorrect.

(C) is correct.

Question 21

Phil, a photographer, was employed by an agency. His job was to take pictures at weddings and other events. The agency provided him with an expensive camera which he used occasionally to take pictures for his personal use in addition to his paid assignments. One day, when he had no assignments and was short of cash for rent, Phil took the camera to a local camera shop and sold it. The suspicious owner of the shop called the agency when he saw its name on the bottom of the camera. Phil was arrested and charged with larceny in a jurisdiction which maintains the common-law distinctions between larceny, embezzlement and obtaining property by false pretenses. His best defense is

(A) his employer lost nothing because the camera wasn't needed when Phil sold it.
(B) the agency was not permanently deprived of its property because the store owner returned the camera.
(C) his employer gave him custody of the camera.
(D) his employer gave him possession of the camera.

Answer to Question 21

(A) and (B) are easily eliminated. (A) suggests that property is not stolen if the owner does not need it. The owner's need is irrelevant to any issue relating to any theft crime.

(B) suggests that the honesty of the store owner could save Phil from the consequences of his illegal act. However, the actual permanent deprivation of property is not the test of whether a theft crime has been committed. The critical test is whether the defendant possesses the appropriate *mens rea* for a theft crime, which is the intention to permanently deprive the owner of the property. It appears that Phil had this intent. Therefore, the fact that the property was returned is not a defense to the larceny crime.

The issue in this question is the quality of Phil's possessory interest. If he is considered a low level employee who uses the personal property of the employer in a strictly regimented format, then he will have the lowest form of possessory interest, namely "custody." The conversion of the camera to his personal use, by selling it, would then be considered a "trespassory taking" and therefore common-law larceny. If, on the other hand, he is considered a higher level employee, and has greater control over the camera, then he will be considered to have "possession" of the camera. If he sells the camera when he has possession of it, then he has converted the personal property of another and is guilty of common-law embezzlement instead of larceny. The level of control Phil had over the camera indicates he had possession, not merely custody. Therefore, (C) is incorrect and (D) is correct.

Question 22

The crime of burglary in State X has been extended to all buildings and to all hours of the day or night. Barbara entered the Shop and Save supermarket in State X to do her weekly grocery shopping and to steal some expensive steaks. She put some bread and milk in her shopping basket and then went to the meat department, picked up a package of steaks and put them in her coat pocket. When she was standing in the check-out line, the manager approached her and said, "I know you have a package of steaks in your pocket. If you will pay for them, I will forget about it, but if I ever catch you again, I will turn you over to the police." Barbara then paid for the steaks as well as the bread and milk.

If the manager changes his mind, and criminal charges are brought against Barbara, the most serious crime (listed in order of seriousness) of which she can be found guilty is

(A) burglary.
(B) larceny.
(C) attempted larceny.
(D) no crime.

Answer to Question 22

(A) can be eliminated because Barbara did not break into the store. There can be no breaking when one enters a store open to the public.

(B) is correct and (C) and (D) are incorrect because at the time that she picked up the steaks intending to steal them, Barbara had committed all of the elements of larceny. An attempt crime merges into the substantive crime if the attempt is successful. The fact that she paid for the steaks does not negate the elements of the crime.

Question 23

Jean and Jerry were coworkers. Jean frequently bragged about her wine cellar full of rare imported vintages. Jerry told Jean that he was inviting his fiancé's parents over for dinner at his apartment and wanted to impress them by showing them a bottle of truly expensive wine in his liquor cabinet. Jean permitted him to take a bottle of Latrec 1939, which was worth $700, to his apartment for the dinner. He promised to return it the next morning. Jerry was actually not engaged, but planned to propose to his girlfriend, Elaine, at a romantic dinner. When his girlfriend arrived, Jerry told her that this dinner was such a special occasion that he had purchased a truly vintage wine which they could enjoy with the meal. Jerry uncorked the wine and they drank it with their filet mignon. After dinner, Jerry proposed marriage and Elaine accepted. The next day Jerry told Jean that he had been mugged on his way home, and that the muggers made off with the wine. Suspicious, Jean examined the trash from Jerry's apartment the next day and found the empty bottle of Latrec 1939. If Jerry is charged with theft in a common-law jurisdiction, he is most likely to be convicted of

(A) embezzlement.
(B) larceny by trick.
(C) larceny.
(D) no crime.

Answer to Question 23

(A) is incorrect because, although Jerry had possession of the wine (which would normally indicate embezzlement), he obtained that possession by fraud. Since he never obtained rightful possession of the wine, he could not be guilty of embezzlement.

Although there was a taking, it was not a true trespassory taking of the kind needed for a common-law larceny. Jean gave possession of the bottle of wine to Jerry, but clearly did not give up ownership. Since it is fairly clear that it was Jerry's intent to drink the wine all along, the possession was obtained by fraud and the crime is larceny by trick. (B) is correct and (C) and (D) are incorrect.

Question 24

In which of the following fact situations would the defendant be guilty of the crime charged?

(A) Fisher takes his friend's outboard motorboat from the dock on a fishing trip without permission and returns it to the dock three hours later. Fisher is charged with common-law larceny.
(B) Fisher obtains permission to use his friend's boat, promising to return it as soon as the fishing trip is concluded, a promise he did not then intend to keep. The boat springs a small leak while Fisher is fishing and he decides to return the boat as promised, and does in fact return it. Fisher is charged with common-law larceny by trick.
(C) Fisher borrows his friend's boat to go on a fishing trip, promising his friend he will return it by sunset. The fishing is excellent and Fisher stays out all night. When he returns the boat the next morning, he is charged with embezzlement.
(D) Fisher rents a boat for cash from an agency, giving false information about his name, address, and occupation on the rental application form. When he returns the boat, he is charged with obtaining property by false pretenses.

Answer to Question 24

Both (A) and (C) involve theft crimes, larceny and embezzlement, which require a specific intent. They are both incorrect because it does not appear that Fisher had the specific intent to steal in either fact situation. The intention required is an intent to deprive another of property permanently, or for an unreasonable period of time. The most reasonable inference to be drawn from the facts of (A) is that Fisher did not act with the intent to deprive his friend of his property permanently. In (C), even though Fisher did not return the boat as soon as he had promised, he never formed an intent to deprive his friend of it permanently.

In (D), Fisher is charged with obtaining property by false pretenses, which requires that the defendant obtain title to the property by means of a knowingly false representation of a material present or past fact which causes the victim to pass title to his property to the defendant. Here, even if the misrepresentation was material, Fisher never obtained title to the property, and so cannot be guilty of obtaining property by false pretenses. (D) is incorrect.

(B) is a classic case of larceny by trick. Larceny by trick occurs when the defendant obtains possession of another's property by lying or trickery. The fraud vitiates the legality of the possession and the crime is a larceny crime even though there was a consensual transfer of possession. In (B), Fisher did not intend to return the boat at the time he took it. Therefore, he is guilty of larceny by trick, even though, because of a change of circumstances, he returned the boat. The critical time for the intent to be judged is at the time possession is transferred. (B) is correct.

Question 25

Eva borrowed Elizabeth's mammoth diamond ring, promising to return it after she wore it to a celebrity gala the following Saturday. Eva sold the ring two days after she borrowed it. If she is charged with common-law larceny,

(A) she will not be guilty because she obtained rightful possession at the time it was loaned to her.
(B) she will not be guilty because a misrepresentation of intent is the crime of obtaining property by false pretenses, not larceny.
(C) she will be guilty only if she had no intention of returning the ring at the time she borrowed it.
(D) she will be guilty no matter when she formed the intent to sell it.

Answer to Question 25

If Eva had no intention of returning the ring at the time she borrowed it, then she obtained possession by fraud because she misrepresented to Elizabeth her intention with respect to the ring, telling Elizabeth that she only wanted to borrow it, when in fact she planned to sell it and deprive Elizabeth of the ring permanently. The timing of the formation of Eva's intent is critical. If Eva did not form the intent to steal until **after** she obtained possession of the ring, then she obtained possession of the ring and converted the ring from her rightful possession. The crime would then be embezzlement, not larceny. Therefore, (D) is incorrect.

(A) is incorrect because the facts in this case do not clearly indicate that Eva obtained rightful possession of the ring at the time Elizabeth gave it to her. If she had an intent to steal the ring at that time, she would have obtained possession by fraud, and therefore would be guilty of larceny by trick, a situation set forth in (C).

(B) is incorrect because to be found guilty of obtaining property by false pretenses, the defendant must obtain **title** to the property by means of a false representation of a material fact which causes the victim to pass title to the property to the defendant. Eva's misrepresentations only gained her possession. She never obtained title to the ring.

In this case, Eva obtained possession of the ring and may be guilty of a special form of common-law larceny, larceny by trick, if she intended to permanently deprive Elizabeth of her property at the time she obtained possession. If the choices of the question do not distinguish between larceny and larceny by trick, then you should consider larceny by trick a form of larceny. (C) is correct.

Question 26

In which of the fact situations below would Dan be guilty of embezzlement?

(A) Dan goes to a construction site. He picks up two pieces of copper pipe, intending to

steal them. Before he has left the premises, he sees a security guard, drops the pipe, and flees.
(B) Dan was shopping for a new automobile. He found one that he liked and asked the salesman if he might take it for a test drive. The salesman assented and gave him the keys. Dan, after driving the car for a while, decided to keep it and never brought it back.
(C) Dan approaches Ellen and succeeds in borrowing $250, telling Ellen that he needs the money to pay bills and that he will pay her back on payday. In fact, he had the intention to do neither. Instead, he lost the money at the racetrack and disappeared.
(D) Dan goes into a department store, takes a camera from the shelf, and replaces its $100 price tag with a $50 price tag, which he obtained from an adjacent camera. He then pays $50 and takes the camera.

Answer to Question 26

All the elements of common-law larceny are present in (A). The defendant engaged in a trespassory taking of the copper pipe and carried it away some distance (even though not off the construction site), at a time when he had an intent to steal the pipe. The crime of common-law larceny was therefore completed. The crime cannot be embezzlement because the defendant never obtained lawful possession of the pipe.

In (C), the physical transfer of the cash from Ellen to Dan transferred **title** of the money to Dan because it was transferred with the intent that Dan could spend the money. Therefore, the crime is obtaining property by false pretenses. (If possession, not title to the money was transferred, the crime would be embezzlement.)

In (D), when Dan paid the incorrect amount of money and went through the checkout stand, he obtained title to, not mere possession of, the camera. Therefore, he is not guilty of embezzlement, but he is guilty of obtaining property by false pretenses because the switching of the price tags was a fraudulent representation of a material fact, namely the price of the camera.

(B) is correct. Dan obtained physical control over the car from the salesman, and later converted it to his own use with the intention of permanently depriving the owner of the car. Since this crime was a conversion by someone who was in rightful possession, the crime is embezzlement. (This crime is not larceny by trick because the defendant did not have an intention to convert the car at the time he was given possession. The facts indicate that he formed that intent later. By the same token, it does not appear that Dan engaged in fraud to obtain possession.)

Question 27

King, Queen, Jack and Joker gathered for an evening of poker at King's house. Just before the last hand, King produced a new deck of cards that were marked in a way that allowed King to determine the cards held in each player's hand. After all the cards were dealt, King determined that he held three tens and that Jack held three nines. Queen and Joker quickly dropped out of the bidding, but King and Jack raised the pot to $500 before King won the hand and $300 of Jack's money. If King is convicted of common-law larceny by trick, rather than obtaining property by false pretenses, it will be because

(A) his conduct was not fraudulent.
(B) he obtained title to the money in the pot once he took possession of it.
(C) his conduct only gave him possession of the money in the pot.
(D) there was no trespassory taking.

Answer to Question 27

The essential elements of larceny by trick are that possession, not title, is obtained, and that it is obtained by fraud, which vitiates the consent and makes it a trespassory taking. Larceny by trick cannot occur unless there is fraudulent conduct that induces the victim to part with possession of the property. Therefore, (A) is incorrect.

(B) is incorrect because if King obtained title to the money in the pot rather than mere possession, the crime would be obtaining property by false pretenses, not larceny by trick.

Another essential element of larceny by trick is a trespassory taking. The fraud vitiates the consent to possession, making the transfer of physical possession a trespassory taking. If the taking were not deemed trespassory, there would be no crime of larceny by trick. (D) is incorrect.

If there is larceny by trick in this case, it is because King's conduct gave him possession, not title, to the money. Therefore, (C) is correct.

Question 28

Rosa bought a ticket that provided admission to the five World Cup soccer games being played in Metropolis, primarily because she wanted to see the Brazilian national team play in games three and four. Because her roommate Sophia was Italian, Rosa let her borrow the ticket for the first two games, which featured the Italian national team. When Sophia was leaving to go to the second game, she had a serious argument with Rosa. After the game was over, she left town for a week, and did not return the ticket to Rosa until the day after the fourth game. Rosa attended the fifth game of the series. If Sophia is charged with embezzlement of the ticket in a common-law jurisdiction, she will be found

(A) not guilty because her conduct constituted larceny by trick.
(B) not guilty because she intended to return the ticket and did return it in time for the fifth game.
(C) guilty only if she formed the intent to deprive Rosa of the ticket at the time she obtained possession of it from Rosa.
(D) guilty because she intended to deprive Rosa of the value of the ticket.

Answer to Question 28

Sophia apparently did not have the intent to convert at the time she received the tickets, the mental state that would be necessary if her conduct were to be found to be larceny by trick.

Therefore, (A) is incorrect. (C) is incorrect because if Sophia formed the intent to convert the ticket at the time she obtained possession of it, she would have been guilty of larceny by trick, not embezzlement.

Sophia is guilty of embezzlement because she started with rightful possession of the ticket. It does not appear from the facts that she formed the intent to withhold the ticket from Rosa until after the argument, and therefore did not take it with the intention of not returning it in time for the third game. By deliberately failing to return the ticket in time for the third game, she converted it so as to deprive Rosa of substantially all its value, since being able to go to the third and fourth games was the principal reason that Rosa bought the ticket. The fact that Rosa was able to attend the fifth game does not change the fact that the substantial value was lost to her because of Sophia's actions. Therefore, (B) is incorrect and (D) is correct.

Question 29

The police, pursuant to a valid search warrant, searched Arnold's home and found a brand new big screen TV that had a list price of $3,000. The set had been stolen from Terry's TV Shop and was in its original carton. Arnold maintains that he purchased the set from a TV repairman for $150. Arnold is charged with receiving stolen goods. He should be found

(A) not guilty if the jury finds that the defendant believed the set was not stolen, even if that belief was unreasonable.
(B) not guilty only if the jury finds that the defendant's belief was honest and reasonable.
(C) guilty even if the jury finds that Arnold believed the set was not stolen.
(D) guilty because the disparity between the retail price and the price paid is enough to prove conclusively that he knew the set was stolen.

Answer to Question 29

The *mens rea* that the jury must find to convict a defendant of receiving stolen goods is that the defendant actually believed the goods to be stolen. If the jury finds Arnold actually held the belief (subjectively) that the goods were not stolen, it must find Arnold not guilty. Thus, (C) is incorrect.

The disparity between value and purchase price may allow the jury to find that Arnold knew the goods were stolen. But that fact alone is not sufficient to **require** a finding that Defendant is guilty. Therefore, (D) is incorrect.

To acquit here, the jury must find that Arnold believed the set was not stolen. The jury need not find that Arnold's belief was reasonable. Therefore, (B) is incorrect, and (A) is correct.

Question 30

Butler stole an antique silver coffee urn from the home of his employers. Later, the police arrested Butler in his home and located the coffee urn in Butler's dining room. In an attempt to achieve a lenient sentence, Butler told the police that he has sold other goods stolen from his current and former employers to Fred, a prominent antiques dealer, and would be willing to sell the silver coffee urn to him to help the police catch him. The police agreed to the plan and informed Butler's employers, who also agreed. The police watched as Butler sold the pitcher to Fred and then charged Fred with receiving stolen goods. On that charge, Fred is

(A) not guilty, unless he knew the urn was stolen.
(B) not guilty, because the urn lost its character as stolen goods when found by the police.
(C) not guilty, because he has the defense of entrapment.
(D) guilty, if he purchased the urn for significantly less than its retail value.

Answer to Question 30

In order to be guilty of receiving stolen goods, the defendant must know that the goods are stolen, and the goods must in fact be stolen. The goods in this case lost their character as stolen goods because the police recovered them and allowed them to be sold to Fred after their owners in effect regained constructive possession of them and consented to the sale. (A) is incorrect because Fred's knowledge is insufficient here, where the goods are not in fact stolen. The fact that Fred purchased the goods at significantly less than retail value would only be a fact from which the jury could infer that Fred knew that they were stolen, but it is not conclusive on this issue. (D) is incorrect for that reason as well as the fact that the goods were no longer stolen goods, eliminating an essential element of the crime.

(C) is incorrect because it sets forth the wrong reason why Fred is not guilty. Since Fred appeared to be in the business of receiving stolen goods, the police did not induce an otherwise innocent person to engage in criminal activity. Therefore, there is no entrapment.

Since they were not actually stolen, Fred is not guilty of receiving stolen goods, even though he probably believed they were stolen. (B) is correct.

Question 31

DeNiro worked for a "protection service" which demanded money from small shopkeepers in exchange for not harming their person or their property. He approached Barry, a small baker, in Barry's shop on June 1 and demanded that $500 be paid to him on June 8. He threatened to break Barry's fingers on that date if the money was not paid. When DeNiro arrived at the shop June 8, accompanied by a large man with numerous facial scars, Barry gave DeNiro $350 and said that was all he could pay. DeNiro made a phone call, and after conferring with his boss, grabbed Barry's apron and told him to have another $250 ready to pay when they returned next week or DeNiro's scar-faced friend would "take care of" Barry at that time.

By his conduct on June 8, DeNiro is guilty of

(A) battery only.
(B) robbery only.
(C) robbery and battery.
(D) neither battery nor robbery.

Answer to Question 31

This question raises a merger issue. A person cannot be convicted of both a battery and a robbery which arise from the same acts. Thus, battery would merge into the robbery if it preceded or was contemporaneous with it.

When Barry, responding to DeNiro's threats, gave him $350, there was a completed robbery -- here, a larceny committed by intimidation. After the completion of that crime, DeNiro grabbed Barry's apron and thereby committed a battery. Since the battery was committed **after** the robbery was completed, the criminal acts were separate and DeNiro can be independently prosecuted and punished for both. (C) is correct and the other choices are incorrect.

Question 32

A statute in State X provides: "Arson shall be punishable by a sentence of not more than ten years in state prison." Erik, during the daytime, went to a house in his neighborhood that was vacant because the previous owners had moved out and the new owners had not yet moved in. He put a lighted match onto the wooden porch of the house, and shortly after the porch ignited, he became afraid and extinguished the fire. The fire only slightly burned the porch.

Erik is charged with arson. He is

(A) not guilty, because the activity took place during the daytime.
(B) not guilty, because the house was unoccupied at the time.
(C) not guilty, because there was not sufficient burning.
(D) guilty.

Answer to Question 32

When a question names a common-law crime but the statute given only prescribes a penalty for it, assume that the crime retains all of its common-law elements. At common law, arson is the malicious (intentional) burning of the dwelling of another.

Common-law arson, unlike common-law burglary, can occur in the daytime as well as the nighttime. Thus, (A) is incorrect.

A house once used as a dwelling house and which will be used as a dwelling house in the future retains its status as a dwelling house even if it is temporarily unoccupied. Thus, (B) is incorrect.

The burning does not need to be extensive, as long as there is combustion on some part of the structure that constitutes real estate. A slight burning of the porch is sufficient. Thus, (C) is incorrect.

Erik is guilty of arson because he intentionally burned the dwelling house of another. (D) is correct.

Question 33

During the nighttime, Darlene broke into the Vanderbilt house while the family was on vacation with the intention of stealing a ruby ring she had seen Victoria Vanderbilt wear at a party. When she could not find the ring, Darlene became angry, lit a match to a newspaper and threw it on Victoria's bed, setting the mattress on fire. The flames destroyed the bed and burned part of the floor under the bed before a sprinkler system put the fire out.

In a common-law jurisdiction, Darlene is guilty of

(A) burglary only.
(B) arson only.
(C) burglary and attempted arson.
(D) burglary and arson.

Answer to Question 33

Darlene is guilty of burglary because she broke and entered into the dwelling house of another during the nighttime to commit a felony. The fact that she was not successful in committing the crime she intended or that she in fact committed another felony is irrelevant to her guilt for burglary; it is the intent to commit a felony at the time of the breaking and entering which is critical.

Darlene is also guilty of arson because she deliberately set a fire that, in addition to burning the mattress, also burned part of the dwelling house of another, namely the floor.

Thus, (D) is correct.

Question 34

In a jurisdiction in which the "retreat doctrine" is in effect, Rep and Dem are at a neighborhood bar. Rep hits Dem with his fist during an argument about presidential politics, knocking him to the floor. As Dem gets up, Rep is standing nearby, ready to punch him again. Dem is next to the entrance door and could easily walk out to end any fight. Instead, he leaps at Rep and punches him in the stomach.

Dem is charged with assault and battery and raises the defense of self-defense. At the conclusion of the trial where the above facts were proven, the prosecutor requests the trial judge to instruct the jury that Dem had an obligation to retreat and that self-defense is not available. That instruction

(A) should be refused, because there is no duty to retreat in a public place such as a restaurant or bar.
(B) should be refused because Dem did not use deadly force.
(C) should be given, because Dem had the obligation to retreat.
(D) should be given, because the jury is entitled to be instructed on all of the issues in the case.

Answer to Question 34

The duty to retreat before using force in self-defense exists in all situations, regardless of whether the assault took place in public or not. Thus, (A) is incorrect. The only exception to the duty to retreat before using deadly force is in the defendant's own residence, where there is never a duty to retreat. However, the duty applies only in situations in which the defendant uses deadly force. In this case, Dem did not use deadly force, and so had no duty to retreat. (B) is correct and (C) is incorrect.

It would, therefore, be improper for the court to instruct the jury on the duty to retreat. A jury should not be instructed on an issue which is inapplicable to the case. Such inapplicable instructions could only serve to confuse the jury. Thus, (D) is incorrect.

Questions 35 and 36 are based on the following fact situation.

Mannie was the manager of a local bank. One morning, while Mannie was in his office at the bank with Ace, the assistant manager, Darien burst into Mannie's office, pointing a gun at Mannie and Ace. Darien told Mannie that he was going to stay in the office with Ace and would kill him if Mannie did not return immediately with $100,000. Mannie went to the bank vault, took $100,000 in cash and gave it to Darien. Darien escaped with the money but was later apprehended.

35. If Mannie is charged with embezzlement of $100,000 of bank funds, he would be

(A) not guilty, because he did not have the *mens rea*.
(B) not guilty, because he was coerced to take the money by the substantial threat to use unlawful force against another person.
(C) guilty, because the defense of duress is unavailable to such a serious crime as embezzlement.
(D) guilty, because there was no substantial threat to use force against Mannie or a member of his household.

36. If Darien were charged with the crime of kidnapping Ace, he would be

(A) guilty, because Ace was imprisoned against his will.
(B) guilty, because Darien used unlawful force to imprison Ace.
(C) not guilty, because Ace was neither secretly imprisoned nor carried away.
(D) not guilty, because Darien did not demand a ransom.

Answer to Question 35

Mannie had the appropriate *mens rea* for embezzlement. He was in possession of the money and did intend to hand it over to a criminal, which would likely permanently deprive the owners of the money. Thus, (A) is incorrect.

However, the defense of duress is available for a crime (other than a homicide) if there is a substantial threat of force against the defendant, or any other person, which a reasonable person could not resist. (C) is incorrect.

(D) is incorrect because it too narrowly limits the availability of the defense of duress. There is no requirement that the threat of force be against the defendant or a member of his family.

Since a threat of substantial force was used against Ace, the defense of duress is available. Therefore, (B) is correct.

Answer to Question 36

Ace was falsely imprisoned by Darien, because he was unlawfully confined to the office by threat of force without his consent. However, the additional element of either asportation or secret confinement of the victim must be present for false imprisonment to be escalated to kidnapping.

(A) and (B) are incorrect because the use of force and the lack of consent only prove false imprisonment.

(D) gives the correct result, but the wrong reason. A demand for a ransom is an element of an aggravated form of kidnapping, but is not necessary for the crime of kidnapping itself. Darien could still be guilty of kidnapping even if the prosecution failed to prove that Darien demanded a ransom.

(C) is correct. In this case, neither of the additional elements of the crime of kidnapping is present.

Question 37

Bill, age 16, drove his mother, Martha, to the mall in her new car. He told his mother that he wanted to listen to the radio while she went shopping. She left him with the keys in the ignition. Bill spotted Rocky, the 18-year-old neighborhood bully who had terrorized him for years, walking toward the car. To hide from Rocky, Bill immediately popped open the trunk, crawled in, and partially closed the lid. Rocky watched with amusement, went up to the car and closed the trunk lid so that it locked. Ten minutes later, Davey, another 18-year-old, walked past the car, saw the keys in the ignition, and drove it off without realizing that Bill was locked in the trunk. Martha returned to the parking lot twenty minutes later to find both the car and her son missing.

Davey decided he could make an easy profit on the car if he held it for ransom. He therefore identified Martha from the car registration papers, called her up, and told her that he had her car and if she wanted it back, she should leave $2,000 in cash at a designated drop-off spot. Martha complied, and received a subsequent telephone call telling her where she could retrieve her car. When she found it, she heard a pounding on the trunk lid, opened it and found Bill.

If Rocky and Davey are each charged with kidnapping,

(A) only Rocky should be found guilty.
(B) only Davey should be found guilty.
(C) both Davey and Rocky should be found guilty.
(D) both Davey and Rocky should be found not guilty.

Answer to Question 37

Rocky is guilty of the crime of false imprisonment of Bill because his act of closing and locking the car trunk intentionally confined him. However, the crime of kidnapping requires either asportation or secret confinement in addition to false imprisonment. Rocky did not move Bill, nor did he take any affirmative steps to keep Bill's location secret. Therefore, Rocky is not guilty of kidnapping. Thus, (A) and (C) are incorrect.

Davey should also be found not guilty. While Davey did transport Bill, and did demand

and receive a ransom for the car, he did not **know** that he was either confining or transporting Bill, and therefore does not possess the *mens rea* for kidnapping. Thus, (B) is incorrect and (D) is correct.

Question 38

Maiden is the lead singer of a nationally known rock band. Natalie is an aspiring vocalist who frequents the same clubs. She is married to Harold, a prosperous businessman. When the band was planning a week's engagement at an out-of-town hotel, Maiden offered to take Natalie on the trip, let her stay in Maiden's hotel suite, and let her sing with the band. Maiden promised Natalie a permanent position with the band if the audiences liked her. Maiden required that Natalie tell no one of the trip, not even Harold. In fact, Maiden had no intention of offering Natalie a permanent position with the band.

One night, while Natalie was performing with the band in the hotel lounge, Maiden called Harold, told him that she had abducted his wife, and demanded $50,000 for her safe return. Harold arranged to drop the money at the designated spot the next evening. As Maiden approached the pick-up spot, she was arrested by the police. Natalie returned to the hotel suite after the show, unaware of Maiden's dealings with her husband.

Maiden is guilty of

(A) attempted extortion only.
(B) attempted kidnapping and attempted extortion.
(C) kidnapping and attempted extortion.
(D) neither kidnapping nor attempted kidnapping, nor attempted extortion.

Answer to Question 38

Maiden is guilty of attempted extortion because she threatened Harold with future harm to Natalie for the purpose of obtaining Harold's property, and she took substantial steps toward the completion of the crime. However, Maiden is not guilty of either kidnapping or attempted kidnapping. Natalie voluntarily went to the hotel room, even though she was induced to go there by a misrepresentation. She was not confined or restricted in her movement in any way. Since Natalie consented to the confinement, there was no false imprisonment. Therefore, Maiden is not guilty of kidnapping or attempted kidnapping. (A) is correct, and all other responses are incorrect.

Question 39

Ramond is charged with the rape of Amelia, age 21. He raises the defense of consent. In which of the following cases is he most likely to be found guilty?

(A) Amelia is a prostitute. Ramond agrees to her price of $100 for sex and offers to pay by credit card. Ramond signs a credit card charge slip for $100 for Amelia's services. Ramond knows that his credit card has been terminated by the bank because of nonpayment of prior balances. Amelia and Ramond have intercourse. The credit card charge slip is later rejected by the bank.
(B) Amelia and Ramond had been dating for a year, during which time Amelia insisted on remaining a virgin. Ramond asked her to marry him and she agreed. Ramond told her that he knew a minister that could marry them that evening. Ramond's friend, pretending to be a minister, performed the ceremony. Raymond and Amelia have intercourse.
(C) Amelia, although an adult, has only a third-grade education, is not intelligent, and has never had sex before, although she knows what it is. Raymond tells her that she should have intercourse soon to avoid contracting cancer. Raymond and Amelia have sexual intercourse.
(D) Amelia meets Ramond at a college fraternity party. Amelia is upset because she has just learned that she is pregnant. Ramond tells her that she will surely abort if she has sexual intercourse in a certain manner he can show her, a statement which Ramond knows is false. Amelia and Ramond then have intercourse.

Answer to Question 39

Rape can be committed by the use of fraud or trickery. It is rape when one person obtains sex by a lie or trick designed to convince another person that intercourse is not occurring or that the intercourse is valid marital intercourse (fraud in the factum). If the fraud only relates to some collateral matter -- such as the effect of the intercourse on a pregnancy (fraud in the inducement) -- but the victim knows he or she is agreeing to extramarital intercourse, the consent is valid and no rape has occurred.

In (A), (C) and (D), the fraud is fraud in the inducement. Amelia knows that she is consenting to extramarital intercourse and therefore Raymond is not guilty of rape in those cases.

In (B), however, Raymond goes through a marriage ceremony which he knows is invalid in order to procure Amelia's consent to sex. This constitutes fraud in the factum, which vitiates her consent and makes Raymond guilty of rape. (B) is correct.

Question 40

Freeman, who lived in a remote wilderness location, hated Scribe, a reporter for a regional newspaper who had commented unfavorably on some of Freeman's political activities. Freeman called Scribe, asked Scribe to visit his outpost to discuss their differences, and offered to let Scribe use Freeman's private plane which was parked at an airport approximately 100 miles away from Freeman's home. Freeman altered the airplane so that it would crash about 50 miles from the airport, on a wooded mountain. Scribe went to the airport, but the fog was so thick that the plane was not allowed to take off, and he therefore abandoned the trip. If Freeman is charged with attempted murder, he will most likely be found

(A) not guilty, because the plane could not take off.
(B) not guilty, because his plan to kill was inherently impossible to execute.
(C) guilty, even if he did not intend to kill Fed.
(D) guilty, because he had taken the last step he had to take to make the plan operative.

Answer to Question 40

Factual impossibility will not be a defense to an attempt. Factual impossibility refers to a situation in which the intended act is criminal and a crime would be committed if the defendant were successful, but the defendant cannot accomplish his crime because of facts unknown to him at the time he acts. This question presents a situation of factual impossibility because Freeman would have succeeded in the crime of murder but for facts unknown to him (bad weather). Therefore, (A) is incorrect.

Inherent impossibility would be a defense to an attempt. Inherent impossibility refers to the situation in which the defendant intends to commit a crime but chooses means obviously incapable of bringing about the criminal act. This defense negates the element of attempt which requires that the defendant have the apparent ability to complete the crime. Here, deceiving the victim into operating an airplane altered so as to crash is not an infeasible method of killing. In fact, it might well have worked, if not for intervening events. Therefore, (B) is incorrect on these facts.

(C) states the correct conclusion but the rest of the answer is wrong. An attempt is an intentional crime. To be guilty, the defendant must intend to commit the crime which he is attempting. If the intended crime is one requiring specific intent, that intent is also a prerequisite to the crime of attempt. Murder is always a specific intent crime. For attempted murder, there must be an actual intent to kill.

An attempt requires a substantial step in the direction of committing a crime, coupled with the intention to commit that crime and the apparent ability to complete the crime. The "substantial step test" requires the legal conclusion that the defendant's conduct goes beyond mere preparation to commit the crime. A defendant who has done all that he needs to do to perpetrate the crime has always gone beyond the preparatory stage. Freeman did perform the last act required on his part to realize his plan to kill

Scribe. He has therefore clearly taken a substantial step toward perpetration of the crime and is therefore guilty of attempted murder. Therefore, (D) is correct.

Question 41

Edward has a long criminal record as a jewel thief, and is currently under indictment for robbery of a jewelry store. In order to carry out his part of a plea bargain, Edward persuades his friends, Damon and Dorian, other notorious jewel thieves with long criminal records, to break into Trudy's jewelry store after hours and steal their diamonds. The government provided some sophisticated burglary tools and equipment to disable the burglar alarm to assist Edward in carrying out the job. As Edward, Damon, and Dorian arrive at Trudy's with the equipment in hand, they are apprehended by the officer on the beat, who happened to notice their suspicious activity.

Damon and Dorian are charged with attempted burglary in a jurisdiction where the limitations on common-law burglary have been removed by statute. What is the most likely finding of the court?

(A) They will be found not guilty because the excessive participation of the government in the case violated fundamental fairness.
(B) They will be found not guilty because they were arrested prior to the substantial step needed for attempt.
(C) They will be found not guilty because they have the defense of entrapment.
(D) They will be found guilty because their acts went beyond mere preparation.

Answer to Question 41

This question deals with separate issues of entrapment and attempt.

The defense of entrapment is designed to prevent the government from "manufacturing" the crime. The majority view focuses on whether the defendant is predisposed to commit the crime; the defendant's past criminal record is relevant to prove predisposition. The entrapment defense has been rejected because of a defendant's predisposition, even where the government has supplied something which is key to the commission of the crime. These defendants were not entrapped, because their long criminal records for this same type of crime show that they were predisposed to commit the crime. Also, the government's acts do not constitute any overwhelming impetus for the crime; the government only supplied the means. Therefore, (C) is incorrect.

(A) is incorrect because, although a violation of fundamental fairness might constitute a deprivation of substantive due process, there is no such rule of law. Therefore, response (A) is either a vague, policy-based answer which should be avoided if there is a better answer (as there is here), or it is an attempt to rephrase an entrapment defense. If that is the case, then entrapment would be a better answer because it is more specific, but the applicable standards for entrapment are not met here.

An attempt requires a substantial step in the direction of committing a crime, coupled with the intention to commit that crime and the apparent ability to complete the crime. The "substantial step test" requires the legal conclusion that the defendant's conduct goes beyond mere preparation to commit the crime. In making the distinction between mere preparation and actual perpetration, courts look to several factors, including: (1) the defendant's proximity in time and place to the scheduled execution of the criminal act; (2) whether the defendant has taken all the actions he can to perpetrate the crime; (3) whether the defendant has already progressed so far in the commission of a crime that he is unlikely to stop without outside interference; and (4) the seriousness of the crime attempted.

Burglary is a serious offense and, for serious offenses, preparation ends and perpetration begins earlier. Damon and Dorian were in immediate proximity, in time and space, to perpetration of the burglary -- they were on the scene. It is probable that they would have carried out the crime immediately but for the outside interference. Therefore, it should be held that their acts went beyond mere preparation. (B) is incorrect and (D) is correct.

Question 42

The state of Idamont has adopted the Model Penal Code. Section 5.01 of that Code provides:

> A person is guilty of an attempt to commit a crime if, acting with the kind of culpability otherwise required for commission of the crime, he or she (a) purposely engages in conduct which would constitute a crime if the attendant circumstances were as he or she believes them to be. ...

In which of the following cases is the defendant most likely to be found not guilty of an attempt crime in the state of Idamont?

(A) Drug X is a controlled substance in Oregonia; criminal penalties are imposed for the possession or sale of Drug X in that state. There are no restrictions on the sale or distribution of Drug X in Idamont. Debbie, a resident of Oregonia, travels to Idamont and sells three kilos of Drug X to Bonnie, an Idamont resident who believes that Drug X is a controlled substance carrying criminal penalties for its sale and distribution in Idamont. Bonnie in turn distributes the three kilos of Drug X to her friends in Idamont, and is charged with attempted sale of a controlled substance.

(B) Jim is caught burglarizing the home of Melissa in Idamont. He has Melissa's diamond tennis bracelet in his possession. The bracelet is returned to Melissa. Jim, in exchange for the prosecutor's promise to recommend leniency on the burglary charge, enters into an agreement with the police that he will take Melissa's bracelet and turn it over to Fenton, the fence with whom he regularly does business. Once Fenton has received the bracelet, the police arrest Fenton for the crime of attempting to receive stolen goods.

(C) The police in the state of Idamont persuade Elaine to answer an ad placed in the local paper by Carter offering expensive wrist watches for sale at bargain prices. The watches are in fact virtually worthless imitations of expensive wrist watches. In response to Elaine's inquiry, Carter comes to Elaine's house and shows Elaine the watches, which Carter misrepresents as being valuable watches. Elaine, knowing of Carter's misrepresentations, gives Carter $500 and receives a wrist watch. The police then arrest Carter and charge him with an attempt to obtain property by false pretenses.

(D) Morticia has been watching her mother, who is terminally ill with cancer, slowly die. She anguishes over the suffering which her mother is enduring. Intending to end her mother's suffering, Morticia enters her hospital room in Idamont and injects what is clearly a lethal dose of morphine into her mother's arm. Morticia did not know that her mother had died from the cancer just before Morticia's arrival. Morticia is charged with attempted murder.

Answer to Question 42

A defendant cannot be guilty of the crime of attempt if, by completing the conduct contemplated, she would not be committing a crime. (Guilty intent alone will not make otherwise legal actions illegal even under the Model Penal Code, just as good intentions or naiveté will not make an illegal action legal.) The Model Penal Code rule regarding the defense of impossibility to the crime of attempt is quite different from the common law rule. At common law, there was a distinction between factual impossibility (such as trying to steal a wallet from an empty pocket) where impossibility would not be a defense, and legal impossibility (such as attempting to receive goods which were not in fact stolen) where the defense of impossibility would succeed. The language of the Model Penal Code was designed to deny the defense of impossibility in both cases. Under the Model Penal Code, impossibility is a defense to attempt only if the conduct contemplated is not a crime.

In (B), Fenton cannot be convicted of the crime of receiving stolen goods because the owner had given the police permission to use the goods, so they were not in fact stolen. However, when the goods were delivered to Fenton, he believed that they were stolen and intended to receive stolen goods. Fenton intended to take an action which he correctly understood to be criminal. If the circumstances were as Fenton believed them to be, i.e., if the bracelet was in fact stolen, he would have committed a criminal act by accepting the bracelet, the receiving of stolen goods. Therefore, he is *guilty of an attempt to receive stolen goods* under the Model Penal Code. (Under the common law, he would have had a valid defense of legal impossibility, because the fact that the bracelet was not stolen made the receiving of it not a crime.)

Carter in (C) also faces conviction for attempt under the Model Penal Code. Carter is not guilty of obtaining property by false pretenses because an essential element of the crime, reliance by the victim, is missing. However, his intended conduct was criminal and he believed at the time that he took the money that the victim was relying on his misrepresentations so he is *guilty of attempt*. (At common law, Carter would have had the defense of legal impossibility. If an element of the substantive crime was missing, a conviction for attempt would be impossible.)

(D) is incorrect. The defendant could not be charged with murder because the victim was dead at the time the defendant acted. However, the defendant would have been guilty of murder if the circumstances were as she believed them to be (i.e., if her mother had been alive), and therefore is *guilty of attempted murder* under the Model Penal Code. (Under the common law, the fact that murder was a legal impossibility when Morticia acted presents her with a valid defense to the charge of attempted murder.)

Bonnie knew she was selling Drug X and she believed that doing so was a crime in Idamont, but it was not a crime. Therefore, she has the defense of impossibility and is *not guilty of an attempt*. (A) is correct.

Question 43

Smith, desiring to harm George, pays Walker to administer a severe beating to George. In the course of administering the beating, Walker causes injuries which prove fatal to George three weeks later. Smith is guilty of

(A) solicitation.
(B) murder.
(C) both solicitation and murder.
(D) neither solicitation nor murder.

Answer to Question 43

In hiring Walker to beat George, Smith solicited a crime. However, once the solicited person agrees to commit the crime, then a conspiracy has been formed and the crime of solicitation merges into conspiracy. Likewise, because the crime was carried out, the solicitation was merged into the solicitor's liability for the target crime. Since Smith is guilty of the substantive crime, as discussed below, he is not guilty of solicitation. (A) and (C) are incorrect.

Smith and Walker entered into an agreement to unlawfully cause great bodily harm to George. Thus, Smith and Walker have entered into a conspiracy and Smith is liable for every crime committed as part of that conspiracy. Smith intended to have Walker inflict great bodily harm (which constitutes malice) and George died as a result. Therefore, this is murder. The killing occurred within the scope of the conspiracy. Since each conspirator is liable for every offense committed pursuant to the conspiracy, Smith is liable for murder.

(B) is correct and (D) is incorrect.

Question 44

When Diane's mother Margaret died, her will left the family's silver candleholders to Diane's sister, Susan. Diane was very unhappy because Margaret had always told Diane that she would be given the candleholders at Margaret's death. Diane was determined to take the candleholders, which were prominently displayed in Susan's dining room.

Diane approached Bob and asked him to break into Susan's house, remove the candleholders, and deliver them to her. Bob agreed to the plan. Diane then drove Bob to the street in front of Susan's house and told him that she would pick him up in one hour. Diane had second thoughts about the plan after dropping Bob off. She went directly home and did not return to pick Bob up.

Bob tripped an alarm upon entering Susan's house and was apprehended by the police when he emerged with the silver candleholders. At the police station, Bob told the police of Diane's involvement.

In addition to the substantive crimes of which Diane can be convicted, she could also be convicted of

I. solicitation.
II. conspiracy.
III. attempt.

(A) I and II only
(B) II only
(C) III only
(D) II and III only

Answer to Question 44

This question requires an understanding of inchoate crimes and the doctrine of merger.

Diane can be convicted of conspiracy, but not solicitation or attempt. Diane combined with Bob to burglarize Susan's house and to steal the silver candleholders and therefore is guilty of conspiracy. Conspiracy, unlike solicitation and attempt, does not merge with the substantive crimes of which Diane can be convicted. Therefore, (B) is correct because conspiracy is the only additional crime she could be convicted of.

All of the other choices are incorrect as a matter of law because solicitation and attempt always merge into the substantive crimes, once committed.

Question 45

Ollie is the owner of an expensive home and needs cash for its upkeep. He approaches his friend Fred and asks Fred to help him break into Ollie's house and "steal" the high-quality stereo equipment because it is insured. Fred agrees. As they approach Ollie's house, they observe a policeman and abandon their plan. Ollie and Fred are

(A) not guilty of conspiracy because there is no multiplicity of persons.
(B) not guilty of conspiracy because the plan was abandoned before the substantive crime was accomplished.
(C) guilty of conspiracy to defraud the insurance company.
(D) guilty of conspiracy to defraud the insurance company and conspiracy to commit burglary.

Answer to Question 45

There is clearly a multiplicity of persons - Ollie and Fred. The crime of defrauding an insurance company or burglary does not necessarily require at least two persons. Thus, the *Wharton* Rule does not apply, and (A) is incorrect.

Ollie and Fred agreed to commit an unlawful act. Their later abandonment of the plan does not affect their liability for the crime of conspiracy. (B) is incorrect.

There was a conspiracy to defraud the insurance company. Under the majority rule, the crime of conspiracy is complete upon the parties' agreement. (Even in those jurisdictions requiring an overt act, the act required need only be something which corroborates the agreement, some small step towards the unlawful goal. The required steps were clearly taken here.)

There was no conspiracy to commit burglary, however. The act Ollie and Fred agreed to undertake, pretending to break into Ollie's house and, once there, remove the silver, is not burglary because breaking and entering one's own house (here, Ollie's house) cannot be burglary. Fred was invited to enter the premises by Ollie, so his entering would also have been lawful. Thus, (D) is incorrect and (C) is correct.

Question 46

In State X, arson has been extended by statute to include the burning of any building. In that jurisdiction, Andie and Bill were fired from their jobs in an oil refinery. They decided to go back at night and destroy a key part of the system that fed crude oil into the refinery. Andie took an ax and punctured some feeder pipes, causing a massive leakage of oil. As Andie and Bill were leaving the plant, Andie threw a lighted match into the doorway, causing an explosion and fire. Bill has been charged with three crimes:

I. conspiracy;
II. malicious destruction of property;
III. arson.

Of which crime(s) is he guilty?

(A) I only
(B) I and II
(C) I, II, and III
(D) I and III

Answer to Question 46

Note that the question asks only for Bill's crimes. Bill is guilty of conspiracy (I) because he entered into an agreement with Andie to commit a crime, the destruction of property. Once a conspiracy has been found, the conspirators are deemed agents of each other. The general rule is that each conspirator, while a member of the conspiracy, is liable for every offense committed by all other conspirators in pursuance or furtherance of the conspiracy, even if the particular conspirator did not participate in the offense. Therefore, Bill is also guilty of malicious destruction of property (II) because of Andie's deliberate act of wrecking the pipes with an ax. Conspiracy and the substantive crime do not merge, so if the crime is completed, the conspirators are guilty of both.

However, conspirators are only liable for crimes committed by their cohorts in pursuance of the conspiracy. An offense must be foreseeable as a natural consequence of the common design. Where one conspirator goes entirely outside the scope of the conspiracy in committing a crime, he alone is guilty of the crime. The arson crime (III) in this case is beyond the scope of the conspiracy because Bill only agreed to wreck the feeder pipes. Therefore, Bill is not guilty of arson.

Question 47

Heather approached Bud and said, "I need someone to come with me and break into Elizabeth's house and retrieve my fur coat, which she borrowed from me but never returned." The coat in fact belongs to Elizabeth, but Bud doesn't know this. Bud agrees, and pursuant to Heather's plan, both Heather and Bud enter Elizabeth's house through an unlocked door, seize the fur coat and are about to leave when they are arrested by the police, who were tipped off and have been waiting in hiding.

Who can be convicted of conspiracy?

(A) Heather
(B) Bud, in a jurisdiction which recognizes unilateral conspiracy.
(C) Both
(D) Neither

Answer to Question 47

A conspiracy under the common law requires an agreement to accomplish an unlawful purpose. The Model Penal Code has modified the elements of conspiracy by adopting the rule of unilateral conspiracy. Under the theory of unilateral conspiracy, a defendant can be held guilty of conspiracy, even if the other person never intended to commit the crime, as long as the defendant (1) intended to commit the target crime, (2) committed some overt act, and (3) believed that the other party also intended to commit the crime. Unilateral conspiracy would allow **Heather** to be convicted, since she **did** agree to commit an act she knew to be illegal. However, unless the choice or the question specifically states that the Model Penal Code applies, you should assume that it does not, so in considering (A) we must apply the common law. (A) is incorrect because the common law requires a multiplicity of persons for conspiracy and if Bud thought that the coat belonged to Heather, which at least arguably is the case, then Bud cannot be convicted of conspiracy. Under the common law, if Bud is not guilty of conspiracy, Heather cannot be guilty.

If the unilateral conspiracy theory applies, it would not permit a conviction of Bud if he did not intend to commit a crime. Therefore, (B) and (C) are incorrect.

(D) can then be chosen as the correct answer by process of elimination.

Question 48

Bob and Chuck hated Howard and agreed to start a fight with Howard, and if the opportunity arose, to kill him. Bob and Chuck met Howard in the street outside a bar and began to push him around. Ray, Phil, and Ted, who also hated Howard, stopped to watch. Ray threw Bob a knife. Phil told Bob, "Kill him." Ted, who made no move and said nothing, hoped that Bob would kill Howard with the knife. Chuck held Howard while Bob stabbed and killed him.

On a charge of murdering Howard, Phil is

(A) guilty, because, with the intent to have Bob kill Howard, he shouted encouragement to Bob.
(B) guilty, because he aided and abetted the murder through his mere presence plus his intent to see Howard killed.
(C) not guilty, because his words did not create a "clear and present danger" not already existing.
(D) not guilty, because mere presence and oral encouragement, whether or not he had the requisite intent, will not make him guilty as an accomplice.

Answer to Question 48

One who aids, counsels or encourages the commission of a crime with the intent that the crime be committed is guilty under a theory of accomplice liability. Under the common law, such an accomplice who is present at the scene of the felony would be considered a principal in the second degree and punished to the same extent as a perpetrator.

(B) is incorrect because a person's mere presence at the scene of a felony does **not** constitute aiding and abetting the crime. Even if that presence is coupled with intent, it is not sufficient to cause criminal liability.

The "clear and present danger" test is a test used in First Amendment analysis. Specifically, a person's right to free speech may not be curtailed or punished unless the words used are used in such circumstances and are of such a nature as to create a clear and present danger that the words will bring about some substantive evil that the government has a right to prevent. On the other hand, expression which encourages a breach of the peace is **not** protected by the First Amendment. The facts make clear that Phil, in fact, did encourage a breach of the peace. Therefore, the test does not apply and (C) is incorrect.

Phil intended that the crime be committed and shouted encouragement. He had the appropriate *mens rea*; shouting encouragement was the *actus reus*. Therefore, as a matter of substantive criminal law, Phil is guilty of murdering Howard. Therefore, (D) is incorrect and (A) is correct.

Question 49

On the way home from a party one night, a group of teenage boys passes through the retail district of Smalltown, discussing the type of security protecting the stores. The oldest boy, Tom, dares the others to attempt to evade the security guards. Huck opens the side window of a shoe store which had warnings that the store was protected by a security system and intruders would be prosecuted, gains entrance and crawls along the floor to a shoe rack facing the display window containing expensive basketball shoes. He takes a pair of shoes off the rack, stands up and waves them in front of him. Soon thereafter, he is arrested by the security guards and is subsequently indicted for burglary and larceny.

At his trial, he testifies that he broke into the store only to show that the security system could be beaten and that he waved the shoes at his friends to celebrate his short-lived triumph.

The jurisdiction has enacted a criminal trespass statute prohibiting entry on the property of another after notice forbidding such entry.

If Huck is tried as an adult and the jury believes Huck's story, he can be convicted at most of

(A) criminal trespass.
(B) burglary only.
(C) larceny only.
(D) burglary and larceny.

Answer to Question 49

Burglary and larceny are both specific intent crimes. In all specific intent crimes, both the intent to do the act and an additional specific intent to cause the harmful consequences are required.

To be guilty of burglary, Huck had to break and enter a dwelling in the nighttime with the intent of committing a felony inside. While some jurisdictions have extended burglary to include the breaking and entering of any building, you must assume that the common law applies in a Multistate question that makes no reference to a statute. This store is not a dwelling. Furthermore, although Huck intentionally broke into and entered the store, he did not possess the specific intent to commit a felony while inside and therefore did not have the *mens rea* for burglary, so another element necessary for a burglary is also not found. Thus, (B) and (D) are incorrect.

To be guilty of larceny, one must take and carry away the property of another with the intent to steal. That intent is more precisely described as intending to deprive the owner of possession of the property permanently or for an unreasonable length of time. Since the question asks you to assume that the jury believes Huck (including that he had no intent to take the jacket), they cannot find the required *mens rea*. There was no intent to steal. Therefore, Huck is not guilty of larceny and (C) is incorrect.

Huck can, however, be convicted of criminal trespass. The statute described in the question sets out the elements of a criminal trespass as (1) entry (2) on the property of another (3) after notice forbidding such entry. Huck's entry point contained a posted warning notice forbidding entry and he intentionally entered the property. He committed the *actus reus* while possessing the required *mens rea*. Therefore, (A) is correct.

Question 50

Donna took Vickie's boat without Vickie's permission at a time when Donna was drunk. She intended to go for a short ride and return it to the dock. On the way back to the dock, Donna crashed into a piling, causing the boat to take on a considerable amount of water. Donna is charged with larceny. The court should find her

(A) not guilty, because drunkenness is a defense to a specific intent crime.
(B) not guilty, because she did not have the required specific intent.
(C) guilty, because she did not return the boat in the condition it was in at the time she took it.
(D) guilty, because the intent to borrow is the functional equivalent of the intent to steal.

Answer to Question 50

Voluntary intoxication is only a defense to a criminal charge if it negates the existence of a specific element of the crime charged. If Donna's drunkenness made it impossible for her to form the specific intent to steal the boat, then it is a defense to the crime of larceny. However, that does not appear to be the case here. Donna simply did not have the intent to steal; her intoxication had nothing to do with it. Therefore, (A) is incorrect.

(C) is incorrect because the fact that Donna encountered an accident does not change the evaluation of her intent at the time she took the boat.

(D) is incorrect because the intent to borrow is not equivalent to the intent to steal if there is a substantial capacity to return the property within a reasonable time.

Larceny is a theft crime and therefore requires a specific intent to steal (i.e., an intent to deprive another of her property permanently). If there is an intent and a substantial capacity to return the property within a reasonable time, the intent to steal is not present. The intent at the time of taking determines criminal liability. Donna took the boat intending to return it. Accordingly, she lacked the intent to steal and is not guilty of larceny. Therefore, (B) is correct.

Question 51

Vic offered Dick $1,000 if Dick could deliver one ounce of cocaine to Vic's home. Dick delivered the cocaine, but Vic refused to pay because he said the product was adulterated. Enraged at what he considered to be a falsehood and a theft of his property, Dick went to Vic's home one night and took $1,000 from Vic's safe. Dick's best defense to a charge of burglary is that

(A) the original contract was illegal, so the law will leave the parties in the status quo.
(B) he was so upset that he acted under an irresistible impulse.
(C) he did not know the elements of the crime of burglary.
(D) he lacked the specific intent to commit the crime.

Answer to Question 51

A court will not decline to convict a defendant just because he might try to defend himself by referring to a contract that was made for an illegal purpose. If a crime was committed, the prosecution would proceed even if the victim was also a criminal. (A) is incorrect.

The "irresistible impulse" test holds that a person is not guilty by reason of insanity if it is determined that he had a mental disease which kept him from controlling his conduct. It is not enough to have such an irresistible impulse: it must also be the product of mental illness. Since there is no suggestion here that Dick suffered any mental illness, (B) is incorrect.

A defendant who has made a "mistake of law" in the sense that he was unaware that a particular act was criminal, does not have a defense. A mistake of law can constitute a defense regarding a specific intent crime, but only if it negates a required element of the crime. The intent required for burglary is only the intent to commit acts which constitute a felony. It is not required that the actor know that those acts constitute a felony. Therefore, it is no defense in this case that Dick did not know the elements of the crime and so did not know that it was a felony. (C) is incorrect.

Common-law burglary is the breaking and entering of the dwelling house of another in the nighttime with the specific intent to commit a felony therein. Thus, the *mens rea* of burglary is the intent to commit a felony. If Dick sincerely believed that he had a claim of right to the money he took, he lacked the specific intent necessary for burglary. Since the question indicates that this retrieval of money was Dick's only intent in entering Vic's house, he did not form the specific intent necessary for burglary. Therefore, (D) is correct.

Question 52

A federal regulatory statute requires that all PCB's, a dangerous chemical that is released upon the dismantling of a transformer, be placed in special drums, labeled conspicuously as hazardous waste and disposed of in an approved hazardous waste facility. The Electric Company was charged with a violation of the labeling portion of this statute.

Which of the following set of circumstances, if true, would be most likely to result in a not guilty verdict?

(A) The employee who dismantled the transformer mistakenly believed that the liquid in the transformer was not a PCB and therefore did not label the drum properly.
(B) The company diligently informed its employees of the necessity of properly affixing labels to drums of PCB's, but an employee forgot to do so.
(C) The company employee affixed the label, but the label became dislodged when the common carrier who was transporting the drum to a hazardous waste site encountered a pothole.
(D) The liquid taken from the transformer contained only one percent PCB's. The company had received an opinion from its environmental counsel that labeling was not required unless the concentration of PCB's in the liquid was more than two per cent. That opinion was erroneous.

Answer to Question 52

Whenever a statute is referred to as a regulatory offense, you should assume it is a strict liability crime unless the text of the statute contains language which makes fault (e.g., knowledge) an element of the crime created. The statute in question is a regulatory statute, creating a strict liability crime requiring neither intent nor criminal negligence. The crime is committed by merely performing the *actus reus*, in this case the failure to affix the label to the hazardous waste material.

Commonly, strict liability crimes will be construed to impose vicarious liability in an employer-employee relationship. An employer will thus be vicariously liable for regulatory crimes which are committed by an employee in the course of employment. Strict liability offenses impose liability without regard to intent and therefore the absence of any *mens rea* is not a defense. In (A), (B) and (D) the action required by the statute was not taken, so the *actus reus* was committed.

The fact that in (B) the omission was attributable to an employee's carelessness will not help the employer avoid liability. Construction of the statute as to the issue of vicarious liability will include consideration of such factors as the degree of harm to the public incurred by failure to comply and the severity of punishment. This regulation is likely to impose such liability. Therefore, the fact that the statute was violated will lead to liability for Electric Company.

Neither a mistake of law (regardless of whether it is based on advice from an attorney or not) as in (D), nor a mistake of fact, even if reasonably held as in (A), will free Electric Company of strict liability.

The only possible defense to the violation of a regulatory statute is that the *actus reus* was not performed. In (C), the label was affixed, so the statute was not violated. Therefore, (C) is correct.

Question 53

A West Carolina statute provides "It shall be unlawful to sell alcoholic beverages to any person under twenty-one (21) years of age," and imposes a fine of $1,000 for violation of the statute. The state courts have interpreted the statute as creating strict liability.

Reggie, the regional manager of a chain of retail package liquor stores known as Better Beverage Inc., chose Marie to manage the Metropolis store in the state of West Carolina. Reggie delegated all decisionmaking concerning operations to Marie.

Marie hired Cecile as a clerk to sell liquor during the afternoon shift. She told Cecile to check the identification of all prospective purchasers and to refuse to sell to anyone under age 21. One afternoon Scott, who was 18 but looked older, purchased a bottle of scotch without showing any identification. An inspector from the state liquor commission was watching the store and, by checking Scott's age, established a violation of the statute.

Reggie was convicted by the trial court of violating the statute and has appealed on the ground that his personal conviction would violate the Due Process Clause of the U.S. Constitution. The appellate court should

(A) uphold the conviction, because he was in a position to exercise control over the sale of liquor by employees of Better Beverage Inc.
(B) uphold the conviction, because regulatory offenses are not subject to due process limitations.
(C) reverse the conviction, because criminal liability is personal and Better Beverage Inc. is the seller, not Reggie.
(D) reverse the conviction, because it is a violation of due process to punish without a voluntary act.

Answer to Question 53

The Due Process Clause issue here relates to vicarious liability. Two of the responses are overbroad in attempting to identify the issue and inaccurate statements of law as well. (B) is incorrect because all of the due process safeguards due to a criminal accused must be accorded a person charged with a regulatory offense. (D) is incorrect because it is not a violation of due process to punish without a voluntary act. A failure to act where there is a legal duty to act may be punished as well.

The statute in question deals with the kind of offense and imposes the type of penalty for which strict liability statutes are constitutional. Statutes imposing vicarious liability upon the innocent employer for the illegal acts of an employee in the scope of employment are generally upheld as constitutional. In evaluating the constitutionality of imposing vicarious liability, the issue of control over employees is the most important consideration. Supervisors with authority over the persons who actually commit the offense can constitutionally be held vicariously liable. Note that the supervisor need not in fact exercise control over the sale; the power and responsibility to control sales is sufficient.

Criminal liability thus is imposed here based upon the power of Reggie to control conduct and his responsible, supervisory relationship as employer with his employees. It is not based upon personal involvement in a sale. Reggie can be held criminally liable, even though Better Beverage will likely be held liable to indemnify him for the fine. Therefore, (A) is correct and (C) is incorrect.

Question 54

Germaine is the personnel manager of Techtronics Inc., a company which assembles personal computers in the state of Kennessee. Company policy is to employ working mothers and require them to stay in the plant for the shortest possible time. The Kennessee Occupational Health and Safety Act, which has been interpreted as a strict liability statute, makes it a criminal offense to employ assembly line workers for an eight-hour shift without granting them one 30-minute break during the shift. Germaine did not know of the law. Without consulting the workers, she chose to require that the workers work eight consecutive hours, because she knew that many were working mothers who did not want to remain away from their children any longer than necessary.

Germaine has been charged with violating the statute and the above-stated facts have been proven. The court should find her

(A) guilty, because she should have inquired as to the preferences of the workers before requiring them to work without a break.
(B) guilty, because she required the workers to work without a break.
(C) not guilty, because Techtronics Inc., not Germaine, is the employer of the workers and sets company policy.
(D) not guilty, because she believed she was following company policy and was not aware of the violation.

Answer to Question 54

The question states that the statute in question has been construed as creating a strict liability offense. Since the statute in question is a strict liability statute, Germaine is guilty of the offense if she engages in the prohibited conduct. Since she required the workers to work eight hours without a break, she has performed the *actus reus*. Whether the workers wanted a break or not is immaterial to the issue of Germaine's guilt. The statute does not provide an exception based on the consent of the protected class. Therefore, (A) is incorrect.

(C) is incorrect because Germaine was in control of working conditions and is therefore liable under the statute, irrespective of the ownership of the company. Although Techtronics Inc. would also be responsible under a theory of vicarious liability, that does not affect Germaine's liability. A person who engages in criminal conduct is personally liable notwithstanding the fact that she acts on behalf of her employer. Germaine will likely be able to recover from the company for any fines she is forced to pay if she was furthering the company's interests or policies in breaking the law, but she can still be held personally liable.

(D) is incorrect because no mistake of fact or law provides a defense to a strict liability offense. (Ignorance of the law is not a defense to any type of crime.) Nor is Germaine's adherence to company policy a defense to criminal liability. Statutes always take precedence over company policy, and Techtronics' liability will not preclude Germaine's.

(B) is correct.

Question 55

State X, by statute, requires an itemized bill of out-of-pocket expenses on each invoice submitted by a consultant. Connie, a consultant to the State of X on health care issues, submits to the State X health department a bill for her consulting work, together with itemized expenses which Connie actually incurred for other work during the relevant time period, but which were not incurred on any state job. Connie is charged with obtaining property by false pretenses. Her defense is that her two-year-old son ransacked her desk and mixed up all of her records, and that she made an honest mistake in submitting the expenses. The court should rule that defense

(A) insufficient, because the mistake was due to Connie's own carelessness.
(B) insufficient, because mistake is not a valid defense to a white-collar crime.
(C) sufficient if she did not know that the expenses attached to the invoice were not incurred on the state job.
(D) sufficient only if her mistake was reasonable.

Answer to Question 55

The crime of obtaining property by false pretenses is a specific intent crime. The defendant must know that his representation is false and intend thereby to defraud the owner. The defendant's knowledge of falsity is measured subjectively. The defendant's belief that her representations are true need only be honest; it need not be reasonable. Thus, if a court finds that Connie's mistake was indeed honest, then she has a sufficient defense. Anything which in fact prevents the defendant from knowing that she is making false representations prevents her formation of an intent to defraud. Thus, (C) is correct.

(A) is incorrect because there is no special mistake doctrine for white-collar crimes.

(B) and (D) are incorrect because Connie's mistake, if it was honest, is a defense even if it was unreasonable and even if it was caused by carelessness.

Question 56

In comparing the Model Penal Code test for insanity (exclusive of its provisions for diminished responsibility) on the one hand, with a combination of the *M'Naghten* and irresistible impulse tests on the other, which of the following statements is most accurate?

(A) The Model Penal Code test incorporates the *M'Naghten* and irresistible impulse tests, and provides an additional test for insanity.
(B) The Model Penal Code test is a refinement and restatement of the *M'Naghten* and irresistible impulse tests in terms more compatible with modern psychiatry.
(C) The Model Penal Code test is a refinement of the *M'Naghten* test, but abandons the concept of the irresistible impulse test for insanity.

(D) The Model Penal Code test abandons the *M'Naghten* and irresistible impulse tests, and substitutes a different test for insanity.

Answer to Question 56

The drafters of the Model Penal Code (MPC) combined and made refinements to both the irresistible impulse test and the *M'Naghten* test. The two-pronged nature of the MPC test means that a defendant is insane if she lacked *either* the requisite cognitive ability (the *M'Naghten* test) *or* the requisite behavioral ability (the irresistible impulse test). The MPC test may be said to refine these two tests because it requires lack of "substantial capacity" to control oneself or to appreciate the wrongful nature of the act. The *M'Naghten* and irresistible impulse tests require **complete** impairment of those capacities.

(B) is correct and the other choices are incorrect because the MPC abandons neither *M'Naghten* nor the irresistible impulse test, and it contains no new tests for insanity.

Question 57

Art and Ben together entered Candace's apartment and each had sexual intercourse with Candace against her will. If Ben is to raise successfully the defense of insanity in a jurisdiction which recognizes only the *M'Naghten* test, which of the following would be most helpful to him?

(A) Ben is mentally retarded, and Art convinced him that this was just a new way of kissing Candace.
(B) Ben is a member of a religious cult; Art, the leader, told him that his act was necessary to purify Candace, and Ben believed Art.
(C) Ben's act was caused by a severe paranoid condition.
(D) Ben does not have the capacity to control his sexual behavior.

Answer to Question 57

The *M'Naghten* test of criminal insanity requires that, to establish insanity sufficient to relieve the defendant of guilt, it must be proved that the defendant: (1) suffered from a mental disease or defect, and (2) because of that defect, was not able to understand either the nature of the act or that the act was legally or morally wrong.

The facts provided in response (B) do not satisfy either prong of the *M'Naghten* test. Belonging to a religious cult does not constitute a mental disease or defect, and there is no other indication that mental illness or mental retardation caused Ben's criminal act. Furthermore, the fact that Ben acted under orders from a religious authority does not necessarily mean he did not know the nature of his act or its illegality. (B) is incorrect.

(C) merely asserts that a mental illness is the cause of the crime. That is not sufficient to establish an insanity defense in a jurisdiction which has adopted the *M'Naghten* test. Proving that one suffers from severe paranoia does not necessarily establish that one cannot know the nature and lawfulness of one's actions. Since the facts provided by (C) do not satisfy the *M'Naghten* test, (C) is incorrect.

Inability to control one's behavior speaks to the "irresistible impulse" test. That test states that a defendant is not guilty by reason of insanity if his acts were the product of a mental disease which rendered the defendant unable to control his conduct. Thus, response (D) would be correct if the irresistible impulse test were applicable and the defendant could show a mental disease was the cause of his lack of control. But that test does not apply and it does not appear that a mental disease caused Ben's lack of control. Since it is quite possible that Ben knew what he was doing and knew it was wrong, while nevertheless being unable to control himself, these facts do not satisfy the *M'Naghten* test. Therefore, (D) is incorrect.

Mental retardation is a mental "defect" which can be the cause of an incapacity to distinguish the nature and quality of the defendant's act. If Ben believed he was just kissing Candace, he did not know what he was doing and did not know that what he was doing was wrong. Therefore, (A) is correct.

Question 58

Daniel inflicted several stab wounds on Veronica and killed her. He believed that Veronica was a drug pusher, and that it was his moral duty to kill her. In fact, Veronica was a law-abiding citizen. When interrogated by the police, Daniel said that he was aware of the fact that Veronica died as a result of the stab wounds, and that he expected the police to prosecute him for murder, but that he was acting according to a higher law.

Dr. Smith, a psychiatrist who examined Daniel for the prosecution, wrote a report saying that Daniel suffered from a form of schizophrenia with delusions and hallucinations, and that he had hallucinations of hearing voices saying that Veronica was a drug pusher and should be killed. Daniel was charged with first-degree murder.

In a jurisdiction which has adopted the *M'Naghten* test for insanity, assuming that the testimony of the psychiatrist is believed, the defense of insanity will

(A) be unsuccessful, because his act was not the product of an irresistible impulse.
(B) be unsuccessful, because he was able to appreciate the criminality of his act.
(C) be successful, because Daniel, as a result of a defect of reason, did not know the nature of his act.
(D) be successful, because Daniel, as a result of a defect of reason, did not know that the act he was committing was a crime.

Answer to Question 58

Under *M'Naghten*, it must be proved that, at the time of the commission of the act, the defendant was laboring under such a defect of reason from a disease of the mind as not to know the nature and quality of the act he was doing, or if he did know it, that he did not know that what he was doing was wrong. Thus, the *M'Naghten* rule requires that a defendant be rendered completely incapable of knowing the nature and quality of his actions or of distinguishing right from wrong.

(A) is incorrect because the "irresistible impulse" test used in other jurisdictions is very different from the *M'Naghten* test applicable here. Under the irresistible impulse test, Daniel would be found not guilty by reason of insanity if he could show that, at the time he acted, he had a mental disease which kept him from controlling his conduct. Under that test, Daniel could be found insane even if it were shown that he knew what he was doing and knew that it was wrong. This does not comport with the *M'Naghten* rule.

In this case, Daniel knew he was stabbing Veronica. Also, Daniel clearly stated that he expected to be charged with murder for his acts. This shows that Daniel knew that his acts were illegal and would lead to his prosecution for murder. Since Daniel knew the nature of his act and he knew it was a crime, he meets neither of the *M'Naghten* criteria of insanity, and will be unsuccessful in his assertion of an insanity defense here. Therefore, (B) is correct and (C) and (D) are incorrect.

Question 59

While testifying as a witness in a civil trial, Whitney was asked on cross-examination if he had been convicted in the district court of Culpepper County of attempted robbery. Whitney said, "No, I have never been convicted of any crime." In fact, Whitney had pleaded guilty to such a charge and had been placed on probation.

Whitney was then charged with perjury on the ground that his statement denying the conviction was false. A statute in the jurisdiction defines perjury as knowingly making a false statement while under oath.

At his trial for perjury, the state proved Whitney's statement and the prior conviction. Whitney testified that the attorney who represented him in the robbery case had told him that, because he had been placed on probation, he had not been convicted of a crime. The advice of the attorney was incorrect.

If the jury believes Whitney, it should find him

(A) not guilty, because he lacked the necessary mental state.
(B) not guilty if the jury also finds that his reliance on the attorney's advice was reasonable.
(C) guilty, because his mistake was one of law.
(D) guilty, because reliance on the advice of an attorney is not a defense.

Answer to Question 59

This perjury statute creates a specific intent crime; the *mens rea* required for that crime is that the defendant must have knowledge that his statements are false. (B) is incorrect because the reasonableness of Whitney's reliance on his attorney's advice is not relevant. The test is entirely subjective. If Whitney's reliance on his attorney's advice prevented him from forming the required *mens rea*, it doesn't matter if that belief was reasonable or not. He need only show that he honestly believed that his statement was not false.

This does not mean he made a "mistake of law" -- nothing indicates that Whitney did not know that perjury was a crime. Thus, (C) is incorrect.

(D) is incorrect because his reliance could negate the *mens rea*.

Whitney will allege that his reliance on his attorney's advice kept him from knowing that his testimony was false. If Whitney did not know his testimony was false, then he could not form the specific intent required by the statute to commit perjury. He is not guilty because his honest belief that his statement was not false precludes the *mens rea* required for this crime - that he **knowingly** made a false statement. Therefore, (A) is correct.

Question 60

In which of the following situations is Dan's claim of intoxication most likely to result in a verdict of not guilty?

(A) Dan is charged with assault with intent to kill Sandra as a result of his wounding Sandra by shooting her. Dan claims he was so drunk that he did not realize anyone else was around when he fired the gun.
(B) Dan is charged with statutory rape after he has sexual intercourse with a girl aged 15, in a jurisdiction where the age of consent is 16. Dan claims he was so drunk that he did not realize the girl was a minor.
(C) Dan is charged with armed robbery. He claims he was so drunk that he did not know whether the gun was loaded.
(D) Dan is charged with manslaughter for a death resulting from an automobile accident. Dan, who was the driver, claims he was so drunk that he was unable to see the other car involved in the accident.

Answer to Question 60

In each of the choices, Dan argues he should be excused from liability for his actions because he was intoxicated. However, **voluntary** intoxication is a defense only if it negates the specific intent required to commit a crime.

Statutory rape is, in most states, a strict liability crime. Therefore, in (B), mistake as to age is not a defense to such a crime. Since the mistake is irrelevant, its cause (intoxication) is likewise irrelevant.

Since it is armed robbery to carry out a larceny even with an unloaded gun, it makes no difference in (C) whether Dan knew the gun was loaded or not. Although Dan was so drunk he did not know the gun was loaded, he has not established that he was so drunk he did not know he was using a gun to commit robbery. Thus, Dan's intoxication has not negated a required element of the crime, and it is therefore not a valid defense.

(D) is incorrect because if Dan, knowing he was intoxicated, nonetheless operated a car, he acted with reckless indifference to a serious danger. That is sufficient for manslaughter. The underlying gross negligence was in driving the car while intoxicated, not in failing to see the other vehicle. In most jurisdictions, even if a defendant is unaware of the risk his recklessness creates due to his voluntary intoxication, he is nonetheless guilty of the recklessness which is an element of the crime charged.

However, if Dan is charged with assault with intent to kill but was too drunk to know there was anyone around, he could not have formed the intent to kill. Although Dan might be convicted of another crime, the *mens rea* required for assault with intent to kill cannot be established. Dan's intoxication has made him incapable of completing the crime. Therefore, (A) is correct.

Question 61

Mindy was 15 years old, but she appeared and acted older. When asked, she always said she was 21, and she carried false identification saying she was that old. She frequented taverns and drank heavily. One evening in a bar, she became acquainted with Daryl. He believed her when she told him her claimed age. They had several drinks and became inebriated. Later, they drove in Daryl's car to a secluded spot. After they had necked for a while, Daryl attempted to achieve penetration. At that point, Mindy changed her mind, saying, "Stop! Don't touch me! I don't want to do it." When Daryl persisted, Mindy started to cry and said, "I am only 15." Daryl immediately jumped from the car and ran away. Daryl was indicted for attempted rape, assault with intent to rape, contributing to the delinquency of a minor, and attempted statutory rape. The age of consent in the jurisdiction is 16.

The charge of contributing to the delinquency of a minor is based on a statute reading, "Whoever shall commit an act affecting the morals of a minor under sixteen years of age shall be deemed guilty of contributing to the delinquency of a minor and shall be punished by imprisonment in the state penitentiary for a period not to exceed five years."

With respect to the contributing charge under the statute, proof by Daryl that he was so inebriated that he could not have formed a criminal intent would be a

(A) poor defense, because contributing to the delinquency of a minor is an offense against a child.
(B) poor defense, because the state of mind of the defendant is irrelevant to this offense, so long as he is legally sane.
(C) good defense, because at least a general criminal intent is required for every offense.
(D) good defense, because the charge requires a specific intent.

Answer to Question 61

The language of this statute, "whoever shall commit an act affecting the morals of a minor...", does not require specific intent. All that is required is that the defendant commit the proscribed act. An argument may be made that this creates either a general intent offense or a public welfare offense imposing strict liability. Under either construction, intoxication is not a defense. If this is a general intent crime, only an intent to do the act is required. If no intent is required, then intoxication has no effect on liability.

(A) is incorrect because the minority status of the victim is not relevant to the intent required to commit the crime; the statute imposes liability without intent or with only an intent to do the stated act.

(C) is incorrect because some statutes impose criminal liability without fault and do not require even a general criminal intent, and (D) is incorrect because the charge clearly does not require specific intent.

(B) is the best statement of the effect of the intoxication defense on this type of crime.

Question 62

Hal had a heart ailment so serious that his doctors had concluded that only a heart transplant could save his life. They therefore arranged to have him flown to Metropolis to have the operation performed.

Ned, Hal's nephew, who stood to inherit from him, decided to poison him before he could be saved. The poison produced a reaction which required postponing the journey. The plane on which Hal was to have flown crashed, and all aboard were killed. By the following day, Hal's heart was so weakened by the effects of the poison that he suffered a heart attack and died. If charged with criminal homicide, Ned should be found

(A) not guilty, because the deceased was already suffering from a fatal illness.
(B) not guilty, because his act did not hasten the deceased's death, but instead prolonged it by one day.
(C) not guilty, because the poison was not the sole cause of death.
(D) guilty.

Answer to Question 62

A homicide crime is committed when one person causes another person to die before he otherwise would, even though the victim would have died of natural causes within a brief period of time. Where the defendant's conduct is a substantial factor in bringing about the victim's death, it is a cause in fact of the death. Thus, (A) is incorrect.

The fact that Ned's conduct may have prolonged Hal's life does not excuse that conduct when it also causes Hal's subsequent death. Thus, (B) is incorrect.

(C) is incorrect because the victim's heart condition is not a superseding cause such that there is no proximate causation between the poisoning and the death. The fact that Hal's heart "was so weakened by the effects of the poison that he suffered a heart attack and died" states a clear causal connection.

Despite the fact that the poison was the cause of Hal's avoidance of death by plane crash, it was also a substantial factor in his death and thus the cause in fact of that event as well. Therefore, Ned is guilty of murder. (D) is correct.

Question 63

Harry, Sally, and their six-month-old baby lived in North Carolina. Sally was a devoted baseball fan. When the Orioles won the American League pennant, Sally announced that she was going to Baltimore for four days to see the third, fourth, and fifth games of the World Series. Harry was angry that he was left with the baby-sitting chores. After Sally had been gone for one day, Harry left with his friends on a fishing trip, leaving Baby in the crib. The Orioles won the World Series in four games, so Sally came home the day after Harry left. She did not find Harry home, did not look in the crib, where Baby was alive and well, and went to Florida for two weeks to visit her mother. Baby died of starvation before Harry returned from his fishing trip, and he was charged with manslaughter. He should be found

(A) not guilty, because his actions were not the proximate cause of Baby's death.
(B) not guilty, because Sally had a duty to check on Baby when she came home.
(C) not guilty, because he knew his wife was coming home soon, and she in fact came home early.
(D) guilty.

Answer to Question 63

Where there is a legal duty to act - as there is between parent and child - inaction causing death can be manslaughter. Whatever Sally's duty initially was, it was Harry who left Baby alone, causing its death. Harry's inaction was the actual ("but for") cause of the child's death. That inaction is also the direct, hence proximate, cause of the child's death. Harry's abandonment of the child without provision for its care continued until the child's death. Her failure to care for the child upon her return cannot be said to be an independent intervening cause which would relieve the defendant of liability since she had no reason to expect that Harry would leave without Baby. Harry is guilty because his own behavior was an actual and substantial cause of death. (D) is correct.

Question 64

Duke sold heroin to Harold. Harold was later stopped by police for speeding. The police searched Harold's car and found the heroin concealed under the rear seat. Harold fingered Duke. Duke is charged with illegally selling heroin. Duke's motion to prevent introduction of the heroin into evidence will most probably be

(A) denied, because the search was proper as incident to a valid, full, custodial arrest.
(B) denied, because Duke has no standing to object to the search.
(C) granted, because the heroin was not in plain view.
(D) granted, because the scope of the search was excessive.

Answer to Question 64

(A), (C) and (D) are all incorrect because they analyze the validity of the search. This analysis is rendered unnecessary by the fact that Duke has no standing to make an objection to the admission of this evidence in the first place. (A) is also incorrect because it incorrectly asserts that the search was proper pursuant to an arrest. The issue that controls the ruling on the motion is whether Duke has standing to object to the admission of the evidence. Defendants may only claim the benefits of the exclusionary rule if their own Fourth Amendment rights have been violated. In this case, the only person that can challenge the propriety of the search is Harold. Duke has no expectation of privacy in Harold's vehicle and no possessory interest in the car or the heroin. See *Rawlings v. Kentucky*, 448 U.S. 98 (1980). Therefore, (B) is correct.

Question 65

Fred was about to take a trip abroad and went to the local federal building to obtain the required passport. His son, Erik, who was home from college, agreed to accompany him. To gain entry to the building, both were required to pass through a metal detection device. A sign was posted saying that it was illegal to carry a firearm in the building. Fred passed through without difficulty, but the alarm sounded when Erik passed through. The security officer on duty searched Erik's person. In Erik's pocket, the security guard found a white envelope. He opened the envelope and found a small amount of cocaine. Erik was arrested and arraigned in the federal district court. His attorney moved to have the evidence suppressed. The prosecution's best argument is that

(A) the officer conducted only a stop and frisk.
(B) there was no search.
(C) although there was a search, no warrant was required because it was incident to a lawful arrest.
(D) the search was a reasonable one.

Answer to Question 65

It is important to note that this question asks what the prosecution's **best** argument is, not whether they will in fact prevail. In analyzing a search and seizure question, you must ask (1) was there a search, (2) was there a warrant and if there was, was it a valid warrant, (3) if there was no warrant, was there an exception to the warrant rule such as probable cause or consent, and (4) was the search reasonable.

An officer who does not have probable cause to arrest may make a limited search of the person, but only a pat-down of the outer clothing for concealed weapons (if he has reasonable suspicion that the suspect is armed and dangerous and that the frisk is necessary for the preservation of his safety and that of others). *Terry v. Ohio*, 392 U.S. 1 (1968). Since the metal detector sounded when Erik passed through it, the security officer had a reasonable suspicion sufficient to frisk Erik for weapons in the interest of security. However, the security officer went beyond a pat-down for weapons and searched Erik's pocket, which is beyond the permissible *Terry* stop and frisk. Therefore, (A) is incorrect. Because there clearly was a search, (B) is also incorrect.

A warrantless search may be conducted as an incident to a lawful arrest. However, the search must come **after** the arrest. In this case, there was no basis for an arrest until the police found the cocaine during the search. Therefore, the arrest may not serve as a basis for the original search. Therefore, (C) is incorrect.

Although (D) is general and conclusory, it does state the core requirement of the Fourth Amendment - the lawfulness of reasonable searches. As such, this is the best choice, if only because the other choices are clearly wrong.

Question 66

There was a fire during the night of September 4 in a building located at 1000 Main Street. The fire crews extinguished the flames at 11:00 p.m., but stayed at the scene until 2:00 a.m. on September 5 in case new fires erupted, and returned that morning at 8:00 a.m. to make sure that the fire was out. Ivy, a police arson investigator, accompanied the firefighters at 8:00 a.m. and noticed the smell of kerosene near the origin of the fire in the basement. He returned to the basement the next day, September 6, took some charred boards for analysis, and found that they had traces of gasoline and other chemicals used by arsonists. Smith, the owner of the building, has been indicted for arson.

At the trial, Ivy is called to the stand and is asked to produce the boards he took from the basement on September 6. Assuming that counsel for Smith (not knowing in advance of Ivy's possession of the boards) properly objects, the trial judge should rule the prosecution's offer

(A) inadmissible, because the September 6 search was the fruit of the illegal search conducted the morning after the fire.
(B) inadmissible, because a search warrant was required for the search on September 6.
(C) admissible, because it is a search of the scene of a crime.
(D) admissible, because once the building burned, the defendant had no justifiable expectation of privacy.

Answer to Question 66

There is no general exception to the warrant requirement that permits warrantless searches at the scene of the crime. Thus, (C) is incorrect. However, the crime might serve as justification for government officials to be present on the premises without a search warrant. For example, in *Michigan v. Tyler*, 436 U. S. 499 (1978) (a case on which this question is based), the Court upheld a warrantless search by fire officials of the scene of the fire, as soon as the fire was extinguished. However, a search without a warrant made several days later specifically to determine if arson was committed was held illegal.

(A) is incorrect because, on the morning after the fire, Ivy was legally on the property. Officials had a right to be there the next day to make sure that the fire was out and to determine the cause of the fire. Therefore, the evidence obtained from the September 6 search is not inadmissible for this reason.

Although Ivy had a valid firefighting reason to be on the property on September 5, once the fire was completely out, he needed a warrant to search the property for evidence of a crime, because he no longer had a valid reason for a search other than to gather evidence. Thus, the September 6 search was unlawful because the defendant had a justifiable expectation of privacy at that time, and there was no consent, exigent circumstance or likelihood of the fire rekindling to justify a warrantless search. As a result, the boards are the fruit of an illegal search and, therefore, inadmissible. (B) is correct and (D) is incorrect.

Question 67

Two police officers stopped an automobile driven by Davis for improperly proceeding through a red light. When Officer Mike approached the car, he observed some hand-rolled cigarettes on the dashboard. He ordered Davis out of the car, examined the cigarettes and determined that they were joints of marijuana. Officer Mike then arrested Davis and guarded him in the back seat of the police cruiser while Officer Mack searched the entire car, including the trunk. In the trunk, he found two rare paintings that had recently been stolen from the city's art museum.

Davis was charged with possession of stolen goods and brought a motion to suppress the introduction of the paintings into evidence.

This motion is most likely to be denied because Officer Mack properly conducted

(A) an automobile search.
(B) an inventory search.
(C) a search incident to an arrest.
(D) a custody search.

Answer to Question 67

A lawful search of a vehicle incident to an arrest is a search of the person and only the area of the vehicle within the defendant's control. *New York v. Belton*, 453 U.S. 454 (1981). In this case, since the trunk is outside the defendant's area of control, the search went beyond the scope of a proper search incident to an arrest. Therefore, (C) is incorrect.

(D) is incorrect because there is no such thing as a custody search. The correct term is an inventory search. An inventory search occurs when the officers properly impound a car and search it while it is in their control to make sure that the assets of the owner of the car are fully accounted for. *South Dakota v. Opperman*, 428 U.S. 364 (1976). In this case, the police did not take custody of the car, so (B) is also not the best reason to deny the motion.

By process of elimination, (A) is correct. Because of a lessened expectation of privacy in a car (as compared to a home) and because of the inherent mobility of a car which can prevent the police from easily obtaining a search warrant and searching it, the police are permitted to make a complete search of an automobile, if there is probable cause to believe that the car contains the fruits, evidence or instrumentalities of a crime. *Carroll v. United States*, 267 U.S. 132 (1925). When the police have probable cause to search an entire vehicle, they may conduct a warrantless search of every part of the vehicle and its contents. *United States v. Ross*, 456 U.S. 798 (1982). While it is doubtful that the marijuana joints provided sufficient probable cause to search the entire vehicle, this is the best reason to deny the motion, because all of the other choices are clearly incorrect.

Question 68

Two agents of the Federal Drug Enforcement Agency were stationed at LaGuardia Airport observing the passengers who arrived from Miami. It was well known that southern Florida drug wholesalers shipped their cocaine to the northeastern states via couriers who travel by plane. Don and Miguel, dressed in flashy, casual clothes, disembarked from the plane carrying hand luggage and made their way quickly from the gate to a nearby telephone. When the telephone conversation was completed, the DEA agents asked them if they would consent to a search of their hand luggage in a nearby DEA office. Both consented. After a search of the luggage produced no narcotics, the agents patted down Don and felt some bulk around his abdomen. Don's person was then searched carefully and a packet containing a kilo of cocaine was found taped to his abdomen. Don and Miguel were then charged with possession of a controlled substance with intent to distribute. Their attorneys made a pretrial motion to suppress the goods. At the pretrial hearing, Miguel admitted that he was the owner of the kilo of cocaine.

Which of the following propositions with respect to the trial of Miguel are correct?

I. The search of Don which resulted in the production of the cocaine was an invasion of Miguel's right of privacy.
II. Miguel's admission of his ownership of the cocaine is admissible against him at trial.

(A) I only
(B) II only
(C) both I and II
(D) neither I nor II

Answer to Question 68

Defendants charged with crimes of possession may only claim the benefits of the exclusionary rule if their own Fourth Amendment rights have been violated. There is no automatic standing for possessory offenses.

United States v. Salvucci, 448 U.S. 83 (1980). To prove that his Fourth Amendment rights have been violated, a defendant must show that he not only had a possessory interest in the items seized, but that he also had a legitimate expectation of privacy in the premises searched. *Rawlings v. Kentucky*, 448 U.S. 98 (1980) (a defendant who placed controlled substances in a companion's purse was denied standing based upon a lack of a legitimate expectation of privacy in the area searched). Miguel had no legitimate expectation of privacy in Don's person and, therefore, proposition (I) is incorrect.

When a defendant testifies at a suppression hearing in order to establish standing, his testimony cannot be admitted against him at trial. *Simmons v. United States*, 390 U.S. 377 (1968). As a result, Miguel's admission of ownership of the cocaine at the suppression hearing is inadmissible in the prosecution's case in chief. Therefore, proposition (II) is also incorrect.

(D) is the correct choice.

Question 69

Two agents of the Federal Drug Enforcement Agency were stationed at the Interstate Bus Terminal in Manhattan observing the passengers who arrived from Miami. It was well known that southern Florida drug wholesalers ship their cocaine to the northeastern states via couriers who travel by bus. Molly, whose appearance was consistent with a general DEA profile of drug couriers, alighted from the bus carrying a handbag. She claimed no luggage, and immediately went to the telephone. When the telephone conversation was completed, the DEA agents asked her if she would consent to a search of her handbag in a nearby DEA office. Molly consented. After a search of the handbag produced no narcotics, the agents patted down Molly's clothing and felt some bulk between Molly's thighs. Molly's person was then searched carefully and a packet containing a kilo of cocaine was found taped to her leg. Molly was charged with possession of a controlled substance with intent to distribute. Her attorney has made a pretrial motion to suppress the goods. The judge should

(A) deny the motion because the agents had probable cause to search without consent.
(B) deny the motion because Molly consented to the search.
(C) allow the motion because the search was beyond the scope of consent.
(D) allow the motion because consent was invalidly obtained.

Answer to Question 69

(A) is incorrect because there was no probable cause to search Molly's person. While she may have fit the drug profile because she was traveling from Miami, carried no luggage and immediately made a phone call upon reaching the terminal, the officers were only permitted to stop Molly to investigate their suspicions. Since they only had a reasonable suspicion, and not probable cause, they were not permitted to conduct a search of her person. See *United States v. Mendenhall*, 446 U.S. 544 (1980). Moreover, since a search of her bag, which Molly consented to, turned up nothing, the search by definition did not unearth any additional evidence to support probable cause for a search of her person.

When a defendant effectively consents to a search, the search may be conducted without a warrant or probable cause, because the defendant's consent operates to waive his or her Fourth Amendment rights. To be effective, the consent must be voluntary and given under no threat or compulsion. In this case, Molly voluntarily consented to the search of her bag, but the police went on to search her person as well. In other words, the search of her person went beyond the scope of the search to which Molly consented. Therefore, (C) is correct and (B) and (D) are incorrect.

Question 70

Grace and Victor, two lawyers, share office space on the 20th floor of the Lawyers' Building, but are otherwise independent practitioners. Grace's secretary, Penny, and Victor's secretary, Kim, work in a common reception room. Each lawyer has a private office. Snitch, a window washer employed by the building management, is on a scaffold washing the window of Victor's private office and sees a marijuana plant growing. During his lunch break, he tells Officer O'Mally about the marijuana plant and brings him up on the scaffold to look at it through Victor's window. After observing the plant, O'Mally goes to the offices of Grace and Victor and asks Penny, who was alone on the premises, if he might take a look in Victor's office. She permits him to do so; he seizes the marijuana plant, and charges Victor with illegal possession of marijuana. Prior to trial, Victor brings a motion to suppress. The judge should

(A) deny the motion because the plant was in plain view.
(B) deny the motion because there was consent to the search.
(C) grant the motion because O'Mally did not have a search warrant.
(D) grant the motion because O'Mally's conduct violated Victor's right of privacy.

Answer to Question 70

(A) is incorrect because the plain view doctrine is inapplicable in this case. A police officer may seize an item in plain view only if (1) the police officer is validly in the position to see the evidence and (2) probable cause to seize the item is immediately apparent. *Texas v. Brown*, 460 U.S. 730 (1983). This seizure was invalid because the police officer did not have a right to search the office from the window. The lawyer had a reasonable expectation of privacy in his office because only via these extraordinary measures was the plant visible to the public. Therefore, the plant is not admissible under the plain view doctrine.

(B) is incorrect because there was no valid consent to the search. In the absence of the defendant, a third party who has joint access or control with the defendant over the premises to be searched can consent to a search over those areas where she has joint control, but not over areas where the defendant has exclusive control. *United States v. Matlock*, 415 U.S. 164 (1974). Here, Penny, Grace's secretary, lacked standing to consent to the search of the office of Victor, who was not even her employer. Her association with Victor was merely that she shared a common reception area with Victor's secretary. At most, she might have had authority to consent to the search of the common reception room, and maybe even Grace's private office, but clearly not Victor's private office.

(D) reaches the right result, but speaks in too abstract and general terms of a "right of privacy" whereas (C) more specifically identifies the Fourth Amendment warrant requirement as the specific ground for suppression. There were no exigent circumstances excusing O'Mally from obtaining a search warrant, such as a risk that the evidence would imminently be removed or destroyed.

Question 71

Debbie's car was parked in front of a fire station. Pursuant to a valid municipal ordinance, the police towed the car to a police garage. At the garage, the police searched the glove compartment and found a pistol. They traced the identification number, found it to be stolen, and charged Debbie with possession of stolen goods. If Debbie's attorney makes a pretrial motion to suppress the gun, the judge should

(A) deny the motion because there is no legitimate expectation of privacy in an automobile.
(B) deny the motion because the search was a legitimate police procedure.
(C) grant the motion because the search was an unconstitutional invasion of a private area.
(D) grant the motion because the search invaded the legitimate expectation of privacy of the defendant.

Answer to Question 71

(A) erroneously states that the Fourth Amendment has no application to automobile searches. Although it has been held in many cases that there is a diminished expectation of privacy in an automobile as compared to a residence, automobile searches are nonetheless subject to some Fourth Amendment limitations.

The privacy of an automobile can be invaded for good cause. As a result, the expectation of privacy in an automobile is subject to legitimate police procedures. The police are authorized to make a warrantless, routine inventory search of the contents of any vehicle that lawfully comes into police custody as part of the police caretaking functions, e.g., seizure for parking in front of a fire station. The warrantless search is authorized because an inventory search furthers the legitimate goals of protecting the police from claims. The police must encounter the evidence while conducting routine inventory procedures. *South Dakota v. Opperman*, 428 U.S. 364 (1976).

In this case, the police properly obtained custody of the car and, therefore, were authorized to conduct an inventory search. Part of such a search is presumably an inventory of the contents of the glove compartment. Since their search of the glove compartment was lawful, the motion to suppress the gun should be denied. Therefore, (B) is correct and (C) and (D) are incorrect.

Question 72

Federal regulations require that all property carried onto a regularly scheduled airline carrier be searched before a passenger is permitted to board. Deirdre, a ticketed passenger, was refused permission to board an airplane because she would not consent to a search of her pocketbook. Finally, over protest, in order to board the aircraft, she permitted a search. The search was conducted by a private security officer, who found cocaine. At a trial where Deirdre was charged with illegal possession of a harmful drug, her attorney moved to suppress the fruits of the search. The trial judge should

(A) overrule the motion because there was no government action involved in the search.
(B) overrule the motion because Deirdre consented.
(C) allow the motion because consent was coerced.
(D) allow the motion because the regulations requiring the search are an invalid invasion of privacy.

Answer to Question 72

(A) is eliminated relatively easily. While it is true that in order to invoke the protections of the Fourth Amendment, there must be state action, state action need not necessarily be carried out by an official state employee. Although a private security officer conducted the search in this case, the search was conducted under color of federal law in the execution of federal regulations, and thereby satisfied the state action requirement.

(D) can be easily eliminated on the basis of everyday experience. Searches of boarding passengers are routine. In fact, the courts have sustained searches of airline passengers, even where there is no probable cause, if the search is confined to a search for weapons and explosives. Such searches further an important governmental interest to ensure the safety of the flying public.

When a defendant effectively consents to a search, it may be conducted without a warrant or probable cause because the defendant has waived his or her Fourth Amendment rights. To be effective, the consent must be voluntary and given under no threat or compulsion. An individual has the right to refuse to submit to an airline search by simply not entering the restricted area. In this case, despite Deirdre's protest, she did have a choice between allowing the search and foregoing her airplane trip, and she chose to submit to the search. Because she had a choice, the consent is not coerced. Therefore, (C) is incorrect and (B) is correct.

Question 73

When the Pluto family left for a weekend trip to Disneyland, they asked Donald, a teenage boy who lived on their street, to come to their house each day to feed the tropical fish which were kept in a tank in the den, and to water the plants kept in the bedrooms and kitchen. The police, suspicious that Mr. Pluto was a counterfeiter, came to the Pluto house while

Donald was there and asked if they might look around. He gave permission and the police went to the basement, where they found illegal printing equipment and counterfeit bills. The equipment was clearly visible to anyone looking in the basement window from the Plutos' backyard. After Mr. Pluto was indicted for counterfeiting, he brought a motion to suppress the evidence found in the basement. The trial judge should

(A) suppress the evidence because the police did not have a search warrant.
(B) suppress the evidence because, even though a basement is not a protected area, the search violated the defendant's reasonable expectation of privacy.
(C) refuse to suppress the evidence because Donald consented to the search.
(D) refuse to suppress the evidence because it was in plain view.

Answer to Question 73

(B) reaches the right result but is an incorrect statement because the basement is part of the defendant's dwelling and, therefore, is a protected area. The defendant has a reasonable expectation of privacy there. Since the basement is a protected area in which the defendant has a reasonable expectation of privacy, a search warrant must be executed or an exception to the warrant requirement must exist.

(D) is incorrect because the plain view doctrine does not apply to this situation. A police officer may seize an item in plain view if (1) he is validly in the position to see the item and (2) probable cause to seize the item is immediately apparent. *Texas v. Brown*, 460 U.S. 730 (1983). In this case, the police officers did not satisfy the first requirement of the plain view doctrine in that their intrusion was invalid under the Fourth Amendment. The fact that the equipment could be seen from a basement window is not determinative, because an officer would have to enter the curtilage of the dwelling to view the equipment through the basement window. Since the curtilage is a protected area, a warrant or an exception to it would be required for that search as well.

In the defendant's absence, a third party who has joint access or control with the defendant over the premises to be searched can consent to a search over those areas where he has joint control, but not over areas where the defendant has exclusive control. *United States v. Matlock*, 415 U.S. 164 (1974). In this case, one could conceivably argue that Donald temporarily had joint access and control over the bedrooms, kitchen and den of the house, but such control clearly did not extend to the basement. If Donald had gone into the basement himself, he would have exceeded the scope of his license and would have been a trespasser. As a result, there was no valid consent to search the basement and (C) is incorrect.

Without consent or the plain view doctrine, and with no other exigent circumstances to excuse the absence of a search warrant, the evidence should be suppressed. Therefore, (A) is correct.

Question 74

Dick has been convicted of a crime in a state court. All appeals within the state court system have been exhausted, and Dick is confined in a state jail. Which of the following events occurring at his state court trial would most likely entitle him to federal habeas corpus?

(A) His conviction was based upon the testimony of an eyewitness to the crime. Evidence discovered after the trial proves that the eyewitness lied.
(B) His conviction was based upon the introduction of evidence which had been seized in violation of the Fourth Amendment.
(C) His conviction was based upon an erroneous instruction to the jury on the issue of entrapment.
(D) His conviction was based upon an involuntary confession.

Answer to Question 74

(A) does not involve a federal constitutional right and, therefore, cannot serve as the basis for federal court jurisdiction. State remedies are available for a miscarriage of justice based upon perjury.

Although a violation of certain fundamental rights guaranteed by the federal Constitution will grant a federal court jurisdiction in a habeas corpus proceeding, (B) is incorrect because a violation of the Fourth Amendment's provisions regarding searches will not. Since the rights protected under the Fourth Amendment are federal constitutional rights, the federal appellate court **in a direct appeal** has the right to review the record to determine if state courts have applied the proper standards in ruling upon the admissibility of evidence following a claim of an illegal search. However, because the purpose of the exclusionary rule is to deter unlawful police conduct, a review of the defendant's Fourth Amendment rights is **not** available by federal habeas corpus proceedings. *Stone v. Powell*, 428 U.S. 465 (1976).

(C) is incorrect because the content of jury instructions is governed by state law and generally is not reviewable in the federal system. The only time they are subject to federal review is when they implicate a federal constitutional right. There is no showing that this is the case here and, therefore, this is not the best reason to seek federal habeas corpus.

Only (D) articulates a fundamental federal constitutional right which provides a federal court with jurisdiction in a habeas corpus proceeding. This federal constitutional right is based on the Fifth Amendment privilege against compelled self-incrimination. *Brown v. Mississippi*, 297 U.S. 278 (1936).

Question 75

Uriah, a convicted methamphetamine dealer and user, convinced the judge that he was a prime candidate for a special supervision program under the state's probation department. One of the requirements of the program was to provide a daily urine sample for drug analysis. Shortly after entering the program, a urine sample provided by Uriah showed evidence of methamphetamine use. Unbeknownst to Uriah's probation officer, Guy, Uriah was suffering from a serious bout with the flu and was taking over-the-counter cold medication. These medications will give a false-positive test result for methamphetamines and a special test is required to determine exactly which drug a probationer is ingesting. Uriah was so debilitated by the flu that he was unable to leave his bed to report to Guy as required and Guy was not able to perform additional testing.

After a week without contact from Uriah, Guy called the police and asked if they would accompany him to Uriah's house to see if they could help find him. Guy told them he had reason to believe that Uriah was probably dealing and using again, because he was testing positive for methamphetamines and had not reported to the office in a week. When they got to Uriah's house, Guy identified himself to Uriah's wife, Myrtle. Myrtle let Guy in and the police followed. Guy looked through the rooms of the house, but he did not see Uriah. Thinking that he might be hiding, Guy looked in the hall closet and found a hunting rifle in the corner. Uriah then came out from one of the bedrooms where he was sleeping under a stack of blankets to keep warm. The police arrested Uriah and charged him with being a felon in possession of a firearm.

At a pre-trial hearing, Uriah's public defender makes a motion to suppress the gun. The judge should

(A) deny the motion, because there was probable cause to conduct the search.
(B) deny the motion, because Myrtle consented to the search.
(C) grant the motion, unless there were reasonable grounds to conduct the search.
(D) grant the motion, because the police did not have a search warrant.

Answer to Question 75

Uriah is a probationer, and as such does not enjoy the same constitutional protections enjoyed by a pre-conviction defendant. In *Griffin v. Wisconsin,* 479 U.S. 1053 (1987), the Court upheld a state regulation allowing a warrantless search by a probation officer by replacing probable cause with a reasonable grounds standard that contraband was present in the probationer's home. The Court held that the "special needs" of the state in supervision of probationers justify a lesser protection of the probationer's Fourth Amendment interests. (A) is incorrect because the probable cause standard does not apply.

(B) is incorrect. Myrtle did not consent to the search. If a person allows a police officer into the house, permission to conduct a search is not automatically granted. There must be a specific request and permission to conduct the search. Here, there was no request to conduct a search. (However, if Guy and the police had requested permission to conduct the search, Myrtle, as Uriah's wife and, therefore, presumably in joint control of the house, could have effectively consented to the search.)

(D) is incorrect because a warrantless search is permitted in these circumstances.

In this case, Uriah's test results, coupled with his failure to report, gave Guy reasonable grounds to believe that contraband was present in the home and thereby provided justification for the warrantless search. The gun was the product of a lawful search and, therefore, is admissible. Since there were reasonable grounds, (C) is correct.

Question 76

Doreen lives in a two-bedroom apartment in Metropolis with her roommate, Rebecca. Lynda, a narcotics detective on the Metropolis police force, suspecting that Doreen is dealing in cocaine, induces Rebecca to enter Doreen's bedroom and look for cocaine under Doreen's bed. Rebecca finds a kilo of cocaine in that location and delivers a sample to Lynda.

When Doreen later finds some cocaine missing, she confronts Rebecca. Rebecca says that she is about to appear before a grand jury investigating Doreen to identify the cocaine and describe where she found it.

Doreen's lawyer immediately files a motion with the judge supervising the grand jury to suppress both Rebecca's testimony and the introduction of the cocaine which she took from Doreen's room.

How should the judge decide the motion?

(A) She should grant it because, if there was no probable cause, the grand jury should not consider the evidence.
(B) She should grant it, because Rebecca was acting as a police agent and her seizure of the cocaine without a warrant was unconstitutional.
(C) She should deny it, because Rebecca had the right to search in her own apartment.
(D) She should deny it, because the exclusionary rule does not apply in grand jury proceedings.

Answer to Question 76

(A) is incorrect because it is the function of the grand jury to determine whether there is probable cause to indict based on the evidence. It is not the function of the judge to take this matter away from the grand jury.

(B), which goes to the legality of the seizure, is also incorrect. Although Rebecca is a private person (to whom the exclusionary rule would not ordinarily apply), in this case she acted in cooperation with the police, so there is state action and there is a privacy interest protected by the Fourth Amendment. The fact that Rebecca was in her own apartment would not give her authority to search in Doreen's room, so (C) is incorrect even if the legality of the seizure were at issue.

The issue in this question is not whether the seizure of the cocaine was valid, but whether this is the appropriate time to raise the issue of its validity. Illegally seized evidence is admissible in grand jury proceedings, so (D) is correct. *United States v. Calandra*, 414 U.S. 338 (1974). A pretrial motion to suppress is the appropriate vehicle for a test of the constitutionality of a seizure.

Question 77

Jay Carson owned a summer home on an exclusive island off the coast of the state of Califaii. The only transportation to the island is by regular ferry service from the shore. Three masked men broke into Carson's home, held him hostage, and robbed him of many valuable jewels. Carson overheard one robber tell another that they "had to be out of the house in ten minutes." When the robbers left, Carson phoned the local police and told them that the robbers were probably on the 6:30 ferry because the timing of their departure from his house coincided with the departure of that ferry.

When the ferry arrived at the opposite shore, the police stopped each car and searched the driver and the trunk. Thief, one of the robbers traveling alone in the car, was required to open the trunk of his car, where the police found the stolen jewels. If Thief brings a motion to suppress the jewels found in the trunk, the court should

(A) grant the motion because the police did not have a search warrant.
(B) deny the motion because the search of all the cars leaving the ferry was permissible under the Constitution.
(C) deny the motion because the search was made with probable cause.
(D) deny the motion because the police had a reasonable basis to search Thief's car.

Answer to Question 77

The fact that the police had a reasonable basis to believe that the jewel thieves and their car were on a particular ferry does not give them the right to search all of the cars leaving that ferry. Under a fixed checkpoint analysis, the police can only stop and ask questions. See *United States v. Martinez-Fuerte*, 428 U.S. 543 (1976). Thus, (B) is incorrect.

A full-scale search of a vehicle at such a checkpoint must be based upon probable cause. *United States v. Ortiz*, 422 U.S. 891 (1975). There is no probable cause as to any given car sufficient to justify a search of that car. Thus, (C) is incorrect.

Further, there was not even a reasonable basis to search Thief's car because the police had no description of the car or the occupant. Thus, (D) is incorrect.

Thus, this search was constitutionally invalid and (A) is correct.

Question 78

The police validly arrest Doug for the armed robbery of the Fifth National Bank and bring him to the police station. There, he is permitted one telephone call. He elects to call his brother Bill and asks him to come to the police station to post bail for him. Bill is unable to go to the police station. Instead, without informing Doug, he calls Larry, a lawyer who had represented the family in the past, and asks Larry to go to the police station and represent Doug. Larry is at home, approximately two hours away from the police station, at the time he receives the call from Bill. He immediately calls the station where Doug is being held and tells the officer on duty that he has been retained to represent Doug and will be at the police station in approximately two hours. The police then approach Doug in his cell, carefully explain his *Miranda* rights and ask him if he will waive those rights and submit to questioning, but do not tell him of the telephone call from Larry. Doug agrees, and after one hour of questioning, admits that he committed the armed robbery of the Fifth National Bank. If Doug's lawyer moves to suppress Doug's statement, the court should

(A) allow the motion because the police did not tell Doug that Larry was coming to represent him.
(B) allow the motion because once a lawyer has been retained for a defendant, the police cannot question him until after he has consulted with his lawyer.
(C) deny the motion because Doug had not hired Larry as his attorney.
(D) deny the motion because the statement was given after a knowing and valid waiver of Doug's *Miranda* rights.

Answer to Question 78

After *Moran v. Burbine*, 475 U.S. 412 (1986), there is no requirement that police either tell a defendant that a lawyer is coming to represent him or stop questioning him until his lawyer arrives. Unless the defendant invokes his

Miranda rights to remain silent or consult with counsel, the police are free to question the defendant without informing him of the fact that a lawyer has been retained to represent him. Therefore, (D) is correct and (A) and (B) are incorrect.

(C) is incorrect because the fact that Doug did not "hire" Larry does not control the ruling on the motion. The issue that controls the outcome is whether Doug invoked or waived his *Miranda* right to counsel before participating in the interrogation.

Question 79

Dan met Jane for the first time at a single's bar and she invited him to her house for a drink after the bar closed. Dan decided to have sexual intercourse with Jane, who resisted with all her strength. Dan finally banged her head against the headboard until she was unconscious, finished raping her and left.

A neighbor, Nelly, heard the noise, saw Dan leave and was able to get the license number of Dan's car. She then discovered Jane unconscious in her bed and rushed her to the hospital. With the information supplied by Nelly, the police traced the car. Dan was apprehended by the police early the following morning. He was taken to police headquarters, given *Miranda* warnings, and asked if he wished to make a statement about the prior evening's events. The police did not mention that Jane had been seriously injured and was in the hospital. Dan said he understood his rights and was willing to talk. He then admitted that he had had intercourse with Jane. The following day, Jane died from injuries caused by the blows to her head.

If, at Dan's trial for murder, Dan moves to prevent introduction of the confession into evidence, his motion should most probably be

(A) denied, because failure of the police to advise Dan of Jane's condition was harmless error since felony murder does not require intent to kill or injure.

(B) denied, because Dan's waiver of his rights did not depend upon the nature of the charges that were later filed against him.

(C) granted, because Dan could not make a knowing and intelligent waiver unless he had information concerning Jane's condition.

(D) granted, because the use of a confession to rape in a prosecution for murder violates due process where the police withheld information about the potential seriousness of the offense.

Answer to Question 79

(A) contains two incorrect assertions. First, there was no "error" at all in failing to warn Dan of all possible charges. Second, felony murder is not the only available murder theory here; Dan may well be charged with murder based on an intent to do great bodily harm.

(C) is incorrect because Dan's lack of knowledge about Jane's condition does not make his statements inadmissible as long as he made a valid waiver of his *Miranda* rights.

A waiver of *Miranda* rights must be knowing and intelligent. A waiver is knowing and intelligent if the defendant knows the rights which he is waiving, namely, his right to remain silent and his right not to incriminate himself. A suspect's advance awareness of all possible criminal charges is not relevant to the validity of the suspect's waiver of the privilege against self-incrimination and the right to remain silent. *Colorado v. Spring*, 479 U.S. 564 (1986). In this case, Dan effectively waived his *Miranda* rights and, therefore, his confession is admissible, regardless of what charges are ultimately brought against him. (D) is incorrect and (B) is correct.

Question 80

The police arrived at the Santa Maria Hotel, the scene of Marilyn's death. They learned that she had entertained three dinner guests, Jack, Bob and Ted. The circumstances of Marilyn's death clearly indicated that one of them was the murderer. The police questioned Jack and asked him if he had been alone with Marilyn at any time that evening, but he remained silent. The next day, they picked Jack up at his apartment and, against his will, brought him to the interrogation room of the police station. Bob and Ted were in the same room and two police officers guarded the door. In the presence of Jack and in response to police questions, both Bob and Ted said that Marilyn was last seen alive in the company of Jack. At that point, Jack said, "I killed Marilyn." Jack was tried for the murder of Marilyn. At his trial, Jack did not testify. At that trial, the prosecution sought to introduce evidence of both

I. the questions asked by the police of Jack at the hotel, together with his silence, as an adoptive admission that he was alone with Marilyn on the night of the murder, and
II. the statement made by Jack the following day at the police station.

The trial judge should admit

(A) I only.
(B) II only.
(C) both I and II.
(D) neither I nor II.

Answer to Question 80

When Jack was questioned at the Santa Maria Hotel, it was not a custodial interrogation because he had the right to leave. However, even when a criminal defendant is not undergoing custodial interrogation, he has a right to remain silent and not incriminate himself. Pre-arrest silence in the face of an accusation is admissible only for impeachment - i.e., after the defendant testifies, which is not the case here. Since the traditional admission by silence rule does not apply, the questions asked by the police and Jack's silence in response to these questions is inadmissible. As a result, the evidence described in (I) should not be admitted.

As for the statements in (II), a suspect has *Miranda* rights at any time that there is custodial interrogation. Custody need not equal arrest. A suspect is in custody any time that there is a significant deprivation of freedom - such as when he is brought to the police station and held there against his will, as here. Likewise, interrogation refers not only to express questioning, but also to any words or actions that the police knew or should have known were likely to elicit an incriminating response from the suspect. *Brewer v. Williams*, 430 U.S. 387 (1977). In such a circumstance, any statements made by the suspect are subject to the *Miranda* exclusionary rule. In this case, Jack was subject to custodial interrogation and thus entitled to *Miranda* warnings, which he was not given. Although Jack was not questioned directly, the officers knew or should have known that their questions and Bob's and Ted's responses were likely to elicit a response from Jack and thereby constituted a *Brewer*-type interrogation. Since Jack's statement was the result of an improper custodial interrogation, the evidence described in (II) is also inadmissible.

Since both types of evidence are inadmissible here, (D) is correct.

Question 81

Dennis was arrested on a charge of burglary. At his arraignment, he exercised his right to counsel and Laurie was appointed to represent him. Dennis pleaded not guilty and bail was set at $10,000.

When he was returned to custody pending the posting of bail, police officer Polly gave him *Miranda* warnings. Dennis agreed to be questioned. Outside of Laurie's presence, Polly asked Dennis if he had committed the burglary for which he had been charged. Dennis admitted the crime to Polly. Polly then asked him if he had been on the corner of Central Avenue and First Street selling cocaine the previous evening. Dennis admitted that he had. The police promptly charged Dennis with possession of cocaine with intent to distribute. Dennis was brought up for trial on the burglary and possession charges at the same time.

At her trial, Laurie has brought a motion to suppress

I. Dennis's statement regarding the burglary.

II. Dennis's statement with respect to the cocaine.

The trial judge should grant the request with respect to

(A) I only.
(B) II only.
(C) both I and II.
(D) neither I nor II.

Answer to Question 81

To answer this question correctly, you must understand the law governing the right to counsel under the Sixth Amendment versus a *Miranda* right to counsel.

With respect to the burglary charge, Dennis requested counsel. Since adversary judicial proceedings had begun, this is a right to counsel under the Sixth Amendment. Once he had exercised his right to counsel under the Sixth Amendment, further interrogation concerning the offense which was the subject of the judicial proceeding was not permissible without counsel present or a waiver of the right to counsel. *Minnick v. Mississippi*, 112 L.Ed.2d 489 (1990). Since counsel was not present and the right to counsel was not waived, the admission concerning the burglary, (I), is inadmissible and should be suppressed.

With respect to the cocaine charge, the United States Supreme Court held in *McNeil v. Wisconsin*, 115 L.Ed.2d 158 (1991), that the invocation of the right to counsel under the Sixth Amendment at a judicial proceeding does not create a right to have counsel present at an interrogation regarding other unrelated and uncharged crimes. Since the interrogation on the cocaine charge was a custodial interrogation, Dennis was given his *Miranda* rights. However, since he waived those rights, his statement concerning the cocaine (II) is admissible and should not be suppressed.

Since only (I) is inadmissible, (A) is correct.

Question 82

Two police officers in a squad car received a radio message from headquarters to be on the lookout for a large black sedan occupied by a man and a woman who had just committed a bank robbery. An hour later they saw a car answering this description traveling down a main boulevard leading out of town. They pulled the car to the side of the road and walked over to the car. One of the officers told the occupants that they were under arrest for bank robbery. The same officer observed a brown paper bag on the floor behind the front seat. He opened the rear door and grabbed the paper bag, causing bundles of paper money to spill out into the view of both officers. At that point Davis, the driver, suddenly put the car in gear and drove off. One officer clung to the car door, partly in and partly out of the vehicle. The other officer pursued in the squad car. Unable to overtake the car and afraid he would lose sight of it in the heavy traffic, the officer fired, first a warning shot and then at the car. He struck Debbie, the passenger sitting next to Davis. At about the same time, Davis, by swerving and sudden acceleration, succeeded in throwing the officer from the car; the officer fell to the road and was run over and killed by the pursuing squad car.

Davis was caught five minutes later by another squad car, to whom the remaining officer had radioed the alarm. Debbie died from loss of blood. Davis was taken to the police station.

About an hour after his capture, Davis was required, over his protest, to participate in a lineup with five other men. The lineup was attended by two of the bank employees who had witnessed the robbery. They identified Davis by his appearance.

Davis was charged with the murders of both the officer and Debbie, and with bank robbery. At trial, the prosecution put on the witness stand one of the bank employees who had identified Davis in the lineup and asked him whether he had identified Davis in the police lineup as one of the men who had committed the robbery. On appropriate objection, the court should rule the answer as

(A) inadmissible, because it may tend to be incriminating.
(B) inadmissible, because no foundation was laid showing that the lineup was fairly conducted.
(C) inadmissible, because Davis was not given the opportunity to have counsel present at the lineup.
(D) admissible.

Answer to Question 82

The defendant is not incriminating himself in the constitutional sense by standing for identification as suggested in (A). Self-incrimination must be testimonial.

(B) is incorrect because **the defendant** has the burden of showing that the lineup was conducted unfairly; the prosecution need not establish a foundation that it was conducted fairly.

This is a pre-indictment lineup and therefore there is no requirement that counsel be present. *Kirby v. Illinois*, 406 U.S. 682 (1972). Thus, (C) is incorrect. Since it appears that the lineup was conducted fairly, the identification will be admissible and (D) is correct.

Question 83

Darcy was captured in a high speed police chase five minutes after a robbery at the Fifth National Bank. The robbers had handed the teller a handwritten note demanding the money. Darcy was taken to the police station where, over her protests, she was required to write out the words of the note. After introducing the robbers' note to the teller, the prosecution also offered in evidence the writing which Darcy had been required to make by the police. On appropriate objection, the court should rule the writing to be

(A) admissible.
(B) inadmissible, because she was not advised that her handwriting sample could be admitted into evidence against her.
(C) inadmissible, because she was not advised of her right to refuse to give a handwriting sample.

(D) inadmissible, because she had not been informed she had a right to have counsel present.

Answer to Question 83

Assuming the **content** of the writing is not used against the defendant, the evidence is not testimonial. Since the evidence is not testimonial, the procedure does not require Fifth or Sixth Amendment protections such as *Miranda* warnings or the presence of counsel. (B) and (D) are incorrect.

Nor is the defendant permitted to refuse. (If she refuses the request of the police, the court can order the defendant to submit the writing sample.) (C) is incorrect.

Therefore, as long as the evidence is relevant, it is admissible. (A) is correct.

Question 84

Vanessa and Victor got lost and could not find their way to the Chicago airport. When they stopped to ask directions, two young men broke the windows of their car, took Vanessa's purse and told Victor to get out of the car. Then they beat him and stole his watch. Vanessa was so frightened by the attack that she looked away so that she would not have to look at what the men were doing to Victor. The men ran when they saw a police car approach. Seeing what had happened, one of the officers chased the men while the other radioed for an ambulance. One of the suspects, Darth, was apprehended and arraigned the next morning.

Victor was taken to the hospital where he was listed in critical condition due to internal injuries caused by the beating. When the police were advised that Victor was near death, they took Darth to the hospital, where Victor identified Darth as one of his assailants. Victor died before trial and the prosecution seeks to admit his identification of Darth as one of the attackers. Darth's lawyer objects. The objection will be sustained because

I. this method of identification is inherently prejudicial and violates due process standards.
II. the identification violated the defendant's right to counsel.

(A) I only
(B) II only
(C) both I and II
(D) neither I nor II

Answer to Question 84

Due process requires fundamental fairness of all identification procedures used as evidence at trial. Identifications made other than at a lineup or the like are particularly susceptible to misidentification. One-on-one identifications, whether they be a suspect brought before the victim or a single photograph shown to him, are generally unnecessarily suggestive. However, there are exceptions to the rule that one-on-one identifications violate due process. For example, when a victim is near death in a hospital room and a lineup is impractical, a showup identification will be permitted. *Stovall v. Denno*, 388 U.S. 293 (1967). In this case, Victor was near death and the only person who clearly saw the attackers. Under *Stovall*, a showup identification does not violate due process in these circumstances. Thus, statement (I) will not support the objection, making (A) and (C) incorrect.

On the other hand, the right to counsel attaches at the initiation of adversarial proceedings. The Court has held that the right to counsel attaches when a defendant is arraigned. See *Moore v. Illinois*, 434 U.S. 220 (1978). Once the right to counsel attaches, the defendant has a right to counsel at all critical stages of the criminal proceedings, including identifications. See *Kirby v. Illinois*, 406 U.S. 682 (1972) and *United States v. Wade*, 388 U.S. 218 (1967). When Darth was arraigned, his right to counsel attached. However, his counsel was not present at the showup identification in Victor's hospital room. As a result, Victor's identification is inadmissible because the identification procedure violated Darth's Sixth Amendment right to counsel. Statement (II) alone should be the basis for sustaining the objection. (B) is the correct answer and (D) is an incorrect answer.

Question 85

Pursuant to a state statute, defendant was tried by a six-person jury and convicted of a crime carrying a maximum penalty of twelve months imprisonment, and was sentenced to six months in prison. If she should appeal on the basis that her trial before a six-person jury is unconstitutional, the appellate court would uphold the conviction because

(A) the federal constitutional requirement of trial by jury is not applicable to the states.
(B) a jury of six is all that is constitutionally required.
(C) the right to a jury trial is not applicable when the maximum penalty is one year or less imprisonment.
(D) the right to jury trial is not applicable when the sentence imposed is less than six months.

Answer to Question 85

The Seventh Amendment jury trial guarantee has been held to be within the Fourteenth Amendment due process guarantee and thus applicable to the states. *Duncan v. Louisiana*, 391 U.S., 145 (1968). Thus, (A) is incorrect.

In determining when the right to a jury trial attaches, the court will look to the maximum allowable sentence. If the maximum allowable sentence is more than six months, the defendant is entitled to a jury. *Baldwin v. New York*, 399 U.S. 66 (1970). Conversely, there is no right to a jury trial if the maximum punishment is six months or less. It is only for offenses with no prescribed maximum penalty, like criminal contempt, that the courts look to the actual sentence imposed to determine if there was a right to a jury trial. *Bloom v. Illinois*, 391 U.S. 194 (1968). Therefore, (C) and (D) are incorrect.

However, *Williams v. Florida*, 399 U.S. 78 (1970), held that, in a noncapital case, a jury of six is constitutionally proper as long as the verdict must be unanimous. Therefore, (B) is correct.

Question 86

Fence was tried and convicted of receiving stolen goods in State X by a jury of six, only five of whom voted for conviction, and was sentenced to the maximum penalty of two years in prison. Both procedures are authorized by a State X statute for all crimes where the maximum penalty is less than five years imprisonment. If Fence should appeal his conviction on the ground that the statute is unconstitutional, the appellate court should

(A) reverse the conviction, because the right to a jury trial is not met unless the verdict is unanimous.
(B) reverse the conviction, because a six-person jury does not foster the type of group deliberation that is constitutionally required.
(C) reverse the conviction, because a unanimous verdict is required if the jury consists of only six persons.
(D) affirm the conviction.

Answer to Question 86

A non-unanimous verdict is permissible as long as there are more than six members of a jury. See *Apodaca v. Oregon*. (A) is incorrect.
A jury of six is constitutionally permissible in some circumstances. *Ballew v. Georgia*, 435 U.S. 223 (1978). Thus, (B) is incorrect. But, if a six-person jury is used, a unanimous verdict is constitutionally required. *Burch v. Louisiana*, 441 U.S. 130 (1978). Since Fence was convicted by a less-than-unanimous six-person jury, his conviction cannot stand. Therefore, (C) is correct and (D) is incorrect.

Question 87

Which of the following cases is **not** a violation of the constitutional right to effective assistance of counsel?

(A) Alan, a criminal defendant, is on the witness stand on his own behalf at the end of a day at trial. The justice orders him not to confer with his counsel during the overnight recess.
(B) Brian, an indigent criminal defendant, lost his appeal to the highest court in the State of Delirium. The state refuses to pay for counsel to prepare a writ of certiorari to the United States Supreme Court.
(C) Connie, a criminal defendant, desires to testify in her own behalf. Connie's counsel wants her to testify after all other defense witnesses. The court orders that if she is going to testify, she must testify before other defense witnesses.
(D) Dorothy and Elaine are charged with the illegal sale of drugs. Elaine is an undercover agent. Dorothy and Elaine attend a conference with Dorothy's lawyer to plot trial strategy. Elaine reports the results of the conference to the prosecutor.

Answer to Question 87

(A) is incorrect because the Sixth Amendment right to counsel includes the right of the defendant to confer with counsel, including during an overnight recess. *Geders v. United States*, 425 U.S. 80 (1976).
(C) is incorrect because, as part of conducting a proper defense, counsel for the defendant has the right to determine when to put the defendant on the stand. *Brooks v. Tennessee*, 406 U.S. 605 (1972).
(D) is incorrect because, under *Weatherford v. Bursey*, 429 U.S. 545 (1977), the presence of a government informer at a pretrial conference between the defendant and the defendant's attorney violates the right to the assistance of counsel if the informer reports the conversations to the prosecutor.
The state does not have to provide counsel for a discretionary appeal (such as a writ of certiorari) to the U.S. Supreme Court. *Ross v. Moffitt*, 417 U.S. 600 (1974). Therefore, (B) is correct.

Question 88

Barbara and Bonnie were arrested at the scene of a bank robbery during which Bonnie shot and killed a teller who threatened to push the alarm button. Barbara and Bonnie were sisters who looked very much alike. They were charged with armed robbery and felony murder. Bonnie entered into a plea bargain and signed various sworn statements covering the events leading to the robbery and the robbery itself. Soon thereafter, Bonnie killed herself. Barbara pleaded not guilty and, in preparation for trial, her attorney requested from the prosecution copies of Bonnie's sworn statements. The prosecution immediately sent them to her, but inadvertently omitted the statement containing Bonnie's confession that she had killed the teller.

At trial, Barbara took the stand and admitted her participation in the robbery, but testified that she did not participate in the shooting and that the killing was outside the scope of the conspiracy to rob the bank. Some witnesses testified, though, that, although they could not be sure, they thought that it was Barbara who had shot the teller. In her closing argument, Barbara's attorney requested that the jury take into account Barbara's lack of culpability in regard to the shooting. The jury was not impressed with this argument, convicted Barbara of first-degree murder, and sentenced her to death by lethal injection.

Shortly after the trial, Barbara's attorney uncovered Bonnie's confession and requested a new trial. The court should

(A) grant the request.
(B) grant the request only if the prosecution acted in bad faith.
(C) grant the request because the confession was material evidence which would create a reasonable doubt of guilt.
(D) deny the request only because omission of the confession was inadvertent.

Answer to Question 88

The controlling issue is whether the suppressed evidence is material to either the guilt or punishment of the defendant. *Brady v. Maryland*, 373 U.S. 83 (1963). While Bonnie's confession might be material in the punishment phase of the trial, it would not exonerate Barbara for the murder of the teller because she participated in a violent felony during which a murder was committed. For this reason, (C) is incorrect.

(B) and (D) are incorrect because the reasons for the omission are irrelevant. The important question is the relationship of the suppressed evidence to the issues of guilt and punishment.

If the jury had known that Bonnie had actually admitted that she had done the killing, they might have imposed a more lenient sentence on Barbara. The court should deny a new trial on the issue of guilt, but should order a new trial on the punishment issue. Therefore, (A) is the correct answer.

Question 89

Duane, an African-American, has been indicted for first-degree murder in a jurisdiction where the death penalty can be imposed by the jury upon conviction of that offense. When the jury panel was assembled, the trial judge asked each juror if the juror could be fair and impartial, and each juror answered in the affirmative. Duane's attorney then requested that the judge ask each juror if the juror would always impose the death sentence on a defendant held guilty of first-degree murder regardless of the mitigating factors. The trial judge refused the request, ruling that the previous question concerning fairness and impartiality was sufficient to cover the issue. Duane's attorney appealed from this ruling.

The petit jury, after the prosecution's peremptory challenges, consisted of six African-American women, three African-American men, and three Caucasian men. Duane's attorney used four peremptory challenges to first challenge the three Caucasian men and subsequently to challenge the one Caucasian man who was chosen to replace one of the three men initially challenged. At this point, the petit jury consisted entirely of African-Americans and the prosecution challenged its composition. Duane's counsel asserted its right to use peremptory challenges to further its trial strategies. The trial judge nullified Duane's peremptory challenges and restored the three Caucasian men to the jury. Duane's attorney appealed from this ruling.

The jury subsequently convicted Duane and sentenced him to death. The state supreme court affirmed the conviction. On certiorari to the United States Supreme Court, Duane's attorney raised as constitutional questions

    I.   the failure of the trial judge to ask the jury the question concerning their willingness to consider mitigating factors, and
    II.   the trial judge's action in removing three African-American jurors and substituting three Caucasian jurors.

The Supreme Court will likely reverse because of

(A) I only.
(B) II only.
(C) both I and II.
(D) neither I nor II.

Answer to Question 89

(I) will provide grounds for reversal. In the case of *Morgan v. Illinois*, 119 L.Ed.2d 492 (1992), the United States Supreme Court held that a trial judge is required to ask a juror who has the power to impose the death penalty whether the juror would impose that penalty in a particular type of case regardless of mitigating factors.

However, (II) is not grounds for reversal. The Fourteenth Amendment Equal Protection Clause prohibits either side from using peremptory challenges solely because of race. *Georgia v. McCollum*, 120 L.Ed.2d 33 (1992). Thus, the prosecution had grounds to object and the trial judge was constitutionally justified in undoing the effect of the defendant's discriminatory use of peremptory challenges.

Therefore, (A) is the correct answer.

Question 90

Dan was charged with the rape of Chrissie, age 5. With the consent of the defense, the prosecution moved to bar the press and the public from the courtroom during Chrissie's testimony. The Daily Monitor, the local newspaper, which regularly covered trials at the courthouse, objected. How should the trial judge rule on the motion?

(A) He should deny the motion because the public has an absolute right to attend criminal trials.
(B) He should allow the motion because the defense and the prosecution are the only parties with standing to require that a trial be public, and both have waived that right.
(C) He should allow the motion because the state has a substantial interest in preventing further trauma and embarrassment to the child rape victim.
(D) He should allow the motion if there are special circumstances in this case that justify denying the public access to the trial.

Answer to Question 90

The public and the press have a First and Fourteenth Amendment right to attend a criminal trial unless there is a compelling state interest in closing the trial, e.g., a substantial likelihood of prejudice to the defendant or disruption of the orderly administration of justice. *Richmond Newspapers, Inc. v. Virginia*, 448 U.S. 555 (1980).

Since there are situations in which the press and the public may be excluded from a criminal trial, (A) is incorrect.

(B) is incorrect because the prosecution and defendants are not the only parties with constitutionally protected interests in the proceedings. While it is not an absolute right, the press and the public do have a First and Fourteenth Amendment right to attend this trial, regardless of any agreement between prosecution and defense. See *Gannett Co. v. DePasquale*, 443 U.S. 368 (1979).

Although the interest in protecting the child is an important one, it is not a concern which will be considered, as matter of law, to override all other interests and justify the complete exclusion of the public from every trial where a child might be traumatized or embarrassed by the evidence to be offered. Therefore, (C) is incorrect.

The court must articulate an overriding interest, not just a substantial one, that justifies closing the trial to the public. (D) is correct, because it most accurately states the rule.

Question 91

Three men invaded the home of the Walters, and at gunpoint tied up Mr. and Mrs. Walter, took their money and jewelry, and fled in a Ford Taurus station wagon.

Art, Bart, and Carter were arrested for the crime. At the station house, Officer Dickens said to the three, "You have the right ..." Bart interrupted him, saying, "Shut up. We know our rights." Neither Art nor Carter said anything. Dickens then asked Bart, "Did you rob the Walters?" Bart replied, "Yes, we did." The three were then taken from the room to jail to await trial or bail.

That night, Art's friend, Shifty, a police informer, visited Art in his cell. The next day, Officer Dickens went to see Shifty, and Shifty told Dickens that Art had admitted to him that the three men had robbed the Walters. Art, Bart and Carter have been indicted for the robbery of the Walters. If all three defendants indicated that they were not going to testify at their trial and Carter brought a motion for a severance of his trial from that of Art and Bart, the trial judge

(A) should not grant a severance, because there is no prejudice if proper instructions are given to the jury.
(B) should not grant a severance, because of the expense of the several trials.
(C) should edit the statement of Shifty if possible; if not, sever the trials.
(D) is constitutionally required to grant a severance.

Answer to Question 91

(A) is incorrect because the Supreme Court has held that a limiting instruction could not alleviate the prejudicial impact of the admission of a co-defendant's confession. The limiting instruction is constitutionally inadequate because of the difficulty the jury has in understanding and applying it

(B) is incorrect because the expense of separate trials is not a consideration where separate trials are constitutionally mandated.

Where one co-defendant is implicated by the confession of another co-defendant and the confessing defendant will not take the stand, the other defendant has a constitutional right to have the confession edited so that it does not implicate him. If this cannot be effectively accomplished, the nonconfessing defendant has the right to exclude the confession or have a severance of the trials. *Bruton v. United States*, 391 U.S. 123 (1968). (C) is correct and (D) is incorrect because (C) better reflects the applicable rule in all its complexity.

Question 92

Diane was on trial for the murder of Vanessa. To prove that Diane actually stabbed Vanessa, the prosecution called Wilga, who testified that she was outside Vanessa's house on the night of Vanessa's death when Vanessa's sister Natalie ran from the house and said to her in a hysterical voice, "Diane has just stabbed Vanessa." If the defense attorney objects to Wilga's testimony, the court will rule that it is

(A) inadmissible unless Natalie is unavailable.
(B) inadmissible because Wilga's proposed testimony deprives Diane of her constitutional right to confront Natalie, the witness against her.
(C) admissible if the trial judge determines that Wilga's testimony comes within a hearsay exception.
(D) admissible if the trial judge determines that Wilga is testifying to an excited utterance.

Answer to Question 92

In the case of *White v. Illinois*, 116 L.Ed.2d 848 (1992), the United States Supreme Court held that the admission of hearsay statements which come within the "well rooted" exceptions to the hearsay rule do not violate the Confrontation Clause, even if the declarant is available. Thus, (A) and (B) are incorrect.

Both (A) and (B) give correct statements of the law. However, the correct choice is the best answer and the best answer is the most specific answer. (D) is the correct answer since it states not only that a hearsay exception will preserve the testimony, but it also states which hearsay exception is applicable. The excited utterance exception is a well rooted exception to the hearsay rule which does not require unavailability. Therefore, if Wilga is testifying to Natalie's excited utterance, her testimony is admissible and does not violate the Confrontation Clause.

Question 93

At the end of a criminal case, the defendant, having submitted evidence of an alibi, entrapment, infancy, and insanity requests that the jury be instructed as to each issue. The court instructs the jury, over the defense's objection, that the defendant has the burden to prove, by a preponderance of the evidence, his alibi, entrapment, infancy, and insanity. These instructions are most likely unconstitutional as to which defense?

(A) alibi evidence
(B) entrapment
(C) infancy
(D) insanity

Answer to Question 93

An affirmative defense relieves a defendant of criminal responsibility although all the elements of the crime are present. In *Patterson v. New York*, 432 U.S. 197 (1977), the Court held that the state may place the burden of proving an affirmative defense on the defendant. Since entrapment, insanity and infancy are all affirmative defense, the judge's instructions as to these defenses were constitutionally permitted. Therefore (B), (C) and (D) are incorrect.

The due process requirement of a fair criminal trial requires that the prosecution prove all elements of the case beyond a reasonable doubt. *Speiser v. Randall*, 358 U.S. 860 (1958). Alibi evidence refers to proving one's factual innocence by evidence one was elsewhere than the scene of the crime. The alibi defense is used to negate the prosecution's case in chief, and therefore the burden of persuasion remains with the prosecution. As a result, it is unconstitutional to shift that burden to the defendant. Therefore, (A) is correct.

Question 94

Manning was indicted for manslaughter. At trial, the prosecution sought to introduce evidence concerning similar crimes committed by the defendant. When the judge sustained the defendant's objection to this evidence, the prosecution sought to make an offer of proof. The prosecuting attorney spoke in a loud voice while making the offer of proof, and the jury heard of the defendant's prior crimes. The defense moved for a mistrial, which the judge granted, and ordered the defendant retried. The defendant objected to the retrial on the grounds of double jeopardy.

At the second trial, Manning was convicted, and the defense appealed. The appellate court has found that, although the prosecution at the retrial presented sufficient evidence to avoid a judgment as a matter of law, the verdict was against the weight of the evidence. That court should

(A) enter judgment for the defendant because the evidence introduced at the trial was insufficient.
(B) enter judgment for the defendant because the prosecution's conduct caused the mistrial.
(C) send the case back for a new trial.

(D) sustain the jury's verdict of guilty because the appellate court does not judge the weight of the evidence.

Answer to Question 94

(A) is incorrect because it does not accurately portray the finding of the appellate court.

(B) is incorrect because, while it is true that the prosecutor's misconduct caused the mistrial, the misconduct was inadvertent. Deliberate misconduct would bar a retrial only if it was intended to cause the defendant to seek a mistrial.

The court found that the verdict was against the weight of the evidence, in which case the appellate court can only send the case back for a new trial. An appellate court, as "thirteenth juror," may judge the weight of the evidence to determine if the verdict was against the weight of the evidence. In acting as the "thirteenth juror," the court determines that, even though reasonable jurors could have found guilt beyond a reasonable doubt, the court believes that the verdict went against the weight of the evidence. Therefore, (D) is incorrect. In such a case, retrial due to a verdict against the weight of the evidence is constitutionally permitted. *Tibbs v. Florida*, 457 U.S. 31 (1982). Therefore, (C) is correct. (On the other hand, if the appellate court had found that the evidence presented by the prosecution was completely insufficient to sustain the conviction, then the Double Jeopardy Clause would prohibit a retrial and the defendant would have to be acquitted. *Burks v. United States*, 437 U.S. 1 (1978).)

Question 95

Duane and Wayne planned to break into a federal government office to steal food stamps. Duane telephoned Lane one night and asked whether Lane wanted to buy some "hot" property. Lane, who understood that "hot" meant stolen and had purchased the stamps from Duane before, said, "Sure, bring them right over." Duane and Wayne then successfully executed their scheme. That same night, they delivered the food stamps to Lane, who paid them $700. Lane did not ask when or by whom the stamps were stolen. All three were arrested. Duane and Wayne entered guilty pleas in federal court to a charge of larceny in connection with the theft. Lane was brought to trial in the state court on a charge of conspiracy to steal food stamps.

If Duane and Wayne are charged with conspiracy to steal the stamps in the state court, they should, on the evidence stated, be found

(A) not guilty, because the state prosecution is barred by the prosecution in the federal court.
(B) not guilty, because the charge of conspiracy is a lesser included offense in the charge of larceny.
(C) not guilty, because to charge them with conspiracy after their conviction of larceny would constitute double jeopardy.
(D) guilty, because they planned and conspired to steal the stamps.

Answer to Question 95

(A) incorrectly applies the Double Jeopardy Clause to prosecutions in the state and federal courts for the same conduct. The Double Jeopardy Clause only bars the second prosecution of an offense **in the same jurisdiction**. A prior federal prosecution, even for the same offense, does not bar a subsequent state prosecution. *Bartkus v. Illinois*, 359 U.S. 121 (1959).

(B) incorrectly states that conspiracy is a lesser included offense of larceny. Conspiracy and larceny each have elements that are not in common. Either can be committed without committing the other. Conspiracy requires an agreement, and larceny requires a taking away with intent to steal, for example. Unlike attempt and solicitation, conspiracy does not merge into the completed substantive crime. Under *Blockburger v. United States*, 284 U.S. 299 (1932), for purposes of double jeopardy, a crime is a lesser included offense within another only if every element of the former offense are also elements of the latter. Therefore, the suggestion in (C) that a conviction of larceny bars a charge of conspiracy is incorrect.

(D) is the only answer which states correctly that Duane and Wayne are guilty of both larceny and conspiracy. Conspiracy does not merge into the substantive target crime. Conspiracy and the substantive target crimes are also not the same offense for double jeopardy purposes.

Question 96

The police suspected that Amos, Andy and Alice were the criminals who had robbed the Third National Bank of Oldtown in State X. During the course of the robbery, one of the robbers fired a bullet from his gun which killed Tom, a teller, and wounded Mark, the bank manager. Pat, a police officer who rushed to the scene of the holdup, was also shot and killed by the robbers.

Amos was indicted by State X for the murder of Tom. At the trial, the only substantial issue was the identification of Amos as one of the robbers. Amos was acquitted by the jury. Subsequently, he was indicted on the charge of assault and battery with a dangerous weapon on Mark. At his trial on the charge, there was substantially more evidence of his identity than at the previous trial and he was convicted. Amos's attorney properly preserved all issues for appeal and appealed the conviction. The appellate court should

(A) reverse the conviction, because Amos was put in jeopardy twice for the same crime.
(B) reverse the conviction, because of the doctrine of collateral estoppel.
(C) sustain the conviction, because the battery on Mark is a distinct crime from the death of Tom, despite the fact that the same act was responsible for causing both crimes.
(D) sustain the conviction, because the additional evidence of identity introduced at the second trial makes the defense of collateral estoppel inapplicable.

Answer to Question 96

(A) is incorrect because assault with a dangerous weapon is not the "same offense" as felony murder; each crime has at least one element not included in the other. Also, the victims of the two crimes were different. Thus, Amos was not put in jeopardy twice for the same crime.

The doctrine of collateral estoppel operates to prevent introduction of certain evidence where the admission of the evidence would violate the Fifth Amendment's guarantee against double jeopardy. Thus, if there is a finding in favor of the defendant on an issue actually litigated between the prosecution and the defendant, the prosecution is precluded from relitigating that issue in any subsequent prosecution, even for another offense ("issue preclusion").

(C) is incorrect because the fact that Amos was not put on trial twice for the same **crime** is not dispositive; the Double Jeopardy Clause will also prevent a second trial on the same **issue**.

(D) is incorrect, because the discovery of new evidence does not avoid the operation of collateral estoppel. *Harris v. Washington*, 404 U.S. 55 (1971).

Here, the issue of Amos's identity as one of the robbers was litigated and resolved in Amos's favor at the murder trial. It could not constitutionally be relitigated at the assault trial, even though there was new evidence against Amos. Therefore, (B) is correct.

Question 97

Roberta held up a gasoline station. Immediately after the robbery, she shot and killed a customer who attempted to pursue her. Roberta was prosecuted for premeditated murder and convicted.

Thereafter, she was indicted for armed robbery of the station. Before the trial, her attorney moved to dismiss the indictment on the ground that further proceedings were unconstitutional because of Roberta's prior conviction.

The motion to dismiss should be

(A) denied, because there is no constitutional requirement that all known charges against Roberta be brought in the same prosecution.
(B) denied, because estoppel does not apply when the defendant is charged with violating two different statutes.
(C) granted, because once Roberta was convicted on any of the charges arising out of the robbery, the prosecution was constitutionally estopped from proceeding against Roberta on any charge stemming from the same transaction.
(D) granted, because the Double Jeopardy Clause prohibits a subsequent trial on what is essentially a lesser included offense.

Answer to Question 97

There are two possible murder charges which could have been brought against Roberta. She could have been prosecuted for felony murder, in which case proof that she was in the commission or attempted commission of a felony would be a required element of the offense. If this were the theory of murder, then double jeopardy would preclude a second prosecution on the underlying armed robbery charge. In this case, however, the question states that Roberta was prosecuted for premeditated murder. There is no element of that crime which is in common with the armed robbery charge, and therefore double jeopardy is not a bar to the armed robbery prosecution. Even though the armed robbery charge arose out of the same transaction, there is no estoppel. The motion to dismiss should be denied. Thus, (A) is correct and (C) and (D) -- which would allow the motion based on Double Jeopardy theories -- are incorrect.

(B) is incorrect for two reasons. First, there is no indication in the question that premeditated murder and armed robbery are statutory crimes. Second, the Double Jeopardy Clause **would** bar prosecution of the second of two statutory crimes if all elements of the first crime were also elements of the second or vice versa. Therefore, this is an incorrect statement of law.

Question 98

Cayne became incensed when he saw his brother Able pasting political bumper stickers on his brand new Pathfinder. When Cayne confronted Able, they argued and eventually started throwing punches. Cayne was charged and tried for assault and battery. At the trial, no one knew that one of the punches caused a blood clot which later traveled to Able's brain and killed him.

After Able died, Cayne was charged with murder. The charge will be

(A) upheld if Cayne was convicted of assault and battery.
(B) upheld whether or not Cayne was convicted of assault and battery.
(C) dismissed if Cayne was convicted of assault and battery.
(D) dismissed whether or not Cayne was convicted of assault and battery.

Answer to Question 98

The general rule is that, if two different crimes are committed in one criminal transaction, they will be deemed to be the same offense only if all of the elements of one offense are also contained within the other offense. The lesser included offense merges into the greater offense, and they become the same offense for purposes of double jeopardy. *Blockburger v. United States,* 284 U.S. 299 (1932). The exception to this rule is that, if all the elements that constitute the second offense have not occurred at the time of the trial of the lesser offense, the defendant may be tried later for the greater offense. That is the case in this question. Since Able died after the first trial, the state could still prosecute Cayne for murder, even if he was convicted of assault and battery. The death resulted from the same criminal activity, but did not occur until after the first trial, and the prosecution could not foresee its occurrence at the time of the first trial. Therefore, (C) is incorrect.

However, if Cayne was **acquitted** of assault, he could not be tried for murder. First, the fact that Cayne's actions did not rise to the level of criminal assault and battery, a lesser included offense of murder, would mean that, as a matter of law and practicality, his actions also did not rise to the level of murder. Second, the state is barred under the Double Jeopardy clause from relitigating the holding that Cayne was not criminally liable for Able's injuries. Therefore, Cayne can be charged with murder only if he was found guilty of assault and battery. Thus, (A) is correct and (B) and (D) are incorrect.

Question 99

Martha had worked and saved for the past ten years so that she could move her family to a "good" part of town. Shortly after she took title to her new home, she discovered that her next door neighbor, Dog, was a drug dealer, small time, but a dealer nevertheless. She was concerned about the effect this would have on her children and eventually on the value of her new home. She contacted the police and advised them of Dog's activities. The police told her they would look into it. Martha also tried to organize a neighborhood task force, but there wasn't much interest because people were afraid of retaliation. Martha had decided to let the police deal with the problem, until she found her 12-year-old daughter smoking a "joint" of marijuana. Martha asked her where it came from and she told her Dog gave it to her as a "housewarming" present. Martha then decided to take matters into her own hands.

For a week, Martha observed Dog's comings and goings and determined that Dog was always at home at noon for lunch. On the eighth day, Martha donned a ski mask, took some rope and a can of gasoline, and forced her way into Dog's house. She caught Dog taking a nap and tied him to the bed. She intended no harm to Dog, but did want to give him a good scare, so she poured the gasoline on the mattress around Dog and for good measure poured some on Dog as well. Assuming someone would come by soon, she left Dog tied to the bed and went home. Shortly after Martha left, a high-wattage light bulb exploded and the gasoline ignited. Dog was able to free himself, but not until the fire caused second-degree burns to his legs. Martha was arrested soon after and charged with arson and false imprisonment.

At trial, Martha insisted she was innocent of the arson and raised crime prevention as her defense to the remaining charge. The jury found her guilty of arson and assault and battery, but not guilty of false imprisonment. Martha appealed the convictions. The appellate court found that there was not enough evidence to support the arson charge, but found an error in the jury instructions as to the assault and battery conviction. Martha was retried on the two original charges.

On retrial, which of the following jury verdicts is permitted by the Double Jeopardy Clause?

(A) guilty of assault and battery
(B) guilty of arson and assault and battery
(C) guilty of arson, assault and battery, and false imprisonment
(D) guilty of assault and battery or false imprisonment

Answer to Question 99

The best method for analyzing this question is to consider the original charges and their results separately.

(B) and (C) are incorrect because Martha cannot be tried a second time for the arson. A retrial is not permitted when the appellate court reverses a conviction due to insufficiency of the evidence. *Burks v. United States*, 437 U.S. 1 (1978). Thus, when the appellate court reversed the arson charge due to insufficiency of the evidence, the Double Jeopardy Clause barred a retrial on the arson count.

(D) is correct because Martha may be convicted of assault and battery **or** false imprisonment, but not both. A key to analyzing this question is knowing that assault and battery is a lesser included offense of false imprisonment. When a defendant is charged with a greater offense, but convicted of a lesser included offense, the conviction on the lesser included offense is an implied acquittal of the greater offense. *Green v. United States,* 355 U.S. 184 (1957). Moreover, if in a second trial after the conviction on the lesser offense, the defendant is retried for the greater offense, but reconvicted on the lesser offense, his conviction is invalid because the presence of the greater offense before the jury might have influenced them to compromise on the lesser offense conviction. *Price v. Georgia*, 398 U.S. 323 (1970). Here, Martha was convicted of assault and battery at the first trial, which was an implied acquittal of the false imprisonment charge. Further, the false imprisonment charge at the second trial may have caused the jury to reach a compromise verdict by convicting for assault and battery, and such a verdict is impermissible.

However, in *Morris v. Matthews*, 475 U.S. 237 (1986), the Court found an exception. If the defendant is retried on the greater offense and convicted of both that offense and the lesser included offense, the appropriate remedy is to strike the conviction of the barred offense, but uphold the conviction of the lesser offense, because a conviction of both shows that the conviction on the lesser charge was not an impermissible compromise verdict. Therefore, in this case, although the false imprisonment conviction will be stricken, the jury verdict itself is permissible.

(A) is partially correct in that Martha could be convicted of assault and battery. However, it is not the best choice because (D) covers both the assault and battery and the original false imprisonment charge.

Question 100

Which of the following is LEAST likely to be the underlying felony in a prosecution for felony murder?

(A) arson
(B) manslaughter
(C) attempted rape
(D) burglary

Answer to Question 100

This question requires only a little common sense to answer. Manslaughter cannot be the underlying felony which forms the basis for a felony-murder conviction. If the death is classified as manslaughter, it is a homicide with mitigating circumstances. If there are mitigating circumstances, there is no basis for a murder conviction. The two charges cannot logically apply to the same action by the same defendant. Therefore, (B) is correct.

This question could also be answered by eliminating the obviously incorrect answers. Burglary, rape and arson are all common-law felonies that are part of the group known as "MRS. BAKER" felonies that serve as the underlying felony crimes for felony murder at common-law. The other crimes in this group are mayhem, robbery, sodomy, kidnapping and escape. If a crime qualifies as an underlying crime, an attempt to commit that crime also qualifies as an underlying crime. Therefore, attempted rape can also be the underlying felony for a felony-murder prosecution.

Question 101

Dunbar and Balcom went into a drugstore, where Dunbar reached into the cash register and took out $200. Stone, the owner of the store, came out of the back room, saw what had happened, and told Dunbar to put the money back. Balcom then took a revolver from under his coat and shot and killed Stone.

Dunbar claims that Stone owed her $200 and that she went to the drugstore to try to collect the debt. She said that she asked Balcom to come along just in case Stone made trouble, but that she did not plan on using any force and did not know that Balcom was armed.

If Dunbar is prosecuted for murder on the basis of felony murder and the jury believes her claim, she should be found

(A) guilty, because her companion, Balcom, committed a homicide in the course of a felony.
(B) guilty, because taking Balcom with her to the store created the risk of death that occurred during the commission of a felony.
(C) not guilty, because she did not know that Balcom was armed and thus did not have the required mental state for felony murder.

164

(D) not guilty, because she believed she was entitled to the money and thus did not intend to steal.

Answer to Question 101

    A defendant may successfully defend against a charge of felony murder by proving that he is not guilty of the underlying felony. If the jury believes Dunbar, it must find that she had no intent to steal, but only an intent to collect, in a nonviolent manner, money she believed Stone owed her. Without a finding of intent to steal, she cannot be found guilty of larceny. If she is innocent of larceny, she is also innocent of robbery, since larceny is an essential element of robbery. If she is not guilty of the underlying felony, she cannot be guilty of felony murder. Therefore, (D) is correct.

    Most likely, if you decided that Dunbar was guilty, it was a maddening effort to choose between (A) and (B). This is because both (A) and (B) state a proper basis for felony murder if in fact there was an underlying felony. This question illustrates the rule that if it is impossible to distinguish between two choices on one side of an issue, the correct answer will probably be on the other side. Here, (A) and (B) are in fact both incorrect.

    (C) states the correct conclusion, but gives the wrong reason. The required mental state for felony murder has nothing to do with the armed state of a companion, but rather with the state of being engaged in the commission or attempted commission of a dangerous felony. If Dunbar was in fact attempting to rob the drugstore, she would be guilty of felony murder even if she did not know that Balcom had a gun.

Questions 102 and 103 are based on the followng fact situation.

    Victor and Defendant were 16 and 17, respectively. Both were old enough to be legally responsible for a crime in the jurisdiction. By prearrangement, they met at the Dairy Shoppe, a teenage hangout. They were depressed. It had been raining for some days, and school had been out for several weeks. Defendant asked Victor if he would like to play Russian Roulette. They had played with a revolver before. The cylinder of the revolver had six chambers, from which they would remove all but one cartridge. One of them would then spin the cylinder, point the revolver at the other's head, and fire it. With six chambers and one cartridge, the odds were 5 to 1 that the revolver would not fire.

    Defendant obtained the revolver from his parents' bedroom. Adam, his father, kept the revolver in the bedroom at all times. Adam repeatedly bragged that he kept a loaded revolver in his room. Defendant took the revolver from the bedroom. He had done this before. He took out all but one cartridge, placed the others in his pocket, and then proceeded to the Dairy Shoppe.

    Victor agreed to play Russian Roulette. Defendant, pointing the revolver at Victor's head, pulled the trigger. Nothing happened. Victor then spun the cylinder and pointed the revolver at Defendant's head. He pulled the trigger. Nothing happened. Defendant spun the cylinder and pointed the revolver at Victor's head. He pulled the trigger. The gun fired. He was heard to exclaim: "Victor, Victor, I didn't think it would shoot! I'm sorry!" Victor died en route to the hospital.

    The homicide statute in this jurisdiction reads in part as follows:

> Murder is the unlawful killing of a human being with malice aforethought. Such malice may be express or implied. It is express when there is manifested a deliberate intention unlawfully to take away the life of a fellow creature. It is implied when no considerable provocation appears or when the circumstances attending the killing show an abandoned and malignant heart.

102.   Defendant is charged with murder. The trial judge can properly charge the jury on which of the following theories?

(A) involuntary manslaughter only
(B) murder and involuntary manslaughter
(C) murder only

(D) voluntary manslaughter and involuntary manslaughter

103. Defendant is charged with first-degree murder. Which of the following is Defendant's soundest theory of defense?

(A) Laws making a 17-year-old liable for any homicide are unconstitutional as imposing a cruel and unusual punishment.
(B) A revolver with only one of its six chambers loaded is not a deadly weapon, and its use therefore cannot prove deliberate killing.
(C) Defendant, because of his youth, could not have the malice aforethought required for murder.
(D) Defendant is guilty of murder, but his deed does not fall within the definition of first degree murder.

Answer to Question 102

The focus of this question is not on the one crime for which the Defendant is most likely to be convicted, but on all of the possible crimes of which a jury could find him guilty. When a killing is unintentional, as here, both involuntary manslaughter and murder (under the depraved heart doctrine) should be considered. Involuntary manslaughter is a lesser included offense to murder, and the jury is entitled to an instruction on that crime if there are facts to convict him of it.

However, they could also find him guilty of murder, even though he did not intend to kill Victor, on a theory of extreme reckless conduct which carried a high risk of death with no counterbalancing benefit. The pulling of a trigger in a game of Russian Roulette causes a high risk of death for no socially important purpose. On these facts, the jury could find the extreme degree of reckless conduct necessary to convict the defendant of murder under the abandoned and malignant heart doctrine. On the other hand, if the jury finds the defendant's conduct to be only grossly negligent or willful and wanton, they should convict the defendant of involuntary manslaughter. Therefore, (B) is correct.

The jury should not be instructed concerning voluntary manslaughter as suggested in (D) because that crime requires an intention to kill, a state of mind which cannot be reasonably inferred from these facts.

Answer to Question 103

Defendant's age is irrelevant to the analysis of this question. A rebuttable presumption exists that a person under 14 years old is incapable of malice aforethought. Since Defendant is over 14, (C) is incorrect.

(A) is incorrect for two reasons. First, as a general rule, an answer which gives a constitutional argument for a defense to a criminal charge is rarely correct. Second, 17-year-olds are universally considered responsible for their crimes, although they may be tried as juveniles rather than adults. The constitutional claim would clearly fail.

Common sense dictates that (B) is incorrect. A loaded gun, even with only a one-in-six chance of discharging when the trigger is pulled, is a dangerous weapon.

By process of elimination, (D) is correct. Defendant's best argument for acquittal of first-degree murder is that the circumstances of the game suggest recklessness, but not an actual intent to kill or an abandoned and malignant heart, at least one of which is necessary for first-degree murder under the statute.

Question 104

A state statute divides murder into degrees. First-degree murder is defined as murder with premeditation and deliberation or a homicide in the commission of arson, rape, robbery, burglary or kidnapping. Second-degree murder is all other murder at common law.

In which of the following situations is Defendant most likely to be guilty of first-degree murder?

(A) Immediately after being insulted by Robert, Defendant takes a knife and stabs and kills Robert.

(B) Angered over having been struck by Sam, Defendant buys rat poison and puts it in Sam's coffee. Sam drinks the coffee and dies as a result.
(C) Intending to injure Fred, Defendant lies in wait and, as Fred comes by, Defendant strikes him with a broom handle. As a result of the blow, Fred dies.
(D) Defendant, highly intoxicated, discovers a revolver on a table. He picks it up, points it at Alice, and pulls the trigger. The gun discharges, and Alice is killed.

Answer to Question 104

The statute defines first-degree murder as a homicide committed as part of one of the enumerated felonies or committed with a specific intent to kill the victim formed after deliberation and premeditation. Under this statute, the killing in (B) was a first-degree murder, because (B) describes an intentional killing with premeditation and deliberation. An intentional killing committed in the heat of passion after adequate provocation is voluntary manslaughter, but in this case, Defendant went out and bought rat poison, and then put it in Sam's coffee. The fatal act of putting the poison in the coffee took place long after the heat of any passion had cooled. The passage of time indicates that the killing was deliberate and premeditated.

The killings described in the other choices are not first-degree murders under the statute. In (A), Defendant clearly committed an intentional killing with malice, but did not commit first-degree murder under this statute, because there was no interval between the insult (before which Defendant had no intent to kill) and the actual killing. Therefore, there was no time during which Defendant could have deliberated and planned his act. Without premeditation or deliberation, the homicide in (A) must be classified as a second-degree murder.

The facts in (C) state that Defendant intended to "injure" Fred, not to "kill" him. A death resulting from an act committed only with the intention to inflict serious bodily harm is simply not within the statutory definition of first-degree murder.

Under the statute, the killing in (D) was also not a first-degree murder. Voluntary intoxication is not a defense to murder, but a highly intoxicated person can be deemed unable to form a specific intent, which reduces a first-degree murder charge to at least second-degree murder, if not manslaughter.

Question 105

Defendant lived in an apartment complex in the city of Newbury where the walls lacked soundproofing. The city of Newbury has an ordinance which makes it a misdemeanor to discharge a firearm within city limits.

Defendant was studying for his bar examination, which was two days away. His neighbors in the next apartment were throwing a birthday party and the stereo was turned up to a loud volume. There was a great deal of loud singing. Unable to study, Defendant knocked on the door of the apartment and asked the occupants to reduce the noise level. They agreed, but the noise of the party continued unabated.

After Defendant made one more fruitless trip to his neighbor's apartment in his quest for peace and quiet, he took his pistol and fired it into the wall which separated the two apartments, in an attempt to convince his neighbors to reduce the level of noise. The bullet went through the wall and struck Vic in the apartment next door. Vic was rushed to the hospital. On the way, the ambulance crashed into a car driving on the wrong side of the road and Vic was killed.

If it can be proven that Vic died solely because of the gunshot wound, the most serious crime of which Defendant can be convicted (listed in the order of seriousness) is

(A) murder.
(B) voluntary manslaughter.
(C) involuntary manslaughter.
(D) discharging a firearm within municipal boundaries.

Answer to Question 105

The killing in this case was unintentional. When a killing is unintentional, the defendant can only be guilty of either murder (under a depraved heart theory) or involuntary manslaughter. Involuntary manslaughter is a killing caused by gross negligence or recklessness, both of which may be said to be present in this case. However, Defendant's activity in shooting a bullet through a thin wall into a room where Defendant knew there was a large number of people is an act which carries a high likelihood that someone will be killed and shows an extreme disregard for human life. Defendant could be found to be aware of the risk, and the social utility of his conduct (even though he was trying to study) is doubtful. Therefore, if (as the query suggests) there is a causal connection between Defendant's act and Vic's death, Defendant's act, though not an intentional killing, indeed constituted murder. The fact that Vic died after the car accident is irrelevant because, according to the facts, the accident was not causally related to Vic's death. Therefore, (A) is correct and (C) is incorrect.

(B) is incorrect because Vic could not be convicted of voluntary manslaughter. An intentional killing, if committed either in the heat of passion after adequate provocation or with the aid of an imperfect defense, is voluntary manslaughter. The killing in this case was not intentional, so the analysis required to reduce an intentional murder to manslaughter is irrelevant. Even if it were relevant, the fact that the room contained noisy partygoers is not sufficient provocation for the action taken by Defendant.

(D) is incorrect because a homicide is a considerably more serious crime than the discharge of a firearm.

Question 106

John was fired from his job. Too proud to apply for unemployment benefits, he used his savings to feed his family. When one of his children became ill, he did not seek medical attention for the child at a state clinic because he did not want to accept what he regarded as charity. Eventually, weakened by malnutrition, the child died as a result of the illness. John has committed

(A) murder.
(B) involuntary manslaughter.
(C) voluntary manslaughter.
(D) no form of criminal homicide.

Answer to Question 106

A parent has a duty to feed his children if he is reasonably capable of doing so. John breached that duty, and arguably acted in a grossly negligent manner by failing to obtain available food to discharge that duty. Therefore, he could be guilty of the crime of involuntary manslaughter. The difficult judgment call is whether his actions were outrageous enough to constitute depraved heart murder. There are three reasons why they probably did not. He was probably unaware that his child was about to die from malnutrition. He also seems to have acted out of moral purpose in refusing to accept welfare, and therefore his conduct had some redeeming social value. Finally, the risk of bodily harm was not clearly "high." These three factors, on balance, would point to involuntary manslaughter rather than depraved heart murder in this case. Therefore, (B) is correct and (A) is incorrect.

(C) should be easily eliminated. Voluntary manslaughter occurs when an intentional killing is committed in the heat of passion or accompanied by an imperfect defense. Since John did not intentionally cause the death of his child, his actions did not constitute voluntary manslaughter. (C) is incorrect.

John failed to feed his children when he knew that support in the form of state aid or charity was available. His conduct is at least grossly negligent, which would provide the mens rea for involuntary manslaughter, which is a homicide crime. (D) is incorrect.

Question 107

Dent, while eating in a restaurant, noticed that a departing customer at the next table had left a five-dollar bill as a tip for the waitress. Dent reached over, picked up the five-dollar bill, and put it in his pocket. As he stood up to leave, another customer who had seen him take the money ran over to him and hit him in the face with her umbrella. Enraged, Dent choked the customer to death.

Dent is charged with murder. He requests the court to charge the jury that they can find him guilty of voluntary manslaughter rather than murder. Dent's request should be

(A) granted, because the jury could find that Dent acted recklessly and not with the intent to cause death or serious bodily harm.
(B) granted, because the jury could find that being hit in the face with an umbrella constitutes adequate provocation.
(C) denied, because the evidence shows that Dent intended to kill or to cause serious bodily harm.
(D) denied, because the evidence shows that Dent provoked the assault on himself by his criminal misconduct.

Answer to Question 107

The question does not ask whether Dent must be found guilty of voluntary manslaughter as a matter of law, but only whether that verdict is one which a jury might reasonably return. If there are any facts to support the argument, the jury should be instructed on voluntary manslaughter. (C) would preclude such an instruction and thereby prevent the jury from deciding between the two charges. Whether there was sufficient provocation to support a finding of voluntary manslaughter instead of murder is a question of fact for the jury to answer. A court may not prevent the jury from making such a decision unless the facts clearly fail to support the requested instruction.

(B) correctly asserts that being hit in the face can be considered by the jury as adequate provocation. Since the killing took place immediately, the jury could find that it was in the heat of passion, and thus might properly return a voluntary manslaughter verdict. The force used was clearly excessive, so the defendant probably has no right to an instruction on the complete defense of self-defense, but an argument can be made that the defendant is only liable for voluntary manslaughter.

(A) states the right result for the wrong reason. Dent requested a jury instruction with respect to voluntary manslaughter, not involuntary manslaughter. Voluntary manslaughter always involves an intentional killing which is reduced in seriousness because of provocation or an imperfect defense. It never involves an unintentional killing, even a reckless one.

Note that the facts do not suggest that the homicide victim was using privileged force, e.g., to make a citizen's arrest; therefore, Dent's apparent crime of larceny is irrelevant. (D) is therefore incorrect.

Question 108

The prosecution in this case has been brought in a jurisdiction which follows the prevailing common-law position on the issues presented.

Fenn commenced an unprovoked attack upon Hall with his fists. Barnes came upon the scene after the attack was under way and, noting that Fenn was getting the better of the fight, came to Hall's aid and struck Fenn with his fists. Fenn fell back onto the sidewalk and struck his head, causing his death. In a homicide prosecution of Barnes, Barnes has

(A) no defense unless Hall is a member of his family.
(B) no defense because he used force resulting in death.
(C) no defense because he did not know for certain that Fenn was the aggressor.
(D) a valid defense.

Answer to Question 108

The question concerns the grounds and scope of "defense of others" as a justification for homicide. In this case, the force used was nondeadly force, even though death did in fact result, because the force used was not likely to result in death. Moreover, the force used by

Barnes was an appropriate response to the attack made on Hall, if Barnes had a right to come to Hall's defense at all. Unless limited by statute, the law does not restrict the privilege to use force to defend others to any particular class of persons. Thus, the fact that Hall was or was not a member of Barnes' family does not change the result. Therefore, (D) is correct and (A) and (B) are incorrect.

(C) is incorrect because Barnes was not required to know anything for certain. In this case, Fenn was the aggressor and Hall clearly had the right to use nondeadly force in his own defense. The standard is broader for the defense of others. It is available if the third party reasonably believes that the person he is attacking is the aggressor. The defender is protected by the "mistake of fact" doctrine, which allows him to act upon the situation as it reasonably seems to be. Thus, even if he aids the aggressor in the reasonable but mistaken belief that the aggressor is the victim, he still has a valid defense. Thus, it is incorrect to imply, as (C) does, that the defender must ascertain for certain which of the combatants was the aggressor before intervening.

Question 109

Defendant, a worker in a metal working shop, had long teased Vincent, a young colleague, by calling him insulting names and ridiculing him. One day Vincent responded to the teasing by picking up a metal bar and attacking Defendant. Defendant could have escaped from the shop. He parried the blow with his left arm, and with his right hand struck Vincent a blow on his jaw from which the young man died.

Select the most serious offense of which Defendant could be properly convicted.

(A) involuntary manslaughter
(B) voluntary manslaughter
(C) murder
(D) none of the above

Answer to Question 109

Vincent's physical attack on Defendant, even though it was in response to Defendant's teasing, gave Defendant the right to use nondeadly force in his defense, a right which he retained so long as the necessity existed. Since Vincent seemed intent on continuing his attack, Defendant clearly acted out of necessity and had the right to use at least nondeadly force to defend himself. His response with a punch by his fist was an appropriate use of nondeadly force, even though it caused Vincent's death. That amount of force was neither likely to nor intended to cause death. Therefore, the Defendant is not guilty of any homicide crime. (D) is correct.

An involuntary manslaughter is an unexcused, unjustified homicide committed with criminal negligence or in the course of an unlawful act. However, a homicide is justifiable if it occurs as a result of an act committed in self-defense. (A) is incorrect.

The only viable argument that Defendant is guilty of voluntary manslaughter is that he intentionally killed Vincent using deadly force at a time when he only had a right to defend himself with nondeadly force, and therefore only has an imperfect defense of self-defense which will reduce murder to voluntary manslaughter. This argument fails because Defendant did not use deadly force. (B) is incorrect.

The only viable argument that Defendant is guilty of murder is that, without justification or excuse, he hit Vincent intending to do great bodily harm which in fact resulted in death. This argument fails because, at the time he hit Vincent, Defendant had the right to use nondeadly force to defend himself from Vincent's attack. (C) is incorrect.

Question 110

D takes a book from V's library. D is not guilty of larceny in which of the following situations?

(A) V consented to D's borrowing the book, but D did not intend to return it.

(B) V did not consent to D's borrowing the book, and D did not intend to return it.
(C) V did not consent to D's borrowing the book, and D intended to return it the next day.
(D) V had stolen the book and did not own it.

Answer to Question 110

(C) is correct. While there was clearly a trespassory taking in this case since D took the book without V's permission, the mens rea necessary for larceny is not present because D did not intend to deprive V of the book permanently at the time he took it. He intended only to borrow the book and to return it. If, when he took the book, he had the intent to deprive V of it, as in choice (B), D would be guilty of larceny.

The question presented in (A) is whether the consent to the taking gives D possession, making the crime embezzlement rather than larceny. D formed the intent to permanently deprive V of the book at the time he received possession. V only consented to D's borrowing the book, and D made an implied representation at that time that he would return the book. This representation was false. Therefore, the fraud vitiates the transfer of possession, transforming the receipt of the book into a trespassory taking, and making the crime a form of larceny crime: larceny by trick.

(D) incorrectly focuses on the quality of V's title. While a thief does not have rightful possession with respect to the true owner, he has superior possessory rights to everyone else. The trespassory taking from a thief in possession with the intent to deprive him of the property permanently is larceny as long as the intent is not to return the property to the true owner.

Questions 111 and 112 are based on the following fact situation.

Johnson took a diamond ring to a pawnshop and borrowed $20 on it. It was agreed that the loan was to be repaid within 60 days, and if it was not, the pawnshop owner, Defendant, could sell the ring. A week before expiration of the 60 days, Defendant had an opportunity to sell the ring to a customer for $125. He did so, thinking it unlikely that Johnson would repay the loan and if he did, Defendant would be able to handle him somehow, even by paying him for the ring if necessary.

Two days later, Johnson came in with the money to reclaim his ring. Defendant told him that it had been stolen when his shop was burglarized one night and that therefore he was not responsible for its loss.

Larceny, embezzlement, and false pretenses are separate crimes in the jurisdiction.

111. It is most likely that Defendant has committed which of the following crimes?

(A) larceny
(B) embezzlement
(C) larceny by trick
(D) obtaining property by false pretenses

112. Suppose that, instead of denying liability, Defendant told Johnson the truth -- that he sold the ring because he thought Johnson would not reclaim it -- and offered to give Johnson $125. Johnson demanded his ring. Defendant said, "Look buddy, that's what I got for it and it's more than it's worth." John reluctantly took the money. Defendant could most appropriately be found guilty of

(A) larceny.
(B) embezzlement.
(C) obtaining property by false pretenses.
(D) none of the above.

Answer to Question 111

In this fact pattern, Defendant had rightful possession of the property when it was turned over to him, but he had no right to convert it during the 60-day period of the agreement. Therefore, his sale of the property before the end of the redemption period is embezzlement and (B) is correct.

In analyzing any theft crime which begins with a lawful transfer of the property, it is important to first determine the possessory interest obtained by the defendant. In this case Defendant had only possession of the ring. To be guilty of obtaining property by false pretenses, the defendant must obtain title to the property by means of a false representation of a material fact. Defendant here is not guilty of obtaining property by false pretenses and, therefore, (D) is incorrect.

If Defendant had obtained possession by misrepresentation he could be guilty of larceny by trick. The fraud vitiates the legality of the possession, and the crime is a larceny crime even though there was a consensual transfer of possession. In this case, Defendant had rightful possession of the ring and did not use fraud or trickery to obtain it. Therefore, Defendant is not guilty of larceny by trick and (C) is incorrect.

(A) is incorrect because when Johnson deposited the diamond ring with the Defendant for the purpose of obtaining a loan, he transferred possession of the ring to Defendant and Defendant then had control of the ring. None of the special common-law rules that reduce possession to custody are present here. Therefore, Defendant's conversion of the ring by selling it did not constitute a trespassory taking, a necessary element of larceny.

Answer to Question 112

When Johnson deposited the diamond ring with the Defendant for the purpose of obtaining a loan, he transferred possession of the ring to Defendant and Defendant then had control of the ring. The crime of embezzlement was complete when Defendant committed the actus reus, namely transferring the ring from his rightful possession to that of the purchaser with the intent to convert the property and permanently deprive the owner of that property. Defendant's honesty and payment of money to the former owner do not alter the fact that when he wrongfully sold the property he had only possession, not ownership. None of the special common-law rules that reduce possession to custody are present here. Therefore, Defendant's conversion of the ring by selling it did not constitute a trespassory taking and was embezzlement rather than larceny. Therefore, (B) is correct and (A) and (D) are incorrect.

The fact that he had possession and not title also means Defendant did not commit the crime of obtaining property by false pretenses, which requires that title be obtained. He also did not commit this crime because he did not use a false representation to obtain the property. Therefore, (C) is incorrect.

Question 113

Young, believing that Brown suffered from arthritis, told her that for $100 he could cure her with a device he had invented. The device was a large box with a series of electric light bulbs along the sides. Brown, after examining the device, agreed to take the treatment, which consisted of placing her hands inside the box for several ten-minute periods. Brown gave Young $100 and went through the treatment. Young is charged with obtaining money by false pretenses.

Young is most likely guilty of obtaining money by false pretenses if

(A) Young honestly believed that the device would cure arthritis, but his belief was unreasonable.
(B) Brown honestly believed that the device would cure arthritis, but her belief was unreasonable.
(C) Young was playing a practical joke on Brown and intended to return the money.
(D) Brown was an undercover police officer and did not believe that the device would cure arthritis.

Answer to Question 113

The facts in this question permit the inference that Brown's representation about the capabilities of the device is in fact false. Therefore, the crime of false pretenses would be committed if it could also be shown that:
(1) Young knew that the representation was false, (2) Brown relied on the representation, and

(3) Young intended to deprive Brown of his money permanently.

(B) is correct because the additional facts set forth in (B) will not help absolve Young. An honest belief by the victim qualifies as the reliance necessary to constitute the crime of obtaining property by false pretenses, even if that belief is unreasonable. In contrast, each of the other responses contains facts which would help acquit Young. The facts in (A), if true, would show that Young did not know that his representation was false. The facts in (C), if true, would show that Young lacked a specific intent to permanently deprive Brown of his money. Finally, the facts in (D), if true, would show that Brown did not rely on Young's false statement.

Question 114

Driving down a dark road, Defendant accidentally ran over a man. Defendant stopped and found that the victim was dead. Fearing that he might be held responsible, Defendant took the victim's wallet, which contained a substantial amount of money. He removed the identification papers and put the wallet and money back into the victim's pocket. Defendant is not guilty of

(A) larceny, because he took the papers only to prevent identification and not for his own use.
(B) larceny, because he did not take anything from a living victim.
(C) robbery, because he did not take the papers by means of force or putting in fear.
(D) robbery, because he did not take anything of monetary value.

Answer to Question 114

Larceny is defined as a trespassory taking with the intent to permanently deprive the victim of the property. Robbery is defined as a larceny accomplished by violence or intimidation. Ownership need not be held by a living person. It is possible for a corporation, an estate or the government to be the victim of larceny.

In this case, there was clearly a trespassory taking of the identification papers. Thus, Defendant is guilty of larceny, making (A) and (B) incorrect. However, there was no violence or intimidation involved. The taking was done after the victim was already dead. Furthermore, any violence directed at the victim happened before the defendant formed an intent to steal the papers and was therefore unrelated to the trespassory taking. (C) is correct.

(D) is incorrect because the property need not have monetary value to be the proper subject of a larceny or robbery.

Question 115

James and Mary Green were walking to their car one evening after having seen a movie. As they were passing a dark alleyway, Dave leaped out brandishing a gun. He pushed Mary against the wall of a nearby building, held the gun to her head, and demanded money from James. James handed over his cash. Dave grabbed the cash and ran away.

Which of the following, listed in descending order of seriousness, is the most serious crime for which Dave may be convicted?

(A) robbery from James Green
(B) larceny from James Green
(C) assault on James and Mary Green
(D) assault on Mary Green

Answer to Question 115

The most serious crime for which Dave could be convicted is robbery of James Green. Dave committed larceny from James Green by taking his money through fear and intimidation. At the time he took the money, he was engaged in an assault on Mary Green in the presence of James Green and was using that threat of inflicting serious bodily harm on Mary as a means to coerce James into handing over his cash. That is sufficient. The force or threat need not be directed at the person from whom the money was taken, so long as there is a causal connection.

Dave could be found guilty of larceny from James and assault on James and Mary (although multiple convictions could present merger issues). However, robbery is a more serious crime than larceny or assault and therefore (A) is correct.

Question 116

Defendant was tried for robbery. Victim and Worth were the only witnesses called to testify. Victim testified that Defendant threatened her with a knife, grabbed her purse, and ran off with it. Worth testified that he saw Defendant grab Victim's purse and run away with it, but that he neither saw a knife nor heard any threats. On this evidence, the jury could properly return a verdict of guilty of

(A) robbery only.
(B) larceny only.
(C) either robbery or larceny.
(D) both robbery and larceny.

Answer to Question 116

The jury is entitled to believe either Worth's testimony that the Defendant took the purse without either violence or intimidation (which would lead to a verdict of the lesser offense of larceny) or Victim's testimony about a threat with a knife (which would lead to a verdict of the more serious offense of robbery). Therefore, it could properly return a verdict on either robbery or larceny, so (A) and (B) are incorrect. But the jury could not return a verdict of guilty on both crimes, because the underlying larceny is a lesser included offense to robbery, and that crime would be merged into the more serious offense of robbery. A defendant can never be convicted of both larceny and robbery for the same act. Therefore, (C) is correct and (D) is incorrect.

Questions 117 and 118 are based on the following fact situation.

Harry met Bill, who was known to Harry to be a burglar, in a bar. Harry told Bill that he needed money. He promised to pay Bill $500 if Bill would go to Harry's house the following night and take some silverware. Harry explained to Bill that, although the silverware was legally his, his wife would object to his selling it.

Harry pointed out his home, one of a group of similar tract houses. He drew a floor plan of the house that showed the location of the silverware. Harry said that his wife usually took several sleeping pills before retiring, and that he would make sure that she took them the next night. He promised to leave a window unlocked.

Everything went according to the plan except that Bill, deceived by the similarity of the tract houses, went to the wrong house. He found a window unlocked, climbed in and found silver where Harry had indicated. He took the silver to the cocktail lounge where the payoff was to take place. At that point, the police arrested the two men.

117. If Harry is charged with burglary, his best argument for acquittal will be that

(A) there was no breaking.
(B) he consented to the entry.
(C) no overt act was committed by him.
(D) there was no intent to commit a felony.

118. If Harry and Bill are charged with a conspiracy to commit burglary, their best argument for acquittal is that

(A) Bill was the alter ego of Harry.
(B) they did not intend to commit burglary.
(C) there was no overt act.
(D) there was no agreement.

Answer to Question 117

If Harry is to be convicted of burglary, it will be because he is a conspirator with Bill and Bill is guilty of burglary. The fact that Harry committed no overt act is immaterial. At common-law, no overt act was necessary for a conspiracy to exist. Even in jurisdictions that require an overt act before there is a conspiracy, there is no requirement that each conspirator engage in an overt act. Since Harry and Bill are acting in concert, anything which Bill did pursuant to the plan will be attributed to Harry. Thus, (C) is incorrect.

While there would be no breaking if Bill acted according to the plan, Bill actually broke into a house that did not belong to Harry by raising the unlocked window and thereby satisfying the breaking element of the burglary crime. Therefore, Harry's consent to "break into" Harry's house is inapplicable. (A) and (B) are thus incorrect.

(D) presents Harry's best defense. When Bill went to the wrong house and raised the window, he satisfied the breaking and entering of a dwelling house in the nighttime elements of common-law burglary. However, he only had an intent to pick up property that belonged to Harry, and Harry had given him permission to do this. Therefore, Bill had no intent to commit a felony. Without that specific intent, he cannot be guilty of burglary, and therefore the crime cannot be imputed to Harry.

Answer to Question 118

To have a conspiracy, there must be a combination by two or more persons to commit an unlawful act or a lawful act by unlawful means. Harry and Bill in these facts are separate individuals who would satisfy the multiplicity of persons requirement of a common-law conspiracy. Therefore, the argument that one person is the alter ego of the other is not justified on these facts. (A) is incorrect.

They also clearly had an agreement. Thus, (D) is incorrect. However, just because there were enough people to have a conspiracy and they had an agreement, does not mean that there was a conspiracy. Harry and Bill entered into an agreement that is legal because Harry is the owner of the silverware and owns or has a right to possession of the house. Since the purpose of the agreement was not unlawful, there is no combination of two or more persons to commit an unlawful act and therefore there is no crime of conspiracy. Therefore, (B) is correct.

(C) is incorrect because at common law, and under the majority rule today, a conspiracy is complete at the time the agreement was made. No overt act is required to complete the crime.

Question 119

Jim watched a liquor store furtively for some time, planning to hold it up. He bought a realistic-looking toy gun for the job. One night, just before the store's closing time, he drove to the store, opened the front door, and entered. He reached in his pocket for the toy gun, but then became frightened and began to move back toward the front door. However, the shopkeeper had seen the butt of the gun. Fearing a hold-up, the shopkeeper produced a gun from under the counter, pointed it at Jim, and yelled, "Stop!" Jim ran to the door and the toy gun fell from his pocket. The shopkeeper fired. The shot missed Jim, but struck and killed a passerby outside the store.

A statute in the jurisdiction defines burglary as "breaking and entering any building or structure with the intent to commit a felony or to steal therein." On a charge of burglary, Jim's best defense would be that

(A) the intent required was not present.
(B) the liquor store was open to the public.
(C) he had a change of heart and withdrew before committing any crime inside the store.
(D) he was unsuccessful, and so at most could only be guilty of attempted burglary.

Answer to Question 119

Burglary is defined as a breaking and entering for the purpose of committing a felony therein. In this case, there was no breaking. Since the liquor store was open to the public, the required trespass has not taken place, even though Jim opened the door to the store to gain entry. Therefore, (B) is correct.

(A) and (C) are incorrect because Jim's change of heart is irrelevant. It is clear that he possessed the requisite specific intent to steal at the time he entered the liquor store. His change of heart and abandonment of the planned robbery after entering is not a defense to the burglary crime.

Jim cannot be properly charged with attempted burglary as suggested in (D) because a completed burglary could not have occurred without a breaking. If he were to be charged with an attempt, it would be attempted robbery, not attempted burglary.

Question 120

Defendant visited a fellow college student, James, in James' dormitory room. They drank some beer. James produced a box containing marijuana cigarettes, and asked if Defendant wanted one. Defendant, afraid of being caught, declined and urged James to get rid of the marijuana. James refused.

Shortly thereafter, both went out to get some more beer, leaving the door to James's room standing open. Making an excuse about having dropped his pen, Defendant went back into James's room. Still apprehensive about their being caught with the marijuana cigarettes, he took the cigarettes and flushed them down the toilet. He was sure James was too drunk to notice that the cigarettes were missing.

Defendant is charged with larceny and burglary (defined in the jurisdiction as breaking and entering the dwelling of another with intent to commit any felony or theft). He should be found guilty of

(A) burglary only.
(B) larceny only.
(C) both burglary and larceny.
(D) neither burglary nor larceny.

Answer to Question 120

The marijuana cigarettes, even though an illegal controlled substance, are the personal property of James. When Defendant picked up the marijuana cigarettes and brought them to the toilet, he engaged in a trespassory taking and asportation. The intent to destroy them is the equivalent to an intent to deprive the owner of them permanently, even though Defendant gains no economic benefit from them. Therefore, he is guilty of larceny. But, Defendant is not guilty of burglary because he entered the dormitory through a door that was "standing open," and a person who can and does move through an open door without touching or moving the door does not commit a "breaking." (B) is correct and the other choices are incorrect.

Question 121

Statutes in the jurisdiction define criminal assault as "an attempt to commit a criminal battery" and criminal battery as "causing an offensive touching."

As Edward was walking down the street, a gust of wind blew his hat off. Edward reached out, trying to grab his hat, and narrowly missed striking Margaret in the face with his hand. Margaret, fearful of being struck by Edward, pushed Edward away.

If charged with criminal assault, Edward should be found

(A) guilty, because he caused Margaret to be in apprehension of an offensive touching.
(B) guilty, because he should have realized he might strike someone by reaching out.
(C) not guilty, because he did not intend to hit Margaret.
(D) not guilty, because he did not hit Margaret.

Answer to Question 121

An attempt requires an intent to the commit the criminal act. In this case assault is defined as an attempt to commit a battery. There is no evidence here that Edward intended to commit a battery. Edward was concerned about his hat, and did not intend to cause an offensive touching of Margaret, even though she might have been fearful that he would touch her. There cannot be an attempt to commit a crime where the state of mind required is negligence or recklessness. (Criminal negligence can provide the general criminal intent for a battery, but such negligence is not presented by these facts and such a standard does not apply to an assault crime.) Therefore, (C) is correct and (B) is incorrect.

(A) makes reference to another common definition of assault, i.e., an intentional placing of another in apprehension of receiving an immediate battery. Even under that type of statute, the defendants' conduct must be intentional.

(D) makes no sense given the definitions in the question. Whether or not Edward actually hit Margaret would be relevant only if he were charged with battery. However, assault by its very definition does not require any physical contact, only the attempt to come into physical contact.

Question 122

Jasper telephoned his friend Carl. Believing the person who answered to be Carl, Jasper said, "Listen, Carl, next Friday morning Bill will steal a shipment of diamonds from the Acme Company's mailbox. If we play it right, we can have those diamonds with very little risk. Think it over. I'll call you again tomorrow." With no further explanation, Jasper hung up.

The person at the other end was not Carl, but Andy, whom Jasper did not know. Immediately after calling, Jasper was seriously injured in an automobile accident. Andy told Carl what he had learned about Bill without revealing the source of his information. Together they followed Bill on Friday morning. After Bill broke open the mailbox and removed a package, they waylaid him, knocked him out, and took away the package.

As Carl and Andy ran from the scene, they were apprehended by a policeman. Andy told the policeman that Jasper had planned the whole thing. Jasper was arrested in the hospital. The package contained fake diamonds worth not more than $25.

If, in addition to other defenses, Jasper contended that, if he had ever become a party to a conspiracy to rob, he had withdrawn by reason of the accident, that defense would

(A) be good, because he did not participate in any overt act.

(B) be good, because he was too seriously injured to have the requisite intent.
(C) not be good, because the conspiracy was complete when he finished talking to Andy.
(D) not be good, because Andy and Carl became his agents to rob Bill.

Answer to Question 122

Under federal criminal law and in many jurisdictions, an overt act in furtherance of the intended objective is necessary to complete the crime of conspiracy. But even where an overt act requirement exists, it never applies to each of the conspirators. When the jurisdiction requires an overt act, such an act by any of the conspirators is sufficient to make all conspirators liable for conspiracy. Thus, (A) is incorrect.

Moreover, at common law, and in the majority of the states, a conspiracy is a completed inchoate offense at the time the agreement is made. An effective withdrawal is not a defense to the charge of conspiracy. Jasper had already committed the crime of conspiracy at the time of his accident. Withdrawal only precludes liability for any substantive crimes committed by the other conspirators after the withdrawal. For one conspirator to withdraw from a conspiracy, it is generally held that the one withdrawing must take an affirmative action which communicates the withdrawal to the other conspirators. The notice must be made in time for the other conspirators to abandon the conspiracy before the attempt stage has been reached. Also, the notice must be given to all conspirators. Jasper made no such communications. Therefore, (C) is correct.

Question 123

Adam and Bailey, brothers, operated an illicit still. They customarily sold to anyone unless they suspected the person of being a revenue agent or an informant. One day when Adam was at the still alone, he was approached by Mitchell, who asked to buy a gallon of liquor. Mitchell was in fact a revenue officer. After Adam had sold him the liquor, Mitchell revealed his identity. Adam grabbed one of the rifles that the brothers kept handy in case of trouble with the law, and shot and wounded Mitchell. Other officers, hiding nearby, overpowered and arrested Adam.

Shortly thereafter, Bailey came on the scene. The officers in hiding had been waiting for him. One of them approached him and asked to buy liquor. Bailey was suspicious and refused to sell. The officers nevertheless arrested him.

Adam and Bailey were charged with conspiracy to violate revenue laws, illegal selling of liquor, and battery of the officer.

On a charge of battery, which statement concerning Adam and Bailey is true?

(A) Neither is guilty.
(B) Both are guilty.
(C) Adam is guilty but Bailey is not, because the conspiracy had terminated with the arrest of Adam.
(D) Adam is guilty but Bailey is not, because Adam's act was outside the scope of the conspiracy.

Answer to Question 123

Adam is clearly guilty of a battery of the police officer. Thus, (A) is incorrect. The issue to be resolved is whether Adam's battery will be imputed to Bailey, who did not actually assault the officer.

Where one conspirator knows the other is carrying a deadly weapon, the unarmed conspirator with such knowledge will usually be held accountable for the use of that weapon in the commission of a crime; each conspirator can be convicted of the crime. Also, these facts state that "the brothers" (plural) kept a gun handy in case of trouble with the law. Thus, the battery was apparently within the scope of this conspiracy. Their criminal enterprise was not only to make illegal whiskey, but also to assault any law officers who attempted to interfere with the enterprise. Since the battery was within the scope of the conspiracy, Bailey is also guilty of battery as a conspirator. Thus, (D) is incorrect.

The fact that the conspiracy may have terminated when Adam was arrested is irrelevant, since the battery took place before the arrest. Therefore, the crucial acts occurred during the time the conspiracy was still in existence. Therefore, (B) is correct and (C) is incorrect.

Question 124

Jackson and Brannick planned to break into a federal government office to steal food stamps. Jackson telephoned Crowley one night and asked whether Crowley wanted to buy some "hot" food stamps. Crowley, who understood that "hot" meant stolen, said, "Sure, bring them right over." Jackson and Brannick then successfully executed their scheme. That same night, they delivered the food stamps to Crowley, who bought them for $500. Crowley did not ask when or by whom the stamps were stolen. All three were arrested. Jackson and Brannick entered guilty pleas in federal court to a charge of larceny in connection with the theft. Crowley was brought to trial in the state court on a charge of conspiracy to steal food stamps.

On the evidence stated, Crowley should be found

(A) guilty, because when a new confederate enters a conspiracy already in progress, he becomes a party to it.
(B) guilty, because he knowingly and willingly aided and abetted the conspiracy and is chargeable as a principal.
(C) not guilty, because, although Crowley knew the stamps were stolen, he neither helped to plan nor participated or assisted in the theft.
(D) not guilty, because Jackson and Brannick had not been convicted of or charged with conspiracy, and Crowley cannot be guilty of conspiracy by himself.

Answer to Question 124

Locating the correct answer to this question requires that you first determine the dimensions of the conspiracy or conspiracies involved. Jackson and Brannick conspired to steal the stamps. Crowley was not part of this conspiracy. There is no factual basis to assume that Crowley joined that conspiracy. The facts do not describe any intent by Crowley to combine with Jackson to accomplish a theft of food stamps. There was no participation by Crowley in the first crime (i.e., to steal food stamps) nor was there any indication at the time of Crowley's agreement that the first crime was not yet completed; in fact, Crowley's statement, "bring them right over," implies that he believed that the crime had already taken place. There was a conspiracy to steal food stamps in progress, but Crowley did not enter into it.

However, there was also a second conspiracy, namely, to receive stolen goods. Crowley was part of that conspiracy. It was formed when Jackson and Crowley agreed that Jackson would sell and Crowley would buy stolen food stamps. Response (C), which states the principle of law which properly defines the scope of the theft conspiracy, is therefore correct; and (A) is incorrect.

(B) describes the common-law standard for determining the liability of an accomplice as an accessory before the fact to a substantive crime. In every instance, an accessory before the fact is also a conspirator because he has entered into an agreement to commit a crime. Since, as discussed above, there is no factual basis to assume that Crowley joined the conspiracy to steal food stamps, (B) is incorrect.

(D) is incorrect because Crowley can be convicted by himself. Each conspirator need not be charged with the crime of conspiracy for one conspirator to be convicted. If co-conspirators are charged, then the rule of consistency requires that the acquittal of all but one would require that the final conspirator also be acquitted as a matter of law. However, the same rule does not apply if only one conspirator is charged. For example, all conspirators but one might agree to testify for the prosecution in another case, in exchange for the state's agreement not to prosecute them. In that case, the remaining conspirator can still be convicted of conspiracy.

Question 125

Bill and Chuck hated Vic and agreed to start a fight with Vic, and if the opportunity arose, to kill him. Bill and Chuck met Vic in the street outside a bar and began to push him around. Ray, Sam, and Tom, who also hated Vic, stopped to watch. Ray threw Bill a knife. Sam told Bill, "Kill him." Tom, who made no move and said nothing, hoped that Bill would kill Vic with the knife. Chuck held Vic while Bill stabbed and killed him. On a charge of murdering Vic, Tom is

(A) not guilty, because mere presence, coupled with silent approval and intent, is not sufficient.
(B) not guilty, because he did not tell Bill ahead of time that he hoped Bill would murder Vic.
(C) guilty, because he had a duty to stop the killing and made no attempt to do so.
(D) guilty, because he was present and approved of what occurred.

Answer to Question 125

(A) is correct. A crime is committed when an actus reus is accomplished by a person simultaneously possessing the required mens rea. Although Tom was present at the scene of the murder, and possessed the required mens rea, he did not aid and abet the commission of the crime. He, therefore, committed no crime. For the same reasons, (D) is incorrect.

If Tom had provided some aid, counsel or encouragement to any of the principals in this crime, he would have been an accessory and a conspirator with the same liability as the principals. However, it is unclear whether a statement that Tom wished Bill would kill Vic would constitute counsel or encouragement. Moreover, the statement would not be necessary to convict Tom if he was ready to aid. In that case, Tom could be held liable as an accomplice even if he did not tell Bill that he hoped Bill would murder Vic. (B) is incorrect because it suggests that the statement would be necessary for a conviction.

(C) is incorrect because Tom had no duty to act. One may commit a crime by failing to act when a legal duty to act exists. Such duties may arise out of statutes, contracts, relationships, or an individual's own actions. Here, the question presents no facts to suggest such a relationship between Tom and Vic.

Question 126

Alan, who was already married, went through a marriage ceremony with Betty and thereby committed bigamy. Carl, his friend, who did not know of Alan's previous marriage, had encouraged Alan to marry Betty and was best man at the ceremony. If Carl is charged with being an accessory to bigamy, he should be found

(A) not guilty, because the encouragement and assistance were not the legal cause of the crime.
(B) not guilty, because he did not have the mental state required for aiding and abetting.
(C) guilty, because he encouraged Alan, and his mistake as to the existence of a prior marriage is no defense to a charge of bigamy.
(D) guilty, because he was present when the crime occurred and is thus a principal in the second degree.

Answer to Question 126

To be guilty as an accessory, a person must intend to aid and abet someone in the commission of a crime. If the alleged accessory does not know the facts which make the action of the principal criminal, then that person does not have the requisite mental state to be guilty of that crime as an accessory. Ignorance or mistake of fact is a defense when it negates the existence of the mental state essential to the crime charged. In this case, Carl did not know of the prior marriage. If the facts were as Carl reasonably thought them to be (i.e., that Alan was not married) there would be no crime. Thus, he lacked the required mental state and is not guilty of being an accessory to bigamy. Therefore, (B) is correct and (C) is incorrect.

(A) is incorrect because a person may be an accessory even if his encouragement and assistance is not the "legal cause" of the crime.

(D) is incorrect because mere presence at the scene of a felony, without the required intent, does not make a person a principal in the second degree.

Question 127

Dunbar and Balcom went into a drugstore, where Dunbar reached into the cash register and took out $200. Stone, the owner of the store, came out of the back room, saw what had happened, and told Dunbar to put the money back. Balcom then took a revolver from under his coat and shot and killed Stone.

Dunbar claims that Stone owed her $200 and that she went to the drugstore to try to collect the debt. She said that she asked Balcom to come along just in case Stone made trouble, but that she did not plan on using any force and did not know that Balcom was armed.

If Dunbar is prosecuted for murder on the basis of being an accessory to Balcom in committing a murder and the jury believes her claim, she should be found

(A) guilty, because in firing the shot, Balcom was trying to help her.
(B) guilty, because she and Balcom were acting in concert in a dangerous undertaking.
(C) not guilty, because she had no idea that Balcom was armed and she did not plan to use force.
(D) not guilty, because she was exercising self-help and did not intend to steal.

Answer to Question 127

One who is present at the scene of a felony and aids and abets its commission with the intent that the crime be committed is guilty as a principal. Dunbar intended to take the money owed her in a quiet, nonviolent manner which was not dangerous. Furthermore, taking money openly and without force in repayment of a debt is not a theft crime. If Dunbar's story is believed, she did not intend to use force and did not undertake the risk of going to the store with a person who was armed. Dunbar did not aid or encourage Balcom's criminal enterprise, nor did she possess any intention that his crime be completed. A finding that a person was merely present at the scene of a crime is not sufficient to allow imposition of criminal liability. (C) is correct.

(D) is incorrect because the mere fact that she could not have had an intent to steal does not exempt Dunbar from liability. If Dunbar intended that Balcom employ the use of force to obtain money, even though the money rightfully belonged to her, the action would be unlawful. Even without an intent to steal, Dunbar and Balcom might have acted in concert to commit a crime. Intent to kill or to do serious bodily harm (or at least the intent to commit a battery) may be inferred from the intentional use of a deadly weapon on another. If that intention were formed or attributed to Dunbar, she would be liable as an accomplice.

(A) is incorrect because it is Dunbar's mental state which will resolve the question of her accomplice liability; Balcom's intent is not determinative of this issue. Response (A) focuses on the wrong party and tries to find liability in one defendant based upon the mental state of the other.

We are asked to assume that the jury believes Dunbar's claims. Therefore, since it is factually incorrect to describe the actions undertaken by Dunbar as a "dangerous undertaking," (B) is incorrect.

Question 128

Jasper telephoned his friend Carl. Believing the person who answered to be Carl, Jasper said, "Listen, Carl, next Friday morning Bill will steal a shipment of diamonds from the Acme Company's mailbox. If we play it right, we can have those diamonds with very little risk. Think it over. I'll call you again tomorrow." With no further explanation, Jasper hung up.

The person at the other end was not Carl, but Andy, whom Jasper did not know. Immediately after calling, Jasper was seriously injured in an automobile accident. Andy told Carl what he had learned about Bill without revealing the source of his information. Together they followed Bill on Friday morning. After Bill broke open the mailbox and removed a package, they waylaid him, knocked him out, and took away the package.

As Carl and Andy ran from the scene, they were apprehended by a policeman. Andy told the policeman that Jasper had planned the whole thing. Jasper was arrested in the hospital. The package contained fake diamonds worth not more than $25.

A charge of being an accessory to the robbery of Bill would not be sustainable against Jasper because

(A) Jasper was in the hospital at the time of the robbery.
(B) robbery was outside the scope of Jasper's talk to Andy.
(C) there would be no proof of aiding, abetting, counseling, or commanding the robbery.
(D) the property obtained from Bill was not what Jasper intended.

Answer to Question 128

The question requires you to select the best argument against accomplice liability, even though (1) it may appear that a stronger argument can be made in support of such liability, and (2) you may be able to formulate a better defense than any of the choices given.

(C) describes the elements of factual proof which must be established to sustain a charge of accessory before the fact to this crime. Although it appears from the question that there is proof of aiding, abetting, counseling or commanding the robbery, if these facts are not be established at trial, Jasper's liability as an accomplice would be negated. Thus, (C) is the correct answer. The other options can be eliminated as erroneous in law or fact.

(A) misstates the substantive law concerning accessory liability. An accessory does not have to be present at the scene of a felony to share liability for the commission of a crime. An accessory is liable for aiding, abetting, counseling or commanding the crime, even if he or she is not present at its commission.

(B) is incorrect because robbery is, or could well have been, what Jasper proposed to the person he supposed to be Carl. Although he did not elaborate, Jasper seemed to imply that he intended to commit larceny by stealing by force or intimidation from Bill, the carrier of the diamonds. His comments could be interpreted as a solicitation of the person he spoke with to commit the crime. Once Andy decided to commit the crime, that solicitation merged into the crime of conspiracy. Conspirators need not know each other's identities, nor do they need to know the details of the criminal plan. By providing the information which constituted a plan for the commission of the crime of robbery, Jasper clearly aided, counseled and encouraged the commission of that crime and a charge against him of being an accessory is certainly sustainable.

(D) is incorrect because a conspiracy need not successfully meet its goal to be a chargeable offense. The crime of conspiracy, and therefore the action that led to the charge of accessory, was complete before Bill was actually assaulted. Whether or not Carl and Andy got anything at all from Bill is irrelevant to Jasper's liability.

Question 129

A state statute makes it a felony for any teacher at a state institution of higher education to accept anything of value from a student at the same institution. Monroe, a student at the state university, offered Professor Smith, his English teacher, $50 in exchange for a good grade in his English course. Smith agreed and took the money. Professor Smith and Monroe are tried jointly for violation of the state statute. Professor Smith is charged with violating the statute and Monroe with aiding and abetting him.

Monroe's best argument for a dismissal of the charge against him is that

(A) a principal and an accessory cannot be tried together, since the principal must be convicted first.
(B) he cannot be an accessory, since he is the victim of the crime.
(C) the legislature did not intend to punish the person giving the thing of value.
(D) he did not assist Professor Smith in violating the statute.

Answer to Question 129

This question presents another example of a question that requires you to choose the best defense offered regardless of whether better answers exist.

It would appear that the purpose of this statute is to protect students from extortion by teachers. It is also apparent that the legislature, by placing the emphasis in the statute on the accepting of anything of value, did not intend to punish the giving. In that case, a student cannot be convicted of violating the statute, but would be considered a member of the legislatively protected class. (C) is not a sure defense, but is the best answer because it is a better choice than any of the others.

(B) presents a similar choice. However, it would be inaccurate to call Monroe a "victim" when in fact he did aid and abet the violation of the statute with the intent that the crime be committed. This is not the best defense of those offered because it does not state the principal of law on which Monroe must rely as accurately as does another choice.

(A) is an incorrect statement of the law. At common law, an accessory could be convicted only if the principal had been apprehended, charged, and convicted. Under the majority rule today, the common-law distinctions between principals and accessories before the fact have been abolished, treating all as principals. Therefore, they can be tried together.

(D) is a factual impossibility. To violate the statute, a student had to give something of value so that Smith might accept it. This is the only way a crime could occur. Someone had to "assist" as a matter of fact. The question clearly establishes that Monroe offered Smith money in exchange for a good grade and then gave Smith the money. The act of accepting $50 from Monroe was the action prohibited by the statute. It is clear that Monroe did assist Smith in violating this statute. The only issue is whether a student can be held liable under the statute at all.

Question 130

The State A statute defining the crime of bigamy reads:

I. Every person having a husband or wife who marries any other person, except in the cases specified in the next section, is guilty of bigamy.
II. The last section does not extend to any person
   (A) whose prior spouse is dead;
   (B) whose prior spouse has been absent for five years without being known to such person to be living;
   (C) whose prior marriage was dissolved by divorce or annulment;
   (D) who reasonably believes that his prior marriage was dissolved by divorce or annulment in another state.
III. Every unmarried person who marries another under circumstances known to him which would render the other person guilty of bigamy under the laws of this state is also guilty of bigamy.
IV. Bigamy is punishable by a fine of not more than $2,000, imprisonment in the county jail not exceeding 6 months, or both.

Betty, lawfully married to John, flew to Mexico and obtained a "quickie" divorce; John was aware of this. Thereafter, John married Lois, but not before consulting an attorney, who advised him that the Mexican divorce would be recognized in State A. John told Lois what his attorney had told him, but she sought another opinion from her own attorney, who erroneously told her that the Mexican divorce would not be recognized in State A. Lois decided to keep that information to herself and proceeded to marry John without telling him what her attorney had advised her. Under these circumstances, if John and Lois are charged with bigamy, the statute should be applied so that

(A) neither John nor Lois is guilty.
(B) both John and Lois are guilty.
(C) only John is guilty.
(D) only Lois is guilty.

Answer to Question 130

To answer this question correctly it is first important to note that, at the time of his marriage to Lois, John was not, in fact, married to Betty. (The facts state that the lawyer's opinion that State A would not recognize John's divorce was erroneous.) Therefore, John's status falls within exception II(c) of the statute (prior marriage dissolved by divorce). John cannot commit bigamy. Thus, (B) and (C) are incorrect.

As a previously unmarried person, Lois can only commit bigamy by marrying a married person who does not fall within any exception under Section II of the statute. Since John does fall within an exception, Lois has not committed bigamy either. Her guilty intent is not sufficient to hold her liable, since in fact no crime was committed. Therefore, (A) is correct and (D) is incorrect.

Question 131

This question is based on the following statute.

> Vehicular Manslaughter. Whoever, in the course of driving a motor vehicle as defined in the Vehicle Code, is criminally negligent in driving such vehicle or omits to do anything that is his duty to do and shows wanton and reckless disregard for the safety of other persons and as a result of such act or omission causes the death of a human being is guilty of vehicular manslaughter.
>
> Vehicular manslaughter is punishable by a sentence of not more than 10 years in the state prison or not more than one year in the county jail.

In this jurisdiction, there are no statutory standards for the amount of alcohol required to be in the blood to create a presumption that a person is under the influence of alcohol. Defendant, an alcoholic, while driving his motor vehicle, collided with another vehicle. A passenger was killed. Defendant is charged with vehicular manslaughter. Experts will testify that a person with blood alcohol of 0.00 to 0.05 percent is not under the influence. From 0.05 to 0.10 percent, he may be under the influence. Most of those with 0.10 to 0.15 percent are under the influence. All of those with over 0.15 percent are under the influence. Defendant consented to and was given a blood alcohol test 60 minutes after the accident. The test showed 0.11 percent alcohol. Of the following, what is Defendant's most appropriate argument to the jury?

(A) Assuming the jury finds that Defendant was driving under the influence of alcohol, they cannot convict him if he lacked the capacity to have the mental state of criminal negligence.
(B) The results of the blood tests were improperly admitted in evidence because there are no statutory standards for the interpretation of such tests.
(C) The blood test should merely be one factor in the jury's determination, along with such things as the police officers' opinion as to sobriety.
(D) Any statute which makes it a crime to kill someone while under the influence of alcohol is invalid under the United States Constitution; alcoholism is a disease and cannot be punished any more than narcotic addiction.

Answer to Question 131

The question asks for the most appropriate argument to the jury. (C) is correct because it presents an argument as to the weight to be assigned to the evidence, a proper matter for the consideration of the jury as trier of fact.

(B) and (D) are incorrect because they argue points of law, which ought to be made to the trial judge. They are not arguments to the jury as to what the evidence shows. Questions concerning the admissibility of evidence are for the trial judge to consider. Moreover, (D) is substantively incorrect. While it would be unconstitutional to make status (e.g., alcoholism or drug addiction) a crime, it is not unconstitutional to make related conduct (e.g., driving under the influence, or possession of narcotics) criminal.

(A) also misstates the substantive law. While most jurisdictions require that a defendant be aware of the risk his conduct creates in order to be guilty of criminal negligence and recklessness, most of those jurisdictions hold that, if the only reason a defendant is not aware of the riskiness of his conduct is that he is voluntarily intoxicated, then he is guilty of the recklessness the crime requires. The required intent may be found in the defendant's decision to drink when he would be driving, thereby creating a risk to others by his intoxication.

Question 132

A state statute requires any person licensed to sell prescription drugs to file with the State Board of Health a report listing the types and amounts of such drugs sold if his sales of such drugs exceed $50,000 during a calendar year. The statute makes it a misdemeanor to "knowingly fail to file" such a report.

Nelson, who is licensed to sell prescription drugs, sold $63,000 worth of prescription drugs during the year but did not file the report. Charged with committing the misdemeanor, Nelson testifies that he did a very poor job of keeping records and did not realize that his sales of prescription drugs had exceeded $50,000. If the jury believes Nelson, he should be found

(A) guilty, because this is a public welfare offense.
(B) guilty, because he cannot be excused on the basis of his own failure to keep proper records.
(C) not guilty, because the statute punishes omissions and he was not given fair warning of his duty to act.
(D) not guilty, because he was not aware of the value of the drugs he had sold.

Answer to Question 132

The key to choosing the correct answer here is the language which appears in quotes. The statute prescribes the mens rea for the misdemeanor as "knowingly failing to file" a report. Thus, knowledge is an element of the specific intent required for this crime. However, the test for knowledge in this case is subjective. If the defendant's lack of knowledge was bona fide, it does not matter that he was negligent in failing to discover the truth. Here, the prosecution cannot prove the required mens rea (that he knowingly failed to file) if the jury believes Nelson's testimony. His failure to realize that he sold over $50,000 of drugs prevents him from having the mens rea necessary to be guilty of the crime. (D) is correct.

(A) is incorrect because Nelson is not charged with a public welfare offense. The statute requires a specific intent, which means this is more than a public welfare offense (also called a strict liability crime).

(B) is incorrect. If Nelson honestly believed that he had not sold more than $50,000 of drugs, even if his negligence in failing to keep proper records helped cause him to form that belief, he lacked the required specific intent, and must be acquitted.

An "honest belief" that the law does not punish a particular act, however, is just ignorance of the law, and is no defense. In this case, Nelson may be said to have had a duty to keep informed about the legal regulations governing his profession. If Nelson had been aware of the value of the drugs he had sold, his failure to file would not be excused or justified by the fact that he was not given "fair warning" of the law that punishes that act. Since a "mistake of law" that is really just "ignorance of the law" is no defense, (C) is incorrect.

Question 133

Which of the following is most likely to be found to be a strict liability offense?

(A) a city ordinance providing for a fine of not more than $200 for shoplifting
(B) a federal statute making it a felony to possess heroin
(C) a state statute making it a felony to fail to register a firearm
(D) a state statute making the sale of adulterated milk a misdemeanor

Answer to Question 133

In the construction of a statute which does not include language requiring fault, a court may impose liability without fault (i.e., strict liability) after consideration of a number of factors. These factors include legislative history, the severity of the punishment for the crime, the seriousness of harm to the public created by the criminal activity, a defendant's opportunities to be informed of the facts which lead to an offense, the difficulty of proving a mens rea, and the number of violations and prosecutions likely to occur.

The seriousness of the penalty is always a very important factor in determining if a crime is a strict liability offense. A strict liability offense usually imposes a light penalty. Where legislative history or other factors do not suggest otherwise, the degree of punishment might be determinative. The crime in (D) is a misdemeanor, not a felony. Also, the statute in (D) regulates a kind of commercial activity which is typically regulated by statutes concerned entirely with actus reus, i.e. strict liability statutes. Therefore, one might reasonably expect the punishment to be relatively light - probably only a fine. Since all of the other choices involve felonies or crimes typically considered specific intent offenses, (D) is correct.

The statute in (A) imposes a $200 penalty for shoplifting. This is not severe, but it is a larceny-type crime. It is likely to be interpreted as requiring the same specific intent necessary to commit larceny as an essential element of the crime. Since strict liability offenses impose liability without fault, any crime which requires specific intent cannot be a strict liability crime. (A) is incorrect.

The statutes in (B) and (C) both concern felonies. Moreover, a person in violation of either of these statutes is probably subject to a

185

jail sentence. These are therefore unlikely to be strict liability offenses. (B) and (C) are therefore incorrect.

Question 134

"A person is not responsible for criminal conduct if, at the time of such conduct, as a result of mental disease or defect, he lacks substantial capacity either to appreciate the wrongfulness of his conduct, or to conform his conduct to the requirements of law."

This quotation is basically a statement of the

(A) M'Naghten rule.
(B) right and wrong plus irresistible impulse test.
(C) Durham rule.
(D) Model Penal Code provision.

Answer to Question 134

The standard stated in the facts reflects the Model Penal Code test for insanity. This test is based upon both the M'Naghten test and the irresistible impulse test, but it is much more sophisticated than either. The irresistible impulse test requires a complete impairment of the capacity to control oneself. The M'Naghten rule requires that a defendant be rendered completely incapable of knowing the nature and quality of the actions or of distinguishing right from wrong. The Model Penal Code test requires only a lack of "substantial capacity" to appreciate the wrongfulness of one's conduct, or to conform one's conduct to the requirements of law. Therefore, (D) is correct and (A) and (B) are incorrect.

(C) is incorrect because the Durham Rule, also called the "product rule," provides simply that an accused is not criminally responsible if his unlawful act was the product of a mental disease or defect. All that is required under the Durham Rule is that there be a causal connection between the mental disease or defect and the behavioral consequences.

Questions 135 through 137 are based on the followng fact situation.

The bigamy statute of State A reads as follows:

I. Every person having a husband or wife who marries any other person, except in the cases specified in the next section, is guilty of bigamy.
II. The last section does not extend to any person
   (A) whose prior spouse is dead;
   (B) whose prior spouse has been absent for five years without being known to such person to be living;
   (C) whose prior marriage was dissolved by divorce or annulment;
   (D) who reasonably believes that his prior marriage was dissolved by divorce or annulment in another state.
III. Every unmarried person who marries another under circumstances known to him which would render the other person guilty of

bigamy under the laws of this state is also guilty of bigamy.

IV. Bigamy is punishable by a fine of not more than $2,000, imprisonment in the county jail not exceeding 6 months, or both.

135. Fred, lawfully married to Agnes, left his home to purchase an evening paper in 1986 and did not return. He was not heard from thereafter. Agnes concluded that Fred was dead, and in 1990 married Clyde; Agnes told Clyde that she had previously been married but that her husband was dead. Fred reappeared in 1991. Under these circumstances, if Agnes and Clyde are charged with bigamy, the statute should be applied so that

(A) neither Agnes nor Clyde is guilty.
(B) both Agnes and Clyde are guilty.
(C) only Agnes is guilty.
(D) only Clyde is guilty.

136. Roger was lawfully married to Ann in State A. With Roger's knowledge, Ann commenced divorce proceedings within State A. After several months, Roger received from the court a document phrased in obscure legalese which he erroneously interpreted as the final divorce decree. In fact, the document merely indicated that the divorce would become final after the passage of three months. Six weeks after receipt of the document, Roger married Nancy. If Roger is now prosecuted for bigamy, the statute should be applied so that Roger is

(A) not guilty of bigamy if his misinterpretation of the document is properly characterized as a mistake of law.
(B) not guilty of bigamy if his misinterpretation of the document is properly characterized as a mistake of fact.
(C) not guilty of bigamy if his misinterpretation of the document is characterized as either a mistake of fact or a mistake of law.
(D) guilty of bigamy whether his misinterpretation of the document is properly characterized as either a mistake of fact or a mistake of law.

137. Victor was lawfully married to Susan, who left him and moved to another city. Victor proposed to Peggy and misled her into believing that Susan was dead. Irwin, another suitor of Peggy, told her that Susan was still alive and produced a recent letter from and photograph of Susan to support his contention. However, Peggy was intoxicated at the time and thus did not understand what Irwin was telling her. Thereafter, Peggy married Victor. On these facts, if Peggy is charged with bigamy, she is

(A) not guilty only if her intoxication was voluntary.
(B) not guilty only if her intoxication was involuntary.
(C) not guilty whether her intoxication was voluntary or involuntary.
(D) guilty whether her intoxication was voluntary or involuntary.

Answer to Question 135

The bigamy statute set out in this question establishes a strict liability offense in Section I to create criminal liability in a married person. Strict liability crimes do not require that a person have any particular mental state, only that the defendant engage in the conduct which is prohibited by the statute. Because Agnes is a "person having a husband," she is subject to the provisions of Section I. In Section II, the statute provides exceptions whereby a person subject to Section I may lawfully marry another person. Section II(b) is the only exemption which could be applicable to Agnes, but it is not in this case, because her husband was not absent for five years at the time of the marriage to Clyde. Even if Agnes' belief that her husband Fred was dead was reasonable, she is guilty of bigamy. She performed the actus reus when she married Clyde and the statute does not require a mens rea for this crime to be completed. When she married Clyde, she already had a husband and therefore is liable under Section I of the act. Thus, (A) and (D) are incorrect.

Unlike Section I, Section III creates a bigamy offense that is a specific intent crime. Under Section III of the statute, the second spouse of a person who is married twice is guilty of bigamy only if he or she knows of the circumstances which make the spouse guilty of bigamy. This offense is not a strict liability crime, and can only be completed if the defendant acts with the knowledge that the prospective spouse is already married. Where knowledge is an element of a specific intent crime, it must be measured subjectively. If a defendant's lack of knowledge is bona fide and reasonably held, then that element of the crime cannot be established. In this case, Clyde was told and could reasonably believe that Agnes' former spouse, Fred, was dead. Therefore, (C) is correct and (B) is incorrect.

Answer to Question 136

Since Roger, lawfully married to Ann, married another person, Nancy, he is guilty of bigamy under section I of the statute unless he falls within an exception under section II. The only exceptions which might apply here are II(c) or (d). II(c) does not apply because the facts state that the prior marriage to Ann was not yet dissolved by divorce when Roger married Nancy. II(d) does not apply because reasonable belief that the prior marriage was dissolved by divorce or annulment applies only to such proceedings "in another state." Here, the marriage and divorce proceedings both took place in State A.

The bigamy offense proscribed in section I of this statute is likely to be construed a general intent or strict liability crime since it does not specifically require knowledge or any mens rea. A mistake of law is generally never a defense to a general intent or strict liability crime. Thus, Roger's mistake as to his marital status at the time of his marriage to Nancy is not a defense. The mens rea required for a general intent crime is present because Roger knows he is performing the specified act, marrying another person. The act itself, without any mens rea, would be sufficient if this is a strict liability offense. Thus, (A) is incorrect.

As a general rule, mistake of fact also is not a defense to a strict liability crime. It is a valid defense to a general intent crime if it is honestly held, based on reasonable grounds, and of such a nature that the conduct would have been lawful if the facts were as they were reasonably believed to be. Roger's mistake cannot be deemed reasonable merely because he found the court decree to be difficult to read. Because a mistake of fact for a general intent crime will be judged by an objective standard, it is likely that this mistake will not be a good defense. Thus, (B) and (C) are incorrect and (D) is correct.

Answer to Question 137

As a previously unmarried person, Peggy's guilt or innocence is determined under Section III of the statute. That section renders an unmarried person guilty of bigamy when "under circumstances known to" the unmarried person, the already married person would be committing bigamy. That requirement of knowledge creates a specific intent crime. The important fact to resolve here is whether Peggy knew that Victor was already married. She lacked that knowledge because she believed Victor when he told her Susan was dead. And she presumably continued to believe this because her intoxication made her incapable of understanding Irwin's explanation of the true situation. Therefore, she lacked the specific intent to be guilty of bigamy. Therefore, (C) is correct and (D) is incorrect.

It is irrelevant whether Peggy's intoxication was voluntary or involuntary, if it prevented her from having the requisite knowledge which is necessary for the completion of the crime. Thus, (A) and (B) are incorrect.

Question 138

Assume that this prosecution has been brought in a jurisdiction which follows the prevailing common-law positions on the issues presented.

Uniformed Officer Gary was attempting to arrest Mug, when Mug fled. Gary called down the street to private citizen Black, "Stop that robber!" Black tackled Mug and, in the process, broke Mug's leg. If Black is charged with battery, he will have a valid defense

(A) only if Mug was in fact guilty of robbery.
(B) only if Gary actually had grounds to arrest Mug.
(C) unless he knew that Gary was not authorized to arrest Mug.
(D) unless it is shown that he was not in fear for his own safety.

Answer to Question 138

A private citizen's right to arrest on police orders does not depend on the legality of an arrest by the officer. A private person may be justified in using the force a police officer directs him to use, even if it turns out that the officer was exceeding his authority and would not himself be permitted to use that same force. Thus, (A) and (B) are incorrect.

To have the defense of justification, making his use of force privileged, it is only necessary that the private person have no knowledge that an officer's action to arrest the suspect is unlawful. Since Black is liable for battery if and only if he knew that Gary was not authorized to arrest Mug, the reverse is true - Black is not liable for battery unless he knew that Gary was not authorized to arrest Mug, as (C) states. Therefore, (C) is correct.

Black's fear for his own safety would be required for him to claim self-defense as justification for his use of force in this situation. However, his right to act under the direction of a police officer is a better basis for his defense. Thus, (D) is not the best answer.

Question 139

Two police officers in a squad car received a radio message from headquarters to be on the lookout for a large green sedan occupied by two men who had just committed a bank robbery. An hour later, they saw a car answering this description traveling down a main boulevard leading out of town. They had the car pull to the side of the road and walked over to the car. One of the officers told the occupants that they were under arrest for bank robbery. The same officer observed a brown paper bag on the floor behind the front seat. He opened the rear door and grabbed the paper bag, causing the bundles of paper money to spill out into the view of both officers. Thereupon Dean, the driver, suddenly put the car in gear and drove off. One officer clung to the car, partly in and partly out of the vehicle. The other officer pursued in the squad car. Unable to overtake the car and afraid he would lose sight of it in the heavy traffic, the officer fired, first a warning shot and then at the car. He struck Evans, the passenger sitting next to Dean. At about the same time, Dean, by swerving and suddenly accelerating, succeeded in throwing the officer from the car. The officer fell to the road and was run over and killed by the pursuing squad car.

Dean was caught five minutes later by another squad car, to which the remaining officer had radioed the alarm. Evans died from loss of blood.

If Dean, by the appropriate procedure, seeks to suppress the brown paper bag and its contents on the ground that they were the fruits of an unreasonable search and seizure, the court should rule that the evidence is

(A) admissible, because there was a valid stop.
(B) admissible, because the brown paper bag was in plain sight.
(C) inadmissible, because the arrest was unlawful.
(D) inadmissible, because, although the arrest was lawful, the search was not incident thereto.

Answer to Question 139

There was no probable cause for arrest. "A large green sedan occupied by two men" is not a sufficiently distinguishing description to constitute probable cause for arresting persons fitting that description. Therefore, the arrest was unlawful. Since the search and seizure were incident to the unlawful arrest, the evidence is inadmissible. Therefore, (C) is correct and (D) is incorrect.

(A) is incorrect because a stop does not necessarily create a basis for a valid search. A "stop" is a limited and temporary intrusion on an individual's freedom short of full custodial arrest. *I.N.S. v. Delgado*, 466 U.S. 210 (1984). A stop is justified if there is a reasonable suspicion, based on an articulable set of facts, that the detainees are presently involved in planning or executing a crime. *Terry v. Ohio*, 392 U.S. 1 (1968). This stop seems justified under this standard. However, when there is a valid stop but the officer does not have probable cause to arrest, he may only conduct a limited pat-down of the person for weapons, if he has reasonable suspicion to believe that the person is armed and dangerous and a threat to others. *Terry v. Ohio*. Therefore, a search of the car is not permitted under a stop theory.

(B) is incorrect because the plain view doctrine does not apply here. A police officer may seize an item in plain view only if (1) the officer is validly in a position to see the item, and (2) probable cause to seize the item is immediately apparent. *Texas v. Brown*, 460 U.S. 730 (1983). In this case, the officer was validly in a position to see the evidence, since this "stop" was pursuant to a reasonable suspicion based on articulable facts. The fact that the police could not arrest for want of probable cause is of no relevance, since they had the authority to be where they were on the basis of a stop. However, probable cause must exist before seizure under the constitutional scheme. In this case, probable cause was not apparent on first sight of the evidence. A brown paper bag is not obviously the fruits, evidence or instrumentality of a crime. It was only upon seizing the bag that probable cause was apparent.

Question 140

Jack and Paul planned to hold up a bank. They drove to the bank in Jack's car. Jack entered while Paul remained as lookout in the car. After a few moments, Paul panicked and drove off.

Jack looked over the various tellers, approached one and whispered nervously, "Just hand over the cash. Don't look around, don't make a false move - or it's your life." The teller looked at the fidgeting Jack, laughed, flipped him a dollar bill and said, "Go on, beat it." Flustered, Jack grabbed the dollar and left.

Soon after leaving the scene, Paul was stopped by the police for speeding. Noting his nervous condition, the police asked Paul if they might search the car. Paul agreed. The search turned up heroin concealed in the lid of the trunk.

The prosecution's best argument to sustain the validity of the search of Jack's car would be that

(A) the search was reasonable under the circumstances, including Paul's nervous condition.
(B) the search was incident to a valid arrest.
(C) Paul had, under the circumstances, sufficient standing and authority to consent to the search.
(D) exigent circumstances, including the inherent mobility of a car, justified the search.

Answer to Question 140

(C) is correct. Proper consent to a search obviates the need for any Fourth Amendment analysis. It is not necessary that the suspect know or be informed of his right to refuse, and even a suspect in custody can voluntarily consent. A person who has joint access or control over the vehicle can consent to the search of the vehicle. See *United States v. Matlock*, 415 U.S. 164 (1974). Here, Paul consented to the search of a car belonging to Jack. Because Paul was rightfully in possession of Jack's car, he had authority to consent to its search. Therefore, this is the prosecution's best argument.

While (A) presents an argument that could be used by the prosecution, it is incorrect because the question asks for the best argument. An argument that the search was "reasonable" is imprecise, at best. A better argument would be any one that speaks to a recognized legal doctrine, such as (C).

(B) is incorrect on the facts and the law. First of all, Paul was not arrested prior to the search. He was only stopped for speeding. This would not automatically constitute an arrest.

Furthermore, if Paul were arrested, a lawful search of a vehicle incident to an arrest is a search of the person and only the area of the vehicle within the defendant's control. *New York v. Belton*, 453 U.S. 454 (1981). The trunk is beyond the driver's reach, so a search of the trunk is never valid pursuant only to arrest.

(D) is incorrect because there were no exigent circumstances to validate the search. The lessened expectation of privacy in a car (as compared to a home), and the inherent mobility of a car, which can prevent the police from easily obtaining a search warrant and searching it, permit the police to make a complete search of an automobile without a warrant, only if there is probable cause to believe the car contains the fruits, evidence or instrumentalities of a crime. *Carroll v. United States*, 267 U.S. 132 (1925). When the police have probable cause to search an entire vehicle, they may conduct a warrantless search of every part of the vehicle and its contents. *United States v. Ross*, 456 U.S. 798 (1982). In this case, even exigent circumstances would not justify a full search of car without probable cause to search the entire vehicle. Paul's speeding and nervous behavior alone are not sufficient to establish probable cause to believe that there are the fruits, evidence or instrumentalities of a crime in the vehicle. Many persons suffer from anxiety when they are stopped by the police.

Question 141

Police were concerned about an increase in marijuana traffic in Defendant's neighborhood. One night, police officers, accompanied by dogs trained to sniff out marijuana, went into the backyard of Defendant's house and onto his porch. Defendant and his friend were inside having dinner. The dogs acted as if they smelled marijuana. The police officers knocked on the back door. Defendant answered the door and let them in. Defendant was immediately placed under arrest. After a brief search, the police officers confiscated a large quantity of marijuana which they found in Defendant's linen closet.

Defendant's motion to prevent introduction of the marijuana into evidence will most probably be

(A) denied, because the search was incident to a valid arrest.
(B) denied, because Defendant permitted the police officers to enter his house.
(C) granted, because under the circumstances, the police activity violated Defendant's reasonable expectation of privacy.
(D) granted, because this kind of detection by trained dogs has not been scientifically verified and cannot be the basis for probable cause.

Answer to Question 141

The police conducted a search without a warrant of the defendant's backyard and porch, which are within the curtilage of the defendant's home. These are protected areas in which the defendant has a reasonable expectation of privacy. A warrantless search is invalid unless it falls within the exceptions enunciated by the courts. In this case, the defendant did not consent to the search of his backyard and porch. Thus, (B) is incorrect.

Further, if an officer is making an arrest in a home, even with an arrest warrant, most states and federal law require that he announce his purpose before entering; failure to do so renders the arrest invalid. Thus, (A) is incorrect.

The use of the dogs may be enough to establish probable cause. Thus, (D) is incorrect as a matter of law. However, the presence of the dogs in the backyard was illegal and could not serve as the basis for probable cause.

Since there was no exception to the warrant requirement, the search was unlawful. The arrest was made as a result of the unlawful search and was therefore also unlawful. Moreover, since there were no exigent circumstances, the police probably could not have arrested the defendant in his home without an arrest warrant. Since the arrest was invalid, no valid search can be made incident to it. Therefore, (C) is correct.

Question 142

Detective received information from Informant, who had given reliable information many times in the past, that Harry was a narcotics dealer. Specifically, Informant said that, two months before, he had visited Harry's apartment with Bill and that on that occasion he saw Harry sell Bill some heroin. Detective knew that Informant, Harry, and Bill were friends. Thereafter, Detective put all this information into affidavit form, appeared before a magistrate, and secured a search warrant for Harry's apartment. A police search turned up a supply of heroin. Harry's motion to suppress introduction of the heroin into evidence will most probably be

(A) granted, because a search warrant cannot validly be issued solely on the basis of an informant's information.
(B) granted, because the information supplied to Detective concerned an occurrence too remote in time to justify a finding of probable cause at the time of the search.
(C) denied, because the magistrate issued a search warrant.
(D) denied, because Informant had proven himself reliable in the past and the information he gave turned out to be correct.

Answer to Question 142

This question provides an example of the good faith exception to the exclusionary rule in search and seizure cases. See *United States v. Leon*, 468 U.S. 897 (1984). Here, the police prepared affidavits, went before a magistrate, received a search warrant, and executed it. The magistrate was probably incorrect in issuing the warrant because the information was stale. Nevertheless, the issuance of a facially valid warrant makes the search valid unless the police acted in bad faith. There are no facts to support such a charge here. Therefore, (B) is incorrect and (C) is correct.

In addition, (A) is incorrect because a search warrant may be issued solely on information from an informant, if that information is trustworthy. In this question, the facts specifically state that Informant gave reliable information in the past, so the information for this warrant was probably trustworthy as well.

(D) is incorrect. Although Informant has proven to be reliable in the past, his information is stale on this occasion. A heroin sale two months earlier does not establish probable cause that there is now heroin at the location. The warrant was wrongly issued, but that does not affect the validity of the search in this case, where the officers acted in good faith. Moreover, the validity of the search cannot be judged in hindsight. The fact that the information turned out to be correct will not retroactively validate an invalid warrant.

Question 143

Donna was arrested and taken to police headquarters, where she was given her Miranda warnings. Donna indicated that she wished to telephone her lawyer and was told that she could do so after her fingerprints had been taken. While being fingerprinted, however, Donna blurted out, "Paying a lawyer is a waste of money because I know you have me."

At trial, Donna's motion to prevent the introduction of the statement she made while being fingerprinted will most probably be

(A) granted, because Donna's request to contact her attorney was reasonable and should have been granted immediately.
(B) granted, because of the "fruit of the poisonous tree" doctrine.
(C) denied, because the statements were volunteered and not the result of interrogation.
(D) denied, because fingerprinting is not a critical stage of the proceeding requiring the assistance of counsel.

Answer to Question 143

The Miranda exclusionary rule applies only to statements made during custodial interrogation. Donna was in custody and, when warned of her Miranda rights, attempted to exercise one of them by asking to consult with a lawyer. Therefore, any statement made by her which was the product of interrogation would be inadmissible. However, the statement at issue was not the product of interrogation. Rather, it was volunteered, or in the words of the question, "blurted out." A voluntary confession even after Miranda warnings have been given is not inadmissible. Therefore, (C) is correct.

(A) correctly states that Donna had a right to contact her attorney promptly, but the only sanction imposed upon the police for denying that right is to render inadmissible statements made by her that are the product of interrogation. Since the statement was not a result of interrogation, the failure to permit contact with a lawyer would not render her voluntary statement inadmissible.

(B) is incorrect because there is no evidence of a poisonous tree. *Wong Sun v. United States*, 371 U.S. 471 (1963), held that a confession while in custody following an illegal arrest was the fruit of that illegal arrest, and on that ground alone was inadmissible. However, Donna's voluntary statement is not the result of any improper police conduct since the question implies that she was legally arrested. Therefore, the statement is not inadmissible under the "fruit of the poisonous tree" doctrine.

(D) correctly states that there is no constitutional requirement that counsel be present during fingerprinting. Nevertheless, it is incorrect because the critical issue is not the admissibility of the fingerprints but the statement made during the fingerprinting. Since Donna had exercised her Miranda right to the assistance of counsel, any statements made by her as a result of interrogation would be inadmissible, regardless of the stage of the proceedings.

Question 144

Darlene was arrested on a murder charge. She was given Miranda warnings and refused to talk further with the police. At trial, she testified in her own defense. She recounted in some detail her whereabouts on the day of the crime and explained why she could not have committed the crime. On cross-examination and over defense objection, the prosecution emphasized the fact that she did not tell the police this story following her arrest. The prosecution thereby suggested that her testimony was false.

Darlene was convicted. On appeal, she claims error in the prosecutor's cross-examination. Her conviction will most probably be

(A) affirmed, because her silence at the time of arrest is tantamount to a prior inconsistent statement, giving rise to an inference that the story was fabricated.
(B) affirmed, because her silence was not used as direct evidence but only for impeachment, a purpose consistent with legitimate cross-examination.
(C) reversed, because post-arrest silence constituted defendant's exercise of her Miranda rights and use of that silence against her at trial violated due process.
(D) reversed, because to require the defense to acquaint the prosecution with defendant's testimony prior to trial would constitute unconstitutional pre-trial discovery.

Answer to Question 144

To answer this question correctly, you must understand the distinction between the use of post-arrest statements versus post-arrest silence to impeach a testifying defendant. *Harris v. New York*, 401 U.S. 222 (1971), permits statements taken in violation of Miranda to be used to impeach the credibility of a criminal defendant, if he takes the stand and gives testimony at variance with those statements. On the other hand, the prosecution may not use the defendant's post-arrest silence as a prior inconsistent action, if the accused at trial takes the stand and denies her guilt. *United States v. Hale*, 422 U.S. 171 (1975). The arrested defendant has a right to remain silent and that right cannot be compromised by use of that silence against the defendant. (Note, though, that pre-arrest silence in the face of an accusation is admissible for impeachment purposes because the defendant's Miranda rights do not apply until he is in custody.) Therefore, (C) is correct and (A) and (B) are incorrect.

(D) is incorrect because pre-trial discovery can be constitutional in a criminal case if both sides have the right to it, and the defendant's privilege against self-incrimination is not infringed. Thus, if the defendant is going to testify (e.g., to alibi), the defense can be required to divulge the nature and basic facts of the defendant's testimony prior to the trial.

Questions 145 and 146 are based on the following fact situation.

Two police officers in a squad car received a radio message from headquarters to be on the lookout for a large green sedan occupied by two men who had just committed a bank robbery. An hour later they saw a car answering this description traveling down a main boulevard leading out of town. They had the car pull to the side of the road and walked over to the car. One of the officers told the occupants that they were under arrest for bank robbery. The same officer observed a brown paper bag on the floor behind the front seat. He opened the rear door and grabbed the paper bag, causing bundles of paper money to spill out into the view of both officers. Thereupon Dean, the driver, suddenly put the car in gear and drove off. One officer clung to the car, partly in and partly out of the vehicle. The other officer pursued in the squad car. Unable to overtake the car and afraid he would lose sight of it in the heavy traffic, the officer fired, first a warning shot and then at the car. He struck Evans, the passenger sitting next to Dean. At about the same time, Dean, by swerving and sudden acceleration, succeeded in throwing the officer from the car; the officer fell to the road and was run over and killed by the pursuing squad car.

Dean was caught five minutes later by another squad car, to whom the remaining officer had radioed the alarm. Evans died from loss of blood. Dean was taken to the police station.

The bank robbers had handed the teller a handwritten note, demanding the money. Dean was required, over his protest, to write out the words of the note and have his fingerprints taken.

About an hour after his capture, Dean was required, also over his protest, to participate in a lineup with five other men. The lineup was attended by two of the bank employees who had witnessed the robbery. They identified Dean by his appearance.

Another employee said she had not seen the robbers' faces well enough to identify either of them, and thus she did not view the men in the lineup. Because she had heard one of the robbers say, "Put it in the bag" in a peculiarly raspy voice, she thought she could recognize his voice if she heard it again. Dean was required to repeat the words, and the bank employee identified his as the voice she had heard.

Dean was charged with the murders of both the officer and Evans, and bank robbery.

145. The prosecution, after introducing evidence of fingerprints on the robbers' note, offers the fingerprints obtained from Dean. Over the appropriate objection, the court should rule this

(A) admissible.
(B) inadmissible, because he was not advised that his fingerprints could be admitted into evidence against him.
(C) inadmissible, because he was not advised of his right to refuse to give his fingerprints.
(D) inadmissible, because he had not been informed he had a right to have counsel present.

146. At trial, the prosecution puts on the stand the bank employee who had identified Dean by his voice. She testifies that she heard one of the robbers say, "Put it in the bag." She is then asked whether she had later heard the same voice. At that point, defense counsel objects to her answering the question. On appropriate objection, the court should rule the bank employee's answering of the question as

(A) admissible.
(B) inadmissible, because it tends to incriminate Dean "out of his own mouth."

(C) inadmissible, because the evidence was obtained by an unlawful search and seizure.
(D) inadmissible, because Dean was not given the opportunity to have counsel present at the voice identification.

Answer to Question 145

(A) is correct. The Fifth Amendment privilege against self-incrimination protects only testimonial evidence, not physical evidence such as fingerprints or a handwriting sample. See *United States v. Wade*, 388 U.S. 218 (1967). Therefore, Dean does not have the right to refuse to be fingerprinted, and (C) is incorrect. Nor is a Miranda warning needed prior to taking fingerprints and there is no requirement that Dean be advised that the fingerprints can be used against him, making (B) incorrect. Further, the defendant has no Fifth Amendment right to counsel in these circumstances. Even under a Sixth Amendment analysis, the taking of fingerprints is a scientific investigation technique which is not a critical stage of prosecution requiring the presence of defense counsel, because the test and the results are available for scrutiny later. Thus, (D) is incorrect.

Answer to Question 146

(A) is correct. A person who is lawfully in custody may be required to provide a voice sample without violating any Fifth Amendment rights. The privilege against self-incrimination protects only testimonial evidence. See *United States v. Wade*, 388 U.S. 218 (1967). By giving a voice sample, the defendant is not incriminated by the meaning of his words, but rather by the way in which he speaks. Only the substance of his words is protected by the privilege against self-incrimination. Thus, (B) is incorrect. Nor is the defendant's Fourth Amendment right to be free from unreasonable searches involved since the procedure is not invasive in such a way as to be categorized as a search. Thus, (C) is incorrect. Since there is no constitutional right implicated by the procedure, there is no Fifth Amendment requirement that counsel be present at a voice identification. Further, even under a Sixth Amendment analysis, the taking of a voice sample is a scientific investigation technique which is not a critical stage of prosecution requiring the presence of defense counsel. *Gilbert v. California*, 388 U.S. 263 (1967). Thus, (D) is incorrect.

Question 147

A robber held up the First National Bank. The teller handed him currency coated with an invisible chemical substance called "No-Bounce" which remains on the skin for seven days after the skin has touched the currency. The day after the robbery, the police saw a man matching the description of the robber given by the bank teller in a supermarket near the bank, and immediately arrested Burt. They took him to police headquarters, tested his hands and found evidence of "No-Bounce" on them. Burt was indicted for the bank robbery and brought a motion to suppress the admission of the test results. The trial court should hold that they are

(A) admissible as a proper investigatory procedure.
(B) inadmissible, because counsel for Burt was not present at the time the test was taken.
(C) inadmissible, because the test violated the defendant's Fifth Amendment rights.
(D) inadmissible as an improper search of Burt's person, because he was arrested without a warrant.

Answer to Question 147

The chemical test is admissible as a proper investigative procedure. When a suspect is in lawful custody, the police may require that the suspect submit to certain tests to gather evidence. Such tests as handwriting samples, blood samples or the chemical test in this case are permissible as proper investigative procedures. These tests are not subject to Fifth Amendment limitations. The Fifth Amendment privilege against self-incrimination protects only testimonial evidence, not physical evidence such as blood samples, a handwriting sample, or the chemical test results here. See *United States v.*

Wade, 388 U.S. 218 (1967). Thus, (C) is incorrect.

Because the tests are not subject to the Fifth Amendment there is no right to counsel on these facts. There is no requirement under the Fifth Amendment that counsel be present because this test does not involve the privilege against self-incrimination. Further, even under a Sixth Amendment analysis, this chemical test is a scientific investigation technique which is not a critical stage of prosecution requiring the presence of defense counsel. There is no right to counsel during scientific investigative procedures, the results of which are available for subsequent scrutiny. *Gilbert v. California*, 388 U.S. 263 (1967). Therefore, (A) is correct and (B) is incorrect.

(D) is incorrect because the police did not need a warrant to arrest the defendant. If the police have a reasonable suspicion that a felony has been committed by a person, they may make an arrest outside the defendant's home without a warrant. In this case, a felony had been committed and Burt fit the description of the bank robber and, therefore, the police had a reasonable suspicion to arrest Burt in public without a warrant.

Question 148

Two police officers in a squad car received a radio message from headquarters to be on the lookout for a large green sedan occupied by two men who had just committed a bank robbery. An hour later, they saw a car answering this description traveling down a main boulevard leading out of town. They had the car pull to the side of the road and walked over to the car. One of the officers told the occupants that they were under arrest for bank robbery. Thereupon Dean, the driver, suddenly put the car in gear and drove off. One officer clung to the car, partly in and partly out of the vehicle. The other officer pursued in the squad car. Unable to overtake the car and afraid he would lose sight of it in the heavy traffic, the officer fired, first a warning shot and then at the car. He struck Evans, the passenger sitting next to Dean. At about the same time, Dean, by swerving and sudden acceleration, succeeded in throwing the officer from the car. The officer fell to the road and was run over and killed by the pursuing squad car.

Dean was caught five minutes later by another squad car, to whom the remaining officer had radioed the alarm. Evans died from loss of blood. Dean was taken to the police station.

Dean was charged with murder of both the officer and Evans.

Suppose the jury finds Dean guilty of the murder of Evans. Before passing sentence, the judge hears argument by both parties. The prosecutor introduces the criminal record of Dean, showing two prior convictions for felonies. Defense counsel admits the correctness of the record. The court imposes the maximum sentence of life imprisonment. On appeal, the appellate court should hold that this sentence

(A) violated Dean's right to due process, in that it deprived him of a fair and unbiased tribunal.
(B) was in error because the introduction of new evidence after the trial deprived Dean of a fair trial.
(C) was not in error.
(D) deprived Dean of the right to confront the witnesses against him.

Answer to Question 148

(C) is correct because the defendant's criminal record is admissible at the sentencing stage. In determining the appropriate sentence, the judge is allowed access to all relevant information concerning the defendant, provided that it is reliable. An official record of prior convictions is generally considered to be reliable.

(A) and (B) are incorrect because the evidence was not introduced at trial, where it could have influenced the factfinder, and could, therefore, not affect Dean's right to a fair trial. Note also that (A) and (B) are very similar answers. When it is difficult to distinguish between two or more answers, they are usually all incorrect.

(D) raises an irrelevant issue, the right of confrontation. That right is a trial right, not a right which exists at the sentencing stage. Further, Dean either had a right to confrontation or waived that right at the trials resulting in the convictions.

Question 149

At the trial of Davis for a murder that occurred in Newtown, the prosecution called Waite, who testified that she saw Davis kill the victim. Davis believed that Waite was 600 miles away in Old Town, engaged in the illegal sale of narcotics, on the day in question. On cross-examination by Davis, Waite was asked whether she had in fact sold narcotics in Old Town on that date. Waite refused to answer on the ground of self-incrimination.

The judge, over the prosecutor's objection, ordered that if Waite did not testify, her direct testimony should be stricken. The order to testify or have the testimony stricken can best be supported on the basis that

(A) Waite had not been charged with any crime and, thus, could claim no privilege against self-incrimination.
(B) Waite's proper invocation of the privilege prevented adequate cross-examination.
(C) the public interest in allowing an accused to defend himself or herself outweighs the interest of a nonparty witness in the privilege.
(D) the trial record, independent of testimony, does not establish that Waite's answer could incriminate her.

Answer to Question 149

This question deals with two distinct constitutional principles - the Fifth Amendment privilege against self-incrimination and the Sixth Amendment Confrontation Clause. Both rights are equally important. The privilege against self-incrimination not only permits a person to refuse to testify against herself at a criminal trial in which she is a defendant, but also permits her to refuse to answer any questions which might incriminate her in future criminal proceedings. *Minnesota v. Murphy*, 465 U.S. 420 (1984). Although Waite has not been charged with any crime, her testimony about drug sales might incriminate her in a future proceeding and, therefore, she may claim the privilege. Thus, (A) is incorrect. Invoking the privilege does not require establishing by independent proof that the answer would be incriminating. Thus, (D) is incorrect. All that is required is a reasonable possibility that the statement could be incriminating for a witness to claim the privilege.

On the other hand, the accused's right to confront witnesses has been found to require that the witness's testimony against him be stricken if the witness's invocation of the privilege prevents cross-examination. Since Waite chose to exercise her privilege against self-incrimination, it effectively denied Davis his right to confront her as a witness. If Waite does not testify as to her whereabouts, then her previous testimony must be stricken, because to do otherwise would violate Davis' Sixth Amendment right of confrontation. (B) is correct.

(C) is incorrect because no balancing test is applicable. The conflict between the rights of the parties involved is resolved by striking the witness's testimony.

Question 150

Davis decided to kill Adams. He set out for Adams' house. Before he got there, he saw Brooks, who resembled Adams. Thinking Brooks was Adams, Davis shot at Brooks. The shot missed Brooks but wounded Case, who was some distance away. Davis had not seen Case.

In a prosecution under a statute that proscribes attempt to commit murder, the district attorney should indicate that the intended victim(s) was (were)

(A) Adams only.
(B) Brooks only.
(C) Case only.
(D) Adams and Brooks.

Answer to Question 150

This question tests what is required to constitute an attempt. To answer it, a student must decide if Davis is guilty of attempted murder of Adams, Brooks, and Case.

Davis is not guilty of the attempted murder of Adams. Even though he **intended** to kill Adams, he never got close enough so that his actions constituted an attempt.

Davis is likewise not guilty of the attempted murder of Case, even though he wounded him, because Davis never had any **intent** either to kill or to seriously harm Case. Attempt is a specific intent crime requiring that the defendant intend to commit the specific act that he is charged with attempting to commit. The doctrine of transferred intent does not apply.

Davis is guilty of attempted murder of Brooks even though he was mistaken about Brooks' identity. Davis saw a human being who was in fact Brooks. He shot at that human being **intending** to kill him. That is sufficient for attempt.

Since Davis is guilty of the attempted murder of Brooks, but neither Adams nor Case, (B) is the correct answer.

Question 151

In which of the following situations is Defendant most likely to be guilty of common-law murder?

(A) During an argument in a bar, Norris punches Defendant. Defendant, mistakenly believing that Norris is about to stab him, shoots and kills Norris.
(B) While committing a robbery of a liquor store, Defendant accidentally drops his revolver, which goes off. The bullet strikes and kills Johnson, a customer in the store.
(C) While hunting deer, Defendant notices something moving in the bushes. Believing it to be a deer, Defendant fires into the bushes. The bullet strikes and kills Griggs, another hunter.
(D) In celebration of the Fourth of July, Defendant discharges a pistol within the city limits in violation of a city ordinance. The bullet ricochets off the street and strikes and kills Abbott.

Answer to Question 151

In each of the choices except (A), the death occurs accidentally. (A) is not correct, however, because the defendant believes that the victim is about to kill him. Even if that mistake is reasonable, then the defendant may utilize the defense of self-defense. If that belief is unreasonable, the imperfect self-defense defense will reduce what would otherwise be murder to manslaughter.

(B) is correct. Even though accidental, this is a killing in the course of a felony, and the homicide crime is felony-murder.

(C) is incorrect because the defendant does not intend to kill. At most, his conduct was grossly negligent and he is guilty of voluntary manslaughter.

(D) is incorrect because there is no intention to kill and the conduct does not rise to that level of recklessness required to invoke the depraved heart doctrine.

Question 152

In which of the following situations is Defendant most likely to be guilty of larceny?

(A) Defendant took Sue's television set with the intention of returning it the next day. However, he dropped it and damaged it beyond repair.
(B) Defendant went into Tom's house and took $100 in the belief that Tom had damaged Defendant's car in that amount.
(C) Mistakenly believing that larceny does not include the taking of a dog, Defendant took his neighbor's dog and sold it.
(D) Unreasonably mistaking George's car for his own, Defendant got into George's car in a parking lot and drove it home.

Answer to Question 152

Defendant is unlikely to be convicted of larceny in (A) because at the time he took the television set he had an intention of returning it, and thus did not have an intent to steal. The subsequent destruction of the television set does not affect his criminal liability, because it is the intent at the time the set is taken which is critical. (A) is therefore incorrect.

Defendant is unlikely to be convicted of larceny in (B) because his intent to collect what he honestly believed he was owed negates an intent to steal. (B) is therefore incorrect.

Defendant is likely to be convicted of larceny in (C) because he took the dog with the specific intent of permanently depriving the owner of his property. His mistaken belief that his activity was not criminal is not a defense, and does not negate the required specific intent. In this case, mistake of law is not a defense to larceny, and (C) is correct.

Defendant is unlikely to be convicted of larceny in (D) because his mistake of fact, even though unreasonable, means that he did not form the required specific intent to commit larceny. (D) is therefore incorrect.

Question 153

In which of the following situations is Defendant most likely to be **not guilty** of the charge made?

(A) Police arrested Thief and recovered goods he had stolen. At the direction of the police, Thief took the goods to Defendant. Defendant, believing the goods to be stolen, purchased them. Defendant is charged with attempting to receive stolen property.

(B) Defendant misrepresented his identity to secure a loan from a bank. The banker was not deceived and refused to grant the loan. Defendant is charged with attempting to obtain property by false pretenses.

(C) Believing that state law made it a crime to purchase codeine without a prescription, Defendant purchased, without a prescription, cough syrup containing codeine. Unknown to Defendant, the statute had been repealed and codeine could be legally purchased without a prescription. Defendant is charged with attempting to purchase codeine without a prescription.

(D) Defendant, intending to kill Selma, shot at Selma. Unknown to Defendant, Selma had died of a heart attack minutes before Defendant shot at her. Defendant is charged with attempted murder.

Answer to Question 153

In each case the defendant is charged with an attempt crime. In each case the defendant intended to commit a crime. In each case the commission of the crime was not possible.

(B) is an example of factual impossibility. This type of impossibility is not a defense to the crime of attempt. The crime would have been committed were it not for the action of the bank officer, so this defendant is guilty of attempt. Therefore, (B) is incorrect.

(C) is the best answer because to be guilty of an attempt, the intent must be to commit an act which is a crime. Since purchasing codeine without a prescription is not a crime, there is true legal impossibility here. There can be no *actus reus* despite the most malevolent intent. Therefore, (C) is the best choice and would not even constitute an attempt if the Model Penal Code was in effect.

There is case law which classifies the type of impossibility in (A) as legal impossibility because the goods were not legally stolen at the time the fence, Defendant, purchased them. However, this result has been criticized because the fence thought they were stolen and they once were stolen property. In any event, the result in this case is not as clear as it is in (C), and therefore (A) is not the best answer. (A) would clearly be an attempt under the Model Penal Code definition of impossibility.

It is legally impossible to kill a person who is already dead. Case law has held that there is no crime of attempted murder under the circumstances of (D). However, this result has been criticized because the defendant had the required evil intent and, except for a fact which he did not know, would be guilty. (D) would clearly be an attempt under the Model Penal Code definition of impossibility.

Questions 154 and 155 are based on the following fact situation.

Adams, Bennett, and Curtis are charged in a common law jurisdiction with conspiracy to commit larceny. The state introduced evidence that they agreed to go to Nelson's house to take stock certificates from a safe in Nelson's bedroom, that they went to the house, and that they were arrested as they entered Nelson's bedroom.

Adams testified that he thought the stock certificates belonged to Curtis, that Nelson was improperly keeping them from Curtis, and that he went along to aid in retrieving Curtis' property.

Bennett testified that he suspected Adams and Curtis of being thieves and joined up with them in order to catch them. He also testified that he made an anonymous telephone call to the police alerting them to the crime and that the call caused the police to be waiting for them when they walked into Nelson's bedroom.

Curtis did not testify.

154. If the jury believes Bennett, it should find him

(A) guilty, because there was an agreement and the entry into the bedroom is sufficient for the overt act.
(B) guilty, because he is not a police officer and thus cannot claim any privilege of apprehending criminals.
(C) not guilty, because he did not intend to steal.
(D) not guilty, because he prevented the theft from occurring.

155. If the jury believes both Adams and Bennett, it should find Curtis

(A) guilty, because there was an agreement and the entry into the bedroom is sufficient for the overt act.
(B) guilty, because he intended to steal.
(C) not guilty, because a conviction would penalize him for exercising his right not to be a witness.
(D) not guilty, because Adams and Bennett did not intend to steal.

Answer to Question 154

Bennett never intended to combine with Adams and Curtis for the purpose of committing larceny. He therefore is not guilty of conspiracy. (C) is thus the correct answer.

Bennett would be guilty of conspiracy if, at the time he reached agreement with Adams and Curtis, he intended to steal Nelson's property because, at common law, the crime is complete at that time. If he subsequently prevented the crime from happening and withdrew from the conspiracy, it would not be a defense to the conspiracy crime. (D) is therefore incorrect.

(B) is incorrect because Bennett's testimony indicates that he never intended to combine for an unlawful purpose or to accomplish the purposes of the conspiracy, and he is not relying on any lawman's privilege as a defense in this case.

(A) is incorrect because no overt act is necessary for conspiracy at common law, but an intent to steal must be proven.

Answer to Question 155

If the testimony of Adams and Bennett is believed, neither of them is guilty of conspiracy and Curtis cannot be guilty of *conspiracy* unless he combined with another human being who could be convicted of the crime. Therefore, (D) is correct.

(C) is incorrect because his failure to take the stand is totally irrelevant to the reason Curtis is not guilty, and he is not being penalized for exercising that right.

(B) is incorrect because, even though Curtis intended to steal and could probably be convicted of attempted larceny, he cannot be convicted of conspiracy unless the multiplicity requirement is met.

(A) is incorrect because an overt act is not required for common law conspiracy and because it does not address the lack of multiplicity of persons.

Question 156

Defendant was driving his automobile at a legal speed in a residential zone. A child darted out in front of him and was run over and killed before Defendant could prevent it. Defendant's driver's license had expired three months previously; Defendant had neglected to check when it was due to expire. Driving without a valid license is a misdemeanor in the jurisdiction. On a charge of manslaughter, Defendant should be found

(A) guilty under the misdemeanor-manslaughter rule.
(B) guilty, because the licensing requirements are to protect life, and failure to obey is negligence.
(C) not guilty, because the offense was not the proximate cause of the death.
(D) not guilty, because there was no criminal intent.

Answer to Question 156

For the defendant to be guilty of manslaughter, the death must have occurred in the course of a misdemeanor **malum in se,** or as a result of the criminal negligence or willful, wanton conduct of the defendant.

(A) is an incorrect answer because driving without a license is a misdemeanor **malum prohibitum,** not **malum in se.** There is no moral turpitude involved. This act is criminal only because the legislature has so defined it. This cannot be the basis for a misdemeanor-manslaughter argument.

(B) is incorrect because failure to obey licensing requirements, which are primarily designed to assure a minimum competence of drivers, is not negligence, particularly where the driver was driving nonnegligently.

(C) is the correct answer because the only manslaughter theory which is applicable, namely negligence, must be supported by a causal connection between the negligence and the death, something which does not exist here.

(D) is incorrect because if the misdemeanor-manslaughter theory were applicable, the criminal intent would be inferred from the commission of the misdemeanor.

Question 157

In which of the following cases is a conviction of the named defendant for robbery LEAST likely to be upheld?

(A) Johnson forced his way into a woman's home, bound her, and compelled her to tell him that her jewelry was in an adjoining room. Johnson went to the room, took the jewelry, and fled.
(B) A confederate of Brown pushed a man in order to cause him to lose his balance and drop his briefcase. Brown picked up the briefcase and ran off with it.
(C) Having induced a woman to enter his hotel room, Ritter forced her to telephone her maid to tell the maid to bring certain jewelry to the hotel. Ritter locked the woman in the bathroom while he accepted the jewelry from the maid when she arrived.
(D) Hayes unbuttoned the vest of a man too drunk to notice and removed his wallet. A minute later, the victim missed his wallet and accused Hayes of taking it. Hayes pretended to be insulted, slapped the victim, and went off with the wallet.

Answer to Question 157

The elements of robbery are a larceny from the *person* by violence or intimidation.

All property over which a person has dominion and control is considered to be on her person for purposes of the definition of robbery. In (A), the property in the adjoining room was the subject matter of larceny. Since it was taken through intimidation, there is robbery, and (A) is incorrect.

The violence can be caused by a confederate, and need not put the victim in fear if its purpose is to facilitate the robbery. Therefore, Brown is probably guilty of robbery, and (B) is incorrect.

In (C), the force and intimidation caused the woman to bring the jewelry within her control. When it was taken from the maid, it was constructively taken from the woman's person, and Ritter is guilty of robbery. (C) therefore is incorrect.

In (D), Hayes is guilty of larceny from the person, but not robbery, because he did not employ either violence or intimidation when he took the wallet. The violence which took place after the larceny was completed is not sufficient to cause the crime to be robbery because it did not facilitate the larceny in any way. (D) is therefore correct.

Question 158

Harry met Bill, who was known to him to be a burglar, in a bar. Harry told Bill that he needed money. He promised to pay Bill $500 if Bill would go to Harry's house the following night and take some silverware. Harry explained to Bill that, although the silverware was legally his, his wife would object to his selling it.

Harry pointed out his home, one of a group of similar tract houses. He drew a floor plan of the house that showed the location of the silverware. Harry said that his wife usually took several sleeping pills before retiring, and that he would make sure that she took them the next night. He promised to leave a window unlocked.

Everything went according to the plan except that Bill, deceived by the similarity of the tract houses, went to the wrong house. He found a window unlocked, climbed in and found silver where Harry had indicated. He took the silver to the cocktail lounge where the payoff was to take place. At that point, the police arrested the two men.

Bill's best argument for acquittal of burglary is that he

(A) acted under a mistake of law.
(B) had the consent of the owner.
(C) reasonably thought he was in Harry's house.
(D) found the window unlocked.

Answer to Question 158

Bill would not be guilty of burglary if he had taken the silver from Harry's house. Since burglary is a specific intent crime, his belief that he was in Harry's house prevented him from having the specific intent to commit a crime in the property. His mistake of fact is therefore a defense, and (C) is the correct answer.

Bill's mistake was a factual one - which house was Harry's. It was not a mistake of law. Therefore, (A) is incorrect.

(B) is incorrect because he did not have the consent of the owner of the house into which he broke. This choice can be eliminated because it is not consistent with the facts of the question.

(D) is incorrect because the raising of an unlocked window constitutes a breaking.

Question 159

Defendant was charged with murder. His principal defense was that he had killed in hot blood and should be guilty only of manslaughter. The judge instructed the jury that the state must prove guilt beyond a reasonable doubt, that the killing was presumed to be murder, and that the charge could be reduced to manslaughter (and Defendant accordingly found guilty of this lesser offense) if Defendant showed by a fair preponderance of the evidence that the killing was committed in the heat of passion on sudden provocation. Defendant was convicted of murder. On appeal, he seeks a new trial and claims error in the judge's instructions to the jury.

Defendant's conviction will most probably be

(A) affirmed, because the judge carefully advised the jury of the state's obligation to prove guilt beyond a reasonable doubt.
(B) affirmed, because Defendant's burden to show hot blood was not one of ultimate persuasion but only one of producing evidence to rebut a legitimate presumption.
(C) reversed, because the instruction put a burden on Defendant which denied him due process of law.
(D) reversed, because presumptions have a highly prejudicial effect and thus cannot be used on behalf of the state in a criminal case.

Answer to Question 159

In a criminal case, the state is required to prove all of the essential elements of a crime, including the lack of the mitigating circumstances necessary to reduce murder to manslaughter, beyond a reasonable doubt. In this case, the trial judge placed that burden on the criminal defendant. Therefore, the conviction will be reversed because the defendant was denied a fair trial, which is an essential element of due process. (C) is correct.

(D) is incorrect because presumptions are permissible in criminal cases on behalf of the state as long as there is such a close nexus between the fact that the state must prove and the presumed fact that the proof of the basic fact is likely to lead a factfinder to the presumed fact.

(A) is incorrect because the trial judge did not correctly instruct the jury regarding the obligation of the state to prove each element of the case beyond a reasonable doubt.

(B) is incorrect because, under the Due Process Clause, neither the burden of production nor the burden of persuasion beyond a reasonable doubt can be placed upon the defendant for an essential element of the case.

Note that while *Mullaney v. Wilbur* established the necessity of the state's proving the lack of mitigation necessary to reduce murder to manslaughter, it is constitutionally permissible to require that the defendant go forward with producing evidence of insanity.

Question 160

Two police officers in a squad car received a radio message from headquarters to be on the lookout for a large green sedan occupied by two men who had just committed a bank robbery. An hour later, they saw a car answering this description traveling down a main boulevard leading out of town. They had the car pull to the side of the road and walked over to the car. One of the officers told the occupants that they were under arrest for bank robbery. The same officer observed a brown paper bag on the floor behind the front seat. He opened the rear door and grabbed the paper bag, causing bundles of paper money to spill out into the view of both officers. Thereupon Dean, the driver, suddenly put the car in gear and drove off. One officer clung to the car, partly in and partly out of the vehicle. The other officer pursued in the squad car. Unable to overtake the car and afraid he would lose sight of it in the heavy traffic, the officer fired, first a warning shot, and then at the car. He struck Evans, the passenger sitting next to Dean. At about the same time, Dean, by swerving and suddenly accelerating, succeeded in throwing the officer from the car; the officer fell to the road and was run over and killed by the pursuing squad car.

Dean was caught five minutes later by another squad car, to which the remaining officer had radioed the alarm. Evans died from loss of blood.

Dean was charged with the first degree murder of Evans. Of the following, his strongest argument is

(A) the death of Evans was not murder, but was justifiable homicide.
(B) the death of Evans was not murder, but was excusable homicide.
(C) Dean did not intend to kill Evans.
(D) the officer did not intend to kill Evans, but only arrest him, and thus Dean cannot be convicted of murdering him.

Answer to Question 160

The *Redline* case is the best theory for holding one conspirator not guilty when the police kill the other conspirator. Here, the killing by the police officer was justifiable homicide, since he had the right to use deadly force to stop a felon fleeing from a serious felony. Therefore, (A) is the correct answer.

(B) is incorrect because the death caused by the police officer was a justifiable, not an excusable, homicide.

(C) and (D) are not correct, because intent to kill is not an element in the crime of felony-murder. All that need happen is that the death occur in the course of the felony.

Question 161

Dobbs, while intoxicated, drove his car through a playground crowded with children just to watch the children run to try to get out of his way. His car struck one of the children, killing her instantly.

Which of the following is the best theory for finding Dobbs guilty of murder?

(A) transferred intent
(B) felony murder, with assault with a deadly weapon as the underlying felony
(C) intentional killing, since he knew that the children were there and he deliberately drove his car at them
(D) commission of an act highly dangerous to life, without an intent to kill but with disregard of the consequences

Answer to Question 161

The fact pattern of this question is an excellent example of the application of the abandoned and malignant heart theory of murder. Dobbs did not intend to kill anyone, but his act was highly dangerous and he had no regard for the consequences of his act. (D) is therefore the correct answer.

(C) is incorrect because he neither desired that any child die nor did anything which made the death of any child inevitable.

(B) is incorrect because it is not possible to use the underlying battery as the felony in a felony-murder prosecution.

(A) is incorrect because Dobbs never had the intent to kill one person which could be transferred to another person.

Question 162

Police Officer stopped Dexter for speeding late one night. Noting that Dexter was nervous, he ordered him from the car and placed him under arrest for speeding. By state law, Police Officer was empowered to arrest Dexter and take him to the nearest police station for booking. He searched Dexter's person and discovered a package of heroin in his jacket pocket.

Dexter is charged with possession of heroin. At trial, Dexter's motion to prevent introduction of the heroin into evidence, on the ground that the search violated his federal constitutional rights, will most probably be

(A) denied, because the search was incident to a valid custodial arrest.
(B) denied, because Police Officer acted under both a reasonable suspicion and a legitimate concern for his own personal safety.
(C) granted, because there was no reasonable or proper basis upon which to justify conducting the search.
(D) granted, if the Police Officer was not in fear and had no suspicion that Dexter was transporting narcotics.

Answer to Question 162

A police officer who validly arrests a motorist for a traffic violation has the right to make a full search of the person incident to that arrest. In this case, Police Officer had grounds to arrest and authority to take Dexter into custody. Therefore, the search was incident to a valid arrest, and (A) is correct.

(B) is incorrect because it describes the standard applicable to an investigatory stop, where an officer may stop and frisk, but not make a full search of the person. However, here, Dexter was validly arrested and the officer may conduct a full search. If the pat-down, stop-and-frisk search was all that was authorized, Police Officer would not have been able to open the package and discover the heroin, since the package presented no risk to the officer's safety.

(C) is incorrect because the arrest was a reasonable and proper basis for conducting a search.

(D) is incorrect because the officer need neither be in fear nor have suspicion that narcotics were being transported to search incident to an arrest.

Question 163

Jack and Paul planned to hold up a bank. They drove to the bank in Jack's car. Jack entered while Paul remained as lookout in the car. After a few moments, Paul panicked and drove off.

Jack looked over the various tellers, approached one and whispered nervously, "Just hand over the cash. Don't look around, don't make a false move - or you will die." The teller looked at the fidgeting Jack, laughed, flipped him a dollar bill, and said, "Go on, beat it." Flustered, Jack grabbed the dollar and left.

Soon after leaving the scene, Paul was stopped by the police for speeding. Noting his nervous condition, the police asked Paul if they might search the car. Paul agreed. The search turned up heroin concealed in the lid of the trunk.

Paul's best defense to a charge of robbery would be that

(A) Jack alone entered the bank.
(B) Paul withdrew before commission of the crime when he fled the scene.
(C) Paul had no knowledge of what Jack whispered to the teller.
(D) the teller was not placed in fear by Jack.

Answer to Question 163

Jack and Paul are guilty of conspiracy to rob the bank and have each taken enough affirmative action towards commission of that crime so that the criminal act of one will be imputed to the other. Therefore, Paul's best defense must be based upon facts which would render Jack not guilty of the robbery.

(A) is an incorrect answer because if Jack were guilty of robbery, Paul would be guilty, even though he did not enter the bank.

(B) is incorrect because Paul's withdrawal is not effective, since it was not communicated to Jack.

(C) is incorrect because whatever was whispered to the teller was within the scope of the conspiracy, and if it completed the crime of robbery, Paul would also be guilty.

(D) is the correct answer because Jack is not guilty of robbery unless he commits a larceny through force or violence. If the teller is not put in fear, there is no force aiding in the larceny, and therefore no robbery. If Jack is not guilty of robbery, then Paul is not guilty.

Question 164

Donaldson broke into Professor Ruiz' office in order to look at examination questions. The questions were locked in a drawer, and Donaldson could not find them. Donaldson believed that looking at examination questions was a crime, but in this belief he was mistaken.

Charged with burglary, Donaldson should be

(A) acquitted, because he did not complete the crime and he has not been charged with attempt.
(B) acquitted, because what he intended to do when he broke in was not a crime.
(C) convicted, because he had the necessary mental state and committed the act of breaking and entering.
(D) convicted, because factual impossibility is not a defense.

Answer to Question 164

The crime of burglary requires that the defendant break and enter with the intent to commit a felony or larceny. It is not possible to intend to commit a felony or larceny if the very act one intends to commit is not a crime, even though one thinks that the act intended is a crime. Therefore, Donaldson should be acquitted because he lacked the requisite specific intent, and (B) is correct.

(A) is incorrect because there is no requirement in burglary that the felony or larceny be either attempted or completed, as long as the defendant intended to commit a felony or larceny at the time of breaking and entering.

(C) is incorrect because Donaldson could not have the necessary mental state if the act he intended to commit was not in fact a crime.

(D) is incorrect because there is a difference between factual impossibility, where the act one intends to commit is a crime but the circumstances prevent him from committing it, and where one cannot commit a crime even if he is successful in doing exactly what he intended to do. Factual impossibility is not a defense to a burglary charge, but the fact that the act to be committed after entrance was not a crime defeats a necessary element of the crime.

Questions 165 - 167 are based on the following fact situation.

Brown suffered from the delusion that he was a special agent of God. He frequently experienced hallucinations in the form of hearing divine commands. Brown believed God told him several times that the local Roman Catholic bishop was corrupting the diocese into heresy, and that the bishop should be "done away with." Brown, a devout Catholic, conceived of himself as a religious martyr. He knew that shooting bishops for heresy is against the criminal law. He nevertheless carefully planned how he might kill the bishop. One evening, Brown shot the bishop, who was taken to the hospital where he died two weeks later.

Brown told the police he assumed the institutions of society would support the ecclesiastical hierarchy, and he expected to be persecuted for his God-inspired actions. Psychiatrist Smith examined Brown and found that Brown suffered from schizophrenic psychosis, that in the absence of this psychosis he would not have shot the bishop, and that because of the psychosis Brown found it extremely difficult to determine whether he should obey the specific command that he do away with the bishop or the general commandment, "Thou shalt not kill." Brown was charged with murder.

165. If Brown interposes an insanity defense and the jurisdiction in which he is tried has adopted only the *M'Naghten* test of insanity, then the strongest argument for the defense under that test is that

(A) Brown did not know the nature of the act he was performing.
(B) Brown did not know that his act was morally wrong.
(C) Brown did not know the quality of the act he was performing.
(D) Brown's acts were the product of a mental disease.

166. If Brown interposes an insanity defense and is tried in a jurisdiction which has also adopted the so-called "irresistible impulse" test of insanity, then, with respect to that part of the test, it is most likely that the jury will be instructed that for the defense to prevail, it must appear that the

(A) defendant lacked both cognition and control.
(B) defendant lacked the capacity for self-control and free choice.
(C) killing was an impulsive act which was not planned in advance.
(D) killing was the product of the defendant's psychosis.

167. Brown is **LEAST** likely to be found to have been the legal cause of the bishop's death if the evidence shows that, after the bishop was taken to the hospital,

(A) prompt medical attention would have saved his life, but no doctor was then on duty in the emergency room.
(B) he would not have died except for the negligent medical treatment given by the doctor in the emergency room.
(C) he contracted a rare disease from another patient and died from the disease.
(D) an earthquake destroyed the wing of the hospital in which the bishop was lying, killing the bishop instantly.

Answer to Question 165

This question requires a thorough knowledge of the *M'Naghten* test of insanity.

(B) is correct. The *M'Naghten* test is two-pronged. First, as a result of a mental disease or defect, did the defendant know of the nature and quality of his act; and second, if he did know its nature and quality, did he know that his act was wrong? The fact pattern clearly indicates that the defendant did know that he was killing another human being, but there is a good factual question of whether he knew his act was morally wrong.

(A) is incorrect. Brown realized that he was killing someone and therefore knew the nature of his act.

(C) is incorrect. Brown recognized that his act would result in the taking of the life of another person and therefore he knew the quality of his act.

(D) is incorrect. Whether the defendant's act was the product of a mental disease is not the *M'Naghten* test, but rather is the *Durham* test.

Answer to Question 166

This question requires a knowledge of the "irresistible impulse" test of insanity.

(A) is incorrect. The concept of cognition - the defendant's knowledge - is not involved in the irresistible impulse test.

(B) is correct. The irresistible impulse test looks at the defendant's ability to control himself and freely choose whether or not to commit the act.

(C) is incorrect. That the act was not premeditated is not probative of whether or not Brown was able to control the impulse to kill, but rather deals with the degree of murder.

(D) is incorrect. This answer applies the *Durham* test and not the "irresistible impulse" test.

Answer to Question 167

This question requires a knowledge of proximate and intervening cause. Proximate cause is the legal conclusion that the defendant's actions were connected closely to the crime and that he is therefore legally responsible. An intervening cause, one which is operative between the time of the defendant's actions and the harm to the victim, can in some cases relieve the defendant of criminal liability by preventing his act from being the "proximate" cause.

(A) is incorrect. That prompt medical attention might not be available is a foreseeable circumstance and is within the risk of the harm caused by Brown; hence, it is not an independent intervening cause that would relieve Brown of liability for the killing.

(B) is incorrect. Again, the negligence of the doctor is foreseeable and is within the risk of the harm caused by Brown.

(C) is incorrect. The possibility that the bishop would contract a fatal disease while in the hospital is within the realm of foreseeability.

(D) is correct. Even though the bishop would not have been in the hospital without Brown's act, the earthquake was an unforeseeable independent intervening cause of the bishop's death.

Question 168

In which of the following situations is Defendant most likely to be guilty of common-law murder?

(A) Angered because his neighbor is having a noisy party, Defendant fires a rifle into the neighbor's house. The bullet strikes and kills a guest at the party.

(B) During an argument, Harry slaps Defendant. Angered, Defendant responds by shooting and killing Harry.

(C) Defendant drives his car through a red light and strikes and kills a pedestrian who is crossing the street.

(D) Using his fist, Defendant punches Walter in the face. As a result of the blow, Walter falls and hits his head on a concrete curb, suffers a concussion, and dies.

Answer to Question 168

Defendant in each case has caused the death of another human being. Murder occurs when that killing is accomplished with malice.

Defendant is not guilty of murder in (D) because he did not intend to kill Walter nor did he intend to inflict serious bodily harm. The fatal blow occurred because Walter hit his head on the concrete curb, an event not foreseen by

Defendant. (D) is therefore not the best answer and is incorrect.

The necessary malice is not present in (C). While Defendant may have been reckless, the conduct was not intentional and did not so far depart from the standard of care as to constitute the equivalent of malice. Therefore, (C) is incorrect.

In (B), Defendant intentionally killed Harry. However, Harry had slapped Defendant and caused him to be angry just before the shooting. This may be sufficient provocation to reduce the crime to voluntary manslaughter instead of murder. Therefore, (B) is not the best answer and is incorrect.

Even though Defendant did not intend to kill a guest at the party in (A), his action in firing a rifle through a wall into a room full of people was such a departure from the standard of care and carried with it such a high risk that it would cause death that he is deemed to have possessed the appropriate malice under the abandoned and malignant heart doctrine, and is guilty of murder. Therefore, (A) is the correct answer.

Questions 169-171 are based on the following fact situation.

Defendant became intoxicated at a bar. He got into his car and drove away. Within a few blocks, craving another drink, he stopped his car in the middle of the street, picked up a brick, and broke the display window of a liquor store. As he was reaching for a bottle, the night watchman arrived. Startled, Defendant turned, struck the watchman on the head with the bottle, killing him. Only vaguely aware of what was happening, Defendant returned to his car, consumed more liquor, and then drove off at a high speed. He ran a red light and struck and killed a pedestrian who was crossing the street.

Relevant statutes define burglary to include "breaking and entering a building not used as a dwelling with the intent to commit a crime therein." Manslaughter is defined as the "killing of a human being in a criminally reckless manner." Criminal recklessness is "consciously disregarding a substantial and unjustifiable risk resulting from the actor's conduct." Murder is defined as "the premeditated and intentional killing of another or the killing of another in the commission of rape, robbery, burglary, or arson." Another statute provides that intoxication is not a defense to a crime unless it negates an element of the offense.

Defendant was charged with the murder of the watchman and manslaughter in the death of the pedestrian. Assume that he is tried separately on each charge.

169. At Defendant's trial for the murder of the watchman, the court should charge the jury on the issue of the defense of intoxication that

(A) intoxication is a defense to the underlying crime of burglary if Defendant, due to drunkenness, did not form an intent to commit a crime within the building, in which case there can be no conviction for murder unless Defendant intentionally and with premeditation killed the watchman.

(B) voluntary intoxication is no defense to the crime of murder.

(C) Defendant is guilty of murder despite his intoxication only if the state proves beyond a reasonable doubt that the killing of the watchman was premeditated and intentional.

(D) voluntary intoxication is a defense to the crime of murder if Defendant would not have killed the watchman but for his intoxication.

170. At Defendant's trial on the charge of manslaughter in the death of the pedestrian, his best argument would be that

(A) he was too intoxicated to realize he was creating a substantial and unjustifiable risk in the manner in which he was operating his car.

(B) when he got in the car his acts were not voluntary because he was too intoxicated to know where he was or what he was doing.

(C) the pedestrian was contributorily negligent in failing to see Defendant's car approaching.
(D) he was too intoxicated to form any intent to voluntarily operate the automobile.

171. The state's best argument to counter Defendant's argument that intoxication prevented him from realizing that his driving created a substantial and unjustifiable risk to the pedestrian, if he is charged in the manslaughter death of the pedestrian, is that

(A) intoxication is no defense to the crime charged, because manslaughter is historically a general intent crime.
(B) intoxication is a defense only to a specific intent crime, and no specific intent is involved in the definition of the crime of manslaughter.
(C) conscious risk-taking refers to the Defendant's entire course of conduct, including drinking with the knowledge that he might become intoxicated and seriously injure or kill someone while driving.
(D) whether Defendant was intoxicated or not is not the crucial issue here; the real issue is whether the manner in which Defendant was operating his car can be characterized under the facts as criminally reckless.

Answer to Question 169

For the defendant to be guilty of murder, he must have either engaged in an intentional killing or a killing in the course of a burglary. Burglary is a specific intent crime. To commit burglary, the defendant had to have the intent to commit the crime of larceny. Drunkenness can prevent him from having that specific intent. If he does not have it, he is not in the commission of the crime of burglary, and cannot be guilty of felony-murder. However, he still might have formed a premeditated intent to kill the watchman, in which case he would be guilty of murder despite his drunkenness. (A) is therefore correct.

(B) is incorrect because drunkenness could negate the specific intent necessary for the underlying felony, and thus be a defense to felony murder. It might also prevent the defendant from having a premeditated intent to kill.

(C) is incorrect because it says that defendant is guilty of murder **only** if the state proves a premeditated intent to kill. This choice leaves out the possibility of felony-murder if the defendant did intend to steal the liquor.

(D) is incorrect because a defendant who becomes voluntarily intoxicated is responsible for his actions while in that state, and cannot avoid criminal responsibility merely because he would not have committed the crime if he were sober.

Answer to Question 170

The statute in this question defines manslaughter as the killing of a human being in a criminally reckless manner, and criminal recklessness as "consciously disregarding a substantial and justifiable risk resulting from the actor's conduct." When the question quotes a statute and asks for the best defense, the answer usually is that the defendant has not violated some element of the statute. The defendant is engaged in reckless conduct as that term is defined if he **consciously** disregards the risk. If drunkenness prevented him from realizing the risk, he has an argument that he did not consciously disregard it, and (A) is the correct answer.

(B) is incorrect because it does not deal with the statutory standard, and his acts were in fact voluntary in the sense that they were not accomplished by an overpowering force.

(C) is incorrect because contributory negligence of the victim is not a defense to manslaughter.

(D) is incorrect because it does not deal with the statutory standard of conscious risk-taking, and factually is not true because he clearly had the intent to operate the car.

Answer to Question 171

The specific intent required for manslaughter is defined in the statute. A state of mind that is criminally reckless is required. Therefore, (A) and (B) are incorrect because a specific intent is required. If manslaughter were a general intent crime, it would not be possible to choose intelligently between (A) and (B).

(D) is incorrect because the issue of recklessness turns on whether the defendant **consciously** disregarded a risk. Intoxication can be relevant on that issue.

(C) is the correct answer because conscious risk-taking can be expanded to the choice of getting drunk, knowing that his conduct is likely to depart seriously from the standard of care when he is drunk.

Question 172

Defendant is charged with assault and battery. The state's evidence shows that Victim was struck in the face by Defendant's fist. In which of the following situations is Defendant most likely to be **not guilty** of assault and battery?

(A) Defendant had been hypnotized at a party and ordered by the hypnotist to strike the person he disliked the most.
(B) Defendant was suffering from an epileptic seizure and had no control over his motions.
(C) Defendant was heavily intoxicated and was shadow boxing without realizing that Victim was near him.
(D) Defendant, who had just awakened from a deep sleep, was not fully aware of what was happening and mistakenly thought Victim was attacking him.

Answer to Question 172

An individual who voluntarily loses his ability to control his actions cannot use that loss of ability as an excuse when charged with criminal conduct. Therefore, since assault and battery are general intent crimes, the voluntary act of submitting to hypnotism will not relieve the defendant of liability for criminal acts committed while hypnotized. Therefore, (A) is incorrect.

(C) is incorrect for the same reason. Voluntary intoxication which induces an unreasonable mistake of fact is not a defense to a general intent crime.

In (D), the defendant might have the defense of self-defense if his belief was reasonable. The facts do not tell us whether they were reasonable or not. Therefore, (D) is incorrect because it is not as clear-cut a case as (B).

In (B), the defendant had no intent to strike Victim, and did not voluntarily put himself in the position that caused the disease. Since his action was not voluntary, there is no *mens rea* and therefore no crime.

Question 173

Statutes in the jurisdiction define criminal assault as "an attempt to commit a criminal battery" and criminal battery as "causing an offensive touching."

As Edward was walking down the street, a gust of wind blew his hat off. Edward reached out, trying to grab his hat, and narrowly missed striking Margaret in the face with his hand. Margaret, fearful of being struck by Edward, pushed Edward away.

If charged with criminal battery, Margaret should be found

(A) guilty, because she intentionally pushed Edward.
(B) guilty, because she caused the touching of Edward whether she meant to do so or not.
(C) not guilty, because a push is not an offensive touching.
(D) not guilty, because she was justified in pushing Edward.

Answer to Question 173

Margaret intentionally pushed Edward. Such a push was not consented to and was probably offensive. However, since his hands were threatening her, she had the right of self-defense. She exercised that right in a reasonable manner. Therefore, her push was justified, and (D) is correct.

(C) is incorrect because a push is often an offensive touching. Unless justified, it could be the basis of a battery.

(A) correctly states that she intentionally touched Edward, but is incorrect because no crime of battery is committed where that touching is justified by the doctrine of self-defense.

(B) is incorrect because she did intend to touch him and because the touching is not a crime if the touching is justified.

Question 174

Alford was a suspect in a homicide committed during a robbery of a liquor store. Barber was a friend of Alford. Police telephoned Barber and asked if he would help locate Alford. Barber agreed and met the police officers at headquarters later that night.

After a discussion during which police asked questions about Alford and the homicide, Barber said that he wanted to get something "off his chest" and advised the officers that he was in on the robbery but that Alford had shot the owner of the store without his permission or prior knowledge. The officers then for the first time gave Barber his *Miranda* warnings.

Barber was indicted for felony-murder. He moved to prevent the introduction of his statement into evidence. His motion should be

(A) granted, because Barber was effectively in custody and entitled to receive *Miranda* warnings at the beginning of the discussion.
(B) granted, because Barber's rights to counsel and to due process were violated by the interrogation at police headquarters.
(C) denied, because his statement was freely and voluntarily given and he was not entitled to *Miranda* warnings.
(D) denied, because by visiting headquarters voluntarily, Barber waived his right to have *Miranda* warnings at the beginning of the discussion.

Answer to Question 174

For *Miranda* to apply, custodial interrogation is necessary. While it is arguable that Barber was effectively in custody while at police headquarters, the statement made by Barber was not the product of interrogation, but was freely given. Barber may not have realized that his statement would incriminate him in the crime of felony murder, but that does not make the statement inadmissible. (C) is therefore the correct answer.

(D) is incorrect because Barber would have possessed *Miranda* rights as soon as he was in custody and was interrogated. Merely visiting police headquarters does not mean that he was not in custody and not under interrogation. It also does not mean that he **waived** his *Miranda* rights.

(A) is incorrect because it only contains half of the requirements for the applicability of *Miranda*. Even if he was in custody, the statement was volunteered and not the product of interrogation.

(B) is incorrect because a defendant can waive his right to counsel and answer questions. There is no violation of the right to counsel if a person volunteers a statement before any *Miranda* warnings must be given.

Questions 175 and 176 are based on the following fact situation.

While Defendant was in jail on a procuring charge, his landlord called the police because rent had not been paid and because he detected a disagreeable odor coming from Defendant's apartment into the hallways. The police officer who responded to the call knew that Defendant was in jail. He recognized the stench coming from Defendant's apartment as that of decomposing flesh, and without waiting to obtain a warrant, entered the apartment with the landlord's consent and passkey. The lease to these premises gave the landlord a right of entry, at any reasonable hour, for the purposes of making repairs. The police officer found a large trunk in the bedroom which seemed to be the source of the odor. Upon breaking it open, he found the remains of Marzipan, Defendant's former mistress.

175. The landlord's consent to the police officer's search of Defendant's apartment is

(A) a waiver of Defendant's Fourth Amendment rights, because a landlord has implied consent to enter a tenant's apartment.

(B) a waiver of Defendant's Fourth Amendment rights, because the lease gave the landlord express authority to enter the premises.

(C) not a waiver of Defendant's Fourth Amendment rights, because the landlord lacked probable cause to believe a crime was then in the process of commission.

(D) not a waiver of Defendant's Fourth Amendment rights, because the landlord had neither actual nor apparent authority to permit the entry.

176. If Defendant undertakes to challenge the search of his apartment, he has

(A) standing, because the items seized in the search were incriminating in nature.

(B) standing, because he still has a sufficient interest in the apartment even while in jail.

(C) no standing, because his landlord authorized the search.

(D) no standing, because he was out of the apartment when it occurred and had not paid his rent.

Answer to Question 175

(A) is incorrect because, absent an agreement between the landlord and tenant, a landlord does not have implied consent to enter a tenant's apartment.

(B) is incorrect because the lease specifically says that the landlord has a right to enter at any reasonable hour, but only for the purpose of making repairs. The lease does not permit the landlord to allow entry for a police search.

(C) is incorrect because probable cause does not determine whether or not the landlord has the right to enter. The issue is whether the landlord-tenant relationship gave the landlord the right to enter. The police might have a right to enter on an emergency basis if they had such probable cause, but not the landlord.

The correct answer, (D), deals with the landlord's authority to allow entry. The landlord's consent is not a waiver of Defendant's Fourth Amendment rights because the landlord had neither actual nor apparent authority to let a police officer enter the apartment. Therefore, there is no consent attributed to Defendant as a result of the landlord's consent, and there is no waiver of his Fourth Amendment rights.

Answer to Question 176

(B) is the correct answer because the fact that Defendant is in jail does not abrogate his right to exclusive possession of the apartment. This right to exclude all others exists for the full term of the lease; it is not diminished by his absence. Therefore, he has standing to challenge the search.

(A) is incorrect because it does not matter whether the items found were incriminating. Defendant's standing is derived from his right to exclusive possession, not from the nature of the items found.

(C) is incorrect because the landlord had no right to authorize a search.

(D) is incorrect because the landlord had not legally evicted Defendant from the apartment. Therefore, the right to possession remained in Defendant, even though he had not paid his rent. It is the right to possession, not actual physical possession, that is determinative.

Question 177

On a foggy night, Vera was clubbed from behind by a man wielding a blackjack. Damon was arrested in the vicinity shortly thereafter. As they were booking Damon, the police took his photograph. They promptly showed that photograph, along with the photographs of seven people who have the same general features as Damon, to Vera. Vera identified Damon as the culprit.

At trial, Damon objects to the introduction into evidence of his out-of-court identification. His objection should be

(A) sustained, because Vera did not have a good opportunity to observe the culprit.
(B) sustained, because Damon was not represented by counsel at the showing of the photographs to Vera.
(C) sustained, because the action of the police in showing the photographs to Vera was unnecessarily suggestive.
(D) denied.

Answer to Question 177

Under *Manson v. Braithwaite,* the only time an out-of-court identification by a witness at a trial is inadmissible under a constitutional due process standard is when the pre-trial identification is both suggestive and unnecessary. The pre-trial identification in this case was not suggestive because the persons in the photos had the same general features as the defendant. The identification was necessary so that the police could ascertain that they had captured the criminal and could abandon their search. Therefore, the objection to the out-of-court identification should be denied, and (D) is correct.

(C) is incorrect because it is factually wrong. The defendant's photo was shown with seven other photos of persons who had the same general features.

(B) is incorrect because counsel need only be present when there is a **post-indictment** line-up. This activity occurred before any indictment.

(A) is incorrect because the issue of the witness's opportunity to observe relates to the evidentiary weight to be given the identification by the factfinder. It is not relevant at this stage, unless it indicates that the line-up was suggestive.

Questions 178 and 179 are based on the four case summaries below. For each question, select the case that would be most applicable as a precedent.

(A) Defendant hit a fellow worker on the head with an iron crowbar, crushing his skull. Although Defendant testified he did not intend to kill, his conviction of murder was affirmed.

(B) Defendant and Doaks held up a bank and tried to escape in their car. Shots from pursuing police disabled the car, and Defendant was captured. Doaks fled on foot, commandeered a passing car, and at gunpoint, forced the driver to drive off. A chase extending over 20 miles followed. In an exchange of shots, a policeman was killed and Doaks escaped. Defendant's conviction of murder was affirmed.

(C) Smythe owed Defendant $500. Impatient at Smythe's failure to pay, Defendant went to Smythe's home. He demanded payment, brandished a revolver, and threatened to shoot Smythe if he did not pay up. All this occurred in the presence of Smythe's aged aunt, who as a result of the excitement, died of heart failure on the spot. Defendant's conviction of manslaughter was affirmed.

(D) Defendant saw his wife and Ares go into the woods under circumstances which made him suspect adultery. While following them after they came out of the woods, Defendant was told by Brent that he [Brent] had seen them commit adultery the day before. Defendant got a rifle and shot Ares dead. Defendant's conviction of murder was reversed, as the evidence showed guilt only of manslaughter.

178. Policeman undertook to arrest Fan for throwing a pop bottle and hitting a baseball umpire. Fan was innocent and indignantly objected to being arrested.

Since Policeman had no warrant, the arrest was illegal. Fan, forcibly resisting Policeman, finally succeeded in seizing Policeman's revolver and shot him dead.

179. Policeman, having a warrant for Defendant's arrest for a felonious assault, went to his home to arrest him. Defendant, however, resisted, and during the ensuing struggle, stabbed Policeman fatally with a butcher knife.

Answer to Question 178

Fan was the victim of an unlawful arrest, but the killing of the police officer was voluntary manslaughter on one of two theories. The better theory is that Fan had the right to use reasonable (probably nondeadly) force to defend himself from the assault and battery committed by the police officer. Fan's use of excessive force in self-defense did not constitute murder because there was a right of limited self-defense, but it is voluntary manslaughter because the force used was excessive. The other theory is that the unlawful battery committed by the police officer was sufficient provocation to reduce the intentional killing to voluntary manslaughter. Therefore, (D) is the most appropriate precedent.

Answer to Question 179

Since the police officer here had a warrant for defendant's arrest, the defendant had no right to resist that arrest, and any battery inflicted by the officer did not give a right to self-defense. Nor could there be the provocation which would reduce murder to manslaughter. Therefore, the use of a deadly weapon raises an inference of intention to kill or do great bodily harm, both of which are sufficient *mens rea* for murder. Therefore, (A) is the most appropriate precedent

PROPERTY QUESTIONS

Question 1

Owen deeded Blackacre "to Alan and his heirs, but if Alan dies survived by Wife and Child, then upon Alan's death to Wife for life and remainder to Child; and if Alan dies survived by Wife only and not Child, then the property shall revert to the grantor."

Shortly thereafter, Owen by a second deed conveyed any interest he might have in Blackacre to Alan. Alan died, survived by Wife and not Child and willed Blackacre to Wife.

In a contest over Blackacre between Wife and Owen,

(A) Owen will prevail because all that Alan had was a life estate.
(B) Owen will prevail because his interest in the property is inalienable.
(C) Wife will prevail because deed #1 was an invalid attempt to restrain the disposition of property by will.
(D) Wife will prevail because the second deed conveyed the interest of Owen in the property to Alan.

Answer to Question 1

(A) is incorrect. Alan's interest in the property is a fee simple subject to a condition subsequent, not a life estate. In addition, Alan received, by the second deed, Owen's right of entry. By combining the terms of the original conveyance with the second deed we can see that if Alan died survived by Child only or neither Wife nor Child, Alan's estate would become a fee simple absolute.

(B) is incorrect. Even in a jurisdiction where Owen's right of entry is inalienable, it is at least releasable to the present possessor of the property, Alan.

(C) is incorrect. It is not against public policy for an owner to control the disposition of granted property by granting one grantee a partial interest in the property and a second grantee another partial interest. Well established property interests such as life estates and remainders have long been used to accomplish such objectives.

(D) is correct. The second deed conveys the critical interest, namely Owen's right of entry for condition broken. After the first conveyance, Owen owned a right of entry for condition broken if Alan died survived by Wife but not by Child. Such a right can at least be released to the present possessor of the property, even if it is inalienable under the laws of this particular jurisdiction. Therefore, the second deed was at least a release of the grantor's right of entry for condition broken. Since the grantor released his right of entry for condition broken to the grantee, and since Child, the only other person to hold an interest, is not alive, the grantee now holds a fee simple interest. The grantee therefore can dispose of the property by will, and Wife will prevail.

Question 2

In 1940 O, who had good title in fee simple absolute, conveyed Blackacre "to A, for so long as alcoholic beverages are not served upon the premises." O is still alive and alcoholic beverages have not been served upon the premises. A has entered into a contract to sell the property to B. After examination of title, B refuses to purchase the property, alleging that as a result of the 1940 conveyance, A does not have marketable title. If A brings suit for specific performance,

(A) A will prevail because O's interest is void under the Rule Against Perpetuities.
(B) A will prevail because O's interest in the property does not destroy the marketability of title.
(C) B will prevail because O has a valid possibility of reverter.
(D) B will prevail because O has a valid right of entry.

Answer to Question 2

(A) is incorrect because the Rule Against Perpetuities does not apply to interests held by the grantor, including possibilities of reverter. Therefore, O's future interest is valid even though it might not vest within lives in being plus 21 years.

In order to have marketable title, the seller must be able to convey a fee simple absolute. In this case, A has only a fee simple determinable. O retains a valid possibility of reverter. Therefore, A cannot convey a fee simple absolute unless O joins in the conveyance. O's future interest destroys the marketability of A's title. Therefore, (B) is incorrect.

While choice (D) correctly states that B will prevail, it is incorrect because it incorrectly names the interest which O possesses. In this case, since A's interest is a fee simple determinable, rather than a fee simple subject to a condition subsequent, the appropriate reversionary interest in O is a possibility of reverter, not a right of entry for condition broken.

The grantor in this case possesses a valid possibility of reverter, because the prior estate created by the instrument was a fee simple determinable, not a fee simple subject to a condition subsequent. The words used were "so long as" instead of "but if." Such a grant creates a fee simple determinable and the grantor's interest following a fee simple determinable is a possibility of reverter, not a right of entry. (C) is the correct answer.

Question 3

Peter deeded Blackacre to the Episcopal Diocese "so long as the premises are used for church purposes." As a result of gold strikes in the area, a group of parishioners started to dig in the church basement and fortunately struck a rich vein. The church has mined the gold on a regular basis and used the proceeds of its sale for church charities. Peter has brought suit against the church to enjoin the church's activity in mining gold. Which of the following is the strongest argument for the church?

(A) Peter has no interest in the property.
(B) The church has a fee interest, even though it is not a fee simple absolute interest.
(C) The church is performing a useful economic function because the gold will help with the U.S. balance of payments.
(D) Courts should be reluctant to enforce a forfeiture against a charity.

Answer to Question 3

(A) is incorrect. Peter has created a fee simple determinable in the Episcopal Diocese. This is not a complete disposition of the property, since it did not convey the rights to the property in the event that it is not used for church purposes. That interest is retained in the grantor as a possibility of reverter which is valid because it is not subject to the Rule Against Perpetuities.

(C) is incorrect. The answers to questions on the Multistate Bar Examination are rarely determined by broad policy issues, such as the economic value of the activity conducted on property here. Instead, you should look to the application of the appropriate substantive rules to the facts presented. Here, there is a strong argument that the terms of the condition have not been violated.

(D) is incorrect. The charitable status of a church would not prevent a forfeiture if the church were in breach of the condition. Here, however, the covenant has not been breached.

(B) is correct. The condition on which the Diocese holds the property is that it be "used for church purposes." Note that it does not say "and for no other purpose." In this case, the church's interest remains vested so long as the premises are used for church purposes, even if some of the land is also used for other purposes. Thus, the church continues to hold a fee simple (albeit a fee simple determinable). As the holder of a fee, the church cannot be held liable for waste as it would be if it only had a life estate. Therefore, because the church has a fee interest, Peter has no right to take the property or prohibit the church from mining.

Question 4

Black was the owner of a 100-acre parcel of land near the Twinbrook nuclear power plant. At the time the plant was built in 1960, Black sold a 10-acre strip of land known as Greenacre, which was located in the middle of that parcel, to the Edison Electric Company, the owner of the plant, so that the Company could erect a transmission line across Blackacre. The deed contained the following language.

"To the Edison Electric Company, its successors and assigns, so long as the premises are used for the transmission of electricity."

In 1995, a routine inspection of the plant by the Nuclear Regulatory Commission found serious deterioration of the plant. The Commission ordered the plant decommissioned and closed permanently. The transmission lines from the plant were dismantled.

Because there was a substantial amount of radioactive waste stored on the site, the state took all land within one-half mile of the plant site, including Greenacre, by eminent domain.

Is Edison Electric Company entitled to any compensation for the taking of any interest it has in Greenacre?

(A) No, because Black's possibility of reverter is possessory.
(B) No, because an easement holder is not entitled to compensation in an eminent domain proceeding.
(C) Yes, because Edison may again use the premises for electrical transmission purposes.
(D) Yes, because the holder of an easement is entitled to compensation for the value of the lost easement right.

Answer to Question 4

The interest held by Edison was a fee simple determinable. The language of the condition clearly implies a reasonable continuity of use of the property for electric transmission purposes. The permanent closing of the plant and the removal of the transmission lines caused Black's possibility of reverter to become possessory. Therefore, Edison had no estate and no compensable interest. Black is now the owner of the property and entitled to the compensation to be awarded from the state. Therefore, (A) is correct and (C) is incorrect.

The facts specifically state that the property was "sold" to Edison. Since the grant was not drafted in terms of mere use of the property, Edison obtained a fee simple determinable interest in the property, not an easement interest. Thus, (D) is incorrect. Moreover, as a matter of law, an easement holder **is** entitled to compensation if there is a taking of the property by eminent domain. Thus, (B) is incorrect on both the facts and the law.

Question 5

Able conveyed Blackacre to Baker for life, then to the heirs of Charlie (a living person). The interest in the heirs of Charlie can be characterized as

(A) a contingent remainder before the death of Baker, because the heirs of Charlie must survive Baker in order to take Blackacre.
(B) a springing use if Charlie dies before Baker.
(C) a vested remainder if Baker dies before Charlie.
(D) a contingent remainder before the death of Charlie because those who will take have not been ascertained.

Answer to Question 5

Although (A) correctly states that Charlie's heirs hold a contingent remainder, the interest is contingent because the heirs of Charlie cannot be ascertained until Charlie dies. Therefore, the choice does not correctly state why the interest is contingent. The heirs of Charlie need not survive Baker in order to take an interest; they need only survive Charlie - at that point, their interests vest. If an heir of Charlie survives Charlie, but predeceases Baker, the heir's interest will pass to the heir's estate.

(B) is incorrect. A springing use is a form of executory interest which occurs when there is a gap between the time when a present possessory interest ends and the future interest becomes possessory. For example, in this case, if Baker died before Charlie, there would be no heirs of Charlie at that time because heirs are not ascertained until death. Therefore, the interest would revert to the grantor until Charlie dies and his heirs are ascertained, at which time the interest would "spring" from the grantor to the heirs. This choice is incorrect because there is no gap if Charlie dies before Baker, because Charlie's heirs would be ascertained at Charlie's death and would be able to take in possession at Baker's death.

(C) is incorrect. The interest in the "heirs" of Charlie will not vest until Charlie's death, because they are unascertained until that time. If Baker predeceases Charlie, the contingent remainder which is held by the descendants of Charlie will be transformed into a springing executory interest which will become possessory at the death of Charlie. Therefore, the interest in the heirs of Charlie does not vest at Baker's death because the interest is not contingent on those persons surviving Baker. Rather, the interest is contingent until those persons survive Charlie.

(D) is correct. The interest in Charlie's heirs is contingent until Charlie's death because, until Charlie's death, his heirs cannot be determined. Charlie's relatives must survive Charlie in order to be considered his heirs. Thus, survival past Charlie's death is a condition precedent to the vesting of this interest.

Questions 6 and 7 are based on the following fact situation.

O, in his will, specifically devised Blackacre "to A for life, and then to the children of B and their heirs." At O's death, C, the only child of B, was alive but C predeceased A, dying intestate. B survived A and is capable of having children.

6. The interest of the heirs of C after O's death, but before A's death, could best be described as

(A) a contingent remainder.
(B) a vested remainder.
(C) an executory interest.
(D) a vested remainder subject to open.

7. If, at A's death, B is still alive, who is entitled to possession of Blackacre?

(A) the residuary beneficiaries of O's estate
(B) C's heirs and any additional children of B, whenever born
(C) C's heirs
(D) C's heirs and any additional children of B born before the death of A

Answer to Question 6

(A) is incorrect. At O's death, C had a vested remainder in Blackacre because he was ascertained and there was no condition precedent (such as survivorship) to his taking. (Note that the grant was to the "children" of B, not the "heirs" of B, and not the "surviving children" of B.)

There are two forms of executory interests. The first form, a shifting use, follows immediately upon a qualified fee simple. Since the prior estate in this question is a life estate, that type of executory interest is not present here. The other form of executory interest, a springing use, is one which is not ready to take upon the termination of the preceding estate. Since C's heirs would be ready to take upon A's death, that type of executory interest is not present either, and (C) is incorrect.

This grant creates a life estate in A and a remainder in fee simple in a class defined as "the children of B and their heirs." The interest of each child of B vests at O's death (or at the child's birth if born after O's death). C's death does not divest the interest in C; the interest passes to C's heirs, since C died intestate. However, since B is still alive, the interest in C's heirs is a vested remainder subject to open, since B could still have other children who would share in the gift. Therefore, (B) is incorrect. (D) is the correct answer. The class will not close until either the death of B (as a practical matter) or the death of A, if someone's interest is already vested and possessory (under the rule of convenience).

Answer to Question 7

(A) is incorrect. O's estate would take Blackacre only if no one were capable of taking Blackacre after the life estate. For that to occur, the remainder interest in B's children would have had to fail completely, which could only happen if B died and never had any children. In this case, C was a child of B and C's heirs can legally take possession, so O's reversionary interest is defeated.

This grant creates a life estate in A and a remainder in fee simple in a class defined as "the children of B and their heirs." (C) is incorrect because it fails to recognize that the gift is a class gift, where the class does not close until the death of either A or B. Any children born to B before the death of A will share in the gift with C's heirs. B has not died yet, so this class will not close for the first reason. However, since there is no precondition that a child of B survive A (or B or O, for that matter), the interest of a child of B vests and becomes legally capable of possession at its birth. Thus, C's interest vested at C's birth. At the death of A, C's heirs can go into possession. Therefore, the class closes at A's death. Therefore, (B) is incorrect. Only C's heirs and any other children born to B before A's death will share in the gift. The rule of convenience with respect to the closing of the class is only a rule of presumed intention. However, there is nothing in the question to indicate that the testator (O) intended to include all of B's children, whenever born, in the gift. (D) is the correct answer.

Question 8

Oscar conveyed Blackacre to Able for life, then to Baker and his heirs. Baker died before Able, survived by Charlie as his heir. Baker left a will devising his interest in Blackacre to Doug. At the death of Able, who is entitled to possession of Blackacre?

(A) Oscar, because Baker's contingent remainder terminated when he failed to survive Able.
(B) Charlie, because Baker's interest devolves to his heirs.
(C) Charlie, because he has an alternative contingent remainder which became vested at the death of Baker.
(D) Doug, because Baker had a vested remainder.

Answer to Question 8

(A) is incorrect. Baker's remainder is not contingent, because there is no express condition of survivorship for his interest to become effective, nor is such a condition implied merely because there is a remainder interest in a named individual following a life estate. Baker's vested remainder becomes possessory at the end of Able's life, even if Baker is no longer alive to enjoy it.

The grant in question creates a life estate in Able and a remainder in fee simple in Baker. The phrase "Baker and his heirs" is a term of art that creates a vested remainder in fee simple in Baker. The words "and his heirs" are not words of conveyance, and so Baker's heirs take no immediate interest in Blackacre. Charlie, as Baker's heir, would take Blackacre only if Baker failed to convey or devise it. Therefore, (B) is incorrect.

(C) is incorrect. Charlie does not hold an alternative contingent remainder. An alternative contingent remainder can only be created by the terms of a grant. Moreover, Charlie does not take at all because Baker conveyed his remainder in fee simple absolute to Doug.

Since Baker held a vested remainder in fee simple, he had the power to convey or devise his interest. He devised his interest in Blackacre to Doug by his will. Therefore, Doug takes Blackacre after Able's death, and (D) is correct.

Question 9

Oscar conveyed Blackacre "to Arthur, his heirs and assigns, but if Arthur dies and is not survived by children by his present wife, Genevieve, then to Lance and his heirs and assigns." Shortly after taking possession, Arthur drilled for oil on the land, was successful and began pumping oil. Arthur has no children. Arthur, Genevieve, and Lance are all still living. Lance brought an action in equity for an accounting of the value of the oil removed and for an injunction against further pumping.

Arthur's best defense to this action is

(A) Lance has no interest in Blackacre.
(B) the right to take oil is an incident of a defeasible fee simple.
(C) the right to take oil is an incident of the right to possession.
(D) when Arthur has a child by Genevieve and the child survives him, Lance will have no interest in Blackacre.

Answer to Question 9

(A) is incorrect. Lance has a valid executory interest in the property. The estate conveyed to Arthur is a fee simple subject to an executory condition. The conveyance to "Arthur, his heirs and assigns" creates a fee simple. However, the remaining part of the conveyance completely divests Arthur and his successors of the property at Arthur's death if he is not survived by children by his present wife Genevieve, and creates a valid executory interest after the fee simple in Lance. Lance's interest is not invalidated by the Rule Against Perpetuities because it will vest at the end of a life in being, either Genevieve or Arthur, whichever comes first. The estate conveyed to Arthur is a fee simple subject to an executory condition, otherwise known as a defeasible fee. Unlike a life tenant, the owner of any fee estate (even a qualified or defeasible fee) cannot generally be prevented from committing waste. During the estate, a qualified fee owner is treated as though she held a fee simple absolute. Therefore, (B) is correct and (D) is incorrect.

(C) is incorrect because it is too broad. The right to possession alone, such as that of a life tenant or a tenant for years, does not give the present possessor the right to commit waste on the property. The landlord or the remainderperson has a cause of action to prevent waste by such tenant.

Question 10

Olga was the record owner of Blackacre in fee simple. Olga's neighbor Alice was having trouble obtaining pure water from her well. Olga orally agreed to let Alice take water from Olga's well for a period of 11 months (the time it would take to remove the impurities from Alice's well water) for a fee of $20 per month.

Olga strongly believed that her daughter should serve her country in the military service. One month after Olga's transaction with Alice, on the occasion of her daughter Donna's eighteenth birthday, Olga presented Donna with a deed to Blackacre duly signed by Olga and properly acknowledged. The deed read as follows:

> I convey Blackacre to my daughter Donna subject to the condition precedent that she satisfactorily complete two years of military service before she reaches age 28. If she fails to complete military service by that time, I convey Blackacre to my son Harold.

Donna immediately recorded the deed.
Donna had long disliked Alice. Immediately after recording the deed, she wrote Alice a letter as follows: "Your rights to take water from my well on Blackacre are immediately terminated."

When Alice continued to take water from Blackacre, Donna brought suit to enjoin her activity. In that suit,

(A) Alice will prevail because her right to take water did not terminate until the end of the 11-month term.

220

(B) Alice will prevail because only Olga, not Donna, has the right to terminate Alice's rights to take water.
(C) Donna will prevail because she has a fee simple subject to divestment.
(D) Donna will win because the right to take water was only a license and terminable at will.

Answer to Question 10

(A) correctly states that Alice will prevail, but states the wrong reason. The right given by Olga to Alice to take water from the well was given orally. Therefore, because of the Statute of Frauds, it could not be either an easement or a profit a prendre, estates in land which are not revocable at will. It could only be a license. A license is revocable at will. However, the revocation must come from Olga, the person who has a present possessory interest in the property, not Donna, who only has a future interest.

(C) is incorrect. The language of the conveyance in this question contains the words "subject to the condition precedent." This means that Donna has an executory interest in the form of a springing use which will become possessory at the time she satisfies the condition precedent. A fee simple subject to divestment would give Donna immediate possession and then oust her if the condition is not satisfied at the specified time. The language here is explicitly that of a condition precedent, not subsequent.

Even though (D) correctly states that Alice had only a revocable license, it is the wrong answer because only Olga (the holder of the present possessory interest in the property), not Donna (the holder of only a future interest), has the power to terminate. Since Olga has not terminated, Alice will prevail.

(B) is the correct answer. The deed in this question did not vest either immediate title or right of possession in Donna. Title only vests at such time as the condition precedent is satisfied, that is, upon her completion of two years military service before she reaches age 28. In the meantime, title and possession remain in Olga. Therefore, Olga is the only person who has the right to terminate Alice's right to take water.

Question 11

Grace desired to leave her property in Philadelphia so that her two oldest children, Albert and Caroline, would have the right to occupy the property during their joint lives. To that end, Grace left her property to Caroline and Albert as tenants in common on the condition that neither can sell his or her interest during their joint lives. If Caroline deeded her interest in the property to Stephanie while Albert was alive, the conveyance would be

(A) valid, because the restriction is an invalid restraint on alienation.
(B) valid, if properly recorded.
(C) void, because it violates the restriction.
(D) void, because Stephanie had record notice of the condition.

Answer to Question 11

(B) is incorrect. A deed which is in proper form and is delivered from the grantor to the grantee conveys title from the grantor to the grantee whether or not it is recorded. Recording is never an issue as between the grantor and grantee, only as between a grantee and other grantees.

Grace left her property to her children as joint tenants in fee simple. She placed a condition on their estates, though, that purported to prevent them from selling their interests during their lives. Such a restriction on a fee owner's right of alienation is prohibited, even if it is limited to a relatively short period of time. Therefore, Caroline's conveyance to Stephanie is valid. (C) is incorrect and (A) is correct.

(D) is incorrect. Since the restriction itself is invalid, the notice of the attempted restraint is irrelevant.

Question 12

Grandpa was the owner of Blackgoldacre and leased it three years before his death to the Wildcat Oil Company. The lease gave the lessee the right to drill for oil and gas for a period of 25 years and provided for the payment of a royalty for oil and gas removed. While Grandpa was alive, no oil or gas was discovered. Upon his death, he devised Blackacre to Son for life, remainder to Grandson. The residue of his estate was left to Grandma. The year after Grandpa died, oil was discovered on Blackgoldacre, and royalties became due. They should be paid to

(A) Grandma, because the right to receive royalties was a contract right belonging to Grandpa's residuary estate.
(B) Son, because the life tenant has the right to the income from Blackacre.
(C) Grandson, because removal of oil and gas constitutes waste, and therefore the proceeds belong to the remainderperson.
(D) Son and Grandson, in a proportion calculated by comparing the actual value of Son's life estate and Grandson's remainder interest.

Answer to Question 12

(A) is incorrect. The right to receive royalties from minerals extracted from a parcel of land is appurtenant to the right of ownership of that land, and therefore goes to the current possessor of the real estate, rather than the residuary legatee of the estate. Therefore, Grandma takes no interest in the royalties.

Although, in general, a life tenant does not have the right to remove a nonrenewable resource from the property, the life tenant may do so if it was the grantor's intent that the life tenant be allowed to do so. If the grantor has depleted the property's resources while the grantor owned the real estate, it is implied that the grantor intended the person to whom the grantor devised a life tenancy to receive the kind of income benefit the grantor received. In this case, since Grandpa gave the license to drill (in a sense, beginning to use the land's resources) before he died, the life tenant (Son) has the right to continue that exploitation even though no income was produced during Grandpa's lifetime. (B) is correct.

(C) is incorrect in these circumstances, although it is a correct statement of the general rule.

(D) is incorrect. This is the kind of compromise which might be reached between a life tenant and remainderperson if the property had not been dedicated to removal of oil. However, the law would not impose this result. At best, the law can only stop the waste and award any profits resulting from the waste to the remainderperson as damages.

Question 13

Owen grants Blackacre, "to L for life, remainder to R." R, with L's permission, builds a house on Blackacre and lives in it without paying rent for 25 years, at which time L brings an action to evict R. The most likely result in that action is

(A) L will prevail because he is entitled to possession.
(B) L will prevail only if he reimburses R for the cost of the house.
(C) R will prevail because R has acquired title by adverse possession.
(D) R will prevail because L surrendered his life estate.

Answer to Question 13

(B) is incorrect. Although R may be able to make a claim against L for some of the benefit conferred on L by R's construction of the house, R certainly cannot recover the full cost of the house. R has already benefited from the use of the house and will regain possession of the house once L dies and the life estate terminates. If R were to recover anything, courts would require R to show some type of injustice or implied contract in this enrichment of L before R could recover. In this case, a court is more likely to hold that R took the risk of L's wanting to take possession of Blackacre.

(C) is incorrect. R did not obtain title to Blackacre by adverse possession, because R's possession was not adverse; R built the house and occupied the land with L's permission. The fact that R did not pay rent does not make the possession adverse.

The facts in this question indicate that L merely gave R permission to build and occupy a house on Blackacre during the term of L's life estate. There was no conveyance of or surrender of the entire estate which L held to R. Thus, (D) is incorrect. Equitable principles might be invoked to prevent an estate holder from claiming rights which he had voluntarily waived, but these facts do not amount to an intentional waiver by L of his possessory rights.

This grant creates a life estate in L and a remainder in R. The fact that L permitted R to occupy Blackacre during part of L's life estate will not affect L's status and rights as a life tenant. L is entitled to possession of Blackacre and can recover the property from R, along with the improvements in question. Therefore, (A) is the correct answer.

Question 14

Oscar, the owner of Blackacre, deeded Blackacre "to A for life and then to B and C in equal shares." The grant also provided that "A shall not have the power to alienate his life estate. In the event that either B or C shall attempt to alienate her remainder interest before it becomes possessory, then the remainder interest shall vest entirely in the person who did not attempt to alienate her interest." One year after the deed, A deeded his life estate to D, and B deeded her remainder interest to E. What is the state of the title to Blackacre after the actions by A and B?

(A) A is the holder of a life estate, and C holds a vested remainder.
(B) A is the holder of a life estate, and E and C hold a vested remainder as tenants in common.
(C) D is the holder of a life estate per autre vie, and C holds a vested remainder.
(D) D is the holder of a life estate per autre vie, and E and C hold a vested remainder as tenants in common.

Answer to Question 14

A disabling restraint on alienation is always invalid, even as against a life estate. Therefore, A's transfer to D creates in D a valid life estate per autre vie, a life estate with A's life as the measuring life.

On the other hand, while forfeiture restraints are valid in general, any restraint on the alienability of a fee simple is invalid. Therefore, the transfer of B's vested remainder to E is effective.

(B) is incorrect because the attempted disabling restraint on the transfer of A's life estate is invalid. Therefore, the transfer of that life estate to D is valid.

Thus, D is the holder of a life estate per autre vie for the life of A, and E and C hold a vested remainder as tenants in common. Thus, (A) is incorrect and (D) is correct.

(C) is incorrect because any attempt to restrain the alienability of fee simple is invalid, even a remainder in fee simple. Therefore, E now holds B's vested remainder.

Question 15

William died and by will left Blackacre to his widow for life and the remainder to his children, provided they reached age 35; and if they died prior to reaching 35, to the children of his children by right of representation. William died survived by his widow, three children, and two grandchildren. In a jurisdiction where the common law Rule Against Perpetuities is in effect, what is the status of the testamentary disposition?

(A) The entire disposition is valid.
(B) The disposition to the children and the grandchildren is invalid because it is

possible that William's widow was not a life in being at the time of the execution of the will.
(C) The dispositions to the widow and children are valid, but the disposition to the grandchildren is invalid because it is possible that more grandchildren may be born after the death of the testator.
(D) The disposition is valid except as it applies to grandchildren born after the date the will was executed.

Answer to Question 15

(B) is incorrect. There cannot be an unborn widow problem in this question because the interests created by William's will are not subject to the Rule Against Perpetuities at the time of the execution of his will, but at the time the will becomes effective, i.e., upon William's death. William's widow is the only widow involved in the question. To be his widow, she had to be married to William at the time of his death and therefore had to be alive at the time of the creation of the interest.

(A) is correct. At William's death, his widow took a life estate and each of his children took a contingent remainder in the property since their interest was subject to the condition precedent that the child reach age 35. The grandchildren of each child also took a remainder contingent on the child's parent dying prior to attaining age 35. The interest of the widow is clearly valid because she takes a possessory life estate at William's death. The interests of William's children is likewise valid because the condition precedent must be satisfied, if it is ever to be satisfied, during the life of each child. Each child is by definition a life in being at the time of the creation of the interest (William's death). The interests of the grandchildren, whenever born, are also valid under the Rule Against Perpetuities. If their alternative contingent remainder is ever to vest, it must vest by the time their parent dies before reaching age 35. These grandchildren, even those unborn at the death of Grandfather, must be born and therefore identified during lives in being, namely the lives of their parents, and the condition precedent to their taking must be satisfied at the death of their parent, a life in being. Therefore, all interests must vest, if they are ever going to vest, either during the life of or at the death of one of William's children, who are lives in being at William's death, and all interests are valid. Therefore, (C) and (D) are incorrect.

Question 16

Owen owned Beachacre in fee simple. He conveyed it "to A, his heirs and assigns; but if B shall be living thirty years from the date of this deed, then to B, his heirs and assigns." The limitation "to B, his heirs and assigns" is

(A) valid, because the interest will vest, if at all, within a life in being.
(B) valid, because B's interest is vested subject to divestment.
(C) valid, because B's interest is a reversion.
(D) invalid.

Answer to Question 16

(B) is incorrect. An executory interest is not considered by the law to be vested until it becomes possessory. Therefore, it is incorrect to say that B's interest is vested subject to divestment.

(C) is incorrect. This question tests the application of the Rule Against Perpetuities to executory interests. Because the interest in B, a third person, was created in the same conveyance as the fee simple subject to a condition subsequent in A and his heirs, B's interest is an executory interest, not a reversion.

B's interest is an interest granted to a third person after a qualified fee simple and is therefore an executory interest, which is subject to the Rule Against Perpetuities. In this case, the interest is valid under the Rule because, if B's interest is ever going to vest, it must vest within his lifetime. Therefore, (D) is incorrect. B is obviously a life in being at the time of the creation of the interest, since he is named in the grant. (A) is the correct answer.

Questions 17 and 18 are based on the following fact situation.

Bill owned Hilltop in fee simple. By his will, he devised as follows: "Hilltop to such of my grandchildren who shall reach the age of 21; and by this provision I intend to include all grandchildren, whenever born." At the time of his death, Bill had three children and two grandchildren.

17. Courts hold such a devise valid under the common-law Rule Against Perpetuities. What is the best explanation of that determination?

(A) There is a rule of construction that dispositive instruments are to be interpreted so as to uphold interests, rather than to invalidate them under the Rule Against Perpetuities.
(B) All of Bill's children would be measuring lives.
(C) The rule of convenience closes the class of beneficiaries when any grandchild reaches the age of 21.
(D) There is a presumption that Bill intended to include only those grandchildren born prior to his death.

18. Which of the following additions to or changes in the facts stated above would produce a violation of the common-law Rule Against Perpetuities?

(A) The instrument was an inter vivos conveyance rather than a will.
(B) Bill's will expressed the intention to include all afterborn grandchildren in the gift.
(C) Bill had no grandchildren living at the time of his death.
(D) A posthumous child was born to Bill.

Answer to Question 17

(A) is incorrect. At common law, the Rule Against Perpetuities was applied with rigor, and there was no rule of construction which was used to save gifts which violated the Rule. Moreover, the interests created in this case do not violate the Rule Against Perpetuities and need no rule of construction to save them. Also, as a general principle, this type of vague, policy-based answer should be avoided, especially in an area like the Rule Against Perpetuities, where the Multistate examiners expect a detailed knowledge of the law and a detailed analysis.

The rule of convenience is a rule of construction which, based on the grantor's presumed intent, closes the class when the first member of the class is capable of taking a possessory interest. That is when the first grandchild reaches age 21. In this case, though, the facts indicate that Bill intended to include all grandchildren whenever born in the gift. Therefore, the rule of convenience does not apply, and (C) is incorrect.

(D) is incorrect because there is no presumption that a testator who uses the word "grandchildren" only intends to mean those grandchildren born prior to his death. Even if there were such a presumption, it would be negated by the testator's language which clearly indicates an intent to include all grandchildren whenever born.

(B) is correct. The will does not become effective until Bill's death and so it does not create any interests until that time. Therefore, the Rule period is measured from Bill's death. At that time, all of Bill's children must be alive. The children thus may act as the measuring lives. The interests in the grandchildren, whenever born, must vest, if they are ever to vest, within 21 years of the death of the last measuring life. Again, by definition, the last grandchild must be born by the end of the last child's life. Therefore, this interest, which vests when each grandchild reaches the age of 21, must vest within 21 years of the death of the last measuring life, a child of Bill's.

Answer to Question 18

(B) is incorrect. This is a choice which can be eliminated even if your knowledge of perpetuities is limited. The focus of the question asks what **additions or changes** in the preceding paragraph will cause a violation of the Rule. This choice does not represent an addition or change. Bill's will already expresses the intent to include afterborn grandchildren. That fact did not cause a violation of the Rule.

(C) is incorrect, as the fact that Bill had no grandchildren alive at his death is not relevant, because the grandchildren are not the measuring lives, Bill's children are. Since the will does not become effective until Bill's death, it does not create any interests until that time. Therefore, the Rule period is measured from Bill's death. At that time, all of Bill's children must be alive. The children may thus act as the measuring lives. Therefore, the interests of the grandchildren, which vest when each grandchild reaches the age of 21, must vest within 21 years of the death of the last measuring life, a child of Bill's.

The fact that a child was born to Bill after his death would not invalidate the disposition under the Rule Against Perpetuities. The Rule provides that all children conceived at the time of a person's death are eligible to be treated as lives in being at the time of the testator's death for the purpose of computing the time limits under the Rule. Therefore, an afterborn child is a life in being to the same extent as a child born before the death of Bill. Thus, (D) is incorrect.

(A) is correct. If this grant were made inter vivos, the time for the running of the Rule would commence at the date of the gift, rather than at the death of Bill. It is possible that another child could be born to Bill after the date of the gift who would then not be a life in being for purposes of computing the time limits under the Rule Against Perpetuities. It is possible that the child born after the date of the deed would have a child whose interest would still be contingent because the child had not yet reached age 21 at the death of the last of Bill's children alive at the date of the deed. Because that child would be a member of the class of grandchildren, the gift would be invalid at common law as to all members of the class.

Question 19

Husband and Wife, legally married to each other, own Blackacre as tenants by the entirety. Husband agrees to sell the property to Buyer. At the closing, Husband brings Girlfriend and introduces her to Buyer as Wife. Husband signs a deed to Buyer. Girlfriend signs Wife's name to the deed. Buyer pays consideration to Husband, does not know that Girlfriend is not Husband's wife, and duly records the deed. If Wife brings an appropriate action to challenge the title of Buyer, what is the most likely state of the title?

(A) Wife and Buyer own the property as tenants in common.
(B) Wife has the entire title because of Husband's fraudulent act.
(C) Husband and Wife are still the legal owners of Blackacre.
(D) Wife has no title at all because Buyer is a bona fide purchaser.

Answer to Question 19

(B) is incorrect. There is no doctrine which allows or requires the interest of a cotenant to be automatically transferred to the other cotenants based on the fraud of the cotenant.

(D) is incorrect. Wife cannot be divested of her interest by this conveyance. A forged deed does not convey any interest of the person whose signature is forged, even if the grantee pays consideration for the deed and believes that the forged signature is genuine. The fact that Buyer is a bona fide purchaser will not give Buyer any greater rights in this property.

The tenants' interest in a tenancy by the entirety cannot be conveyed to a third person by the unilateral act of one cotenant. Therefore, the signature of Husband on the deed does not convey Wife's, or for that matter Husband's, interest in the property. Wife's interest was not conveyed because the deed was not signed by Wife or her authorized agent. Therefore, (C) is correct and (A) is incorrect.

Question 20

A and B are tenants in common in Blackacre. A spends $50,000 on improvements to Blackacre, which increases its market value by $30,000. If A sues B for reimbursement for these expenditures, A would receive

(A) $30,000.
(B) $25,000.
(C) $15,000.
(D) nothing.

Answer to Question 20

(D) is correct. A cotenant who makes **necessary repairs** to property can usually recover from a noncontributing cotenant, but the cotenant who **improves** property has **no** right to contribution from noncontributing cotenants. At best, he can recover the value of those improvements in an action for partition or accounting for profits. Since there is no partition or accounting involved in this question, A can recover nothing in a suit for reimbursement. Therefore, (A), (B), and (C) are incorrect.

Question 21

John and Mary believed that they were married to each other. However, John's previous marriage to Beth was still in effect and therefore John and Mary were not legally married. John and Mary bought Blackacre, located in State X, from Owen and received a deed to "John and Mary, husband and wife, as tenants by the entirety." A statute in State X provided that every conveyance to two unmarried persons is presumed to create a tenancy in common. What is the state of the title to Blackacre?

(A) John and Mary own Blackacre as tenants in common because of estoppel by deed.
(B) John and Mary own Blackacre as joint tenants because there was an intention to create a right of survivorship among the cotenants.
(C) John and Mary own Blackacre as tenants by the entirety because the deed created that relationship.
(D) John and Mary own Blackacre as tenants by the entirety because they believed they were married when they took title.

Answer to Question 21

(A) is incorrect. The doctrine of estoppel by deed has nothing to do with the analysis of this question. Estoppel by deed only applies when a grantor does not have title at the time of the conveyance but later acquires it. That is not the case here; there are no facts indicating that Owen was not the true owner of Blackacre.

(D) is incorrect. A tenancy by the entirety cannot be created between unmarried persons, even if they honestly believe that they are married.

Because John and Mary are not legally married to each other, they cannot own Blackacre as tenants by the entirety. Thus, (C) is incorrect. The only two forms of ownership available are tenants in common and joint tenants with the right of survivorship. The statute of State X creates a **presumption** that John and Mary hold as tenants in common, but that statute does not say that this presumption is irrefutable. Therefore, the presumption can be overcome by the facts showing that John and Mary wanted to take as tenants with a right of survivorship, which would mean that they would take as joint tenants. The fact that they chose the words of a conveyance which would provide for a right of survivorship most likely rebuts the presumption that they intended to hold as tenants in common (which has no right of survivorship) and makes it more likely that they intended to hold the property as joint tenants. (B) is the correct answer.

Question 22

Oscar deeded Blackacre to Art, Bob, Chuck, and Don as joint tenants.

If Art built a house on a portion of Blackacre, fenced off a yard, and lived in it

227

during that year, what would he owe to his cotenants?

(A) three-fourths of the fair rental value of the land, less three-fourths of the real estate taxes on the land
(B) three-fourths of the fair rental value of the house and land
(C) three-fourths of the fair rental value of the land
(D) nothing

Answer to Question 22

Each cotenant has a right to occupy the entire premises. Therefore, Art is not liable to account to his cotenants for the fair rental value of his own personal use of the property unless he ejects them. Art owes nothing to the other cotenants for his use of the land. (D) is correct and all of the other choices are incorrect.

Question 23

Abbott and Bergen are owners of Blackacre as joint tenants. Abbott entered into a lease of Blackacre to Costello for a term of ten years. In the fifth year of the lease, Abbott died intestate, survived by his son Edgar as his sole heir. Edgar deeded all his right, title and interest in and to Blackacre to the tenant Costello. Bergen has brought an action against Costello to oust him from possession. The best argument that Bergen will prevail is

(A) Abbott breached his fiduciary duty to Bergen by leasing Blackacre to Costello.
(B) Costello had no right to rely on Abbott's representation that he owned Blackacre.
(C) a joint tenancy cannot be transformed into a tenancy in common.
(D) the lease is insufficient to cause a severance.

Answer to Question 23

(A) is incorrect. A cotenant holding an interest in a joint tenancy has the right, without violating any fiduciary duty to his cotenant, to alienate his interest to the same extent as any fee owner. Therefore, a lease of a cotenant's right of possession could not be considered a breach of any fiduciary duty.

(B) is incorrect. Costello is not relying on Abbott's representation that he owned Blackacre. Costello is relying on the deed from Edgar to establish his right to possess Blackacre, not on Abbott's lease. Therefore, Costello's knowledge of Abbott's cotenancy at the time Costello took the lease is irrelevant.

(C) is incorrect as a matter of law. A joint tenancy is quite easily transformed into a tenancy in common (e.g., if one of the joint tenants alienates his interest in the joint tenancy to a third party).

(D) is the correct answer. In order to prevail, Bergen must establish that Edgar inherited nothing from Abbott and therefore had nothing to convey to Costello. To accomplish this, Bergen must argue that his joint tenancy with Abbott was not severed prior to Abbott's death. In order to do this, Bergen will have to argue that Abbott's lease to Costello does not constitute a conveyance that would sever their joint tenancy and turn it into a tenancy in common, an issue of law on which jurisdictions are split.

Question 24

Olga in 1975 deeded Blackacre to A, B, C, and D, unrelated individuals, as joint tenants. In 1977, A died intestate. In 1988, B died intestate. In 1989, C deeded all of his right, title, and interest in Blackacre to Z, who died intestate in 1995.

If you were an attorney for a buyer who was about to take title to Blackacre in 1997, the least you should require to assure your client good title is

(A) a duly executed deed from D.

(B) a duly executed deed from D and the heirs of Z.
(C) a duly executed deed from the heirs of B, the heirs of Z, and D.
(D) a duly executed deed from the heirs of A, the heirs of B, the heirs of Z, and D.

Answer to Question 24

A deed from D alone is not sufficient to convey marketable title, because C's one-half interest in the property was effectively conveyed to Z and her heirs. Thus, (A) is incorrect.

A deed from the heirs of B is likewise not required. The death of A did not sever the joint tenancy. B continued to hold his one-third interest as a joint tenant with right of survivorship after A's death. Since nothing disturbed that joint tenancy before the death of B, his interest passed to C and D, and a deed from B's heirs is not required. Thus, (C) is wrong.

No event occurred which would cause a severance of the joint tenancy before the death of A. Therefore, when A died, his interest passed by right of survivorship to B, C, and D, who then held undivided one-third interests as joint tenants. Therefore, A's heirs have no interest in the property, and a deed from them is not required. Thus, (D) is incorrect.

The deaths of A and B during the existence of a joint tenancy mean that their heirs take no interest in the property. Although C and D originally held as joint tenants after the death of A and B, this joint tenancy was converted into a tenancy in common between Z and D when C conveyed to Z. Therefore, the heirs of Z received her interest when she died, and the least requirement is a deed from the heirs of Z and D. (B) is correct.

Question 25

In 1975, Oliver deeded Blackacre as follows: "as tenants in common, an undivided one-half interest to A and B as joint tenants, and the other undivided one-half interest to C and D as joint tenants."

In 1987, A died intestate. In 1988, B died intestate. In 1989, C deeded all of his right, title, and interest in Blackacre to Z, who died intestate in 1993.

In 1995, D entered into a contract to sell Blackacre to X in fee simple. After examining title, X refused to perform on the ground that D could not give good title. In addition to his own deed what else must D produce to convey good title?

(A) a deed of the interest of the heirs of B
(B) a deed of the interest of the heirs of Z
(C) a deed of the interests of the heirs of B and the heirs of Z
(D) nothing

Answer to Question 25

The original conveyance in this case is of two joint tenancies which hold with respect to each other as tenancies in common. A deed from the heirs of B is required because, after A's death, B alone held the undivided one-half interest which was originally deeded to A and B as joint tenants. B's interest did not pass to his other cotenants when he died because, as to them, he was only a tenant in common (with no right of survivorship). Rather, B's heirs succeeded to B's interest when B died. Thus, (B) is incorrect.

When C deeded his interest to Z, the joint tenancy between C and D was transformed into a tenancy in common between Z and D. When Z died, her heirs succeeded to her interest and must therefore join in the deed. (A) incorrectly omits the need for a deed from the heirs of Z.

A deed of both the heirs of B and the heirs of Z is required (in addition to D's deed) to convey title to Blackacre. (C) is correct and (D) is incorrect.

Question 26

Able, the owner in fee simple absolute, deeded Blackacre to Baker and Charlie as joint tenants. Baker, in order to secure a promissory note to Max, executed a mortgage to Max of the entire fee in Blackacre. The state of the title after the mortgage is

(A) a joint tenancy with right of survivorship in Baker and Charlie subject to a mortgage on the interest of Baker, in a state which adheres to the title theory of mortgages.
(B) a tenancy in common between Baker and Charlie with a mortgage on Baker's undivided half interest, in a state which adheres to the lien theory of mortgages.
(C) a joint tenancy with right of survivorship in Baker and Charlie subject to a mortgage on Baker's interest, in a state which adheres to the lien theory of mortgages.
(D) a joint tenancy with right of survivorship in Baker and Charlie subject to a mortgage on Baker's interest if Baker survives Charlie and inherits the entire fee, in a state which adheres to the title theory of mortgages.

Answer to Question 26

Baker and Charlie held Blackacre as joint tenants prior to the granting of the mortgage. A conveyance by either party would sever their joint tenancy and convert it into a tenancy in common. In a title theory state, a mortgage by Baker of his interest in the property would be a conveyance which would convert their cotenancy into a tenancy in common, irrespective of which joint tenant survives. Therefore, (A) and (D) are incorrect.

In a lien theory state, a mortgage would not constitute a conveyance and severance would not occur until foreclosure of the mortgage.
Therefore, (C) is correct and (B) is incorrect.

Question 27

Able is the owner of Highland, a large tract of land which forms the headwaters of Bear Creek, a nonnavigable watercourse which flows through Highland and thence through Lowland, an abutting 100-acre parcel owned by Baker. Both Highland and Lowland are in the watershed of Bear Creek. The period required to obtain prescriptive rights in the jurisdiction is 20 years.

When Baker purchased Lowland in 1960, she cleared the land and established a vegetable farm. Starting in 1961 and continuing to the present, Baker irrigated her crops with water taken from Bear Creek.

In 1990, Able built her residence on Highland and began using water from Bear Creek for domestic purposes. During 1990 and 1991, the water in the creek was more than adequate to supply all of the needs of both Able and Baker.

In 1992, the area experienced a severe drought. The water in the creek could only supply either:
(1) all of Able's needs and half of Baker's needs, or
(2) all of Baker's needs.

Able has continued to draw water from Bear Creek as it passes through Highland, sharply limiting the water available for Baker's farming operation.

If Baker brings an appropriate action to enjoin Able's use of water from Bear Creek to the extent that such use deprives Baker of the quantity of water which she has historically used in her farming operation on Lowland, she will prevail

(A) only if the property is located in a jurisdiction which follows the common-law doctrine of riparian rights.
(B) only if the property is located in a jurisdiction which follows the doctrine of prior appropriation with respect to riparian rights.
(C) in either a common-law jurisdiction or a prior appropriation jurisdiction.
(D) in neither a common-law jurisdiction nor a prior appropriation jurisdiction.

Answer to Question 27

Baker will not prevail in a common-law jurisdiction. In a common-law jurisdiction, "reasonable use" is the appropriate standard for adjudicating water rights between competing riparian owners. Under this doctrine, water for domestic use, as required by Able, has superior rights to the agricultural use of the water required by Baker. Such domestic use is, by definition, reasonable. Also, water rights cannot be acquired by prescriptive use under the common law. Therefore, in such a jurisdiction, Baker will not be successful in obtaining an injunction. Thus, (A) and (C) are incorrect.

In a jurisdiction which follows the doctrine of prior appropriation, Baker's continuous use of the water for beneficial farming use since 1961 gives her the right to continue to use the same quantity of water from the creek before Able has any right to use water. Baker will therefore prevail in a prior appropriation jurisdiction. Therefore, (B) is correct and (D) is incorrect.

Question 28

Amelia and Bedelia are the owners of adjoining parcels of land. In 1990, a road was built along the edge of both Amelia's land and Bedelia's land. The grade of the highway was approximately 10 feet lower than the grade of Amelia's and Bedelia's land.

In 1991, Bedelia decided to develop her property commercially. She excavated her entire property down to the grade of the road in a careful manner and built a restaurant and parking lot.

At the time Bedelia excavated, Amelia and Bedelia agreed that for themselves, their heirs and assigns, in lieu of any obligation for lateral support, Bedelia would build and maintain a retaining wall near the boundary between the two properties. That agreement was recorded. Bedelia built the retaining wall and then sold her property to Clarice. Thereafter, the retaining wall deteriorated and Amelia's property started to fall onto Clarice's land. In a suit by Amelia against Clarice to require her to rebuild the wall,

(A) Amelia would win because, as a successor to Bedelia, Clarice is required to maintain the wall.
(B) Amelia would win because Clarice, as abutting landowner, has an absolute duty to provide lateral support for Amelia's land in its natural state.
(C) Clarice would win because Bedelia's obligation is personal and does not bind Clarice.
(D) Clarice would win because she has no obligation to provide artificial support for her neighbor's land.

Answer to Question 28

The agreement between Amelia and Bedelia was in writing, was intended to run with the land, touches and concerns both properties, and was recorded so that successors to the original contracting parties had notice of the agreement. The covenant is more than a personal agreement between Amelia and Bedelia. Therefore, the covenant is enforceable by way of injunctive relief as an equitable servitude against Bedelia's successor in interest, Clarice. Thus, (C) and (D) are incorrect and (A) is correct.

(B) is incorrect in these circumstances. Amelia gave up the common-law right for lateral support in exchange for Bernice's agreement to build and maintain a retaining wall between the two properties. Therefore, the common-law rights of support are irrelevant to the resolution of the problem.

Question 29

Blackacre and Whiteacre are adjacent one-acre lots zoned for single or multifamily use. Whiteacre, owned by White, is improved by a single-family house. Its water supply, which is furnished by a well drilled on the property, is sufficient to service the property. Blackacre, a vacant parcel, was purchased by Developer, who received all necessary permits to erect a six-story 100-unit apartment house with a swimming pool on the property. To supply water to the new development on Blackacre, Developer drilled a large-diameter well on the property. The well drew water from underneath both Blackacre and Whiteacre, was serviced by a high-powered pump, and was 50 feet deeper than White's well. When the apartment house and swimming pool were fully operational, the water drawn from the well on Blackacre caused the water table to drop below the level of White's well, depriving Whiteacre of its water supply.

White has brought suit against Developer to enjoin her from operating the well on Blackacre in a manner which deprives White of a reasonable water supply on Whiteacre. In that lawsuit, Developer will

(A) prevail only in a jurisdiction which follows the reasonable use doctrine with respect to underground water.
(B) prevail only in a jurisdiction which follows the absolute ownership doctrine with respect to underground water.
(C) prevail in either a reasonable use jurisdiction or an absolute ownership jurisdiction.
(D) not prevail.

Answer to Question 29

A general principle of American water law is that a landowner has an ownership interest in water lying under her land which she can recover by drilling a well. This law is very different than the more limiting doctrines with respect to the right to take water from a watercourse on the surface of the property. In a reasonable use state, the only limitation on a property owner's rights to underground water is that the water must be used reasonably in connection with the property. Developer has met this standard in this case since she is using the water for domestic use in the apartment house and for the swimming pool, a reasonable amenity on the land.

In an absolute right state, the water could also be used off of the premises, in addition to all of the uses made on the premises themselves. Developer would clearly prevail in a jurisdiction which has adopted this standard. Thus, Developer can prevail in either jurisdiction, and (C) is the correct answer.

Question 30

Able is the fee simple owner of Blackacre, on which his principal residence, a seven-bedroom house, is located. Able lives on his Blackacre estate during spring, summer and fall and spends winters in Florida. Baker owns Greenacre, which is adjacent to Blackacre. Greenacre is undeveloped.

Baker discovers that there may be treasure buried under his land when he finds an old pirate's map hidden under a rock on Greenacre. Baker begins excavating on Greenacre, looking for the buried treasure. Baker's excavation causes Blackacre to subside and Able's house collapses while Able is away. Able brings an action against Baker. The most that Able can recover is

(A) the damage to the land and the house, if Able can show that the land would have subsided even without the construction of the house.
(B) the damage to the land, if Able can show that the excavation was done negligently.
(C) the damage to the house and the land, as the harm was caused by Baker's acts.
(D) nothing.

Answer to Question 30

An adjacent landowner has an absolute duty to support a neighbor's land in its natural state. However, if the plaintiff can show that the land would have subsided in its natural state, the plaintiff can recover for any damages to buildings resulting from the subsidence. A consideration of the land in its natural state is necessary to establishing liability, but does not limit the damages recoverable. If the proper showing is made, Able can recover for the damages to the house and the land, regardless of the negligence of Baker. Thus, (A) is correct. (D) is incorrect because it fails to recognize that Able can recover in the circumstances outlined in (A).

The same damages could be collected if the plaintiff could prove that the defendant was negligent in excavating, but (B) implies that damages can only be obtained for the land, not the building, which is not true.

(C) speaks only to causation, when a duty must also be shown. There is strict liability for damages to structures, which might be implied by this choice, only in the limited cases where it can be shown that the land would have subsided even if unimproved.

Question 31

Able and Baker, adjacent property owners, executed and recorded reciprocal easements to five-foot strips of land on the border of their properties for the purpose of constructing a ten-foot-wide common driveway to School Street, on which each of them had only five feet of frontage. After the driveway had been constructed, the town constructed a new road, Church Street, abutting Able's property in the rear. Able constructed a new driveway to Church Street, and soon thereafter ceased using the common driveway. One year later, Able sold the property to Charlie, who used the driveway to Church Street for four years. Charlie then commenced using the entire ten feet of the School Street driveway, and Baker commenced an action to prevent Charlie's use of the five feet of the driveway on Baker's land. In that suit,

(A) Baker will prevail because the easement was abandoned by Able and Charlie because they failed to use it for five years.
(B) Baker will prevail only if the period required for adverse possession is five years or less.
(C) Charlie will prevail because non-use is insufficient to cause abandonment of the easement.
(D) Charlie will prevail because he is a bona fide purchaser.

Answer to Question 31

The easement in this case is an easement by grant. That easement was not used for five years, but non-use alone does not terminate an easement. For the easement to be terminated by non-use, it would have to be accompanied by an intention to abandon the easement, or the fee owner (Baker) would have to exclude Charlie from using the easement in an open and notorious manner for the period necessary to acquire an easement by prescription. (B) is incorrect because the acts of Baker do not constitute the open and notorious blocking of the easement which is required to terminate an easement by adverse possession, even if the period required to acquire a property interest by adverse possession was five years or less.

(D) is incorrect because Charlie's success does not depend upon his status as a bona fide purchaser. Charlie holds the easement solely because it is appurtenant to the land which he purchased. His good faith in purchasing the land and paying value for it did not enlarge his rights.

The easement was not terminated by mere non-use, and Charlie will prevail as the successor to the easement granted to Able. Thus, (C) is correct and (A) is incorrect.

Question 32

Oscar owned two one-acre parcels of land, Frontacre and Backacre. Frontacre was bounded on the east by 200 feet of state highway. Backacre was directly to the west of Frontacre, was improved by an office building, and obtained access to the highway by a 20-foot-wide driveway on the southerly boundary of Frontacre. Oscar sold Frontacre to Able and reserved in the deed an easement to use the 20-foot-wide driveway. Oscar then built a second office building on Backacre. If Able sues Oscar for a determination of the scope of the easement, the court should hold that

(A) the easement may be used by the tenants in both buildings, and Able is required to keep the easement in repair.
(B) the easement may be used by the tenants in both buildings, and Oscar must keep the easement in repair.
(C) the easement was destroyed because of the increase in use.
(D) the easement is only available for the use of the tenants in the building existing at the time of the conveyance of Frontacre to Able.

Answer to Question 32

(A) improperly states that the holder of the servient estate must keep the easement in repair. That obligation belongs to the holder of the easement, the owner of the dominant estate.

(C) is incorrect. As long as Oscar was using the easement for the benefit of the dominant estate (Backacre) and for a use contemplated at the time of the reservation, an increase in use of the scope described in this question is permissible. Moreover, an easement is usually not destroyed by misuse.

(D) is incorrect. The concept of overburdening of an easement applies when the easement is used for purposes other than the service of the dominant estate. Here, the second office building is on Backacre and the use is not different than that contemplated when the easement was reserved. This is not an easement by necessity, implication, or prescription where the necessity or the prior use would define the scope of the easement; this is an express easement and Oscar should be allowed to use the easement according to the terms of the reservation. Therefore, the easement can be used by occupants of both office buildings.

(B) correctly states that there was no misuse or overburdening of the easement by the construction of a second building on the dominant estate, and properly states that the holder of the easement and the dominant estate (Oscar) must keep the easement in repair.

Question 33

Owen inherited Lots 1 and 2, which were adjacent to each other, from his mother in 1972. In 1978, he sold Lot 2 to Able. At that time, Owen also conveyed to Able an easement over the 15 yards in the eastern portion of Lot 1 for Able to use as a driveway. Lot 2 is north of Lot 1. Able never used, paved or improved the easement. There was another access road from the north leading to the highway which Able used.

In 1985, Owen, seeing that Able never used the easement anyway, decided to build a porch which would extend 8 feet into the easement. Owen approached Able about the porch, to which Able replied, "That's okay. I don't think I'll ever use that driveway you laid out." Owen built the porch as planned.

In 1992, the city took the land north of Able's house for use as a reservoir, cutting off any access to the highway he may have had in that direction. Able is now suing Owen to remove the portion of the porch extending into the easement. Able's request will be

(A) granted because of an implied easement by necessity.
(B) granted because of the express easement.
(C) denied because of extinction of the easement by non-use and obstruction.
(D) denied because of estoppel.

Answer to Question 33

(A) is incorrect. This could not be an implied easement by necessity because the facts state that Able had access to the highway via another road. Where there is an express easement by grant, there cannot be a similar implied easement by necessity, because an easement is implied only under limited circumstances when there is no express easement.

(C) is incorrect. The original easement was not extinguished because of non-use. An intent to abandon must accompany the non-use for it to terminate the easement. There is no such intent apparent on the facts. The obstruction of the easement by the porch, if done adversely to the holder of the easement, would terminate the easement if it lasted for the period required by the statute of limitation (presumably 20 years). However, that is not the case here, where the obstruction was permissive and has persisted for only seven years.

The grant in 1978 created an express easement in favor of Able. However, under the circumstances of this case, where Able orally relinquished the easement knowing that Owen would rely on it, and Owen built a porch in reliance on that release, the easement is terminated because Able is estopped from enforcing it. Thus, (B) is incorrect and (D) is correct.

Question 34

Ollie owned two parcels of land: Eastacre, which was bounded on the east by 200 feet of state highway; and Westacre, an unimproved parcel directly to the west of Eastacre, the only access to which, other than across Eastacre, was from a winding dirt road. Ollie conveyed Westacre to Deborah by a duly recorded deed which also contained the grant of an easement to use a strip of land 40 feet wide on the southerly boundary of Eastacre for access to the highway.

In which of the following situations would the owner of Eastacre lose in her effort to enjoin the attempted use of the easement across Eastacre?

(A) One year later, Deborah conveyed Westacre to Edward by a duly recorded deed which did not refer to the easement. Two years later, Ollie conveyed Eastacre to Edward by a duly recorded deed which did not refer to the easement. Three years later, Edward conveyed Westacre to Frank by a duly recorded deed which did not refer to the easement. Frank then commenced to build a house on Westacre and a driveway in the purported easement area across Eastacre. Edward brought an action to prevent Frank from using the easement.

(B) Deborah assigned her interest in the easement to Greta, the owner of Southacre, which abutted both Westacre and the southerly side of Eastacre, so that Greta could cross Eastacre to get to Southacre. Deborah then built a house on Westacre and commenced building a driveway in the easement area on Eastacre. Ollie then brought an action to prevent Deborah from using the easement.

(C) Shortly after he sold Westacre to Deborah, Ollie built a six-foot-high chain-link fence around the perimeter of his property. Twenty-two years later, Deborah started to build a house on Westacre, tore a portion of the fence down, and commenced building a driveway in the easement area across Eastacre. Ollie then brought an action to prevent Deborah from using the easement.

(D) Deborah sold Westacre to Hal, who also owned Farwestacre, a parcel of land abutting Westacre on the west. Hal built a house on Farwestacre and commenced building a driveway across Westacre and across the easement portion of Eastacre. Ollie then brought an action to prevent Hal from using the easement.

Answer to Question 34

When Ollie conveyed Eastacre to Edward and Deborah conveyed Westacre to Edward, the servient and dominant estates were in common ownership, and the easement was thereby destroyed by merger. To recreate the easement, Edward would have been required to specifically grant it to Frank. The easement is not automatically revived by Edward's conveyance of Westacre unless an easement by implication or necessity applies, which is not the case here, since there is other access available. Therefore, Edward would prevail in a suit to prevent Frank from using the easement on the theory that it was extinguished by merger. (A) is therefore incorrect.

An easement can be terminated if the owner of the servient estate acts in a continuous, open and notorious manner to prevent the holder of the easement from using it for the statutory period of adverse possession, presumably 20 years. Ollie has more than complied with all of these requirements of adverse possession by maintaining a fence across the easement for a 22-year period. Therefore, Ollie would prevail against Deborah on the theory that the easement was extinguished by adverse possession. (C) is therefore incorrect.

The use of the easement to service a parcel other than the dominant estate automatically overburdens the easement. Thus, Ollie would prevail in an effort to enjoin Hal from using the easement to service a house on Farwestacre and (D) is therefore an incorrect answer.

The attempted alienation of the easement from Deborah to Greta, the owner of Southacre, is ineffective because the owner of an appurtenant easement cannot convey it except in conjunction with a conveyance of the dominant estate. However, this conveyance does not destroy the easement, which can still be used by Deborah, the holder of the dominant estate. Therefore, Ollie would not prevail in a suit against Deborah to enjoin use of the easement. Thus, (B) is the correct answer. (Ollie could, though, prevail against Greta in such a suit, but that is not asked here.)

Question 35

Peggy is the owner of an historic ten-story office building in the business district of the city. The offices on the southern side of the building have had the benefit since the building was built of a beautiful view, over the adjacent vacant lot, of a riverside park and the adjoining river. The zoning by-law in effect for the district permits buildings to be built right up to the lot line, and Peggy's building covers its entire 10,000 square foot lot to its full ten-story height.

Elvira, the owner of the adjacent lot to the south of Peggy's building, acquires all necessary government approvals and constructs a 12-story office building covering her entire lot. When Elvira's building is completed, it totally blocks the view, the light and the air from the southern windows of Peggy's building.

Peggy can no longer rent the space on the southern side of her building for anything except storage, and has experienced a dramatic drop in the income derived from her building. If Peggy sues Elvira for damages and injunctive relief, and is successful in proving the above-stated facts, the court would most likely hold that

(A) Peggy is entitled to a mandatory injunction requiring Elvira to provide access for light and air to the windows on the south side of her building.
(B) Peggy is entitled to damages for losses suffered to the date of trial and may sue in the future for additional damages, but is not entitled to injunctive relief.
(C) Peggy is entitled to recover permanent damages for the difference between the value of Peggy's building before Elvira constructed the neighboring building and the value of Peggy's building after the construction, but she is not entitled to injunctive relief.
(D) Peggy is entitled to neither damages nor injunctive relief.

Answer to Question 35

There is no cause of action for an implied easement for view, light and air, nor can such rights be acquired by prescription. Thus, Peggy has no cause of action at all. (D) is the correct answer. Neither a mandatory injunction nor damages can be awarded, making (A), (B) and (C) all incorrect.

Question 36

Oscar was the owner of two adjacent parcels of land, Blackacre and Whiteacre. Each parcel was improved by adjacent three-story buildings. A stairway which was entirely in the building on Blackacre was the only stairway used by Oscar to reach the upper floors of both buildings. Oscar sold Whiteacre to White by a quitclaim deed which made no mention of the stairway. He then sold Blackacre to Black. The stairway fell into disrepair because Black was not using the upper floors of his building. White demanded the right to repair and use the stairway. Black refused and White has brought suit to enforce the demand. In that suit,

(A) White will prevail because he has an implied right to use the stairway and keep it in repair.
(B) White will prevail because he has prescriptive rights to use the stairway and keep it in repair.
(C) Black will prevail because the deed from Oscar to White did not grant White an easement to use the stairway.

(D) Black will prevail because he is a bona fide purchaser taking without knowledge of an easement to White.

Answer to Question 36

(B) is incorrect. There has been no adverse use of the stairway. When the property was held in common ownership, Oscar's use of the stairway for the purposes of benefiting Whiteacre was not adverse because he owned Blackacre. Therefore, there is no easement by prescription.

(C) is incorrect. An easement by implication exists without a formal written grant of easement. The transfer of Whiteacre from Oscar to White created an easement by implication which is appurtenant to Whiteacre to use the stairway in Blackacre for the purposes of reaching the upper floors of Whiteacre.

(D) is incorrect. The easement was not created by deed. The very nature of an easement by implication is that it is not expressly granted by deed; it is implied from the facts of the situation.

Any time two parcels of land are held in common ownership and an easement on one parcel is necessary to the enjoyment of the other parcel, an easement by implication or necessity may arise. The easement in this case is an easement by implication because the grantor used the stairway on the servient estate to benefit the dominant estate during his ownership of both parcels and the use of the stairway is reasonably necessary for the continued enjoyment of the parcel conveyed. Absolute necessity is not required. The holder of an easement has a concomitant right to keep the stairway in good repair for his use. Thus, (A) is the correct answer.

Question 37

Ollie owned Frontacre and Backacre, abutting two-acre parcels of land in the Town of Falmouth. Frontacre was bounded on the north by Pondview Street, a town road. Backacre was bounded on the north by Frontacre and on the south by a duck pond, a public body of water approximately five feet deep which also abutted a public dock near the center of Falmouth. On the west, both Frontacre and Backacre are bounded by an unimproved pasture.

On the east, both Frontacre and Backacre abutted Perimeter Drive, a road which intersected Pondview street. It was constructed by the owner of Exclusive Estates, a private residential subdivision. The construction of Perimeter Drive was approved by the Falmouth Planning Board, but the road is owned and maintained by the lot owners in the subdivision.

Two years ago, Ollie constructed a house on Backacre which was connected by a path across Frontacre to Pondview Street. While she used the path occasionally, she regularly used Perimeter Drive for access to Backacre.

Ollie sold Backacre to Backrach and then sold Frontacre to Fontaine. Neither deed included easement rights. Each promptly and properly recorded their deeds. The trustees of Exclusive Estates then forbade Backrach from using Perimeter Drive and Fontaine then forbade him to cross Frontacre.

What is the best description of Backrach's rightful access to Backacre?

(A) an easement by necessity over Frontacre
(B) an implied easement to use the path across Frontacre
(C) an easement by dedication to use Perimeter Drive
(D) access only by water across the duck pond to the town dock

Answer to Question 37

While Backacre abuts Perimeter Drive, Backrach has no right to use it. It is privately owned and maintained, and has never been dedicated to public use. Ollie's use of that road for two years creates no rights prescriptive or otherwise to use that land. No easement by necessity or implication exists because Exclusive Estates was not held in common with Backacre. Thus, (C) is an incorrect answer.

(A) is incorrect because the facts do not support an easement by necessity. While there is no access to Pondview Street from Backacre, and the deprivation of access occurred because of the subdivision of Ollie's property, Backacre has access via water across the duck pond to a public dock, and therefore there is not the absolute necessity needed to support an easement by necessity. There is also a better argument that an easement by implication exists, so this choice is incorrect, even if an argument could be made that an easement by necessity exists.

(B) is correct. While the facts in this question do not support an easement by necessity, because there is water access to the property, they are sufficient to support an easement by implication. Backacre was deprived of direct access to Pondview Street by a conveyance from a commonly owned parcel. There existed a quasi-easement over Frontacre at the time of the conveyance in the form of the path from the house on Backacre to Pondview Street. There is a reasonable necessity to continue the use of that path for access to Backacre. Therefore, there is an easement by implication to use that path in favor of the owner of Backacre.

(D) is incorrect because an easement by implication over the pathway on Frontacre exists, in addition to the rights of access by water.

Question 38

Blackacre, owned by Black, is a 300,000 square-foot parcel of unimproved land, bounded on the north by 300 feet of state highway. Blackacre runs back from the highway to a depth of 1,000 feet. Towards the rear of the parcel, Blackacre is abutted on the west by a one-acre landlocked parcel, Whiteacre, owned by White. Black orally grants White permission to construct and use a paved road, 800 feet long and 20 feet wide, along the westerly boundary of Blackacre connecting Whiteacre to the state highway.

White builds a house on Whiteacre and constructs the road in accordance with the agreement. One year later, Black and White have a violent argument and Black blocks access to the road at the point where it abuts Whiteacre.

If White brings an action to enjoin Black from obstructing his use of the road,

(A) Black will prevail because of the Statute of Frauds.
(B) Black will prevail because no easement was created in favor of White to use the road.
(C) White will prevail because he holds an implied easement.
(D) White will prevail because he holds an executed license.

Answer to Question 38

It is true that no easement was granted because such a grant must be in writing because of the Statute of Frauds, but White will have the right to continue to use the road because he holds an executed license. The Statute of Frauds does not apply to licenses. Therefore, (A) and (B) are incorrect.

The only time that either an implied easement or an easement by necessity can be created is when there is a division of a parcel of land, and one parcel after the conveyance lacks an essential service (such as access) which is available only from the other portion of the common parcel. In this case, there is an agreement between two abutting owners, not a division of a common parcel. Thus, (C) is an incorrect answer.

When oral permission is given by one landowner to another landowner to use land, the grant is a license, which is usually revocable because it is not an interest in land. That license becomes irrevocable by estoppel if, with the knowledge and consent of the licensor, the licensee expends substantial sums in reliance on the grant of the license. The license at that time is called an executed license, and is irrevocable. That is the case here, because White has spent a substantial amount in building the road, with the knowledge of Black. Therefore, Black is estopped from revoking the license and (D) is the correct answer.

Question 39

There are three abutting farms on the easterly side of Route 28, a rural part of State X. Each farm is rectangular in shape, has approximately 1,000 feet of frontage on Route 28 and is 3,000 feet deep. No express or implied easement rights existed over any of the parcels.

The northernmost farm, Northacre, is owned and occupied by Nancy. The middle farm, Middleacre, is owned and occupied by Mary. The southernmost farm, Southacre, is owned by Sally.

Each day for 25 years, Sally, after finishing her farming chores, crossed Middleacre along a cart path between Southacre and Northacre for the purpose of visiting Nancy in her house in Northacre. Sally never sought nor received Mary's permission to use the path.

After farming for 25 years, Sally retired and sold Southacre to Sam. The deed conveyed "Southacre in fee simple together with an easement to use the cart path across Middleacre." Mary immediately brings an action to enjoin Sam from using the cart path.

The issue which will determine the outcome of that lawsuit is

(A) the adequacy of the description of the cart path in the deed from Sally to Sam.
(B) the character and frequency of the use which Sam will make of the cart path.
(C) if the easement in Sally is appurtenant.
(D) if Sally can create an easement in a third person by a deed.

Answer to Question 39

If the easement is appurtenant, it need not even be described in the deed; the easement passes to the grantee automatically. If the easement is in gross, it cannot be passed by a deed, no matter how perfectly the easement is described. Therefore, the adequacy of the description in the deed will not be determinative of the outcome. (A) is incorrect.

The issue in this suit is whether the easement by prescription can be transferred to Sam as appurtenant to a conveyance of Southacre. The future proposed conduct of Sam with respect to the easement is irrelevant to that issue. Sam need not continue to use the easement for it to remain valid. Since Sally used the property for at least 20 years, that use has ripened into an easement by prescription, which remains valid even if it is never used again. Likewise, an overburdening of the easement by the grantee could be the subject matter of a later suit, but is not an issue in a suit concerning the existence of the easement. Therefore, (B) is incorrect.

(D) is wholly irrelevant because Sally is not trying to create an easement in a third person by a deed. She is merely trying to convey an easement which she owns to the grantee of her property. This choice would only apply if Sally had tried in her deed to Sam to convey the easement to someone other than Sam.

It is clear from the facts of this case that Sally has acquired, by her conduct, a prescriptive easement to travel across Middleacre. The key issue is whether the easement created in Sally by her conduct was created by virtue of her ownership of Southacre, in which case it is an appurtenant easement, or whether it was a personal easement (called an easement in gross). If the easement was created in her capacity as owner of Southacre, then it is automatically transferred with the transfer of her dominant estate to her successor in title, even if it is not mentioned in the deed. If it was an easement in gross, the usual rule is that it is not alienable. Therefore, the appurtenance of the easement is the controlling issue. (C) is correct.

Question 40

Piedmont and Delta are owners of adjoining 40-acre dairy farms. Piedmont's land has access to a state highway, whereas the land of Delta abuts an unimproved dirt road which is frequently impassable. For a period of 21 years, Delta traveled across the land of Piedmont to get to the state highway as his usual means of access by foot, by farm tractor, and by automobile. Because Piedmont's property was all grazing land, Delta followed no particular route and left no trail. After 21 years, Piedmont for the first time actually observed Delta crossing his land, made an investigation of the extent of the activity, and brought suit to permanently enjoin Delta from crossing his land. In that lawsuit,

(A) Delta will prevail because the activity need not be open and notorious.
(B) Delta will prevail because the activity is open and notorious.
(C) Piedmont will prevail because Delta did not use the same kind of transportation nor the same route during the 21-year period.
(D) Piedmont will prevail because he did not have actual notice until shortly before he commenced suit.

Answer to Question 40

For the user of land to obtain an easement by prescription, the owner of the land must be put on notice that she has a cause of action for trespass, since the expiration of the statute of limitations is the basis for the easement. Absent actual notice, open and notorious use of the property will be enough to give the title owner constructive notice of the use, which is sufficient. Therefore, (D) is an incorrect answer.

(A) is incorrect because, as stated above, since Piedmont did not have actual notice of Delta's trespass until just before bringing suit, Delta's conduct must be open and notorious for Delta to prevail. Thus, (A) is incorrect.

(C) is incorrect. To obtain an easement by prescription, a person must use the land of another for a specific purpose on a continuous basis for the statutory period without the permission of the owner. The requirement that the use be continuous means primarily that the use cannot be interrupted by the true owner, not that the use occur every day in precisely the same manner. There is no requirement that the same form of transportation or the same route be used.

This use was sufficiently open and notorious because an owner paying attention to the land would have noticed this use. Therefore, (B) is correct.

Question 41

Black owned Blackacre. In 1966, he placed a large sewer line (to service a single-family house he built on the property) across Whiteacre, the abutting property, without the permission of White, the owner. In 1985, Black tore down the single-family house in preparation for the construction of an apartment house on Blackacre, and made an agreement with municipal authorities to take an easement across Whiteacre and install a new sewer line to service the property. The municipal authorities failed to perform their agreement, and Black constructed the apartment house in 1987 using the existing sewer line. If White should attempt to enjoin the use of the sewer line to service the apartment house,

(A) White would be successful because the agreement in 1985 with the municipal authorities estopped Black from using the existing line to service the apartment house.
(B) White would be successful because the increased flow of sewage from the apartment house was beyond the prescriptive rights acquired.
(C) White would lose because the original sewer line was a license which ripened into an implied easement.
(D) White would lose because the use was within the scope of the prescriptive easement acquired.

Answer to Question 41

By 1986, Black had maintained the sewer line across Whiteacre for the statutory period and therefore had acquired an easement by prescription to continue to use that line. Once Black obtained an easement by prescription over Whiteacre, that property right persists despite any actions by the municipal authorities with regard to Whiteacre, or any actions by Black with regard to the authorities. Thus, (A) is incorrect.

(B) is incorrect. The scope of Black's easement is determined by the nature of the adverse use. In this case, Black adversely maintained a pipe across Whiteacre and put sewage through that pipe. That same pipe in the same location will be used for the apartment house. The amount of sewage through that pipe will not affect White's property and so is not overburdening the easement. This is not a case where Black is using the easement to benefit a different parcel of land, only a new building on the land benefited by the easement.

(C) is incorrect. Black never had a license. A license is a permissive use of property. Black placed the sewer line across the property without White's permission. Moreover, the use never ripened into an implied easement. Such an easement can only occur when there is a division of a large parcel of property into smaller parcels and there is a reasonable necessity for the owner of one of the parcels to continue to use rights over another part of the larger parcel. There is no such division of property here. Instead, the adverse use by Black ripened into an easement by prescription.

(D) is the correct answer. Black has made an adverse use of Whiteacre since the sewer line was first constructed across it. The fact that Black tore down the house on Blackacre does not stop the prescriptive period from running, since the mere existence of the sewer line was an adverse use and there was no intent to abandon it. Therefore, Black's use ripened into a prescriptive easement 20 years after that use first began. Moreover, the use of the line to service the apartment house is within the scope of the easement by prescription because the same pipe in the same location will be used for the apartment house and the amount of sewage through the pipe will not affect White's property.

Question 42

The time limit necessary to obtain an easement by prescription in this jurisdiction is 20 years. In 1974, Olivia was the owner of Blackacre and Clara was the owner of an adjoining property, Whiteacre. An unpaved driveway running from the main road across a portion of Whiteacre gave Clara access to her residence. However, Clara decided that it would be more convenient for her to use the paved driveway on Blackacre and, in January of 1974, Clara began to use this paved driveway without making any effort to obtain Olivia's consent.

Olivia also used the paved driveway as access to Blackacre, but did not discover that Clara was using it until two years later. At that time, she wrote a letter to Clara protesting the use of the driveway, but Clara continued that use until February 1994, at which time she filed an action for declaratory judgment, declaring that she had a prescriptive right to use the driveway on Blackacre.

Which of the following is the most accurate statement with regard to Clara's use of the driveway in 1994?

(A) Clara could not acquire a prescriptive easement in Blackacre because her original use beginning in 1974 was wholly trespassory and without any claim of right.
(B) The prescriptive period began to run in 1974 because Clara was in open and notorious possession, despite the fact that Olivia did not know of it.
(C) The prescriptive period began to run in 1974 despite the fact that, at that time, Clara was sharing her use with Olivia.
(D) The prescriptive period did not begin to run until two years later, at the time Clara's use of the driveway was contested.

Answer to Question 42

(A) is incorrect. The only way in which a prescriptive easement can be obtained is for a person to trespass on land and to continue to trespass for the statutory period. The fact that the use was wholly trespassory in fact gives Olivia the cause of action and starts the clock running on the statute of limitations. Whether the use was undertaken under a claim of right is wholly immaterial to the analysis. The statute of limitations runs whether or not the trespasser thinks the use is lawful.

(D) is incorrect. Clara's use of the driveway in 1974 was open and notorious and without Olivia's permission, which is all that is required to start the prescriptive period running. The actual protest by Olivia in 1976 was not necessary to start the prescriptive period. An adverse use can ripen into a prescriptive easement even if the fee owner never notices or complains.

There is no requirement of exclusive use for Clara to obtain an easement by prescription. Exclusivity is only required in cases of adverse possession. Adverse possession is not at issue here because Clara has not "possessed" any part of Blackacre, and does not require title to continue her use of the property, which is all she seeks. Thus, (C) is correct.

Likewise, (B) is incorrect because Clara was not in open and notorious possession; she was merely using Olivia's driveway. The distinction is important because exclusive possession for the statutory period leads to title by adverse possession, while adverse use will only result in a prescriptive easement. Clara does not need to and could not live up to the more exacting standard of adverse possession in this case.

Question 43

Able purchased two acres of land which were part of an estate, and subdivided it into two one-acre lots, Blackacre and Whiteacre. An old fieldstone wall crossed the property in the area on Blackacre where Able wanted to erect a house. Before he dug the foundation, the contractor moved the fieldstones to Whiteacre so that they could be used in building a retaining wall at the time the house was landscaped. While the house on Blackacre was under construction, Able needed additional funds and therefore sold Whiteacre to Baker. When he was ready to commence building the retaining wall, Able started to take the fieldstones off of Whiteacre and Baker brought suit to enjoin him from doing so. In that lawsuit, the court is most likely to decide for

(A) Able, because the stones are personal property.
(B) Able, because he did not intend to convey the stones when he conveyed Whiteacre.
(C) Baker, because the stones are part of the real estate conveyed.
(D) Baker, because Able did not reserve a right to enter at the time he sold the property.

Answer to Question 43

This question turns on the characterization of the fieldstones as either real or personal property. Whether the fieldstones are part of the real estate conveyed is determined by the law of fixtures. If they are a fixture, they are considered part of the real estate and title would pass with a conveyance of the real estate. While the stones were not physically affixed to the land, they are indigenous to land and would clearly be considered part of the real estate, conveyed with the land just as the soil would be. Therefore, unless there was a specific agreement to the contrary, the stones would be considered real estate, not personal property. Thus, (A) is incorrect and (C) is correct.

(B) is incorrect. The ordinary expectation of the buyer of property is that she would be getting title to the stones which were physically on the property. While that expectation could be altered by a specific agreement between the parties, the subjective intention of the grantor that he was not conveying something which is ordinarily part of the real estate would not be sufficient to permit him to retain title.

(D) is incorrect. If Able **had** retained the fieldstones as his personal property, he would have had an automatic and irrevocable license to come on the land to recover the stones, even after title to the land passed to Baker. The stones belong to Baker, but it is not solely because Able has no right to go onto Baker's land to get them.

Question 44

Rita is the owner of Blackacre in fee simple subject to a purchase money mortgage in the amount of $100,000 given to the Family Savings Bank. Because the kitchen in the house on Blackacre was installed when the house was built in 1925, Rita undertakes the remodeling of the kitchen. As part of the remodeling, she removes

242

the original gas stove (which is still in working order) and stores it in the cellar. In its place, she installs a countertop stove connected to the gas pipe which originally served the old stove. The stove is secured to the counter with four screws and can be removed without damage to the countertop.

When Rita bought the stove on credit for $1,000, she gave a purchase money security interest to the seller, Appliance Mart. Appliance Mart filed a notice of a security interest with the Secretary of State, the appropriate place to file security interests under the local version of Article 9 of the Uniform Commercial Code, and a notice in the appropriate registry of deeds within ten days of the installation of the stove. When Rita failed to make the required installment payments on the stove, Appliance Mart attempted to repossess it. Family Savings Bank has brought suit to enjoin Appliance Mart from removing the stove.

In that action,

(A) Appliance Mart will prevail, because the stove is personal property on which it holds a valid security interest and Family Savings Bank has no lien on the stove.
(B) Appliance Mart will prevail because it holds a valid security interest which is superior to that of Family Savings Bank.
(C) Family Savings Bank will prevail, because the stove has been incorporated into the real estate, voiding the personal property lien held by Appliance Mart.
(D) Family Savings Bank will prevail, because Appliance Mart's lien is junior to the bank's lien.

Answer to Question 44

The stove is not personal property, but rather a fixture because of the intention to make it a permanent part of the real estate at the time it was affixed. Rita was not a tenant affixing the stove to the real estate for the limited term of her lease, but rather the owner of the property in fee simple. The fact that the stove could be easily detached is not a sufficient reason to classify it as personalty when there was a clear intention to permanently affix it. Therefore, the better analysis is that her intention was to incorporate the stove permanently into the realty. Thus, (A) is incorrect in saying that the stove is personalty. It is also incorrect in saying that Family Savings Bank has no lien on the stove. The stove has become a fixture and so is subject to Family Savings Bank's mortgage. The question is now one of priority.

A security interest in personal property is not automatically defeated when it becomes part of the real estate because it is a fixture, except in the rare case where the fixture is such an integral part of the realty (e.g., bricks) that it cannot be removed without substantial structural damage to the realty. Under UCC §9-313(4), when personal property which becomes affixed to real estate is subject to a valid purchase money security interest under Article 9 of the Uniform Commercial Code, the seller can maintain the priority of that security interest over an existing mortgagee by recording the security interest in the appropriate registry within ten days of the time the personal property is affixed to the real estate. The seller can remove the property and sell it as personal property if the buyer defaults and the seller can remove the personalty without damaging the real estate. That appears to be the case here. Therefore, (B) is correct and (D) is incorrect.

(C) is incorrect. The security interest in the personalty will remain valid, and Appliance Mart may remove the stove and sell it without compensating the bank for the diminution in value of the real estate.

Question 45

Developer owns a large tract of land on which he plans a residential subdivision. The subdivision is unique because it will contain an airstrip which will abut the rear of each house lot in the subdivision. Developer wants to ensure that the owner of each house lot will have a right to use the airstrip, that the right cannot be taken away inadvertently and that the successor in title of each lot will have the right to use the airstrip in perpetuity. The best device to accomplish these objectives is

243

(A) an appurtenant easement.
(B) an undivided fee ownership.
(C) an equitable servitude.
(D) a profit a prendre.

Answer to Question 45

(B) is incorrect. A fee ownership might at first seem like the best option, since it is the most comprehensive package of property rights available in property law. However, the cotenants of the property would have, as an incident of that co-ownership, the right to partition the property. If the property were partitioned by a physical division among the co-owners, the benefits of the airstrip would be lost because each co-owner could bar the other from the property he owned. If the partition took place by auctioning the property to the highest bidder, some of the lot owners could be barred from using the airstrip.

(C) is incorrect. An equitable servitude would serve the purpose of granting use rights to the subdivision owners, but its enforcement would be subject to equitable defenses to which an easement would not be subject. For example, a court has the discretion to refuse enforcement because of changed circumstances, such as the abandonment of the airstrip by a substantial majority of owners of the benefited estates. Moreover, an easement, which is a limited right to use the land of another indefinitely, is more functionally suited to accomplishing the purposes which the developer desires.

(D) is incorrect. A profit a prendre is an easement right to come onto land, sever a part of it, and carry that part away. While the easement portion of the profit is the best way to accomplish the developer's goals, there is no need for the easement holder to sever and keep a portion of the realty. Therefore, a profit a prendre is not appropriate.

(A) is correct. An appurtenant easement is most suited to Developer's purpose. It conveys a perpetual right to use the land without conveying any other unnecessary ownership rights, and cannot be terminated by the unilateral act of the fee owner. Because the easement is appurtenant, it would run with each parcel of land so that each subsequent owner would have the same right to use the airstrip as his predecessor.

Question 46

Blackacre is a magnificent Victorian mansion which has been Oscar's family homestead for 100 years. It is in an area of the city which is zoned for apartment houses, and many homes in the area have been torn down to build new apartment structures. Oscar wants to sell Blackacre, but does not want the house torn down nor the land used for an apartment house. If he should convey, which of the following will most successfully accomplish his objective?

(A) a covenant running with the land preventing the property from being used except as a single-family dwelling
(B) a negative easement preventing the property's use except as a single-family dwelling
(C) a fee simple determinable giving the property to the grantee so long as it is used as a single-family residence
(D) a right in Oscar and his assigns to purchase the property at the price at which it is sold by Oscar if the property is to be used for other than a single-family dwelling

Answer to Question 46

To answer this question, you must focus on Oscar's sole objective, which is to sell Blackacre but prevent the purchaser or his successors from tearing down the house thereon. A covenant running with the land would not be the most effective way to achieve this result for two reasons. First, a covenant will not run with the land and bind successive owners of the mansion as an equitable servitude unless there is a benefited estate. Here, there is no such estate, since it appears that the mansion is the only property owned by Oscar in the neighborhood. Therefore, if the buyer of the property should resell it, the new owner would not be bound by the covenant in equity. Second, a covenant would only be effective in accomplishing Oscar's purpose if a court of equity would specifically enforce it. If there is a significant change in circumstances between the time the easement is granted and the time when the owner wants to tear the property down, a court might deny specific enforcement of the covenant and enforce it only by way of money damages. Therefore, (A) is incorrect.

(B) is incorrect. A negative easement is not the best option because it would serve only to prevent particular uses by the owner. Thus, it could be used to prevent the owner from building an apartment building, but it would be difficult to draft a negative easement that would require the new owner to maintain the house on the property. An easement simply is not appropriate to accomplish this result. Moreover, since Oscar does not appear to hold any land which would be benefited by this easement, it would have to be construed as an easement in gross. Such an easement would terminate at Oscar's death and would be inalienable. Even if Oscar does own benefited land, the easement would attach to the land and would be transferred with it. Then, Oscar would lose control over the enforcement of the easement if he sold or lost title to the dominant estate.

(C) is the correct answer. A fee simple determinable will best accomplish Oscar's objectives. If the current owner attempted to tear the building down, the property would revert to Oscar by virtue of his possibility of reverter, an estate which lasts indefinitely because a reversionary type interest is not subject to the Rule Against Perpetuities. The termination of the fee simple determinable would be automatic. It does not depend on equitable discretion and does not require that Oscar own a benefited estate. The major drawback of a qualified fee, the unmarketability of the title created by it, is not a consideration in this question.

(D) is incorrect. This buyback arrangement would be an invalid restraint on alienation, and would violate the Rule Against Perpetuities. A right to buy the property at a fixed price (especially the price originally paid for the property) would inhibit the alienation of property because the original price probably would not reflect its current market value. Therefore, a fixed price arrangement, in contrast to a right of first refusal, is an invalid restraint on alienation. In addition, rights to purchase property are subject to the Rule Against Perpetuities. Since, in order to achieve Oscar's goal, the right proposed in this case would have to be unlimited in time, it therefore could be exercised more than 21 years beyond lives in being at the time of the creation of the interest, and thus would violate the Rule.

Question 47 skip

Angela is the owner of Blackacre, a lot of land in a subdivision in the state of Pencilvania. All deeds from the common grantor of the lots in the subdivision imposed a restriction prohibiting any structures within fifteen feet of the sideline. The local zoning ordinance prohibits structures within ten feet of the sideline. There are no restrictions concerning rear yard setbacks in either the deed from the common grantor or in the local zoning ordinance.

The statute of limitations for adverse possession in Pencilvania is twenty years; for contracts, it is six years; and for enforcement of zoning violations, it is two years.

Angela has sold Blackacre to Bonnie. Bonnie has constructed a garage at the rear of her property. It is within seven feet of the sideline and encroaches two inches over the rear lot line.

What is the minimum amount of time that the garage must be on Blackacre before Bonnie will have a valid defense (other than the defense of laches) in a suit requiring her to remove her garage from its present location?

(A) no time, because all persons who would be attempting to require removal would be estopped from bringing the action
(B) more than two years
(C) more than six years
(D) more than twenty years

Answer to Question 47

The proper approach to answering this question, since it asks how long the building must be on the land before it is not subject to **any** claims for removal, is to first deal with the longest time period to see if anyone has the right to have the building removed within that period. If they do, then the longest time period is the correct answer. If they do not, then proceed to the next longest period and perform the same analysis until you reach a period where someone has a right to have it removed.

The longest time period, 20 years, is the period which an adjoining landowner would have to force the removal of a trespassing structure. In this case, that time period would be inapplicable, even though there is an encroachment, because the encroachment is only two inches. A court of equity would not force removal over an encroachment which is *de minimis*. Therefore, (D) is an incorrect answer.

The second time period is six years, the statute of limitations on a contract action. There is a breach of the covenant in the deed because the structure is within fifteen feet of the sideline. Any lot owner in the subdivision would be able to bring suit within the six-year period, and would be successful in obtaining injunctive relief to prevent continuation of the violation of the covenant. Therefore, (C) is the correct answer.

The two-year period for enforcement of the zoning ordinance is not correct, even though there is clearly a zoning violation, because a cause of action may be brought within six years to have the building removed. Therefore, (B) is an incorrect answer.

There is no basis in the facts of this question to find that any person has taken a position inconsistent with the position they would have to take to require removal of the structure, and therefore, the potential plaintiffs will not be estopped from bringing their actions. Therefore, (A) is an incorrect answer.

Question 48

Able and Baker each owned one-story buildings on adjacent lots on Main Street. A common wall which was half on the land owned by Able and half on the land owner by Baker was an integral part of both buildings. Able and Baker each held a recorded easement on the land of the other which was under the wall. Baker desired to add a second story to her building, and Able and Baker entered into a written party wall agreement (which was duly recorded), for themselves, their successors and assigns, whereby Baker was permitted to increase the party wall at her cost and Able agreed to reimburse her one-half of the cost at such time as Able extended his building to two stories. Able then sold his lot to Charlie and Baker sold her lot to Doug. If Charlie now decides to construct a second story on the building and Doug sues him for half the original cost of the wall,

(A) Charlie will prevail because he is not in privity of contract with Doug.
(B) Charlie will prevail because Able's agreement does not touch and concern the land.
(C) Charlie will prevail because the benefit of Baker's contract is personal to him.
(D) Doug will prevail because both the benefit and the burden of the contract between Able and Baker run with the land.

Answer to Question 48

Historically, some cases held that any contract which only requires the payment of money cannot touch and concern the land. More modern cases hold that a contract to pay money which is intimately associated with the land will meet the touch and concern requirement. When Charlie built on his property, he gained a benefit which was directly related to the land, and he clearly should be obligated to pay. While it can be argued that Baker should be the payee since she paid for the wall, it must also be noted that she conveyed the wall at the time she sold the lot to Doug. Since the agreement bound the original parties, their successors and assigns, the right to payment also ran with the land. Since the better argument is that the touch and concern requirement is met, the covenant will run with the land. Therefore, (B) and (C) are incorrect and (D) is correct.

(A) is incorrect because the original Able-Baker contract runs with the land and binds their successors. The fact that two parties are not in privity of contract does not mean that the contract is not enforceable against them as a covenant running with the land.

Question 49

Abigail was the founder of a religious sect known as the Saints, She was the owner of Blackacre, on which the Saints' church was built, and Whiteacre, the adjoining parsonage. Blackacre and Whiteacre are located in State X, which provides that all interests in real estate are devisable and descendible. When she retired as the leader of the sect, she deeded the church to her successor minister, Beatrice, "for so long as the property is used for church purposes." She also inserted in the deed, "The grantee and her heirs shall use the premises only for purposes of religious worship."

Abigail continue to live in the parsonage.

Shortly after Abigail retired, the church fell on hard times and Beatrice therefore sold the church property by warranty deed to the Adventist Church in fee simple.

Abigail died one year later and left all of her property, both real and personal, to her beloved friend Beatrice.

The Adventist Church has likewise fallen on hard times. It has obtained an appropriate license, and now uses the church property for bingo games five nights a week and for nothing else. When patrons leave the bingo games late at night, they make noise which sometimes disturbs Beatrice, who now lives in the parsonage.

What is the best theory under which Beatrice might prevent the use of the church hall solely for bingo games?

(A) a suit in contract to specifically enforce the covenant with respect to the use of the premises
(B) take possession of the property pursuant to the possibility of reverter which she inherited from Abigail
(C) a suit on an equitable servitude
(D) a suit in tort to enjoin a nuisance

Answer to Question 49

(A) is incorrect. There is no covenant in the deed from Beatrice to the Adventist Church restricting the use of the property to church purposes. Since there is no privity of contract between them, Beatrice will not be successful on a contract theory. She can only pursue a theory of a covenant running with the land, which this choice does not address.

(B) is incorrect. Beatrice will not be successful in taking control of the property pursuant to the possibility of reverter which she inherited from Abigail. Although she did inherit it, she had previously given a warranty deed to the Adventists that she owned the property in fee simple. Under the doctrine of estoppel by deed, the possibility of reverter which she inherited from Abigail went directly to the Adventist Church by virtue of her warranty deed. Therefore, she cannot now use that reverter to repossess the property.

(C) is correct. The deed from Abigail to Beatrice contains not only a fee simple determinable, but also a covenant concerning the use of the property which benefited Abigail's remaining land, the parsonage. Abigail could have enforced that covenant against Beatrice and her successors in title. When Beatrice succeeded to ownership of the parsonage at Abigail's death, she owned the benefited land which held the equitable servitude. It is clear that the possibility of reverter which Beatrice inherited from Abigail went to the Adventist Church under the doctrine of estoppel by deed because of the warranty deed given by Beatrice. However, the same is not true with respect to the right to enforce the covenant, which is an incident of land which Beatrice still clearly owns. Therefore, her best argument is to enforce the covenant as an equitable servitude.

(D) is incorrect. While a suit to enjoin a nuisance is a possible cause of action when the owner of one parcel of land interferes with the use and enjoyment of a neighbor's land, the interference here seems to be minimal and not of sufficient magnitude to warrant injunctive relief. The parsonage is directly next to a building which is used for meetings. It is likely that, even when it was used for a church, there was noise when the parishioners left the premises. Injunctive relief under these circumstances is unlikely.

Question 50

Developer owned a 30-acre parcel of land which he subdivided into 20 residential house lots. In the deeds of lots one through ten, Developer included a covenant which prohibited the buyer from erecting a fence more than five feet in height along the side or rear lot lines. Developer then sold lot 11, which abutted a commercial strip of land at the edge of the subdivision, to Anita. Before Developer started his subdivision, Helga, the owner of the commercial land next to Anita's lot, had erected a seven-foot-high picket fence along their common rear boundary. Anita was told of the height restriction of fences at the time she agreed to purchase lot 11, but by inadvertence, no restriction concerning fences was placed in her deed. Developer placed the fence restriction in the deeds to lots 12 through 20. All deeds were promptly and properly recorded.

Anita constructed a house on lot 11 and thereafter sold the property to Brenda. The deed conveying lot 11 contained no restrictions. Brenda then constructed a seven-foot-high picket fence along the sideline between her lot and lot 10. Felicia, the owner of lot 10, has commenced suit against Brenda to require her to reduce the height of her fence to five feet.

If Brenda prevails it will be because

(A) Felicia's lot was not owned by Developer at the time he conveyed lot 11 to Anita.
(B) The seven-foot-high rear yard fence represents a changed circumstance which makes it inequitable to enforce the covenant.
(C) The fence restriction was not binding on Anita, Brenda's predecessor in title, because it was not placed in the deed she received from Developer.
(D) Decisions interpreting the recording statute of the jurisdiction hold that Brenda does not have constructive notice of the deeds of Developer to lots 1-10 and 12-20.

Answer to Question 50

Developer has placed the same restriction in the deeds to all of the lots in the subdivision except for lot 11, where the restriction was omitted by inadvertence. Therefore, there is a common scheme. One of the incidents of a common scheme is that any lot owner burdened by the restriction can sue any other lot owner within the common scheme, irrespective of whether the land of the plaintiff was owned by the developer at the time the restriction was placed on the land of the defendant. Therefore, the fact that Developer did not own lot 10 at the time of the deed to Anita of lot 11 is irrelevant and (A) is incorrect.

One of the other incidents of a common scheme is that the developer is under an implied obligation to impose the same restriction on all other lots in the subdivision. Then, under the doctrine of negative reciprocal covenants, Anita's lot is bound by the restriction because she had notice of it. Thus, (C) is incorrect. The only issue is whether her successor in title has notice so that she is also bound.

Jurisdictions are split on the issue of whether the purchaser of a lot has constructive notice of all restrictions placed in other deeds by a common grantor. If the courts of the jurisdiction do not find constructive notice in the deeds of Developer to the other lots in the subdivision, then Brenda does not have notice of the restriction and would take free of it. (D) is therefore the correct answer.

(B) is incorrect because the seven-foot-high fence was in place at the rear of Anita's lot before Developer began work on the subdivision. It cannot therefore be a **changed** circumstance which will justify not enforcing the restriction.

Questions 51 and 52 are based on the following fact situation.

Olga, the owner of a 200-acre tract of land, laid out and obtained the necessary approvals for a 250-lot subdivision known as Tall Oaks. All of the lots in the subdivision were conveyed during the ensuing two years. The deeds contained provisions, expressly stated to be binding upon the grantees, their heirs and assigns, requiring the lots to be used only for single-family, residential purposes. The deeds expressly stated that these provisions were enforceable by the owner of any lot in the Tall Oaks subdivision. The land is located in a jurisdiction where restrictions in prior deeds are in the chain of title.

The 200 acres in Tall Oaks have been zoned for residential use in a classification which permits both single-family and multiple-family use.

Thereafter, a spontaneous organization of the owners of lots 1 to 249 agreed and duly recorded a signed declaration of agreement that no house more than one story in height shall be built on any lot. The owner of Lot 250, Zack, refused to sign the agreement.

51. Zack, who purchased Lot 250 from Olga, thereafter conveyed his property to Zeb by a deed containing no restrictions. Which of the following statements is most accurate?

(A) Andrew, the owner of Lot 1, may enjoin the building of a house more than one story in height on Lot 250.
(B) Andrew, the owner of Lot 1, may enjoin the construction of an apartment house on Lot 250.
(C) Olga may enjoin Zeb from building an apartment house on Lot 250.
(D) Olga may sue Zack for damages if Zeb constructs an apartment house on Lot 250.

52. Ed, the owner of adjacent lots numbered 5 and 6, sells Lot 5 to Elaine. The deed to Elaine contains only covenants by Elaine that any building shall be set back 20 feet from the road and that Elaine will plant a lawn between his house and the street. Ed then sold Lot 6 to Fred. If Elaine were to commence the construction of a one-story, single-family house closer than 20 feet to the streetline, who would be successful in enforcing an equitable servitude?

(A) only Fred

(B) both Fred and Ed
(C) Fred and any lot owner in Tall Oaks
(D) Fred, Ed, and any lot owner in Tall Oaks

Answer to Question 51

(A) is incorrect. The agreement among the owners of lots 1 through 249 restricting the height of buildings on their lots created a valid covenant running with the land enforceable by and against the parties to the agreement and their successors in title. Zack is not a party to that agreement and it is not enforceable against Zack or his successors. Therefore, Andrew cannot restrict Lot 250 to a single-story residence.

However, Zack took a deed which expressly limited the use of the property to a single-family residence. That restriction is a valid covenant, in writing, which touches and concerns the land and is expressly intended to bind successors in title. The covenant runs with the land and is enforceable by any other similarly burdened lot owner under a common scheme theory. Though Zeb took a deed without restrictions, the covenant was in the chain of title and thus the recording system provided him with notice. Andrew is a lot owner who may enforce the restrictions in Zack's original deed against his successors in title. The construction of an apartment house would violate that covenant. The declaration of agreement among owners of Lots 1 through 249 is not needed to enjoin this construction. (B) is correct.

(C) is incorrect. Although Zack originally took the deed containing the covenant from Olga as grantor, she owns no benefited land. Olga has no right to sue a subsequent owner in equity for breach of a covenant once she no longer holds any benefited land. If a covenant runs with the land (as it does here), the right to enforce the covenant is conveyed with the benefited land such that the grantor no longer has that right after that conveyance. Here, Zeb may be enjoined from building the apartment house, but Olga is not a proper plaintiff.

(D) is incorrect. The covenant in the original deed from Olga to Zack created a binding contract between them. That contract would have been enforceable between them by

249

an action for damages, even after Olga had conveyed all the land which benefited from the covenant, if Zack were still the owner of the burdened land and violated the covenant in that capacity. However, Zack no longer owns Lot 250 and has no control over Zeb's actions on that lot. Therefore, courts will not hold him liable for breach of the contract contained in his deed from Olga.

Answer to Question 52

Ed cannot sue to obtain equitable relief because he does not now own any land benefited by the covenant in the deed. Most courts would hold that if a covenant runs with the land (as it does here), the right to enforce the covenant is conveyed with the benefited land such that the grantor no longer has that right after that conveyance. Thus, (B) and (D) are incorrect answers.

When a lot owner places new restrictions on the land as part of a deed, those restriction do not become part of the common scheme. The restriction contained in the common scheme which limit the property to single-family residences has not been violated. Therefore, in this case, the other lot owners in Tall Oaks cannot prevent Elaine from undertaking her planned construction, since it only violates a covenant in her deed, not the common scheme. Thus, (C) is an incorrect answer.

(A) is correct. Only Fred can sue to enforce the covenant. The covenant in Elaine's deed that he would only build 20 feet from the road only inured to the benefit of the other lot then held by Ed, which was later sold to Fred. That benefit was conveyed, with the land, to Fred.

Question 53

Developer is the owner of 750 acres of land in an area where there is a great interest in horses. Except for 30 acres near the main road at the edge of the parcel, which he reserved for commercial development, Developer laid out the remainder of the property for house lots.

In addition, Developer constructed on land retained by him a series of bridle paths connecting each lot to a central area of five acres, also retained by him, improved by an outdoor area with a grandstand in which horses could perform.

He sold the lots both with a covenant that each lot would be located on a bridle path and with a provision in the deed requiring that the lots be used only for residential purposes. The lots were deeded by reference to a plan which showed the bridle paths.

Over time, the underbrush grew into the bridle paths, making them unusable. A fire partially destroyed the performing ring and grandstand, and that part of the structure still remaining was in great danger of collapsing.

Developer plans to tear down the half-burned grandstand and performing ring, and in response to a large demand for retail stores, plans to erect a small shopping center in its place and use some of the area previously occupied by bridle paths for parking.

If a suit were brought by 10 owners of lots in the subdivision who had purchased their lots from original purchasers, seeking to enjoin Developer from using the bridle paths for parking purposes, their best theory would be that

(A) each had an implied easement.
(B) the deeds gave each lot owner a warranty of access.
(C) there was an implied covenant as a result of Developer's common scheme.
(D) each lot owner had an easement by prescription.

Answer to Question 53

(A) is incorrect. In order for the lot owners to hold implied easements, a quasi-easement must be in existence at the time the property was divided and the use of the bridle paths must be reasonably necessary to the enjoyment of the dominant parcels. A bridle path is a luxury, not a necessity, and the lots in question may still be used for residential purposes without the paths. Therefore, no implied easement would be found.

(B) is incorrect. While a warranty of access may be implied from the fact that the deeds contain reference to a plan which shows the bridle path, the issue is not access alone, but the use of the entire bridle path free from parked cars. A right of access will not accomplish this goal.

(C) is correct. The facts describe a development scheme which consists of residential, commercial and other specific uses. At the time the lots were conveyed, their deeds made reference to a plan which laid out the bridle paths, one part of the scheme. Each deed also contained a covenant that they would be located on a bridle path. It could be argued that the reference in each deed to the plan amounted to a covenant that each owner would have a right to use of the bridlepaths and performing area as such. Since such a covenant would touch and concern the land and appears to be intended to run with the land, the current lot owners have at least a colorable argument that they have a right to enjoin any change in use of the property. Under a common scheme theory, the current owners who are burdened by the restrictions concerning the bridle paths should be able to enforce related burdens on Developer, whose land is logically part of the scheme.

(D) is incorrect. The lot owners could not have obtained an easement by prescription because, until recently, their use was permissive. Also, an easement by prescription requires continuous use and the facts indicate that the use of the bridle paths may have been abandoned before the prescriptive period ended.

Question 54

Oprah, the owner in fee simple, laid out a subdivision of 325 lots on 150 acres of land. During the ensuing two years, she sold 200 lots and inserted in each deed a restriction limiting the use of the land to residential purposes.

Because of difficulty encountered in selling the remaining lots for single-family use, Oprah advertised the remaining lots with prominent emphasis: "These lots are not subject to any restrictions and purchasers will find them adaptable to a wide range of uses."

Oprah sold the remaining lots in the subdivision, imposing no restrictions in the deeds to those lots. Donohue, a subsequent owner of one of the 200 lots originally sold during the first two years, proposed to erect a grocery store on his lot.

In a suit by Oprah to enforce the restriction, Donohue's best defense would be that

(A) the facts do not establish a common building or development scheme for the entire subdivision.
(B) the burden of the covenant does not run with the land.
(C) the plaintiff is not the owner of land benefited by the restriction.
(D) the plaintiff is estopped because he failed to place restrictions on the lots sold after the first two years.

Answer to Question 54

(A) is incorrect. Oprah owned land which had the benefit of the residential restriction, whether or not there was a common scheme. Moreover, it appears that a common scheme is in fact present.

(B) is incorrect because the burden of a use restriction prohibiting commercial development touches and concerns the land and meets the other requirements necessary for the covenant to run with the land. Therefore, an individual who owned land having the benefit of the restriction could enforce the restriction against a subsequent owner of a burdened lot.

The question asks what is the best defense of an owner of a lot which is bound by the restriction. Since the defendant is a subsequent purchaser of the lot, he is not bound to Oprah on a contractual basis. Oprah's suit must proceed on the theory of a covenant running with the land. To enforce such a covenant, Oprah must be the owner of a parcel benefited by the restriction. Otherwise, Oprah would have conveyed his cause of action with the land. Since Oprah has sold all of the remaining land, he is not an owner of benefited land and therefore would not be successful in enforcing the restriction against Donohue. Therefore, (C) is the correct answer.

(D) is incorrect because Oprah's failure to place restrictions on later lots does not necessarily estop him from suing to enforce an earlier restriction, if he owns land which is clearly benefited.

Question 55

Sue, the owner of Blackacre, has entered into an oral agreement to sell Blackacre to Pat for $20,000. Pat has delivered the purchase price to Sue, who deposited it in her bank account. Sue then changes her mind about selling the property, sends back the purchase price plus interest, and refuses to give Pat a deed. Pat sues for specific performance. In that suit,

(A) Pat will win because he performed his obligation.
(B) Pat will win because a court of equity will specifically enforce an oral contract when there has been part performance.
(C) Sue will win because she sent the purchase price back and therefore has clean hands.
(D) Sue will win because of the Statute of Frauds.

Answer to Question 55

Usually, in an action for specific performance, an agreement to convey land must satisfy the Statute of Frauds. The Statute is satisfied if the contract to convey is evidenced by a writing or writings containing the essential terms of a purchase and sale agreement and signed by the party against whom the contract is to be enforced. If there is no written agreement, as here, a court of equity can specifically enforce an oral agreement to convey only if the part performance doctrine is satisfied. In a majority of jurisdictions, part performance is proven when the purchaser pays the purchase price, has possession of the land, and makes improvements on the land, all with the permission of the seller. No jurisdiction is satisfied by payment of the purchase price alone. Since all Pat did is pay the purchase price, he is not entitled to specific performance. Thus, (A) and (B) are incorrect and (D) is correct.

(C) is incorrect. Return of the purchase price will not preclude enforcement of a purchase and sale agreement **if** the agreement is otherwise enforceable either under the Statute of Frauds or the part performance doctrine. Also, "clean hands" are required of the **plaintiff** in an equity action. The cleanliness of the defendant's hands is irrelevant.

Question 56

P and S entered into a written purchase and sale agreement for the purchase of Blackacre. The only copy of the agreement was retained by P and was destroyed through no fault of P. P delivered a check for the required deposit to S. S then decided he did not want to sell, and offered to return the deposit check. P made a tender of the remaining portion of the purchase price and thereafter sued for specific performance. In that suit,

(A) P will prevail because the deposit check was not destroyed.
(B) P will prevail because the destruction of the purchase and sale agreement is not controlling.
(C) S will prevail because of the parol evidence rule.
(D) S will prevail because of the Statute of Frauds.

Answer to Question 56

(A) is incorrect. In general, an agreement to convey land is enforceable only if it is evidenced in a writing or writings that will satisfy the Statute of Frauds. The writing or writings will satisfy the Statute of Frauds if the following elements are included: a) the vendor and purchaser must be identified, b) the land must be identified, c) it must contain words of sale, d) if the parties have agreed on a purchase price, the agreement must include the purchase price, and e) it must be signed by the party to be charged. From the facts given, it does not appear that the deposit check contained the essential terms as required by the Statute of Frauds and therefore does not constitute an enforceable agreement to convey land.

However, the Statute of Frauds only requires that certain agreements be reduced to writing; it does not require that the writing or writings actually be produced. If the writings are lost or destroyed, or some other exception to the best evidence rule is applicable, oral evidence can be used to prove the existence and contents of the writings satisfying the Statute. Therefore, since a written purchase and sale agreement existed, P can try to prove the existence and contents of that agreement, despite its destruction. Thus, (B) is correct and (D) is incorrect.

(C) is incorrect. The parol evidence rule will not prevent the introduction of evidence regarding the existence and contents of a written document. The rule prohibits only evidence (oral or written) of statements made by either party prior to or contemporaneous with the signing of the contract which vary or contradict the writing. Here, P is attempting to prove the existence and contents of a written purchase and sale agreement and not introducing statements which contradict the writing.

Question 57

Barbara and Sally had been in the business of buying and selling apartment houses in Metropolis for many years. Each had sold the other five separate properties. They would meet for lunch, agree on a price, and two weeks later would meet at the registry of deeds, where the seller would deliver the deed and the other the purchase price which they had orally agreed upon.

At lunch at the Metropolis Women's Business Club, Sally asked Barbara if she would like to repurchase the ten-unit apartment building on Main Street which Barbara had sold to Sally two years earlier. Barbara said, "I will pay you one million dollars for it." Sally said, "Its a deal." Barbara gave Sally a check for $10,000 on which she made the notation, "deposit Main Street apartments." Sally then said, "I'll meet you at the registry in two weeks. Bring your checkbook."

The next week, an arson fire burned down one of Barbara's apartment building, which was underinsured. Barbara will be forced to spend substantial sums to rebuild it. She therefore called Sally and said, "Because of the fire I can't go through with the purchase of Main Street. Please send my deposit back."

Sally refused to return the deposit, appeared at the registry on the appointed date, and tendered a valid deed. Sally then sued Barbara for specific performance, asking for $990,000 in exchange for a deed to the Main Street property and Barbara counterclaimed for the return of her $10,000. In those lawsuits,

(A) Sally will prevail on both the claim and the counterclaim, either because the signed deposit check constituted a memorandum, or because their course of dealings is a substitute for a writing.
(B) Barbara will prevail on both the claim and the counterclaim because of the Statute of Frauds.
(C) Barbara will prevail on both the claim and the counterclaim because the change of circumstances caused by the fire relieves her of the obligation to buy.
(D) Neither will prevail on their claims; Barbara will not be required to purchase the property and Sally will keep the $10,000.

Answer to Question 57

(A) is incorrect because **Barbara** will prevail on both the claim and the counterclaim because of the Statute of Frauds, as explained below.

(C) correctly states that Barbara will prevail, but states the wrong reason. The fire did not relate to the property in question. A fire on another property has simply affected Barbara's ability to pay. This is not a change of circumstances which would excuse Barbara's performance of this agreement, if there were a sufficient memorandum to make it enforceable.

Sally cannot enforce an agreement to sell real estate in these circumstances unless she has a memorandum signed by the party to be charged. The deposit check does not constitute a sufficient memorandum because it does not contain a notation of the purchase price, which has been agreed upon. The course of dealings between the parties is not a substitute for a writing. Since there is no enforceable agreement, Barbara is entitled to the return of her deposit. (B) is correct. Barbara will prevail on both the claim and the counterclaim because of the Statute of Frauds.

Since there is no enforceable agreement, there is no basis under which Sally is entitled to keep the $10,000. Sally will be required to return the deposit on a theory of unjust enrichment, or the like. The seller is usually only allowed to keep the deposit in the case of a contract breached by the buyer where the contract provided that the deposit would constitute liquidated damages. That is not the case here because there was no enforceable contract, and, even if there were, there is no indication that the contract provided for liquidated damages. (D) is therefore incorrect.

Question 58

Bertha, an avid sailor, was about to cross the Atlantic alone in her 40-foot sailboat, when she heard that Seaview, the house next to the Regal Yacht Club owned by Sal, might be coming on the market. Before departing on her trip, she authorized Laura, her lawyer, by a written power of attorney, to negotiate for her and purchase Seaview on her behalf. She also placed $250,000 in Laura's escrow account to complete the purchase.

Bertha left the east coast of the United States on February 1.

Seaview came on the market on March 1.

Laura (as attorney for Bertha) and Sal entered into a written purchase and sale agreement on April 1 whereby Bertha agreed to purchase Seaview.

Laura paid the $250,000 from her escrow account to Sal on May 1 in return for a deed to Seaview naming Bertha as grantee, which was recorded by Laura on May 15.

Bertha's body was found lashed to her overturned sailboat on June 1.

Sal learned of Bertha's death and had second thoughts about selling Seaview. He therefore tendered $250,000 to Laura, who was the executrix of Bertha's estate, and brought suit to declare the deed to Bertha a nullity. In that lawsuit, Sal will be

(A) successful only if Bertha died before April 1.
(B) successful as long as Bertha died before May 1.
(C) successful even if Bertha died between May 1 and May 15.
(D) unsuccessful no matter when Bertha died.

Answer to Question 58

Laura was acting for Bertha as her agent under a power of attorney. That agency terminated at Bertha's death. If that death occurred prior to the time that Laura and Sal signed the purchase and sale agreement, then the agreement is a nullity and the deed given by Sal to a dead person is also a nullity. Therefore, if Bertha died before the purchase and sale agreement was signed on April 1, Sal will be successful in regaining the property by returning the purchase price. Therefore, (A) is correct and (D) is incorrect.

Sal will not be successful if Bertha died after April 1, because Laura would then have validly entered into a binding purchase and sale agreement. Then, under the doctrine of equitable conversion, Bertha (and later her estate) were the owners of Seaview. Therefore, if Bertha died after April 1, Sal will be unsuccessful in rescinding the transaction. Therefore, (B) is an incorrect answer. The fact that Bertha was not alive on the date that the deed was delivered is not determinative, because of the doctrine of equitable conversion. The deed to Bertha is a nullity because Bertha was dead; but Bertha's estate can still force a conveyance of title by an appropriate court action.

(C) is incorrect. If Bertha was alive at the time the deed was delivered on May 1, she held title to the property in her own name at the time

254

of her death, even if the deed was not recorded until May 15. The delivery of a valid deed passes title to the property even if it is not recorded. Therefore, Sal will be **un**successful if Bertha lived until May 1.

Question 59

Seller, the owner of Blackacre, has entered into a written contract to sell it to Buyer for $50,000. Title is to be conveyed two years from the date of the agreement. The agreement provides that Buyer will maintain the roads on the property, and will pay all real estate taxes assessed to the property between the date of the agreement and the date for the conveyance. If the agreement is silent on the matter, which of the following is the best argument that Buyer is entitled to possession before the date of the conveyance?

(A) Buyer has equitable title under the doctrine of equitable conversion.
(B) It is presumed that the buyer under a valid purchase and sale agreement is entitled to possession.
(C) The obligation of the buyer to pay taxes and maintain the road implies that he has a right to possession.
(D) The length of time between the date of the agreement and the time for conveyance implies that Buyer has the right to possession.

Answer to Question 59

(A) is incorrect. The doctrine of equitable conversion does not give the purchaser a right to possession prior to the time of performance of the contract.
(B) is incorrect. It is not ordinarily presumed that the buyer under a purchase and sale agreement is entitled to possession. The usual purchase and sale agreement is simply an agreement to convey land containing the terms of that conveyance. Without a specific grant of right of possession within the agreement, one cannot be implied or presumed.

(D) is incorrect. The length of time alone between the date of the purchase and sale agreement and the date of conveyance will not establish a right to possession in the purchaser.
(C) is correct. The fact that the buyer must perform duties, particularly the payment of taxes, which usually indicate and require possession is the best argument.

Question 60

Owens contracted to sell a scenic tract of land, Giverny, to Painter by general warranty deed. However, at the closing, Painter did not carefully examine the deed and accepted a quitclaim deed without covenants of title. Painter later attempted to sell Giverny to Developer, who refused to perform because Owens had conveyed an easement for a highway across Overlea before Painter bought the property.

Painter sued Owens for damages. Which of the following arguments will most likely succeed in Owens's defense?

(A) The existence of the easement does not violate the contract.
(B) The mere existence of an easement which is not being used does not give rise to a cause of action.
(C) The proper remedy is rescission of the deed.
(D) Painter's cause of action must be based on the deed and not on the contract.

Answer to Question 60

An easement destroys the marketable title of the land if it actually or potentially interferes with the reasonable use of the land or would violate the covenant against encumbrances of a general warranty deed. This easement clearly interferes with the reasonable use of the land. Therefore, (A) is incorrect, as the terms of the contract were violated.

(B) is incorrect. An easement destroys the marketable title of the land if it actually or

potentially interferes with the reasonable use of the land or violates the covenant against encumbrances of a general warranty deed. This easement potentially interferes with the reasonable use of the land because a third party has a right to build a highway on the land at any time.

(C) is incorrect. Although Owens promised a general warranty deed, Painter accepted the quitclaim deed and the purchase and sale agreement was thereby satisfied. Painter could have rescinded the purchase and sale agreement only **prior** to acceptance of the quitclaim deed, because Owen failed to deliver a general warranty deed as promised in the purchase and sale agreement.

A deed is generally held to satisfy all the requirements of the purchase and sale agreement, except for any provisions of the agreement which are expressly made to survive the closing. Thus, once there is a conveyance, the grantee can usually only sue on the basis of the covenants in the deed. In this case, Owens's promise to convey by a general warranty deed is not expressly made to survive the closing. Therefore, Painter can only sue on the basis of the deed. Since Painter accepted a quitclaim deed which made no covenants as to title or encumbrances, Owens will prevail in a lawsuit resulting from the easement. (D) is the correct answer.

Question 61

Lana is the owner of a three-story office building which has one tenant on each floor. The first floor tenant is a restaurant which holds a ten-year lease. The tenants on the second and third floors hold periodic monthly tenancies. Both of the tenants have told Lana that they will be leaving in about three months because of the cockroaches generated by the restaurant. These conditions could not be found by a reasonable inspection of the property.

Lana asks her property manager, Mandy, to put a "for sale" sign in the window and show the building for her. Mandy is aware of the cockroach problem and is informed by Lana that two tenants intend to leave in the near future.

Tess responds to the sign, and Mandy shows her the building. Tess does not ask about the condition of the building, nor the status of the tenancies, and Mandy does not volunteer any information.

Tess decides to buy the building. Lana draws up a purchase and sale agreement which annexes the first floor lease and describes the two other tenancies as "periodic tenancies." The agreement specifies that no representations or warranties concerning the periodic tenancies or the condition of the property were made.

Two months after Tess took title, the two upstairs tenants terminated their periodic tenancies and moved out. The floors were vacant for six months and Tess incurred the cost of exterminating the cockroaches. Tess then brought suit against Lana for damages because of the losses she suffered and for the cost of exterminating the cockroaches.

If the court finds for the defendant, it will be because

(A) Tess would have discovered the problems if she had made a serious investigation prior to purchase.
(B) the provision of the contract that there were no warranties or representations controls the rights of the parties.
(C) Lana's duty to disclose problems and defects was satisfied because she informed Mandy, who showed the building to Tess, of them.
(D) the seller of a commercial building which has been inspected by the purchaser has no responsibility toward the purchaser.

Answer to Question 61

(C) is incorrect. Under general principles of the law of agency, a principal is responsible for the acts or omissions of her agent. Since Lana told Mandy that her tenants intended to vacate the premises and Mandy was aware of the cockroaches, Lana is liable for Mandy's failure to disclose the problems if there was an obligation

256

to do so. Disclosure to the seller's agent is not a substitute for disclosure to a buyer.

Absent a specific disclaimer in the contract, there is a strong argument that a seller **is** required to disclose known defects and problems which would not readily be discoverable by inspection. Thus, (A) is incorrect. The fact that a more thorough investigation would have revealed problems does not relieve the seller of the disclosure responsibility. In this case, moreover, the facts specifically state that "these conditions [cockroaches and the intent of the tenants to vacate the premises] could not be found by a reasonable inspection of the property." Therefore, (D) is incorrect.

(B) is correct. In the absence of fraud, the terms and conditions of the purchase and sale agreement will control the rights of the parties. Lana's strongest argument is that the purchase and sale agreement contained a clause disclaiming warranties and representations about the status of the tenancies and the condition of the building, and therefore she is not liable to Tess for any damages caused by existing conditions.

Question 62

Ryan, a homebuilder, constructed a single-family home on Blackacre. Soon after it was finished, water leaked during a heavy rainstorm through an improperly installed sliding glass door, staining the adjacent floor. Ryan did not disclose the problem to any prospective purchasers. Patsy inspected the house and made an offer to purchase, which was accepted by Ryan. At the closing, Ryan delivered a quitclaim deed. During the first heavy rainstorm after the closing, the sliding glass door leaked again, further staining the adjacent floor. Patsy spent $1,000 to properly install the door and refinish the adjacent floor area, and has brought suit against Ryan to recover these expenditures. In that lawsuit,

(A) Patsy will prevail because Ryan failed to disclose the problem with the sliding glass door.
(B) Patsy will prevail on a breach of warranty theory despite the fact that Ryan delivered a quitclaim deed.
(C) Patsy will prevail both because Ryan breached his warranty and because he failed to disclose the defect.
(D) Ryan will prevail.

Answer to Question 62

There is no tort liability for a defect which is in plain view because there is no misrepresentation. The stained floor makes the defect - the leaking glass door - obvious. Thus, there is no liability here based on a misrepresentation theory, that Ryan failed to disclose the defect. Thus, (A) and (C) are incorrect.

However, while there is ordinarily no implied warranty concerning the condition of real estate when it is sold, there is an exception when a builder constructs and sells a new home. Thus, Ryan is liable for breach of warranty, making (B) the correct answer and (D) an incorrect answer. The fact that Patsy received a quitclaim rather than a warranty deed is irrelevant because the warranties in a deed deal with the quality of title rather than the condition of the real estate.

Question 63

Omar, the owner of Blackacre, a two-acre commercial parcel lying between Main Street and School Street, subdivided it into six lots and constructed a retail store on each lot. Each store fronted on a private pedestrian road, Back Way, which connected Main and School Streets and was built on part of each of the lots. The deed to each lot granted an appurtenant easement to each of the lot owners over Back Way.

Omar sold lot 2 to Sally who operated a cosmetics store on the premises. Sally then entered into a written contract with Barbara to

257

sell lot 2 to her. The agreement did not specify the quality of title to be conveyed and did not provide that title was to be conveyed subject to the easements over Back Way.

Soon after the purchase and sale agreement was signed, Ginny, the owner of lot 1, where she had operated a gift shop, sold the premises to Marlene, who opened a pawn shop. The change in use on lot 1 hurt the remaining retail businesses on Back Way.

On the day appointed for the closing, Barbara wrote to Sally saying that she refused to close both because the easement destroyed marketable title and because of the change in the nature of the retail business next door. Sally tendered the deed at the appointed time and sued Barbara for specific performance.

In that lawsuit,

(A) Barbara will prevail because the easement destroys marketable title.
(B) Barbara will prevail even though Barbara possesses marketable title because the adverse change in the retail use of the adjoining property between the time of the signing of the purchase and sale agreement and the closing is a basis for rescission.
(C) Sally will prevail because the easement for Back Way on lot 2 does not destroy marketable title.
(D) Sally will prevail because the agreement did not require her to deliver marketable title.

Answer to Question 63

(B) correctly states that Sally possesses marketable title. However, the change in ownership and quality of the retail establishment next door does not provide a basis for rescission. No representations were made by Sally about the retail establishment next door, and she had no control over it. The nature of the establishment next door does not form the basis of the bargain, so a mutual mistake with respect to it would not form the basis for rescission.

(D) is incorrect because, if a purchase and sale agreement is silent on the quality of title required, a requirement of marketable title is implied. (In this case, Sally possesses marketable title, as discussed above.)

Generally, the presence of an easement will destroy the marketability of title if the easement actually or potentially interferes with the reasonable use of the land (unless the contract specifies that the property is to be sold subject to the easement). Another exception to this general rule applies when the easement is visible and beneficial to the property. Both criteria are met here. A simple inspection of the property would reveal that pedestrians are passing over Back Way in order to reach the retail shops. This easement is beneficial and essential for the operation of a retail shop on lot 2. Therefore, the easement does not destroy marketable title, even though the easement was not specifically provided for in the purchase and sale agreement. Thus, (C) is the correct answer and (A) is an incorrect answer.

Question 64

Black and White entered into a written purchase and sale agreement by the terms of which "Black agrees to convey Blackacre to White on March 15. Black shall convey marketable title to Blackacre."

White searched title and found that record title was in Green, not in Black. When questioned about this discrepancy, Black replied that he had been in adverse possession of Blackacre for twenty-five years, five years longer than was required under the applicable statute, and submitted to White convincing affidavits and other documentary evidence to establish his title by adverse possession.

White informed Black that he would not purchase Blackacre from him and Black brought suit against White for specific performance of the agreement.

In that action,

(A) Black will prevail because he has marketable title.
(B) Black will prevail because the validity of his title by adverse possession will be established in the suit for specific performance.

(C) White will prevail because the dispossessed record owner, Green, has an equitable lien on the property.
(D) White will prevail because he cannot be required to purchase property if he will run the risk of defending a lawsuit, even if it is likely he will prevail.

Answer to Question 64

Black must establish that he has marketable title to prevail. A marketable title is one reasonably free from doubt both in fact and in law. It is a title which a prudent businessperson purchasing the property would accept. Unless there has been an adjudication that good title is in the adverse possessor, title acquired by adverse possession does not meet the standard of marketable title. The purchaser might have to prove all of the elements of adverse possession sometime in the future and might lose because he does not have the necessary evidence. It is not reasonable to expect White to assume the burden of potential future litigation and therefore he will prevail. Until Black obtains a judicial decree that he has title to Blackacre by adverse possession, he does not have marketable title. Thus, (A) is incorrect and (D) is correct.

(B) is incorrect. There will not be a binding adjudication of the validity of Black's title by adverse possession in a suit for specific performance of the purchase and sale agreement between Black and White, because Green, the record owner, will not be a party. Therefore, the judgment will not be binding on Green and Black will not have marketable title.

(C) is incorrect. Green, the record owner, does not have an equitable lien without benefit of a court decree. Any possibility of obtaining an equitable lien would be defeated if Black is successful in establishing adverse possession.

Question 65

A ten-lot subdivision was approved by the proper governmental authority. The authority's action was pursuant to a map filed by Dietz, which included an undesignated parcel in addition to the ten numbered lots. The shape of the undesignated parcel is different and somewhat larger than any one of the numbered lots. Subdivision building restrictions were imposed on "all the lots shown on said map."

Dietz contracts to sell the unnumbered lot, described by metes and bounds, to Butch. Is title to the parcel marketable?

(A) Yes, because the undesignated parcel is not part of the subdivision.
(B) Yes, because the undesignated parcel is not a lot to which the subdivision building restrictions apply.
(C) No, because the map leaves it uncertain whether the unnumbered lot is subject to the building restrictions.
(D) No, because the undesignated parcel has never been approved by the proper governmental authority.

Answer to Question 65

(A) is incorrect because it is not at all clear that the unnumbered lot is not subject to the subdivision building restrictions. This reasonable doubt is sufficient to destroy its marketable title.

The issue presented in this question is whether the undesignated parcel might be considered a lot and thus subject to the building restrictions. The restrictions state that they are imposed on "**all** the lots shown on said map." Thus, if the unnumbered parcel is a lot, it would be subject to the restriction. Since the subdivision plan is ambiguous on this issue, there is a reasonable doubt about the applicability of the restrictions. This reasonable doubt would cause a prudent businessperson not to accept the title. Therefore, the seller does not possess marketable title, and (B) is incorrect.

The issue in this question is whether restrictions destroy marketable title to a parcel of land, not governmental approval of the lot for a subdivision. Title to the lot is marketable if it is free from the building restrictions, even if it has not been approved as a lot in a subdivision. Therefore, (D) is incorrect.

(C) is the correct answer. Restrictions destroy marketable title if they are more burdensome than the zoning ordinances applicable to the land. Restrictions also would render the title unmarketable if the property was to be sold "free of all encumbrances." There is a possibility that the restrictions apply to the unnumbered parcel because it might be considered a lot and the restrictions are imposed on "**all** the lots shown on said map." This creates a doubt as to whether the restrictions apply to the unnumbered lot. That doubt is sufficient to destroy marketable title.

Question 66

On January 15, Sarah entered into a purchase and sale agreement to sell Blackacre, a vacant parcel of land zoned for business purposes, to Betty on June 15 for $200,000 by good and clear marketable title. On January 15, the property was free from all liens except a $100,000 first mortgage.

Betty examined title and found that, in 1900, Oscar owned Blackacre and deeded it to Sarah's grandmother "as long as alcoholic beverages are not sold on the property." Betty also discovered that Sarah inherited the property from her grandmother in 1960. A search of the property records and vital statistics reveals no information about Oscar or his heirs.

On the day appointed for the closing, Sarah tenders a deed to Blackacre in fee simple to Betty, and presents a letter from the first mortgagee to Betty in which the mortgagee agrees to discharge the first mortgage upon payment of $100,000. Sarah asks Betty to pay off the mortgage from the proceeds of the closing.

Betty refuses to close, alleging that the outstanding first mortgage lien and the 1900 conveyance destroy marketable title.

Sarah sues Betty for specific performance. In that lawsuit,

(A) Betty will prevail only because Sarah has failed to produce a discharge of the first mortgage at the closing.

(B) Betty will prevail only because there is a chance that she will be dispossessed if she sells alcoholic beverages on the property.

(C) Betty will prevail, either because Sarah failed to produce a discharge of the first mortgage at the closing or because there is a chance that she will be dispossessed if she sells alcoholic beverages on the property.

(D) Sarah will prevail.

Answer to Question 66

The existence of a lien which will be discharged out of the proceeds of the closing will not destroy marketable title. Sarah is not required to produce a discharge of the mortgage at the closing, but is entitled to use the proceeds for the discharge. Therefore, (A) and (C) are incorrect answers.

On the other hand, the 1900 conveyance creating a fee simple determinable will destroy marketable title because there is a possibility that it could become possessory if alcoholic beverages were served on the property. The statute of limitations has not yet begun to run because there has been no breach of the condition. The Rule Against Perpetuities will not invalidate the interest because it is reversionary in nature. While the possibility that someone will come to claim the property is remote because Oscar is almost certainly dead and his heirs cannot be found, the possibility of reverter is still outstanding and creates a risk that a reasonable businessperson would not accept. Thus, title to the parcel is not marketable. (B) is the correct answer and (D) is an incorrect answer.

Question 67

Pierre was the owner of Blancacre. He gave a promissory note secured by a first mortgage on Blancacre to Savings Bank. Pierre then sold Blancacre to Danielle subject to the mortgage. Danielle failed to make the payments on the mortgage note and Savings Bank sued Pierre for the unpaid balance on the note. Pierre paid Savings Bank in full. If Pierre now attempts to foreclose the mortgage on Blancacre, it will be under the doctrine of

(A) subrogation.
(B) novation.
(C) assignment.
(D) estoppel.

Answer to Question 67

(B) is incorrect. A novation occurs when the mortgagee agrees to substitute the grantee as the obligor on the note and releases the grantor-mortgagor from any liability. To do this, the mortgagee and the grantee have to enter into a new contract. Here, there was no novation between the bank and Danielle and so Pierre remained liable. If there had been a novation, Pierre would not have had to pay the note and, therefore, would have no basis to foreclose.

(C) is incorrect. An assignment is a transfer of rights under a contract. Savings Bank did not assign their rights to Pierre. Pierre paid the note and discharged his obligation. Therefore, Pierre cannot foreclose on the property on the theory that he is the assignee of the note.

(D) is incorrect. Estoppel means that a party is prevented by his own acts or representations from claiming a right to the detriment of the other party who was entitled to rely on such conduct or representations and has acted accordingly. Estoppel is a doctrine which is simply not applicable to this case.

(A) is correct. Subrogation means that the grantor-mortgagor in effect buys the mortgage and steps into the shoes of the mortgagee. Thus, Pierre may sue to foreclose on the mortgage if the grantee, Danielle, does not reimburse him. This situation arises when property is sold subject to the mortgage and the grantee fails to pay the mortgage. In that case, the grantee has no personal obligation, either to the grantor or to the mortgagee, to pay the mortgage note. Therefore, if the grantor-mortgagor pays the obligation, he has no direct cause of action against the grantee for reimbursement. The grantor-mortgagor has, however, in effect bought that portion of the note and mortgage and is

subrogated to the rights of the mortgagee. As a result, the grantor may foreclose on the property if the grantee does not pay him back. In this case, Pierre's payment on the note is treated as a purchase of the note, meaning that he has also acquired the rights of the mortgagee and can foreclose on the property.

Question 68

Bart, the owner of Blackacre in fee simple, borrowed $50,000 from Mort. Bart gave Mort a promissory note for $50,000 and secured the payment of the note by giving Mort a mortgage on Blackacre which was duly recorded. One year later, Bart sold Blackacre to Wart, giving him a quitclaim deed which was promptly recorded. While Wart was the owner of Blackacre, the mortgage note was not paid when it became due.

If, at the time of the conveyance from Bart to Wart, the deed contained no reference to the mortgage, and Mort sues Wart on the promissory note, Mort will most likely

(A) win, because Mort is a third-party beneficiary of the conveyance from Bart to Wart.
(B) win, because an implied delegation of duties resulted from the conveyance from Bart to Wart.
(C) lose, because Wart did not promise to pay the mortgage debt.
(D) lose, unless Wart had constructive notice of the existence of the mortgage.

Answer to Question 68

(A) is incorrect. There is no third-party beneficiary contract unless the grantee promises to assume the debt. If a grantee assumes the mortgage obligation, the grantee expressly promises the grantor-mortgagor to pay the mortgage obligation. The mortgagee then becomes a third-party beneficiary of this promise to pay and can then sue the grantee directly if the grantee fails to pay. However, the mortgagee obtains no such right by virtue of the conveyance alone. There must be an express promise to pay to trigger the personal liability of the grantee. Here, Wart made no promise to pay on the note and, therefore, Mort does not have the rights of a third-party beneficiary.

(B) is incorrect. Delegation is a transaction whereby a person who has a contractual obligation gets someone else to perform the obligation, usually for consideration. However, a delegation cannot be implied from a conveyance of the property alone without an express promise by the grantee to assume the duty to pay on the note.

(D) is incorrect. Since the mortgage was properly recorded, the grantee had constructive notice of the mortgage. The grantee thus took the property subject to the mortgage, but only incurs personal liability on the note if the grantee agrees to assume the mortgage.

(C) is correct. In this question there is no agreement by the grantee to assume the mortgage. Thus, the grantee only takes the property subject to the mortgage. Since the grantee did not promise to pay the debt, the grantee is not personally liable. Only the grantor is personally liable on the note. Therefore, in the event of default, the grantee risks the loss of the property by foreclosure, but is not liable on the note.

Question 69

Owen owned Blackacre, which is located in State X, in fee simple free of any encumbrances. Owen signed a promissory note for $10,000 to Mike, and secured the note by a mortgage of Blackacre to Mike. The mortgage was duly recorded. Owen then sold Blackacre to Pete who assumed and agreed to pay the mortgage to Mike on Blackacre. Pete did not make payments on the mortgage note to Mike. Mike, following appropriate statutory procedures, foreclosed the mortgage and gave notice to both Owen and Pete that he intended to sue for any deficiency. At the foreclosure sale, Terry was the successful high bidder at $6,000. Mike now sues both Pete and Owen for $5,000, which is the remaining amount of the unpaid principal and interest on the note

plus costs of foreclosure. He will be successful in obtaining a judgment against

(A) Owen only.
(B) Pete only.
(C) either Owen or Pete.
(D) both Owen and Pete.

Answer to Question 69

Mike will be successful in obtaining a judgment against both Owen and Pete, although he may only collect once. When a grantee assumes the mortgage, the grantee expressly promises the grantor-mortgagor that he will pay the mortgage obligation as it becomes due. The mortgagee then becomes a third-party beneficiary of the grantee's promise to pay and can sue the grantee directly if the grantee fails to pay. After the assumption, the grantor-mortgagor becomes a surety who is secondarily liable to the mortgagee on the note if the grantee fails to pay. Owen and Pete are jointly liable, even though Pete is primarily liable and Owen is secondarily liable as a surety. Therefore, (D) is correct. (A) and (B) are incorrect.

(C) is incorrect. Since Pete assumed the mortgage obligation, Mike can sue Pete, but he can also sue Owen in the same action as the surety.

Question 70

Olive, the owner of Blackacre in fee simple, executed a mortgage to Mary, securing a note for one hundred thousand dollars ($100,000) payable in equal monthly installments over a 20-year period, together with interest at the rate of 11 percent per annum. The note and mortgage each contained the following provisions.

In the event that the mortgagor alienates the mortgaged premises, the mortgagee shall have the right to declare the note due and payable at her option.

No forbearance on the part of the mortgagee in the exercise of her rights shall be deemed a waiver of those rights.

One year later, Olive sold Blackacre to Ann for $150,000. Ann paid Olive $52,000 in cash. The balance of the purchase price was represented by Ann taking the property subject to the existing mortgage, which then had an unpaid balance of $98,000. For the next year, Ann made the payments in accordance with the note and Mary accepted them because mortgage rates had fallen to nine percent.

One year after Ann bought the property, mortgage interest rates rose to 13 percent. Mary sent Ann a letter demanding that the unpaid balance of the mortgage be paid in full. When Ann refused, Mary commenced foreclosure proceedings and an action for a declaration that Ann was liable for any deficiency judgment resulting from the foreclosure.

In that lawsuit,

(A) Ann will prevail in both actions because the due on sale clause is invalid.
(B) Ann will prevail in both actions because Mary waived her rights to accelerate the note by accepting payments from Ann for one year.
(C) Mary will prevail with respect to her right to foreclose, but will not be able to obtain a deficiency judgment against Ann.
(D) Mary will prevail with respect to her right to foreclose, and will be able to obtain a deficiency judgment against Ann.

Answer to Question 70

(A) is incorrect. A due on sale clause is a valid and enforceable provision and is a common term in a mortgage and a mortgage note. Therefore, Mary had the right to accelerate the note and declare the balance due on the transfer of the property to Ann.

Parties to a mortgage and a note may agree to various terms and conditions. Since the mortgage documents in this case specifically provide that forbearance in the exercise of a right will not be deemed a waiver of that right, Mary's acceptance of payments on the note from Ann for one year will not be deemed a waiver of the right to accelerate payment of the note pursuant to the due on sale clause. Thus, (B) is incorrect.

When a grantee takes property "subject to a mortgage," the grantee does not promise to pay the mortgage and only the grantor is personally liable on the note. However, if there is a "due on sale" clause, the mortgagee has the right to foreclose on the property if the note was not paid at the time of the sale. The question specifically states that Ann took the property subject to the mortgage and, therefore, did not agree to assume and pay the mortgage. Therefore, Mary does not have a direct cause of action against Ann for the amount due on the note because Ann is not personally liable on the note, but Mary does have the right to foreclose on the property by virtue of the "due on sale" clause. Although Mary did not exercise her right to declare the note due and payable at the time of the sale, her right to do so was preserved by the no-waiver clause in the agreement. Therefore, (C) is correct and (D) is incorrect.

Question 71

Seller, the owner of Blackacre, entered into a written contract with Buyer to purchase Blackacre for $124,000, payable in monthly installments of $1000 per month for twenty years. Buyer had the right to immediate possession. The contract was not recorded. In the fifteenth year of the contract, Buyer broke his leg and did not make three consecutive payments. If Seller brings an action to evict Buyer, Buyer's best defense would be

(A) Buyer defaulted because of a medical disability.
(B) the equities of the transaction favor Buyer.
(C) mortgage moratorium laws would protect Buyer.
(D) the agreement has not been recorded.

Answer to Question 71

Generally, the purchaser under an installment contract is obligated to make payments on a timely basis. If the purchaser fails to do so, he is in breach of the contract and may lose possession of the property and the payments made to date. However, courts will sometimes not permit such a result to occur and can be persuaded by equitable principles. Here, Buyer paid on the contract for 15 of the 20 years and did not maliciously default on the contract. Buyer's best defense is that termination of the contract at this time would unjustly enrich seller and, therefore, the equities of the transaction favor Buyer. (B) is correct.

Because (A) only provides one example of the general rule stated in (B), (B) is the better answer.

(C) is incorrect. There was no mortgage on Blackacre. Buyer and Seller entered into an installment contract and Seller retained the title to the property. Therefore, mortgage moratorium laws are inapplicable in this case. A mortgage moratorium law is a legislative act designed to grant mortgagors a period after they are in default to bring their mortgage up to date to avoid foreclosure. During that time, the mortgagee is forbidden from foreclosing his mortgage lien on the property. Note that you should not choose an answer that deals with a legal principle which you have never heard of before. Such choices are usually drafted as filler and are incorrect.

(D) is incorrect. The purpose of a recording system is to give stability to titles by providing a method of verifying a grantor's title and protecting the title of a purchaser who has bought land without knowledge of any prior grantee. Here, recording is irrelevant, since Seller and Buyer are the original parties to the agreement and no subsequent purchaser is involved.

Question 72

Lorraine owned Blackacre, a single-family residence. She financed the purchase of the property with a first mortgage loan of $125,000 from First Bank. Soon thereafter, a job offer in a distant city caused her to sell Blackacre to Barbara for $200,000. Because she was anxious to close and because Barbara paid the asking price, Lorraine conveyed the property to Barbara subject to the $125,000 mortgage. Barbara financed $50,000 of the remaining $75,000 purchase price by granting a second mortgage to Melissa.

Barbara then lost her job and became delinquent on both the first and second mortgages. First Bank accelerated the mortgage note and made demand on Lorraine. To protect her credit standing, Lorraine sent the bank a check in the amount of the unpaid principal balance of the mortgage.

Melissa has commenced foreclosure of her mortgage and claims that her mortgage is superior to any claim that Lorraine has against Blackacre. Which of the following is her strongest argument?

(A) The payment by Lorraine to First Bank discharged the debt and therefore the mortgage no longer secures an obligation.
(B) Any assignment which Lorraine obtained of First Bank's mortgage was later in time and therefore junior to Melissa's lien.
(C) The fact that Lorraine conveyed Blackacre to Barbara subject to the mortgage prevents Lorraine from being subrogated to the rights of First Bank.
(D) Lorraine can sue Barbara personally on any amount she paid, whereas Melissa must rely solely on the property for repayment.

Answer to Question 72

While the assignment from First Bank to Lorraine may be later in time than Melissa's mortgage, the date of the original mortgage establishes the priority of the liens. The mortgage from Lorraine to First Bank was earlier than Melissa's mortgage from Barbara, and Lorraine as assignee of the mortgage would have the right to the priority established at the time that the mortgage was granted. Therefore, (B) is incorrect.

The correct rule of law is exactly contrary to that stated in (C). Because the conveyance to Barbara was "subject to" the mortgage, Barbara has no personal liability to Lorraine to pay the mortgage. Lorraine's only remedy to recoup her money, if she is required to pay off the mortgage, is to be subrogated to the rights of the bank and obtain repayment by foreclosure of the property.

(D) is incorrect on the law on both counts. Because Lorraine conveyed the property "subject to" the mortgage, she has no personal right of action against Barbara. Her only rights are against the property, as a subrogee on the bank's rights as mortgagee. On the other hand, Melissa holds a mortgage note directly from Barbara and can sue her personally on that personal obligation.

The only theory by which Melissa can reasonably assert that her mortgage is ahead of any lien that Lorraine has on the property is that the payment by Lorraine to the First Bank was a discharge of the first mortgage. A mortgage is only security for an obligation. If the obligation is discharged, then the mortgage is no longer valid. It is unlikely that a court would find that the payment to the bank was intended to discharge the obligation, but it is the only theory by which Melissa can obtain priority over Lorraine. Therefore, (A) is the best answer.

Question 73

Bonnie borrowed $65,000 from Primo Bank, secured by a first mortgage on Bonnie's only piece of real property. That mortgage was properly executed and recorded. Bonnie then borrowed $35,000 from Segundo Bank, secured by a mortgage on the same piece of property. This mortgage was also properly executed and recorded.

Soon thereafter, Bonnie found herself unable to make the required payments on the loan from Primo Bank and Primo brought foreclosure proceedings. Notice of these foreclosure proceedings was published in local newspapers, as required by law, and delivered personally to Bonnie, but not Segundo Bank. At the foreclosure proceedings, Primo Bank was the highest bidder, and purchased the property for $65,000. Segundo Bank then learned of the purchase by Primo and brought suit to establish the following rights, in the alternative, with respect to the property:

I. the right to tender $65,000 to Primo Bank in exchange for a deed to the property.
II. the right to foreclose its second mortgage, subject to an outstanding (rather than foreclosed) mortgage to Primo Bank.

The court will most likely find that Segundo has the right to

(A) I only.
(B) II only.
(C) either I or II.
(D) neither I nor II.

Answer to Question 73

When the property is foreclosed upon by a senior mortgagee without notifying a junior mortgagee, the junior mortgagee can pursue either of two options.

First, the junior mortgagee can step into the shoes of the mortgagor and redeem the property by paying off the debt owed to the senior mortgagee at the time of the foreclosure. Thus, Option I is available to Segundo.

Second, the junior mortgagee can continue to pursue its own mortgage and foreclose on the property if the debt is not properly paid. The purchaser at the senior mortgagee's sale takes subject to the junior mortgage if the junior mortgagee was not informed of the sale. Thus, Option II is available to Segundo.

Therefore, in this case, Segundo has both a right of redemption and the right to foreclose on its own mortgage. (C) is correct.

Question 74

Ozzie held title to Blackacre, a parcel of land the fair market value of which is $200,000, in fee simple free from all encumbrances. Harriet agreed to lend Ozzie $200,000, provided that Ozzie deliver to her a deed to Blackacre. Ozzie executed a promissory note by which he promised to pay Harriet the entire principal balance and interest at 5% per annum in one year. He also delivered a deed to Blackacre, which Harriet promptly recorded.

Soon after the loan was made, the value of Blackacre increased sharply. Harriet conveyed Blackacre to Ricky, who did not know of the arrangements between Ozzie and Harriet, for $300,000.

Upon learning of the conveyance to Ricky, Ozzie brought suit against Ricky for an order that he convey Blackacre back to Ozzie in exchange for the balance of principal and interest due on the promissory note, and against Harriet for damages in the amount of difference between $300,000 and the balance due on his loan to her.

The results of the litigation should be that Ozzie will

(A) only prevail in his suit against Harriet.
(B) only prevail in his suit against Ricky.
(C) prevail in both suits and may chose either remedy but not both.
(D) not prevail, because Harriet paid him fair market value for a conveyance of Blackacre.

Answer to Question 74

Ozzie will not be successful in regaining the property from Ricky because Ricky is a bona fide purchaser. He paid value for the property to the record owner without notice of the equitable mortgage arrangement that Harriet and Ozzie had negotiated. Therefore, Ricky will prevail over Ozzie. Therefore, (B) and (C) are wrong.

The conveyance to Harriet from Ozzie, although absolute on its face, was only an equitable mortgage because it was given only as security for the repayment of a debt. Upon payment of the note by Ozzie, Harriet was obliged to reconvey Blackacre to him. She cannot now perform that obligation because she no longer owns Blackacre, but can be made to respond in damages in the amount she received

for the property less the amount due on her promissory note. Therefore, (A) is the correct answer.

The fact that the loan was equal to the fair market value of the property does not change its character from a loan transaction to an absolute conveyance. Thus, (D) is an incorrect answer.

Question 75

Saul and Isaac are about to enter into a purchase and sale agreement for Blackacre, a ten-acre farm. The purchase price agreed upon was $150,000. The agreement provides that Isaac was to pay Saul 10% of the purchase price upon the signing of the agreement, at which time he was entitled to take possession of the land. Isaac was required by the agreement to pay 10% of the purchase price on each anniversary date of the agreement. Saul was required to deliver a deed at the time that the purchase price was paid in full. Which of the following steps would not be helpful to ensure that Isaac will obtain good title to the farm at the time he pays the full purchase price?

(A) Record the purchase and sale agreement at the registry of deeds.
(B) Insert a grace period for the payment of installments in the purchase and sale agreement.
(C) Examine Saul's title prior to signing the purchase and sale agreement.
(D) Insert a provision in the purchase and sale agreement requiring Saul to keep the property insured during the term of the agreement.

Answer to Question 75

(A) is incorrect because recording the purchase and sale agreement would be to Isaac's benefit. Unless the agreement provides otherwise, the seller only has to produce marketable title at the closing and does not have to have marketable title at the time that the purchase and sale agreement is executed. One of the greatest dangers in using the purchase and sale agreement as a financing device is that the seller may not be in a position to convey good title at the time all of the installments are paid. To lessen that danger, Isaac should, among other things, record the purchase and sale agreement, so that any person who attempts to purchase or encumber the property thereafter will have notice of Isaac's right to purchase and thus will not be able to gain rights as bona fide purchasers which are superior to Isaac's rights.

Similarly, (B) is incorrect because including a grace period in the purchase and sale agreement **would** be to Isaac's benefit. If there is no provision for a grace period in the contract and Isaac is in default, even only once, Isaac may not be able to require performance by Saul and Saul will be able to terminate the agreement for breach, keeping the property and the money paid. A grace period will prevent Isaac from being in default if he makes the required payment within that grace period and, therefore, would help ensure that he can enforce the agreement against Saul even if every payment has not been made on time but has been made within the grace period.

Again, (C) is incorrect because examining Saul's title **would** be to Isaac's benefit. Isaac should, among other things, examine the seller's title at the time the agreement is signed to ensure that there are no existing encumbrances which would prevent the seller from giving good title when required.

(D) is the correct answer. A purchaser who has a valid and binding agreement to convey has an insurable interest in the property. Therefore, Isaac can insure the property himself and protect against loss. He need not rely on Saul to do so. Moreover, even if Saul insures the property, there is no reason to believe that that will benefit Isaac unless the insurance proceeds are paid to Isaac to compensate him for his equity in the property. Further, the presence or absence of insurance against loss has no bearing on Saul's ability to convey good title.

Question 76

Brenda agreed to buy Blackacre from Sarah for $150,000. Brenda agreed to pay $80,000 in cash and pay the remainder by a $70,000 promissory note secured by a mortgage on Blackacre. Brenda borrowed $50,000 needed for the purchase from Michelle, delivered to her a $50,000 promissory note, and executed a mortgage to secure the obligation.

Brenda met with Sarah to execute documents necessary to close the transaction. Sarah delivered a deed to Brenda which was "subject to a purchase money mortgage." Brenda, in turn, executed and delivered a promissory note for $70,000 and $80,000 in cash to Sarah. Brenda also executed a mortgage to secure the $70,000 promissory note and told Sarah she would record it with her deed. Brenda then went to the registry of deeds, recorded the deed and then recorded mortgages on Blackacre in favor of Sarah and Michelle in that order.

The jurisdiction has a notice recording statute.

When Brenda failed to pay either note, both Sarah and Michelle accelerated the notes and brought actions to foreclose their respective mortgages. If Sarah's mortgage is held to have priority over Michelle's mortgage, it will mostly likely be because

(A) Sarah's mortgage was recorded first.
(B) a purchase money mortgage from a seller prevails over all other mortgages.
(C) Sarah did not have notice that the down payment came from another lender.
(D) Michelle's mortgage fails because it was executed before a deed to Blackacre was delivered to Brenda.

Answer to Question 76

(B) is incorrect. There is no doctrine which makes a purchase money mortgage a first lien. Ordinarily, this is a matter for explicit negotiation by the parties. If the buyer is also to obtain institutional financing, the purchase money mortgage is ordinarily a second mortgage, because institutions ordinarily only take first mortgages. On the other hand, a seller can require that any purchase money financing be a first lien. In this case, the position of the lien was not explicitly negotiated.

The only way that Sarah could assure herself that the purchase money mortgage was a first lien would be to negotiate its priority in the purchase and sale agreement and make sure that it was recorded first. Her lack of knowledge about the source of funds for the down payment does not automatically assure her a first lien in the purchase money mortgage. Therefore, (C) is an incorrect answer.

While it is true that the mortgage to Melissa was signed at a time that Brenda did not own Blackacre, a standard mortgage has covenants in which the mortgagee warrants that they are the owners of the property. When Brenda became the owner, that warranty became true and Melissa's mortgage properly attached to Blackacre, as in the case with estoppel by deed. Therefore, (D) is incorrect.

However, both Sarah and Michelle authorized Brenda to record their mortgages, and neither explicitly specified that her mortgage be a first lien on the property. Therefore, the fact that Sarah's mortgage was recorded prior to Michelle's could be held to mean that, at the time that the mortgages were filed, Michelle had constructive notice that there was a superior mortgage on record. Under that reasoning, her mortgage lien could be held to be junior to the lien of Sarah. Therefore, (A) is correct.

Question 77

Oscar is the record owner of Blackacre in a jurisdiction where the statute of limitations to recover possession of real property is 20 years and the age of majority is 18 years. In 1970, Addie went into possession adversely to Oscar and was still in possession in 1985 when Oscar died, leaving Blackacre to his seven-year-old son Sam. Addie remained in possession between 1985 and 1995. In 1995, Sam's guardian discovered Addie's possession and brought an action to evict Addie. In that action, the court should find

(A) for Sam, because the adverse possession started running again at Oscar's death in 1985 and has not been continuous, open and notorious for 20 years.

(B) for Sam, because Oscar's death and the inheritance of Blackacre by Sam tolled the running of the statute until Sam reaches the age of majority.

(C) for Sam, because Addie cannot obtain title by adverse possession while Sam is under a disability,

(D) for Addie, because she has acquired title by adverse possession.

Answer to Question 77

Addie went into adverse possession in 1970. At that time, the property was owned by Oscar, a person who was not under a disability. The statute of limitations to recover possession of the property started to run immediately. The statutory period of 20 years was not interrupted by the death of Oscar. Thus, (A) is incorrect. The death of an owner starts the statute anew only if that owner was only a life tenant. Here, it appears that Oscar held a fee simple.

The statutory period also was not tolled by the inheritance by Sam, a minor. The statute of limitations is tolled only where the owner of the land at the time of the commencement of the adverse possession, and not a subsequent owner, is under a disability. Once the statute starts to run, it cannot be stopped by a subsequent disability. If Sam had owned the property at the time possession started, the statute would have been tolled, but that did not occur here. Therefore, title by adverse possession ripened in Addie in 1990, even though the property was at that time held by a minor. Thus, (D) is correct and (B) and (C) are incorrect.

Question 78

Oscar owned a large estate, which contained a small lake, in a Southern state. There was an island in the middle of the lake. Frequently Juliet, a prominent married politician, and her lover, Romeo, would swim to the island in a very surreptitious manner, and make love in a small shelter which they had constructed on the island. Although they thought that their activity went unnoticed, Oscar observed them one day

268

after they first went to the island, and made it a point to watch them at regular intervals thereafter. Twenty-one years after Romeo and Juliet had constructed their shelter on the island, Juliet was turned out of office by the voters. She thereupon divorced her husband, married Romeo, and claimed ownership of the shelter on the island. In an action to establish title, she should

(A) prevail, because her possession was open and notorious, even though Juliet did not know that Oscar was aware of her activity.
(B) not prevail, because her possession was not open and notorious.
(C) not prevail, because she had unclean hands.
(D) not prevail, because her use was permissive.

Answer to Question 78

(A) is correct. To satisfy the open and notorious requirement of adverse possession, the owner must have actual or constructive knowledge of the possessor's occupancy of the property. The statute of limitations begins to run when the owner knows or should know of the possession. Despite the fact that Juliet and Romeo thought that their activities were secretive, Oscar (the record owner of the land in question) did in fact know of their possession. Therefore, since he had actual notice, the statute of limitations started to run against him and at the end of the period (presumably 20 years) Oscar lost title to Romeo and Juliet under the doctrine of adverse possession.

(B) is incorrect. Although the activity of Romeo and Juliet was not open and notorious in the sense that they publicly displayed their romantic hideaway, it was open and notorious in a legal sense because their use conveyed actual notice to the owner of the property.

(C) is incorrect. Unclean hands is a defense to an action for equitable relief, which is not applicable here. The doctrine means that a person who has defrauded the other party in the subject matter of the action will not be able to assert any rights in equity. The party's wrongdoing must have some proximate relation to the subject matter of the controversy. Here, Juliet's activities on the island might raise some moral questions, but they do not give rise to a defense of unclean hands, as they were not inequitable in regard to Oscar.

(D) is incorrect. In an action to establish title by adverse possession, the possession must be "hostile." This requirement is satisfied as long as possession is had without permission of the owner. Although Oscar was aware of Juliet and Romeo's use of the island, the use was not permissive because they made no attempt to obtain Oscar's permission, nor did he voluntarily give his permission.

Question 79

Amy was the owner of a houselot which abutted a beach owned by her neighbor, Bernie. In 1972, Amy constructed a house on her land. During the summer of 1972, Amy fenced off Bernie's beach from abutting landowners so that it was only accessible from Amy's property and the water. During the summer months from 1972 through 1993, Amy and her family regularly used the beach on Bernie's land for swimming and sunbathing. In the spring and fall, Amy used the beach for fishing. If other people tried to walk, sit, or fish from the beach, Amy told them to "Get off my beach."

In the summer of 1988, Bernie, who had not visited his property since 1972, used his beach on a regular basis, but made no effort to prevent Amy's use of the beach in her customary manner. In 1989, Bernie sold his property to Daryl, who did not even set foot on the property until 1993. In that year, he brought an action of ejectment against Amy. In that action,

(A) Daryl will prevail only because the 1989 transfer of title interrupted Amyl's possession.
(B) Daryl will prevail only because of Bernie's joint possession in 1988.
(C) Daryl will prevail, either because the 1989 transfer of title interrupted Amy's possession or because of Bernice's joint possession in 1988.
(D) Amy will prevail.

269

Answer to Question 79

The statute of limitations is not tolled by a transfer of title after possession has begun. Thus, (A) and (C) are both incorrect. Assuming the other requirements for adverse possession are met, the statute of limitations which first began to run against Bernie continues to run against Daryl.

Adverse possession must be exclusive of the owner to ripen into title. Thus, if the owner goes into possession, the statutory period is terminated, even if the owner's possession is short-lived and she does not eject the possessor. Here, Amy's possession was not exclusive because Bernie used the beach in the summer of 1988. Thus, the statutory period terminated at that time. As a result, Amy will not be able to establish title by adverse possession because she did not adversely possess the property for a continuous 20-year period. Thus, (D) is incorrect and (B) is correct.

Question 80

Developer owned Blackacre, a large parcel of land with 1,000 feet of frontage on Spring Street. He laid out and sold a number of lots with frontage on Spring Street, but retained a 40-foot strip of land between two lots so that he would be able to build a road to the rear of the property at a later date. He sold the lot immediately south of the strip to Stan and the lot immediately north of the strip to Nina. Developer lost interest in the rear portion of the property when he discovered that it was covered with a subterranean ledge of rocks. To prevent the strip of land which was between them from becoming an eyesore, Stan and Nina planted a vegetable garden on it each spring, sold the vegetables at the local farmers market, and split the proceeds. After Stan and Nina repeated the process each spring for 21 years, what is the state of title to the strip of land?

(A) Developer has an exclusive interest in the strip, because the seasonal use by Nina and Stan does not constitute continuous use.
(B) Developer has an exclusive interest in the strip, because neither Nina nor Stan possessed the strip exclusively.
(C) Nina and Stan each own a portion of the strip which is 20 feet wide and which abuts his/her property.
(D) Nina and Stan own the strip as tenants in common.

Answer to Question 80

The possession of the strip by Nina and Stan was not exclusive of each other, but it was exclusive with respect to the true owner, Developer, which is all that is required for adverse possession. Therefore, (B) is incorrect.

Nina and Stan, acting in concert, occupied the strip of land by growing vegetables on it for the statutory period necessary to acquire title by adverse possession. Their common possession of the produce grown on the property and the manner in which they possessed Developer's land means that the only way in which they could meet the exclusivity requirement to acquire title by adverse possession is if they are considered as a unit. Their possession was adverse to Developer and adverse to the rest of the world, but not adverse to each other, so they achieve title by adverse possession as tenants in common. Since each of them copossessed the property for the statutory period, the adverse title which they will acquire will be as tenants in common. Therefore, (D) is the correct answer.

If Nina and Stan had each grown their own vegetables on one half of the property, then each would have acquired a 20-foot strip by adverse possession because each would have possessed a portion of Developer's land continuously, openly and notoriously, exclusively, and adversely for the statutory period. The facts in this case, however, indicate that they exclusively possessed the entire 40-foot strip **together** and that neither exclusively possessed any portion of the strip. Therefore, they will not each own one half of the strip. Therefore, (C) is an incorrect answer.

While Nora and Sally did not physically occupy the strip all winter, they did occupy it consistent with the purpose for which it was suited, namely a vegetable garden during the warm weather. That is sufficient possession to meet the continuity requirement to acquire title by adverse possession. (C) is therefore incorrect.

Question 81

Borg and Connors owned adjoining parcels of land. In 1972, Borg decided to build a tennis court. He laid out the court with an observation booth built on the top of the fence along one side. Connors observed the layout and complained that the fence was on his land. Borg said that he had the property surveyed and the fence was definitely on his land. In 1993, Connors sold his property to Graf, who had the property surveyed and found that, although the fence was on Borg's land, the observation booth, with an expensive video system installed, was overhanging her land by two feet. If Graf brings an action to require Borg to remove the observation booth from her land,

(A) Graf will prevail but must bear the costs of removing the offending structure.
(B) Graf will prevail and may remove the booth, and Borg must bear the cost of removal.
(C) Borg will only be liable for the diminution in value of Graf's land caused by the overhang.
(D) Borg will prevail.

Answer to Question 81

Borg will prevail because Borg adversely possessed the airspace over the neighboring land for the statutory period of 20 years. Since an owner of land has a right to exclusive possession of the airspace above the land, Borg's possession of the airspace was hostile to Connors in that Borg did not have Connors' permission to possess the airspace. Further, the fact that Connors sold the land to Graf does not affect Borg's rights to the airspace. Borg adversely possessed the airspace for the required 20-year period by the time of the conveyance to Graf and, since Connors no longer had a cause of action against Borg, Graf did not obtain one with the transfer of title. Therefore, (D) is correct, and (A) and (B) are incorrect.

(C) is incorrect. Once title is established by adverse possession, the possessor is not in trespass and is not liable to the owner for any damages.

Question 82

At a time when Son, a small businessman, is close to insolvency, Father, the owner of Blackacre, prepares and signs a deed of Blackacre to Son and shows it to Son. Son says that he does not want the deed because he is sure that his creditors will get the property. Crud, a substantial creditor of Son, was visiting Father one day when he saw the deed on Father's desk. He took the deed from the desk, recorded it, and brought suit against Son, eventually obtaining Son's interest in Blackacre in satisfaction of his debt. In a suit by Father against Crud to establish his interest in Blackacre, judgment will be for

(A) Father, because Crud had no right to record the deed.
(B) Father, because there was no delivery.
(C) Crud, because recording satisfies the condition that a deed must be delivered.
(D) Crud, because acceptance is presumed when a validly executed deed has been tendered.

Answer to Question 82

Since there was no delivery, there was no passage of title and recordation by Crud would have no effect, at least as long as no bona fide purchaser is involved. Recording may create a presumption of acceptance, especially if it is the grantee who records. However, recordation does not replace the requirement of delivery and acceptance. Thus, (A) and (C) are incorrect.

(D) is incorrect. Acceptance may be presumed when there are no facts showing the contrary. Here, however, Son has expressly refused title. In such a case, there is no acceptance, even if there was delivery.

(B) is correct. There must be a "delivery" and acceptance of the deed for title to be conveyed. The delivery requirement is an intent issue; the grantor must intend to confer an immediate, irrevocable interest on the grantee. Father properly executed a deed to Blackacre but merely "showed" it to Son, which may not constitute a delivery. Moreover, Son clearly refused to accept it. Since there was no delivery of the deed, there was no passage of title. Crud's actions of taking the deed and recording it are legally void and title remains in Father.

Question 83

Able owned Blackacre. He prepared and signed a deed, containing an adequate description of Blackacre, in which the grantees were named as his nephews, Bob and Clark, as joint tenants. He mailed the deed to Clark with a note saying, "I always wanted you and your brother to own Blackacre." Before the letter arrived, Clark died, survived by his son, Sam, his sole heir. Then Able died, survived by a daughter, Dora, his sole heir.

Who owns Blackacre?

(A) Dora alone
(B) Bob alone
(C) Dora and Bob
(D) Bob and Sam

Answer to Question 83

(A) is incorrect. Able effectively conveyed Blackacre before he died, so Dora did not inherit any interest in the property.

(C) is incorrect. Bob **is** the surviving joint owner of the property, but Dora has no interest in it, as shown above, because Able effectively conveyed Blackacre before he died.

(D) would be correct only if Bob and Clark were tenants in common at Clark's death. This is not the case, because Able effectively conveyed Blackacre to Clark and Bob as joint tenants (which includes a right of survivorship). Therefore, Clark's interest passed to Bob at Clark's death.

(B) is correct. A grantor can "deliver" the deed without physically giving it to the grantees. All he need do is execute the deed and somehow manifest an intent to make the conveyance effective immediately. When Able placed a valid deed in the mail, delivery was complete because he thereby manifested an intent to make the conveyance effective immediately. He could not thereafter stop delivery. As a result, when the deed was mailed, title to Blackacre vested in Bob and Clark as joint tenants. Clark was designated the agent of Bob to accept delivery of the deed. Further, the deed was accepted because acceptance is presumed, unless the grantee specifically rejects the deed. When Clark died, Bob took exclusive title to Blackacre as the surviving joint owner of Blackacre.

Question 84

Molly, the owner of Blackacre, the family homestead, planned to retire to a warmer climate. She had two children: Addie, a successful accountant, and Al, a troubled son who has had trouble with alcohol.

Molly executed a deed of Blackacre and delivered it to Addie. In addition to a description of the property, the deed contained the following language: "Grantee, by acceptance of this deed, agrees to provide a bedroom in the property known as Blackacre for the use of my son Al during his lifetime."

Molly died soon after moving, leaving her entire estate to her daughter Addie and son Al in equal shares. Al, upset by his mother's death, sank deeper into alcoholism. Addie, unwilling to tolerate Al's behavior, prohibited him from entering Blackacre.

Al then brought a suit against Addie to establish a one-half interest in Blackacre. In that lawsuit,

(A) Addie will prevail, because Molly retained no interest in Blackacre.
(B) Addie will prevail, because Al's conduct terminated the rights he had to an interest in Blackacre.
(C) Al will prevail, because Addie breached her contractual obligation to him.
(D) Al will prevail, because the condition in the deed to Addie was broken.

Answer to Question 84

The language of the deed from Molly to Addie does not create a conditional fee simple. Rather, it contains language of contractual obligation which creates a covenant. Therefore, Al will not prevail on the basis of a broken condition and a breach of covenant will not give him a right to take any interest in the title. At most, it will give him a right to sue for breach of the contract on a third-party beneficiary theory. Therefore, (C) and (D) are incorrect.

(A) is correct. The deed from Molly to Addie created a fee simple in Addie. Therefore, Al has no claim on the property, even if Addie breaches her contractual obligation to him.

Thus, Al did not lose his claim on the property by his behavior. He simply never had a claim. (B) is therefore incorrect.

Question 85

Able and Baker owned Blackacre as joint tenants. Baker entered into an oral agreement to sell his interest in Blackacre to Perry for $10,000. On June 8, Baker delivered a deed to Earl, an escrow agent, with instructions that he should deliver it to Perry on June 15, when Perry paid Earl the $10,000 purchase price. Baker died on June 10, and Perry delivered $10,000 to Earl on June 15. What interest does Able have in Blackacre on June 16?

(A) The entire fee simple interest, because the deed to Perry was not recorded prior to Baker's death.
(B) The entire fee simple interest, because the transfer from Baker to Perry was not completed until after Baker's death.
(C) An undivided one-half interest as tenant in common, because the delivery of the deed into escrow coupled with the fulfillment of the escrow agreement by Perry terminated the joint tenancy.
(D) An undivided one-half interest as tenant in common, because the purchase and sale agreement between Baker and Perry terminated the joint tenancy.

Answer to Question 85

A deed need not be recorded to convey valid and good title. Recording is not a requirement to sever a joint tenancy; the conveyance alone is sufficient. Thus (A) is incorrect.

(B) is incorrect. As a general rule, an attempt to transfer a joint tenant's interest after his death is ineffective because, upon a joint tenant's death, that tenant's interest immediately passes to the surviving joint tenants. However, in this case, the transfer was complete prior to Baker's death.

(D) states the correct outcome, but the wrong reason. Able and Baker originally owned Blackacre as joint tenants. Baker's oral agreement to convey his interest in Blackacre did not sever the joint tenancy because the Statute of Frauds provides that an oral agreement to convey land is unenforceable. A joint tenancy is not severed by a purchase and sale agreement unless it is enforceable.

Generally, a deed delivered to a third party which is only effective on the fulfillment of a condition is ineffective to pass title until the condition is fulfilled. An exception to this rule is when the deed is delivered to an escrow agent to be delivered to the grantee upon fulfillment of the grantee's obligations under the sales contract. When a deed is properly put into escrow and the escrow agreement is properly executed, the date of the conveyance relates back to the date the deed was originally put into escrow. Therefore, when Perry delivered the purchase price to Earl, the conveyance took effect as of the date Baker put the deed into escrow. Thus, the law would hold in this situation that there was a conveyance of Baker's interest to Perry prior to Baker's death, which conveyance severed the joint tenancy. Therefore, Able has only an undivided one-half interest in Blackacre as a tenant in common with Perry, and (C) is the correct answer.

Question 86

Grantor deeded adjoining lots Blackacre and Whiteacre to Alicia by warranty deed. Under the law of the jurisdiction, a warranty is considered a contractual obligation governed by a six-year statute of limitations. At the time the deed was delivered, Grantor owned Blackacre but did not own Whiteacre because he had previously deeded it to Harold. Harold had properly recorded his deed but had made no improvements on the lot. Alicia built her house on Blackacre and planted a flower garden on Whiteacre.

Eight years later, Alicia gave her property to her daughter Dolly by executing and delivering to her a quitclaim deed describing both Blackacre and Whiteacre. Dolly continued to plant the flower garden for one year. At that time, Harold commenced construction of a house on Whiteacre and successfully terminated Dolly's rights in Whiteacre. Dolly examined title and found that Grantor did not own Whiteacre at the time that he had deeded that property to Alicia. She then brought suit for breach of warranty against both Alicia and Grantor. In those suits,

(A) Dolly would prevail against Grantor but would not prevail against Alicia.
(B) Dolly would prevail against both Grantor and Alicia.
(C) Dolly would not prevail against Grantor because of the statute of limitations and would not prevail against Alicia.
(D) Dolly would not prevail against Grantor because remote grantees cannot sue on covenants and would not prevail against Alicia.

Answer to Question 86

Dolly will prevail against Grantor. The covenant breached by Grantor in this question is the covenant of quiet enjoyment, since the successor grantee was deprived of her possession of Whiteacre by one claiming superior title. This covenant runs with the land, as do all future covenants. Therefore, Grantor is liable, not only to his immediate grantee, but to all successor grantees, for a breach of that covenant. Thus, (D) is incorrect. The cause of action accrued, not when he conveyed the property, but when the grantee was ousted from possession and thus deprived of quiet enjoyment. Therefore, the statute of limitations is no defense to Grantor. Thus, (C) is incorrect. Grantor is liable to Dolly as a remote grantee for breach of a future covenant even though she took by quitclaim deed because that deed conveys whatever rights her grantor (Alicia) had at the time of the conveyance. The future covenants in a warranty deed run to all subsequent grantees, no matter what type of deed they took personally.

On the other hand, Alicia is **not** liable to Dolly; she made no independent promises to Dolly because she gave only a quitclaim deed, i.e., one without covenants. A grantor can only be sued on the covenants he or she made. Thus, (A) is correct and (B) is incorrect.

Question 87

Oscar deeded Blackacre to Able in 1990 by a general warranty deed. At the time Able purchased the property, there was on it a railroad track on Blackacre running parallel to its rear border, connecting the properties to the north and south of Blackacre. The track had not been used since the gravel pit on the abutting land to the north had closed down in 1980. Prior to the real estate closing, Able inquired about the railroad line and Oscar told him not to worry about it.

In 1992, Able noticed that Nancy, his abutter to the north, had reopened the gravel pit and was using the railway to haul gravel to a processing plant south of Able's property. Able ordered Nancy to stop using the line. He then rechecked his title and discovered that an owner of Blackacre prior to Oscar had given Nancy an easement 15 feet in width for the railroad track, which had been properly recorded. Nancy sued Able for a declaration that the easement was valid and prevailed.

Able then brought suit against Oscar to recover the diminution in the value of his property because of the presence of the easement. In that suit, he will

(A) win because this was a visible encumbrance which Able knew about.
(B) win because Oscar breached his warranty against encumbrances.
(C) lose because the easement was created by Oscar's grantor, not Oscar.
(D) lose because the easement was a matter of record and, therefore, Able is not a bona fide purchaser.

Answer to Question 87

(A) is incorrect. Able might **not** be able to prevail on a breach of warranty theory if there was a plainly visible and plainly valid easement which he knew about at the time he took title. That is not a reason for the grantee, Able, to prevail, as this choice states.

(C) is incorrect. When the grantor gives a general warranty deed (rather than a **special** warranty deed), this warranty extends to all encumbrances, whether created by the grantor or by a predecessor in the chain of title. (Able would lose if Oscar had conveyed the property by a special warranty deed. In this type of deed, the grantor is only liable for defects or encumbrances incurred during his ownership and he does not warrant against any encumbrances created by his predecessors in title.)

The fact that Able is not a bona fide purchaser does not defeat Able's right to sue on the covenants in Oscar's deed to Able. The fact that Able is not a bona fide purchaser is the reason Nancy was successful in establishing the validity of the easement, but it does not control the outcome of his case against Oscar. Thus, (D) is incorrect.

(B) is the correct answer. Oscar deeded Blackacre to Able by a general warranty deed, and a warranty against encumbrances is a covenant of such a deed. In a covenant against encumbrances, one of the things the grantor warrants is that there are no easements which will diminish the ownership rights of the grantee, except those listed in the deed. Such a warranty is breached by an existing easement over the property not mentioned in the deed. Although Able had notice of the railway, Oscar told him not to worry about it and did not include it as an existing encumbrance in the deed. Therefore, Oscar breached his warranty against encumbrances.

Question 88

A particular piece of land is described in a deed as being "that parcel of land being 80 acres which is the north half of the northwest quarter of Section 5" with a reference to the geographical survey. There is only one median line and one base line in the relevant area. This description is

(A) sufficient only if the boundary lines of the property are also described.
(B) sufficient only if the geographical survey is recorded with the deed.
(C) sufficient without any additional data.
(D) insufficient because no reference is made to the median line and the base line.

Answer to Question 88

The description of the property in a deed need only be such as would remove any reasonable doubt as to what land is being conveyed. Reference to a survey, map or plat is an effective means of describing land without references to boundaries and monuments. Therefore, (A) is incorrect. Reference to the geographical survey is all that is required to have it be incorporated by reference into the deed. It is not necessary that the survey, map or plat be recorded at all, much less recorded with the deed. (B) is therefore incorrect. Since there is only one median and base line in the area, this description should be a sufficient description of the property. Therefore, (D) is incorrect and (C) is correct.

Question 89

Alice was the fee simple owner of Blackacre in Floribama, which has a race type of recording statute. The following transactions took place with respect to Blackacre:

January 2: Alice delivers a properly executed deed to Charles as a gift. Charles does not record the deed.

February 1: Charles gives the deed he received back to Alice.

April 1: Alice deeds Blackacre to Eager, who has knowledge of the Alice-Charles deed and who records immediately.

If Eager should sue Charles concerning the ownership of Blackacre, the court will most likely

(A) find for Eager, because returning the unrecorded deed to Alice extinguished Charles's interest.
(B) find for Eager, because of the recording statute.
(C) find for Eager, because Charles received his deed as a gift.
(D) find for Charles, because he received a valid deed prior to the time Eager received one.

Answer to Question 89

(A) is incorrect. A valid deed was delivered to Charles and therefore transfers Alice's interest in Blackacre to him even if it is not recorded. Acceptance of the deed is presumed because Charles did not expressly reject it at the time. Therefore, the redelivery of that deed to Alice does not transfer title back to Alice. That can only be accomplished by a new deed signed by Charles and delivered to Alice.

(C) is incorrect. It is Charles's failure to record which causes him to lose to Eager, not the fact that he received the property as a gift. If he had recorded first, he would have won even though he received the property as a gift, and, on the other hand, his failure to record would bar him even if he had paid for the property. (Eager's success, however, is dependent upon his deed having been purchased. A subsequent deed delivered as a gift cannot defeat a prior deed. The subsequent grantee must be a bona fide purchaser. Whether or not the first deed was purchased is irrelevant to its status.)

(D) is incorrect. The question states that these transactions took place in a jurisdiction with a race recording system. Under such a system, an unrecorded deed is valid as between the grantor and grantee, but only a properly recorded deed is good against the rest of the world. Charles' receipt of a valid deed from Alice will only protect him against a subsequent bona fide purchaser if he records first.

(B) is correct. In a race jurisdiction, a subsequent grantee (in this case, Eager) from the same grantor (Alice) gets superior title over a prior grantee (Charles) if the subsequent grantee is a purchaser and records before the prior grantee, even if he has notice of the prior deed. Alice appears on record to be the owner of Blackacre and has the power to vest good title in a grantee who records before the first purchaser. Thus, the recording statute is the reason Eager will prevail over Charles.

Question 90

Oprah held, in fee simple, Blackacre, a large tract of vacant land. The state wherein Blackacre is situated has a grantor-grantee index in its registry of deeds and has a statute which provides, in substance, that unless the conveyance is recorded, every deed or other conveyance of an interest in land is void as to a subsequent purchaser who pays value without notice of such conveyance. The following transactions occurred in the order given:

First: Oprah conveyed Blackacre, for a fair price, to Amanda by general warranty deed. Amanda did not immediately record.

Second: Oprah conveyed Blackacre, for a fair price, to Bernice by general warranty deed.

Bernice had no notice of the prior conveyance to Amanda.

Third: Amanda duly recorded her deed from Oprah.

Fourth: Bernice duly recorded her deed from Oprah.

Fifth: Amanda conveyed Blackacre, for a fair price, to Candice by general warranty deed. Candice had no actual notice of the prior conveyance from Oprah to Bernice.

In a suit between Candice and Bernice concerning title to Blackacre,

(A) Bernice will prevail because Candice had constructive notice of Bernice's deed from Oprah.
(B) Bernice will prevail because she paid value for Blackacre without notice of the conveyance from Oprah to Amanda.
(C) Candice will prevail because she paid value for Blackacre without notice of the conveyance from Oprah to Bernice.
(D) Candice will prevail because her grantor, Amanda, recorded first.

Answer to Question 90

(A) is incorrect because Candice did **not** have constructive notice of the deed to Bernice, because Bernice's deed was recorded late (after the deed from Oprah to Amanda) and therefore out of order in the recording system.

(B) correctly states the result in a contest between Bernice and Amanda, but fails to recognize that Candice is also a bona fide purchaser and so will prevail over Bernice.

Candice will prevail over Bernice, as (D) correctly states, but not because her predecessor in title (Amanda) would have prevailed. In fact, as explained above, Amanda would have lost to Bernice. Priority is not necessarily a function of who records first, except in a pure race jurisdiction. Recording is only constructive notice of a prior claim. A subsequent purchaser can always take good title before a prior grantee records, as here.

Because the jurisdiction has a notice type recording system, Bernice, who paid value without notice of the deed from Oprah to Amanda, would prevail over Amanda even though she did not record first. However, her deed was recorded late (after the deed from Oprah to Amanda) and therefore out of order in the recording system; a person examining title would search the grantor index under Oprah's name until she found the deed from Oprah to Amanda on record, and then would search under Amanda's name in the grantor index and never find the Oprah-Bernice deed. Therefore, Candice does not have constructive notice of the Oprah-Bernice deed, and purchased title without notice of any adverse claims, from a person who appeared to be the record owner of Blackacre. Therefore, Candice will prevail over Bernice, even though Candice's grantor, Amanda, would have lost to Bernice. Bernice lost her favored status as a bona fide purchaser because she failed to record immediately, and as a result, lost her title to a subsequent bona fide purchaser. Therefore, (C) is correct.

Question 91

Orrin held, in fee simple, Blackacre, a large tract of vacant land. The state wherein Blackacre is situated employs a grantor-grantee index at its registry of deeds and has a statute which provides, in substance, that unless the conveyance is recorded, every deed or other conveyance of an interest in land is void as to a subsequent purchaser who pays value without notice of such conveyance and who first records.

The following transactions occurred in the order given:

First: Orrin conveyed Blackacre, for a fair price, to Al by general warranty deed. Al did not immediately record.

Second: Orrin conveyed Blackacre, for a fair price, to Barbara by general warranty deed. Barbara had no notice of the prior conveyance to Al and promptly and properly recorded the deed.

Third: Barbara conveyed Blackacre to Connie as a gift. Connie knew of the unrecorded prior deed to Al at the time she received the deed from Barbara. Connie did not immediately record.

In a suit between Connie and Al concerning title to Blackacre,

(A) Connie will prevail because her grantor, Barbara, would prevail over Al.
(B) Connie will prevail unless Al recorded before Connie recorded.
(C) Al will prevail because Connie is a donee, not a purchaser.
(D) Al will prevail because Connie knew of the Orrin-Al deed before she received her deed from Barbara.

Answer to Question 91

Barbara purchased Blackacre from Orrin without knowledge or constructive notice of the earlier deed from Orrin to Al, and recorded her deed. She, therefore, was a bona fide purchaser and was the record and actual owner of Blackacre. As a bona fide purchaser, under the doctrine of shelter, Barbara could thereafter convey her title and her status as a bona fide purchaser to almost anyone. Connie does not have to conform to the requirements of a bona fide purchaser in the recording statute to prevail. She, in effect, purchased that status from Barbara, under the shelter doctrine. Therefore, the facts that Connie had knowledge of the Orrin-Al deed, received the property as a gift, and might not have recorded before Al are irrelevant. The doctrine of shelter gives Connie the title which Barbara had. Thus, (A) is correct and (C) and (D) are incorrect.

(B) is also incorrect. To get a better handle on any choice in which the operative qualifier is "unless," it is best to turn the result around and substitute "if and only if" for "unless." This choice would then read "Al will prevail if and only if Al recorded before Connie recorded." That statement is not true. For Al to prevail, he would have to have recorded her deed prior to **Barbara**, thus preventing Barbara from becoming a bona fide purchaser. Once Barbara, a bona fide purchaser, recorded before Al, Barbara became the actual and record owner of Blackacre and Al could do nothing to take the property from Barbara or any of her successors and assigns, because of the doctrine of shelter.

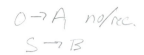

Question 92

Oscar deeded Blackacre to Able, who failed to record in a jurisdiction with a notice type recording statute. Oscar died intestate leaving Sonny as his sole heir. Sonny, for valuable consideration, gave a deed to Blackacre to Baker, who did not know of the deed to Able. Baker did not record his deed. In a suit between Able and Baker over title to Blackacre,

(A) Able will prevail because heirs cannot be bona fide purchasers.
(B) Able will prevail because the holder of the earlier deed prevails when both parties fail to record.
(C) Baker will prevail because the deed from Sonny starts a new chain of title.
(D) Baker will prevail because a purchaser without notice need not record.

Answer to Question 92

Baker **purchased** from Sonny without notice of Able's interest. It is Baker's rights as a bona fide purchaser that are at issue here, not Sonny's rights as a donee. Therefore, (A) is incorrect.

Priority of recording is irrelevant. A subsequent bona fide purchaser prevails over a prior unrecorded interest, even if the second interest is never recorded. Thus, (B) is incorrect. The common law rule concerning titles was first in time, first in right. The first grantee to receive a deed would prevail over a subsequent purchaser. Modern recording systems modify that rule and provide a method of verifying a grantor's title and protecting the title of a purchaser who buys land without any knowledge of a prior grantee. In a jurisdiction with a recording system, that system will govern the conveyance of land whether or not the various grantees seek its protection. The fact that neither Able nor Baker recorded does not take their transactions out of the recording statute, as this answer suggests.

(C) reaches the correct conclusion for the wrong reason. This answer is an incorrect statement of the law. The deed from Sonny does **not** start a new chain of title. It continues the old chain of title through Oscar's probate, which transmits the title from Oscar to his heir. Able will not win because his failure to record allows any purchaser of Blackacre from its record owner (now Sonny) without actual knowledge of Able's deed to prevail as a bona fide purchaser.

This is a notice jurisdiction. Under this system, a subsequent purchaser takes good title by merely purchasing without notice of the prior conveyance. The subsequent purchaser need not record to prevail over a prior conveyance. Able failed to record his first deed from Oscar. Therefore, any bona fide purchaser will be able to prevail over Able. Sonny took as an heir, so he is not a purchaser and cannot prevail. However, Baker purchased from Sonny without notice of Able's interest. A bona fide purchaser from a donee is protected by the recording statute. Baker will prevail over Able because this is a notice jurisdiction and he is a purchaser without notice. He need not record. Thus, (D) is the correct answer.

Question 93

Alpha, the owner of Blackacre, in a jurisdiction which has a race-notice recording statute, decided he wanted to sell Blackacre. After attempting unsuccessfully to sell the property without a broker for two months, he employed the services of Beta to help him sell the property.

Soon after Beta started looking for a buyer, Beta located Phi, who wanted to buy Blackacre. Phi executed an offer to purchase the property and Beta brought the written offer to Alpha. Upon receiving the offer, Alpha called Phi and told him that he accepted the offer. Alpha then prepared a written purchase and sale agreement for Blackacre, signed it, and delivered it to Beta with instructions to deliver the agreement to Phi upon receipt of the required deposit.

Before Beta had delivered the agreement to Phi, Alpha received a better offer for the property from Kappa, and explained to her that he would accept her offer and tell Beta not to deliver the signed purchase and sale agreement to Phi. In the meantime, Alpha deeded Blackacre to Kappa, who paid consideration and recorded her deed. Phi is now suing Alpha and Kappa, requesting a decree in equity that the court order Blackacre be deeded to him. In that suit,

(A) Phi will lose because Alpha's offer to sell the property was properly revoked.
(B) Phi will lose because Kappa recorded her deed.
(C) Phi will lose because of the Statute of Frauds.
(D) Phi will prevail.

Answer to Question 93

(C) is incorrect. The Statute of Frauds requires that an agreement to convey land be evidenced by a writing signed by the party to be charged. The signed purchase and sale agreement which Alpha deposited with Beta is a memorandum, signed by the party to be charged, which is evidence of the agreement reached between Alpha and Phi. (Delivery of that document by Beta to Phi is not a prerequisite to the enforceability of the contract it memorializes. "Delivery" is required of a deed for it to be enforceable, but not a purchase and sale agreement.)

(B) is incorrect. Since Kappa knew of the facts which constituted the binding purchase and sale agreement between Alpha and Phi, she is not a bona fide purchaser and therefore cannot take free of the rights of Phi. Therefore, under the race-notice type recording system in force, Kappa's deed would not prevail because she had notice, even though she paid consideration and recorded her deed. (Kappa would prevail only in a pure race jurisdiction, where her knowledge is irrelevant.)

(A) is incorrect. The attempted revocation of the contract by Alpha was ineffective because the contract had been concluded orally and there was a memorandum signed by Alpha which satisfied the Statute of Frauds. Under the doctrine of equitable conversion, Phi would already be deemed to be the equitable owner of Blackacre.

Thus, (D) is correct. The purchase and sale agreement between Phi and Alpha is valid and enforceable.

Question 94

Owen is the owner of Blackacre in fee simple absolute. He delivered to Paul a properly executed quitclaim deed of Blackacre for valuable consideration. Paul kept the deed but did not record it. One year later, in satisfaction of a prior debt, Owen gave Charles a warranty deed to Blackacre. Charles did not know of the Owen-Paul deed and recorded his deed. What is the best statement of the relative rights of Paul and Charles in a jurisdiction where good faith and value are the two requirements necessary for a second grantee to take over the prior grantee?

(A) Charles could not prevail because he did not give current consideration.
(B) Charles could not prevail because Owen had nothing to give at the time he gave Charles the deed.
(C) Charles could not prevail unless he could prove he ran the records at the registry before accepting the conveyance.
(D) Charles could prevail because of the failure of Paul to record.

Answer to Question 94

The question states that all that is required for Charles (the second grantee) to prevail over Paul (the first grantee) is that Charles have purchased in good faith and for value (i.e., a typical notice system - Charles prevails if he is a bona fide purchaser).

Charles purchased in good faith, because apparently he had no actual knowledge of the prior deed to Paul and because Paul's failure to record means that Charles had no constructive notice of Paul's interest.

Charles purchased for value because he took the deed in exchange for cancellation of a debt owed by Owen to him. The cancellation of a prior debt qualifies as consideration. A deed given in such an exchange is purchased for value and entitled to the protection of the recording system. Thus, (A) is incorrect and (D) is correct. Charles is a subsequent bona fide purchaser for value and his title receives the protection of the recording system.

(B) is incorrect. This answer describes the rationale behind the common-law rule of "first in time, first in right." Under modern notice recording laws, though, subsequent grantees **can** take good title if they take a deed in exchange for value at a time when they have no notice of the prior deed. It does not matter that their grantor may have previously deeded away the property, unless the subsequent purchaser has actual knowledge or constructive notice of that fact.

(C) is incorrect. The recording system described here is a typical notice system. Any subsequent purchaser is held to have notice of a properly recorded conveyance in the chain of title, whether or not he actually checks the registry of deeds. By the same token, a subsequent purchaser is held not to have notice of an unrecorded deed, whether or not he actually checks the registry. Therefore, a subsequent purchaser need not actually check the registry of deeds to attain the status of a bona fide purchaser. In this case, checking at the registry would be irrelevant because the prior deed was unrecorded and so was not constructive notice. Unless Charles has actual or inquiry notice, he will qualify as a bona fide purchaser, regardless of whether or not he examined the records at the registry before purchasing Blackacre.

Question 95

Buyer and Seller entered into a purchase and sale agreement concerning Blackacre, located in State X. Buyer paid Seller a deposit of $10,000, and Seller deposited a signed deed with Easy, the escrow agent, to be released when the remaining $90,000 of the purchase price was paid. Buyer paid the remaining $90,000 to Easy, who turned it over to Seller. Through inadvertence, Buyer did not take possession of his deed, and therefore did not record it. In State

X, only subsequent purchasers and their mortgagees are entitled to the protection of the recording statute. One year thereafter, a judgment creditor of Seller, Champ, attempted to enforce his judgment by selling Blackacre, and Buyer brought suit to enjoin him. In that lawsuit,

(A) Champ will prevail because there was no delivery of the deed.
(B) Champ will prevail because Buyer did not record.
(C) Buyer will prevail because title has passed to him.
(D) Buyer will prevail because Champ did not rely on Seller's title to Blackacre when he obtained the judgment.

Answer to Question 95

The general rule is that physical transfer of a deed to a third party only qualifies as a delivery of that deed if the grantor thereby intends to create an irrevocable and immediate interest in the grantee. One exception to this rule is that a deed may be placed in commercial escrow as part of a binding purchase and sale agreement and still be deemed delivered. Such an escrow must require that the deed be handed over to the grantee on fulfillment of the grantee's obligations. The deed must not be otherwise revocable by the grantor. Seller's deposit of a signed deed with Easy, an escrow agent over whom he had no apparent control, pursuant to a valid purchase and sale agreement, is sufficient to satisfy the delivery requirement. Thus, (A) is incorrect.

The fact that Buyer did not record is of no relevance as between Buyer and Champ because the facts specifically state that the recording statute of the jurisdiction protects only subsequent bona fide purchasers and mortgagees. Champ is a judgment creditor, not a purchaser or mortgagee. Therefore, he cannot prevail over Buyer, and (B) is incorrect.

Buyer is the owner of Blackacre as soon as he has performed his payment obligations under the purchase and sale agreement. Thus, (C) is correct. Champ is a judgment creditor, not a purchaser or mortgagee. Therefore, Champ cannot prevail over Buyer, even though record title to the property is in Seller's name at the time Champ tried to sell it. Someone who purchased at the foreclosure sale could prevail in these circumstances, but Champ cannot, because he is not a purchaser under the terms of the statute.

(D) is incorrect. Champ cannot prevail over Buyer even if he had made a title search and obtained a judgment against Seller for the purpose of foreclosing on this specific property.

Question 96

The recording statute of jurisdiction X reads as follows:

> Deeds, mortgages and leases for more than seven years shall not be valid as against any person, except the grantor, mortgagor or lessor, his heirs and devisees and persons having actual notice of them, unless they are recorded in the Registry of Deeds for the county in which the land lies.

The recording statute of jurisdiction Y reads as follows:

> Every conveyance of real estate within the state hereafter made, which shall not be recorded as provided in this chapter, shall be void as against any subsequent purchaser in good faith and for a valuable consideration, of the same real estate or any portion thereof, whose conveyance shall be first duly recorded.

Anne is the owner of Blackacre, an undeveloped parcel of land. Anne executed and delivered a deed of Blackacre to Beth. Beth did not promptly record.
Anne then executed and delivered a deed of Blackacre to Clarice, who did not know of the delivery of the deed from Anne to Beth. Beth then recorded her deed before Clarice recorded her deed.
Assume that Beth and Clarice are purchasers for value. In a contest between Beth and Clarice over ownership of Blackacre, Clarice would prevail over Beth

281

(A) in jurisdiction X.
(B) in jurisdiction Y.
(C) in both jurisdiction X and jurisdiction Y.
(D) in neither jurisdiction X nor jurisdiction Y.

Answer to Question 96

The statute in jurisdiction X establishes a notice system of recording. The state Y statute creates a race-notice system because it requires that the bona fide purchaser also record first in order to prevail. Clarice will prevail over Beth in a notice jurisdiction such as jurisdiction X because she took her deed without knowledge or notice of Beth's interest. In this system, a subsequent bona fide purchaser need not record to prevail over a prior deed. However, Clarice cannot prevail in a race-notice jurisdiction such as jurisdiction Y because she did not record her deed before Beth recorded her deed. Therefore, Clarice can prevail only in jurisdiction X. (A) is correct and the other choices are incorrect.

Question 97

Larry entered into a written residential lease with Tom on June 1. The demised premises consisted of a single-family house and surrounding land. Tom paid the first and last month's rent at the time that the lease was signed. The lease term was for one year commencing July 1. At the time the lease was signed, the premises were occupied by William under a lease expiring on June 30. William remained in possession after his lease expired, leaving only after he had been evicted on August 15.

Tom's best theory for a cause of action against Larry for his failure to deliver possession by July 1 would be

(A) Larry had an immediate right to possession on July 1 and should have thrown William out bodily on that date.
(B) Larry was negligent in his failure to remove William on or before July 1.
(C) Larry breached the covenant of quiet enjoyment which is implied in every lease.
(D) William's continued possession constitutes a trespass.

Answer to Question 97

(A) is incorrect because the landlord could not resort to self-help to regain possession. William was originally a tenant under a lease and became a tenant at sufferance at the expiration of the lease. His possession is therefore not a trespass and can only be terminated by a court-ordered eviction, not by self-help.

(B) is incorrect. A claim of negligence will not be the best argument for Tom, because it appears that Larry acted diligently and quickly to pursue the legal means available to remove a holdover tenant at sufferance.

(D) is incorrect. William's continued possession is as a tenant at sufferance since he held rightfully until June 30 as a tenant under a lease. Therefore, he is not a trespasser. Moreover, even if he were a trespasser, this would not be the basis for a cause of action by the tenant against the landlord. In fact, just the opposite: if the possessor is a trespasser, the landlord is **not** responsible for that possession at common law. In that case, the tenant would have to evict the trespasser, and the landlord would not be in violation of the covenant of quiet enjoyment (as he might be if the tenant holds over as a tenant at sufferance).

(C) is correct. A covenant of quiet enjoyment is implied in every lease. The tenant has paid rent for a term commencing July 1 and has a right to possession on that date. The landlord breaches that covenant if he permits a person with a greater possessory right (e.g., a holdover tenant at sufferance who has not yet been evicted) to deny possession to a tenant who has a right to it. The majority position in the United States today supports this position, even though the traditional "American Rule" is that the landlord only owed the tenant the right to possession at the beginning of the term, not possession itself. Under that rule, landlords were not liable for failure to evict third parties; they breached the covenant only if they themselves or their agents were in possession.

Question 98

Laura leased a retail store to Teresa by a written lease for a term of two years for rent of $500 per month payable on or before the first day of each month. The lease contained no provisions for extensions or renewals.

Shortly before the term of the lease expired, Laura sent Teresa a new lease for a two-year term to commence at the expiration of the original term. The rent reserved in the new lease was $600 per month, which was the fair rental value of the property at the time the lease was to commence. Teresa did not sign the new lease, remained in possession after the original lease terminated on June 30, and sent Laura a rent check on July 1 for $500 marked "July rent." Laura deposited the check immediately. What is the status of the parties as of July 2?

(A) Teresa has a periodic month-to-month tenancy at $600 per month.
(B) Teresa has a periodic month-to-month tenancy at $500 per month.
(C) Teresa has a two-year lease at $600 per month.
(D) Teresa is a tenant at sufferance and can be immediately evicted with an appropriate rebate on her rent if she leaves before August 1.

Answer to Question 98

There is no two-year lease because neither party signed a written document, which would be required for a new lease to arise. It does not arise automatically because the tenant holds over, unless the original lease specifically so provides. Here, the facts state that the lease was silent as to extensions or renewals. (C), therefore, is an incorrect answer.

When Teresa stayed in possession of the premises after the lease between Laura and Teresa ended on June 30, Teresa became a tenant at sufferance. However, when Laura accepted Teresa's check for a month's rent, she started a new periodic tenancy, which ended the tenancy at sufferance. (D) is therefore incorrect.

The rent for the monthly rental period is $600, not $500, because that is the rent proposed by Laura. Teresa is deemed to have accepted the proposal for the increased rent by staying in possession. The terms of the prior lease no longer apply to their relationship. Therefore, (A) is the correct answer and (B) is an incorrect answer.

Question 99

Larry leased a restaurant to Terry for a period of seven years. The lease contained the following provision: "No subleasing or assignment will be permitted unless with the written consent of the lessor." One year later, Terry assigned all interest in the lease to Albert, who assumed and agreed to perform the lessee's obligations under the terms of the lease. Larry learned of the assignment and wrote to Terry that he had no objection to the assignment to Albert and agreed to accept rent from Albert instead of Terry.

Thereafter, Albert paid rent to Larry for a period of three years. Albert then defaulted and went into bankruptcy. In an appropriate action, Larry sued Terry for rent due.

If Larry loses, it will be because there was

(A) a novation.
(B) laches.
(C) an accord and satisfaction.
(D) a subrogation.

Answer to Question 99

When the tenant in a landlord-tenant relationship assigns her lease to a third party, the tenant remains contractually liable to the landlord even if the assignee agrees to pay and the landlord agrees to accept the rent from the assignee. The landlord and tenant remain in privity of contract. In the fact pattern presented in this question, Larry should be successful in collecting the rent from Terry after Albert defaulted. The only circumstances under which Larry would lose is if he agreed to accept Albert's performance in place of Terry's and to release Terry (in other words, if the parties entered into a novation). Thus, (A) is the correct answer.

(B) is incorrect. Laches is the failure to assert a right for an unreasonable period of time when the delay has been prejudicial to the adverse party, rendering it inequitable to enforce the right. Here, Larry is not guilty of laches since he sued promptly after Albert went into bankruptcy. Moreover, laches is an equitable defense, and a suit for rent is an action at law.

Accord occurs when parties to a contract subsequently make an agreement which they intend as a substitute for the original contract. The performance of that subsequent agreement is the satisfaction. An accord does not discharge the original duty until it is performed. If an accord is breached, the obligee may enforce either the original duty or any duty under the accord. Even if these facts could be construed to show an accord between Larry and Terry regarding payment of the rent by Albert, that accord was not performed and thus satisfaction did not occur. Larry remains free to sue under the original agreement. Therefore, (C) is incorrect.

The circumstances of a subrogation are not present here. If Terry had paid the rent for the remainder of the term and was suing Albert for the rent, the principle of subrogation would be a theory on which Terry could recover against Albert because he would be stepping into the shoes of the landlord. That fact pattern is not present here. Therefore, (D) is incorrect.

Question 100

The following events took place with respect to Blackacre in the order mentioned:

First: Landlord, the fee simple owner of Blackacre, leased it under a written document to Tenant for 3 years at a rental of $12,000 per year.

Second: Tenant assigns the lease to Able.

Third: Able assigns the lease to Baker, who is insolvent.

Fourth: Baker subleases the property to Able, reserving the last day of the term.

Fifth: Able abandons the property before his sublease expires and pays no further rent.

Which of the following statements is LEAST accurate?

(A) Tenant is liable to Landlord for the rent for the entire term.
(B) Able is responsible to Baker for rent while the sublease is outstanding, even though he is not in possession.
(C) Baker is liable to Landlord for the rent during Able's subtenancy.
(D) Able is responsible to Landlord for the rent during his subtenancy when he was not in possession.

Answer to Question 100

This question asks for the **least** accurate statement. Therefore, if the statement is a correct statement, it is a wrong answer. Because (A) is a true statement, it is an incorrect answer. Tenant is liable to Landlord for the rent for the entire term because Tenant is bound by the original contractual obligation. In their lease, Tenant agreed to pay the rent for the entire term. A tenant cannot discharge the rent obligation by either a sublease or an assignment.

Because (B) is a true statement, it is an incorrect answer. Able has signed a lease with Baker and is therefore liable to Baker for the rent for the entire term of the sublease because he is bound to Baker by a contractual obligation. Therefore, Able is responsible for any rent due under his lease with Baker, even if Able is no longer in possession.

Because (C) is a true statement, it is an incorrect answer. Able is only a sublessee, so he is not in privity of estate with Landlord. A sublease creates a second tenancy between a tenant and the subtenant. The subtenant's landlord is the tenant (here, Baker) while the tenant remains in a landlord-tenant relationship with the owner. The creation of this subtenancy does not break Baker's privity of estate with Landlord. Therefore, Baker is liable to Landlord for the rent even during Able's sublease.

Because (D) is an incorrect statement, it is the correct answer. At the time he abandoned Blackacre, Able was not in a landlord-tenant relationship with Landlord. Able was in privity of estate with Landlord during his assignment from Tenant, but that privity of estate was terminated by his assignment to Baker. When Able ended his possession by an assignment to Baker, he was no longer liable on the rent obligation to Landlord. Then, Able did not become liable to Landlord by virtue of his subtenancy from Baker, because a subtenant is neither in privity of estate nor privity of contract with the landlord. Able's only rent obligation at that time was to Baker based on his contractual obligation to Baker.

Question 101

Andres conveyed Applewood Farm "to Bogatz, her heirs and assigns, so long as the premises are used for residential and farm purposes, then to Cohen and his heirs." The common law Rule Against Perpetuities, unmodified by statute, is part of the law of the jurisdiction in which Applewood Farm is located. As a consequence of the conveyance, Cohen's interest in Applewood Farm is

(A) nothing.
(B) a valid executory interest.
(C) a possibility of reverter.
(D) a right of entry for condition broken.

Answer to Question 101

(A) is correct. An interest created in a third party after a fee simple determinable is an executory interest. Such an interest is subject to the Rule Against Perpetuities and so must vest within the period of the Rule or it is invalid. The interest in this case vests only after the premises are no longer used for residential and farm purposes. Since there is no time limit on the occurrence of the condition in the document itself and since the premises could be used for residential and farm purposes for an indefinite period, the executory interest can vest in possession beyond lives in being plus 21 years. Therefore, the executory interest is invalid and Cohen takes nothing.

(B) is incorrect because the executory interest is invalid as a result of the Rule Against Perpetuities and Cohen takes nothing.

(C) is incorrect because a possibility of reverter is an estate which can only occur in the grantor, Andres, not in a third party such as Cohen.

(D) is incorrect because a right of entry for condition broken is a right reserved in the grantor, not a third person. Moreover, if this right had been retained by the grantor it would be a possibility of reverter, rather than a right of entry for condition broken, because the fee interest is a fee simple determinable, not a fee simple subject to a condition subsequent.

Questions 102 to 104 are based on the following fact situation.

In 1991, Owen, owner of Blackacre, executed and delivered a deed by which he conveyed the tract of land as follows: "To Alpha and his heirs as long as it is used exclusively for residential purposes, but if it is ever used for other than residential purposes, to the American Red Cross."

In 1993, Owen died leaving a valid will by which he devised all of his real estate to his brother, Bill. The will had no residuary clause. Owen was survived by Bill and by Owen's son, Sam, who was Owen's sole heir.

The common law Rule Against Perpetuities applies in the state where the land is located and the state also has a statute providing that, "All future estates and interests are alienable, dependable, and devisable in the same manner as possessory estates and interests."

102. In 1994, Alpha and Sam entered into a contract with John, whereby Alpha and Sam contracted to sell Blackacre to John in fee simple. After examining title, John refused to perform on the ground that Alpha and Sam could not give good title. Alpha and Sam joined in an action against John for specific performance. Prayer for specific performance will be

(A) granted, because Alpha and Sam together own a fee simple absolute in Blackacre.
(B) granted, because Alpha alone owns the entire fee simple in Blackacre.
(C) denied, because Bill has a valid interest in Blackacre.
(D) denied, because the American Red Cross has a valid interest in Blackacre.

103. In 1992, the interest of the American Red Cross in Blackacre could be best described as a

(A) valid contingent remainder.
(B) void executory interest.
(C) valid executory interest.
(D) void contingent remainder.

104. In 1994, the interest of Bill in Blackacre could best be described as

(A) a possibility of reverter.
(B) an executory interest.
(C) an executory interest in a possibility of reverter.
(D) nothing.

Answer to Question 102

The conveyance to Alpha is a fee simple determinable with a gift over to the American Red Cross. The gift over to the Red Cross is known as a "shifting executory interest." Since this interest is not expressly or inherently limited as to when it may become possessory, it violates the Rule Against Perpetuities. Because Alpha holds a fee simple determinable, a possibility of reverter in the grantor remains after the executory interest is destroyed. This future interest is not subject to the Rule Against Perpetuities because it is a reversionary interest in the grantor. We are now left with a fee simple determinable to Alpha and his heirs, with a possibility of reverter in the grantor, Owen. Owen dies, devising all of his real estate to Bill. Bill thus takes Owen's possibility of reverter by the terms of Owen's will. Therefore, Bill owns a valid possibility of reverter interest in Blackacre. (C) is correct.

(A) is incorrect because Bill (not Sam) owns the possibility of reverter. Sam takes no interest whatever.

(B) is incorrect. Alpha alone does not own a fee simple absolute in Blackacre because Bill owns a valid possibility of reverter.

(D) is incorrect because the interest of the American Red Cross is invalid since it violates the Rule Against Perpetuities. This future interest is not saved from the operation of the Rule by the "charity-to-charity" exception because that exception only applies, as its name indicates, if both the present possessory estate and the future interest are held by charities, which is not the case here.

Answer to Question 103

For an interest in land to be a remainder it must be created in the same instrument as the prior possessory interest, which must be an interest of limited duration (e.g., a life estate), and it must be capable of taking effect in possession when the prior estate terminates. The interest in the American Red Cross does not qualify as a remainder because it follows an estate of potentially unlimited duration, the fee simple determinable in Alpha. Thus, (A) and (D) are incorrect.

The conveyance to Alpha is a fee simple determinable with a gift over to the American Red Cross. The gift over to the Red Cross is known as a "shifting executory interest." Vesting and possession occur at the same time with respect to a shifting executory interest which follows a fee simple determinable. Thus, the American Red Cross's interest in Blackacre may not vest until an indeterminate time in the future and is a void executory interest due to the Rule Against Perpetuities. (The fact that the American Red Cross is a charity will not save its future interest from the operation of the Rule because the "charity-to-charity" exception only applies, as is indicated by its name, if both the prior estate and the future interest are held by charities.) Thus, (B) is correct and (C) is incorrect.

Answer to Question 104

The conveyance to Alpha is a fee simple determinable with a gift over to the American Red Cross. The gift over to the Red Cross is known as a "shifting executory interest." With respect to a shifting executory interest, vesting does not occur until the interest becomes possessory. Since this interest is not expressly or inherently limited as to when it may become possessory, it violates the Rule Against Perpetuities. Therefore, we must delete the part of the grant that deals with the American Red Cross. However, because Alpha holds a fee simple determinable, a possibility of reverter in the grantor remains after the executory interest is destroyed. This future interest is not subject to the Rule Against Perpetuities because it is a reversionary interest in the grantor. We are now left with a fee simple determinable to Alpha and his heirs, with a possibility of reverter in the grantor, Owen. Owen dies, devising all of his real estate to Bill. Since a possibility of reverter is a devisable interest in real estate, Bill inherits Owen's possibility of reverter. The characterization of the future interest does not change because it is now held by someone other than the grantor; its characterization is fixed at the time of the original deed. Therefore, Bill owns a valid possibility of reverter interest in Blackacre. Thus, (A) is correct and (D) is incorrect.

(B) is incorrect because Bill's interest in Blackacre comes not from a conveyance by Owen, but rather as a devise of Owen's interest. Therefore, it retains the same title as it had in the hands of Owen. Bill takes Owen's possibility of reverter by the terms of Owen's will.

(C) is incorrect. There is no future interest which is both an executory interest and a possibility of reverter and Bill does not have an executory interest, as explained above.

Question 105

Anders conveyed her only parcel of land to Burton by a duly executed and delivered warranty deed, which provided:

> To have and to hold the described tract of land in fee simple, subject to the understanding that within one year from the date of the instrument said grantee shall construct and thereafter maintain and operate on said premises a public health center.

The grantee, Burton, constructed a public health center on the tract within the time specified and operated it for five years. At the end of this period, Burton converted the structure into a senior citizens' recreational facility. It is conceded by all parties in interest that a senior citizens' recreational facility is not a public health center.

In an appropriate action, Anders seeks a declaration that the change in the use of the facility has caused the land and structure to revert to her. In this action, Anders should

(A) win, because the language of the deed created a determinable fee, which leaves a possibility of reverter in the grantor.
(B) win, because the language of the deed created a fee subject to a condition subsequent, which leaves a right of entry or power of termination in the grantor.
(C) lose, because the language of the deed created only a contractual obligation and did not provide for retention of a property interest by the grantor.

(D) lose, because an equitable charge is enforceable only in equity.

Answer to Question 105

Courts avoid finding that a grant creates a qualified fee estate whenever possible. Thus, since the grantor did not use the words recognized at common law as creating a fee simple determinable or fee simple subject to a condition subsequent and did not expressly reserve any future interest, a court will find that this grant did not create a qualified fee, but instead a contractual obligation, which may be enforced by an action for an injunction or damages, but which will not result in a forfeiture. All Anders might be able to do is to force Burton to continue to use the property as a public health center or collect damages for the breach of the covenant. Thus, (A) and (B) are incorrect and (C) is correct.

(D) is incorrect. An equitable charge is not the relief which Anders is seeking. Anders is seeking possession of the land, the remedy to which he would be entitled if he had created either a fee simple determinable or a fee simple subject to a condition subsequent.

Question 106

Homer conveyed his home to his wife, Wanda, for life, remainder to his daughter, Dixie. There was a $20,000 mortgage on the home, requiring monthly payments covering interest to date plus a portion of the principal. Which of the following statements about the monthly payment is correct?

(A) Wanda must pay the full monthly payment.
(B) Wanda must pay a portion of the monthly payment based on an apportionment of the value between Wanda's life estate and Dixie's remainder.
(C) Wanda must pay the portion of the monthly payment which represents interest.
(D) Dixie must pay the full monthly payment.

Answer to Question 106

Where a life tenant and a remainderperson have an interest in real property, the life tenant must bear the current operating expenses of the property. On the other hand, the remainderperson must make any payments required which are capital in nature. The monthly payments on the mortgage are partly current expense (the interest portion) and partly capital (the principal portion). The life tenant therefore must pay the interest portion of the mortgage payment, and the remainderperson the principal portion. (C), which correctly states one-half of this concept, and says nothing which is incorrect, is the best answer.

(A) is incorrect. Wanda need not pay that portion of the mortgage which represents principal payments.

(B) is incorrect because the appropriate apportionment is based upon the principal and interest portions of the mortgage payment, and not the relative values of the interest of the life tenant and the remainderperson in the property.

(D) is incorrect. Dixie need not pay that portion of the mortgage which represents interest payments.

Question 107

In 1960, Hombre, the owner in fee simple absolute, conveyed Stomacher, a five-acre tract of land. The relevant, operative words of the deed conveyed to "Church [a duly organized religious body having power to hold property] for the life of my son, Carl, and from and after the death of my said son, Carl, to all of my grandchildren and their heirs and assigns in equal shares; provided, Church shall use the premises for church purposes only."

In an existing building on Stomacher, Church immediately began to conduct religious services and other activities normally associated with a church.

In 1975, Church granted to Darin a right to remove sand and gravel from a one-half-acre portion of Stomacher upon the payment of royalty. Darin has regularly removed sand and gravel since 1975 and paid royalties to Church. Church has continued to conduct religious services and other church activities on Stomacher.

All four of the living grandchildren of Hombre, joined by a guardian ad litem to represent unborn grandchildren, instituted suit against Church and Darin seeking damages for the removal of sand and gravel and an injunction preventing further acts of removal. There is no applicable statute. Which of the following best describes the likely disposition of this lawsuit?

(A) The plaintiffs should succeed, because the interest of Church terminated with the first removal of sand and gravel.
(B) Church and Darin should be enjoined, and damages should be recovered but impounded for future distribution.
(C) The injunction should be granted, but damages should be denied, because Hombre and Carl are not parties to the action.
(D) Damages should be awarded, but the injunction should be denied.

Answer to Question 107

Church did not lose its life estate when it removed the gravel; it merely violated a covenant. Church has a life estate for the life of Carl, and the grandchildren as a class have a vested remainder. The deed does not create a life estate which will be lost if the condition is broken because courts are reluctant to enforce a forfeiture unless such a result is clearly called for in the language of the grant. Instead, the court will enforce this language as a covenant. Note, also, that the grandchildren are not asking to obtain the property in their suit; they are only asking for damages and an injunction. Therefore, (A) does not apply at all to the call of the question.

(B) is correct. Church has violated the covenant by removing sand and gravel from the property, since under the covenant they were only supposed to use the property for church purposes. Moreover, as a life tenant, Church committed voluntary waste by taking a nonrenewable resource (sand and gravel) from the property, thereby permanently reducing the value of the remainder interest. Hombre's grandchildren, as a class, have a remainder interest in fee simple at the expiration of Church's life estate. Since this is a class gift which does not become possessory until Carl's death, the class will remain open until then. Therefore, the plaintiffs are clearly entitled to an injunction to stop further violations of the covenant and to prevent waste. They are also entitled to damages for the breaches of the covenant which have already occurred. Since the precise identity of the persons who will constitute the remainder class will not be known until Carl's death, the damages should be held for distribution to the class as it is constituted when the class closes and the remainder interest becomes possessory.

(C) is incorrect. It correctly states that an injunction should be granted because Church has violated and, absent an injunction, will continue to violate a covenant running with the land. However, neither Hombre nor Carl have an interest in the property, and need not be parties. Hombre is the grantor of the interest to Church and to his grandchildren, but since there are grandchildren who are capable of taking, Hombre holds no remainder interest in the property. Carl never had an interest in the property. His life is merely the measuring life for Church's life estate per autre vie.

(D) is incorrect. The grandchildren, as remainderpersons, have the traditional common-law equitable remedy to restrain waste on the property based on the fact that Church is permanently depleting a nonrenewable resource on the property by removing sand and gravel, thereby diminishing the value of the remainder interest. In addition, as owners of a remainder interest in the land, they have the right to equitable, injunctive relief to prevent Church from violating the covenant which prevents Church from using the property for anything but church purposes.

Question 108

For a valuable consideration, Amato, the owner of Riveracre, signed and gave to Barton a duly executed instrument that provided as follows: "The grantor may or may not sell Riveracre during her lifetime, but at her death, or if she earlier decides to sell, the property will be offered to Barton at $500 per acre. Barton shall exercise this right, if at all, within 60 days of receipt of said offer to sell." Barton recorded the instrument. The instrument was not valid as a will.

Is Barton's right under the instrument valid?

(A) Yes, because the instrument is recorded.
(B) Yes, because Barton's right to purchase will vest or fail within the period prescribed by the Rule Against Perpetuities.
(C) No, because Barton's right to purchase is a restraint on the owner's power to make a testamentary disposition.
(D) No, because Barton's right to purchase is an unreasonable restraint on alienation.

Answer to Question 108

(A) is incorrect. The instrument is valid, but the recording of that instrument is irrelevant to its validity. There has been no conveyance of the property to a third party who would not be bound by the Amato-Barton agreement unless it was recorded. This contest is between the original parties to the option contract and, in those circumstances, recording is irrelevant.

(B) is correct. An option agreement is subject to the Rule Against Perpetuities. The option must be exercisable under all circumstances, if it is ever to be exercised, within lives in being at the time of the granting of the option plus 21 years. In this case, the latest time the option can be exercised is within 60 days of the death of Amato, who is a life in being at the time of the granting of the option.

(C) is incorrect because Amato, for valid consideration, contracted to give a right to Barton to buy the property, and thereby voluntarily gave up her right to dispose of the property by will. While one of the incidents of property ownership is the right to dispose of it by will, an owner has the right to give up that right by contracting it away for valuable consideration.

(D) is incorrect because Amato, the owner of the property, by a valid option contract, gave up his right to alienate the property. This limitation was not imposed on Amato by his grantor. Therefore, the rules concerning the invalidity of restraints on alienation are inapplicable, and the length of the option is limited only by the time restraints of the Rule Against Perpetuities.

Question 109

The following events took place in a state that does not recognize common-law marriages, and which follows the common law with respect to tenancies by the entirety.

Wade Sloan and Mary Isaacs, who were never formally married, lived together over a seven-year period. During this time, Mary identified herself as "Mrs. Sloan" with the knowledge and consent of Wade; Wade and Mary maintained several charge accounts at retail stores under the names "Mr. and Mrs. Wade Sloan"; and they filed joint income tax returns as "Mr. and Mrs. Sloan."

Within this period, Wade decided to buy a home. The deed was in proper form and identified the grantees as "Wade Sloan and Mary Sloan, his wife, and their heirs and assigns forever as tenants by the entirety." Wade made a down payment of $10,000, and gave a note and mortgage for the unpaid balance. Both Wade and Mary signed the note and mortgage for the unpaid balance as husband and wife. Wade made the monthly payments as they became due until he and Mary had a disagreement and he abandoned her and the house. Mary then made the payments for three months. She then brought an action against Wade for partition of the land in question. The prayer for partition should be

(A) denied, because a tenant by the entirety has no right to partition.
(B) denied, because Wade has absolute title to the property.
(C) granted, because the tenancy by the entirety that was created by the deed was severed when Wade abandoned Mary.
(D) granted, because the estate created by the deed was not a tenancy by the entirety.

Answer to Question 109

Wade Sloan and Mary Isaacs were not married to each other since the jurisdiction does not recognize common-law marriages. As they were not married, they could not hold property as tenants by the entirety, since that form of ownership can only exist between married couples while they are actually married. Therefore, (A) is incorrect.

(B) is incorrect. The grantees on the deed were Wade and Mary, indicating some form of co-ownership, even though it could not be a tenancy by the entirety. Mary is a co-owner either as a tenant in common or as a joint tenant.

(D) is correct. A tenancy by the entirety is the only cotenancy which cannot be partitioned. Since there is no tenancy by the entirety, a partition can be granted.

(C) is incorrect. A co-ownership is not terminated because one of the co-owners abandons the property.

Question 110

Lawnacre was conveyed to Celeste and Donald by a deed which, in the jurisdiction in which Lawnacre is situated, created a cotenancy in equal shares and with the right of survivorship. The jurisdiction has no statute directly applicable to any of the problems posed.

Celeste, by deed, conveyed "my undivided one-half interest in Lawnacre" to Paul. Celeste has since died. In an appropriate action between Paul and Donald in which title to Lawnacre is at issue, Donald will

(A) prevail, because he is the sole owner of Lawnacre.
(B) prevail if, but only if, the cotenancy created in Celeste and Donald was a tenancy by the entirety.
(C) not prevail if he had knowledge of the conveyance prior to Celeste's death.
(D) not prevail, because Paul and Donald own Lawnacre as tenants in common.

Answer to Question 110

(A) is correct only if the interest created was a tenancy by the entirety; it is incorrect if the form of cotenancy in equal shares was a joint tenancy. Likewise, (D) is correct only if the interest created was a joint tenancy; it is incorrect if the form of cotenancy in equal shares was a tenancy by the entirety. The facts only state that Celeste and Donald owned a cotenancy in equal shares with a right of survivorship. That cotenancy could either be a joint tenancy or, if Celeste and Donald were married, it could be a tenancy by the entirety. If it were a joint tenancy, the conveyance from Celeste to Paul would have severed the joint tenancy, creating a tenancy in common between Paul and Donald. On the other hand, if Celeste and Donald held as tenants by the entirety, the unilateral conveyance by Celeste to Paul would be a nullity and Donald would inherit Celeste's interest by right of survivorship. (A) and (D) are tempting choices, because they are each correct under one possible scenario. However, they are still wrong because another choice correctly incorporates both rules.

(B) is correct because it correctly limits the situation in which Donald will prevail to the case where Donald and Celeste held as tenants by the entirety.

(C) is incorrect because knowledge of the conveyance by the other cotenant is irrelevant in determining if the right of survivorship has been terminated. If the interest was a tenancy by the entirety, the right of survivorship would not have been terminated, even if Donald knew of Celeste's deed to Paul. On the other hand, if the interest were a joint tenancy, the right of survivorship would have been terminated even if Donald were ignorant of Celeste's deed.

Question 111

The following transactions occurred with respect to Blackacre.

(1) In 1980 Oleg, the owner, conveyed his interest in fee simple "to my brothers Bob and Bill, their heirs and assigns as joint tenants with right of survivorship."
(2) In 1985 Bob died, devising his interest to his only child, "Charles, for life, and then to Charles's son, Sam, for life, and then to Sam's children, their heirs and assigns."
(3) In 1990 Bill died, devising his interest "to my friend, Frank, his heirs and assigns."
(4) In 1992 Frank conveyed by quitclaim deed "to Paul, his heirs and assigns whatever right, title, and interest I own."

Paul has contracted to convey marketable title in the land to Patrice. Can Paul do so?

(A) Yes, without joinder of any other person in the conveyance.
(B) Yes, if Charles, Sam, and Sam's only child (Gene, aged 25) will join in the conveyance.
(C) No, regardless of who joins in the conveyance, because Sam may have additional children whose interests cannot be defeated.
(D) No, regardless of who joins in the conveyance, because title acquired by quitclaim deed is impliedly unmerchantable.

Answer to Question 111

The answer to this question depends upon the disposition of Bob's interest in the property at his death. Since Bob and Bill held the property as joint tenants and nothing was done to sever the joint tenancy before Bob's death, Bob's interest passed to Bill by right of survivorship at Bob's death. Therefore, the provisions of Bob's will are irrelevant, and the entire interest in the property passed at Bill's death to Frank and, by Frank's deed, to Paul. Therefore, Paul can convey without any other person, and (A) is the correct answer. (B) and (C) are incorrect, as Bob's devisees have no interest in the property.

(D) is incorrect because a quitclaim deed conveys all of the title which a grantor has in the property conveyed. If the grantor has marketable title, the grantee acquires marketable title from a quitclaim deed.

Question 112

After Amy had built a four-story building on her own land, an accurate survey revealed that one of the eaves extended about six inches over the land of her neighbor, Bonnie. The guttering and spouting were so constructed that no water from the house fell upon Bonnie's land.

Bonnie sued Amy in trespass, praying for damages caused by the overhanging eaves. Judgment for

(A) Amy, because Bonnie has suffered no damages.
(B) Amy, because Amy acted in good faith and was unaware of the overhang until after the building was completed.
(C) Amy, because the overhang does not touch or concern any present or contemplated use of Bonnie's land.
(D) Bonnie, without regard to whether or not Bonnie is able to show any actual harm to herself.

Answer to Question 112

The overhanging eaves constitute a trespass on Bonnie's land. Actual damages are not necessary for a landowner to recover in trespass. She is entitled to recover nominal damages if she has suffered no actual damages. Thus, (A) is incorrect and (D) is correct.

Good faith is not a defense to a trespass action. If a person is unjustifiably on someone else's property, even unknowingly, the person is a trespasser and is liable for at least nominal damages. Thus, (B) is incorrect.

(C) is incorrect because a landowner is not required to show she is using or intends to use the particular piece of land in question in order to sue for trespass and win.

Question 113

Allen owned a lot of land improved with a four-story building. Bates, Allen's abutting landowner, began the erection of a two-story building on his land. In doing so, he excavated to a depth of several feet up to, but not over, the line between Allen and Bates. Bates did not give Allen any advance notice of the excavation. The excavation was performed in a careful and workmanlike manner, except that no steps were taken to shore up Allen's building.

As a result of the excavation, Allen's building settled and cracked and was seriously damaged before the excavation came to Allen's personal attention.

In an action brought by Allen against Bates for damage to Allen's building, it was shown that, even if there had been no building on the land, Allen's land would have subsided as a result of Bates's excavation. This was because of an especially pliable clay soil condition of which Bates was unaware prior to the excavation. Judgment for

(A) Allen, because Allen is entitled to support for his land in its natural condition.
(B) Allen, because Allen is entitled to support for his land in its improved condition.
(C) Bates, because Bates is not liable for the peculiar condition of the soil.
(D) Bates, because he was not negligent in the way he excavated.

Answer to Question 113

(A) is correct. For Allen to recover without proving negligence, he would have to prove that there would have been a failure to support the land even if it had been in its natural state. Land which is in its natural state is entitled to absolute support from adjoining land. If that support is removed, the adjoining landowner is liable for damages in strict liability, without proof of negligence. This strict liability standard also applies to improved land if it can be shown that there would have been damage even if the land had been in its natural state, a fact given in the question.

(B) is incorrect because it is too broad to say that Allen is entitled to support for his land in its improved condition. This would wrongly apply a strict liability standard to improved land.

(C) is incorrect because Bates assumes the consequences of the peculiar condition of the soil in applying the strict liability standard, as here. If the unimproved land would have settled, even due to the peculiar condition of the soil, the neighboring landowner is strictly liable.

(D) is incorrect because, even aside from negligence, a landowner can recover under a strict liability theory if the land would have subsided in its natural, unimproved state, a fact given in the question.

Question 114

Anna owned a lot of land improved with a building. Betty, Anna's abutting landowner, began the erection of a building on her land. In doing so, Betty excavated to a depth of several feet on her land in a careful and workmanlike manner.

There was no settling or subsidence of Anna's land at the time of Betty's excavation. However, as a result of a carefully designed drainage system on Betty's land, percolating water was drained from Anna's land. As a result, Anna's building settled and cracked. Anna sued Betty for the resulting damage. Judgment for

(A) Betty, because there has been no trespass upon Anna's land.
(B) Betty, because she has drained away only water and has not drained away any sand, silt, or other substance of the soil.
(C) Anna, because Betty's act is the proximate cause of Anna's damage as a matter of law.

(D) Anna, because Betty has no right to improve her own land in a manner that causes harm to the land of another.

Answer to Question 114

(A) is incorrect. Under the common law, a landowner excavating on his or her own land is under an absolute duty to support the land of the abutters in its natural state and to avoid negligence which could cause subsidence in the abutter's improved land. Therefore, there can be liability without an actual trespass on a neighbor's land.

(B) is correct. The common law of underground water rights permits a landowner to secure underground water from his or her own land even if the water is drawn from under a neighbor's land. Unlike the excavation of earth, the removal of water from underneath one's own land does not cause liability for failure to give lateral support.

(C) is incorrect. Proximate causation is only one element of liability. There must be some basis for liability - a contract or a duty which has been breached. As explained above, no such basis exists here.

(D) is incorrect. A landowner has a right to improve his or her land with some limitations that do not amount to an absolute bar on harming abutting land. For example, a landowner may excavate on the property, even if it causes a building on a neighbor's land to subside, as long as the excavation was not done in a negligent manner. The only time strict liability applies is if land of an abutter would have subsided in its natural state.

Questions 115 and 116 are based on the following fact situation.

Ogden was the fee simple owner of three adjoining vacant lots fronting on a common street in a primarily residential section of a city which had no zoning laws. The lots were identified as Lots 1, 2, and 3. Ogden conveyed Lot 1 to Akers and Lot 2 to Bell. Ogden retained Lot 3, which consisted of three acres of woodland. Bell, whose lot was between the other two, built a house on his lot. Bell's house included a large window on the side facing Lot 3. The window provided a beautiful view from Bell's living room, thereby adding value to Bell's house.

Akers then erected a house on his lot. Ogden made no complaint either to Akers or Bell concerning the houses they built. After both Akers and Bell had completed their houses, the two of them agreed to and did build a common driveway running from the street to the rear of their respective lots. The driveway was built on the line between the two houses so that one-half of the way was located on each lot. Akers and Bell exchanged right-of-way deeds by which each of them conveyed to the other, his heirs and assigns, an easement to continue the right of way. Both deeds were properly recorded.

After Akers and Bell had lived in their respective houses for thirty years, a new public street was built bordering on the rear of Lots 1, 2, and 3. Akers informed Bell that, since the new street removed the need for their common driveway, he considered the right-of-way terminated; therefore, he intended to discontinue its use and expected Bell to do the same.

Thereafter, Ogden began the erection of a six-story apartment house on Lot 3. If the apartment house is completed, it will block the view from Bell's window and will substantially reduce the value of Bell's lot.

115. In an action brought by Bell to enjoin Akers from interfering with Bell's continued use of the common driveway between the two lots, the decision should be for

(A) Akers, because the termination of the necessity for the easement terminated the easement.
(B) Akers, because the continuation of the easement after the change of circumstances would adversely affect the marketability of both lots without adding any commensurate value to either.

(C) Bell, because an incorporeal hereditament lies in grant and cannot be terminated without a writing.
(D) Bell, because the removal of the need for the easement created by express grant does not affect the right to the easement.

116. In an action brought by Bell to enjoin Ogden from erecting the apartment building in such a way as to obstruct the view from Bell's living room window, the decision should be for

(A) Bell, because Ogden's proposed building would be an obstruction of Bell's natural right to an easement for light and air.
(B) Bell, because Bell was misled by Ogden's failure to complain when Bell was building his house.
(C) Ogden if, but only if, it can be shown that Ogden's intention to erect such a building was made known to Bell at or prior to the time of Ogden's conveyance to Bell.
(D) Ogden, because Bell has no easement for light, air, or view.

Answer to Question 115

(A) is incorrect. This cannot be an easement by necessity because such an easement arises only when a parcel of land is subdivided, and one of the parcels needs an easement from the other in order to make any use of the land. These characteristics are not present here. While it is true that the end of the necessity terminates an easement by necessity, that proposition is irrelevant because this is not an easement by necessity.

This is an easement by grant because it creates the right to use the land of another with the formalities necessary to convey an interest in land. (D) correctly states the law concerning termination of an easement by grant. An easement created by express grant is a permanent property interest which can only be terminated by very specific situations (e.g., a written release or estoppel). The end of the need or motivation for the easement is not sufficient to terminate a granted easement.

A change in circumstances will **not** cause the termination of an easement by grant. The equities of the situation are not a factor in the enforceability of an easement. While changed circumstances can be grounds for refusing to enforce a covenant, they are not a ground for terminating an easement. Thus, (B) is incorrect.

(C) is incorrect. An incorporeal hereditament means an interest in land which does not have a physical presence, namely an easement. While an easement by grant must always be created by a writing, it can be terminated by actions other than a writing, such as the merger of the dominant and servient estates, adverse possession, or estoppel.

Answer to Question 116

Absent an express agreement by the parties, a negative easement for light and air will not be created by implication because it is not apparent and would create uncertainty in titles and hamper development. There is no "natural right" to an easement for light and air. That right can only be created by an express easement. Thus, (A) is incorrect and (D) is correct.

(C) misplaces the burden between the parties. If Bell wanted to protect his view, he could have obtained an express "view easement," in which Ogden would have given up his right to build on a portion of his lot.

(B) is incorrect. Ogden had no reason to complain while Bell was building his house because the construction was within Bell's rights. Ogden did not have to put himself on record concerning his intentions regarding building on his lot in order to preserve the right to do so. There is no indication of fraud or misrepresentation in Ogden's conduct.

Question 117

Oxnard owned Goldacre, a tract of land, in fee simple. At a time when Goldacre was in the adverse possession of Amos, Eric obtained the oral permission of Oxnard to use as a road or driveway a portion of Goldacre to reach adjoining land, Twin Pines, which Eric owned in fee simple. Thereafter, during all times relevant to this problem, Eric used this road across Goldacre regularly for ingress and egress between Twin Pines and a public highway.

Amos quit possession of Goldacre before acquiring title by adverse possession. Without any further communication between Oxnard and Eric, Eric continued to use the road for a total period, from the time he first began to use it, sufficient to acquire an easement by prescription. Oxnard then blocked the road and refused to permit its continued use. Eric brought suit to determine his right to continue use of the road. Eric should

(A) win, because his use was adverse to Amos and once adverse it continued adverse until some affirmative showing of a change.
(B) win, because Eric made no attempt to renew permission after Amos quit possession of Goldacre.
(C) lose, because his use was with permission.
(D) lose, because there is no evidence that he continued adverse use for the required period after Amos quit possession.

Answer to Question 117

The original use of the property by Eric was permissive with respect to Oxnard, the true owner of the property. The fact that it was adverse to a person who was no more than a trespasser (i.e., Amos) is irrelevant. Amos was a trespasser who never acquired title by adverse possession. Thus, (A) is incorrect.

At all times, the true owner of the property was Oxnard and Eric's use with respect to Oxnard was clearly permissive at the start and there is no evidence that it changed. The use remains permissive until Oxnard withdraws permission or is notified that Eric is holding adversely to him, because that would be the only way Oxnard would know that he has a cause of action to prohibit the use of the property. Therefore, the failure to renew permission does not make further use adverse. (B) is incorrect.

So, the adverse element necessary to obtain an easement by prescription is not present and (C) is correct.

(D) is incorrect because it turns on whether Eric "continued" adverse use after Amos quit possession. Because the use never was adverse as to Oxnard, it did not "continue" to be adverse once Amos left and that issue is irrelevant.

Questions 118 and 119 are based on the following fact situation.

Albert, the owner of a house and lot, leased the same to Barnes for a term of five years. In addition to the house, there was also an unattached, two-car brick garage located on the lot. Barnes earned his living as an employee in a local grocery store, but his hobby consisted of wood carving and the making of small furniture. Barnes installed a work bench, electric lights, and a radiator in the garage. He also laid pipes connecting the radiator with the heating plant inside the house. Thereafter, Albert mortgaged the premises to Good Bank to secure a loan. Barnes was not given notice of the mortgage, but the mortgage was recorded. Still later, Albert defaulted on his mortgage payments, and Good Bank began foreclosure proceedings, as it was entitled to do under the terms of the mortgage. By this time, Barnes's lease was almost ended. Barnes began the removal of the equipment he had installed in the garage. Good Bank brought an action to enjoin the removal of the equipment mentioned above. Both Barnes and Albert were named as defendants.

118. If the court refuses the injunction, it will be because

(A) Barnes was without notice of the mortgage.
(B) the circumstances reveal that the equipment was installed for Barnes's exclusive benefit.
(C) in the absence of a contract agreement, a residential tenant is entitled to remove any personal property he voluntarily brings upon the premises.
(D) the Statute of Frauds precludes Good Bank from claiming any interest in the equipment.

119. If the equipment had been installed by Albert, but the facts were otherwise unchanged, the effect on Good Bank's prayer for an injunction would be that the

(A) likelihood of Good Bank's succeeding would be improved.
(B) likelihood of Good Bank's succeeding would be lessened.
(C) likelihood of Good Bank's succeeding would be unaffected.
(D) outcome of the litigation would depend upon whether or not the mortgage expressly mentioned personal property located on the premises.

Answer to Question 118

When personal property is affixed to real property, the question is whether it becomes a "fixture." If it is a fixture, its ownership is automatically transferred as the ownership of the real property is transferred. If it is not a fixture, it can be removed by the person who installed it. Whether a particular object is a fixture is primarily a question of the intention of the parties at the time it was affixed. In the leasehold situation, as here, there is a presumption that there was no intent that easily detachable property would become a fixture, and so it may be removed at the end of the leasehold term. The property involved in this question is the type that can be easily removed without damaging the real estate, and therefore the tenant should have a right to remove it. Thus, (B) is correct. This choice does not spell out the applicable legal theory completely, but the fact that the property was installed for the tenant's exclusive benefit is the foundation for the inference that there never was an intention to leave it there permanently, and this choice comes closer than any other to setting forth the basis on which the property can be removed.

The mortgagee stands in no better position than the owner with respect to the rights of a tenant to remove attached property. The tenant's knowledge of the mortgage is irrelevant because the tenant could prevail even if he knew of the mortgage. Therefore, (A) is incorrect.

(C) is incorrect because it is overbroad. There are situations where a tenant can attach personal property with the intent that it become a fixture and thereby lose title to the personalty. However, such cases are rare and this does not appear to be one of them. If personal property is not removed in a timely fashion, it remains as part of the real estate and the tenant loses his ownership rights in the affixed property.

(D) is incorrect because the bank's interest can only derive from its interest in the property as realty. The bank has a written mortgage which establishes that interest, and complies with the Statute of Frauds.

Answer to Question 119

If the property were installed by a fee owner who planned to own the real estate indefinitely, rather than by a lessee who only had a temporary interest, the intention at the time the property was installed is much more likely that it was to be a permanent part of the real estate. Therefore, the bank, which has a security interest in the real estate, would be more likely to be able to prevent Albert from turning the fixture back into personal property and its chances of obtaining the injunction would be improved. The bank's chances of obtaining the injunction would be improved, not lessened. Therefore, (A) is correct and (B) and (C) are incorrect.

(D) is incorrect. The outcome does not depend on whether personal property is included in the mortgage because the bank's theory would be that the property affixed to the real estate is a permanent part of the realty which cannot be severed.

Question 120

Ohner holds the title in fee simple to a tract of 1,500 acres. He desires to develop the entire tract as a golf course, country club, and residential subdivision. He contemplates forming a corporation to own and to operate the golf course and country club; the stock in the corporation will be distributed to the owners of lots in the residential portions of the subdivision, but no obligation to issue the stock is to ripen until all the residential lots are sold. The price of the lots is intended to return enough money to compensate Ohner for the raw land, development costs (including the building of the golf course and the country club facilities), and his profit, if all of the lots are sold.

Ohner's market analyses indicate that he must create a scheme of development that will offer prospective purchasers (and their lawyers) a very high order of assurance that several aspects will be clearly established:

(1) Aside from the country club and golf course, there will be no land use other than for residential use and occupancy in the 1,500 acres.
(2) The residents of the subdivision will have an unambiguous right of access to the club and golf course facilities.
(3) Each lot owner must have an unambiguous right to transfer the lot to a purchaser with all original benefits.
(4) Each lot owner must be obligated to pay annual dues equal to a pro rata share (based on the number of lots) of the club's annual operating deficit (whether or not such owner desires to make use of club and course facilities).

In the context of all aspects of the scheme, which of the following will offer the best chance of implementing the requirement that each lot owner pay annual dues to support the club and golf course?

(A) covenant
(B) easement
(C) mortgage
(D) personal contractual obligation by each purchaser

Answer to Question 120

(A) is correct. A covenant which runs with the land, obligating the original owner and all subsequent owners while they own the property to pay their shares of the club expenses, is the best way to accomplish the objective. Since the obligation runs with the land, the present lot owners would be liable and could be sued by the club if they failed to pay their obligations. The biggest problem with the enforceability of such a scheme is that historically courts have been reluctant to find that an agreement to pay money touches and concerns the land, a requirement which must be met if the covenant is to bind subsequent lot owners. However, where the covenant is specifically tied to supporting a facility which benefits the land and is necessary for the well-being of the neighborhood, courts have found that the touch and concern requirement is met.

(B) is incorrect. If an easement were to be used to accomplish this goal, the golf club property would have to be the dominant estate and the use of each lot as a servient estate would only be for that lot to generate money to run the golf course. That is not a "use" which an easement would allow. Therefore, an easement is not an appropriate instrument, even though it possesses the very desirable characteristics of being easily enforced and unlimited in time.

(C) is incorrect. A mortgage on each lot to secure the obligation to pay for support of the country club would be the most efficient way to ensure its financial stability, since the mortgage could be foreclosed and the lot sold if the payments were delinquent. However, the development itself is not feasible unless the lot owners can obtain financing for the lots and the homes to be built on them. The lenders will require a first mortgage to secure the financing obligation. If the mortgage to secure the club payments is already a first lien, then financing may be difficult to obtain. While a provision for subordination of the club lien to a mortgage lien is possible, it is cumbersome and unlikely to be acceptable to attorneys for prospective purchasers. Moreover, mortgages are usually only established to secure repayment of a fixed amount. It is unusual to use a mortgage to secure the payment of an annual, eternal obligation.

(D) is incorrect. A personal contractual obligation does not offer the best chance of implementing the requirement, because such a contractual obligation would not run with the land. It will not bind subsequent purchasers and an original purchaser who moves away will have no incentive to continue to make payments. Defaults will be high and this will jeopardize the financial stability of the golf club.

Question 121

Allen and Barker are equal tenants in common of a strip of land 10 feet wide and 100 feet deep which lies between the lots on which their respective homes are situated. Both Allen and Barker need the use of the 10-foot strip as a driveway, and each fears that a new neighbor might seek partition and leave him with an unusable 5-foot strip. The best advice about how to solve their problem is

(A) a covenant against partition.
(B) an indenture granting cross-easements in the undivided half interest of each.
(C) partition into two separate 5-foot wide strips and an indenture granting cross-easements.
(D) a trust to hold the strip in perpetuity.

Answer to Question 121

A covenant against partition is a restraint on alienation of a cotenancy because it restricts the co-owner from selling an individual fee in property and requires that he forever hold the property in a co-ownership form. While the present fee owners might be able to limit their own rights to partition, the rules concerning restraints on alienation would prevent their successors in title from being bound. Therefore, this device would probably not work, and (A) is incorrect.

An easement is an interest to use the land of another in a particular way. An easement cannot be created by fee owners in property which they already own. If the dominant and servient interest in an existing easement come into the same ownership, the easement is terminated.

Therefore, the parties cannot effectively grant cross-easements in the undivided half interest of each, and (B) is incorrect.

(C) is the correct answer. Once the land is partitioned into two separate five-foot strips, it is possible for each party to grant an easement in the portion which he owns to the other party. The cross-easements are then appurtenant to the houselots each owns and cannot be terminated without the permission of both landowners. Easements can exist in perpetuity and, if recorded, will bind a subsequent purchaser.

(D) is incorrect. The trust created would be a private trust, which would be subject to the Rule Against Perpetuities. The trust would violate the Rule because the property would be held in perpetuity and thus would not vest during lives in being plus 21 years.

Questions 122 and 123 are based on the following fact situation.

Oscar, the owner in fee simple, laid out a subdivision of 325 lots on 150 acres of land. He obtained governmental approval (as required by applicable ordinances), and between 1990 and 1992 he sold 140 of the lots, inserting in each of the 140 deeds the following provision:

"The Grantee, for himself and his heirs, assigns, and successors, covenants and agrees that the premises conveyed herein shall have erected thereon one single-family dwelling, and that no other structure (other than a detached garage, normally incident to a single-family dwelling) shall be erected or maintained; and, further, that no use shall ever be made or permitted to be made than occupancy by a single family for residential purposes only."

Because of difficulty encountered in selling the remaining lots for single-family use, in January, 1993, Oscar advertised the remaining lots with prominent emphasis: "These lots are not subject to any restrictions and purchasers will find them adaptable to a wide range of uses."

122. Payne had purchased one of the 140 lots and brought suit against Oscar to establish that the remaining 185 lots, as well as the 140 sold previously, can be used only for residential purposes by single families. Assuming that procedural requirements have been met to permit adjudication of the issue Payne has tendered, which of the following is the most appropriate comment?

(A) Oscar should win because the provision binds only the grantees.
(B) The outcome turns on whether a common development scheme had been established for the entire subdivision.
(C) The outcome turns on whether there are sufficient land areas devoted to multiple-family uses within the municipality to afford reasonable opportunity for all economic classes to move into the area so as to satisfy the standards of equal protection of the law.
(D) Payne should win under an application of the doctrine which requires construction of deeds to resolve any doubt against the grantor.

123. Oscar sold 50 lots during 1993 without inserting in the deeds any provisions relating to structures or uses. Doyle purchased one of the 50 lots and proposes to erect a service station and to conduct a retail business for the sale of gasoline. Pringle purchased a lot from Boyer. Boyer had purchased one of the lots from Oscar in 1990 and the deed contained the provision that is quoted above in the facts. Pringle brings suit to prevent Doyle from erecting the service station and from conducting a retail business. In the litigation between Pringle and Doyle, which of the following constitutes the best defense for Doyle?

(A) Oscar's difficulty in selling with provisions relating to use establishes a change in circumstances which renders any restrictions which may once have existed unenforceable.
(B) Enforcement of the restriction, in view of the change of circumstances, would be an unreasonable restraint on alienation.
(C) Since the proof (as stated) does not establish a danger of monetary loss to Pringle, Pringle has failed to establish one of the necessary elements in a cause of action to prevent Doyle from using his lot for business purposes.
(D) The facts do not establish a common building or development scheme for the entire subdivision.

Answer to Question 122

The question here is whether there is a common development scheme. If there is such a scheme, the provision written into the deeds of the first lots sold will bind the grantor as well as the grantees. Under the theory of negative reciprocal restrictions, a grantee can require the grantor to impose the restriction on all the other lots which are part of the common scheme. Because Oscar restricted the use of a substantial number of subdivision lots with identical provisions written into their deeds, it is arguable that a common development scheme has been established. If there is such a common scheme, any owner burdened by restrictions may enforce them against any land which is part of the common scheme. Thus, (B) is correct.

(A) is incorrect. If a common development scheme has been established, the provision binds the grantor as well as the grantee.

(C) incorrectly states a public policy issue and a Constitutional Law standard. Property questions on the Multistate Bar Exam are rarely determined by broad policy issues such as the availability of affordable housing or a municipality's interest in population distribution. Instead, you should look to the application of property concepts to the facts presented.

(D) is incorrect. There is no doctrine which requires the construction of deeds to resolve any doubt against the grantor. Deeds should be construed in such a manner as to carry out the intent of the parties.

Answer to Question 123

(A) is incorrect on two counts. First, the facts here do not show changed circumstances. Oscar's difficulty in selling the second group of lots does not show a significant change of circumstances which so reduce the benefit of the restriction as to render meaningless the purposes of a common scheme. Second, if the facts did show a significant change of circumstances, then the doctrine of changed circumstances would only preclude equitable enforcement. That doctrine does not act to terminate restrictive covenants. Thus, Doyle might still be liable for monetary damages, even if the covenants were not specifically enforceable due to changed circumstances.

Covenants restricting use are not considered restraints on alienation. Therefore, (B) is incorrect.

(C) is incorrect. Pringle is seeking an equitable remedy in this action. Such a suit in equity to enjoin the use of land in violation of a covenant does not require proof of monetary loss. If these restrictions can be imposed upon Doyle's lot, absence of harm to Pringle might be a cause to deny equitable enforcement of the covenant, but would not defeat the covenant altogether.

The best defense for Doyle is that the facts do not present a common scheme. Pringles' lot was among the first group conveyed by Oscar and is burdened by express provisions in his deed. Doyle's lot, along with the other lots in the second group conveyed, is not expressly burdened by any restrictions. Restrictions which burden the first lots can only be imposed on Doyle's lot if Pringle can show a common scheme which burdens the entire subdivision. The doctrine of negative reciprocal restrictions will not apply unless a common scheme is established. Arguably, these facts do not show such a common scheme because there is no showing that Oscar either intended to restrict **all** of the lots or led early purchasers to believe he so intended. If no common scheme can be shown, Doyle is free to use his lot as he pleases. Therefore, (D) is the correct answer.

Question 124

Fernwood Realty Company developed a residential development, known as the Fernwood Development, which included single-family dwellings, town houses, and high-rise apartments for a total of 25,000 dwelling units. Included in the deed to each unit was a covenant under which the grantee and the grantee's "heirs and assigns" agreed to purchase electrical power only from a plant Fernwood promised to build and maintain within the development. Fernwood constructed the plant and the necessary power lines. The plant did not supply power outside the development. An appropriate and fair formula was used to determine the cost of the power.

After constructing and selling 12,500 of the units, Fernwood sold its interest in the development to Gaint Realty Investors. Gaint operated the power plant and constructed and sold the remaining 12,500 units. Each conveyance from Gaint contained the same covenant relating to electrical power that Fernwood had included in the 12,500 conveyances it had made.

Page bought a dwelling unit from Olm, who had purchased it from Fernwood. Subsequently, Page, whose lot was along the boundary of the Fernwood development, ceased buying electrical power from Gaint and began purchasing power from General Power Company, which provided such service in the area surrounding the Fernwood development. Both General Power and Gaint have governmental authorization to provide electrical services to the area. Gaint instituted an appropriate action against Page to enjoin her from obtaining electrical power from General Power. If judgment is for Page, it most likely will be because

(A) the covenant does not touch and concern the land.
(B) the mixture of types of residential units is viewed as preventing one common development scheme.
(C) the covenant is a restraint on alienation.
(D) there is no privity of estate between Page and Gaint.

Answer to Question 124

Gaint's action against Page is an attempt to enforce a covenant to purchase electricity originally made by prior owners of their respective properties. In order to make a covenant binding by and against successors in interest to the pieces of land which were originally burdened and benefited, it must meet the requirements of a covenant which runs with the land. If Page prevails, it is most likely because not all of those requirements have been met and thus the covenant is not enforceable against a subsequent owner, either at law or as an equitable servitude. There is a strong argument that the purchase of a fungible product like electricity, which could easily be generated hundreds of miles away, does not affect the use of the land and is not closely connected to the parcels of land owned by the plaintiff and defendant. Therefore, the touch and concern requirement for a covenant to run with the land is not met, and (A) is the correct answer.

(B) is incorrect on several counts. First, the statement this answer makes about the common scheme doctrine is incorrect; a common scheme may contain various types of use, residential as well as commercial and industrial, as long as the areas and the scheme itself are clearly set out. Second, a common scheme theory is of no benefit here. A common scheme only allows restrictions to be imposed upon land that is not expressly so burdened. Here, the original deeds all clearly contained the restriction. The issue is whether successors to the lots are bound by these restrictions.

(C) is incorrect. A covenant running with the land is not a restraint on alienation unless it prevents the lot owner from selling the land. A covenant that imposes some restrictions on the use of the property does not so seriously affect the alienability of property as to render it a restraint on alienation. Therefore, a requirement that a landowner purchase electricity at a reasonable price from one company does not amount to a restraint on alienation.

This is a suit to specifically enforce a covenant as an equitable servitude. Horizontal privity is not required for enforcement in equity. Vertical privity is only required for the **right** to be enforceable, and since Gaint is the successor in title to Fernwood, Gaint can enforce the right. Moreover, even if this were an action at law, the greater privity required in such an action is present. Here, the original covenant was imposed in the deed which conveyed the estate from Fernwood to Olm. Therefore, there was horizontal privity between the original promisee and promisor. Page and Gaint derived their titles from the original contracting parties and so there is the vertical privity required for both the right and the duty to run at law, and (D) is incorrect.

Questions 125 and 126 are based on the following fact situation.

Owner held 500 acres in fee simple absolute. In 1990, Owner platted and obtained all required governmental approvals of two subdivisions of 200 acres each.

In 1990 and 1991, commercial buildings and parking facilities were constructed on one, Royal Center, in accordance with the plans disclosed by the plat for each subdivision. Royal Center continues to be used for commercial purposes.

The plat of the other, Royal Oaks, showed 250 lots, streets, and utility and drainage easements. All of the lots in Royal Oaks were conveyed during 1990 and 1991. The deeds contained provisions, expressly stated to be binding upon the grantees, their heirs and assigns, requiring the lots to be used for single-family, residential purposes only until 2025. The deeds expressly stated that these provisions were enforceable by the owner of any lot in the Royal Oaks subdivision. The land is located in a jurisdiction where restrictions in prior deeds are in the chain of title.

At all times since 1959, the 200 acres in Royal Center have been zoned for shopping center use, and the 200 acres in Royal Oaks have been zoned for residential use in a classification which permits both single-family and multiple-family use.

125. In an appropriate attack upon the limitation to residential use by single families, if the evidence disclosed no fact in addition to those listed above, the most probable judicial resolution would be that

(A) there is no enforceable restriction because judicial recognition constitutes state action which is in conflict with the Fourteenth Amendment to the United States Constitution.
(B) there is no enforceable restriction because of Owner's conflict of interest in that he did not make the restriction applicable to the 100 acres he retained.
(C) the restriction on use set forth in the deeds will be enforced at the suit of any present owner of a lot in Royal Oaks residential subdivision.
(D) any use consistent with zoning will be permitted but to the extent that such uses so permitted as are in conflict with the restrictions in the deeds will give rise to a right to damages from Owner or Owner's successor.

126. Owner now desires to open his remaining 100 acres as a residential subdivision of 125 lots (with appropriate streets, etc.). He has, as an essential element of his scheme, the feature that the restrictions should be identical with those he planned for the original Royal Oaks residential subdivision, and further, that lot owners in Royal Oaks should be able to enforce (by lawsuits) restrictions on the lots in the 100 acres. The zoning for the 100 acres is identical with that for the 200 acres of the Royal Oaks subdivision. Which of the following best states the chance of success for his scheme?

(A) He can restrict use only to the extent of that imposed by zoning (that is, to residential use by not more than four dwelling units per lot).
(B) He cannot restrict the 100 acres to residential use because of the conflicting use for retail commercial purposes in the 200 acres comprising the shopping center.
(C) He cannot impose any enforceable restriction to residential use only.
(D) Any chance of success depends upon the 100 acres being considered by the courts as a part of a common development scheme which also includes the 200 acres of Royal Oaks.

Answer to Question 125

(A) is incorrect. A restriction on the use of property has been found not to violate the Fourteenth Amendment unless enforcement of the restriction constitutes state action denying an individual rights guaranteed by that Amendment, such as the racially restrictive covenants struck down in *Shelley v. Kramer*. A restriction to single-family residential use does not violate the Fourteenth Amendment.

(B) is incorrect. The covenants contained in the deeds to the lot owners in the subdivision are intended to run with the land, and touch and concern the land. A common scheme is created because a similar restriction was contained in the deed to each lot. The covenants are specifically enforceable by any lot owner in the subdivision against any other lot owner. A conflict of interest such as that described in the question will not render the covenant enforceable. An owner may freely choose whether or not to encumber particular pieces of land. A restriction on certain lots will not lead to an equitable requirement that the owner encumber other property, unless the common scheme is found to cover the other property also. In this case, the subdivision is large enough to be a cohesive unit without involving an additional 100-acre tract.

(C) is correct. Since Owner imposed identical restrictions on all 250 lots in the 200-acre subdivision, he has created a common scheme. One of the consequences of a common scheme is that the owner of each lot in the subdivision, whether the deed to that lot was received from the original developer before or after the deed to any other lot, may enforce the covenant against the owner of any other lot similarly burdened, whether that owner is an original grantee or a subsequent grantee.

(D) is incorrect. The fact that the zoning laws permit uses prohibited by the covenant does not prevent the covenant from being specifically enforced.

Answer to Question 126

(A) incorrectly states that Owner can restrict the new development only to the extent permitted by zoning laws. Zoning laws and the imposition of restrictions by deed are separate and independent issues. Zoning is not a limitation upon the right to impose restrictions.

(B) is incorrect. The shopping center was planned, approved and created independently of the remaining 100 acres. There is nothing in the facts that indicates the shopping center is integrally tied up with this other land. Moreover, a development scheme may include residential and commercial areas and still amount to a common scheme, as long as a definite plan is set out.

(C) is incorrect. Restrictions on the use of land are commonly achieved with covenants such as the one described here. A restriction to residential use would be said to touch and concern the land, and if it met other requirements, could be enforced as a covenant running with the land at law or as an equitable servitude. Such a restriction is a typical one to be enforced under a theory of common scheme. Here, it would be identical to the provisions restricting another similarly situated group of lots and will provide notice to lot owners to be restricted. This land can be restricted to residential use only.

(D) is correct. If the courts consider the remaining 100 acres to be part of a common scheme which includes Royal Oaks, then the land in Royal Oaks would be legally benefited by restrictions contained in the deeds pertaining to those 100 acres. If this land is located such that it should logically be developed as part of the common scheme, some jurisdiction might include it as restricted land regardless of Owner's actions. Here, the inclusion of uniform, consistent restrictions would give rise to the expectations of the Royal Oaks owners that the new acreage is part of a common scheme and, by virtue of the language in their deeds, the new lot owners will have notice of the enforceability of these restrictions under the existing Royal Oaks development scheme. Therefore, people who own land in Royal Oaks would be allowed to enforce such restrictions.

Questions 127 and 128 are based on the following fact situation.

In 1985, Oscar, owner of a 100-acre tract, prepared and duly recorded a subdivision plan called Happy Acres. The plan showed 90 one-acre lots and a ten-acre tract in the center that was designated "Future Public School."

Oscar published and distributed a brochure promoting Happy Acres which emphasized the proximity of the lots to the school and indicated potential tax savings "because the school district will not have to expend tax money to acquire this property." There is no specific statute concerning the dedication of school sites.

Oscar sold 50 of the lots to individual purchasers. Each deed referred to the recorded plan and also contained the following clause: "No mobile home shall be erected on any lot within Happy Acres." Sarah was one of the original purchasers from Oscar.

In 1991, Oscar sold the remaining 40 lots and the ten-acre tract to Max by a deed which referred to the plan and contained the restriction relating to mobile homes. Max sold the 40 lots to individual purchasers and the ten-acre tract to Pete. None of the deeds from Max referred to the plan or contained any reference to mobile homes.

127. Joe, who purchased his lot from Max, has placed a mobile home on it and Sarah brings an action against Joe to force him to remove it. The result of this action will be in favor of

(A) Sarah, because the restrictive covenant in her deed runs with the land.

304

(B) Sarah, because the presence of the mobile home may adversely affect the market value of her land.
(C) Joe, because his deed did not contain the restrictive covenant.
(D) Joe, because he is not a direct but a remote grantee of Oscar.

128. In 1992, the school board with jurisdiction over the area in which Happy Acres is situated voted to erect a new school on the ten-acre tract. In an appropriate action between the school board and Pete to determine title, the result will be in favor of

(A) Pete, because the school board has been guilty of laches.
(B) Pete, because the deed did not refer to the subdivision plan.
(C) the school board, because Pete had constructive notice of the restricted use of the tract
(D) the school board, because there has been a dedication and acceptance of the tract.

Answer to Question 127

The restriction against mobile homes is in writing, is contained in a deed from Oscar to Max, touches and concerns the land, and arguably is intended to bind successors in title. Thus, the restriction creates a covenant running with the land. It even burdens lots where the restriction has not been explicitly imposed by deed because those lots are part of a common scheme and the doctrine of negative reciprocal servitudes applies. The covenant thus burdens remote as well as direct grantees. A grantee must have notice for a covenant to run against him in equity. That requirement is satisfied in this case because deeds to similar lots in the subdivision have been burdened by a similar covenant, and the restriction is contained in an earlier deed in Joe's chain of title (the deed from Oscar to Max). Thus, (D) is incorrect.

The restrictive covenant forbidding the construction of mobile homes may be enforced against Joe because it is in Joe's chain of title (and so he has at least constructive notice of it) and the covenant runs with the land. Therefore, Joe is bound by the restriction under the doctrine of negative reciprocal servitudes, whether or not the covenant is contained in his deed, because his land is part of a common scheme. Thus, (C) is incorrect. Sarah is a proper plaintiff for this action because the facts present a common scheme which includes the lots owned by both Sarah and Joe. Thus, (A) is the correct answer.

(B) is incorrect. A use of one neighbor's land which reduces the value of another's does not by itself create a right of action. There must be some form of covenant which burdens the land of the defendant and benefits the land of the plaintiff.

Answer to Question 128

The subdivision plan filed by Oscar in 1985 constituted the dedication of the ten-acre site to the municipality as a school site. The school board took control of the site and went forward with plans to build a school, which constitutes acceptance. Thus, (D) is the correct answer.

(C) is the next best answer because it states that the school board will be successful in this case, and the reason stated is not totally wrong. The plan was recorded by Oscar, and Pete did have constructive notice of the dedication, so he cannot claim to hold free of the restriction. However, there is some doubt that a third party, such as the school board, could enforce a restrictive covenant against a landowner in the development. This would work for a neighboring landowner in the development, but is not a sufficient theory for the school board to prevail.

The school board did not sit on its right to the land knowing that Pete was relying on their supposed disinterest in the property in buying the land. Therefore, there are no facts which would constitute laches and (A) is therefore incorrect.

(B) is incorrect. The subdivision plan filed by Oscar in 1985 was recorded and is clearly in Pete's chain of title because it was referred to in Oscar's deed to Max. Therefore, Pete had constructive notice of the plan and the dedication of the site for a school. The fact that his deed does not specifically refer to the plan is irrelevant, and will not be a basis for him prevailing.

Question 129

Blackacre is a three-acre tract of land with a small residence. Olga, the owner of Blackacre, rented it to Terrence at a monthly rental of $200. After Terrence had been in possession of Blackacre for several years, Terrence and Olga orally agreed that Terrence would purchase Blackacre from Olga for the sum of $24,000, payable at the rate of $200 a month for ten years and also would pay the real estate taxes and the expenses of insuring and maintaining Blackacre. Olga agreed to give Terrence a deed to Blackacre after five years had passed and $12,000 had been paid on account and to accept from Terrence a note secured by a mortgage for the balance. Terrence continued in possession of Blackacre and performed his obligations as orally agreed. Terrence, without consulting Olga, made improvements for which he paid $1,000. When Terrence had paid $12,000, he tendered a proper note and mortgage to Olga and demanded the delivery of the deed as agreed. Olga did not deny the oral agreement but told Terrence that she had changed her mind, and she refused to complete the transaction. Terrence then brought an action for specific performance. Olga pleaded the Statute of Frauds as her defense. If Olga wins, it will be because

(A) nothing Terrence could have done would have overcome the original absence of a written agreement.
(B) the actions and payments of Terrence are as consistent with his being a tenant as with an oral contract.
(C) Terrence did not secure Olga's approval for the improvements that he made.
(D) Olga has not received any unconscionable benefit and, therefore, Terrence is not entitled to equitable relief.

Answer to Question 129

Usually, in an action for specific performance, an agreement to convey land must satisfy the Statute of Frauds. The Statute is satisfied if the contract to convey is evidenced by a writing or writings containing the essential terms of a purchase and sale agreement and signed by the party against whom the contract is to be enforced. If there is no written agreement, a court of equity **can** specifically enforce an oral agreement to convey if the part performance doctrine is satisfied. Under the part performance theory of unequivocal referability, the court will order a conveyance only if the conduct of the parties unequivocally proves that an oral agreement to convey existed. In a majority of jurisdictions, part performance is proven when the purchaser pays the purchase price, has possession of the land with the permission of the seller and makes improvements on the land. If Terrence satisfied the requirements for part performance in the particular jurisdiction, he would have overcome the original absence of a written agreement. If Olga is going to win, it is because she can show that there has not been sufficient part performance to take the agreement out of the Statute of Frauds and, therefore, the oral agreement is unenforceable. Thus, (A) is incorrect.

(B) is the correct answer. If the jurisdiction will permit an oral agreement to be enforceable only where the actions of the parties unequivocally refer to the existence of an oral contract to convey land, the only reason Terrence will not prevail is because his actions with respect to the property are as consistent with the continuation of his original tenancy as they are with the existence of a purchase and sale agreement. Of course, an argument can be made that payment of taxes and insurance on the property are not consistent with the terms of Terrence's tenancy, but this choice provides Olga with the best argument to overcome Terrence's argument that there has been part performance.

(C) is incorrect. The fact that Terrence made improvements in reliance upon an oral contract might be sufficient to take the agreement out of the Statute of Frauds whether or not the improvements were made with Olga's approval.

Under the equitable fraud theory of the part performance doctrine, a court will enforce an oral agreement to convey only if the petitioner can show that undue hardship to him or unconscionable gain to his opponent will result from the court's refusal to order specific performance. An argument can be made that Olga's failure to perform under the contract has caused Terrence undue hardship in that he has performed his obligations over a five-year period in reliance on the agreement and Olga has received the benefit of the improvements to her property. On the other hand, Olga has a strong argument that $1,000 in improvements over a five-year period is not an unconscionable benefit. However, the essence of the equitable fraud theory is the harm to the purchaser, not the unconscionable benefit to the seller. Therefore this is not Olga's best defense against the part performance doctrine, and (D) is incorrect.

Question 130

Landover, the owner in fee simple of Highacre, an apartment house property, entered into an enforceable written agreement with VanMeer to sell Highacre to VanMeer. The agreement provided that a good and marketable title was to be conveyed free and clear of all encumbrances. However, the agreement was silent as to the risk of fire prior to the closing, and there is no applicable statute in the state where the land is located. The premises were not insured. The day before the scheduled closing date, Highacre was wholly destroyed by fire. When VanMeer refused to close, Landover brought an action for specific performance. If Landover prevails, the most likely reason will be that

(A) the failure of VanMeer to insure his interest as the purchaser of Highacre precludes any relief for him.
(B) the remedy at law is inadequate in actions concerning real estate contracts and either party is entitled to specific performance.
(C) equity does not permit consideration of surrounding circumstances in actions concerning real estate contracts.
(D) the doctrine of equitable conversion applies.

Answer to Question 130

Where there is no statute governing the subject, the common-law doctrine of equitable conversion applies once the parties have entered into an enforceable purchase and sale agreement with respect to property. This doctrine provides that a purchaser who has a valid and binding agreement to convey should be treated as the owner of the property. Under the doctrine, the purchaser bears the risk of loss if the subject property is destroyed, unless the parties agree otherwise. Since Landover and VanMeer entered into an enforceable purchase and sale agreement which did not provide to the contrary, VanMeer is the equitable owner of the property and bears the risk of loss and cannot refuse to perform because of the destruction of the property. As a result, Landover can specifically enforce the contract despite the fact that the buildings were uninsured and burned down. Thus, (D) is correct.

(A) is incorrect. The enforceability of the contract turns on the issue of who has the risk of loss, not on whether VanMeer insured against that risk. VanMeer had the right, but not the obligation to insure.

(B) is incorrect, even though it is a correct statement of the law. Because all real estate is unique, the nonbreaching party in an enforceable contract to convey usually has the option to pursue a remedy at law for damages or seek specific performance of the contract. So, the argument can always be made that the remedy at law is inadequate, but that does not decide the crucial issue here, which is the determination of which party has the risk of loss.

(C) is an incorrect statement of the law of equity. A court of equity can look at surrounding circumstances and in some cases refuse specific performance. For example, specific performance could be refused if the plaintiff had unclean hands. Reasons for refusing specific performance are not present in this case, however.

Question 131

Seller and Buyer execute an agreement for the sale of real property on September 1. The jurisdiction in which the property is located recognizes the principle of equitable conversion, and has no statute pertinent to this problem.

Seller dies before closing, and his will leaves his personal property to Perry and his real property to Rose. There being no breach of the agreement by either party, which of the following is correct?

(A) Death, an eventuality which the parties could have provided for, terminates the agreement if they did not provide otherwise.
(B) Rose is entitled to the proceeds of the sale when it closes, because the doctrine of equitable conversion does not apply to these circumstances.
(C) Perry is entitled to the proceeds of the sale when it closes.
(D) Title was rendered unmarketable by Seller's death.

Answer to Question 131

Death of a party does not render a purchase and sale agreement void or voidable because the agreement does not relate to the unique personal services of either party, nor does it render title unmarketable. The estate of the decedent is liable with respect to any obligations remaining under the contract. Therefore, (A) and (D) are incorrect.

The doctrine of equitable conversion treats a specifically enforceable contract to convey realty as converting the seller's interest into a vendor's lien for the purchase price of the property and the purchaser's interest into ownership of real property plus a contractual obligation to pay the purchase price. Thus, if the seller dies, the devisees of his realty will be required to convey the property to the buyer, but the devisees of his personalty will receive the vendor's lien on the property and the purchase moneys when paid. Applying these principles to the facts of this question, Buyer is the equitable owner of the property because there is an enforceable purchase and sale agreement and the doctrine of equitable conversion applies. Rose, as devisee of Seller's realty, is obligated to convey the real property pursuant to the purchase and sale agreement, but is not entitled to the proceeds from the sale, because Seller's interest in the property was converted from realty to personalty upon execution of the binding purchase and sale agreement. Therefore, (C) is correct and (B) is incorrect.

Question 132

Seller and Buyer execute an agreement for the sale of real property on September 1, 1993. Buyer dies before closing, there being no breach of the agreement by either party.

What are the rights of the parties after the death of buyer?

(A) Buyer's heir may specifically enforce the agreement.
(B) Seller has the right to return the down payment and cancel the contract.
(C) Death terminates the agreement.
(D) Any title acquired would be unmarketable by reason of Buyer's death.

Answer to Question 132

(A) is correct, assuming that Buyer died intestate, because the doctrine of equitable conversion applies. The doctrine provides that a purchaser who has a valid and binding agreement to convey should be treated as the owner of the property and can compel a conveyance of the land in an action for specific performance. If the purchaser dies, the heir or devisee of the purchaser's realty possesses whatever rights the purchaser had with respect to such property. Here, Buyer had the right to specific performance of the agreement, and Buyer's heir will inherit that right.

The death of a party to a purchase and sale agreement does not terminate the contractual obligations of either party because the agreement does not require any unique personal services of either party to the contract. In this instance, the administrator of Buyer's estate is capable of performing the contractual obligations. Thus, (B) and (C) are incorrect.

Likewise, the death of Buyer has no effect on the marketability of Seller's title. Nothing in the fact pattern indicates that there is a problem with Seller's chain of title and, therefore, the title Seller conveys will be marketable. Thus, (D) is incorrect.

Question 133

Seth owned a vacant lot known as Richacre. Seth entered into a written contract with Bob to build a house of stated specifications on Richacre and to sell the house and lot to Bob. The contract provided for an "inside date" of April 1, and an "outside date" of May 1, for completion of the house and delivery of a deed. Neither party tendered performance by May 1.

On May 3, Bob notified Seth in writing of Bob's election to cancel the contract because of Seth's failure to deliver title by May 1. On May 12, Seth notified Bob that some unanticipated construction difficulties had been encountered, and that Seth was entitled to a reasonable time to complete in any event. The notification also included a promise that Seth would be ready to perform by May 29 and that he was setting that date as an adjourned closing date. Seth obtained a certificate of occupancy and appropriate documents of title, and he tendered performance on May 29. Bob refused. Seth brought an action to recover damages for breach of contract. The decision in the case will most likely be determined by whether

(A) Seth acted with due diligence in completing the house.

(B) Bob can prove actual "undue hardship" caused by the delay.
(C) the expressions "inside date" and "outside date" are construed to make time of the essence.
(D) there is a showing of good faith in Bob's efforts to terminate the contract.

Answer to Question 133

(C) is correct. The determinative issue in this case is whether Seth lost all rights because he did not perform by May 1, or whether he could perform within a reasonable time after that date. That, in turn, is determined by whether the contract is construed such that the use of the words "inside date" and "outside date" made time of the essence. If they did, then Seth would lose all his rights by failing to close on the outside date.

If time was of the essence, then Seth's due diligence would be irrelevant. If time was not of the essence, the issue would be whether Seth was prepared to close within a reasonable time. The diligence in completing the house would only be of marginal relevance on the issue of whether the proposed time was reasonable. Thus, Seth's due diligence would be relevant only **after** it was determined whether time was of the essence and so (A) is incorrect.

(B) is incorrect. Undue hardship to Bob is irrelevant if he had a contract whereby time was of the essence. He would not be obligated to close after that date even if he had suffered no hardship. If, on the other hand, time was not of the essence, the possible hardship to Bob would only be one factor in determining if the closing took place within a reasonable time.

(D) is incorrect. If time was of the essence, then Bob had a right to rescind the contract and refuse to perform because a deed was not delivered on May 1. His good faith in exercising his rights is irrelevant.

Question 134

Chase, as seller, and Smith, as buyer, enter into a written contract for the sale and purchase of land which is complete in all respects except that no reference is made to the quality of title to be conveyed. Which of the following will result?

(A) The contract will be unenforceable.
(B) Chase will be required to convey a marketable title.
(C) Chase will be required to convey only what he owned on the date of the contract.
(D) Chase will be required to convey only what he owned on the date of the contract plus whatever additional title rights he may acquire prior to the closing date.

Answer to Question 134

(A) is incorrect. The Statute of Frauds does not prevent the contract from being enforceable. The Statute requires that the purchase and sale agreement be evidenced by a writing or writings containing the essential terms of the agreement. The quality of title is not an essential term of the agreement. Since this contract is complete in all other respects, it is enforceable.

(B) is correct. If the quality of title is not mentioned in the purchase and sale agreement, the seller must provide marketable title at the closing.

(C) is incorrect. If there are encumbrances on the property at the time of the signing of the agreement which destroy marketability, they must be removed before closing. The quality of title **at closing**, not at the time the sales contract is entered into, is controlling.

(D) is incorrect. If the seller does not have marketable title at the closing, he is in breach of the sales contract, even if he is prepared to convey all of the title he owns at that time. This choice gives Smith only what Chase owned at the closing, if anything. In order to comply with the purchase and sale agreement, Chase must convey marketable title.

Question 135

Arthur owns a farm. He enters into a written agreement with Walter which reads in full as follows:

"I, Arthur, agree to sell my farm to Walter for $50,000. Received $1,000 on account.

Signed: Walter
                Arthur
Dated: June 1, 1993"

Assume the agreement called for settlement on August 1, 1993, and that on June 1, 1993, title to the farm was held by Ralph. At settlement on August 1, 1993, Arthur produces a deed from Ralph to Arthur dated July 1, 1993, and a deed from himself to Walter. Walter refuses to settle. Arthur sues for specific performance. Judgment for

(A) Arthur, because Walter failed to give written notice of his objection to Arthur.
(B) Arthur, because he is not required to deliver marketable title until settlement.
(C) Walter, because Ralph was not a party to the agreement.
(D) Walter, because he was entitled to marketable title on June 1, 1993, even though the agreement was silent as to title.

Answer to Question 135

Unless the contract provides otherwise, the seller must possess and provide marketable title at the closing. If the seller does not possess marketable title at the time the purchase and sale agreement was signed, but does possess marketable title at the time of closing, the seller has complied with the contract. Since Arthur had marketable title at the closing, there was nothing to which Walter could object. Thus, (D) is incorrect. If this had been a case where there was a defect in title, Arthur might have been able to force Walter to consummate the transaction, if Walter had failed to notify Arthur of claimed defects. However, this is not a case where there was any defect in the title. Thus, (A) is incorrect.

(B) is correct. The fact that Arthur did not hold title on the date the purchase and sale agreement was executed is of no importance, because he apparently holds marketable title on the date of the closing and therefore is in compliance with the contract.

(C) is incorrect. Whether Ralph is a party to the agreement is irrelevant. The issue is whether Arthur and Walter have performed under the contract. Arthur has performed his part of the agreement by possessing and providing marketable title and has the right to force Walter to perform his obligations under the contract. From whom Arthur received title, or the fact that Walter could not have obtained title from Ralph if Arthur had not performed is irrelevant.

Question 136

By way of gift, Pat executed a deed properly describing a houselot which he owned on Main Street, naming his son, Mike, as grantee.

Pat handed the deed to Mike who immediately returned it to his father for safekeeping. His father kept it in his safe deposit box. The deed was not recorded.

Pat died, leaving all of his property to his second wife, Sally.

In a suit between Mike and Sally over title to the houselot,

(A) Mike will prevail, because Pat effectively transferred title to the houselot to him.
(B) Sally will prevail, because the deed was not recorded.
(C) Sally will prevail, because Mike never accepted the deed.
(D) Sally will prevail, because the deed was not delivered to Mike since Pat maintained custody of the deed.

Answer to Question 136

Delivery is a question of the grantor's intent, not physical possession. The delivery requirement is met if the grantor intends to confer an immediate, irrevocable interest on the grantee. Since it appears that Pat handed the deed to Mike with the immediate intent to convey title to him and Mike accepted it, the deed was "delivered." Even though Pat kept possession of the document, it was at the request of Mike after delivery and acceptance. Since there was a delivery and acceptance, title passed to Mike and he can enforce his interest against Pat's devisee, Sally. Therefore, (A) is correct and (D) is incorrect.

(C) is incorrect. Absent an express rejection of the deed, acceptance of a deed is presumed. Although Mike handed the deed back to his father, he was not rejecting the deed, but merely leaving it with Pat for safekeeping.

(B) is incorrect. A deed need not be recorded to be effective to pass title from the grantor to the grantee. The purpose of the recording system is to protect the rights of subsequent purchasers, but does not affect the rights of the immediate grantor and grantee. Sally is not entitled to the protection of the recording statute because she is not a purchaser. Therefore, Sally will lose, even if she had no notice of Mike's prior claim to the property.

Question 137

Patricia, the owner of a 40-acre farm, executed a deed naming her daughter Michelle as grantee. The deed contained a description of the land conveyed as follows:

> "All that part of my farm, being a square with 200-foot sides, the southeast corner of which is on the north line of my neighbor, John Brown."

The description of the land conveyed is

(A) sufficient if consideration has been paid.
(B) sufficient because no ambiguity therein appears on the face of the deed.
(C) insufficient because it does not reference a plan.
(D) insufficient because of vagueness.

Answer to Question 137

To be effective, a deed must contain a description of the property sufficient to determine the land to be conveyed. If the description is ambiguous, parol evidence is admissible to assist in determining the intention of the parties concerning the land to be conveyed. However, where the description is so vague that it is impossible to determine the land to be conveyed even with parol evidence, then the inadequacy of the description will invalidate the deed. In this case, the description is of a square parcel with sides of 200 feet in a 40-acre farm. This description would include any square with 200-foot sides as long as the southeast point is on the north line of the neighboring property. It is not possible from that description to accurately determine the land to be conveyed. Thus, (B) is incorrect and (D) is correct.

If the description is inadequate, the amount or absence of consideration has no effect on the validity of a deed. Consideration will not cure a defective description. Thus, (A) is incorrect.

(C) states the correct result but not the right reason. In most modern conveyancing, property is conveyed by reference to a surveyor's plan, but a deed need not refer to a plan in order to be valid, as long as the property can be reasonably identified from the description.

Question 138

Rogers gave Mitchell a power of attorney containing the following provision: "My attorney, Mitchell, is specifically authorized to sell and convey any part or all of my real property." Mitchell conveyed part of Rogers' land to Stone by deed in the customary form containing covenants of title. Stone sues Rogers for breach of a covenant. The outcome of Stone's suit will be governed by whether

(A) deeds without covenants are effective to convey realty.
(B) the jurisdiction views the covenants as personal or running with the land.
(C) Stone is a bona fide purchaser.
(D) the power to "sell and convey" is construed to include the power to execute the usual form of deed used to convey realty.

Answer to Question 138

The principal issue in this case is whether Mitchell bound his principal by the covenants which he gave in the deed. It could be argued in theory that, if deeds without covenants are not effective to convey realty, then it could be inferred that Mitchell had the power to give covenants because that is the only way in which he could carry out the task he was specifically authorized to do. (A) is not the best choice, however, because the law is universal that a deed without covenants **is** effective to convey property.

(B) is incorrect. This is a suit by Stone, the immediate grantee. Therefore, the covenants (if they are authorized) are binding as contracts between the parties whether or not they run with the land. Therefore, that issue is irrelevant to this lawsuit. (In fact, some covenants [those designated as future covenants] do run with the land and can be sued upon by remote grantees. Present covenants, on the other hand, only run to the immediate grantee and do not run with the land.)

(C) is incorrect. One does not have to be a bona fide purchaser in order to obtain the benefit of covenants. Covenants are promises by the grantor that the title is in a certain condition. The grantor is liable on these covenants whether or not the grantee enjoys the status of a bona fide purchaser.

The real issue is whether or not Mitchell, as agent, had the authority to bind his principal to these covenants. In other words, did the words "sell and convey" also confer the authority on

Mitchell to make covenants as to the title of the property. This is a matter of contract and agency law. If Mitchell was authorized, either explicitly or implicitly as an incident to his power to convey, to give covenants of title, then Stone can prevail against Rogers. Thus, (D) is the correct answer.

Questions 139 and 140 are based on the following fact situation.

Owen held in fee simple Farmdale, a large tract of vacant land. The state wherein Farmdale is situated has a statute which provides, in substance, that unless the conveyance is recorded, every deed or other conveyance of an interest in land is void as to a subsequent purchaser who pays value without notice of such conveyance. The following transactions occurred in the order given:

First: Owen conveyed Farmdale, for a fair price, to Allred by general warranty deed. Allred did not immediately record.
Second: Owen executed a mortgage on Farmdale to secure repayment of a loan concurrently made to Owen by Leon. Leon had no notice of the prior conveyance to Allred and promptly and duly recorded the mortgage.
Third: Owen, by general warranty deed, gratuitously conveyed to Niece, who promptly duly recorded this deed.
Fourth: Allred duly recorded his deed from Owen.
Fifth: Niece, by general warranty deed, conveyed Farmdale to Barrett. Barrett had no actual notice of any of the prior transactions, paid full value, and promptly duly recorded the deed.

139. Asserting that his title was held free of any claim by Leon, Allred instituted suit against Leon to quiet title to Farmdale. Judgment should be for

(A) Allred, because Leon is deemed not to have paid value.
(B) Allred, because a mortgagee is not a subsequent purchaser within the meaning of the statute.
(C) Leon, because he recorded before Allred.
(D) Leon, because he advanced money without notice of Allred's rights.

140. Assume for this question only that Niece had not conveyed to Barrett. After Allred recorded his deed from Owen, Allred, asserting that Allred's title was held free of any claim by Niece, instituted suit against Niece to recover title to Farmdale. Judgment should be for

(A) Niece, because she had no notice of Allred's rights when she accepted the deed from Owen.
(B) Niece, because she recorded her deed before Allred recorded his.
(C) Allred, because Niece was not a bona fide purchaser.
(D) Allred, because he paid value for Farmdale and had no actual or constructive notice of the deed to Niece.

Answer to Question 139

A mortgagee is deemed to have paid value for his interest, since he has loaned the mortgagor money in reliance on the mortgagor's title. A deed given as security for a loan is deemed purchased as long as the loan and the deed are simultaneous. Therefore, (A) and (B) are not correct.

(C) states the correct result for the wrong reason. It is critically important in a question like this to test the choices against the description of the applicable statute in the body of the question. The statute is a notice type recording statute because it protects a subsequent purchaser who pays value without notice. It does not require, as a race-notice statute would, that the purchaser also first record. Therefore, Leon prevails over Allred even if Leon doesn't record at all. A subsequent bona fide purchaser takes good title by merely purchasing without notice of a prior conveyance.

(D) is the correct answer. This jurisdiction has a notice type recording statute. A subsequent grantee therefore takes good title by merely purchasing without notice of a prior conveyance - i.e., by being a bona fide purchaser. The facts state that Leon had no actual notice of Allred's claim. Since Allred did not record his deed before Leon gave the mortgage, there is also no constructive notice to Leon. A mortgagee is deemed to have paid value for the mortgage interest, as long as the loan and the mortgage deed are simultaneous. Thus, Leon is a bona fide purchaser from Owen and prevails over Allred.

Answer to Question 140

This is a notice type recording statute. A subsequent bona fide purchaser takes good title by merely purchasing without notice of a prior conveyance. Such a purchaser need not record at all to prevail over a prior deed. Thus, the fact that Niece recorded is not relevant, and (B) is incorrect.

In order to defeat a prior deed, a subsequent deed must have been purchased. A subsequent deed delivered as a gift cannot ever defeat a prior deed. Since Niece took her deed as a gift, she is not a purchaser and so is not protected by the recording statute. Therefore, Allred will prevail over Niece. (C) is the correct answer and (A) is incorrect.

(D) is incorrect. Allred's notice and value paid are irrelevant, since his deed was **first** in time. Notice and value are only relevant when a **subsequent** purchaser tries to take title over a prior conveyance.

Question 141

Owen held in fee simple Farmdale, a large tract of vacant land. The state wherein Farmdale is situated has a statute which provides, in substance, that unless the conveyance is recorded, every deed or other conveyance of an interest in land is void as to a subsequent purchaser who pays value without notice of such conveyance. The following transactions occurred in the order given:

>First: Owen conveyed Farmdale, for a fair price, to Allred by general warranty deed. Allred did not immediately record.
>Second: Owen, by general warranty deed, gratuitously conveyed Farmdale to Niece, who promptly duly recorded this deed.
>Third: Allred duly recorded his deed from Owen.
>Fourth: Niece, by general warranty deed, conveyed Farmdale to Barrett. Barrett had no actual notice of any of the prior transactions, paid full value, and promptly duly recorded the deed.

Asserting that his title was held free of any claim by Barrett, Allred instituted suit against Barrett to quiet title to Farmdale. If Barrett prevails, it will be because

(A) Allred's prior recorded deed is deemed to be outside Barrett's chain of title.
(B) Barrett's grantor, Niece, recorded before Allred.
(C) as between two warranty deeds, the later one controls.
(D) Barrett's grantor, Niece, had no notice of Allred's rights.

Answer to Question 141

The jurisdiction has a notice type recording statute. A subsequent grantee takes good title by merely purchasing without notice of a prior conveyance - i.e., by being a bona fide purchaser. Thus, Barrett prevails over Allred if Barrett paid value with no actual or constructive notice of Allred's prior interest. The facts state that Barrett had no **actual** notice of Allred's interest. Barrett is a bona fide purchaser then, as long as he does not have constructive notice of the deed to Allred. Because deeds are indexed as of the date they are submitted to the registry, not by the date of conveyance, Allred recorded his deed from Owen out of order (after a deed from Owen to Niece). Thus, Barrett could trace his title back from Niece to Owen without ever finding the deed to Allred. The majority of jurisdictions hold that a purchaser does not have constructive notice of a late-recorded instrument which is out of the chain of title. Therefore, if Allred's deed is held to be out of the chain of title, which it likely will, Barrett will not be deemed to have constructive notice and will prevail. Thus, (A) is the correct answer.

(B) is incorrect. The fact that Niece recorded first does not affect her status. Niece is not a purchaser but a donee. If there had been an action between Niece and Allred, Allred would have prevailed. Barrett's status as a possible bona fide purchaser must be determined separately.

(C) is a wholly incorrect statement of law. At common law, the earlier deed prevails. Modern recording statutes dictate the circumstances under which the later deed prevails. It is not the case that the later deed always prevails. The subsequent deed must be to a purchaser who takes without notice (and in some cases, also records first, depending on the type of recording statute) in order for that deed to prevail. Also, the type of deed is irrelevant to priority. A quitclaim deed may prevail over a warranty deed, if the purchaser of the quitclaim deed meets the standards of the recording statute.

(D) is incorrect. This is a notice type recording system. A subsequent bona fide purchaser takes good title by merely purchasing without notice of a prior conveyance. The fact that Niece took her deed from Owen without notice of Allred's claim is not relevant because she is not a purchaser, and so cannot prevail under any recording statute. Barrett must attain the status of a bona fide purchaser on his own.

Question 142

Tess occupied an apartment in a building owned by Len. She paid rent of $125 in advance each month. During the second month of occupancy, Tess organized the tenants in the building as a tenants' association and the association made demands of Len concerning certain repairs and improvements the tenants wanted. When Tess tendered rent for the third month, Len notified her that the rent for the fourth and subsequent months would be $200 per month. Tess protested and pointed out that all of the other tenants paid rent of $125 per month. Thereupon, Len gave the required statutory notice that the tenancy was being terminated at the end of the third month.

By an appropriate proceeding, Tess contests Len's right to terminate. If Tess succeeds, it will be because

(A) a periodic tenancy was created by implication.
(B) the doctrine prohibiting retaliatory eviction is part of the law of the jurisdiction.
(C) the $200 rent demanded violates the agreement implied by the rate charged to other tenants.
(D) the law implies a term of one year in the absence of any express agreement.

Answer to Question 142

The relationship established between Tess and Len as a result of the payment of rent in advance each month was a periodic tenancy in which the rental period was one month. However, such a tenancy can be terminated by either party by notice given prior to the commencement of a rental period, terminating the tenancy at the end of that period. The creation of a periodic tenancy does not protect Tess here, because such a tenancy can be terminated by the notice given by Len. (A) is incorrect.

The periodic tenancy was only for a one-month term because that was the rental interval. No one-year tenancy can be implied under these circumstances. Thus, (D) is incorrect.

(C) is incorrect. A landlord may condition the renewal of a periodic tenancy upon a rent increase. Also, a landlord has a right to charge different rents to different tenants. There is no implied agreement to charge the same rent to all tenants. Len has taken the proper steps both to terminate the tenancy and to obtain a rent increase.

(B) is correct. Tess's only hope is a statute which would prevent retaliatory evictions. She would come within the protection of such a statute because Len's action in raising her rent and trying to evict her seems to be motivated by her activity in forming a tenant's association which made demands on Len.

Question 143

Lester, the owner in fee simple of a small farm consisting of 30 acres of land improved with a house and several outbuildings, leased the same to Tanner for a ten-year period. After two years had expired, the government condemned 20 acres of the property and allocated the compensation award to Lester and Tanner according to their respective interests taken. It so happened, however, that the 20 acres taken embraced all of the farm's tillable land, leaving only the house, outbuildings, and a small woodlot. There is no applicable statute in the jurisdiction where the property is located nor any provision in the lease relating to condemnation. Tanner quit possession, and Lester brought suit against him to recover rent. Lester will

(A) lose, because there has been a frustration of purpose which excuses Tanner from further performance of the contract to pay rent.
(B) lose, because there has been a breach of the implied covenant of quiet enjoyment by Lester's inability to provide Tanner with possession of the whole of the property for the entire term.
(C) win, because of the implied warranty on the part of the tenant to return the demised premises in the same condition at the end of the term as they were at the beginning.
(D) win, because the relationship of landlord and tenant was unaffected by the condemnation, thus leaving Tanner still obligated to pay rent.

Answer to Question 143

Many jurisdictions have extended the applicability of the doctrine of frustration of purpose beyond supervening illegality to encompass acts of God or third parties which make the property unusable for its intended purpose. The doctrine, in those circumstances, would allow a tenant to avoid the lease. The doctrine would not be applicable here, though, because the government has compensated Tanner for the interest taken here. Therefore, there is no frustration of purpose, and Tanner would still be bound by the obligation to pay rent, and (A) is incorrect.

This question is ambiguous with respect to two key issues: the way in which the award was allocated, and the amount of rent for which Lester is now suing. If the government gave Tanner the fair value of the right to occupy for eight years and only paid the landlord on the basis of the reversionary interest, then the tenant would continue to owe rent to the landlord for the remainder of the term. If, however, the landlord's interest were valued as the right to receive rent for eight years plus a reversion, and the tenant were only compensated on the basis of the fair rental value of the possession being greater than the rental obligation, then the landlord would not be entitled to the full rent, but might be entitled to a lesser amount for the property still available.

Since (D) was the correct answer given by the National Conference of Bar Examiners, we must assume that the tenant was compensated for the value of the right to occupy for the next eight years.

(B) is incorrect. The covenant of quiet enjoyment is breached only if the landlord, someone claiming through him, or someone with superior title disrupts the tenant's possession. This covenant is not breached by actions of parties unrelated to the landlord or his title. A taking by eminent domain is not a breach of this covenant, since it originates from the government, not the landlord. The taking of property by eminent domain may terminate the lease, but it is not a breach by the landlord that provides the tenant with a complete defense to the rent obligation.

(C) is incorrect. Lester is not suing for a breach of the covenant to return the property in the same condition as it was at the beginning of the term. He is suing for a breach of the obligation to pay rent. The damages available under the two theories might not be comparable at all. Moreover, it is unclear whether the tenant could be held liable for failure to return the demised premises where the property was taken by the government by eminent domain.

(D) is the correct answer. At common law, the obligation to pay rent was an independent covenant. It continued almost no matter what the circumstances. A breach of a covenant probably would not even discharge the obligation to pay rent. Only if the landlord breached the covenant of quiet enjoyment in such a substantial degree as to qualify as a constructive eviction and the tenant had to vacate, did the tenant have a defense to the rent obligation. That doctrine is not applicable here because the tenant was evicted by the government, not the landlord or someone claiming through the landlord. More recent developments in the law probably also would not aid the tenant here because it appears that the tenant has been compensated for his losses in this case by the government.

Question 144

Homer and Purcell entered into a valid, enforceable written contract by which Homer agreed to sell and Purcell agreed to purchase Blackacre, which was Homer's residence. One of the contract provisions was that, after the closing, Homer had the right to remain in residence at Blackacre for up to 30 days before delivering possession to Purcell. The closing took place as scheduled. Title passed to Purcell and Homer remained in possession. Within a few days after the closing, the new house next door which was being constructed for Homer was burned to the ground, and at the end of the 30-day period, Homer refused to move out of Blackacre; instead, Homer tendered to Purcell a monthly rental payment in excess of the fair rental value of Blackacre. Purcell rejected the proposal and that day brought an appropriate action to gain immediate possession of Blackacre. The contract was silent as to the consequences of Homer's failure to give up possession within the 30-day period, and the jurisdiction in which Blackacre is located has no statute dealing directly with this situation, although the landlord-tenant law of the jurisdiction requires a landlord to give a tenant 30 days notice before a tenant may be evicted. Purcell did not give Homer any such 30-day statutory notice. Purcell's best legal argument in support of his action to gain immediate possession is that Homer is a

(A) trespasser *ab initio*.
(B) licensee.
(C) tenant at sufferance.
(D) tenant from month to month.

Answer to Question 144

If Homer were a trespasser *ab initio*, this would give Purcell a great argument to evict him. However, (A) is clearly wrong because it does not comport with the facts at all. Homer was once in lawful possession, and his remaining in possession did not cause that original possession to be unlawful. Therefore, he was not a trespasser *ab initio*.

(B) is the correct answer. This is a difficult question because Homer's right to remain in residence is probably the right to exclusive possession and therefore a tenancy. However, Purcell did not comply with the statutory requirements to evict a tenant, so he must rely on a theory that Homer was not a tenant. If Homer's occupancy can be characterized only as a contract right to use the property for a limited period of time, then he will only be a licensee and not entitled to the protection of the 30-day notice statute. Since the question describes "a contract provision that he had a right to remain in residence," this is a tenable argument and the only one which might be successful.

The most accurate legal characterization of Homer's interest in Blackacre after he conveyed the property is that he had a term for years for a 30-day period with an option to terminate the tenancy earlier. When the 30-day period expired, he most likely was a tenant at sufferance because he was originally in rightful possession. While the legal analysis concerning the tenancy at sufferance is probably correct, (C) is not

Purcell's best legal argument because a tenancy at sufferance is still a tenancy, and Homer would therefore be entitled to the 30-day notice under the statute.

(D) is incorrect. Because Purcell refused to accept the check after the 30-day period expired, it is clear that a periodic month-to-month tenancy was not created.

Questions 145 through 147 are based on the following fact situation.

Smith, an owner in fee, leased a house and lot to Jones for ten years. By the terms of the lease Jones, for himself, his heirs, executors, administrators, and assigns, expressly covenanted to pay rent and to pay the taxes on the premises during the term of the lease. Two years later, Smith conveyed his interest in the premises to Alpha. About the same time, Jones assigned his lease to Beta by a written assignment which expressly assumed the obligation of the covenant to pay rent, but was silent concerning the payment of taxes.

145. Beta refused to pay taxes and Alpha, after paying the same, brought action against Beta for the amount paid. Judgment for

(A) Beta, because Beta has made no contract concerning payment of taxes and is not liable upon contracts he did not make.
(B) Beta, because the covenant to pay taxes is a collateral covenant not touching or concerning the land.
(C) Beta, because no covenant will run with the land unless the intent that it run is clearly expressed.
(D) Alpha.

146. Beta made regular rent payments for about a year after the assignment and then defaulted. Alpha brought action against Jones for the unpaid rent. Judgment for

(A) Alpha, because the assignment did not terminate Jones's status as a tenant.

(B) Alpha, because Jones's contractual obligation under the lease survived the assignment.
(C) Jones, because the assignment terminated the obligation of Jones to pay rent.
(D) Jones, because Alpha failed to give Jones notice that he had acquired title.

147. All conditions in the lease, including the obligation to pay rent and taxes, were properly complied with for the first four years of the term. At the end of four years, Beta assigned his interest to Gamma, although Beta knew at the time that Gamma was insolvent. Gamma defaulted in the payment of taxes and Alpha, after paying the same, brought action against Beta for the amount paid. Judgment for

(A) Alpha, because Beta's contractual obligation to Alpha could not be terminated by Beta's unilateral act.
(B) Alpha, because of Beta's bad faith in making the assignment to Gamma.
(C) Beta, because Beta's privity of estate terminated when he assigned to Gamma.
(D) Beta, because Beta at no time had any obligation for the payment of taxes.

Answer to Question 145

Even if Beta made no express covenants in his lease, he can be bound to covenants in the lease of his assignor if the covenants run with the land. This covenant to pay taxes is a covenant which runs with the land because it is in writing, touches and concerns the land, and was intended to run with the land. Smith and Jones were in horizontal privity as landlord and tenant when they made these lease covenants, so they will run at law. Since Beta purchased the estate from Jones, there is vertical privity. Beta is the successor to Jones, who made a covenant concerning the payment of taxes which runs with the land and binds Jones's successor in interest, Beta. Thus, (A) is incorrect and (D) is correct.

(B) is incorrect. The covenant to pay taxes is not a collateral covenant. It touches and concerns the land, since it refers to an obligation inextricably associated with the land.

(C) is incorrect because there is a clear expression in the language used here of the parties' intention that this covenant run with the land. Jones made the agreement on behalf of his "heirs, executors, administrators, and assigns."

Answer to Question 146

The assignment **did** terminate Jones's status as a tenant, so (A) is incorrect. The assignment did **not**, however, terminate the obligation to pay rent, because Jones's obligation under the contract remained. A tenant cannot discharge the rent obligation by either a sublease or an assignment. Where a tenant assigns the leasehold, the assignee assumes the primary obligation to pay rent, but the original tenant remains secondarily liable, by virtue of the lease contract, as a surety for that obligation. Thus, (B) is correct and (C) is incorrect.

(D) is incorrect. While a tenant is not liable to a new landlord until notified of the conveyance, failure to give express notification does not discharge the rent obligation. These facts do not present a situation where the tenant paid the rent to the wrong person. Jones has not paid rent to anyone for the period in question. Therefore, Jones was not harmed by Alpha's failure to give notice, so failure to give notice is not a good defense for Jones.

Answer to Question 147

Beta never made a contractual promise to Alpha to pay taxes. Therefore, Beta was obligated to pay the taxes while he was in possession of the premises only because he was a successor in title to Jones and Jones's covenant to pay taxes ran with the land. An assignee's obligation to perform a covenant running with the land is due solely to his ownership of the estate. Once Beta assigned to Gamma, he was no longer in privity of estate with the landlord, and so he was no longer obligated to comply with the covenants in the assignor's lease. Thus, (A) is incorrect and (C) is correct. Beta would

have been personally liable to pay the taxes, aside from his ownership of the land, only if he had expressly agreed to pay the taxes. Then Alpha could have sued on a third-party beneficiary theory.

(D) is incorrect. Although Beta did not expressly assume the obligation to pay the taxes, Beta was in fact obliged to pay the taxes while he was in privity of estate with Alpha, as explained above.

(B) is incorrect. Good faith and bad faith are irrelevant to this issue. All Beta had to do so that he would not be obligated to pay the taxes was to terminate his privity of estate with Alpha. He did this.

Question 148

On the first day of November, 1991, Landlord rents his grocery store on Main Street in Crosstown to Tenant for four years. The parties signed a written lease in which the rent was fixed at $500 per month.

On February 1, 1992, Landlord conveyed the grocery store to Owner subject to the lease.

On July 1, 1992, Tenant entered into a sublease whereby he leased the premises to Subtenant until October 15, 1995. In the absence of an applicable statute, which of the following statements is most accurate?

(A) Tenant could not enforce his sublease because it was not authorized by the lease.
(B) Tenant could enforce his sublease because it was not prohibited by the lease.
(C) The legal status of Subtenant is the same as it would be if Subtenant obtained an assignment rather than a sublease.
(D) Subtenant would be liable to Owner for rent because of his privity of contract with Owner.

Answer to Question 148

If the lease is silent with respect to subleasing or assignment, the tenant has a right to either sublet the property or assign the lease. Only a specific prohibition in the lease against assignment or subletting will bar the tenant from doing so. Thus, (A) is incorrect because it has the law backward and (B) is correct.

(C) is incorrect because the legal status of an assignee and subtenant are quite different. As a sublessee, Subtenant did not take the entire term which Tenant held. Therefore, Subtenant's landlord would be Tenant, with whom he would be in privity of estate. A sublessee is not in privity of estate with the owner of the property, and so cannot be sued by the owner on any covenants in the original lease, unless the sublessee expressly assumed them. Tenant, on the other hand, continues to maintain a landlord-tenant relationship (including privity of estate) with Owner, and therefore Tenant remains liable on all covenants which run with the land. Tenant would retain a reversionary interest in the property which would commence at the end of the sublease. If there had been an assignment, Tenant would have retained no reversionary interest in the property and therefore would not be liable on the lease on a privity of estate theory. Only the assignee would be liable for breach of covenant on that theory.

(D) is incorrect. Subtenant is not in privity of contract with Landlord because he has only entered into a lease contract with Tenant, and is therefore in privity of contract only with Tenant. Because Subtenant is only a sublessee and not an assignee, Owner is not in privity of estate with Subtenant and must pursue Tenant for the rent and the fulfillment of the other obligations of their lease. However, if Tenant fails to pay the rent, Landlord can sue Tenant on the lease and reach and apply Subtenant's rent obligation as a means of getting paid. Landlord can also terminate the lease for nonpayment of rent.

Questions 149 and 150 are based on the following fact situation.

A brother and sister, Bruce and Sharon, acquired as joint tenants a 20-acre parcel of land called Greenacre. They contributed equally to the purchase price. Several years later, Bruce proposed that they build an apartment development on Greenacre. Sharon rejected the proposal but orally agreed with Bruce that Bruce could go ahead on his own on the northerly half of Greenacre and Sharon could do what she wished with the southerly half of Greenacre. Bruce proceeded to build an apartment development on, and generally developed and improved, the northerly ten acres of Greenacre. Sharon orally permitted the southerly ten acres of Greenacre to be used by the Audubon Society as a nature preserve. Bruce died, leaving his entire estate to his son, Stanley. The will named Sharon as executrix of his will, but she refused so to serve.

149. In an appropriate action to determine the respective interests of Sharon and Stanley in Greenacre, if Stanley is adjudged to be the owner of the northerly ten acres of Greenacre, the most likely reason for the judgment will be that

(A) the close blood relationship between Sharon and Bruce removes the necessity to comply with the Statute of Frauds.
(B) Sharon's conduct during Bruce's lifetime estops her from asserting title to the northerly half of Greenacre.
(C) the joint tenancy was terminated by the oral agreement of Sharon and Bruce at the time it was made.
(D) Sharon had a fiduciary obligation to her nephew Stanley by reason of her being named executrix of Bruce's will.

150. In an appropriate action to determine the respective interests of Sharon and Stanley in Greenacre, if Sharon is adjudged to be the owner of all of Greenacre, the most likely reason for the judgment will be that

(A) the Statute of Frauds prevents the proof of Sharon's oral agreement.
(B) Bruce could not unilaterally sever the joint tenancy.
(C) Sharon's nomination as executrix of Bruce's estate does not prevent her from asserting her claim against Stanley.
(D) the record title of the joint tenancy in Greenacre can be changed only by a duly recorded instrument.

Answer to Question 149

Two persons who are co-owners of property as joint tenants can agree to voluntarily partition the property, giving each a total ownership in part of the property. However, since each co-owner is obtaining and transferring an interest in land, such an agreement must ordinarily satisfy the requirements of the Statute of Frauds and the actual voluntary partition must be accomplished by an instrument which satisfies the formalities of a deed.

This question asks the best reason that a partition was successfully accomplished.

(A) is incorrect because the Statute of Frauds applies with equal force to brothers and sisters as it does to strangers.

(C) is incorrect because the oral agreement without more does not terminate the joint tenancy. Unless some additional factors make that oral agreement enforceable, the Statute of Frauds bars it.

(D) is incorrect because it is irrelevant. The naming of Sharon as executrix in Bruce's will imposes no fiduciary duty upon her if she does not accept.

(B) is the correct answer. The substantial reliance by Bruce during his lifetime on the oral agreement and Sharon's conduct in taking control over the southerly portion of the property arguably take the oral agreement out of the Statute of Frauds and make it enforceable.

Answer to Question 150

As the discussion of the previous question indicates, the Statute of Frauds will make the oral agreement between Sharon and Bruce unenforceable unless there is a specific basis to make the agreement enforceable despite the statute. Sharon's best argument is that there is nothing in these facts to prevent the operation of the Statute, and (A) is therefore the correct answer.

(B) is not correct because Bruce did not unilaterally attempt to sever the joint tenancy. He did it by oral agreement.

(C) is not correct because, even though the statement is true, it does not relate to the central legal issue in the problem, namely the enforceability of the oral agreement.

(D) correctly states the law with respect to a change of record title to the property, but the issue in this case is not whether record title has been changed, but rather the rights of the two co-owners among themselves. Their rights in the property with respect to each other could be changed even though record title was not.

Question 151

Talbot and Rogers, as lessees, signed a valid lease for a house. Lane, the landlord, duly executed the lease and delivered possession of the premises to the lessees. During the term of the lease, Rogers verbally invited Andrews to share the house with the lessees. Andrews agreed to pay part of the rent to Lane, who did not object to this arrangement, despite a provision in the lease that provided that "any assignment, subletting or transfer of any rights under this lease without the express written consent of the landlord is strictly prohibited, null, and void."

Talbot objected to Andrews' moving in, even if Andrews were to pay a part of the rent. When Andrews moved in, Talbot brought an appropriate action against Lane, Rogers, and Andrews for a declaratory judgment that Rogers had no right to assign. Rogers' defense was that he and Talbot were tenants in common of a term for years, and that he, Rogers, had a right to assign a fractional interest in his undivided one-half interest.

In his action, Talbot will

(A) prevail, because a cotenant has no right to assign all or any part of a leasehold without the consent of all interested parties.
(B) prevail, because the lease provision prohibits assignment.

(C) not prevail, because he is not the beneficiary of the nonassignment provision in the lease.
(D) not prevail, because his claim amounts to a void restraint on alienation.

Answer to Question 151

A tenant has the right to assign any or all of his interest under a lease unless prohibited by contract. This contract gives the landlord the right to void an assignment or sublease, but does not create such a contract right in a cotenant. Thus, the cotenant has no natural or contractual right to object to an assignment or sublease, and (C) is the correct answer.

(A) is not the correct answer because cotenants can assign or sublease their interests in a leasehold estate. The other cotenants will have a cause of action if the assignment or sublease impinges on their rights (e.g., of enjoyment and use) in the property, but they do not have an automatic right to void an assignment.

Although the lease provision can be read to void this sublease, courts' dislike for restraints on a tenant's right of alienation will lead them to find that Lane has waived his right to void this sublease. Thus, (B) is not a correct answer.

(D) is an incorrect answer because a restraint on alienation of a tenant's interest is permissible in some situations.

Question 152

O'Neal entered into a written contract to sell her house and six acres known as Meadowacre to Perez for $75,000. Delivery of the deed and payment of the purchase price were to be made six months after the contract. The contract provided that Meadowacre was to be conveyed "subject to easements, covenants, and restrictions of record." The contract was not recorded.

After the contract was signed but before the deed was delivered, Electric Company decided to run a high-voltage power line in the area and required an easement through a portion of Meadowacre. O'Neal, by deed, granted an easement to Electric Company in consideration of $5,000; the deed was duly recorded. The power line would be a series of towers with several high-voltage lines that would be clearly visible from the house on Meadowacre but would in no way interfere with the house.

When Perez caused the title to Meadowacre to be searched, the deed of easement to Electric Company was found. O'Neal appeared at the time and place scheduled for the closing and proffered an appropriate deed to Perez and demanded the purchase price. Perez refused to accept the deed. In an appropriate action for specific performance against Perez, O'Neal demanded $75,000.

In this action, O'Neal should

(A) obtain an order for specific performance at a price of $75,000.
(B) obtain an order for specific performance at a price of $70,000.
(C) lose, because Perez did not contract to take subject to the easement to Electric Company.
(D) lose, because his grant of an easement to a third party after entering into a purchase and sale agreement constitutes fraud.

Answer to Question 152

The purchase and sale agreement obligated the vendor to produce title free of all easements, covenants, and restrictions except those recorded at the time of the execution of the purchase and sale agreement. Therefore, O'Neal's grant of an easement after the execution of the purchase and sale agreement breaches her contractual obligations. Thus, Perez cannot be forced to complete the sale and (C) is the correct answer.

(A) would be the correct answer only if O'Neal produced marketable title to the land promised in the purchase and sale agreement.

(B) would be correct only if O'Neal produced marketable title, but a court would order an abatement in price corresponding to the value of property lost. For example, this might be the case if O'Neal could produce marketable title to an area of land less than he had promised in the purchase and sale agreement.

(D) is an incorrect answer because it is not necessary to prove fraud in order to avoid performance of a purchase and sale agreement.

Questions 153 and 154 are based on the following fact situation.

Sue owned a five-acre tract of land, one acre of which had previously been owned by Opal, but to which Sue had acquired title by adverse possession. Sue contracted to convey the full five-acre tract to Peg.

153. Assume that the contract did not specify the quality of title Sue was to convey. At the closing, Peg refused the tendered deed and demanded return of her earnest money. If Peg should bring a lawsuit against Sue for the return of the earnest money,

(A) Sue would prevail because Peg's remedies are limited to either specific performance or damages.
(B) Sue would prevail if her title by adverse possession has been confirmed by judicial decree.
(C) Sue would prevail because she has title to the entire tract, even though not marketable title.
(D) Peg would prevail because Sue does not have record title to the entire tract.

154. Assume that the contract contained a covenant that Sue would provide "a good and marketable title." Pursuant to that contract, Peg paid the purchase price and accepted a deed from Sue containing no covenants of title. Sue's title to the one acre subsequently proved defective and Peg was ejected by Opal. Peg sued Sue. Which of the following results is most likely?

(A) Peg will win because Sue's deed was fraudulent.
(B) Peg will win because the terms of the deed control Sue's liability.
(C) Sue will win because the terms of the deed control her liability.
(D) Sue will win because the deed incorporates the terms of the contract.

Answer to Question 153

This question turns on the type of title which a buyer must take from the seller of property. (A) is a wrong answer because a buyer's remedies in the case of a breach of the obligation to convey marketable title include rescission, as well as specific performance and damages.

(B) is the correct answer because title acquired by adverse possession which is confirmed by judicial decree is thereafter marketable; the previous record owner can no longer challenge the title of the adverse possessor or his successors.

(C) is the wrong answer because marketable title is the standard required where no other standard is specified in the purchase and sale agreement.

(D) is the wrong answer because record title is not an absolute prerequisite to marketable title. Adverse possession confirmed by a judicial decree is an acceptable substitute.

Answer to Question 154

Here, the purchase and sale agreement called for good and marketable title. Sue obviously did not have marketable title to one acre. However, the deed given contained no covenants of title. Since the purchase and sale agreement does not survive the closing and the deed contained no covenants, Sue must prevail.

(A) is incorrect because Sue's deed conveyed all she had, made no representations, and therefore was not fraudulent.

(C) is correct because under the terms of the deed, which do in fact control, Sue made no warranty.

(B) is incorrect because, even though the terms of the deed control liability, Peg will not win since there are no covenants in the deed.

(D) is incorrect because the deed does not incorporate the terms of the contract. If it did, Peg, not Sue, would win.

Question 155

Assume that State X has modified the common law Rule Against Perpetuities by adopting a "wait and see" rule with respect to vesting of interests.

Owen deeded Blackacre "to my daughter Able for life, and then to my daughter's children who reach age 25; provided, however, that no children of Able shall have the power to sell or dispose of their interest in the property before they attain age 30." At the time of the gift, Able had just given birth to a child and had had a hysterectomy. Owen died one year after the gift, and the residuary beneficiaries of his will have brought suit to obtain a declaration that the interest in Owen's grandchildren is invalid, and that they have a reversion in the property. In that suit, the court should hold that

(A) the remainder interest is invalid because it violates the Rule Against Perpetuities.
(B) the remainder interest is invalid because of the disabling restraint.
(C) the remainder interest is valid as written.
(D) the remainder interest is valid but the disabling restraint is invalid.

Answer to Question 155

This question requires a determination of the effect on this conveyance of the Rule Against Perpetuities and the rules concerning restraints on alienation.

The conveyance does not violate the Rule Against Perpetuities in a jurisdiction which has adopted a "wait and see" modification of the common law Rule Against Perpetuities. The conveyance would violate the common law Rule Against Perpetuities because the common law conclusively presumed that Able was capable of having children during her entire lifetime, and that she could have a child after Owen died who was under four years of age at Able's death. The interest of such a child might vest more than 21 years after the death of lives in being at the creation of the interest. Under the wait and see rule, however, the determination of whether there is remote vesting would not be made until the death of Able. Since Able was incapable of having any more children prior to Owen's death, any child of Able's would have to be a life in being at the creation of the interest, and a determination would ultimately be made that the rule was not violated. In any event, a challenge to the gift on perpetuities grounds is premature before the death of Able. Therefore, (A) is incorrect.

The restraint set forth in this question is a restraint on the alienability of a fee simple, albeit a limited restraint on a future interest. Such a restraint on any fee simple is invalid, but it does not invalidate the gift to which it is attached. Therefore, (B) is incorrect.

(C) is incorrect because the disabling restraint is invalid.

(D) is correct because the interest is valid but the disabling restraint is invalid.

Question 156

In 1940, Owens, the owner in fee simple of Barrenacres, a large, undeveloped tract of land, granted an easement to the Water District "to install, inspect, repair, maintain, and replace pipes" within a properly delineated strip of land 20 feet wide across Barrenacres. The easement permitted the Water District to enter Barrenacres for only the stated purposes. The Water District promptly and properly recorded the deed. In 1941, the Water District installed a water main which crossed Barrenacres within the described strip; the Water District has not since entered Barrenacres.

In 1945, Owens sold Barrenacres to Peterson, but the deed, which was promptly and properly recorded, failed to refer to the Water District easement. Peterson built his home on Barrenacres in 1945, and since that time he has planted and maintained, at great expense in money, time, and effort, a formal garden area which covers, among other areas, the surface of the 20-foot easement strip.

In 1986, the Water District proposed to excavate the entire length of its main in order to inspect, repair, and replace the main, to the extent necessary. At a public meeting, at which Peterson was present, the Water District announced its plans and declared its intent to do as little damage as possible to any property involved. Peterson objected to the Water District plans.

Assume that Peterson reserved his rights and, after the Water District completed its work, sued for the $5,000 in damages he suffered by reason of the Water District entry. Peterson's attempt to secure damages probably will

(A) succeed, because his deed from Owens did not mention the easement.
(B) succeed, because of an implied obligation imposed on the Water District to restore the surface to its condition prior to entry.
(C) fail, because of the public interest in maintaining a continuous water supply.
(D) fail, because the Water District acted within its rights.

Answer to Question 156

(A) is incorrect because the easement was properly recorded in Peterson's chain of title and so is enforceable against him, even if it wasn't mentioned in his deed.

(B) is incorrect because the holder of an easement, in the exercise of its rights to inspect, repair, and replace the pipe, has a right to dig and is not responsible to the owner of the servient estate for the damage caused to the property on top of the pipe. While the easement holder might have an obligation to refill the hole and to be careful in its excavation, it would not have to replace the formal gardens.

(D) is the correct answer because one of the rights incident to the easement is the right to dig for the purposes of inspection and repair.

(C) is incorrect because it does not establish a legal basis for the water district's actions, except perhaps the power of eminent domain. If the district proceeded on an eminent domain theory, it would be obligated to compensate the owner for the damage caused. The power of eminent domain is not at issue here, though, because the water district holds an easement by grant.

Question 157

In 1975, Hubert Green executed his will which, in pertinent part provided, "I hereby give, devise, and bequeath Greenvale to my surviving widow for life, remainder to such of my children as shall live to attain the age of 30 years, but if any child dies under the age of 30 years survived by a child or children, such child or children shall take and receive the share which his, her, or their parent would have received had such parent lived to attain the age of 30 years."

At the date of writing his will, Green was married to Susan, and they had two children, Allan and Beth. Susan died in 1980 and Hubert married Waverly in 1982. At his death in 1990, Green was survived by his wife, Waverly, and three children, Allan, Beth, and Carter. Carter, who was born in 1984, was his child by Waverly.

In a jurisdiction which recognizes the common-law Rule Against Perpetuities unmodified by statute, the result of the application of the Rule is that the

(A) remainder to the children and to the grandchildren is void because Green could have subsequently married a person who was unborn at the time Green executed his will.
(B) remainder to the children is valid, but the substitutionary gift to the grandchildren is void because Green could have subsequently married a person who was unborn at the time Green executed his will.
(C) gift in remainder to Allan and Beth or their children is valid, but the gift to Carter or his children is void.
(D) remainder to the children and the substitutionary gift to the grandchildren are valid.

Answer to Question 157

Since the interest in question is created by devise, the period of the Rule Against Perpetuities does not begin to run until the death of the testator. Since all of the testator's children must, by definition, be alive at the testator's death, they may serve as lives in being. Since all interests vest under this devise by the ends of their lives (if not earlier), all interests created by this devise are valid under the Rule Against Perpetuities. Thus, (D) is the correct answer.

(A) and (B) are wrong because this conveyance was testamentary, meaning that Hubert's children could serve as measuring lives. Thus, their interests are valid. The interests of their children (the grandchildren) will vest, if at all, on the death of their parents (the measuring lives) and so are valid. (A) and (B) would have been correct answers only if the conveyance had been inter vivos. Then, a child born after the conveyance would not be a measuring life and, since he might not become 30 until 21 years after any available measuring lives, would void the interests of the children and grandchildren.

(C) would be the correct answer only if the conveyance were inter vivos, Carter was born after the conveyance, and the jurisdiction did not void the gifts to all the children on the basis of the invalidity of the gift to Carter.

Question 158

At a time when Ogawa held Lot 1 in the Fairoaks subdivision in fee simple, Vine executed a warranty deed that recited that Vine conveyed Lot 1, Fairoaks, to Purvis. The deed was promptly and duly recorded.

After the recording of the deed from Vine to Purvis, Ogawa conveyed Lot 1 to Vine by a warranty deed that was promptly and duly recorded. Later, Vine conveyed the property to Rand by warranty deed and the deed was promptly and duly recorded. Rand paid the fair market value of Lot 1 and had no knowledge of any claim of Purvis.

In an appropriate action, Rand and Purvis contest title to Lot 1. In this action, judgment should be for

(A) Purvis, because Purvis' deed is senior to Rand's.
(B) Rand, because Rand paid value without notice of Purvis' claim.
(C) Purvis or Rand, depending on whether a subsequent grantee is bound, at common law, by the doctrine of estoppel by deed.
(D) Purvis or Rand, depending on whether Purvis' deed is deemed recorded in Rand's chain of title.

Answer to Question 158

(C) may, at first, appear to be the correct answer, since this question involves estoppel by deed. However, this is not a question of the effect of the doctrine of estoppel by deed under the common law - Purvis would clearly prevail at common law, since his deed was received first and is valid under the doctrine of estoppel by deed. Rather, the question involves the effect of estoppel by deed under a modern recording statute. Since Rand bought here without any actual notice of the deed to Purvis, he is entitled to the status of a protected bona fide purchaser, unless he is held to have constructive notice of the deed to Purvis. Since the deed from Vine to Purvis was recorded before Vine received title, Purvis' deed would not be within the normal chain of title. Thus, Rand will be held to have constructive notice of Purvis' deed only if the jurisdiction holds that a prior-recorded deed is constructive notice - answer (D).

(B) is a correct answer only in the jurisdictions which hold that a prior-recorded deed is not constructive notice to the subsequent grantee. Thus, it is not the best answer.

As mentioned above, (A) is clearly correct only in a common-law jurisdiction which has no recording statute.

Question 159

Orris had title to Brownacre in fee simple. Without Orris' knowledge, Hull entered Brownacre and constructed an earthen dam across a watercourse. The earthen dam trapped water that Hull used to water a herd of cattle he owned. After twelve years of possession of Brownacre, Hull gave possession of Brownacre to Burns. At the same time, Hull also purported to transfer his cattle and all his interests in the dam and water to Burns by a document that was sufficient as a bill of sale to transfer personal property but was insufficient as a deed to transfer real property.

One year later, Burns entered into a lease with Orris to lease Brownacre for a period of five years. After the end of the five-year term of the lease, Burns remained on Brownacre for an additional three years and then left Brownacre. At that time, Orris conveyed Brownacre by a quitclaim deed to Powell. The period of time to acquire title by adverse possession in the jurisdiction is ten years.

After Orris' conveyance to Powell, title to the earthen dam was in

(A) the person who then held title to Brownacre in fee simple.
(B) Burns, as purchaser of the dam under the bill of sale.
(C) the person who then owned the water rights as an incident thereto.
(D) Hull, as the builder of the dam.

Answer to Question 159

The principal issue tested in this question is whether the earthen dam was realty or personalty. If realty, ownership is in the owner of the real estate. If personalty, it could have been conveyed by a bill of sale. Since the earthen dam is permanently affixed to the real estate and is used in conjunction with the land, it would be properly characterized as real estate, making (A) the correct answer and (B) incorrect.

The ownership of water rights does not also carry with it the ownership of part of the realty and (C) is incorrect.

Since the dam is realty, ownership follows the ownership of the real estate and (D) is therefore incorrect.

Question 160

Arthur and Celia, brother and sister, both of legal age, inherited Goodacre, their childhood home, from their father. They thereby became tenants in common.

Goodacre had never been used as anything except a residence. Arthur had been residing on Goodacre with his father at the time his father died. Celia had been residing in a distant city. After their father's funeral, Arthur continued to live on Goodacre, but Celia returned to her own residence.

There was no discussion between Arthur and Celia concerning their common ownership, nor had there ever been any administration of their father's estate. Arthur paid all taxes, insurance, and other carrying charges on Goodacre. He paid no rent or other compensation to Celia, nor did Celia request any such payment.

Thirty years later, a series of disputes arose between Arthur and Celia for the first time concerning their respective rights to Goodacre. The jurisdiction where the land is located recognizes the usual common-law types of cotenancies, and there is no applicable legislation on the subject.

If Arthur claims the entire title to Goodacre in fee simple and brings an action against Celia to quiet title in himself, and if the state where the land is located has an ordinary 20-year adverse possession statute, the decision should be for

(A) Arthur, because during the past 30 years, Arthur has exercised the type of occupancy ordinarily considered sufficient to satisfy the adverse possession requirements.
(B) Arthur, because the acts of the parties indicate Celia's intention to renounce her right to inheritance.
(C) Celia, because there is no evidence that Arthur has performed sufficient acts to constitute her ouster.

327

(D) Celia, because one cotenant cannot acquire title by adverse possession against another.

Answer to Question 160

A cotenant's exclusive enjoyment of joint property does not constitute adverse possession, as long as it is permissive. A cotenant's possession of joint property becomes adverse only when he ousts his cotenant(s). In order to oust a cotenant, the tenant has to physically eject or bar the cotenant from possession, or explicitly announce the intention to do so to the excluded cotenant. Since this was not the case here, (C) is the correct answer.

(D) is not the correct answer, because a cotenant can gain exclusive title by adverse possession in the limited circumstances described above.

(A) might be the correct answer if this were not a cotenant case, where Arthur had a presumed right to the possession and enjoyment he exercised.

(B) is an incorrect answer, because Celia's allowance to Arthur of exclusive possession of Goodacre is not a renouncement of her interest in the property, just as it does not indicate acquiescence to adverse possession.

Question 161

Seth was an elderly widower who lived alone on a small farm which he owned. Except for the farm, including the house and its furnishings, and the usual items of personal clothing and similar things, Seth owned substantially no property. Under proper management, the farm was capable of producing an adequate family income.

Because of the usual deterioration accompanying old age, Seth was unable to do farm work or even to provide for his own personal needs. Seth entered into an oral contract with his nephew, Jim, by which Seth agreed to convey the farm to Jim and Jim agreed to move into the house with Seth, operate the farm, and take care of Seth for the rest of his life. The oral contract was silent as to when the land was to be conveyed.

Jim, who lived about fifty miles away where he was operating a small business of his own, terminated his business and moved in with Seth. With the assistance of his wife, Jim gave Seth excellent care until Seth died intestate about five years after the date of the contract. In his final years, Seth was confined to his bed and required much personal service of an intimate and arduous sort.

Seth was survived by his only son, Sol, who was also Seth's sole heir and next of kin. Sol resided in a distant city and gave his father no attention in his father's final years. Sol showed up for Seth's funeral and demanded that Jim vacate the farm immediately. Upon Jim's refusal to do so, Sol brought an appropriate action for possession. Jim answered by way of a counterclaim to establish Jim's right to possession and title to the farm.

If the court's decision is in favor of Jim, it will be because

(A) the land is located in a state where the Statute of Frauds will not be applied if there has been such part performance as will result in an irreparable hardship if the contract is not performed.

(B) the land is located in a state where the Statute of Frauds will not be applied if there has been such part performance that is by its very nature unequivocally referable to the contract.

(C) Sol is precluded by the "clean hands" doctrine from enforcing his claim against Jim.

(D) the blood relationship of uncle-nephew is sufficient to remove the necessity for any writing to satisfy the Statute of Frauds.

Answer to Question 161

There are two distinct theories under which an oral agreement to convey land will be enforced. One of those theories is unequivocal referability. It is used when the acts of the parties to the oral contract refer to the existence of the contract. This is not present here, because Seth continued to live on the property, and the presence of Jim on the property is as consistent with an employment relationship as it is with an agreement to transfer title. Therefore, (B) is incorrect.

The second theory is that of equitable fraud. It focuses both on the change of position of the party seeking to enforce the contract which was induced by the owner of the property, and on the hardship that the purchaser would incur if he were not able to obtain title to the land. It is basically an estoppel theory which prevents the seller from taking a position inconsistent with the promise made, upon which the buyer relied. There is such hardship and reliance here, and (A) is therefore correct.

(C) is incorrect because Sol has done nothing which would amount to unclean hands, and thus render him unable to seek equitable relief. Moreover, he needs no assistance from equity, since his title to the property results from his status as Seth's heir.

(D) is incorrect because there is no exception to the Statute of Frauds which permits the enforcement of oral agreements concerning land among blood relations.

Question 162

Testator devised his farm "to my son, Selden, for life, then to Selden's children and their heirs and assigns." Selden, a widower, had two unmarried, adult children.

In an appropriate action to construe the will, the court will determine that the remainder to the children is

(A) indefeasibly vested.
(B) contingent.
(C) vested subject to partial defeasance.
(D) vested subject to complete defeasance.

Answer to Question 162

Selden's two children each take a vested remainder. They are ascertained, and there is no condition precedent to their taking. They will take whether they survive Selden or not, because the property will go to their heirs and assigns. There are no circumstances that will take the interest away from them completely. Therefore, (D) is incorrect because the interest is not subject to complete defeasance, and (B) is incorrect because it is not contingent.

The interest is in fact subject to partial defeasance, however, because Selden can remarry and have more children. If he did so, each of the children now living would then take a lesser interest. Therefore, (C), and not (A), is the correct answer.

Question 163

Venner, the owner of Greenacre, a tract of land, entered into an enforceable written agreement with Brier providing that Venner would sell Greenacre to Brier for an agreed price. At the place and time designated for the closing, Venner tendered an appropriate deed, but Brier responded that he had discovered a mortgage on Greenacre and would not complete the transaction, because Venner's title was not free of encumbrances, as the contract required. Venner said that it was his intent to pay the mortgage from the proceeds of the sale, and he offered to put the proceeds in escrow for that purpose with any agreeable, responsible escrowee. The balance due on the mortgage was substantially less than the contract purchase price. Brier refused Venner's proposal. Venner began an appropriate legal action against Brier for specific performance. There is no applicable statute in the jurisdiction where Greenacre is located. Venner's best legal argument in support of his claim for relief is that

(A) as the seller of real property, he had an implied right to use the contract proceeds to clear the title being conveyed.
(B) the lien of the mortgage shifts from Greenacre to the contract proceeds.
(C) under the doctrine of equitable conversion, title has already passed to Brier, and the only issue is how the purchase price is to be allocated.

(D) no provision of the contract has been breached by Venner.

Answer to Question 163

Venner was required under an enforceable purchase and sale agreement to convey Greenacre free from all encumbrances. At the closing, the mortgage was on the property and was an encumbrance, and at that moment he could not convey free and clear of encumbrances. Therefore, he had possibly violated one of the provisions of the contract, and (D) is not the correct answer.

If the deed had been given and accepted at the closing, the mortgage would have remained as a lien on the property until the note was paid off and the mortgage was discharged. The lien does not shift to the proceeds, and (B) is therefore incorrect.

(C) is incorrect because legal title does not pass under the doctrine of equitable conversion. Title passes only when a valid deed is given. Moreover, it does not address the critical issue, which is the existence of an encumbrance on the property at the time of closing.

(A) is the best argument for Venner, although some jurisdictions would not give him a right to use the purchase money to clear title unless that right were specifically reserved in the contract. It is reasonable to imply such a right, however, because the buyer is not harmed if the seller immediately uses the proceeds to clear liens on the property.

Question 164

Arthur owns a 500-acre farm on which his dwelling is situated. He enters into the following written agreement:

> I, Arthur, agree to sell Walter my dwelling and a sufficient amount of land surrounding the same to accommodate a garden and lawn. Price: $20,000. Received: $1.00 on account.
>
> Signed: Walter
> Arthur

Walter refuses to perform the agreement. Arthur sues for specific performance. Judgment for

(A) Arthur, because he has a written agreement signed by the party to be charged therewith.
(B) Arthur, because the agreement satisfies the Statute of Frauds.
(C) Walter, because the agreement is ambiguous.
(D) Walter, because $1.00 constitutes a nominal consideration which will not support a contract.

Answer to Question 164

The question here is whether or not the written agreement satisfies the Statute of Frauds. For a written agreement to satisfy that statute, it must identify the land to be sold with reasonable precision. The language used here does not identify the land with reasonable precision because there is no definition of how much land is necessary to constitute a lawn and garden. It could be one-half acre. On the other hand, it could be 25 acres. Therefore, the agreement is ambiguous, and (C) is the correct answer.

(A) is incorrect because, even though Arthur has a written agreement signed by the party to be charged, the agreement is too ambiguous to satisfy the Statute of Frauds, and is therefore unenforceable.

(B) is incorrect because the written agreement does not contain a description of the land which is sufficient to satisfy the Statute of Frauds. Moreover, both statements (A) and (B), in which Arthur prevails, say the same thing. If you were to find that the Statute of Frauds was satisfied, you could not properly choose between them. This is an important clue that the drafter of the question thought the agreement was ambiguous, and Walter should prevail.

(D) is incorrect because the dollar is a deposit, not the entire consideration. You do not even need a deposit to support this type of contract. All that is required is a return promise by the buyer to purchase the land for the agreed purchase price.

Question 165

Metterly, the owner in fee simple of Brownacre, by quitclaim deed conveyed Brownacre to her daughter, Doris, who paid no consideration for the conveyance. The deed was never recorded. About a year after the delivery of the deed, Metterly decided that this gift had been ill-advised. She requested that Doris destroy the deed, which Doris dutifully and voluntarily did. Within the month following the destruction of the deed, Metterly and Doris were killed in a common disaster. Each of their successors in interest claimed title to Brownacre. In an appropriate action to determine the title to Brownacre, the probable outcome will be that

(A) Metterly was the owner of Brownacre, because Doris was a donee and therefore could not acquire title by quitclaim deed.
(B) Metterly was the owner of Brownacre, because title to Brownacre reverted to her upon the voluntary destruction of the deed by Doris.
(C) Doris was the owner of Brownacre, because her destruction of the deed to Brownacre was under the undue influence of Metterly.
(D) Doris was the owner of Brownacre, because the deed was merely evidence of her title, and its destruction was insufficient to cause title to pass back to Metterly.

Answer to Question 165

A conveyance of land is complete upon delivery and acceptance of a valid deed. Once a deed has been delivered, its function of transferring title has been completed; thereafter it serves only as evidence of that transaction. To retransfer the property, the grantee or new owner must sign and deliver a new deed to the old owner. Therefore, the destruction of the deed in this case did not retransfer title from Doris to Metterly. Therefore, (D) is correct.

(C) is incorrect because the facts are insufficient to show undue influence; and her destruction of the deed, even if not under undue influence, would not transfer title.

(A) is incorrect because delivery of a quitclaim deed transfers whatever title the grantor has, even if the grantee is a donee.

(B) is incorrect because the destruction of a deed does not cause the title to revert to the grantor.

Question 166

Alice conveyed Twinoaks Farm "to Barbara, her heirs and assigns, so long as the premises are used for residential and farm purposes, then to Charles and his heirs and assigns." The jurisdiction in which Twinoaks Farm is located has adopted the common-law Rule Against Perpetuities unmodified by statute. As a consequence of the conveyance, Alice's interest in Twinoaks Farm is

(A) nothing.
(B) a possibility of reverter.
(C) a right of entry for condition broken.
(D) a reversion in fee simple absolute.

Answer to Question 166

The interest in Charles and his heirs is an invalid executory interest, since there is no assurance that it will vest (in this case, become possessory when the premises are no longer used for residential or farm purposes) within lives in being plus 21 years. It therefore violates the Rule Against Perpetuities. When an interest violates the Rule Against Perpetuities, the instrument is construed with the language which created that interest deleted. Therefore, the conveyance should read "to Barbara and her heirs and assigns so long as the premises are used for residential and farm purposes." Such a conveyance is a fee simple determinable. Alice, as the grantor, has a possibility of reverter, the interest which follows a fee simple determinable. It is valid; an interest retained in the grantor does not violate the Rule Against Perpetuities. Thus, (B) is the correct answer.

(A) is incorrect because a possibility of reverter follows a fee simple determinable when the executory interest over is void.

(C) is incorrect because a right of entry is the interest retained by the grantor after a fee simple subject to a condition subsequent, not a fee simple determinable.

(D) is incorrect because it incorrectly states the name of the interest in the grantor after a fee simple determinable.

Question 167

Johnson and Tenniel owned Brownacre as joint tenants with the right of survivorship. Johnson executed a mortgage on Brownacre to Lowden in order to secure a loan. Subsequently, but before the indebtedness was paid to Lowden, Johnson died intestate with Stokes as her only heir at law. The jurisdiction in which Brownacre is located recognizes the title theory of mortgages.

In an appropriate action, the court should determine that title to Brownacre is vested

(A) in Tenniel, with the entire interest subject to the mortgage.
(B) in Tenniel, free and clear of the mortgage.
(C) half in Tenniel, free of the mortgage, and half in Stokes subject to the mortgage.
(D) half in Tenniel and half in Stokes, with both subject to the mortgage.

Answer to Question 167

This problem involves a joint tenancy where one joint tenant mortgages his interest in the property. Of course, the mortgage only attaches to the interest of the tenant who executes the mortgage; the interests and rights of other cotenants cannot be impinged by the actions of one cotenant. But, more importantly, the majority rule (adopted by all title theory states and some lien theory states) is that a mortgage by one joint tenant converts the joint tenancy into a tenancy in common (with no right of survivorship). Thus, in this case, Johnson's execution of a mortgage converted the tenancy into a tenancy in common, so that when Johnson died, his half interest passed to his heir, Stokes, subject to the mortgage. Thus, (C) is the correct answer.

(A) and (D) are incorrect answers because Tenniel's interest can never be subject to the mortgage, since he didn't join in it. (A) is also wrong because Tenniel's right of survivorship cannot survive Johnson's mortgage of his interest.

(B) would be the correct answer only in a lien theory state that held that one tenant's mortgage does not destroy a joint tenancy. In such a state, the mortgagee's interest in the property would be extinguished with Johnson's death, since his death would also terminate Johnson's estate.

Question 168

In 1977 Owen held Blackacre, a tract of land, in fee simple absolute. In that year, he executed and delivered to Price a quitclaim deed which purported to release and quitclaim to Price all of the right, title, and interest of Owen in Blackacre. Price accepted the quitclaim and placed the deed in his safe deposit box.

Owen was indebted to Crider in the amount of $35,000. In September, 1982, Owen executed and delivered to Crider a warranty deed, purporting to convey the fee simple to Blackacre, in exchange for a full release of the debt he owed to Crider. Crider immediately recorded his deed.

In December, 1982, Price caused his quitclaim deed to Blackacre to be recorded and notified Crider that he (Price) claimed title.

Assume that there is no evidence of occupancy of Blackacre, and assume further that the jurisdiction where Blackacre is situated has a recording statute which requires good faith and value as elements of the junior claimant's priority. Which of the following is the best comment concerning the conflicting claims of Price and Crider?

(A) Price cannot succeed, because the quitclaim through which he claims prevents him from being bona fide (in good faith).
(B) The outcome will turn on the view taken whether Crider paid value within the meaning of the statute requiring this element.
(C) The outcome will turn on whether Price paid value (a fact not given in the statement).
(D) Price's failure to record until December, 1982, estops him from asserting title against Crider.

Answer to Question 168

(A) is incorrect because a quitclaim deed does not prevent Price from being a bona fide purchaser.
(C) is incorrect because the issue is not whether Price paid value, since Price was first in time. The requirement of payment of value is for the subsequent grantee, not the prior grantee.
(D) is incorrect because Price took good title when Owen executed the deed. The question here is whether or not the subsequent grantee takes this good title away from Price because the subsequent grantee was in good faith (i.e., did not know about the deed to Price) and paid value. Price has not done anything to mislead anyone, so the issue of estoppel cannot be raised. Even if Price can be held to be estopped from prevailing on his claim by the fact that he waited so long to record, (B) is a better answer because Crider's rights under the recording statute are much more certain.
(B) is the correct answer. Crider took the deed in consideration for forgiveness of an antecedent debt. If this is value within the meaning of the statute, and he was in good faith, then Crider will prevail. The case probably will be determined in favor of Crider, because he did give up something of value, namely the right to receive $35,000 from Owen, in order to get the deed.

Questions 169 and 170 are based on the following fact situation.

Meadowview is a large tract of undeveloped land. Black, the owner of Meadowview, prepared a development plan creating 200 house lots in Meadowview with the necessary streets and public areas. The plan was fully approved by all necessary governmental agencies and duly recorded. However, construction of the streets, utilities, and other aspects of the development of Meadowview has not yet begun, and none of the streets can be opened as public ways until they are completed in accordance with the applicable ordinances of the municipality in which Meadowview is located.
College Avenue, one of the streets laid out as part of the Meadowview development, abuts Whiteacre, an adjacent one-acre parcel owned by White. Whiteacre has no access to any public way except an old, poorly developed road which is inconvenient and cannot be used without great expense. White sold Whiteacre to Breyer. The description used in the deed from White to Breyer was the same as that used in prior deeds except that the portion of the description which formerly said, "thence by land of Black, northeasterly a distance of 200 feet, more or less," was changed to "thence by College Avenue as laid out on the Plan of Meadowview North 46° East 201.6 feet" with full reference to the plan and its recording data.
Breyer now seeks a building permit which will show that Breyer intends to use College Avenue for access to Whiteacre. Black objects to the granting of a building permit on the grounds that he has never granted any rights to White or Breyer to use College Avenue. There are no governing statutes or ordinances relating to the problem. Black brings an appropriate action in which the right of Breyer to use College Avenue without an express grant from Black is at issue.

169. The best argument for Black in this action is that

(A) Breyer's right must await the action of appropriate public authorities to open College Avenue as a public street, since no private easements arose by implication.
(B) the Statute of Frauds prevents the introduction of evidence which might prove the necessity for Breyer to use College Avenue.
(C) Breyer's right to use College Avenue is restricted to the assertion of a way by necessity and the facts preclude the success of such a claim.
(D) Breyer would be unjustly enriched if he were permitted to use College Avenue.

170. The best argument for Breyer in this action is that

(A) there is a way by necessity over Meadowview's lands to gain access to a public road.
(B) the deed from White to Breyer referred to the recorded plan and therefore created rights to use the streets delineated on the plan.
(C) sale of lots in Meadowview by reference to its plan creates private easements in the streets shown on the plan.
(D) the recording of the plan is a dedication of the streets shown on the plan to public use.

Answer to Question 169

Whiteacre is a completely separate tract of land from Meadowview. From the question it does not appear to have been commonly owned. Therefore, is not possible for the owner of Whiteacre to acquire either an easement by necessity or an easement by implication on any road in Meadowview. Such easements must be acquired incident to a division of commonly held land. The only theory which Breyer would have is that the streets in the subdivision are open to the public. (A), which expresses this idea, is therefore correct.

(B) is incorrect because it is the lack of the element necessary for an easement by necessity, namely commonly owned land, which precludes it from arising. The Statute of Frauds is not a bar to proving an easement by necessity if the essential elements are there.

(C) is correct in that it states that there is no easement by necessity. However, it is incorrect in stating that this is the only theory Breyer has. If the property has been dedicated to public use, then Breyer would have a right to use it.

(D) is incorrect because Breyer's only theory to use the street is as a member of the public when and if it is dedicated. Exercise of such rights does not constitute unjust enrichment.

Answer to Question 170

For the reasons set forth in the previous answer, there is no easement by necessity over Meadowview for the benefit of Breyer. Therefore, (A) is incorrect.

The reference to a recorded plan in a deed can only create rights in land owned by the grantor. Since White did not own the streets in Meadowview when he sold Whiteacre, he can grant no rights to them, and (B) is incorrect.

(C) is true as far as it goes. Lots in Meadowview will have rights in the streets of that subdivision even if the streets remain private ways. However, Whiteacre is not a lot in Meadowview, so no easement in the roads is created for the benefit of Whiteacre, and therefore (C) is incorrect.

(D) is the correct answer. The only theory under which Breyer can obtain a right to use the streets, absent an express easement, is if they are open to the public.

Question 171

Assume for the purposes of this question that you are counsel to the state legislative committee that is responsible for real estate laws in your state. The committee wants you to draft a statute governing the recording of deeds that fixes priorities of title, as reflected on the public record, as definitely as possible. Which of the following, divorced from other policy considerations, would best accomplish this particular result?

(A) Eliminate the requirement of witnesses to deeds.
(B) Make time of recording the controlling factor.
(C) Make irrebuttable the declarations in the deeds that valuable consideration was paid.
(D) Make the protection of bona fide purchasers the controlling factor.

Answer to Question 171

(A) is incorrect because witnessing a deed will not affect priority of title. Additionally, there is no general requirement that deeds be witnessed.

(B) is correct. The type of recording statute in which the priority of title most definitely reflects the public record is a race statute. The public record shows the date and time of every deed recorded. Therefore, priority is determined by the order of recording in the public record and not by extraneous events.

Once a deed is delivered, there is no requirement that the delivery be supported by consideration. In most jurisdictions, recording a deed creates a presumption of delivery and, therefore, a declaration of consideration is irrelevant to a recording statute, and (C) is incorrect.

(D) is incorrect. Protecting the bona fide purchaser requires that the circumstances of the purchase, and not what appears in the public record, determine the priority of title.

Question 172

Owner held 500 acres in fee simple absolute. In 1980, Owner platted and obtained all required governmental approvals of two subdivisions of 200 acres each.

In 1980 and 1981, commercial buildings and parking facilities were constructed on one, Royal Center, in accordance with the plans disclosed by the plat for each subdivision. Royal Center continues to be used for commercial purposes.

The plat of the other, Royal Oaks, showed 250 lots, streets, and utility and drainage easements. All of the lots in Royal Oaks were conveyed during 1980 and 1981. The deeds contained provisions, expressly stated to be binding upon the grantee, his heirs and assigns, requiring the lots to be used for single-family, residential purposes only until 2005. The deeds expressly stated that these provisions were enforceable by the owner of any lot in the Royal Oaks subdivision.

At all times since 1979, the 200 acres in Royal Center have been zoned for shopping center use, and the 200 acres in Royal Oaks have been zoned for residential use in a classification which permits both single-family and multiple-family use.

Assume that Owner now desires to sell the 100 acres which were not included in either of the subdivisions established in 1980. Which of the following is the most appropriate comment about the effect of the 1980-1981 transactions on the title to the 100 acres?

(A) There is assurance that title is clear of encumbrance.
(B) The title is encumbered to the extent that no use can be made of the land except for residential use.
(C) There is a substantial basis for the position that Owner (or his successor) can only continue the present use of the 100 acres and not change same by any further development.
(D) There is a significant doubt as to the exact freedom of choice of development scheme for the 100 acres.

Answer to Question 172

As an owner of a lot in Royal Oaks may be able to argue that the 100 acres is covered by a common scheme restricting the possible uses of the 100 acres, (D) is the correct answer and (A) is an incorrect answer.

An owner may be able to argue that the common scheme included plans that the 100 acres remain undeveloped, but that is a difficult argument to make. Therefore, it cannot be said that there is a "substantial basis" for this proposition. (C) is an incorrect answer.

Likewise, an argument may be made that the common scheme restricts the use of the 100 acres to residential use, but such a restriction must be proven. It cannot be said that the property is certainly so encumbered. Thus, (B) is an incorrect answer.

Question 173

Opus, the owner of Stoneacre, entered into a written agreement with Miner. Under this written agreement, which was acknowledged and duly recorded, Miner, for a five-year period, was given the privilege to enter on Stoneacre to remove sand, gravel, and stone in whatever quantities Miner desired. Miner was to make monthly payments to Opus on the basis of the amount of sand, gravel, and stone removed during the previous month. Under the terms of the agreement, Miner's privilege was exclusive against all others except Opus, who reserved the right to use Stoneacre for any purpose whatsoever, including the removal of sand, gravel, and stone.

One year after the agreement was entered into, the state brought a condemnation action to take Stoneacre for a highway interchange. In the condemnation action, is Miner entitled to compensation?

(A) Yes, because he has a license, which is a property right protected by the due process clause.
(B) Yes, because he has a *profit a prendre*, which is a property right protected by the due process clause.
(C) No, because he has a license, and licenses are not property rights protected by the due process clause.
(D) No, because he has a *profit a prendre*, which is not a property right protected by the due process clause.

Answer to Question 173

There are two determinations necessary to correctly answer this question.

First, what kind of right was created by the written agreement - a license or a *profit a prendre*? The agreement between Opus and Miner created a *profit a prendre* because it was in writing and gave Miner an irrevocable right for five years to enter the land of Opus, sever some of the realty and carry it off as personalty. A license, on the other hand, need not be in writing and is revocable.

Second, a *profit a prendre* is an interest in land. When such an interest, even though not a fee interest, is taken by the state, the Due Process Clause of the Fourteenth Amendment (incorporating the Fifth Amendment) entitles the owner of that right to just compensation. Therefore, (B) is correct.

(A) is incorrect because it improperly characterizes the agreement as creating a license. It is also an incorrect statement of law; a license is a mere contract right and not an interest in land which would require just compensation under the Eminent Domain Clause.

(C) is a correct statement concerning licenses, but incorrectly characterizes this agreement as a license.

(D) is incorrect because a *profit a prendre* is a property right protected by the Eminent Domain Clause.

Question 174

Assume for the purposes of this question that you are counsel to the state legislative committee that is responsible for real estate laws in your state. The committee wants you to draft legislation to make all restrictions on land use imposed by deeds (now or hereafter recorded) unenforceable in the future so that public land-use planning through zoning will have exclusive control in matters of land use.

Which of the following is **LEAST** likely to be a consideration in the drafting of such legislation?

(A) compensation for property rights taken by public authority
(B) impairment of contract
(C) sovereign immunity
(D) police power

Answer to Question 174

(A) is incorrect because an interest restricting the use of land is a property right and eliminating that right may involve problems of eminent domain. This answer is, therefore, likely to be a consideration.

A covenant restricting the use of land is a contract and eliminating the restriction may impair the contract. Therefore, this answer is likely to be a consideration, and (B) is incorrect.

(C) is correct because a state's immunity against being sued is irrelevant to drafting a statute making land use restrictions in deeds unenforceable.

(D) is incorrect because the state's interest in regulating the use of land will be relevant to determining whether the regulation constitutes a valid exercise of the police power.

Question 175

A certain written lease was entered into, the total contents thereof being as follows:

> On the first day of November, 1989, Landlord rents his grocery store on Main Street in Crosstown to Tenant for four years. The rent shall be $100 per month.
>
> Signed: Landlord
> Tenant

On February 1, 1990, Landlord conveyed the grocery store to Owner subject to the lease. Tenant had no notice of the conveyance and continued paying rent to Landlord until July 1, 1990, when he learned thereof and assigned the lease to Assignee without Owner's knowledge. Assignee paid no rent. The Statute of Frauds required a lease for more than three years to be in writing.

In the absence of an applicable statute, the assignment of the lease by Tenant to Assignee was

(A) effective, whether or not it was in writing.
(B) effective, because the lease did not prohibit an assignment.
(C) not effective, because the lease contained no clause permitting assignment.
(D) not effective, because Tenant failed to give notice thereof to Owner.

Answer to Question 175

Unless prohibited by statute or agreement, a tenant has the right to assign the leasehold interest. Since there was no such prohibition here, Tenant's assignment is effective. Since (A) seems to state categorically that an assignment is valid, it is not the best answer. (B), which recognizes that an assignment can be prohibited by the terms of the lease, is the correct answer.

It is not the law that an assignment is allowed only if the lease permits it. In fact, the opposite is true - assignment is permitted unless the lease prohibits it. (C) is an incorrect answer.

Notice to the landlord is not generally required to make an assignment effective. Thus, (D) is an incorrect answer.

Question 176

Santos agreed to sell and Perrine agreed to buy a described lot on which a single-family residence had been built. Under the contract, Santos agreed to convey marketable title subject only to conditions, covenants, and restrictions of record and all applicable zoning laws and ordinances.

The lot was subject to a 10-foot side line setback originally set forth in the developer's duly recorded subdivision plot. The applicable zoning ordinance zones the property for single-family units and requires an 8.5-foot side line setback. Prior to closing, a survey of the property was made. It revealed that a portion of Santos' house was 8.4 feet from the side line. Perrine refused to consummate the transaction on the ground that Santos' title is not marketable.

In an appropriate action, Santos seeks specific performance. Who will prevail in such an action?

(A) Santos, because any suit against Perrine concerning the setback would be frivolous.
(B) Santos, because the setback violation falls within the doctrine *de minimis non curat lex*.
(C) Perrine, because any variation, however small, amounts to a breach of contract.
(D) Perrine, because the fact that Perrine may be exposed to litigation is sufficient to make the title unmarketable.

Answer to Question 176

A seller is required to produce "marketable" title in order to be able to enforce a purchase and sale agreement. In order to be marketable, the title must be reasonably free from doubt both in fact and in law. If there is a reasonable potential for litigation in regard to the property, the title is not marketable. Since the house on the property violates a zoning ordinance and a restrictive covenant, it may be the subject of litigation and renders the title unmarketable. Thus, Perrine cannot be forced to perform the contract and (D) is the correct answer.

(C) is an incorrect answer because a purchase and sale agreement can be enforceable despite minor variations between the title promised in the agreement and the title produced at the closing.

(B) is wrong since the law of conveyancing is that an existing violation of a zoning ordinance is not a minor matter and renders title unmarketable.

(A) is an incorrect answer, because potential litigation is sufficient to render title unmarketable, even if the title conveyed will ultimately prevail.

Question 177

Lord was the owner of a warehouse building and the lot on which it stood. Prior tenants had sublet the building and grounds to companies that had failed to keep up the property adequately. Lord was determined that his next tenant would use the entire premises for the entire term of the lease so his worries as a landlord would be minimized.

Taylor responded to Lord's agent's advertisements for leasing the property. After lengthy negotiations, Lord and Taylor entered into a ten-year lease. The lease contained a clause prohibiting Taylor from subletting his interest. Taylor now desires to assign his interest in the lease and comes to you for your advice regarding this issue. Would you advise him that he may do so?

(A) Yes, because restraints on alienation of land are strictly construed.
(B) Yes, because disabling restraints on alienation of land are invalid.
(C) No, because the term "subletting" includes "assignment" when the term is employed in a lease.
(D) No, because even in the absence of an express prohibition on assignment, a tenant may not assign without the landlord's permission.

Answer to Question 177

There is a distinction between a **sublease,** where the tenant conveys the property for less than the full term and thereby retains a remainder interest in the leasehold, and an **assignment,** where the tenant transfers the entire interest in the leasehold. A prohibition against subletting is not a prohibition against assignment, and (A) is

338

the correct answer because it properly states that restraints on alienation of land are strictly construed.

(B) is incorrect because a disabling restraint, one which prevents alienation of an interest in land, is invalid only with respect to fee simple interest in land. Since Taylor does not hold a fee simple, this rule does not apply. A disabling restraint **could** be placed on this estate, but it has not.

(C) is incorrect because the term "subletting" does not include "assignment." The two are construed as mutually exclusive terms.

(D) is incorrect because, in the absence of an express prohibition, both assignment and subletting of a leasehold interest are permitted.

Made in the USA
Charleston, SC
17 June 2011